ENCYCLOPEDIA OF

WOMEN
IN THE
AMERICAN WEST

To Barbara Jean Farrington, Esq.,
and Erika Lyn and Emily Grace Henderson

ENCYCLOPEDIA OF

WOMEN
IN THE
AMERICAN WEST

EDITED BY

GORDON MORRIS BAKKEN & BRENDA FARRINGTON

California State University, Fullerton   Fullerton College

SAGE Publications
International Educational and Professional Publisher
Thousand Oaks ■ London ■ New Delhi

For information:

Sage Publications, Inc.
2455 Teller Road
Thousand Oaks, California 91320
E-mail: order@sagepub.com

Sage Publications Ltd.
6 Bonhill Street
London EC2A 4PU
United Kingdom

Sage Publications India Pvt. Ltd.
B-42, Panchsheel Enclave
Post Box 4109
New Delhi 110 017 India

Printed in the United States of America

Library of Congress Cataloging-in-Publication Data

Encyclopedia of women in the American West / Gordon Morris Bakken and
Brenda Farrington, editors.
    p. cm.
Includes bibliographical references and index.
ISBN 0-7619-2356-X (cloth)
    1. Women-West (U.S.)—History-Encyclopedias. 2. Women-West (U.S.)—Biography.
I. Bakken, Gordon Morris. II. Farrington, Brenda.
HQ1438.W45E53 2003
305.42´0978—dc21

                         2003006729

Printed on acid-free paper

03   04   05   06   07   08   09   10   9   8   7   6   5   4   3   2   1

Acquiring Editor:	Jerry Westby
Editorial Assistant:	Vonessa Vondera
Production Editor:	Claudia A. Hoffman
Copy Editor:	Barbara Coster
Typesetter:	C&M Digitals (P) Ltd.
Indexer:	Molly Hall
Cover Designer:	Michelle Lee

Contents

Acknowledgments

This encyclopedia was made possible by the willingness of many scholars to write, revise, edit, and ponder the meaning of women in the American West and to give so much of themselves to see this project into print. The professionals at Sage Reference made this volume possible with guidance, enthusiasm, and a critical eye. In particular, we thank Rolfe A. Janke, Jerry Westby, Claudia Hoffman, and Leticia Gutierrez for their support, professionalism, and prompt responses to so many questions over the past three years. Barbara Coster, our copy editor, brought consistency with good questions and professional touches to this volume.

We also thank all the librarians who have made much of this research possible. Bill Stein, the archivist at the Nesbitt Memorial Library in Columbus, Texas, made seemingly difficult research possible for a California researcher. Our author/librarians Debra Gold Hansen at San Jose State, Danelle Moon at Yale, Judy Ruttenberg of the University of California, Irvine, and Jayne Sinegal at Irvine Valley College helped us in many ways and assisted many of our authors. We also thank the professional staff at the Huntington Library, San Marino, California, and the Pollock Library at California State University, Fullerton, for their assistance. We know that no meaningful research can be done without the assistance of professional librarians and we are deeply in their debt.

We remember the sacrifice of our authors in meeting deadlines and committing so much time to entries. Our colleague Clark Davis died at age 36 shortly after completing his entry. His loss is felt by so many and the loss to history and its students is incalculable. Some of our intended authors were prevented by severe illness from completing their promised work. We acknowledge the help of Willis E. McNelly, a World War II veteran and Professor Emeritus of English, California State University, Fullerton, who passed on April 6, 2003, unable to complete his entry. We also acknowledge the professionalism of so many who work outside of academia yet gave so much to their work. Taking time from 50- and 60-hour weeks to work in archival materials, oral histories, and secondary sources speaks loudly to us all. Yet we all heed the same call to bring life to the women who built the American West. It is our hope that this volume advances the cause.

List of Entries

Reader's Guide

To give the reader a quick sense of the topics contained in this work, we have arranged most of the entries in the following topical guide. Broad topical entries such as Kansas and Oklahoma (the study of the women of a state), Women of the Southwest (a regional perspective on women), and Cripple Creek (the women of a city) are included in this encyclopedia to give you an idea of how to structure a work on women in a place. Because of the scope considered by the authors transcending topics, you should consult them for their contents and concepts. The nine topical categories are Agriculture/Ranching, Arts and Letters, Education, Entrepreneurs, Law, Pioneers, Public Performance, Religion, and Women's Organizations. We hope you find this useful, but remind you to use the Index as a finding means.

AGRICULTURE/RANCHING

Cowgirls
Homesteaders
Rindge, Rhoda May Knight
Veterinary Medicine
"Wine, Women, and Song"

ARTS AND LETTERS: ARTISTS, POETS, WRITERS

Anzaldua, Gloria E.
Bird, Gloria
Bower, B. M.
Butler, Octavia
Callahan, Sophia Alice
Cather, Willa
Cleaveland, Agnes Morley
Coel, Margaret
Crow Dog, Mary
Darden, Fannie Baker
Davis, Mollie Evelyn Moore
Farnham, Eliza Wood Burhans
Flanner, Hildegarde
Foote, Mary Hallock
Hale, Janet Campbell
Hasselstrom, Linda M.
Hogan, Linda
Hubble, Grace Lillian Burke

Ivins, Molly
Jackson, Helen Hunt
Jaramillo, Cleofas Martínez
Kingston, Maxine Hong
Naranjo-Morse, Nora
Red Shirt, Delphine
Sandoz, Mari (Marie Susette)
Sewell, Helen Moore
Silko, Leslie Marmon
Sinclair, Bertha Muzzy
St. Johns, Adela Rogers
Stewart, Elinore Pruitt
Tan, Amy
Underhill, Ruth Murray
Wiggin, Kate Douglas Smith
Williams, Jeanne
Winnemucca, Sarah
Woody, Elizabeth

EDUCATION: TEACHERS, LIBRARIANS, PROFESSORS, RESEARCHERS

Brown, Ruth Winifred
Bunzel, Ruth Leah
Burnstad, Hattie
Collins, Audrey B.
Deloria, Ella Cara
Education

Hearst, Phoebe Apperson
Librarianship in California
McGlandrey, Donna Joy
Parsons, Elsie Clews
Reichard, Gladys Amanda
U.S. Air Force Academy

ENTREPRENEURS

Callender, Marie
Clark, Georgie White
Eagle Woman
Ehmann, Freda
Handler, Ruth
Pleasant, Mary Ellen
Scudder, Laura
Summers, Emma A. McCutcheon
Terasawa, Kuniko

LAW/LAWYERS, JUDGES, POLICE, INCARCERATION, CRIME, LEGISLATORS, PUBLIC OFFICIALS

Adams, Annette Abbott
Arizona Political Women
Baird, Lourdes G.
Berzon, Marsha L.
Bird, Rose Elizabeth

Preface

In 1983 the first Western Women's Conference convened in Sun Valley, Idaho, to address the omissions and absence of women in traditional western history. This conference marked the first national meeting devoted to western women's history and launched the publication of *The Women's West,* edited by Susan Armitage and Elizabeth Jameson (1987). These pioneering scholars provided a springboard for future histories focused on western women and laid the foundation for future studies navigating the spectrum and diversity of women's experiences in the West. As noted by Armitage and Jameson, the influence of Frederick Jackson Turner's "frontier thesis" in 1893 portrayed western history as "one-dimensional and historically inaccurate and incomplete" (3-6). The histories of American Indians, Hispanics, Asians, individual families, and all ethnic and social classes of women were left out of Turner's rough-and-tumble "wild West."

The success of western women's history as a separate yet integral part of western history and U.S. history is a testament to the scholarship of these early pioneers. The articles in this encyclopedia contribute to the growing body of literature documenting the diverse lives of women in the West and the nation. Some of the topics explored include the clubwomen's movement, politics, prostitution, women homesteaders, suffrage, mining, agriculture, rodeo women, literary women, conservation, emigrant experiences, librarians, and research strategies locating primary and secondary resources.

Through these articles, the *Encyclopedia of Women in the American West* brings together an array of experiences, and like its predecessor publications, hopes to advance continued scholarship in western women's history, to develop new methodologies for analysis, and to locate new materials that will allow for inclusiveness and a broader, more accurate understanding of women's contributions to western and American history.

— Danelle Moon
Yale University

About the Editors

Gordon Morris Bakken, coeditor of this volume, is Professor of History at California State University, Fullerton, Past President of Phi Alpha Theta, and Founding Vice President and Director of the California Supreme Court Historical Society. He is the author/editor of 15 books and 43 articles and law reviews.

Brenda Farrington, coeditor of this volume, teaches at Fullerton College, Chapman University, Long Beach City College, and Rancho Santiago Canyon College. She is the author/editor of seven books, two book chapters, and numerous reviews.

About the Contributors

Mary Adams is President and cofounder of ISIM University, an online graduate school based in Denver, Colorado. She holds degrees in History and Business.

Elwood Bakken is an independent scholar in Bozeman, Montana, and shipping manager for Action Lighting. He has published in *Montana: The Magazine of Western History* and *Carve*.

Michelle Bean is a California native. In 1991 she graduated from the University of California, Irvine, with a bachelor's degree in Political Science and a minor in History. Currently, she is finishing her secondary school teaching credential at California State University, Fullerton.

Brenda Bitgood is an independent scholar and graduate of California State University, Fullerton, with a B.A. in History and a B.A. in American Studies. She currently resides in Anaheim, California, with her husband and her daughter.

Renae Moore Bredin currently teaches in the Women's Studies Program at California State University, Fullerton. Her publications include essays on Native American women writers, Elsie Clews Parsons, and gender and technology.

Anne M. Butler is the editor of *The Western Historical Quarterly* and Professor of History at Utah State University, Logan. She is the author of *Daughters of Joy, Sisters of Misery: Prostitutes in the American West, 1865-90* (1985), *Gendered Justice in the American West: Women Prisoners in Men's Penitentiaries* (1997), *Uncommon Common Women* (1996) with Ona Siporin, and *The Frontiers and Catholic Identities* (1999) with Michael Engh.

Sharon Snow Carver is Adjunct Professor at Utah State University, Tooele, and holds a Ph.D. from Brigham Young University in American History. She has done extensive research on women's clubs in the Intermountain West and contributed to the *Utah Historical Quarterly* as well as other publications.

Henry Fay Cheung is a doctoral student in history at the University of California, Riverside.

Kevin Christy teaches history in a Christian school in Orange County, California.

Tiffany E. Dalpe is a doctoral student in ethics and the history of philosophy at the University of Memphis.

Maureen Woodard Dana teaches at Sacramento City College and holds a Ph.D. in American Literature from the Claremont Graduate School. Her research includes work on captivity narratives of the 17th and 18th centuries, female short story writers of the 1930s, and late 20th-century feminist fiction and theory.

Clark Davis was Associate Professor of History at California State University, Fullerton, author of *Company Men: White Collar Life and Corporate Cultures in Los Angeles, 1892-1941* (2000), and coeditor of *The Human Tradition in California* (2002). Clark passed on February 4, 2003, at the age of 36.

Susan Badger Doyle is an independent scholar in Pendleton, Oregon, and the author of *Journeys to the Land of Gold: Emigrant Diaries from the Bozeman Trail, 1863-1866* (2000).

Randal Fulkerson is Adjunct Professor of History and Humanities at California Baptist University-High Desert Campus. His graduate education focused on late 19th-century to early 20th-century American and church history.

Victor W. Geraci is Associate Professor of History at Central Connecticut State University, New Britain, and the author of a forthcoming book, *Salud*.

Joan V. Greenwood is Professor Emerita of English and Comparative Literatures at California State University, Fullerton.

Vanessa Anne Gunther teaches history at a variety of institutions in Southern California and holds a Ph.D. in Native American History from the University of California, Riverside. She also works in the medical arts field.

Debra L. Gold Hansen is Associate Professor at San Jose State University's School of Library and Information Science and has a Ph.D. in American History from the University of California, Irvine.

Mary Hardy teaches history in Thailand at Assumption University. She continues to engage in historical research projects and is currently awaiting a publication coauthored with Dr. William Haddad in the journal *Israeli Affair*. She also is working with Dr. B. Carmon Hardy editing a new edition of a world civilizations primary sourcebook.

Angela E. Henderson is Professor of Reading at Fullerton College and author of "Fiction as Reality: 'Lonesome Dove,' the Law, and a Property-Holder's Society," *Journal of the West* (Fall 2000).

Craig Hendricks teaches at Long Beach City College. He received both an M.A. and Ph.D. from the State University of New York, Stony Brook, focusing on modern Latin American history, and has published articles and edited four essay collections.

Lori S. Iacovelli is Lead Archives and Exhibits Assistant at the Whittier, California, Historical Society Museum.

Elizabeth Jameson holds the Imperial Oil & Lincoln McKay Chair in American Studies at the University of Calgary. Her publications include *All That Glitters: Class, Conflict and Community in Cripple Creek,* and two coedited books, *The Women's West* and *Writing the Range: Race, Class and Culture in the Women's West.*

Patricia Jimenez holds B.A.s from the University of California, Riverside, in History and Political Science. She is currently taking time off from graduate work in history. Her areas of interest include the Vietnam War, the antiwar movement, and protest music.

Mary L. Kelley is Assistant Professor of History at Lamar University. Her areas of specialization are modern United States, women, and Texas. She is currently working on a forthcoming book, *Private Wealth, Public Good.*

Scott Kesilis recently graduated with honors from California State University, Fullerton, with bachelor's degrees in Political Science and History. At present, he is taking a sabbatical from his studies.

Alexandra Kindell is a doctoral candidate at Iowa State University. She is interested in women's roles in rural life and agriculture, which she has explored in her teaching and during her tenure as assistant editor of *Agricultural History.*

Renee M. Laegreid teaches at Hastings College in Hastings, Nebraska, specializing in American western and cultural history. She received her Ph.D. from the University of Nebraska in 2002. Her recent publications focus on the evolution of the rodeo queen phenomena, and she is currently preparing a book for publication on that subject.

Neal Lynch is the Technical Services Manager at Cemex Concrete Division in Ontario, California, a graduate student in history at California State University, Fullerton, a member of Toastmasters International, a volunteer docent at the Lincoln Shrine Museum, and a teacher of U.S. citizenship at a local community center.

Sandra K. Mathews-Lamb teaches at Nebraska Wesleyan University, Lincoln. She finished her Ph.D. in 1998 at the University of New Mexico in History (American West and Latin America). Currently, she is completing a biography of Donna Joy McGladrey and a manuscript on Pueblo Indian land grants (1600 to 1870).

Mary M. McCulloch teaches in the undergraduate Religious Studies Department at Mount St. Mary's College, Los Angeles. Prior to receiving her graduate degree, she spent 15 years working for Allstate Insurance Company as an underwriter and marketing manager.

Becky Jo (Gesteland) McShane is Assistant Professor at Weber State University, where she teaches classes in technical communication, literature, and composition. Her publications include articles on women's southwestern autobiographies and case studies of business writing. Her current research explores the professional writing of anthropologists Gladys Reichard and Fanny Bandelier.

Melissa L. Miller is currently pursuing a graduate degree in history from California State University,

Fullerton, while working as a food server at Alcatraz Brewing Company. She received her bachelor's degree from CSUF in 2001.

Linda Frances Mollno is a Lecturer in U.S. History and California History at both California State Polytechnic University, Pomona, and California State University, Los Angeles, and is a doctoral candidate in history at the Claremont Graduate University. She is writing her dissertation on the Pasadena Community Playhouse.

Danelle Moon is Adjunct Professor in the History Department at Central Connecticut State University, teaching U.S. and Women's History, and is Archivist in Manuscripts and Archives, Yale University Library. She is a trained Public Historian, independent researcher and scholar, and most recently published chapters in *Law in the Western United States* (2000) and *California History: A Topical Approach* (2003).

William Allan Myers holds a Ph.D. from the University of California, Riverside, and is the author of *Historic Civil Engineering Landmarks of Southern California* (1974), *Iron Men and Copper Wires: A Centennial History of the Southern California Edison Company* (1983), *Nuclear Pioneer: The Story of San Onofre Nuclear Generating Station's Unit One* (1993), *Ranchos to Residences: The Story of Sunny Slope Water Company* (1994), and numerous articles and reviews.

Jeffrey Nichols is Assistant Professor of History at Westminster College in Salt Lake City, Utah, and a former officer in the U.S. Navy. His research interests include the social and environmental history of Utah and the rest of the American West.

Michelle L. Oropeza, a graduate of California State University, Fullerton, is a student at Whittier Law School.

Shannon Orr holds a B.A. from Humboldt State University (1997) and continues her graduate work while working at the Crown Plaza Irvine Hotel.

Heidi J. Osselaer teaches part time at Arizona State University and the Maricopa County Community College District. She received her Ph.D. in History from ASU in 2001.

Alonso Quezada received his B.A. in History at California State University, Fullerton, and is an M.A. candidate at CSUF.

Jamie Rasmussen was a cadet at the U.S. Air Force Academy.

Glenda L. Riley is Alexander M. Bracken Professor of History at Ball State University and the author of *Inventing the American Woman* (1987, 1995, 2001), *The Life and Legacy of Annie Oakley* (1994), *A Place To Grow: Women in the American West* (1992), and five other books.

Judy Ruttenberg is a librarian at the University of California, Irvine, libraries. Her M.A. in American History is from the University of Massachusetts, Amherst, and her M.L.S. is from the University of Maryland, College Park.

Dale H. Sawyers teaches high school government, economics, and U.S. history, and is pursuing a law degree at Western State University School of Law. He served 8 years on active duty in the U.S. Navy, completed his B.A. in History at the University of California, Riverside, and an M.A. in History from California State University, Fullerton.

Marcus J. Schwoerer is an independent scholar living in Southern California. He has published three articles in the *Welebaethan: Journal of History* and continues work on the American Civil War.

Charles Joseph Sedey is currently finalizing his master's degree in Military History at California State University, Fullerton. He has taught political science and U.S. history at Don Lugo High School for the past 8 years.

Jayne Sinegal is a librarian at Irvine Valley College and a graduate student in History at California State University, Fullerton. She received her A.B. in History in 1975 from the University of California, Berkeley, her M.L.S. in Library Science in 1976, and an M.P.A. in 1978 from Golden Gate University. Her interests include Africa, slavery, women, and World War II.

Christopher Small is an avid reader and collector of Louis L'Amour, married, and a full-time graduate student. His interests are primarily 19th- and 20th-century American history, including the American West and World War II.

Sherry L. Smith is Professor of History at Southern Methodist University. Her research interests include American cultural, Native American, and western history. She is the author of several books, including

Reimagining Indians: Native Americans Through Anglo-Eyes, 1880-1940 (2002).

John Joseph Stanley is a Los Angeles County Deputy Sheriff who has written extensively on the history of Los Angeles County jails. His recent publications on this subject appeared in *Law in the Western United States* (2001) and *California History: A Topical Approach* (2003).

Michelle A. Stretch is an independent researcher living in Yorba Linda, California.

Carolyn Stull joined the U.S. Navy to see the world and saw Norfolk, Virginia, from 1991 to 1995. She is working toward a teaching certificate to teach social sciences to junior high school students.

Trangdai Tranguyen is the Director of the Vietnamese American Project, Center for Oral & Public History, at California State University, Fullerton.

Philip R. VanderMeer is Associate Professor of History at Arizona State University. His areas of expertise include political, legal, and western history. His recent publications include *Phoenix Rising: The Making of a Desert Metropolis* (2002) and "The Historical Patterns of Arizona Leadership" in Building Leadership in Arizona, *Arizona Town Hall 80* (Spring 2002).

Debra A. Viles is a Ph.D. candidate at Wayne State University in Detroit, Michigan. Her dissertation examines the constructions of citizenship in the American antebellum state constitutions and the meaning of this hierarchy of rights and liberties for foreigners, women, and African Americans.

Kelly A. Woestman is Associate Professor of History at Pittsburg (Kansas) State University. She has authored *@history*, a CD-ROM published by Houghton Mifflin, along with several other instructor and student ancillaries. She is a coeditor of *H-Teach* and serves on the Kansas Territorial Sesquicentennial Advisory Committee.

Michael G. Woods is a graduate student at California State University, Fullerton. He edits the *Welebaethan: Journal of History*, has taught history in private education for the last 11 years, and is currently a California Historical Society Whitsett Student Fellow.

Introduction

We are pleased to offer this *Encyclopedia of Women in the American West* as part of the Sage family of reference books. We intend this volume to be used by the reading public in conjunction with other Sage publications, particularly Angela M. Howard & Frances M. Kavenik's *Handbook of American Women's History* (second edition) published in 2000. Because our focus is regional and follows this Sage reference work of greater breadth, we strongly advise our readers to consult both works in terms of fully informing research and knowledge in the growing field of women's studies.

For us the West is west of the 100th meridian. This is where explorers, pioneers, and present-day environmentalists confronted the fact of aridity. We know this is a contested definition, and in our book *Where is the West?* (2001) we set out the scholarly debate regarding the changing definition of what constitutes the West.

Your editors have traveled a long scholarly path to this point. Professor Bakken benefited from the insights of William L. O'Neill in the 1960s as he pioneered women's history at the University of Wisconsin and from the scholarship of and friendships with Anne Butler, Betsy Jameson, Sandra Mathews-Lamb, Glenda Riley, Janet Schmeizer, Sherry L. Smith, Sandra VanBurkleo, and Kelly A. Woestman in the three decades that followed. Professor Farrington studied women's history as part of American legal history in the 1980s and benefited from the counsel of Glenna Matthews and Glenda Riley, who expanded her scholarly reach and inquiry. She has taught women's history at a variety of institutions and continues her scholarly inquiry as part of that instructional enterprise. In 2000 we produced

a six-volume work titled *The American West*, with one of the volumes titled *The Gendered West*. *Encyclopedia of Women in the American West* continues our mutual quest to capture the lives of women in the West and to contextualize their experiences and contributions to American society.

We recognize that our selections for this encyclopedia are limited amid a rapidly growing field of women's history, women's studies, and feminist studies. Even within the West, a field with explosive scholarly tendencies since the 1980s, we have attempted both a selective and a suggestive set of entries. Some of the entries are topical, others biographical. Some entries survey the existing literature and provide a research bibliography. Debra Hansen of the San Jose State University School of Library and Information Science provides such an entry on women's clubs in the American West. Some of the entries pull together existing historiography and put forward research findings. Danelle Moon's work in librarianship in California is suggestive of the potentialities of such research. Our authors have produced some material not in print in any venue. Others have reworked fields of long-term scholarly interest. We trust that the combination will be useful to all readers, and encourage interest in further research. In that light, we have an entry on research strategies in the Appendix and encourage all to read it before entering the pages of our enterprise.

—Gordon Morris Bakken
California State University, Fullerton

—Brenda Farrington
Fullerton College

ADAMS, ANNETTE ABBOTT
(1877-1956)

Annette Abbott Adams is best known as the first female lawyer to hold the positions of Assistant U.S. Attorney, U.S. Attorney, and Assistant Attorney General as well as a temporary judge pro tempore on the California Supreme Court. Adams was born in Prattville, California, in 1877, where she studied to become a teacher at the State Normal School in Chico, graduating in 1897. She taught for a period of years and was also a school principal but decided to further her education by going to the University of California, Berkeley, receiving a law degree in 1904 and a juris doctorate in 1912. She was one of the first women to graduate from Boalt Hall, where she met her future law partner, Marguerite Ogden, the daughter of an Alameda Superior Court judge. Upon completion of her degree, she and Ogden set up a practice, and during one case she was matched against U.S. Attorney John W. Preston. He was impressed enough by her argument in defense of her client that he suggested her nomination for Assistant U.S. Attorney in San Francisco. The Attorney General, James McReynolds, objected strongly to her appointment, and it took a period of 8 months for it to finally be approved, and even then she was paid $200 less per year than the male attorneys. One of her first successful cases, the *Bopp* conspiracy case, involved the violation of U.S. neutrality laws by the German consulate at the beginning of World War I.

During this period, Adams was a strong supporter of the Democratic Party and served as the president of the California Democratic Women's Club. Her friend and supporter Congressman John Raker recruited her to join the campaign of President Woodrow Wilson. She supported Wilson because of his prosuffrage stance in the days before women were given the vote. When Wilson was victorious, Raker worked to get her appointed to the position of U.S. Attorney when he moved on to the position of Assistant U.S. Attorney General. In 1920 she was appointed Assistant U.S. Attorney General and successfully defended the constitutionality of the Eighteenth Amendment and the Volstead Act before the Supreme Court.

Adams left the federal system in 1923 after the Republicans won the White House. After an unsuccessful bid for a seat on the San Francisco Board of Supervisors, she began a private practice. She went on to become a federal judge in 1942 as Presiding Justice of the 3rd District Court of Appeal of California, but retired in 1950 before the end of her 12-year term. She was also honored in 1950, at the celebration of the Court's 100-year anniversary, to sit as judge pro tempore on the California Supreme Court for one case. Her many accomplishments went a long way to breaking down the barriers for women in careers in law and the judiciary.

—Michelle Bean

SUGGESTED READINGS

Franck, Irene M., and David M. Brownstone. *The Wilson Chronology of Women's Achievements*. New York: H. W. Wilson, 1998.

Horton, Joey Dean. "'Girl' Lawyer Makes Good: The Story of Annette Abbott Adams." Retrieved from www.stanford.edu/group/WLHP/papers/aaahtml.html.

O'Dea Schenken, Suzanne. *From Suffrage to the Senate: An Encyclopedia of American Women in Politics.* Santa Barbara, CA: ABC-CLIO, Inc., 1999.

Weatherford, Doris. *A Chronology of American Woman's History.* New York: Facts on File, 1997.

AFRICAN AMERICAN PHYSICIANS

The female African American physician's role in history has not received much attention, as there are few records available on the subject, particularly on those women in the western United States. Statistics regarding physicians emerge after the end of slavery at a time when racial segregation and discrimination were at a high. There were 115 African American women physicians accounted for in the United States at this time. The experiences of these women vary dramatically from that of other physicians and women during the time period. The majority of these women worked within their communities at local hospitals, clinics, and colleges. Many of the contributions that these women made were beneficial to members of both the white and the black community. Homes were established for unwed mothers and poor women, training programs were created to teach health standards, and hospitals and clinics were established to train others interested in the health professions.

The first African American woman in the United States to graduate with a medical degree was Rebecca Lee Crumpler, who graduated in 1863 from the New England Female Medical College in Boston. Rebecca J. Cole was the second African American woman physician in the United States, graduating from the Woman's Medical College of Pennsylvania in 1866. Cole was one of the first women to combine private practice with community services. Working with Elizabeth Blackwell, the first white female physician, Cole became a tenement physician. This position required her to make house calls in slum neighborhoods and to train mothers in family hygiene and basic health care. The early successes of Crumpler and Cole created a foundation for other African American women, showing what strong determined women could achieve in the face of obstacles.

The appearance of the female African American physician in the western United States coincided with the movement of immigrants into the less-developed western territories. The majority of the territories and the states that they entered were antislavery, although many that entered these regions did so as slaves and later as indentured servants. There were many African American women who entered the western states free. Many of these women served as household laborers, cooks, and nannies. African American women in the West and in the South differed in several ways. Western women tended to live in urban areas, had fewer children, and the median age was higher than that of their southern counterparts. Both women in the West and women in the South had to endure similar amounts of racial discrimination. As in the South, educational facilities were segregated. It was difficult for African American women to receive even the most basic education, let alone a specialized education in the field of medicine. For example, the first medical degree awarded to an African American woman in California was in 1918 to Ruth J. Temple.

The number of female physicians increased in the late 19th century. In 1860 there were approximately 200 female physicians. That number rose to 2,423 in 1880 and then to 7,000 in 1890. However, by 1920 the U.S. Census listed only 65 African American female physicians. The number of African American male physicians was much greater than that of the females. In 1920 there were 3,885 male African American physicians. This large number of physicians can be attributed to the increase in medical schools that were founded for African Americans during Reconstruction. Despite the number of schools founded, only Meharry Medical College and Howard University School of Medicine remained open by 1914. Howard University ran a government-supported program that had graduated 552 physicians by 1900; of that number 25 were women. The largest number of female African American physicians who graduated from medical school were from Meharry. The school graduated 39 African American women by 1920. The Woman's Medical College of Pennsylvania was another medical school that was responsible for graduating African American women. Many of the graduates went on to be the first women to practice medicine in their home state.

Many of the women to practice medicine shared similar backgrounds. For the most part, students of medicine came from privileged families. The majority also had more extensive education prior to enrollment. Some women received sponsorship from activists interested in the advancement of African American women. There are instances of former slaves working their way through medical school, but the majority of students were upper-class African Americans.

Mississippi-born Ruth J. Temple is an example of a woman who benefited from activist sponsorship. Temple moved to Los Angeles, California, in 1904. With financial support from a local prominent African American activist, T. W. Troy, Temple was able to receive medical training at Loma Linda University, receiving a degree in 1918. After obtaining her degree, Temple created the Temple Health Institute and the Health Study Club program. This program was an educational collaboration between parents, teachers, and children designed to educate the population on sex education, basic health issues, immunization, and drug-related issues. The program was very successful within the state and beyond.

Women who did receive an education in medicine still had many obstacles to overcome. Due to racial attitudes and customs, African American women physicians primarily practiced among women of their race. Another difficulty involved the patients. Many of the women avoided medical attention because they lacked funds. Also, fear of doctors and superstition forced many physicians to have to expend great effort to treat the ill. Despite these hardships, many women were successful in creating social service agencies and local practices. As a result of segregation within the medical field, the medical needs of African Americans were being met within the community.

Over the years, standards were raised in the medical field. Medical students were expected to serve internships, maintain residencies, and pass the state medical board examinations. Few hospitals around the nation were willing to accept African Americans or women for internships and residencies, and the majority of the hospitals that served the African American community gave men priority. Some states required internships as a prerequisite for obtaining a medical license. The hospitals that accepted women applicants usually only accepted white women. Often racism and sexism were so intense that female physicians would go to extremes to assist patients. For example, May Chinn, the first woman to graduate from Bellevue Hospital Medical College, performed major surgeries in the homes of patients throughout the 1930s because she was unable to gain access to hospitals during that time. Sexual and racial segregation were the two main factors that hindered the aspirations of African American women.

The attitudes that African Americans held toward women working were similar to those held by white Americans. Many felt that educated and professional women lost their femininity to some degree. Women given the opportunity to work in hospitals, colleges, and clinics experienced blatant sexism. Men believed that medicine was a male sphere in which women had no place. The majority of women were underpaid, overworked, and ostracized by their male counterparts. Many times economic necessity and racism dictated whether or not a woman worked. These conditions made working women more acceptable. In fact, African American female physicians were seen as extremely desirable marriage partners.

Prior to World War II, most African American physicians worked in private practices or aided civil organizations in programs benefiting the community, because fewer opportunities were available in other areas of medicine. After World War II, the more lucrative sectors of specialty medicine became available as training opportunities began to open up for African Americans. The latter half of the 20th century was a critical time in which leadership roles became available in the medical profession. In 1985 Edith Irby Jones became the first woman president of the National Medical Association. Five years later, Roselyn Payne Epps became president of the American Medical Women's Association, the first African American to ever do so.

In recent years challenges to affirmative action have risen, creating much controversy. There are those who believe affirmative action is beneficial in that it allows for more minorities to enter institutions that had previously excluded them. This in turn creates a growth of African American doctors, of which there is a critical shortage, which will ease the burden of low-income communities lacking medical attention. Opponents to affirmative action believe that scholastic aptitude should be the only issue in accepting students, not race. Putting the controversy aside, African American enrollment increased as a result of affirmative action. In recent years, institutions that do not enforce affirmative action show a decline in enrollment of female African American medical students. Of the 30,260 women enrolled in medical school for the 2001-2002 school year, only 3,119 were African American.

Since the 1920s the number of female African American physicians has increased. In 1970 the number reached 1,051. This number grew to 3,250 in 1989. By the year 2001 there were 8,370 practicing female African American physicians. This accounts for only 4% of the total female physician percentage in the United States. If the number of African American men and women are combined, they only account for 20,738 physicians in the United States, or 2.5% of the total physician population. Until the creation of affirmative action, the majority of women who graduated from medical schools did so by attending Meharry or Howard.

African American women have challenged race and gender barriers throughout their history. Even today ambitious women attempting to persevere in a career in the medical field are breaking stereotypes.

—Melissa L. Miller

SUGGESTED READINGS

Abram, Ruth J., ed. *Send Us a Lady Physician: Women Doctors in America, 1835-1920*. New York: Norton, 1985.

American Medical Association. *Physician Characteristics and Distribution in the U.S., 2003/2004 Edition*. "Number of Female Physicians by Race/Ethnicity, 2001" retrieved from www.ama-assn.org/ama/pub/print/article/168-185.html.

American Medical Association. Source: Barzansky, B., & Etzel, S. I. Educational programs in U.S. medical schools, 2001-2002. *JAMA*, 288:1067-1072. "Racial and Ethnic Backgrounds of Medical Students—Total Enrollment, 2001-2002" retrieved from www.ama-assn.org/ama/pub/print/article/168-191.html.

Austin, Gail T., comp. "African-American Women in the Sciences and Related Disciplines." Retrieved from www.nau.edu/~wst/access/lcafam.html.

Davis, Marieanna W., ed. *Contributions of Black Women to America: Vol. 2, Civil Rights, Politics and Government, Education, Medicine, Sciences*. Columbia, SC: Kenday Press, 1982.

Gabriel, Barbara A. "In Their Footsteps: The First Women Physicians and the Pioneers Who Followed Them." Retrieved from www.aamc.org/newsroom/reporter/dec01/womenphysicians.htm.

Harding, Jan, ed. *Perspective on Gender and Science*. London: Falmer Press, 1986.

Hine, Darlene Clark, ed. *Black Women in America: An Historical Encyclopedia*, Vols. 1 & 2. New York: Carlson, 1993.

H-Net. Humanities and Social Sciences Online. Retrieved from www2.h-net.msu.edu/~women/bibs. Copyright © 1995-2003, H-Net, Humanities & Social Sciences OnLine.

Horner, Louise L., ed. *Black Americans: A Statistical Sourcebook*. Palo Alto, CA: Information Publications, 1999.

Luchetti, Cathy. *Medicine Women: The Story of Early-American Women Doctors*. New York: Crown, 1998.

PageWise. History: People. Retrieved from www.essortment.com/in/history.people. © 2002 Pagewise, Inc.

Rubio, Philip F. *A History of Affirmative Action, 1619-2000*. Jackson: University Press of Mississippi, 2001.

Sammons, Vivian Ovelton, ed. *Blacks in Science and Medicine*. New York: Hemisphere, 1990.

Smith, Jessie Carney, and Carrell Peterson-Horton, eds. *Historical Statistics of Black America: Media to Vital Statistics*. New York: Gale Research, 1995.

Smith, Jessie Carney, ed. *Notable Black American Women*. Detroit, MI: Gale Research, 1992.

Watson, Wilbur H., ed. *Black Folk Medicine: The Therapeutic Significance of Faith and Trust*. New Brunswick, NJ: Transaction Books, 1988.

Wright, A. J. "Early Black and Female Physicians in Jefferson County. Retrieved from www.anes.uab.edu/jeffcodocs.htm.

ALL-GIRL RODEO

All-girl rodeos, which began in the early 1940s, evolved in response to the removal of professional cowgirl athletes from professional rodeo competition. Since women first began competing in the rodeo arena at Cheyenne Frontier Days in 1903, there had never been a large number of professional women riders. Rodeo promoters advertised women riders, often calling them sweethearts or queens of the rodeo. Beginning in the early 1930s, however, cowgirl participation in rodeos as event contestants—cowgirl athletes—became increasingly restricted, and their roles as nonathlete promoters of rodeos was encouraged. Rather than hiring itinerant cowgirl athletes to promote their rodeos, local rodeo directors increasingly sought out young, unmarried local girls, some with rather questionable riding skills, to serve as rodeo queens.

During World War II some of these cowgirl athletes, both professional and amateur, came together under the banner of patriotism to reestablish their presence and skills in the arena by holding all-girl rodeos. In 1947 two cowgirl athletes and former rodeo queens, Nancy Binford and Thena Mae Farr, took the idea of an all-girl rodeo a step further. In direct contradiction to the trend that regarded queens as society belles and allowed women only cameo appearances in the rodeo arena, they set about to reinstate the definition of rodeo queen as champion rider. As Binford announced to the press, "This is going to be a rodeo, not a social event."

The idea of revisiting an earlier definition of rodeo queen, one based on championship status, took only a short look back in time. In 1927, when the directors of the Pendleton Round-Up in Pendleton, Oregon, selected Mabel Strickland as queen of the rodeo, she was the epitome of a rodeo queen. The Pendleton newspaper described her as a rare example of womanly "beauty and talent." She easily met the current standards of femininity; the papers touted her beauty and grace, noting, "There is nothing masculine in her appearance and she does not wear mannish clothes. She dresses with excellent taste, whether in the arena or on the street." In terms of talent, she was an excellent bronc rider, and held world champion status as a relay rider, trick rider, and steer roper. When Mabel was hired to be the queen of the Round-Up, then, as now, the main role of a rodeo queen was to bring in the crowd. To have a nationally renowned rodeo rider agree to be queen of the Round-Up helped draw widespread attention to their show.

The following year, 1928, was the height of professional rodeo for women, with as many as one third of all rodeos featuring cowgirl events. All that was soon to change. By the end of World War II, the number of contests open to women, as well as the number of women who were still able to make a living in rodeo, had dropped dramatically. As Mary Lou LeCompte writes concerning professional cowgirl athletes, female participation in all areas of rodeo decreased, and events for women were only found in isolated rodeos from Wyoming to Florida. While the exclusion of cowgirl athletes from the rodeo arena is complicated and diverse, it is possible to identify several key factors leading to the decline: a debate over the propriety of women competing, the formation of the Rodeo Association of America (RAA), and the Great Crash, which led to the Great Depression. All three events occurred in 1929, making it a watershed year for cowgirl athletes.

Contributing to the exclusion of women was the death of Bonnie McCarrol, a well-known rodeo rider, at the 1929 Pendleton Round-Up. During the saddle bronc event, McCarrol was thrown from the horse and her foot hung up on a stirrup. The crowd watched in horror as she was dragged around the arena until the horse could be brought to a stop. When she died several days later at the Pendleton hospital, newspapers from around the country discussed the tragedy—and the propriety of women competing in rough-stock events. Until that point, cowgirls were rarely criticized for participating in dangerous events—instead they were praised for their courage and tenacity. Two years earlier, when Queen Mabel Strickland injured her hand in Pendleton during a roping event, the newspapers cheered her plucky attitude, writing that she continued with the steer until the job was finished, then waved a bloodstained hand at the audience and went to the hospital tent. McCarrol's death, however, seemed to unite the growing opposition to women riding bulls and broncs in open competition. Her death spelled the end for women to compete in rough-stock events in rodeos across the West.

The RAA was founded in 1929 to create standards of conduct within the rodeo. An important element in standardizing rodeo was to determine which events to include in all RAA-sanctioned rodeos and which ones not to include. The RAA did not sanction or prohibit women's bronc riding, that is, it was not included as one of the events required for RAA-approved rodeos. Rather, local rodeo committees were left to decide how or if they wanted to feature the event. When the RAA later increased the number of required events from four to eight, member rodeos began to include them all, usually at the expense of both locally popular contests and events for women. The RAA's decision did not lead to an immediate cessation of women's competition, but it encouraged a shift from open competition to hiring well-known cowgirl athletes as exhibition riders. The RAA's decision on women's rough-stock riding was also consistent with the changing attitudes toward women's role in rodeo. Cheyenne Frontier Days ended its long-standing tradition of women competing in rough-stock events in 1928, a year before the RAA was founded and before the tragedy of McCarrol's death.

Economic hardships during the Great Depression also played an instrumental role in limiting opportunities for women to compete in rodeo. For the most part, large rodeos did quite well during the Depression—people wanted entertainment and large rodeos could muster the financial backing to hold them. Smaller rodeos, or rodeos that were only marginally successful, were unable to continue, thus "depriving lower-echelon contestants of opportunities." Therefore, while top professional cowgirl athletes were still able to find work at the major rodeos, predominately as exhibition riders, the Depression reduced the number of overall opportunities, with amateur riders hardest hit.

The death of a famous rodeo queen, the founding of the RAA, and the Depression are all related through their common concern for the proper role for women. In one respect, they all addressed the question, Where do women belong? The major shift in attitudes toward acceptable behaviors and occupations for women that began in the 1880s and continued until the late 1920s was coming to an end. It had not been an easy or complete shift. It was more of a swing in the cultural pendulum, which, in its liberal arc, allowed women access into competitive events during rodeo's formative years. But the economic crisis in the late 1920s swung the pendulum back toward a resurgence of traditional gender roles.

The introduction of the sponsor contest in 1931 at the Texas Cowboy Reunion in Stamford, Texas, exemplified this shift away from serious athletic competition and into more "suitably feminine" roles. From its inception, the Stamford Texas sponsor contest embraced the larger cultural movement toward cultural conservatism, especially in terms of female domesticity, and was instrumental in redirecting the image of a cowgirl queen from one who could compete in contests that focused on usable cowhand skills to that of a beautiful socialite who competed for the title of queen in areas only marginally associated with ranching skills. The concept of a sponsor contest was quickly adopted by other rodeos throughout the region, which included West Texas, Oklahoma, and New Mexico.

In terms of helping the conservative trend along, sponsor girl contests dealt a serious blow to cowgirl athletes, whether they cared for bronc riding or not. The contest was a way of allowing women to compete, because cowgirl athletes had always competed in the arena. However, this contest emphasized appearance, regalia, and appearance of the horse, as well as riding ability. Conducting themselves with grace at social events held in their honor and answering questions by the press, the sponsor girls shifted the role of women away from the sport of cowgirl athletes and into a new direction, one that emphasized the role of promotional figurehead.

Sponsor girl articles typically featured a studio photo of the young woman, followed by a brief story discussing her family, accomplishments, and activities. Typical examples would be the following: "Elizabeth Bowyer rides for the recreation of it," and "Miss Mare Anne Green is a skillful and daring rider but is considered a very graceful dancer and one of the leaders in the younger social set." While the Texas Cowboy Reunion always insisted that the sponsor girls were top-notch riders, and a number did go on to compete in rodeos in the late 1940s, their riding skills were not given top billing and were often not mentioned at all. The changing attitude emphasized the girls' social position, reinforcing the importance of their amateur status as contestants and adherence to community standards of appropriate feminine behavior.

The shift did not go unnoticed by cowgirl athletes. Women who seriously rode as cowgirl athletes, professionally or as amateurs, were a community unto themselves and supported each other's efforts to be taken seriously. An example is seen in the support cowgirl athletes gave to one of their sisters, Isora DeRacy, who was widely recognized for her skills as a calf roper. Steer roping, the event that garnered Mabel Strickland so much fame, was gradually barred from rodeo. Citing the injury it caused to the steers, humane societies pressured most states to eliminate the event and replace it with calf roping. The shift from steer to calf roping was haphazard, and as the switch was made, rules on allowing women to compete in the calf-roping event were also anything but uniform. Calf roping became especially popular in Texas, where women who lived on ranches and roped calves as part of their regular ranch chores were most likely to find avenues to compete. Although not sanctioned by the RAA, cowgirl athletes were sometimes able to compete against cowboys, especially at small nonsanctioned local rodeos. Occasionally, special cowgirl "jackpot" or "challenge" contests were held in connection with larger, professional rodeos.

In rodeo, as in almost every aspect of life, World War II changed the rules. With men off to war, women were called upon to fight the war at home and to participate in society in ways that challenged existing gender expectations. The world of sports was no exception; women began to compete in sports that had either been off limits to them or had been available on a more limited scale.

Scholars generally agree that World War II was devastating to cowgirl athletes in their bid to continue as professional riders. Teresa Jordan writes, "In large part, women's rodeo became a casualty of the war: rodeo stock grew scarce as did transportation and resources. Rodeo producers found it hard to maintain two strings of broncs. There were far fewer women than men, so the producers cut the women's events." However, severely limiting opportunities for top professionals and eliminating lower-level competitors created a vacuum that amateur riders stepped in to fill. In effect, it was not so much the end of women competing as professionals as it was a change in the dynamics of women in the sport of rodeo.

It is difficult to say who held the very first all-girl rodeo. Jimmie Hurley writes, "Women refused to let their interest in rodeo die, continuing to compete on a local, unorganized basis. A group of girls in Texas might get together and compete against each other. Another group in Oklahoma or Arizona, unknown to the Texas girls, would get together to compete in roping and riding events." These informal gatherings were an important first step. The community of women who participated and supported these early all-girl rodeos helped pave the way for the acceptance of larger, well-organized all-girl rodeos that appeared during World War II.

During 1942 Pendleton and so many other rodeos called off their celebrations because of the war. That was also the year when Fay Kirkwood of Fort Worth, Texas, produced the first widely publicized rodeo at the Fannin County Fairgrounds in Bonham, Texas. Because so many cowboys were enlisted to fight the war and regular rodeos were on hold, women could do their part for the war effort by staging a rodeo, which would provide entertainment to soldiers and the community. The newspaper announcement of the rodeo was placed squarely in the middle of the war news. The headline "World's First All-Girl Rodeo to Begin Friday" was placed under the top two headlines, which read: "2 Axis Drives Stemmed Momentarily" and "42 Billion Dollar Bill for Army Reaches House," and surrounded on all sides by news on London, German paratroopers, and the need for more planes. There was even a special rodeo event to pay tribute to the war effort, the article noting, "The program for

the rodeo itself will consist of the cowgirls' drilling a 'V for Victory' formation."

The opening day featured, among other events, "sponsor girls from every town in North Texas" and a "special contest for the sponsor girls and amateur riders." A subtle but important distinction was being made here between sponsor girls—the young women selected by their towns who could ride a horse tolerably well and for whom this might be their only foray into sponsor contests—and amateur riders—the girls sponsored by a town or ranch who competed regularly in sponsor events throughout the region.

At the first all-girl rodeo, perhaps it is not too surprising that it was not as "all-girl" as later ones would be. Half of the rodeo committee was made up of men, and event number 13 was "Presenting as Special Guest—The Only Cowboy to take part in the All-Girl Rodeo," although what that part might be was not revealed. The rodeo also conformed more closely to how professional rodeo defined women's events, with exhibition events rather than women competing in open competition as the men did. For example, of the seventeen events, which included everything from the Grand Entry to the Final V for Victory Formation, only the bulldogging and the sponsor contest were not advertised as exhibition events. For the rest of the events, 15 professional riders entertained the crowd with an assortment of skills. Nevertheless, the rodeo was well attended, women were able to compete, and Fay Kirkwood made plans to hold another rodeo.

LeCompte writes, "Kirkwood was unaware that many of the local cowgirls really wanted to compete in the professional contests, apparently assuming they were satisfied with the sponsor contest. Some of them must have discussed this with her, because her later rodeo included more contests, with the professional events opened to all who wished to compete." Kirkwood did hold two more rodeos. Although no extant information on the second rodeo exists, her last rodeo was held in Wichita Falls, Texas, again with the intent of providing entertainment for the servicemen stationed there. Mary Ellen "Dude" Barton was one of the amateur riders who took advantage of the chance to compete in the other events. A sponsor girl for the Matador Ranch and a frequent competitor in sponsor events around the area, she did very well. Barton's hometown paper announced, "No one in this section, familiar with Miss Barton's rope and saddle ability, was surprised when she returned home with about everything Wichita Falls had on its prize list. . . . To match her with the average satin and gabardine riding girl left the outcome a 'forgone conclusion.'"

Vaughn Kreig, arena director for Kirkwood's rodeo, produced the second all-girl rodeo later that year. A champion cowgirl in her own right, she and her husband produced rodeos at their ranch in Fort Towson, Oklahoma. Kreig's program was more forcefully patriotic than Kirkwood's. The front page of the newspaper read, "The All-Cowgirl Rodeo is formed with the idea of entertainment for our fighting forces. With women taking part in all branches of war work, to the front came the cowgirls riding to the strains of martial music, the American flag held high, and the show is on! The cowgirl's dream a reality. Keep 'Em Flying! Keep 'Em Rolling! Buy War Bonds and Stamps! And On to VICTORY!"

Vaughn Kreig rounded up the top rodeo stars for her rodeo; half of the contestants also participated in Kirkwood's rodeo. But here, 8 out of the 19 listed events were contests. Although advertised as a way to entertain troops, it was clearly organized as a vehicle for women to seriously compete in the arena. In a promotional flyer produced by Kreig, she wrote, "This show was organized because the cowgirls' riding events have been discontinued in the present day rodeos, and as the girls love the rodeo as a sport, love their horses, and have the rodeo spirit, their thought was to form their own rodeo, where they could demonstrate their ability and skill in riding and roping, as well as the other roped events such as Bronc Riding, Bulldogging, Calf Roping, Brahma Bull Riding, Trick Riding, Etc."

The Flying V events included a sponsor contest as well. There was the customary review of the sponsors, but the producers made a point in stating that the horsemanship element—a flag race—would be a timed event. This was an important step in breaking with the tradition of having the entire sponsor subjectively judged.

Neither Kirkwood's nor Kreig's rodeos had rodeo queens. It is quite likely that because these rodeos were held in the same region where sponsor contests proliferated, the producers continued to use sponsors as a means of promoting their rodeo. It is also possible that the exclusion of a rodeo queen was a form of protest against the role of rodeo queens in general. The perception among cowgirl athletes was that queen contests were, if not crooked, then seriously misguided; they did not emphasize the true importance of rodeo—the cowgirl athletes—as much as they did the

lovely daughters of local boosters. At these all-girl rodeos, all attention was focused on the riders. With top performers coming to town and women promoters rallying town support for their rodeo, who needed a "satin and gabardine riding girl" to advertise the show?

One year before the end of World War II, rodeos around the country came back, and came back big. The defense industry in the West had boosted the economy, and people had money in their pockets, but with durable goods and new housing still severely limited, people were eager to spend their money on whatever was available, including entertainment. Rodeos in Pendleton, Oregon, Cheyenne, Wyoming, and the Texas Cowboy Reunion in Stamford, Texas, to name a few, had record attendance. If cowgirl athletes expected to be welcomed back into the arena, however, they were in for a disappointment. The mood of the country was decidedly more conservative than ever; in the postwar rodeo, the main role for women was as promotional figureheads, not athletes. While wartime efforts suggested a possibility of expanding, or at least maintaining, the inroads women had made during the war, they found themselves excluded from the rodeo arena once again, as mainstream American culture moved toward traditional gender expectations.

In 1947 sponsor contests and the occasional calf-roping contest were the only opportunities open for women to compete. It was in this climate that the third major all-girl rodeo made its debut when two West Texas cowgirls, 25-year-old Nancy Binford and 19-year-old Thena Mae Farr, decided to hold an all-girl rodeo. When they created the Tri-State All-Girl Rodeo, they set about to reshape the meaning of the term "rodeo queen" into one that was representative of their cowgirl community but still acceptable to the conservative social norms of mainstream American society.

In an ironic twist, the sponsor contests that originated at the Texas Cowboy Reunion provided the springboard for amateur cowgirl athletes to get back into the ring as serious competitors. These frequently held contests gave women who were seriously interested in competing a chance to get together and develop friendships and a sense of community. At the Texas Cowboy Reunion, the years 1945 through 1947 saw the largest number of ranch sponsors—half of the total number of young women entered. While competing at various sponsor contests, the cowgirl athletes could discuss the relative merits of such contests;

a common complaint noted in one newspaper was that "some of the cowgirls denounced as 'crooked' many sponsor contests where judging is done on riding, girl's appearance, etc." The sponsor contest also gave women like Binford and Farr experience in public relations, which proved useful as they worked to establish their own rodeo.

Binford and Farr were aware that the town of Amarillo was looking for some sort of community event. As Binford recalled, "We talked to the Chamber of Commerce in Amarillo and they said if we thought it was possible, that they would let us put on an all-girl rodeo and see if it would be successful during their state fair." With the approval of the Chamber behind them, Binford and Farr set about to organize the rodeo. When asked in a 1985 interview if she was worried that there would not be enough women to compete in the events, Binford replied, "Oh no—we had asked many girls just to be sure that we would have enough to produce the rodeo. We had eight ropers out the first day and some of them had never thrown a rope in an arena, and there wasn't a calf missed. They were real excited about it, and it turned out real well."

Getting support from their cowgirl community was one task; promoting the rodeo to the public was another. Their experiences as sponsor girls were key for their success in promoting the Tri-State All-Girl Rodeo. Kathy Willis writes, "Basking in the media savvy they learned as beauty queens, Nancy and Thena Mae . . . attracted the attention of the press." And press coverage was extensive. There was, of course, concern over how the public would receive their rodeo. As one newspaper reported, "The rodeo will feature all of the 'rough and ready' events familiar to rodeo fans, except girls will be in the saddle." It was important to both Binford and Farr that the rodeo encouraged their community of riders with traditional rodeo events but without alienating the general public with fears of unwomanly women. After all, they needed paying spectators; this rodeo, like all rodeos, needed to be a financial success.

Photos, interviews, and newspaper clippings depicted the cowgirl athletes as western women in the truest sense—they roped calves, rode bucking broncs, some even rode bulls. But according to the reports, they accomplished these feats looking like ladies. The papers not only described the appearance of the women, but also reported on the personal lives of Binford, Farr, and other cowgirl athletes, describing their after-rodeo hobbies, interests, and family.

One paper reported that "after a day in the arena, [cowgirls] went home to cook dinner for the family, work a little needlepoint, or maybe on a Friday night, get dressed up for a night on the town." This emphasis on femininity and domesticity in postwar print quite likely helped to reassure readers that, to use Susan Cahn's words, "conventional gender distinctions and heterosexuality remained intact even as women competed successfully in work, politics, or sports." This was especially important for a sport like all-girl rodeo that advertised that women would participate in "all the events that made up the best of male rodeos."

Binford was apparently aware of the perceived contradiction between womanly behavior—concern with appearance, femininity, and motherhood—and rodeo. In an article titled "Performers Prove Beauty and Rodeo Can Be Mixed," Binford is quoted as saying, "Look at little Jeanette Campbell. She got married, and now has a baby boy. She'll be here for this show. There are others, too." Reporters also alerted readers about which of the cowgirls were still in the marriage market, noting, as this article did, that not only was Binford an accomplished rider, but "by the way—she is good-lookin' and single, guys."

The Tri-State All-Girl Rodeo, while designed to allow women to compete in traditional events, kept the sponsor contest. Binford and Farr used their position as producers, however, to change a few of the rules of the sponsor contest that, as sponsor contestants themselves, they considered unfair and unnecessary. They eliminated the cowgirl regalia portion of the contest and they also ended the practice of having a panel of male judges subjectively evaluate how the women rode around the barrels. Instead, the contest was objectively evaluated—timed—and the woman who completed the pattern with the fastest time won.

The Tri-State All-Girl Rodeo filled the definition of all-girl rodeo more completely than had any other. With the exception of the announcer, all contestants, judges, promoters, and staff supporters were women. And it was a huge success. Standing-room-only crowds cheered cowgirls as they competed in bareback riding, calf roping, sponsor contest, cutting, team tying, saddle bronc riding, steer riding, and an exhibition bulldogging performance. The newspapers described it as a "knockout," and said that "Nancy and Thena Mae continued to produce the rodeo until both returned to competitive rodeo in 1951." At the Tri-State All-Girl Rodeo there were no social events—no teas, luncheons, or formal dances. At this rodeo, to wear the title of "queen" required champion rider status.

Encouraged by the success of the rodeo, 23 of the cowgirl contestants met immediately afterwards and organized the Girls Rodeo Association (GRA), now known as the Women's Professional Rodeo Association. The newspapers reported, "The main purpose is to standardize rodeo rules applying to girl contestants, and to eliminate unfair practices." Perhaps the most important decision made at the first meeting concerned the sponsor contest; the association stated that it "intended to bar cowgirl sponsor contests from Rodeo Cowboy Association and Girls Rodeo Association-approved rodeos except where it is made a timed event." The Flying V rodeo had insisted on timing its sponsor contest, but with the formation of the GRA, the organization was able to enforce the practice, turning the event into a strictly athletic contest.

GRA members also dropped the regalia portion of the sponsor contest. No longer would the contest be split between clothing and appearance and ability to ride. However, the women recognized the importance of image. According to GRA rules, women participating in GRA-sanctioned contests "had to ride in the opening parades and always be dressed in colorful attire when they appear in the arena." The emphasis on image extended to include ideas of correct feminine behavior as well. According to the 1949 rulebook, sanctions would be applied to members who swore in the arena, drank publicly on the rodeo grounds, or behaved in an otherwise unladylike manner.

The changes in the riding portion of the sponsor contest, initiated by Binford and Farr and adopted by the GRA, were felt throughout the rodeo world, especially in terms of legitimizing the riding portion of the sponsor contest. The changes were key elements for women to spring back into serious rodeo competition. By discarding the subjective elements and focusing on an objective evaluation of horsemanship, the sponsor contest became what is known today as barrel racing, a highly competitive, lucrative, and popular event in professional rodeo.

As members of the sponsor girl generation, Binford and Farr used their public relations experiences to challenge the meaning of rodeo queen and make it their own, but with a conscious effort to assure the public that they were regular women who liked the opportunity to take the skills they learned and used on

their ranches and compete for recognition. They emphasized the fact that they were not social oddities, but normal women who could participate in normal society as wives, mothers, and daughters, as well as compete in rodeos. The efforts of Binford and Farr helped reestablish the distinction between "satin and gabardine riders" as queens and cowgirl athletes competing in the sport of rodeo.

In the long run, the legacy of their effort to reinstate the early definition of rodeo queen was ambiguous. On one hand, the definition of rodeo queen, so self-consciously developed among the community of riders, did not take hold among the general public. Despite their efforts to prove to audiences that the cowgirls were regular women just using their home-grown skills to compete in the arena, their riding was just a little too far from the norm for the conservative postwar era. It could be that, like the rodeo queens they sought to emulate from the 1920s, the cowgirl athletes in the 1940s rode a little beyond the pale. On the other hand, Binford and Farr were able to get women back in the arena to compete in traditional rodeo events. The Women's Professional Rodeo Association continues to support all-girl rodeos and women athletes in the sport.

—Renee M. Laegreid

SUGGESTED READINGS

Jordan, Theresa. *Cowgirls: Women of the American West.* Garden City, NY: Anchor Press, 1982.

LeCompte, Mary Lou. *Cowgirls of the Rodeo: Pioneer Professional Athletes.* Urbana: University of Illinois Press, 1993.

Stoeltje, Beverly. *Females in Rodeo: Private Motivation and Public Representation.* Kentucky Folklore Record 32 n.1-2 (1986): 46.

Wills, Kathy Lynn, and Virginia Artho. *Cowgirl Legends from the Cowgirl Hall of Fame.* Salt Lake City, UT: Gibbs-Smith, 1995.

ANZALDUA, GLORIA E. (1942-)

Originating from humble surroundings in the Southwest, Gloria E. Anzaldua propelled herself into contemporary intellectual scholarship by intertwining her lesbian-feminist ideals into a cultural examination of the Chicano community. Anzaldua incorporates the socially oppressive obstacles that she encountered while developing her feminist-Chicana-lesbian identity into her cultural studies, which has developed as her interpretative signature. As a result, she efficiently characterizes the multilayered identification complexities of being a woman of color in contemporary western society. Her most comprehensive work, *Borderlands/La Frontera: The New Mestiza* (picked as one of the best 38 books of 1984 by *Literary Journal*) interconnects her gender and cultural theories with an introspective historical backdrop of the American Southwest. Anzaldua includes her feminist-Chicana-lesbian identity and ideals into her writing in order to show the socially oppressive obstacles that she and many others have struggled with. As a western author, Anzaldua has influenced western feminism, Chicano/a studies, cultural and ethnic studies, and queer theory. Furthermore, she has developed herself as an intellectual Chicana forerunner theorizing, describing, and attempting to break down the oppressive social barriers that Chicanas, lesbians, and feminists are burdened with in contemporary western society.

On September 26, 1942, Anzaldua's mother gave birth to her on a ranch in the Valley of South Texas. This ranch resembled so many others that her family worked on in order to survive in the migrant farming frontier of the Southwest. Her father saw the importance in education and realized that his four children could not achieve adequate scholastic achievement by migrating each season. The family settled in Hargill, Texas, and shortly afterwards her father abruptly died. Anzaldua, only 15 at the time, had to consistently labor in the fields to survive through this tremulous period. She worked in harsh conditions with her family throughout her high school and undergraduate career. At this time, she began to encounter the oppressive Chicano gender roles that she later describes in her scholarship. In 1969 she earned her bachelor's degree from Pan American University and relinquished the rigorous conditions of the fields. She left the rural community and acquired her M.A. in Education and English 3 years later from the University of Texas. Her distressing adolescent and young adult experiences in the Chicano agricultural communities of the Southwest exposed her to the oppressive gendered roles that she later rebelled against and implemented into her theoretic literature.

The social roles that Anzaldua struggled with early on were the repressive gender roles that ran throughout the Chicano community. The community at this time believed that women belonged at home, in the fields, or performing domestic services to provide a supplemental family income. They definitely did not belong in higher education, where Anzaldua's aspirations lay. She realized the need to break loose from these oppressive barriers during her adolescent development. As a result, she found herself theoretically conflicting with her mother on a variety of culturally established female roles. Her mother also believed in the outlined gendered roles instilled upon the community for generations, which characterized women as childbearing caretakers who have little education but excel in domestic working environments. Anzaldua escaped her exhausting work and conflicting social sentiment by indulging herself in reading, writing, art, and poetry. Her mother, stricken with old-fashioned attitudes, frowned upon Anzaldua's newly discovered escape as laziness and/or weakness. This newfound love for art and literature guided her on a path out of the farming community and into an urban learning environment, where she openly challenged her Chicana role and found her identity as a feminist-Chicana-lesbian.

Anzaldua's exodus from the South Valley of Texas had significant implications for her identity and career. She emerged as the first person to attend college in her rural farming community. The acquisition of her degrees signified that Chicanas of low socioeconomic status could achieve scholastic success. Thus, she denounced the previously conceived cultural and gender roles that her family and community tried to instill upon her and developed an opposite identity as a self-proclaimed "Chicana Dyke." Nevertheless, leaving her established rural habitat for a multiracial urban learning environment left her socially marginalized and oppressed by the predominately Anglo-American community.

During her graduate career at the University of Texas, she collided with an Anglo-American student body and faculty that marginalized her due to her overambitious scholastic interest. She possessed a strong thirst for literature and knowledge outside the designated curriculum that many professors and advisers did not support. Furthermore, her pursuit of a field still in its adolescent stage of development (Chicano Studies), compounded with her profeminist and lesbian ideals, facilitated her further alienation from the academic community. Once again, she stood at the edge of a community's social composition and felt oppressed due to her differing identity and ideals. She enrolled in the comparative literature program at the university after receiving her M.A. She patiently waited for her chance to pursue a theoretical dissertation focused on Chicano or Feminist Studies. Unfortunately, the conservative professors never approved her radical dissertation topics, and she decided to leave the program to further her self-education without the restraints of an unsupportive community in 1977. At this time, she refined her feminist-Chicana-lesbian identity that was subsequently reflected in her literature. In 1979 she emerged at the University of California, Santa Cruz, where she lectured and found a more receptive curriculum. San Francisco State University and Vermont College also invited her to lecture as the feminist and Chicano audience began to proliferate.

Anzaldua discusses at length the impact that writing had on her personal and spiritual development. She strongly believes that writing is the love of her life and that it fills a void that she cannot find anywhere else. Her intellectual literature is fueled by her anger toward the oppressive atmospheres that she encountered while developing and sustaining her feminist-Chicana-lesbian identity. This angry fire that burns within her is exemplified throughout her major compositions as she intertwines her repressed interpersonal identity to depict the complexity of being a women of color in contemporary society.

In *This Bridge Called My Back: Writings by Radical Women of Color,* she joins forces with coeditor and contributing author, Cherrie Moraga. Anzaldua contributes two articles, "La Prieta" and "Speaking in Tongues: A Letter to 3rd World Writers." "La Prieta," meaning "The Dark One," is an autobiographical piece that recounts the oppressive gender roles she struggled with in the Chicano community. She illustrates the interpersonal turmoil she endured while in the process of uncovering her true identity as a freethinking Chicana lesbian. Her family responded negatively because it exposed their private lives and Anzaldua's previously hidden lesbian sexuality. Also, "La Prieta" publicized the oppressive gender roles within the Chicano community. "Speaking in Tongues" is her call for a new methodological approach for feminist-minority writers. She believes that the subject's contemporary literature is burdened with an old approach stricken with objectivity, which she feels clouds the

author interpretation. Furthermore, she describes the necessity to mix theoretical genres to produce effective contemporary interpretations. This approach is exemplified in her principal piece, *Borderlands/ La Frontera.*

In *Cuentos: Stories by Latinas,* Anzaldua collaborates with Cherrie Morgan, Alma Gomez, and Mariana Romo-Carmona to produce a volume that attempts to capture the Chicana's true feminist identity and sentiment that is unique from their Anglo-American counterparts. Anzaldua contributes a fictional narrative titled "El Paisano Is a Bird of Good Omen" that describes a Chicana's turmoil to expose her gay identity. This short story exemplifies the difficulty Chicanas face when trying to express their identities in the midst of being trapped within rigid gender roles. Anzaldua effectively illustrates the narrative from her past experiences, and once again she imposes her personalized familiarity into her writings to show the multilayered complexities of being a women of color in contemporary society.

Last, Anzaldua independently developed a theoretically rich and socially comprehensive volume titled *Borderlands/La Frontera: The New Mestiza.* It rigorously examines Chicanos in Anglo-American society, female gender roles within the Chicano community, and lesbians in a heterosexual world. Once again, she recounts her oppressive past as a vehicle to convey the emotional rage that burns within her. This cultural interpretation sets aside objectivity in order to compound the study with a variety of scholastic fields. Anzaldua intertwines her autobiographic account with philosophy, history, theory, and sociolinguistics. Her article "Speaking in Tongues" previously outlined this new methodological approach, and she cleverly delivers it in her first autonomous volume.

Borderlands is divided into two sections. The first section, "Atrevesando Fronteras/Crossing Borders," consists of seven independent essays that develop a unique interpretation of the Chicana in the Southwest. The second section, "Un Agitado Viento/ Ehecatl, the Wing," is comprised of a series of poems that further describe the hardships Chicanas endure when developing their independent identities. "Crossing Borders" facilitates the new methodological approach to depict the crossing of physical, mental, and spiritual borders in the Southwest. The first chapter of the section primarily discusses the historiography of the borderland region between San Diego, California, and Brownsville, Texas, while implanting her autobiographic insight. The subsequent essays deal heavily with the theoretical and philosophical aspects of crossing linguistic, spiritual, and mental borders. For example, "How to Tame a Wild Tongue" investigates the linguistic barriers that Chicanos face in contemporary society. She says that Anglo-Americans discriminate against Chicano Spanish, and as a result it can hinder socioeconomic advancement or even oppress a child's Chicano identity. Furthermore, she ventures out into deep theoretic territory in her explanation of a new mestiza consciousness in "La conciencia de la mestiza/ Towards a New Consciousness." Anzaldua theorizes on the development of a contemporary Chicana identity that crosses a series of abstract and spiritual borders that will evolve into a new cultural and gendered consciousness for Chicanas.

"Crossing Borders" is intellectually complex, with an abundant amount of philosophy and theory that congests and clutters the clarity of her interpretation. Also, she uses a variety of languages that further facilitates the difficulty of the text. Nevertheless, the poems that formulate "Ehecatl, the Wing" are written extremely lucidly. They paint vividly violent pictures of the oppressive environment that many Chicanas encounter in the West. Anzaldua's paramount work describes the oppressive Chicana world that she encountered. It is compounded with an insightful amount of philosophy and theory; as a result, she produces a theoretically rich volume that investigates vital Hispanic cultural aspects. Even though the text is sometimes difficult, she innovatively illustrates the gendered and cultural differences that many Chicanas struggle with in their pursuit to develop their individualized identities.

Anzaldua has established herself as an intellectual 20th century author who strongly reflects her feminist-Chicana-lesbian identity throughout her writing. Her endeavors have tackled crucial cultural issues that opened new fields of research. Moreover, her work has affected a number of contemporary academic fields. She has received a number of distinguished awards, such as the Lambda Lesbian Small Book Press Award, NEA Fiction Award, Before Columbus Foundation American Book Award, and the Sappho Award of Distinction. Anzaldua currently resides in Santa Cruz, California, where she diligently works on future projects while still lecturing at universities and conferences nationwide.

—Alonso Quezada

SUGGESTED READING

Calderon, Hector, and Jose David Saldivar. *Criticism in the Borderlands.* Durham, NC: Duke University Press, 1991.

ARIZONA POLITICAL WOMEN

Arizona's early history usually conjures up images of mining camps, saloons, gunslingers, cowboys, and Indians—a decidedly male environment. However, a closer look reveals that women played an important role in the development of Arizona, especially in the field of politics. Women's participation in politics began when Arizona was still a territory, rooted in local temperance and suffrage movements.

The first territorial legislature convened in 1864, but Arizona remained sparsely populated, with few Anglo female residents, until the U.S. Army had removed most of the nomadic tribal population to reservations in the 1870s. Soon after white farmers, miners, and ranchers started moving to Arizona, woman's suffrage became an issue. A Mormon attorney from Prescott, Murat Masterson, introduced the first suffrage bill in the territorial legislature in 1881. However, at the time, anti-Mormon sentiment in Arizona was strong. Members of the Church of Jesus Christ of Latter-Day Saints were supporters of a woman's right to vote, but most early woman's suffrage leaders were evangelical Baptists and Methodists who were unwilling to include the Mormons in their campaign because they did not want to be associated with the polygamous practices of some Mormons. Although both Mormons and suffragists were supporters of both temperance and suffrage, they did not work together in the early territorial years.

In the 1880s, a small group of evangelical women in Tucson led by Josephine Brawley Hughes began the first temperance organization in the territory. Hughes helped to fund and build the first Methodist church in Tucson, and in 1884 she invited Frances Willard, president of the National Women's Christian Temperance Union (WCTU), to help organize a territorial WCTU. The Arizona WCTU met with only limited success in obtaining its goals of eliminating drinking, gambling, and vice in the territory, so leaders like Hughes quickly became convinced that women needed the vote to become more effective. Hughes resigned as president of the Arizona WCTU to take up the leadership of the suffrage movement in 1891. Many other woman suffrage leaders, including Pauline O'Neill (the widow of Spanish-American War hero and Populist politician William "Buckey" O'Neill) and Frances Willard Munds (a relative of Frances Willard), came over from the WCTU to hold positions of leadership in the fledgling Arizona suffrage movement.

The first formal suffrage organization was formed in Arizona in 1891 when Laura Johns, a field worker for the National American Woman Suffrage Association (NAWSA), arrived to organize women in the territory and named Josephine Brawley Hughes president. Hughes and a small group of female activists lobbied the legislature while it met in the winter in Phoenix. Although suffrage amendments were introduced annually in the territorial legislature, they met with repeated failure. Many politicians working to prepare Arizona for statehood knew that extending the vote to women could double the Mormon vote, which in the 1890s still seemed a risky proposal if Arizona wanted to obtain congressional approval for statehood. As it turned out, key congressional leaders believed Arizona did not have sufficient schools, resources, or population to warrant statehood, so neither statehood nor suffrage were achieved at this time. However, suffrage leaders used this negative national image of Arizona as a backward place to bolster their own cause, arguing that if women were allowed to vote, they would support the educational and social reform measures necessary to allow Arizona to join the union.

In 1901 Frances Willard Munds assumed the leadership of the Arizona suffrage association, vowing to reach out to Mormon leaders, to enlist women to improve education, and to combat drunk and disorderly behavior in the territory. She was born in Sacramento, California, and grew up on a ranch in Nevada. While attending a Baptist boarding school in Maine, the petite redhead developed an independent streak and was dubbed the Nevada Wild Cat by her classmates. While she was away at school, her father, who was suffering from tuberculosis, began to move his cattle and family to Arizona in search of a better climate. He died en route, but his sons continued the journey with the herd and settled in the Cottonwood region.

Frances's life was dedicated to the twin causes of temperance and suffrage. Her mother, Mary Grace Willard, was a Baptist, an ardent suffragist and temperance advocate, and a crucial early influence in Frances's life. When Frances finished her eastern education in 1885, she joined her family in Arizona and taught in Jerome, a booming mining town. Her schoolroom was a former saloon and was located between two operating saloons. She quickly tired of the drunks who paraded through her classroom, and she finally quit when two students drew knives during an argument in her class and the school board refused her request to expel them.

Shortly after her marriage to John Munds, a rancher and sheriff in Yavapai County, Frances joined Prescott's Monday Club, the first woman's club of Arizona, where she met Pauline O'Neill. The two women shared an interest in both temperance and suffrage. O'Neill, a Catholic, was born in 1865 at the Presidio in San Francisco. Her father, a career army office, was transferred to Fort Whipple near Prescott around 1884, where Pauline worked as a teacher until her marriage to O'Neill in 1885.

Unlike Josephine Brawley Hughes and the early members of Arizona's suffrage movement, Munds and O'Neill welcomed Mormon women into the new Arizona Equal Suffrage Association they led in the early 1900s. Munds's first teaching position had been among Mormon families in the communities of Pine and Payson, Arizona, where she came to admire their hardworking and law-abiding ways. Also, by 1900, anti-Mormon sentiment in the Arizona territory had subsided considerably with the resolution of the polygamy issue. Munds invited Mormon women to hold formal positions in the organization, and worked with Mormon legislators to introduce and support suffrage bills. At least 14 of the 32 Arizona Equal Suffrage Association Campaign Committee members were Mormons. The legislature came under increasing pressure from this united group to address the suffrage issue.

In 1903 a suffrage bill passed in both houses of the Twenty-Second Legislature, but victory quickly evaporated when the governor, Alexander Brodie, a Republican appointee, vetoed the bill. Publicly, Brodie stated he believed the bill was unconstitutional. Privately, he told colleagues that he feared it would give Mormons control of territorial government. The suffrage movement in Arizona was devastated and disbanded as a result of the veto, but leaders had learned a valuable lesson: any chance for future victory would depend on the creation of a larger constituency beyond the Mormon and evangelical reform elements of the territory. Although NAWSA would continue to send workers to the territory, local leaders refused to reengage in the battle until 1909, when Arizona's political leaders once again began to prepare for a constitutional convention and statehood.

In 1909 suffrage leaders implemented a new strategy that included the growing labor movement in the territory. The presence of a large copper mining industry in Arizona demanded the labor of both skilled and unskilled mine workers. Many skilled miners in the territory joined the Western Federation of Miners, considered a radical advocate of industrial socialism. Munds quickly established a strong relationship with many of the territory's most prominent labor leaders, a tactic that would prove vital to the success of the suffrage movement. By 1909, as Arizona once again approached a statehood drive, suffrage women were forging ties with labor unions, promising female support of labor legislation in exchange for labor's support of suffrage.

NAWSA responded to the growing statehood movement in Arizona and sent veteran suffrage organizer and labor advocate Laura Gregg of Kansas to tour the territory during the fall and winter months of 1909 and 1910. Gregg found especially receptive audiences in the Mormon and mining counties of the territory. She stood on soap boxes on the street corners of mining towns like Bisbee and Morenci, exhorting miners to support a woman's right to vote. Her relations with local unions were exceptionally warm; in fact, she married the leader of Arizona's Western Federation of Miners, Joseph Cannon, while they were campaigning for suffrage together.

As the summer of 1910 approached, Labor Party candidates were gaining such popularity in Arizona that they threatened to control the statehood convention. Democrats quickly adopted most of the Labor Party's platform and elected many pro-Labor delegates to the convention. The Arizona Equal Suffrage Association deluged the convention with petitions and speakers, hoping to include suffrage in the new state constitution. Munds presided over the hearing on woman suffrage. Pauline O'Neill argued that women should not be taxed without representation, while other suffragists argued that women voters would erase the state's poor image by supporting legislation to improve schools and social welfare services. It was Ernest J. Liebel of the Labor Party, however, who finally said what was on the minds of suffragists and political leaders when he warned politicians that

women voters would eventually turn antisuffrage men out of office.

Despite these extensive public hearings and efforts by women leaders, suffrage was defeated at the convention by a vote of 30 to 19. Many delegates, including convention president George W. P. Hunt, feared that woman suffrage was "a dangerous and radical thing" to include in the state constitution, and it might jeopardize Arizona's chances for statehood with a Congress not inclined toward suffrage. Also, although Hunt was a close friend of Munds and O'Neill and an ardent suffrage supporter, he believed an issue of this magnitude should not be settled by elected officials, but by the public as an initiative or referendum. Statehood was achieved in 1912, but the women of Arizona still lacked the vote, so women made plans to put the issue before the male voters of the new state.

When the first state legislature met in 1912, newly elected Governor George W. P. Hunt was bombarded with requests and petitions from suffragists to recommend a suffrage amendment to the new constitution. Hunt obliged them in his message to the first state legislature. A suffrage referendum passed in the House, but failed by one vote in the Senate. Once again, the legislature could not bring itself to give women the vote. Subsequently, Munds and O'Neill launched an initiative campaign in the summer of 1912 to collect the 3,342 signatures required by state law to place an initiative on the November ballot. For 6 weeks over 50 Arizona male and female volunteers, many of whom belonged to the Socialist Party, canvassed the state without the assistance of NAWSA. The petition drive was successful and the ballot went before the male voters of the state that fall.

The fall campaign concentrated on turning out the vote in the Mormon counties and winning the endorsement of labor unions and the political parties. By election day, Munds had secured the support of 95% of the labor unions in the state, including the Western Federation of Miners, the American Federation of Labor, and the United Mine Workers of America. Labor's contribution to the campaign in 1912 is undeniable. With the weight of the labor unions behind suffrage, the political parties were forced to reassess their positions on suffrage. When the state Progressive Party came out in favor of suffrage in the fall of 1912, Munds and O'Neill went before the Democratic and Republican conferences, telling leadership they would throw the support of all women voters behind the Progressive Party if the two main parties refused to cooperate. Pressure from the labor unions and the popular Progressive Party forced Democratic and Republican Party leaders to reluctantly support suffrage.

Sixty-eight percent of Arizona voters supported the suffrage initiative on the 1912 ballot, the largest popular victory in the country at the time. As expected, support was highest in the Mormon counties of the state, but every county returned a majority for the amendment, including the mining counties where labor leaders were effective in converting miners to suffrage. Women's leaders like Munds were thrilled, but did not believe their work was done. They believed that this election was a mandate from the male voters of the state for women to enter mainstream politics not just as voters but as politicians as well.

During the drive for statehood, suffrage leaders promised that women voters would bring respectability to Arizona by supporting political reform measures, labor legislation, and laws to improve schools, libraries, and other state institutions. These women indicated that they were interested in running for office as alternatives to male candidates, because the men of Arizona had not sufficiently represented the interests of women and children. They promised that if women were elected to the legislature, they would ensure that Arizona would have protective labor legislation equal to any other state. Suffrage leaders like O'Neill and Munds had learned many political strategies during their campaign—aligning with labor, working with Mormon leaders, trading votes in the legislature—and now were anxious to use those skills in achieving a women's agenda for public office. In other words, they were anxious to engage in the kind of "grubby" politics that women in many other states abhorred. Politicized by the suffrage battles, large numbers of women ran for county, legislative, and state office from 1914 to 1950, but they often had to do so without the blessings of the state's political parties.

The state's political parties were quick to welcome female voters to their rosters but failed to incorporate women as party officials. Unlike most other states, Arizona's Democrats and Republicans did not implement the 50-50 rule, granting women equal representation on party committees. From 1914 to the late 1920s, women rarely attained positions on party committees and, therefore, had little to say about the direction of the parties. When women leaders tried to organize and rally females to partisan causes, newspaper editors and male political leaders ridiculed them and accused them of becoming political bosses to women. Many women interested in political campaigns were veterans of the suffrage battle, but they remained bitter, distrustful, and angry toward male Democratic and Republican leaders who had repeatedly blocked suffrage in the legislature, so most turned away from the male-dominated parties and turned to female organizations as platforms for running for office and for pushing women's issues.

The two major women's organizations in the state, the Arizona Federation of Women's Clubs (AFWC) and the Arizona Federation of Business and Professional Women's Clubs (Arizona BPW), became the two most important agencies for promoting women in politics. Many women candidates developed leadership skills and legislative knowledge from their work within these organizations. In addition, the Arizona BPW clubs actively recruited women to run for office in the state, so a majority of county and state female candidates were members of these organizations.

The Arizona BPW became the dominant voice for political women in the state shortly after its formation in 1919. Its leaders were deeply committed to equality for women in the workplace and did not believe that males could adequately represent women's interests in government, so they actively recruited and supported women candidates for county, legislative, and state office. This organization provided the funding and moral support for female candidates found lacking in most other states and at the federal level, and created a pool of qualified female candidates who had the potential to win public office. Many of the organization's top leaders, including its founder, C. Louise Boehringer, ran for office. These women ran to represent women and children, but also often had experience in business, so they were able to tackle all issues they faced as public officials, blurring the line between male and female politicians.

From 1920 until 1950, the Arizona BPW was also involved in sustained battles to expand the rights of women in Arizona. They boosted the political involvement of women by encouraging them to register and vote and by preparing them for their new rights of citizenship. Foremost among these, they believed, was the right of women to serve on juries. These businesswomen understood they could not receive a fair trial, criminal or civil, if women did not serve as jurors. The Arizona BPW worked for 10 years to get the state legislature to allow women on juries, and was finally successful in 1945. This group also spearheaded campaigns to eliminate economic discrimination against working women and to pass the Equal Rights Amendment and equal pay laws. The Arizona BPW not only lobbied for these issues but also made sure they had their own members in the legislature to introduce the bills in the first place.

The Arizona BPW often recruited members with clerical or educational backgrounds to run for county office. The vast majority, 69%, of professional women in Arizona worked as teachers, but many school districts barred married women from teaching. However, married women were eligible for positions as county school superintendents and, therefore, found running for office a way to continue working after marriage. But the job was not easy in sparsely populated frontier Arizona. County school superintendents logged long hours on Arizona roads to inspect schools, fill vacancies on school boards, and conduct exams for teaching certificates. Gwyneth Ham, a divorced woman with a young child, was appointed as school superintendent in Yuma County in 1942 and served until 1969. Ham kept a complete automobile repair kit in her car for the frequent drives over rough desert terrain in the northern part of her county. Bessie Kidd Best, who served as Coconino County school superintendent from 1928 to 1973, drove an average of 10,000 miles a year on official business during her first 3 years in office while visiting the rural schools spread out over the 18,623 square miles of her county. These women were often deeply committed to improving the county school system, and became well-respected figures in local government, often supervising the growth of the state's schools as they transitioned from rural one-room buildings to large, modern school districts.

Women also ran for positions that required clerical skills, including county clerk and recorder. Because the state's economy was dominated by ranching, farming, and mining—fields that employed few office workers—women with accounting and clerical skills often found their best chances for employment with government agencies or in county offices. Many campaigned "As a Woman for a Woman's Job," implying that the qualities required for these offices were integral parts of a woman's character. Women quickly dominated the educational and clerical offices in most counties, but were slow to run for county treasurer, sheriff, attorney, or board of supervisors until the 1940s. These positions remained controlled by men

who had more training in accounting, law, and law enforcement. The first female deputy sheriff was appointed in 1915, but in 1936 Belle Talley became Arizona's first female sheriff when she was named to replace her deceased husband in Graham County. Jewell Jordan was appointed sheriff of Maricopa County in 1944 when her husband, Lon, an Arizona rancher, died during his third term, and she became the first elected female sheriff in 1946. Jordan remarked after her tenure as sheriff, "It was a man's job. I had some harrowing experiences and really saw all sides of life."

Although women fared well in county offices, they exerted more political clout when they ran for the state legislature. Arizona has always had high levels of female representation in the legislature. Since 1914 Arizona has usually ranked among the top five states in female representation. Women constituted from 5% to 14% of the legislature from 1912 to 1950, and thereafter their numbers have grown steadily. Women did not simply start running for office in large numbers in Arizona in recent decades. Rather, they established a strong basis for women's political involvement immediately following suffrage and have gradually expanded it over the years.

The political party composition of the state from 1900 to 1950 was decidedly lopsided—with approximately 63% of all voters registered as Democrats. Democratic primary elections for the legislature were generally competitive, with three to five candidates for contests, while Republicans often found it difficult to entice candidates to run. Women fared well in Democratic primaries, usually winning elections in roughly the same ratios as men. This suggests that most voters viewed females as well-qualified candidates for the legislature.

In 1914, the first year women were eligible to vote in Arizona, two Democratic women, Frances Willard Munds and Rachel Berry, were elected to the state legislature. Munds, the outspoken suffrage leader, represented Yavapai County in the state senate, while Berry, a Mormon suffrage worker, was unopposed in the general election for Apache County's sole house seat. Their work in the legislature promoting education and social reform was highly praised by the press, and the women who followed them into office through the 1920s continued to position themselves as alternatives to males, highlighting their expertise in education, public health, and social welfare. But two other attributes were also important to female candidates:

Most were business or educational professionals, and most were born or raised in the West. Just over three quarters of the women who ran for Arizona's legislature between 1914 and 1950 had some college or postgraduate education, and a majority worked outside the home, often as partners with their husbands in business. Almost 70% of the women elected were western born or raised, compared to only 26% of males in the legislature. Therefore, women could run on exceptionally strong credentials. They were wives and mothers, often involved in civic work, yet they often also had knowledge of business, mining, ranching, and labor laws through their work experiences. They were long-time residents of the state who, unlike many transitory men, were dedicated to Arizona's future. Additionally, they had grown up in a frontier region, often living for long stretches in tents or log cabins, and doing the work of men. These women were not pampered ladies, but rather were accustomed to working hard alongside their fathers or husbands on their ranches or in their businesses. In addition, many were responsible for the financial survival of their families, either working to support parents and siblings in poor health or as widows raising young families on their own. Both male and female voters recognized the experience and intimacy these women had with the problems facing the new state, and understood that these women were entitled to representation as much as any man.

Initially, women who were elected to Arizona's legislature concentrated on laws of interest to women and children. Roughly half of all bills sponsored by women from 1914 to 1928 were related to issues concerning education, public health and welfare, and pensions for widows. During the Great Depression, women's legislative interests increasingly turned to the economy, but legislation to benefit women and children still represented approximately one third of all bills sponsored by women in the 1930s. They worked to establish a children's colony for troubled youth and county child welfare boards, and bills were introduced to eradicate gambling, to enforce the state prohibition law, and to allow women to serve on juries.

Over the years, many women were quite successful in establishing themselves as leaders in the legislature. Early on, most women chaired the legislative committees on education, public health, and welfare, reflecting their work as teachers or in social welfare. But as the number of women candidates with backgrounds in law, business, ranching, farming, and mining increased in the 1930s, they began chairing committees concerned with these areas as well. Their names became associated with important building projects and tax bills, including appropriations for bridges and creation of the state income tax. The two women who sponsored the most legislation during this period were Lorna Lockwood and Nellie Trent Bush, both graduates of the University of Arizona Law School.

Lockwood was born in Douglas, Arizona, in 1903 and was the daughter of distinguished Arizona jurist Alfred C. Lockwood. After graduation from law school in 1925, Lorna intended to go into practice with her father, but when he was elected to the Arizona Supreme Court, she went into practice by herself. After facing discrimination from clients as a female attorney, Lockwood worked for a while as a legal secretary before her election to the state legislature from Maricopa County in 1938. She sponsored legislation concerned with criminal procedures, including prescribing penalties for child molestation. She helped establish a commission on unemployment compensation and introduced numerous highway and motor vehicle bills. She is best remembered, however, for her accomplishments on the bench. In 1950 she became the first woman to be elected to the Arizona Superior Court, in 1960 she was the first woman elected to the Arizona State Supreme Court, and she later became the first woman to serve as a chief justice of a state Supreme Court in the United States.

Lockwood's classmate in law school was another well-known Arizona politician, Nellie Trent Bush. Born in Missouri in 1888, Nellie arrived in Arizona in 1893 when her family moved to Mesa because of her father's bronchial ailments. Like so many families seeking cures for lung disease, Nellie spent her early life in poverty. The Trent family made its home in a tent in the desert for many years, and as a child, Nellie's clothes were made of flour sacks. After her marriage to Joe Bush, she moved to Parker, where she helped her husband run a ferry business across the Colorado River, worked as a teacher, and was prominent in local women's organizations, including the Parker Business and Professional Women's Club. With the support of women's groups, she was elected justice of the peace in Parker in 1918 and elected to the state legislature in 1920, where she represented Yuma County until the 1940s. Bush chaired numerous committees during her tenure in the House and Senate, including Ways and Means and Judiciary, and she sponsored legislation for the construction of numerous bridges, dams, and roads in the state. Despite her success and tremendous popularity in state politics, Bush was unable to win election to Congress in 1936.

Bush was not alone in her inability to reach office above the state legislature in Arizona: barriers to high office were numerous for women. Competition for state and national office was intense, campaign expenses high, and public attitudes biased against female candidates. An individual legislator does not wield much influence or power, nor does a lone county official. But state executive officers control budgets, hire and fire personnel, and establish policy within their departments. Although many women believed they were entitled to representation in state office, especially as superintendent of public education or as secretary of state, the voting public did not agree. Only three women, Ana Frohmiller, Elsie Toles, and Jewel Jordan, out of a total of 25 female candidates, attained state executive office between 1914 and 1950. Only Frohmiller, who served as state auditor, was successful in holding state office more than one term.

From 1926 to 1950, Ana Frohmiller served as state auditor, the first woman in the nation to hold this position. The Babbitt Brothers Trading Company employed Frohmiller, a Democrat from Coconino County, in her early career. She received support from the Babbitts as well as women's groups in her early campaigns. Catholic and twice divorced, Frohmiller was a founding member of the Flagstaff Business and Professional Women's Clubs. As state auditor, she was a well-known figure in Arizona politics. In 1950 she was the surprising victor over four male Democratic candidates in a tight primary election for governor. In the general election, Frohmiller faced stiff competition from Howard Pyle, a popular radio show host whose campaign was boosted by a recently rejuvenated Republican Party and by his outspoken campaign manager, Barry Goldwater. Despite Frohmiller's qualifications, name recognition, and membership in the still-dominant Democratic Party, she faced strong bias from voters as a female candidate. Many voters, both male and female, believed that a woman was not suited for the job, and she lost a close and bitter race, subsequently retiring from politics.

Prior to 1950, only one woman was able to transcend the prejudice against women in high political office in Arizona and to rise to national prominence: Isabella Selmes Greenway. Greenway emerged as a state Democratic leader in 1928 because of her powerful personal political connections and her own impressive political skills. She was born in Kentucky in 1886 but grew up on a ranch in North Dakota owned jointly by her father and his good friend, Theodore Roosevelt. At school in New York, Isabella became good friends with Theodore's niece, Eleanor Roosevelt, serving as her bridesmaid in her 1905 wedding to Franklin Delano Roosevelt. Isabella moved to Arizona in 1922 with her second husband, John Greenway, a copper mining manager and politician in the Progressive Party.

Through her close affiliation with the Roosevelts and her knowledge of Arizona politics, Greenway was appointed Arizona's Democratic national committeewoman in 1928. For most women, both in Arizona and in other states, the position of national committeewoman held little power. Usually the predominantly male state central committees chose women with strong relationships with prominent male party leaders. Greenway was different because she held power in her own right. The Democrats had neglected their female voters since suffrage, and now these women were drawn to the political clubs formed by Greenway. As membership in the female Democratic clubs soared, women became an important factor in party politics. She found and encouraged a talented pool of candidates to run for the state legislature, to serve on party committees, and to address the issues of the state's female voters. In 1932 her political future was sealed when her close friend, Franklin Roosevelt, was elected president. Her political expertise and connections to Washington dwarfed those of any other state male leader and forced Arizona's Democrats to acknowledge Greenway's power and to invite her to run for higher office.

Greenway quickly gained attention as a state candidate after her successes as Arizona's Democratic national committeewoman. She briefly considered a run for the governorship but eventually succeeded in becoming Arizona's first female congresswoman in 1933. In the House, she worked hard to bring federal funds to Arizona, fighting to keep the state's copper mines open and to increase employment and funding for health care and veterans' benefits. She retired from Congress in 1936. No woman would represent Arizona in Congress again until the 1990s.

Throughout the years from 1900 to 1950, women tested the limits to their power in Arizona politics. Frances Willard Munds, Nellie Trent Bush, Lorna Lockwood, Ana Frohmiller, Isabella Greenway, and numerous other women were political pioneers who set the stage for later generations of women to follow. These women would find access to some county positions and to the state legislature, but faced discrimination for higher office until the modern woman's movement eliminated many biases. The number of women would continue to grow in the state legislature until 1998, when women were elected to 40% of seats in the Arizona legislature. The state legislature was an important proving ground for women in higher office. In the 1970s, Arizona State Senator Sandra Day O'Connor became the first female state majority leader in the United States and went on to become the first female U.S. Supreme Court justice. In 1998 O'Connor returned to Arizona to swear in the five women elected to the top executive positions in Arizona government—a first in the nation's history. These accomplishments were not made in a vacuum, but were the product of a long tradition of female participation in Arizona politics.

—Heidi J. Osselaer

SUGGESTED READING

Osselaer, Heidi J. *"A Woman for a Woman's Job": Arizona Women in Politics, 1900-1950.* Ph.D. dissertation. Arizona State University, 2001.

ARMSTRONG, SAUNDRA BROWN (1947-)

Saundra Brown Armstrong was born in Oakland, California, in 1947. After receiving her associate of arts degree from Merritt College, she transferred to the California State University at Fresno. Following her graduation in 1969, she attended the University of San Francisco School of Law and earned her juris doctor in 1977. She worked as a policewoman for the Oakland Police Department during her time at law school. After graduation, she began as a judicial extern for the California Court of Appeals. She served as the deputy district attorney for Alameda County on two separate occasions: the first from 1978 to 1979 and then from 1980 until 1982. Between her stints as deputy D.A., she was the senior consultant for the California Assembly Committee on Criminal Justice. From 1982 to 1983, she served as a trial attorney for

the Public Integrity Section of the U.S. Department of Justice. From there, she moved on to become the commissioner of the Consumer Product Safety Commission until 1986. For the next 3 years, Armstrong was the commissioner of the U.S. Parole Commission. In 1989 she became a judge in the Alameda Superior Court of California. On April 25, 1991, President George H. W. Bush nominated her for the seat vacated by William A. Ingram on the U.S. District Court for the Northern District of California. The Senate confirmed her nomination on June 14, 1991, and she received her commission on June 18, 1991.

—Marcus Schwoerer

SUGGESTED READING

Saundra Brown Armstrong. Retrieved from http://air.fjc. gov/servlet/tGetInfo?jid=59 via http:// www.fjc.gov, the Web site of the Federal Judicial Center, Washington, D.C. Source: *History of the Federal Judiciary.*

ASIAN WOMEN

The best books on Asian American women focus on narrow issues mostly dealing with perceptions. The scholarly concerns have been how white America has understood Asians or the "oriental problem," how white America has portrayed Asians, how white America has treated Asians, and how Asian Americans have perceived their lives in the United States. Interpretative synthesis has yet to characterize the literature.

Asian American women in the 19th century were a small part of the tiny Asian population. Chinese men arrived during the Gold Rush and flooded the labor market to build the western leg of the Transcontinental Railroad. With the railroad's completion in 1869, the Chinese became a negative reference group for many whites fearing labor competition. Few women immigrated to America during the century, and with the Chinese Exclusion Act of 1882, they were systematically denied entry. The great exception in early California was prostitution. The Hip Yee Tong supposedly started the traffic in 1852 and imported about 6,000 women over the next 22 years. These women were property, had little access to the courts, suffered the loss of family connections, and earned less for their services than did white prostitutes. Yet as Benson Tong has demonstrated, few of the San Francisco prostitutes were hapless victims prone to suicide. Rather, these women adjusted to life in the San Francisco brothels, made resources available to later arriving sisters, and were actors in the frenzied world of commercial vice, bribery, and violence. The quantum of women was similarly low in Boise County, Idaho Territory. In 1870 all 35 of the women in the county were prostitutes, and a decade later, there were 25 women and 27 prostitutes listed among the 1,225 residents tallied in the census. Between 1863 and 1910, women never represented more than 5% of the population. Only 6% of the Chinese population of Los Angeles in 1910 was female. Exclusion had been a very effective mechanism at keeping Chinese women out of the country.

Japanese women were completely different demographically. The first Japanese woman, named Okei, arrived in 1869 as part of the Wakamoto Tea and Silk Farm Colony in California. The venture failed and she died, but after 1900 a stream of Japanese women arrived courtesy of photography. In 1900 there were fewer than 500 married Japanese women in California, but by 1920 there were 22,000. The picture bride industry flourished with the rise of the nisei, or second-generation, male population. In the 1920s the federal government moved to restrict female immigration and male marriage in Japan. Several states passed discriminatory legislation to limit Japanese access to land and businesses, but the picture brides helped to create stable Japanese communities in the West. These women increasingly started working outside the home, and by 1920 over 40% worked in nonagricultural pursuits, particularly domestic service.

Asian communities were spatially segregated. Chinatown, Japantown, Koreatown, and enclaves of South Asians dominated urban life in the West. In the 1970s Vietnamese congregated in ethnic communities like Little Saigon in Orange County, California, within larger white areas. As racial covenants in deeds, redlining, and other racially discriminatory practices fell under constitutional scrutiny starting in the 1950s, some of these ethnic enclaves melted away and others solidified.

For Asian women, America was a land of opportunity. They had "a Chinaman's chance," as Liping Zhu has so aptly put it, to live a life so much better than the one they had in their homeland. Yet they had to struggle with life within their family and culture. Judy Yung has demonstrated that Chinese women moved from a cloistered existence in the 19th century to challenge gender roles in the family and discrimination in the society in the 1920s. In the 1930s they made important strides economically and in terms of power, in labor unions. World War II provided even greater opportunity in defense plants and the public war effort. World War II for Japanese women meant exactly the opposite, as internment camps destroyed family businesses, family life, and family hopes.

The life of Rose Hum Lee was one extraordinary journey of this sort. Her father worked his way through the manual labor markets of the West and used the money he saved to open a general merchandise store in Butte, Montana, in 1900. Returning to China, he was able to use the merchant wife exception to bring his wife to America. Rose Hum was born in Butte in 1904, educated at Butte High School, and, like her three sisters and three brothers, went on to a professional career. Education was a significant family value.

Lee finished her doctorate at the University of Chicago in 1947 with a dissertation titled *The Growth and Decline of Rocky Mountain Chinatowns*. In 1956 she became the first woman and first Chinese American to chair a sociology department at an American university. By the time of her passing in 1964, scholars acknowledged that her assimilation theories had transformed the discipline's research agenda.

March Fong Eu was another educated woman who achieved public acclaim, but in California politics. She earned her bachelor's degree at the University of California, Berkeley, master's degree at Mills College, and a doctorate at Stanford University. Active in women's club activities, the people of Oakland and the Castro Valley sent her to the state assembly in 1966, the first Asian American woman ever to serve in the assembly. After four terms in the legislature, she won the secretary of state office in 1974 by a record-setting 3 million votes. She was the first woman secretary of state and the first Asian American in statewide office. She gained public notoriety by smashing a toilet bowl on the steps of the state capitol building as part of a successful campaign to ban pay toilets, a discriminatory practice. During her tenure, she brought automation to the office, reformed notary public law, implemented the Political Reform Act of

1974, and won legislative approval for the building of the state Archive Plaza, a modern archival system, and a museum displaying the documents of California's history.

In 1994 President Bill Clinton appointed Eu as U.S. ambassador to the Federated States of Micronesia. She returned from federal service, ran a losing campaign for California secretary of state in 2002, and continues an ambitious painting career.

Beulah Ong Kwoh also was an educated woman but turned her attention to acting. Born in Stockton, California, she graduated from the University of California, Berkeley, attended the University of Chicago and roomed with Rose Hum Lee, and entered a doctoral program at the University of California, Los Angeles, prior to starting her movie and television career. With the stage name Beulah Quo, she had minor parts in numerous movies, including *Girls, Girls, Girls, MacArthur,* and *Chinatown.* She retired in 1991 after 6 years of work on the TV serial *General Hospital.*

Setsuko Matsunaga Nishi was born in 1921 in Los Angeles and was a student at the University of Southern California when World War II began. Relocated to Washington University in St. Louis, she completed her B.A. and M.A. there and entered doctoral studies at the University of Chicago studying Japanese American achievements as a cultural response to degradation.

Despite the gains of individuals, Asian American women are small proportions of the business elite. In the mid-1990s Asian women held only 3% of the management or administrative positions in the private sector, as compared with 7% held by African American women and 5% held by Hispanic women.

In terms of entry to university faculty positions, Asian women exceeded only American Indian women in 1996-1997. Of the 12,557 doctorates that women earned, Asians accounted for 569.

In the 106th Congress, the last of the 20th century, there were 56 women representing their constituencies. Only 1 was Asian American.

The good news is that research on Asian American women continues to grow. Some is highly analytical, and other books simply give voice to Asian American women. In time, the voices will be heard and the research will grow in sophistication.

—Gordon Morris Bakken

SUGGESTED READINGS

Bhopal, Kalwant. *Gender, "Race" and Patriarchy: A Study of South Asian Women.* Aldershot, England: Ashgate, 1997.

Chan, Sucheng. *Hmong Means Free: Life in Laos and America.* Philadelphia, PA: Temple University Press, 1994.

Chow, Claire S. *Leaving Deep Water: The Lives of Asian American Women at the Crossroads of Two Cultures.* New York: Dutton, 1998.

Costello, Cynthia B., and Anne J. Stone. *The American Woman, 2001-2002: Getting to the Top.* New York: Norton, 2002.

Diggs, Nancy Brown. *Steel Butterflies: Japanese Women and the American Experience.* Albany: State University of New York Press, 1998.

Espiritu, Yen Le. *Asian American Women and Men: Labor, Laws, and Love.* Thousand Oaks, CA: Sage, 1997.

Kessler, Lauren. *Stubborn Twig: Three Generations in the Life of a Japanese Family.* New York: Random House, 1993.

Lee, Joann Faung Jean. *Asian American Experiences in the United States: Oral Histories of First to Fourth Generation Americans from China, the Philippines, Japan, India, the Pacific Islands, Vietnam, and Cambodia.* Jefferson, NC: McFarland, 1991.

Lee, Josephine Ding. *Performing Asian America: Race and Ethnicity on the Contemporary Stage.* Philadelphia, PA: Temple University Press, 1997.

Lowe, Lisa. *Immigrant Acts: On Asian American Cultural Politics.* Durham, NC: Duke University Press, 1996.

March Fong Eu: A Career of Breaking Barriers. Retrieved from www.smartvoter.org/2002/03/05/ca/state/vote/eu_m/bio.html. Copyright © League of Women Voters of California Education Fund.

Matsumoto, Valerie. *Farming the Home Place: A Japanese American Community in California, 1919-1982.* Ithaca, NY: Cornell University Press, 1993.

Nam, Vickie. *Yell-Oh Girls! Emerging Voices Explore Culture, Identity, and Growing Up Asian American.* New York: Harper Collins, 2001.

Peffer, George Anthony. *If They Don't Bring Women Here: Chinese Female Immigration Before Exclusion.* Urbana: University of Illinois Press, 1999.

Tong, Benson. *Unsubmissive Women: Chinese Prostitutes in Nineteenth-Century San Francisco.* Norman: University of Oklahoma Press, 1994.

Yu, Diana. *Winds of Change: Korean Women in America.* Silver Spring, MD: Women's Institute Press, 1991.

Yu, Henry. *Thinking Orientals: Migration, Contact, and Exoticism in Modern America.* New York: Oxford University Press, 2001.

Yung, Judy. *Unbound Feet: A Social History of Chinese Women in San Francisco.* Berkeley: University of California Press, 1995.

Zhu, Liping. *A Chinaman's Chance: The Chinese on the Rocky Mountain Mining Frontier.* Boulder: University Press of Colorado, 1997.

B

BAIRD, LOURDES G. (1935-)

Lourdes G. Baird was U.S. District Attorney for the Central District of California during some of the most difficult cases that were ever brought before the courts. Her actions in response to the Rodney King beating trial resulted in the conviction of the officers who administered the beating, but most important, resulted in upholding the civil rights of citizens. Her action in that case helped to satisfy the needs of the people who rioted in the streets of Los Angeles in 1992, and showed them that their needs had been noticed. In another case, she was asked to deal with accusations at then Mayor Tom Bradley, which claimed that he had had inappropriate dealings with banks and had perhaps used insider information about stocks.

Before becoming a U.S. District Attorney, Baird received recognition and support from many who had worked with her. Judge Paul Boland, interim U.S. Attorney Robert Brosio, and Assistant U.S. Attorney William Fahey all praised her work and encouraged her appointment to the California position.

Baird began her career as an Assistant U.S. Attorney for the Central District of California in 1977. She entered private practice in 1983 with the firm of Baird, Munger & Myers. In 1986 she started her judicial career as an East Los Angeles Municipal Court judge and in 1988 as a Los Angeles Superior Court judge. In 1992 President George H. W. Bush appointed her to the federal bench as judge of the U.S. District Court for the Central District of California. She was a member of several active groups, including the California Women Lawyers Association, the Mexican-American Bar Association, the Latino Judges Association, and the National Association of Women Judges. She also was the head of the University of California, Los Angeles, School of Law Alumni Association from 1981 to 1984.

Baird was born to a family of seven in Quito, Ecuador. Her parents were James C. Gillespie and Josefina Delgado. Her father moved to California to get work, and she began her education in the Catholic school system, where she developed a strong sense of responsibility, a hard-working attitude, and a love for sports. In 1956 she married William T. Baird and had three children, William Jr., Maria, and John. After her youngest child entered school, she decided to go to school as well. She started at Los Angeles City College and transferred to UCLA, where in 1973 she graduated with a B.A. in sociology and in 1976 with a law degree. She is a great example of a woman who earned her position in life through hard work and determination.

—Kevin Christy

SUGGESTED READINGS

Detroit Free Press. August 6, 1992, p. A3.

Detroit Free Press. August 9, 1992, p. F2.

Kamp, Jim, and Telgen, Dianne. "Lourdes Baird." *Notable Hispanic American Women.* Detroit, MI: Gale Research, 1993.

Los Angeles Times. November 30, 1989, p. B1.

Los Angeles Times. December 4, 1989, p. B6.

Los Angeles Times. May 15, 1990, p. B1.

Los Angeles Times. May 21, 1990, p. B6.

Los Angeles Times. July 11, 1990, p. B6.

Los Angeles Times. July 19, 1990, p. B1.

Lourdes G. Baird. Retrieved from air.fjc.gov/servlet/t GetInfo?jid=77. Source: History of the Federal Judiciary. http://www.fjc.gov. Web site of the Federal Judicial Center, Washington, D.C.

BARNES, FLORENCE "PANCHO" LOWE (1901-1975)

Florence Lowe Barnes, the self-styled "Mother of the Air Force," was born in California on July 29, 1901. She was the second child of Thaddeus Lowe Jr. and Caroline Dobbins, a wealthy Pasadena couple. Her grandfather, Thaddeus Lowe, had been a Civil War balloonist. She attended her first air show at age 9 with her grandfather, but equestrian activities were her first love. She won her first riding trophy at age 5 when she took first prize at the inaugural Pasadena Horse Show in 1906.

A self-centered and spoiled child, Florence was a constant discipline problem in school. Her parents sent her to a convent in Alhambra, California, in hopes of instilling discipline. She ran away at age 15 by riding her horse to Tijuana, Mexico. She was then sent to a strict Episcopalian boarding school in La Jolla, California.

She married Rev. Calvin Rankin Barnes on January 1, 1921. Her parents arranged the marriage, but Florence was a willing bride. Her only child, William, was born in October of 1921. The couple was married in name only as Florence pursued her own activities. She left the care of William to a nanny while she worked in movies as a stunt rider, horse trainer, and script girl.

Barnes organized numerous parties for her Hollywood friends, which she financed from her inheritance. Her wild parties created a local scandal, so she fled to Mexico. She hired out on a banana boat headed for Mexico, not knowing that the boat was providing guns for the Gomez-Serrano Rebellion. When her ship was seized in San Blas, she escaped with helmsman Roger Chute and made her way across Mexico. Roger gave her the nickname "Pancho" during their escape.

In 1928 Barnes began taking flying lessons. She was able to use her great wealth to purchase the finest planes available. She flew her first solo on September 6, 1928. On February 22, 1929, she entered America's first women's air race in Glendale, California, easily taking first place. Later she defeated Roscoe Turner in a well-publicized race from San Francisco to Los Angeles. In 1930 she won the first Tom Thumb 225-mile race. She purchased a Travel Air Model R *Mystery Ship* on August 4, 1930, which she used to shatter the women's speed record with a speed of 196.19 mph.

Her victories led to a lucrative contract with Union Oil. She entered the women's race from Los Angeles to Cleveland, Ohio, in conjunction with the National Air Show, but crashed in Texas. As a publicity stunt, she became the first woman to fly scheduled flights into Mexico. She also served as a test pilot for Bach, Lockheed, and Beechcraft. Her test flights took her over the Mojave Desert, where she discovered her dream airport location near Muroc Dry Lake.

Barnes performed aerial stunts for the movies beginning in the 1920s. Her most famous film was *Hell's Angels.* She helped organize the Motion Picture Pilot's Union, which set daily and stunt rates for pilots. She played hostess to numerous wild parties, which taxed her financial resources. Her position as secretary-treasurer of the union led to an unsuccessful attempt to become a county supervisor in 1932.

Unhappy with women's flying clubs, Barnes organized the Women's Air Reserve in 1931. This was to provide training for pilots and aid for the public in emergencies. She was the general of this militarily organized group. She used the reserves, with a subsidy from Gilmore Oil, to fly cross-country to promote equal rights for women pilots. In reality her purpose was to lobby in Washington for the release of her lover, actor Reynaldo Duncan, from federal prison. Her efforts succeeded when Franklin D. Roosevelt pardoned Duncan.

The Depression and her wild spending habits caused Barnes to lose most of her property. She moved to the Mojave Desert to build her dream airport. In her land adjacent to Muroc Dry Lake, she raised livestock. She collected garbage from the nearby air base, which she fed to the hogs. She then sold the meat back to the military.

When Congress approved Roosevelt's Civilian Pilot Training Program, Barnes secured a contract to provide planes and instructors. Initially she used Palmdale Airport, but later moved the training to her Rancho Oro Verde property.

When World War II began, the Muroc Air Base became a major testing and training center and

Barnes's ranch became an unofficial recreation center for the airmen. She provided food, alcohol, women, and rooms at the ranch but was often the main attraction because of her unique gift for storytelling. Base Commander Clarence Shoop often visited her ranch, giving it a semiofficial status.

After the war, Barnes renamed her operation Pancho's Fly In. She closed her dairy and added rooms and gambling. She promoted rodeos in the valley for added entertainment. The ranch became a watering hole for Hollywood friends and test pilots such as Chuck Yeager, and General Al Boyd used the ranch for official meetings. Barnes changed the name again to the Happy Bottoms Riding Club. Her fourth husband, Eugene McKendry, ran the daily operations.

In the 1950s, Barnes was driven off her property by air base expansion, even though she filed numerous lawsuits to keep her property. An arsonist burned down the ranch, and the culprit remains unknown. The cost of losing her land made life difficult for her. She tried to start a new ranch in Cantil, near Boron, California, but was unable to re-create the old times. In May of 1964 she was honored as the "First Citizen of Edwards Air Base." With the aid of friend Ted Tate, she had a brief lecturing career in the 1970s. In 1975 she died in her Boron, California, home under mysterious circumstances. Her old barnstorming friend Jimmy Doolittle gave her eulogy, and her ashes were spread over the desert near her old ranch.

—Randal C. Fulkerson

SUGGESTED READINGS

Kessler, Lauren. *The Happy Bottoms Riding Club: The Life and Times of Pancho Barnes*. New York: Random House, 2000.

Tate, Grover Ted. *The Lady Who Tamed Pegasus: The Story of Pancho Barnes*. Bend, OR: Maverick, 1984.

BERZON, MARSHA L. (1945-)

Justice Marsha L. Berzon, a former labor lawyer, is a judge of the U.S. Court of Appeals for the Ninth Circuit, which covers eight western states and Guam, and is best known for her 2-year-long confirmation process. Berzon received her law degree from the University of California, Berkeley, Boalt Hall School of Law in 1973. She went on to clerk for the Hon. James R. Browning of the Court of Appeals for the Ninth Circuit from 1973 to 1974 and then clerked for Supreme Court Justice William J. Brennan Jr. until 1975. She went into private practice in Washington, D.C., with the firm of Woll & Mayer until 1977, and joined the notable labor firm of Altshuler, Berzon, Nussbaum, Berzon, & Rubin in 1978. The firm was noted for its big labor clients as well as for taking progressive cases in areas such as health and safety areas. One of these cases involved California Proposition 65 regarding safe drinking water and issues of immigration and environmental safety. In 1991 Berzon argued her most important case before the U.S. Supreme Court in *United Auto Workers vs. Johnson Controls* and successfully prevented employers from discriminating against women of childbearing age for certain hazardous positions. She has also written over 60 appellate briefs, especially for the American Civil Liberties Union (ACLU).

In January 1999 President Bill Clinton nominated Berzon for the position of federal judge for the Court of Appeals for the Ninth Circuit. Her appointment was considered favorable by both parties despite her prolabor record; however, the political temper of the times served to hold her nomination in committee for the next 2 years before it could even come to a floor vote. The Ninth Circuit had a reputation as a very liberal court, and many conservative senators in Washington wanted to change the makeup of the large and influential body. The past 6 years had seen 90% of the court's decisions overturned by the Supreme Court, and in the year 1997, 27 of the 28 decisions were overturned. In addition to the conservative backlash, President Clinton was in the middle of a sordid impeachment scandal and had very little time to promote judicial appointments. That left the process up to Judiciary Committee Chairman Orrin Hatch and Majority Leader Trent Lott, who both favored putting through less controversial appointments first. After a period of 2 years, Democrats began to take actions into their own hands, blocking the nominations of friends of both Hatch and Lott, in order to get the leaders to guarantee dates for the Berzon committee and floor votes. When it was all over, Berzon was confirmed by a vote of 63-34. She went on to write her first published opinion on Indian gaming within 6 months, a record for a first-time judge. She then published a total of 23 opinions and 4 dissents in her first year.

—Michelle Bean

SUGGESTED READINGS

Dewar, Helen. "Senate Starts to Act on Judicial Nominees; Party Leaders Reach Agreement That Breaks Impasse on Confirmation Process." *Washington Post.* October 2, 1999.

Elias, Paul. "Berzon's 9th Circuit Bid Looks Good." *The Recorder.* June 17, 1999.

Grunwald, Michael. "Coming Up Short on an Appeals Circuit; Labor Lawyer's Nomination Is Latest Casualty of Ideological Fight, Clinton Woes." *Washington Post.* October 6, 1998.

Helm, Mark. "Boxer Forces Vote on Stalled Judicial Nominations; Lott Caves In When Friend Became a Casualty." *San Francisco Examiner,* November 13, 1999.

Kisliuk, Bill. "Marsha Berzon Nominated to Ninth Circuit." *The Recorder,* January 28, 1998.

Peters, Alexander. "Creating a Different Kind of Labor Practice; With a Long Roster of Union Clients, Altshuler, Berzon Has Established a Public Interest Practice That Pays the Rent." *The Recorder,* May 10, 1991.

United States Court of Appeals for the Ninth Circuit. Retrieved from www.ca9.uscourts.gov.

BIRD, GLORIA (1951-)

Native American author and poet Gloria Bird was born in Washington State and is a member of the Spokane Tribe of Indians in Wellpinit, Washington. She attended the Institute of American Indian Arts in Santa Fe, New Mexico, while she was in high school. After high school, she attended Portland Community College in Portland, Oregon. She received a bachelor's degree in English from Lewis and Clark College, also in Portland, in 1990. In 1992 she received a master's degree in literature from the University of Arizona.

Bird returned to the Institute of American Indian Arts and taught literature and creative writing for 5 years after graduating from the University of Arizona. During these years she published her first book of poetry, *Full Moon on the Reservation*, which earned her the Diane Decorah Memorial Award for Poetry.

In 1997 Bird published her second book of poetry, *The River of History*. That same year she also published an anthology of writing by Native American women titled *Reinventing the Enemy's Language*, edited with Joy Harjo. In the summer of 1997 Bird

taught a "Subversive Literary Strategies" workshop for other Native American writers at the Fishtrap Gathering in Joseph, Oregon. In addition, Bird continues to work on a collection of poetry on the Nez Perce retreat that she started in 1988 while attending Portland Community College. To date, this manuscript remains unpublished.

Bird is one of the founding members of the Northwest Native American Writers Association. She formerly served as a contributing editor for *Indian Artist* magazine. Currently she is an associate editor for the *Wicazo Sa Review* and also teaches occasionally at the Wellpinit Campus of Salish-Kootenei College.

Bird began writing as a young woman while living on a remote reservation. Writing was a way to find herself: "Out of that isolation came some of my first poems that mark, for me, a beginning. I knew there had to be another Indian woman somewhere who was living like I was, who might hear me and identify." However, she continues to write as a source of power, not only for her but also for all Native American people. When explaining some of the reasons why she writes, she states, "I write because I have to, and because the more I learn the more I believe in the power of the word."

—Brenda Bitgood

SUGGESTED READINGS

Bird, Gloria. *Full Moon on the Reservation.* New York: Greenview Review Press, 1993.

Bird, Gloria. *The River of History.* Portland, OR: Trask House Press, 1997.

Bird, Gloria, and Joy Harjo, eds. *Reinventing the Enemy's Language.* New York: Norton, 1997.

Bird, Gloria, and Karen Strom. "Gloria Bird." Retrieved from www.hanksville.org/storytellers/gbird.

Native American Authors Project. "Gloria Bird." Retrieved from www.ipl.org/cgi/ref/native/browse.pl/A138.

BIRD, ROSE ELIZABETH (1936-1999)

Rose Elizabeth Bird, controversial Chief Justice of the California Supreme Court, was born in Tucson, Arizona, on November 2, 1936. Raised by her mother, Rose came from humble beginnings and moved with

campaign for the governor in 1974, and he appointed her secretary of California's Department of Agriculture and Services. In 1977 Brown appointed her Chief Justice of the California Supreme Court, a position that she was subsequently elected to in 1978 and served until the voters unseated her in 1987. Bird struggled with breast cancer until she succumbed to the disease in 1999.

Bird's professional life was driven by a conviction to do what she believed was right, and thereby she created two distinct legacies for herself. The first was that of the liberal and unpopular Chief Justice of California's highest court at a time when a conservative bent swept the nation's most populist state. Bird's opinion that the popular 1978 Proposition 13—"the taxpayers' revolt"—was unconstitutional demonstrated this. Despite this tax reform's overwhelming support by the voters and the conclusion that it was constitutional by the remaining six members of the Court, Bird remained resolute in her opposition to this law, which would change the way California was governed. Further politically polarizing Bird from California's polity was the perception that she was soft on crime. A firestorm of criticism resulted from the Bird Court's decision against mandatory prison time for the convicted in *People v. Tanner*, even though the state, led by Jerry Brown, championed one of the toughest gun laws on the books that touted "use a gun, go to prison." In addition, of the 58 death penalty cases that came before the Court, she voted against the death penalty in all of them. Eventually, all of these controversial contraindications with the growing conservative mood led to her failed reelection attempt in 1978.

her family to New York City in 1950, where she attended high school. Upon graduating from Long Island University, where she studied English and history, she spent a year as a secretary in New York City before returning to graduate school at the University of California, Berkeley, to study political science. Her studies not only introduced her to California politics and the future governor of the state, Jerry Brown, but they also motivated her to pursue a law degree at Berkeley's Boalt Hall School of Law. After graduating, she worked as a clerk for the Nevada Supreme Court and later for Santa Clara County as a public defender. She aided Brown in his successful

The other less-known legacy left by Bird was that of a woman who either facilitated or was an accomplice to unimaginable change in the state of California. Bird broke the gender barrier that existed in many of the West's male-dominated legal environments. She was the female clerk to the Nevada Supreme Court and Santa Clara County's first female Deputy Public Defender. In 1975 she became the first Secretary of Agriculture, thereby becoming not only the first woman to serve the state in a cabinet position but the leader of a committee dominated by males. Her ascension to the California Supreme Court was unprecedented by any woman and probably thought unimaginable by all at the time Bird graduated from law school.

Although most remembered for her controversial Court, Bird worked to serve the State of California with conviction and tenacity. She fought for women, minorities, farm workers, and the poor from within the state's government, ultimately at the expense of her own political career.

—Michael G. Woods

SUGGESTED READINGS

Barnett, Stephen. "The Supreme Court of California 1981-1982 Forward: The Emerging Court." *California Law Review 71* (July 1983): 1134-1195.

Dobbin, Muriel. "As Voters Try to Overrule a Top Judge." *U.S. News & World Report* (December 2, 1985): 71, 73.

Endicott, William, and Robert Fairbanks. "Supreme Court Decision to Reverse Gun Law Reported." *Los Angeles Times,* November 7, 1978, p. 1.

Farrington, Brenda. "Banking on the Court and Congress," in Gordon Morris Bakken, ed., *Law in the Western United States.* Norman: University of Oklahoma Press, 2000.

Farrington-Myers, Brenda. *Rose Bird and the Rule of Law.* Thesis. California State University, Fullerton. 1991.

Farrington-Myers, Brenda. "Credibility and Crisis in California's High Court," in John W. Johnson, ed., *Historic U.S. Court Cases: An Encyclopedia.* New York: Routledge, 2001.

Lacayo, Richard. "Shaking the Judicial Perch." *Time* (September 15, 1986): 76.

Medsger, Emily. *Framed: The New Right Attack on Chief Justice Rose Bird and the Courts.* New York: Pilgrim Press, 1983.

Putnam, Jackson K. *Modern California Politics* (4th ed). Sparks, NV: MTL, 1996.

Stolz, Preble. *Judging Judges: The Investigation of Rose Bird and the California Supreme Court.* New York: Free Press, 1981.

Traut, Carol Ann, and Craig F. Emmert. "Expanding the Integrated Model of Judicial Decision Making: The California Justices and Capital Punishment." *Journal of Politics, 60*(4). (November 1998): 1166-1180.

Turner, William Bennett. "From the *Tanner* Hearings to the Brethren and Beyond: Judicial Accountability and Judicial Independence." *California State Bar Journal 55* (July 1980): 292-297.

BLANTON, ANNIE WEBB
(1870-1945)

Annie Webb Blanton, the first woman elected to statewide office in Texas, was born on August 19, 1870, in Houston, one of seven children of Thomas Lindsay and Eugenia Webb Blanton. Her twin sister, Fannie, died as a girl. After graduation from La Grange High School in 1886, Blanton began teaching. She attended the University of Texas, Austin, at night and during vacations. She graduated in 1899 with a bachelor's degree in literature. From 1901 to 1918 she was a faculty member of the English Department at North Texas State Normal College (now the University of North Texas) in Denton. During this time she became active in the Texas State Teachers Association (TSTA). In 1916 she became the first female president of the TSTA. She held the post for 2 years. During her tenure she established a fund for financing campaigns for securing more support for public schools.

Blanton's success as president of the TSTA encouraged her to make a bid for the office of State Superintendent of Public Instruction. Her campaign was bitter. She was accused of being an atheist and a tool for others. In 1918, thanks to the support of the State Department of Education, various civic organizations, educators, and legislators, Blanton became the first woman to be elected to statewide office in Texas. She was in office for two terms.

During her tenure as superintendent, Blanton established a system of free textbooks, revised teacher certification laws, raised teachers' salaries, and made efforts to improve rural education. In 1920 she introduced the Better Schools Amendment to remove constitutional limitations on tax rates for local school districts. The voters passed it.

In 1922 Blanton unsuccessfully ran for U.S. Congress from Denton County. After losing her bid for Congress, she returned to the University of Texas and earned her master's degree in 1923. She taught in the University of Texas Education Department until 1926, when she took a leave of absence to complete her Ph.D. at Cornell University. In 1927 she returned to the University of Texas and remained a professor of education for the rest of her life.

Blanton served as vice president of the National Education Association in 1917, 1919, and 1921. In 1929 she founded the Delta Kappa Gamma Society, an honorary society for female teachers that, as of 1988, had an international membership of 162,000. She published several books during her career. These include *Review Outline and Exercises in English Grammar* (1903), *A Handbook of Information as to Education in Texas* (1922), *Advanced English Grammar* (1928), and *The Child of the Texas One-Teacher School* (1936). There are public schools named after her in Austin, Dallas, and Odessa. Blanton, who never married, died on October 2, 1945, in Austin, Texas.

—Tiffany E. Dulpe

SUGGESTED READINGS

Cottrell, Debbie Mauldin. *Pioneer Woman Educator: The Progressive Spirit of Annie Webb Blanton.* College Station: Texas A&M University Press, 1993.

The Handbook of Texas Online. Retrieved from www.tsha.utexas.edu/handbook/online.

Holden, Eunah Temple. *Our Heritage in the Delta Kappa Gamma Society.* Austin, TX: Delta Kappa Gamma Society, 1960; rpt. 1970.

BOWER, B. M., AKA BERTHA MUZZY SINCLAIR (1871-1940)

B. M. Bower was a popular author and screenwriter. Born Bertha Muzzy in Cleveland, she moved to Montana as a small child. In Montana, she was able to experience ranch life firsthand and later put these experiences and people into the characters of her novels. She married Clayton J. Bower at the age of 18

and became a schoolteacher as well as the mother of three children. Her first published work was in the pulp magazine *Popular* in 1904, coming out in serial installments over 6 years. Her work was published under her initials and may have led readers to believe the author was a man, because women authors in the western genre were very rare. She published her first novel, *Chip, of the Flying U,* in 1906 and continued to come back to these characters in several sequels, including *The Happy Family* (1910) and *Flying U Ranch* (1914). She wrote approximately two books a year, with a total of 57 published works in her 40-year career as a western author. Her first collection of short stories, *The Lonesome Trail,* appeared in 1909. Other novels included *Lonesome Land* (1912), *Cabin Fever* (1918), *The Heritage of the Sioux* (1916), and *The Five Furies of Leaning Ladder* (1935). Her first novel about the lives of cowboy Chip Bennett and his group of hands at the Flying U ranch was so popular that it became a standard for many Americans who knew nothing about true life in the West. Popularity led Bower to script several of her novels into Hollywood films and led to a fascination with the film industry that even found its way into her characters and plot lines. Twelve films were made of her works. She spent the final 20 years of her life in Los Angeles, California.

Bower's writing was not always praised by literary critics, who viewed the western genre as sensationalist or melodramatic. Bower geared her writing to the commercial audience of Americans who were eager to learn about the adventures of cowboys and ranchers. She based her characters on the firsthand experience she had growing up in Montana and as the wife of three "cowboys." She married her second husband, Bertrand W. Sinclair, in 1906, and the third, Robert Ellsworth Cowan, wrote a published work, *Range Rider,* of his remembrances of the cowboy life in Texas. However, in Bower's work, the female character was also as developed as that of the male. In *Chip, of the Flying U,* her heroine, Della Whitmore, was a doctor, level headed, and courageous. Critics claimed that Bower still concluded her stories with her female characters giving up their independence to enter the domestic role of wife and mother; however, whether this was Bower's concept of the real world or a desire for happy endings for a romance story is unclear. The theme of adaptation to the different circumstances that western life throws at her characters is also central to her stories.

Bower's work gave the majority of Americans their first look into the workings of a ranch community and the typical hardships that people who endured this lifestyle must face. The warm relationships and humor entertained the reader while involving them in this new landscape.

—Michelle Bean

SUGGESTED READINGS

Guide to Life and Literature of the Southwest. Retrieved from users.erols.com/hardeman/lonestar/olbooks/dobie/dobie21.htm.

Mainiero, Lina, ed. *American Women Writers: A Critical Reference Guide from Colonial Times to the Present: Vol. 4. S-Z.* New York: Frederick Ungar, 1979.

Tuska, Jon, and Vicki Piekarski. *Encyclopedia of Frontier and Western Fiction.* New York: McGraw-Hill, 1983.

Vinson, James, ed. *Twentieth-Century Western Writers.* Detroit, MI: Gale Research, 1982.

BOXER, BARBARA (1940-)

Growing up in Brooklyn, New York, U.S. Senator Barbara Boxer did not originally consider a future political career for herself. She married Stewart Boxer during her senior year at Brooklyn College and immediately went to work to put her husband through Fordham Law School.

After Stewart's graduation from Fordham, the couple relocated to San Francisco and raised two children, Doug and Nicole. During this time Barbara became involved with a program called the Education Corps of Marin, which provided job training to high school dropouts. While this may have been a first step in her interest in activism, her past experiences of sexual discrimination must have been equally important in pushing her into the political realm. While still in New York, she tried to get a job on Wall Street but was told they only hired men. Later in California, she was attacked for not wanting to stay home with her children when she ran for supervisor of the Marin County Board of Supervisors. She lost the election.

After the loss of her first election, Boxer went to work as a reporter at the *Pacific Sun.* Two years later she became an aide for Congressman John Burton.

She decided to once more run for the position of supervisor of Marin County, and this time she won. This victory is recognized as the beginning of her triumphant political career.

Boxer served as Marin County supervisor for 6 years and became the first woman president of the Marin County Board of Supervisors. She was elected to the U.S. House of Representatives in 1983 and served as a congresswoman for 10 years. She was active in the areas of health care, biomedical research, and education. She was recognized with awards from various organizations, including the Anti-Defamation League, National Council of Jewish Women, and Planned Parenthood.

Boxer was elected to the U.S. Senate in 1993 and won a second 6-year term in 1998. As senator, she has concentrated her efforts on education with her Computers in Classrooms program, environmental protection with her successful amendment to the Safe Drinking Water Act, medical research as a leading advocate of AIDS research, and the elimination of violence in America by helping pass the 1994 Crime Bill. She has also been the Senate's leading advocate of a woman's right to choose. She authored the Family Planning and Choice Protection Act.

Boxer's capacity to react to recent issues is evident in her efforts to protect workers' retirement plans in the wake of the Enron scandal. In addition, she responded to the September 11, 2001, attacks by working for increased air safety. In October 2001 she authored a resolution to include women in the temporary government of Afghanistan. She has been working for the rights of Afghani women since 1997, long before the attacks.

Whether in her role as wife, mother, or senator, Boxer has proven herself to be a truly remarkable woman.

—Brenda Bitgood

SELECTED READINGS

Boxer, Barbara. *Strangers in the Senate: Politics and the New Revolution of Women in America.* Washington, DC: National Press Books, 1994.

Official Website of U.S. Senator Barbara Boxer of California. "Senator Boxer's Biography." Retrieved from boxer.senate.gov/about.

BROWN, JANICE ROGERS (1949-)

The first African American woman to sit on the California Supreme Court was born in the small town of Laverne, Alabama, in 1949, the daughter of a sharecropper. Her father joined the U.S. Air Force and the family followed him to his duty station in California. She graduated from California State University, Sacramento, with a B.A. in 1974 and a J.D. in 1977 from the University of California, Los Angeles, Law School. She worked for the California Legislative Counsel's office for 2 years, the Attorney General's office for 8 years, and in private practice at the firm of Nielsen, Merksamer, Parrinello, Mueller & Naylor from 1989 to 1991. In 1991 she became Governor Pete Wilson's legal affairs secretary, and on November 4, 1994, she became an associate justice of the California Court of Appeal, Third Appellate District, in Sacramento. In 1996 Scott Graham, the Court's editor for *The Recorder*, termed her "an emerging intellectual force on the court of appeal and a prime contender for a California Supreme Court vacancy."

Brown filled the vacancy created by the elevation of Ronald George to chief justice to replace retiring Chief Justice Malcolm Lucas. Despite a skirmish with the Commission on Judicial Nominees, she was confirmed in 1996. Four years later commentators thought her to be an "outspoken conservative on a court steering a moderate course." Furthermore, court watcher Gerald Uelmen said that she was "a very gutsy justice." Harriet Chiang, legal affairs writer for the *San Francisco Chronicle,* wrote that "her bare-knuckles style of writing can delight legal experts or make them wince. At the very least, she shakes the stereotype of court opinions as mind-numbingly dull recitations."

She continues as one of three women on the California Supreme Court.

—Gordon Morris Bakken

SUGGESTED READINGS

Judicial Council of California. "Associate Justice Janice Rogers Brown." Retrieved from www.courtinfo.ca.gov/courts/supreme/justices/brown.htm.
Metropolitan News-Enterprise, March 29, 1996.
The Recorder, February 12, March 21, May 3, 1996.
San Francisco Chronicle, April 29, 2001.

BROWN, RUTH WINIFRED
(1891-1975)

Ruth Brown began her career as a librarian in Bartlesville, Oklahoma, in 1919. She was the president of the Oklahoma Library Association in 1931 and was a founding member of the Committee on the Practice of Democracy (COPD) in 1946. The COPD was the only affiliate of the Congress on Racial Equality south of the Mason-Dixon Line at that time.

Brown had two daughters, whom she adopted in 1942 to remove them from an abusive foster home.

Brown came to national attention in early 1950, when the Bartlesville Library Board dismissed her. The official reason given for her dismissal was the Bartlesville Public Library's subscription to subversive and communist literature. Some of the titles cited were *Soviet Russia Today, The Nation, New Republic,* and *Consumer Reports.* However, it was obvious to the citizens of Bartlesville that anticommunism was not the driving force behind her dismissal, but Brown's informal racial integration of the library, her plans to hold an interracial children's story hour, and an appearance in public at a segregated lunch room with two African American teachers, asking to be served lunch.

Brown's dismissal divided the community, several members of which quickly formed a group known as the Friends of Ruth Brown. Phillips Petroleum, the major employer in Bartlesville, abruptly transferred several of the Friends of Ruth Brown. The American Library Association took up her case as a battle against censorship, but Brown never regained her position. She left Bartlesville after her appeals were denied to teach in an African American school in Mississippi, and she moved to Colorado, where she was once again a librarian until her death in 1975.

A film titled *Storm Center,* starring Bette Davis, was made in 1956 based on some of the events surrounding her dismissal, though the controversy over racial integration was not included in that film.

—Tiffany E. Dalpe

SUGGESTED READING

Robbins, Louise S. *The Dismissal of Miss Ruth Brown.* Norman: University of Oklahoma Press, 2000.

BUFFALO CALF ROAD (1850-1879)

Among the patrilineal Cheyenne of the Northern Plains, the place of native women is rarely recognized as anything more than that of helpmate, by either Cheyenne men or later by white researchers. This has led to a dearth of information about Cheyenne women who did not conform to subordinate roles. Despite this propensity to ignore the contributions of native women, the stories of some exemplary women have managed to survive. One such example is Buffalo Calf Road.

Born in the early 1850s, possibly into the band of Dull Knife, Buffalo Calf Road would have spent her early life in the Yellowstone. It is possible that she witnessed the massacre of her people at Sand Creek in 1864. That event may have influenced her later exploits. Buffalo Calf Road enters the written records on June 17, 1876, at the Battle of the Rosebud. At the time of the Battle, she would have been in her mid-20s; she was married to Black Coyote and had a young daughter. She was also the sole Cheyenne woman actively engaged in the fight, and distinguished herself by risking her life to rescue her brother. A week later she fought against Custer at the Little Big Horn. During this second military engagement, she again distinguished herself in battle and earned the name Brave Woman.

Following Custer's disastrous defeat, the Cheyenne broke camp and moved into the Bighorn Mountains to wait out the winter. Buffalo Calf Road was pregnant with her second child when the Cheyenne fled the Little Big Horn. The respite the Cheyenne had hoped for was short lived. On November 25, 1876, Col. Ranald S. MacKenzie led an assault on the band, killing 45 and burning the village to the ground. A second skirmish between the army and the band in January of 1877, coupled with the freezing winter temperatures, forced most Cheyenne to finally surrender. In August of 1877 Buffalo Calf Road and her band were forced to move to Indian Territory in modern-day Oklahoma. Squalid conditions, disease, and starvation caused many Cheyenne to decide to leave the territory and return to the Yellowstone. In September 1878 Buffalo Calf Road and 300 other Northern Cheyenne began their trek. The army pursued the band relentlessly and frequent skirmishes broke out. True to her warrior spirit, Buffalo Calf Road led the women in battle against the army.

During the winter of 1878-1879, the band hid out in the Sandhills of Nebraska. However, a dispute among the remaining members forced Buffalo Calf Road, her family, and four others to leave the safety of the band early in the year. They wandered north until Black Coyote killed a soldier near Fort Keogh. By April 1879 Buffalo Calf Road and the rest of the band had been captured by the army and imprisoned at the fort. While in custody, Buffalo Calf Road became ill with diphtheria and died in June of 1879. Upon hearing of his wife's death, Black Coyote committed suicide.

—Vanessa Anne Gunther

SUGGESTED READINGS

Agonito, Rosemary, and Joseph Agonito. "Resurrecting History's Forgotten Women: A Case Study From the Cheyenne Indians." *Frontiers* 6(3): 8-16.

Berry, Carolyn. "Comenha." *Frontiers* 6(3): 17-19.

Kammen, Robert, Frederick Lefthand, and Joe Marshall. *Soldiers Falling Into Camp: The Battles at the Rosebud and the Little Big Horn.* Encampment, WY: Affiliated Writers of America, 1992.

Liberty, Margot. "Hell Came With Horses: Plains Indian Women in the Equestrian Era." *Montana: The Magazine of Western History* 32 (Summer 1982): 10-19.

Sandoz, Mari. *Cheyenne Autumn.* Lincoln: University of Nebraska Press, 1992.

BULLOCK, GEORGIA (1874-1957)

Georgia Bullock was born in 1874 in Chicago, Illinois. She married and had a son and a daughter. Her husband either died or left while the children were young, and she raised them alone while she went to law school. She helped establish a legal society for women called Phi Delta Delta in 1912 while she was in law school. She volunteered as a juvenile probation officer of Los Angeles County from 1913 to 1914 and graduated from the University of Southern California Law School in Los Angeles in 1914. From 1915 to 1917 she was a referee for women's cases before the Police Court in Los Angeles until she became deputy district attorney in 1917. Bullock was judge pro tem, Superior Bench, in 1922 and the first woman member of the Los Angeles Bar Association. In 1924 she was named police judge in Women's Court, and in 1926 she was named municipal judge.

In 1928 Bullock was appointed judge pro tem of the Los Angeles Superior Court and served from April 1 to July 1. She received an honorary doctor of law degree from Southwestern University that same year. She also ran an unsuccessful campaign for the seat of judge of the Los Angeles Superior Court, even though she was well qualified and had experience. Three years later, on August 14, 1931, Governor James Rolph Jr. appointed her to the Los Angeles Superior Court as a judge, the first woman ever in that position. In 1939 Woodbury Business College in Los Angeles issued her another honorary degree. Bullock was known to the media for her bobbed hair and had a reputation for being tough on men who didn't provide support to their families.

—Carolyn Stull

SUGGESTED READING

Robertson, Cara. "Bobbed-Haired Portia Takes the Bench": Judge Georgia Bullock and Her Campaign for the Los Angeles Superior Court (May 13, 1997). Retrieved from www.stanford.edu/group/WLHP/papers/georgia.html.

BUNZEL, RUTH LEAH (1898-1990)

Ruth Leah Bunzel was born in 1898 to a Jewish family in Manhattan, New York. In 1918 she earned a bachelor's degree in European history from Barnard College. Shortly after her graduation, she began work as a secretary to Franz Boas, who soon launched her anthropological career. In 1924 she accompanied Ruth Benedict to the Southwest, where Boas insisted that she undertake her own project: to understand the relationship between the artist and her work.

In the early part of the 20th century, anthropologists sought to place themselves both inside and outside their objects of study. By means of participant observation—directly participating in a culture *and* observing the habits of people living inside that culture—anthropologists hoped to be able to understand cultures better than their predecessors. Therefore, Bunzel apprenticed herself to the potter Catalina (Lina) Zuni in order to understand Zuni tribal aesthetics and culture. The result of her research was her dissertation and book, *The Pueblo Potter: A Study of Creative Imagination in Primitive Art* (1929), described by two recent scholars as "a landmark in Pueblo ethnoaesthetic studies." This book was the first anthropological text to combine art and psychology.

In 1926 Bunzel returned to the Zuni tribe to study ceremonialism with a Zuni man. She spent her third season learning the language. The result of this latter research is her 1933 collection, *Zuni Texts,* Volume XV in *Publications of the American Ethnological Society,* edited by Franz Boas. In the Foreword to this volume, Bunzel explains how and when she gathered the ethnological texts and tales that constitute her collection. Most of the material was gathered from the Zuni during the summer of 1926, as part of her study of the Zuni language. In 1927 she returned to the Zuni and added an as-told-to narrative from Lina Zuni, modestly titled "An Autobiography." The autobiography is brief, approximately 12 pages, and is presented as a linguistic study: the Zuni narrative and its English translation appear together and include numbered lines to facilitate bilingual readings. The as-told-to narrative functions as the basis for the more fully constructed ethnographic autobiography. It is the form closest to the raw text, the actual transcription taken from the informant by the anthropologist.

Thus this autobiography retains the simple language, repeated phrases and themes, and stream-of-consciousness movement that characterize oral storytelling. In this passage, Lina Zuni movingly yet simply describes the scene of her childhood:

> I and my brother were both small, and we lived alone with our grandmother at her peach orchard. We were very poor. There was no meat. Our grandmother made corn cakes for us, and these we ate. When the corn was ripe, grandmother made us fresh cornbread, and *hepaloka,* fresh corn *hepaloka.* We were very poor. We stayed with her alone at our peach orchard. Every day we ate *hampasa* [Note #1: A yellow flowered herb], dipping it in water. We were living alone with our grandmother; and our grandfather also, poor thing, was living alone. We did not go around with our mother. We always wanted our grandmother and our grandfather. We were very poor.

These short, simple sentences move abruptly from one to the next without apparent transitions—as if a speaker is telling her listeners about her life. Like an oral account, this narrative repeats phrases, such as "we were very poor" and "we lived alone," that serve to bind the passage together and convey a larger message about her people's poverty and isolation. The apparent linear discontinuity (from sentence to sentence) is thus contained by the narrative's circular continuity and its cohesive cultural message. Where and how they lived and what they ate are framed by how they felt: poor and lonely. This emotional structure seems to originate in Lina Zuni's own storytelling voice; the oral narrative moves according to her emotional patterns. We hear no questions, no voice of the listener or interpreter, but the use of the footnote to explain a Zuni word that is untranslatable reminds us that there is someone guiding this narrative, someone translating the actual words of Lina Zuni into English. Bunzel presents the autobiography as a linguistic study that seeks to preserve Lina Zuni's emotions, intentions, and native stylistics.

Critics of Bunzel's text either view "An Autobiography" as accurate, as the actual textual rendering of Lina Zuni's oral story, or they see the narrative as largely the result of Bunzel's manipulation. For example, the anthropologist's questions of the informant are not included in the text; however, these unasked questions are revealed by the kind of information provided. When Lina Zuni explains the origin of a kachina ceremony, she discusses a topic not specifically related to her personal story but one that provides a useful demonstration of the importance of ritual in Zuni society. The life story thus functions as a cultural lesson for someone who does not understand Zuni culture.

Bunzel spent three seasons observing Zuni habits, manners, and speech and participating in cultural activities, thereby creating shared experiences with her informants. Coupled with her extensive cultural contact is the gender connection she forms with her female informant and translator. The all-woman team that created "An Autobiography" included Bunzel, Lina Zuni, and her daughter, Flora, who translated. Bunzel, who was eventually formally adopted into Flora Zuni's family, could claim Flora as a relative. According to Flora, she "was just like a sister to me." This gender connection gave her access to the lives of native women. In a 1985 interview, Bunzel explained her feminist interest in the Zuni: "Zuni is a woman's society. The women have a great deal of power and influence, so it's a good place for women to work." Of her anthropological emphasis she said that she felt that "there was a great lack of knowledge of people's lives—particularly about women."

Except for a visit in 1938, Bunzel did not return to the Zuni after completing her fieldwork in 1929. In the 1930s she conducted field trips to Guatemala, Mexico, and Spain. For the remainder of her life, Bunzel worked on the Research in Contemporary Cultures project and taught at Columbia University. In 1985 she talked about the Southwest sky; she remembered "sleeping on the pueblo roof on summer nights, far from New York, and being awestruck at the spaciousness and beauty and intricacy of nature." She died in 1990 in New York.

—Becky Jo (Gesteland) McShane

SUGGESTED READINGS

Babcock, Barbara A., and Nancy J. Parezo. *Daughters of the Desert: Women Anthropologists and the Native American Southwest, 1880-1980.* Albuquerque: University of New Mexico Press, 1988, 38-43.

Fawcett, David M., and Teri McLuhan. "Ruth Leah Bunzel," in Ute Gacs, Aisha Khan, Jerrie McIntyre, and Ruth Weinberg, eds., *Women Anthropologists: Selected Biographies.* Urbana: University of Illinois Press, 1989, 29-36.

Hardin, Margaret Ann. "Zuni Potters and the Pueblo Potter: The Contributions of Ruth Bunzel," in Nancy Parezo, ed., *Hidden Scholars: Women Anthropologists and the Native American Southwest.* Albuquerque: University of New Mexico Press, 1993, 259-269.

BURNSTAD, HATTIE (1911-1986)

Historically, the West has been a difficult place in which to survive. For the miner, it was a constant boom-or-bust cycle; for the rancher and farmer, it was the natural cycle of weather that plagued them. No matter what the pursuit, nothing escaped the fact that in the West, life does not come easy. To make it in the West you needed a little more spirit or determination and a lot more perseverance than average. Today this spirit or attitude is still very alive and embodied in the saying "cowboy up." The cowboy image is so popular that it can still be found everywhere in the West, for example, in Wyoming, from the "Welcome to Wyoming" signs that greet visitors to the bucking bronco on the state's license plates. To "cowboy up" means you must be able to rise to the occasion no matter what you are provided with. This western attitude is also so popular that you can find it on everything from bumper stickers, T-shirts, and mud flaps throughout the entire West.

Western history gives us many women who have embraced the cowboy spirit and cowboyed up. These women have chosen, through their determination and hard work, to persevere and leave an indelible impression on their surroundings. In fact, the pages of this book are full of these women. They all share one common and central attribute: through their dedication, perseverance, and hard work, they strove to enhance the communities around them. They saw the importance of a strong cultural identity and its relationship to the health and well-being of the community as a whole. Hattie Burnstad, through her teaching, volunteer work, and personal life, constantly worked to enhance her community through the improvement of education and cultural growth. Because of this inspiration, Burnstad received a plethora of awards and recognition from every organization she worked with. Her hard work, dedication to her family, and her community are what make her a great western woman.

Born in a small farmhouse on October 17, 1911, in Winona, North Dakota, Hattie Caroline Feterley's birth involved most of the family—her third aunt performed as a midwife while other family members served as attendants. Hattie's mother understood the importance of education at an early period. During the long North Dakota winters, she would read books to the entire family. Because of this, she enjoyed reading at a very early age. Her early education was typical of rural North Dakota. She attended a small one-room school that was 3 miles from home.

In 1925 the family rented their farm and moved 60 miles to Braddock, North Dakota, to enable Hattie to attend high school. This is very impressive for the time period and reflects the progressive thinking of her parents. In the 1920s most forms of agriculture struggled to survive due to a national farm depression. Even though most of the country was experiencing prosperity, agricultural prices remained low due to overproduction during the war years. Usually if education was of any importance, it was important to male offspring. Also, in the context of an agricultural setting, as opposed to an urban setting, it is even more significant that Hattie's parents found it important for her to be educated instead of learning the ways of the farm.

While in high school, Hattie not only excelled in academics but also was very busy with extracurricular activities. She was the valedictorian of the class of 1929. She was president of the glee club, a member of the debate team, and also active with the Epworth League Organization. She did not just limit herself to her immediate surroundings. She traveled to Chicago to attend the Methodist Youth Conference and the World's Fair. Chicago exposed her to new and different cultures and ideas. She reminisced that the fair was her most interesting experience of that time.

Hattie's success in school is ironic. Her early school experiences were very negative. However, it was because of the encouragement of a friend and Hattie's outstanding character that allowed her to turn a negative experience into something very positive. Grade school was her first separation from her parents and caused her great difficulties. This trend continued through high school. Having recently moved to attend high school made Hattie the obvious target for the older kids. Many of the older kids spent their time pestering her, but one person's encouragement drove her to move forward. High school friend Ed Hixon told her that "there's only one way you're going to beat this bunch. You have to show them you are smarter than they are. You know darn well you really are!" Hattie took this advice to heart, and even though school presented her with a negative experience, she persevered and excelled.

Upon graduation, Hattie pursued her higher education at Jamestown College in North Dakota. College life shared many similarities with high school. Although she was not teased, she was very socially active. She was involved with a group known as "nerds" or "naughty but nice." The group was made up of nine women who were all daughters of preachers. The group's experiences bonded them in such a way that they started a round-robin letter-writing group that stayed in close contact and were still active in 1984.

Upon the completion of college, Burnstad found employment immediately. Her first teaching job was in Seville, North Dakota. The grand salary was $50 a month, but she was lucky to have a job during the Depression. Her next position was in Burnstad, North Dakota, where she taught seventh and eighth grade algebra and political science. From 1937 to 1938 she taught sixth, seventh, and eighth grades and four high school subjects in Jay-Em, Wyoming. Then in 1938 she moved to Solen, South Dakota, where she was promoted to principal of the school. Eventually, marriage and pregnancy caused her to take a short break from her career, and she did not return to the profession until 1957.

Hattie's success as a teacher was mirrored in her personal life. She was married to Mike Burnstad in 1941. It was a small ceremony in Beach, North Dakota, attended only by her mother. Hattie and Mike had three children, Helen Marie, Patrick Manley, and Karen Sue, who were her beaming source of pride. A demonstration of her belief in the importance of education can be found on her resume. She notes in parentheses that all her children were college graduates.

When Hattie returned to teaching, she taught at Worland (Wyoming) Jr. High School from 1957 to 1974. While teaching there, she felt the need to create a better curriculum. There were two manifestations of her improvements to the curriculum. First, she wrote the text titled *Summary of Wyoming Government*, which was used as a textbook for 9 years. Second, she worked on the state's curriculum guide. The core of the guide was the work product of 15 administrators and classroom teachers from all levels. The guide covered all disciplines from kindergarten through 12th grade. It was one of the most challenging activities of her life. She wrote about the experience, "I'm sure I was never in my life presented so many tried and proven truths and concepts in such a short space of time, and to sort and evaluate was a real challenge. The contacts made there as well as the acceptance of the finished product, not only within our state but many places in the nation, was most gratifying."

Hattie continued to teach even after retirement. She taught college credit courses in Wyoming government at Northwest Community College and also lectured for community organizations and at Bethesda Care Center. Her dedication to her students went so far that when she could not make it to class for health reasons, she invited them into her apartment.

Roger Youtz, principal of Worland Jr. High School, described Hattie's dedication and spirit as a teacher:

> To put down in writing or say a few words about Hattie is most difficult. Time and space are too limited. If we could find the perfect procedure to define a master teacher and then put Hattie's name above the definition, the job would be complete. Hattie, you are a 10 in my book. What a joy for a brand new principal to have you on the staff. You were always one hundred percent professional who gave willingly of your time and talents to the youth of Worland.

In her teaching career, spanning 39 years, Hattie achieved many milestones. She was named Washakie County Teacher of the Year 1969, listed in *Who's Who of Western Women 1969*, *Leaders of Elementary and Secondary Education 1971-74*, *Who's Who Honorary Society of America 1975*, and nominated to the Bicentennial National Committee. She was Wyoming's National Education Association delegate to three national conventions, and was involved with the Wyoming Education Association and National Council of Social Studies. She served as president of the Wyoming Council of Social Studies for 1970-1971 and was a member of the state social studies curriculum committee from 1970 to 1972.

Hattie's hard work and determination did not stop when she left the schoolhouse. She volunteered extensively throughout the community. She first became involved with the Boy Scouts and Girl Scouts when her children became active in the groups. She was a scout leader for both of her daughters, and even after they had moved on, she still helped any in need. She helped many scouts receive their government badges. She took full advantage of any opportunity to share Wyoming history and government with any scouts.

Even after Hattie's children left Worland, she continued to give of her own time to other organizations in her community. She was active with the American Association of University Women (the state's first and second vice president, 1968-74), Wyoming State Historical Society (president, 1970), and received achievement awards from Kiwanis, Boy Scouts, Worland Chamber of Commerce, United Nations, and the Wyoming School Board Association.

Hattie's awards demonstrate and compliment her efforts and western spirit. However, her greatest compliment is that an entire community gathered to honor her for her tireless work. On September 27, 1984, the inhabitants of Worland recognized her hard work and dedication in a program titled "Days of Remembrance, Hattie Burnstad." Hundreds illustrating how her life had enhanced the quality of others' lives attended this celebration of her life.

She demonstrated confidence in herself, and that confidence was contagious. Helen Schoeler at "Days of Remembrance, Hattie Burnstad" said,

> The confidence you [Hattie] had in us when sometimes we are reluctant to take a minority stance or sometimes we are reluctant to venture out or sometimes we don't want to try something, I think with both students and adults Hattie silently had a way of saying go for it, do it. And we were always glad she did and she got me into a great many things I was grateful for.

Hattie's life was inspirational. When her life is put into context, it is truly amazing. Her achievements left a very lasting mark on her students, family, and community. Her tireless efforts to constantly improve the cultural area around her makes her a great western woman.

—J. Elwood Bakken

SUGGESTED READINGS

Burnstad, Hattie. Personal papers, private collection in author's possession.

Burnstad, Hattie. *Summary of Wyoming Government.* Worland, WY: Valley Press, 1967.

Northern Wyoming Daily News. "Days of Remembrance. Hattie Burnstad" (video and pamphlet). United Methodist Church RER Building, Worland, Wyoming, September 27, 1984.

BUTLER, OCTAVIA (1947-)

Author Octavia Butler was born into a strict Baptist family in Pasadena, California. Her father died when she was an infant, so her mother and grandmother raised her. She began writing "her own little stories" at the age of 12. She has always described herself as shy.

She attended Pasadena City College and received her associate of arts degree in 1968. She went on to California State University at Los Angeles and then on to the University of California, Los Angeles, for its Open Door Program of the Screen Writers Guild of America. She also went to San Francisco for the Clarion Writers Workshop. Harlan Ellison mentored her.

Her writing consists of an interweaving of African American history and science fiction. She published her first book, *Crossover*, in 1971. Her work has received numerous awards. In 1980 she received the James Tiptree award for *Wild Seed*. In 1993 she won the New York Notable Book of the Year for *The Parable of the Sower*. She received the Hugo award and the Nebula award for *Bloodchild and Other Stories* in 1995. She also received a "genius grant" MacArthur Foundation fellowship in 1995.

—Lori S. Iacovelli

SUGGESTED READINGS

Beal, Frances M. "Black Scholar Interview with Octavia Butler: Black Women and the Science Fiction Genre," *The Black Scholar: The Black Woman Writer and the Diaspora 29* (October 1985): 14-18.

O'Connor, Margaret Anne. "Octavia E. Butler," in Thadious M. Davis and Trudier Harris, eds., *Dictionary of Literary Biography: Afro-American Fiction Writers After 1955: Vol. 33.* Detroit, MI: Gale Research, 1984.

CABRINI, SAINT FRANCES XAVIER
(1850-1917)

Francesca Cabrini was born on July 15, 1850, in San Angelo, a small village about 20 miles south of Milan, in the fertile plain of Lombardy. She was the youngest of 13 children born to Agostino and Stella Cabrini. Agostino, the proprietor of a modest estate, made a living farming. Living in their modest and comfortable home, the Cabrinis were a pious family dedicated to both their children and their church.

A fragile baby at birth, Francesca was taken to the church immediately for baptism. Having been born when her mother was 52 and had 12 other children to tend to, Francesca was left to be cared for by her oldest sister. Rosa, whose career aspirations were to be a teacher, taught Francesca how to knit and sew, and offered her religious instruction.

At the age of 13, Francesca was sent to the Daughters of the Sacred Heart, a private school at which she remained for 5 years. At the age of 18, she passed her teaching examinations with top honors and applied for admission into the convent. Her application was turned down on account of her health, and her hopes of being sent to teach in the Orient were dashed. She soon returned home to care for her parents.

After suffering the loss of her parents, Francesca devoted herself to a life of lay service. When an epidemic of smallpox ran through the village, she dedicated herself to nursing the stricken. Her commitment to helping the sick resulted in her contracting the

disease, but her recovery was prompt and life would soon offer another challenge.

After serving as a substitute teacher for a short time in the village school, Francesca applied once again for admission to the convent of the Daughters of the Sacred Heart. Although her health was much improved, Father Antonio Serrati instructed the mother superior to once again turn her down. Having watched Francesca work dutifully in her voluntary roles, Father Serrati had other plans for her.

For the next 6 years, Francesca was put in charge of reorganizing an orphanage called the House of Providence, in the nearby town of Cadogno, which was run by two laywomen, one of whom had put up the money for its endowment. At the age of 24, Francesca was faced with the task of putting things right in the orphanage. Soon thereafter she began wearing the nun's habit and within 3 years had taken vows and been made mother superior of the orphanage. When the House of Providence was dissolved 3 years later, Mother Cabrini and the seven young nuns she had trained were left homeless.

The women would not suffer long, as the bishop of Lodi soon sent for Francesca and asked her to found a missionary order of women to serve under his diocese. Upon finding a location for the convent, Mother Cabrini opened a day school, once again began receiving orphans, and resumed the position of mother superior. The order was named the Missionary Sisters of the Sacred Heart, and Mother Cabrini selected St. Francis de Sales and St. Frances Xavier as the patron saints. Due to the large number of children asking for admission, it became necessary to expand the order. The nuns responded by building an addition to the first building, and 2 years later Mother Cabrini opened a mission at Cremona and then a boarding school for girls in Milan. Seven more institutions would be opened within the next 7 years, all staffed by nuns who had been trained by Mother Cabrini.

In order to gain papal approval for the order and in an attempt to receive permission to open a house in Rome that might serve as a headquarters for future enterprises, Mother Cabrini in September of 1887 set out on her first trip to Rome. Her trip proved successful; both Cardinal Parocchi and Pope Leo XIII received her well. While her service was of great value in Rome and the surrounding areas, it became clear that Mother Cabrini's next challenge would lie in being a missionary to the United States.

Due to the large immigration of Italians to the United States and the growing concern with their well-being in Italy, the Catholic Church took an active role in attempting to help the immigrants in the New World. Bishop Scalabrini wrote a pamphlet describing the misery of the immigrants and established the Congregation of St. Charles Borromeo in New York City to provide material assistance for those in need. After corresponding with Bishop Scalabrini, Mother Cabrini determined that her next call of duty would be in the United States.

On March 31, 1889, Mother Cabrini and seven nuns arrived in New York to aid Archbishop Corrigan. Quickly establishing the needs of the community, the young women opened an orphanage with the aid of a wealthy Italian woman. It was to mark the beginning of a lifetime of traveling and building in order to spread the word of Christ. For the next 28 years, Mother Cabrini traveled throughout America and in this time founded orphanages, hospitals, and schools throughout New York City, Chicago, Seattle, and New Orleans. Her orphanages and schools reached Argentina, Brazil, Chile, France, Italy, Panama, and Spain. She regularly visited Seattle and worshiped at St. James Cathedral. In 1902 Bishop Nicholas Matz invited her to visit Denver, and in August she traveled to the Mile High City. The Mother Cabrini Shrine is located in Golden, Colorado, and memorializes her visits and contributions to the West.

In 1909 Mother Cabrini became an American citizen and was named general superior for life in 1910. After her death on December 22, 1917, her remains were moved from where she had been buried in Chicago to the chapel at Mother Cabrini High School in 1933. The first American saint to be canonized, she was beatified by Pope Pius XI in 1938 and canonized by Pope Pius XII in 1946. In 1950 the church made her the Patroness of Immigrants.

—Patricia Jimenez

SUGGESTED READING

DiDonato, Pietro. *Immigrant Saint: The Life of Mother Cabrini.* New York: McGraw-Hill, 1960.

CALLAHAN, SOPHIA ALICE
(1868-1894)

Sophia Alice Callahan was born in Sulphur Springs, Texas, on January 1, 1868. Her father was part Creek Indian and had a large farm and cattle ranch in what later became Oklahoma. He became a significant figure, serving the Creek Nation in an official capacity as a representative of the Creek and Seminole Nations to the Confederate Congress during the Civil War. Her mother was a Methodist minister's daughter, so Sophia followed the Protestant religion and was sent to a women's school in Staunton, Virginia, where she became certified as a teacher.

When she was 23 years old, Sophia wrote a romantic fictional account called *Wynema,* about a young Creek girl who becomes a teacher and sets up a school in her village. It was a reform novel intended for a white audience, illustrating the wrongs done to American Indians at the time it was written. Also included are arguments for women's suffrage and records of Creek culture.

In 1892-1893 she was a teacher at Wealaka Mission School and later in 1893 at Harrel Institute High School in Muskogee. She had first planned to finish her own education in Staunton, but was called back to Muskogee because several teachers at Harrel Institute had become ill. She died on January 7, 1894, 2 weeks after contracting pleurisy.

—Carolyn Stull

SUGGESTED READING

Van Dyke, Annette. "An Introduction to Wynema, A Child of the Forest, by Sophia Alice Callahan." *Studies in American Indian Literature* (Summer/Fall 1992).

CALLENDER, MARIE (1907-1995)

Upon tasting one of Marie Callender's home-baked pies that she brought to church and neighborhood gatherings, someone remarked that Marie should consider selling the delicious pies to the public. She did, organizing a small home baking business after World War II that soon turned into gold under the careful management of her husband, Cal Callender. Their son, Don, would expand the business from a single restaurant in Orange County, California, to a chain of over 140 restaurants by the mid-1980s, with annual sales of $175 million. Although the family eventually sold the company, Marie's name remains on all the restaurants as a guarantee to customers that the quality of her pies remains unchanged.

Marie was born in South Dakota in 1907. Her family, as did so many other midwesterners after World War I, migrated westward, ending up in California in the early 1920s. She met and married Cal Callender in 1924. An only child, Don, was born 4 years later. For the better part of the next 2 decades, Marie was a homemaker and mother, focusing on the needs of her husband and son. After the war, California experienced a dramatic population growth as new towns and cities dotted the map. Southern California was an entrepreneurial cradle, producing major lifestyle and consumer changes with the birth of new companies such McDonald's and Carl's Junior restaurants. Marie answered a help wanted ad for a job in a delicatessen. Soon she was making pies, using her own recipes. The owner asked for more of her popular pies, but Marie felt overwhelmed by the logistics of producing several hundred pies every week. After discussions with her husband and son, and a guarantee from the delicatessen owner that he would buy her pies, the family went into the pie-making business.

They raised investment capital by selling the family car, rented a small Quonset hut in Long Beach, California, and began producing pies in 1948. Working through the night, the family baked and then sold several hundred pies a week to local eateries. The key was Marie's pie recipes that she had developed and tested. The demand never slackened, and in 1962 the family, at the urging of son Don, decided to open their own coffee shop in Orange County to enhance their profits. First-time customers got a free slice of pie, and the Callenders put a working pie oven in the front window of the shop.

Within a few years, full menus were added, and the number of locations began to grow. Don Callender began an aggressive expansion into the Southwest in the late 1960s, and soon the chain numbered well over 100 restaurants. The family's original $700 investment in 1948 was now generating over $100 million in sales. Marie's pies became a holiday tradition wherever the pie shops operated. Every major holiday, customers buy thousands of pumpkin, apple, and pecan pies. A typical shop might sell as many as 7,000 pumpkin pies at Thanksgiving. The recipes remain a secret, locked away and carefully guarded. Marie always felt that her pies could withstand any competition and that customers would always return for more once they tasted the product.

Cal Callender died in 1984, and the family sold the company shortly thereafter. Marie became involved in local Orange County charities and religious activities, although she always kept an active interest in how the restaurants were doing. Until her death in 1995, she enjoyed eating at the shops that bear her name, always thinking about ways to improve the operation. There have been several changes of ownership over the last 15 years, but the company still produces hundreds of thousands of Marie's pies, using her recipes developed in that rented Quonset hut in the 1940s.

—Craig Hendricks

SUGGESTED READINGS

Cekola, Anna. "Marie Callender; Turned Pie Shop Into Restaurant Chain." *Los Angeles Times*, November 12, 1995.
Lowe, Jennifer. "Sweetie Pie." *Orange County Register*, November 11, 1998.

CATHER, WILLA (1873-1947)

When 9-year-old Willa Cather moved with her family from Virginia's Shenandoah Valley to the high plains frontier near Red Cloud, Nebraska, in April 1883, she was destined to grow up as a woman of the West. Born on December 7, 1873, the precocious eldest child of Charles and Mary Virginia Boak Cather's seven children, Wilella Cather was always called Willie by family and friends but invented Willa for herself and adopted the middle name Sibert after a Confederate uncle who died at Manassas. Her individual determination and her critical attitude, as well as her creativity, were also evident very early in her ambivalent attitude toward southern manners and traditions. The family that settled in the Back Creek Valley near Winchester a century before the Civil War was divided between the Union and the Confederacy throughout the conflict. Willa's parents tried with some success to mend the rifts; she did not want to leave her first family home to follow her paternal grandparents and aunt and uncle to Nebraska. She could not, of course, foresee that she would become an excellent as well as prolific and popular writer and notably the creator of an extraordinary variety of fictional women of the West, who live on in her dozen novels and more than 60 short stories.

Willa was, as Henry James said in *The Art of Fiction* in 1884, what a writer should be, "one of those on whom nothing is lost." Open to the subtleties and complexities of an environment that many have considered flat and boring, she observed and later described nature on the prairie with interest and in precise detail. While Red Cloud, like other new towns on the plains, had a paucity of cultural amenities, the population of immigrants, including Bohemians, Danes, French, Germans, occasionally Mexicans, Norwegians, Russians, and Swedes, as well as those born in states to the east, made up a surprisingly cosmopolitan community. Young Willa learned much from Bohemian families like the Pavelkas and from the cultured German Jewish neighbors next door. When she went to Europe for the first time just before she turned 30, she felt that she had already been there. As a child she also benefited from the unusually good library in the Cather home.

Still, she lived in a paradoxical situation with which her younger colleague, Wallace Stegner, identified. His childhood on the remote Saskatchewan-Montana border in the 2nd decade of the 20th century was paradoxical in the same way. In 1956, when he lectured on Cather at Stanford, he emphasized that the young would-be artist in Cather's situation or his had challenging and interesting material to work with: the transition from unplowed prairie to cultivated land and the effect of that transition on human beings. But in an area in which Euro-American settlement was new, such would-be artists had limited access to nurturing cultural institutions like libraries and museums.

A corollary irony follows. Willa, after graduating from high school in Red Cloud, where she also studied music, began a long series of eastward moves, first in 1890 to Nebraska's new capital, Lincoln. She needed additional preparatory work before she entered the young University of Nebraska, from which she graduated in 1895. During her almost 5 years in Lincoln, she studied the classics and demonstrated an ability in story writing and journalism, particularly theatrical reviews. For more than a year after her arrival, she kept her hair cut short, as it had been since before she turned 13, and affected a partially masculinized style of dress adopted too by other "new women." She made interesting friends in Lincoln and was not the only distinguished early University of Nebraska graduate; her close companion Louise Pound became the first woman president of the Modern Language Association.

Willa moved to Pittsburgh, Pennsylvania, a year after graduation to accept a position on the *Home Monthly,* from which she moved to the *Pittsburgh Leader* and then to high school teaching in 1901. Within 2 years she published *April Twilights,* a volume of poetry, and 2 years later, *The Troll Garden,* which led to her appointment as managing editor of *McClure's* magazine in New York City. As she moved east again from Pittsburgh, she left behind Isabelle McClung, whose family home she shared for more than 4 years. This personal relationship was almost certainly Willa's most emotionally significant, though whether or not it was lesbian in a physical sense will probably remain unclear. While she was a discreet person, certainly her most important friendships were with women, so the ongoing discussion about her sexual orientation is appropriate.

In 1908, after several years in New York, she took an apartment with Edith Lewis. Having met in 1903 in Lincoln, they lived together amicably until Cather's death on April 24, 1947, and traveled together when Lewis's independent career in publishing and advertising permitted.

Since her university days, Cather had been writing poetry and fiction. Many of her early stories dealt with the material of the high plains frontier, although early in the new century she made it clear that Henry James and Edith Wharton were the American writers of fiction she most admired, as stories like "Flavia and Her Artists" from *The Troll Garden* indicated. But "The Enchanted Bluff," which appeared in *Harper's* in April 1909, portrays a group of boys camping and telling stories by a Nebraska river. The story also contains an inset about Native American villagers in the

Southwest who starve to death after the stairway from their bluff is destroyed in a storm. This lugubrious tale illustrates her fascination with the region and its indigenous inhabitants several years before her first trip to the area to visit her brother Douglass in Flagstaff, Arizona, in 1912. "The Sculptor's Funeral," another story from *The Troll Garden,* presents a grim picture of the lack of understanding of an artist's life in a Kansas high plains town; his mother stands out as a realistically if briefly characterized woman of the West. In "Wagner Matinee," however, she depicts Georgiana, a professionally trained New England pianist, who gave up her career to marry for love and homestead on the high plains. Attending a concert in Boston after a generation, she does not want to return home, but Cather adds resonance to the story when she writes that Georgiana's husband also gave her "a little parlour organ" after 15 years on the prairie. In her early stories, Cather established her recurrent concerns with frontier life and with the problems of the artist.

In 1912 Cather left editing to devote herself entirely to writing, and published her first novel, *Alexander's Bridge,* in which the flawed character of its designer, Bartley Alexander, is analogous to that of his bridge, and his personal affections are divided between two devoted women, his eastern Canadian wife, Winifred, and the vivacious British actress, Hilda Burgoyne. Identifying this novel as Cather's would be difficult without her name on the title page.

Then the next year, with the appearance of *O Pioneers!,* Cather first focused successfully on a full-length work about the high plains frontier. This work is the first of three to emphasize the struggles and eventual successes of young immigrant women. Swedish Alexandra Bergson has the ability to become an innovative farmer, but she must not only contend with her stubborn brothers after their father's death and make good agricultural decisions, but she loses her much younger brother, Emil, when Frank Shabata, the husband of Emil's lover, Marie, shoots them in a jealous rage. Cather presents their deaths graphically; this aspect of the novel serves as a corrective to any thought that success comes without intense loss and pain. Alexandra, who brings beauty and order to the land, is the epitome of the strong female protagonist. Her friend, the engaging and mercurial Marie, is partly responsible for bringing anguish to two families.

In her second novel, Cather writes democratically of Scandinavians and Bohemians; she creates Russian Ivar, thought of as crazy by many neighbors, and Emil's French friends, Angélique and Amédée, whose death from a ruptured appendix, in an ironic contrast to the impending deaths of Emil and Marie, cuts short their happiness. Her characters include well-delineated servant girls, like Signa.

Thea Kronborg's struggle in Cather's next very long novel, *The Song of the Lark,* published in 1915, is to recognize the nature of her musical talent and eventually to become an opera singer. Friends and family realize that this powerful female protagonist has special gifts, though for years she studies piano rather than voice. The physician in Moonstone, Colorado, helps her, as do several teachers, but the horrible death of her admirer, Ray Kennedy, in a railroad accident gives her the inheritance to pursue her dream in Chicago. Once more, a gruesome loss serves as a corrective to sentimentality. The lengthy process through which Thea learns may suggest too the development of Cather as a different kind of artist. Like Cather, Thea finds restorative solace among the Native American ruins of the Southwest. After working in Europe for years, the singer, partially modeled on Cather's friend Olive Fremstad, performs splendidly at the Metropolitan Opera. The powerful Thea must also move east several times to find necessary training. Her mother, Mrs. Kronborg, who misses her, provides an individualistic example of the supportive women in the novel Thea dominates.

Readers see Ántonia Shimerda, the strong Bohemian immigrant protagonist of *My Ántonia,* through the eyes of her younger neighbor, Jim Burden, who arrives in Nebraska on the same train as Ántonia and her family. An orphan from the Shenandoah Valley, Jim admires first Ántonia's zest for life. After her sensitive musical father commits suicide during his initial prairie winter, Jim respects her determination to work as hard as a man on the land, though he regrets that she cannot go to school. The vicissitudes of her life include bearing an illegitimate child, of whom she is proud despite having been deceived by the baby's father. Ántonia, though not always wise, learns, loves, and continues to work hard and persevere. At the end of the novel, Jim finds her, a worn middle-aged woman, happy with her good husband, large family, and productive farm. One section of the book, "The Hired Girls," depicts Ántonia and her peers Lina Lingard and Tiny Soderball, who work as domestic servants, relatively uncommon fictional subjects in 1918. The novel contains an unusual number of other interesting women of the West, such as Jim's grandmother, Ántonia's employer, Mrs. Harling, and the sympathetic Mrs. Steavens.

By the time this novel appeared, however, several events were casting shadows on Cather. Isabelle McClung's marriage to Jan Hambourg, a concert violinist, in April 1916 was a blow to her friend. Although Cather remained on good terms with Isabelle and Jan, her relationship with him was never entirely easy. For some time, moreover, Cather, who returned home to Red Cloud regularly as long as her parents were alive, had been aware that after the heroic cooperative efforts of establishing agriculture and communities on the high plains frontier, residents were becoming more litigious and materialistic. She despaired of the fascination with poorly built and quickly obsolescent machinery and neglect of flora, fauna, and even children. Most seriously, the terrible carnage of World War I horrified her as well as her modernist contemporaries who participated in the conflict. Furthermore, her cousin Grosvenor P. Cather was killed at Cantigny on May 23, 1918. In the wake of this personal loss and in the light of all the war's effects, her sadness deepened. She said that the world broke in two in 1922 or thereabouts. Despite the fact that she and her parents found some solace when they were confirmed in Grace Episcopal Church in Red Cloud on December 27 of that year when T. S. Eliot had published *The Waste Land,* her next four novels were pessimistic in various ways in comparison with the previous three.

One of Ours, another 1922 publication, won the Pulitzer Prize in 1923. This large and in many ways exceptionally interesting novel is somewhat unwieldy and lacks a degree of unity, but its sensitive protagonist, Claude Wheeler, manages to combine a thoroughgoing critical attitude toward the philistinism and banality of the high plains just before the United States enters World War I with, from April 1917 on, enthusiasm about participating in the hostilities and coming to appreciate French culture. On the home front, Cather's social commentary is especially telling; she effectively depicts prejudice against German Americans, for example. Her narrative about the inexorable influenza epidemic on Claude's troop ship en route to France is based on the journal of a physician from Jaffrey, New Hampshire, rather than Cather's experiences, but is nonetheless extraordinary in its frightening details. She did not deserve the castigation she received from some critics for writing

about the wartime pandemic. Furthermore, a remarkable variety of supporting characters interact with Claude. Unforgettable women of the West include his pious mother; the faithful family retainer Mahailey, based in large part on Marjorie Anderson, who moved west with the Cathers; and frigid Enid Royce, who is as mistaken in marrying Claude as he is in marrying her and soon deserts their unconsummated union to join her sister as a missionary in China.

The overwhelming detail of Cather's war novel contrasts sharply with the succinctly evocative *A Lost Lady,* which, coming out in 1923, illustrates her famous essay "The Novel Démeublé," which appeared in *The New Republic* on April 12, 1922. In a beautifully structured and economical narrative, she presents, through the point of view of the boy and then young man Niel Herbert, the lost lady, Marian Forrester, evoked by Cather's memories of Lyra Garber, wife of former Governor Silas Garber and the most socially prominent woman in Red Cloud while Cather was growing up. The effect of the fictional character's charm is inescapable; Niel looks up to her and appreciates her kindness. But unlike the real Mrs. Garber, Marian is unfaithful to Captain Forrester, a man of absolute integrity a generation older than she. When he has a stroke and continues to fail, she cares for him assiduously as she carries on her affair; her complex mixture of gracious and engaging qualities with illicit pleasures and eventually a willingness to do whatever she must to survive as an impecunious widow has generated much discussion. Representing the time after the passing of the frontier when the network of railroads, rife with nepotism, has changed the high plains, Marian, once seemingly the epitome of good taste, accepts the tawdry advances of Ivy Peters, who, as a boy, demonstrated his cruelty by slitting the eyelids of a woodpecker, an act foreshadowing his treatment of Marian, who sells her land to him for enough money to leave Sweet Water and eventually marry again. She is a memorable woman of the West in a way different from the hard-working and humane Alexandra and Ántonia.

Cather's subsequent novels do not contain a major female protagonist who is so clearly a salient figure in the West. Professor Godfrey St. Peter, the main character in *The Professor's House,* lives in a college town on the shore of Lake Michigan; his eight-volume *Spanish Adventurers* has brought him financial success as well as acclaim as an author. But in a work the structure of which indeed suggests that of a house,

St. Peter wants to continue working in the old sewing room of his former rented home; he is as uncomfortable in the new one as he is with the greed and materialism of his daughters and their husbands and the widening distance between him and his wife. Whether or not characters just outside Chicago can be said to be of the West, the famous inset of Tom Outland's story set in the Southwest is pertinent to the novel as a whole. The book includes a few interesting women, though Augusta, the family seamstress, is unusual as well as important to St. Peter.

The professor's quiet ennui pales before the internal bitterness of another Illinois resident, Myra Henshawe, protagonist of *My Mortal Enemy.* This was Cather's shortest individually published entity, the closest she came to implementing her theories on the "novel démeublé." From the point of view of a young woman, the niece of Myra's friend, Cather tells the story of Myra's marrying Oswald despite the disapproval of her uncle and guardian, who disowns her. In several places from New York to San Francisco (barely identifiable because Cather knew little about San Francisco), Myra and Oswald's marriage deteriorates, until, resentful of his lack of money and cancer-ridden, Myra dies overlooking the Golden Gate after calling him her mortal enemy. Whether her brief stay in San Francisco qualifies her as a woman of the West or not, she is memorable for being consumed by a largely intangible unhappiness. The central focus on a marriage in this novella is unusual, too.

By 1927, however, *Death Comes to the Archbishop,* Cather's great work evocative of the human, geographical, and historical complexities of the Southwest, appeared as a reaffirmation of positive possibilities. With an emphasis on the Roman Catholic Church as a cultural vehicle and on the nature of the protagonist, Archbishop Jean Latour, and his vicar general, Father Joseph Vaillant, Cather integrates into one work strong insets from different places and levels of time. This unique book, which she preferred to call a narrative, brought critical, popular, and financial success to her and her publishers. The clerics, based to a considerable extent on the admirable real Archbishop Lamy and Father Machebreuf, unify the novel, in which they cope after the Mexican War with the disarray of a long-neglected church, including people from a very broad moral continuum. Cather includes among their contacts a number of finely drawn women of the West, from aristocratic and vain Doña Isabella, who will do almost anything to conceal her age, to Magdalena, the abused Mexican wife of Yankee murderer Buck Scales.

Once more, in *Shadows on the Rock,* which portrays Quebec in 1697, Cather returns to the issues of the frontier in North America and, as in *Death Comes to the Archbishop,* retreats to a frontier depicted, in this case, long before homesteaders settled on the high plains. In mid-19th-century New Mexico or very late 17th-century New France, she recaptures the hopeful possibilities realized in *O Pioneers!, The Song of the Lark,* and *My Ántonia.* In Quebec, during the long battle between England and France for empire in North America, Cécile Auclair is the 13-year-old daughter of the apothecary Euclide Auclair, who serves everyone, religious or secular, French or Native American, in another society more complex than it at first appears. Cécile functions as an appropriate protagonist through a cycle of the seasons and the liturgical year. Although Cécile is not a woman of the West beyond the Mississippi, already explored by her countrymen, she does grow, like Alexandra, Thea, and Ántonia, into a successful woman on an earlier frontier.

Cather's last novel of the high plains, *Lucy Gayheart,* published in 1935, echoes in a pale way Thea's epic struggle to become an opera singer. But Lucy, lacking Thea's extraordinary talent and drive, returns from Chicago to her small hometown without achieving musical success. This sad young woman of the West, having learned of the drowning in Lake Como of Sebastian, the married man she loves, ironically dies when she skates on thin ice. Her earliest admirer, long since spurned, fails to offer her the ride which would have prevented her from trying to skate to her destination.

In Cather's last novel, *Sapphira and the Slave Girl,* published in 1940, she revisits her Virginia heritage, once again in an earlier time, 1856, also just before American involvement in war. Drawing heavily on family history, she brings to life a conflict between Sapphira, a slave-owning mother, and her husband and daughter, Rachel, over the slave girl Nancy, who reaches safety in Canada by way of the underground railroad. Sapphira, the strong and manipulative protagonist, is morally crippled by the issues of slavery, which Cather's grandmother, very much like the daughter in this novel, opposed.

While Cather was writing her last several novels, she continued to publish short stories, a number of them excellent. Some, like "The Old Beauty," published posthumously in 1948, are set far from the American West, in this case on the Riviera, but in other works Cather returns to the high plains that became her second home. "Neighbour Rosicky," from 1928, emphasizes the end of the life of the Bohemian immigrant Anton, who has in middle age married his countrywoman Mary, fathered a warm, well-cared for family, and established a farm where he respects nature and consistently acts with generosity. Before his heart fails, he brings his American town-bred daughter-in-law Polly fully into the family; she and Mary are loving women of the West who will live on as Anton lies in the nearby graveyard he considered welcoming.

In the longer "Old Mrs. Harris," also found in the 1932 volume *Obscure Destinies,* Cather achieves an extraordinary portrait of a three-generation family from Tennessee that establishes a new life in the high plains. The death of the aged cat foreshadows that of Mrs. Harris, the grandmother, who feels her role is to work hard to manage the home so her daughter, Victoria, can represent the family in the local community. Somewhat self-centered and oblivious to her mother's decline, Victoria can nevertheless be kind, though she does not want the kinder neighbor, Mrs. Rosen, to see how austerely Mrs. Harris lives and works. The Rosens cooperate with Mrs. Harris to make a college education possible for Vickie, the bright but also self-centered eldest child. At the end, Mrs. Harris, who has self-effacingly achieved so much, is laid out properly in Victoria's bed. The echoes of Cather's own family are obvious, though, of course, the raw material from life is reshaped and changed in fiction.

Cather's last story, "The Best Years," published posthumously in *The Old Beauty and Others,* is also a remarkable achievement peopled by three strong women of the West. After a lifetime of moving eastward, traveling in Canada, France, Great Britain, and elsewhere, and establishing a summer home on remote Grand Manan Island in New Brunswick, Cather returns home for the last time in this story in which Lesley Ferguesson, a bright 16-year-old teacher in 1899, shepherds her students safely to a farmhouse in a sudden blizzard but then dies of pneumonia contracted during the crisis. Twenty years later, Lesley's mother and her former school superintendent, Evangeline Knightly Thorndike, reminisce about the promising girl they loved. In Lesley's visits home in the first part of the story are reflected aspects of Cather's family life. In the last of many creative Cather epilogues, Mrs. Ferguesson, looking back, utters what is almost an epitaph for an earlier time on the high plains frontier which she, her daughter, and her devoted friend knew: "Our best years are when we're working hardest and going right ahead when we can hardly see our way out." Perhaps for Willa Cather, the woman of the West writing this last of numerous literary works, so many of which feature complex portrayals of fictional women of the West, this statement is also a fitting epitaph, although the inscription on her gravestone in Jaffrey, New Hampshire, where she did a lot of her best writing, comes from *My Ántonia:* "That is happiness; to be dissolved into something complete and great."

—Joan V. Greenwood

SUGGESTED READINGS

Arnold, Marilyn. *Willa Cather's Short Fiction.* Athens: Ohio University Press, 1984.

Bennett, Mildred. *The World of Willa Cather.* Lincoln: University of Nebraska Press, 1961.

Bloom, Edward A., and Lillian Bloom. *Willa Cather's Gift of Sympathy.* Carbondale: Southern Illinois University Press, 1962.

Brown, E. K., with Leon Edel. *Willa Cather: A Critical Biography.* Lincoln: University of Nebraska Press, 1953.

Callander, Marilyn Berg. *Willa Cather and the Fairy Tale.* Ann Arbor: University of Michigan, 1989.

Cather, Willa. *The Troll Garden.* 1905. In Sharon O'Brien, ed., *Early Novels and Stories.* New York: Library of America, 1987.

Cather, Willa. *Alexander's Bridge.* 1912. In Sharon O'Brien, ed., *Stories, Poems, and Other Writings.* New York: Library of America, 1992.

Cather, Willa. *O Pioneers!* 1913. In Sharon O'Brien, ed., *Early Novels and Stories.* New York: Library of America, 1987.

Cather, Willa. *The Song of the Lark.* 1915. In Sharon O'Brien, ed., *Early Novels and Stories.* New York: Library of America, 1987.

Cather, Willa. *My Ántonia.* 1918. In Sharon O'Brien, ed., *Early Novels and Stories.* New York: Library of America. 1987.

Cather, Willa. *Youth and the Bright Medusa.* 1920. In Sharon O'Brien, ed., *Stories, Poems and Other Writings.* New York: Library of America, 1992.

Cather, Willa. *One of Ours.* 1922. In Sharon O'Brien, ed., *Later Novels.* New York: Library of America, 1992.

Cather, Willa. *April Twilight and Other Poems*. 1923. In Sharon O'Brien, ed., *Stories, Poems, and Other Writings*. New York: Library of America, 1992.

Cather, Willa. *A Lost Lady*. 1923. In Sharon O'Brien, ed., *Later Novels*. New York: Library of America, 1990.

Cather, Willa. "Nebraska: The End of the First Cycle." *The Nation 117* (1923): 236-238.

Cather, Willa. *The Professor's House*. 1925. In Sharon O'Brien, ed., *Later Novels*. New York: Library of America, 1990.

Cather, Willa. *My Mortal Enemy*. 1926. In Sharon O'Brien, ed., *Stories, Poems, and Other Writings*. New York: Library of America, 1992.

Cather, Willa. *Death Comes for the Archbishop*. 1927. In Sharon O'Brien, ed., *Later Novels*. New York: Library of America, 1990.

Cather, Willa. *Shadows on the Rock*. 1931. In Sharon O'Brien, ed., *Later Novels*. New York: Library of America, 1990.

Cather, Willa. *Obscure Destinies*. 1932. In Sharon O'Brien, ed., *Stories, Poems, and Other Writings*. New York: Library of America, 1992.

Cather, Willa. *Lucy Gayheart*. 1935. In Sharon O'Brien, ed., *Later Novels*. New York: Library of America, 1990.

Cather, Willa. *Not Under Forty*. 1936. In Sharon O'Brien, ed., *Stories, Poems, and Other Writings*. New York: Library of America, 1992.

Cather, Willa. *Sapphira and the Slave Girl*. 1940. In Sharon O'Brien, ed., *Later Novels*. New York: Library of America, 1990.

Cather, Willa. *Willa Cather in Europe*, George N. Kates, ed. New York: Knopf, 1956.

Cather, Willa. *Willa Cather on Writing*. Stephen Tennant (Introduction). 1949. Lincoln: University of Nebraska Press, 1988.

Cather, Willa. *Early Stories of Willa Cather*, Mildred R. Bennett, ed. New York: Dodd, Mead, 1957.

Cather, Willa. *Willa Cather's Collected Short Fiction, 1892-1912*, Virginia Faulkner, ed. Mildred R. Bennett (Introduction). Lincoln: University of Nebraska Press, 1965.

Cather, Willa. *The Kingdom of Art: Willa Cather's First Principles and Critical Statements, 1893-1896*, Bernice Slote, ed. Lincoln: University of Nebraska Press, 1966.

Cather, Willa. *Willa Cather: 24 Stories*, Sharon O'Brien, ed. New York: Penguin Meridian, 1988.

Cather, Willa. *The Old Beauty and Others*. 1948. In Sharon O'Brien, ed., *Stories, Poems, and Other Writings*. New York: Library of America, 1992.

Cather, Willa. *Stories, Poems, and Other Writings*, Sharon O'Brien, ed. New York: Library of America, 1992.

Crane, Joan. *Willa Cather: A Bibliography*. Lincoln: University of Nebraska Press, 1982.

Daiches, David. *Willa Cather: Critical Introduction*. Ithaca, NY: Cornell University Press, 1951.

Dennis, Helen May, ed. *Willa Cather and European Cultural Influences*. Studies in American Literature 16. Lewiston, NY: Mellen,1996.

Fryer, Judith. *Felicitous Space: The Imaginative Structures of Edith Wharton and Willa Cather*. Chapel Hill: University of North Carolina Press, 1986.

Gelfant, Blanche. "The Forgotten Reaping-Hook: Sex in *My Ántonia*." *American Literature 43* (1971): 60-82.

Gerber, Philip L. *Willa Cather*. New York: Twayne, 1995.

Giannone, Richard. *Music in Willa Cather's Fiction*. Lincoln: University of Nebraska Press, 1968.

Harvard University's Cather Web Site. Retrieved on January 9, 2003, from lcg.harvard.edu/~cather/home.html.

Howarth, William. "The Country of Willa Cather." Photos by Farrell Grehan. *National Geographic 162* (July 1982): 71-93.

Lee, Hermione. *Willa Cather: Double Lives*. Chapel Hill: University of North Carolina Press, 1989.

Lewis, Edith. *Willa Cather Living*. Lincoln: University of Nebraska Press, 1953.

Lindeman, Marilee. *Willa Cather: Queering America*. New York: Columbia University Press, 1999.

March, John. *A Reader's Companion to the Fiction of Willa Cather*, Marilyn Arnold, ed. Westport, CT: Greenwood, 1999.

McDonald, Joyce. *The Stuff of Our Forebears: Willa Cather's Southern Heritage*. Tuscaloosa: University of Alabama Press, 1998.

Murphy, John J. *Critical Essays on Willa Cather*. Boston: Hall, 1984.

Murphy, John J. *Willa Cather: Family, Community, and History*. Provo, UT: Brigham Young University Humanities Publication Center, 1990.

Nelson, Robert J. *Willa Cather and France: In Search of the Lost Language*. New York: Oxford University Press, 1988.

O'Brien, Sharon. *Willa Cather: The Emerging Voice*. New York: Oxford University Press, 1987.

Randall, John H. *The Landscape and the Looking Glass: Willa Cather's Search for Value*. Boston, MA: Houghton, 1960.

Reuben, Paul P. "Chapter 7: Early Twentieth Century— Willa Cather." PAL: Perspectives in American

Literature—A Research and Reference Guide. Retrieved on January 9, 2003, from www.csustan.edu/english/reuben/pal/chap7/cather.html.

Rosowski, Susan J. *The Voyage Perilous: Willa Cather's Romanticism*. Ithaca, NY: Cornell University Press, 1986.

Rosowski, Susan J. "Willa Cather's Ecology of Place." *Western American Literature 30* (1995): 37-57.

Schroeter, James, ed. *Willa Cather and Her Critics*. Ithaca, NY: Cornell University Press, 1967.

Sergeant, Elizabeth Shepley. *Willa Cather: A Memoir*. Lincoln: University of Nebraska Press, 1963.

Skaggs, Merrill Maguire. *After the World Broke in Two: The Later Novels of Willa Cather*. Charlottesville: University Press of Virginia, 1990.

Slote, Bernice. *Willa Cather: A Pictorial Memoir*. Photographs by Lucia Woods and others. Lincoln: University of Nebraska Press, 1973.

Smith, Patricia Clark. "Achaeans, Americanos, Prelates and Monsters: Willa Cather's *Death Comes for the Archbishop* as New World Odyssey," in E. A. Mares, ed., *Padre Martinez: New Perspectives from Texas*, 101-124. Taos, NM: Millicent Rogers Museum. 1988.

Stouck, David. *Willa Cather's Imagination*. Lincoln: University of Nebraska Press, 1975.

Stout, Janis P. *Willa Cather: The Writer and Her World*. Charlottesville: University Press of Virginia, 2000.

Stout, Janis P., ed. *A Calendar of the Letters of Willa Cather*. Lincoln: University of Nebraska Press, 2002.

Urgo, Joseph R. *Willa Cather and the Myth of American Migration*. Urbana: University of Illinois Press, 1995.

Van Ghent, Dorothy. *Willa Cather*. Minneapolis: University of Minnesota Press, 1964.

Wagenknecht, Edward. *Willa Cather*. New York: Continuum, 1994.

Wasserman, Loretta. *Willa Cather: A Study of the Short Fiction*. Boston, MA: Twayne, 1991.

Willa Cather Pioneer Memorial Web Site. Retrieved on January 9, 2003, from www.willacather.org.

Woodress, James. *Willa Cather: Her Life and Art*. Lincoln: University of Nebraska Press, 1970.

Woodress, James. *Willa Cather: A Literary Life*. Lincoln: University of Nebraska Press, 1987.

CAULFIELD, BARBARA A. (1947-)

Originally from Oak Park, Illinois, Barbara A. Caulfield received her bachelor's degree from Northwestern University in 1969. After graduation, she continued on at the Northwestern University School of Law and graduated in 1972.

Caulfield had a very extensive private professional career before taking a seat on the bench. She was a researcher and attorney for the Northwestern University Center for Urban Affairs from 1972 until 1973, and then became the supervising attorney for the Northwestern School of Law Legal Aid Clinic until 1974. She then applied her talents to teaching and was a professor of law at the University of Oregon Law School from 1974 to 1978 and later a professor of law at the University of California, San Francisco, Hastings College of Law from 1978 to 1983. While at UCSF, she was the academic dean for the years 1980-1981.

On June 27, 1991, President George H. W. Bush nominated Caulfield to the U.S. District Court for the Northern District of California. The Senate confirmed her on October 31, 1991, and she received her commission on November 5, 1991. She served in the Northern District Court until her resignation on September 16, 1994.

After leaving the bench, Caulfield returned to private practice in San Francisco. She currently is the Executive Vice President and General Counsel of Affymetrix Inc. She has represented many high-profile companies such as Microsoft, Hoffman-La Roche, and Apple Computers. In addition, she continues to occasionally return to teaching as a lecturer in law at Stanford Law School, a position she has held since 1988.

—Brenda Bitgood

SUGGESTED READING

Barbara A. Caulfield. Retrieved from air.fjc.gov/newweb/jnetweb.nsf/fjc_bio. Source: *History of the Federal Judiciary*. http://www.fjc.gov. Web site of the Federal Judicial Center, Washington, D.C.

CHESNEY, MAXINE M. (1942-)

Maxine Mackler Chesney was born on October 29, 1942, in San Francisco, California. She earned her bachelor's degree from the University of California, Berkeley, in 1964. She went on to receive her juris doctor from Berkeley's Boalt Hall School of Law in 1967.

Chesney became a trial attorney with the San Francisco District Attorney's Office in 1968. From this start her rise through the ranks was rapid and impressive. She became Senior Trial Attorney in 1968, Principal Trial Attorney in 1971, Head Trial Attorney in 1976, and San Francisco Municipal Court judge in 1979.

Chesney was appointed to the San Francisco County Superior Court by Governor Jerry Brown on January 1, 1983, a post she held until 1995. President Bill Clinton then gave her a lifetime appointment to the U.S. District Court for the Northern District of California, a position she currently holds.

In addition to her judicial duties, she sits on the board of directors of the Federal Judges Association and is active in the National Association of Women Judges and the United States Association of Constitutional Law.

—Neal Lynch

SUGGESTED READING

Maxine M. Chesney. Retrieved from air.fjc.gov/newweb/ jnetweb.nsf/fjc bio. Source: *History of the Federal Judiciary*. http://www.fjc.gov. Web site of the Federal Judicial Center, Washington, D.C.

CHEUNG, KATHERINE (1904-)

On March 4, 2001, the Museum of Flying in Santa Monica, California, honored Katherine Cheung by inducting her into the Women in Aviation International Pioneer Hall of Fame. The ceremony included a play about Cheung titled *Into the Blue*, performed by actress Josephine Chien. The Chinese Consul General participated in the ceremonies, granting this long overdue honor to Cheung.

Cheung was born in Enping, Canton, China, on December 12, 1904. Her given name of Sui Fun is Chinese and signifies courage and long life, a name that certainly befits this gentle aviator. Cheung came by ship to the United States to live with her businessman father in 1921. She married her father's business partner, George Young, in 1926. She kept her maiden name during the marriage. The couple had two

daughters, Doris and Dorothy. They were happily married for 62 years until Mr. Young's death in 1988.

A gifted pianist, Cheung attended the prestigious Los Angeles Conservatory of Music, where she obtained a degree in academic piano. She continued her studies at the University of Southern California and California Polytechnic State University. She later gave up her promising music career in 1932 when she became an aviator. She became fascinated by flying when she was waiting for her father in a parking lot next to Dyser Airfield. She signed up for flying lessons at age 26. She performed her first solo flight after only 12½ hours of lessons. Her first solo landed at Dyser Airfield. After her solo, she earned her private license, becoming the first Chinese woman aviator in history.

After earning her private license, Cheung learned stunt and blind flying. She performed aerial stunts such as rolls and spirals at a variety of air shows. In 1936, after becoming an American citizen, she obtained her commercial pilot's license. That same year she became a member of the prestigious Ninety-Nines, the famous women's flying club. She flew in a number of shows and air races during the 1930s. She was unable to afford the top-flight planes that her competitors flew, which hampered her in competitive flying, so the Chinese community in Los Angeles combined their funds to purchase a plane for her. She frequently spoke in the Chinese community advocating aviation as a career for women.

When Japan invaded China, Cheung decided to return to China to aid her native land in its defense. Her friends purchased a plane for her to fly back to China after she had made the decision to go to China, but during the presentation ceremony, the pilot crashed the plane as he came in to land. The pilot died and the plane was destroyed. When she finally arrived in China, she opened a flying school to teach flying to Chinese volunteers.

Cheung's father became concerned about her flying after this crash. Before he died, Cheung promised him she would retire from flying. In 1942, after training pilots in China for 5 years, she retired from flying, fulfilling her promise to her father.

The Smithsonian National Air and Space Museum recognizes Cheung as the nation's first Asian woman aviator. She has also been honored by the Beijing Air Force Aviation Museum, which officially dubbed her the Chinese Amelia Earhart.

Cheung lived a more quiet life after the war years. In 1981 she visited friends in Hong Kong, where she appeared on television to speak about her career. She postponed a visit to the mainland due to her husband's failing health. After her husband passed away, she became lonely. At this time her family persuaded her to complete the aborted trip to the Chinese mainland. She visited her home village of Enping, where the aviation museum and research institute honored her when she visited.

In December 1999 the citizens of Chinatown in Los Angeles honored Cheung with a banquet. She has also been honored by the Museum of Flying in Santa Monica and the Pacific Asia Museum of Pasadena. As of this writing, Cheung is living in a suburb of Los Angeles and occupies her time with family and friends and engaging in a variety of crafts.

—Randal C. Fulkerson

SUGGESTED READINGS

Douglas, Deborah G. *United States Women in Aviation.* Washington, DC: Smithsonian Institution Press, 1990.

Welch, Rosanne. *Encyclopedia of Women in Aviation and Space.* Santa Barbara, CA: ABC-CLIO, 1998.

CLARK, GEORGIE WHITE
(1910-1992)

Born on November 13, 1910, in Guymon, Oklahoma, Bessie DeRoss, who was later called Georgie, grew up in poverty. Her father, a tenant farmer/miner, was gone most of the time and later divorced her mother. Her mother, who became a laundress, raised her alone. In 1928 Georgie married her first husband, Harold Clark, and had a daughter the next year named Sammona Rose. They divorced in 1941 and Georgie moved to Los Angeles, California. Her daughter stayed with Georgie's mother until Georgie married James Ray White in 1942. Then Sammona came to live with her in Los Angeles, where they became very close, hiking and cycling together. In 1944, while on a cycling trip, Sammona was hit by a drunk driver and killed, and Georgie took her daughter's death very hard. In reaction to her grief, she became active with the Sierra Club and went on her first Colorado River Grand Canyon expedition with Sierra Club speaker Harry Aleson and biologist Gerhard Bakker. She became enamored of the area and went back again and again

until finally establishing her own business called the Royal River Rats raft trips, taking tourists down the Colorado River through the canyon. She became the first woman to lead a boating party through the Grand Canyon and the first woman outfitter. She also was the first woman to swim the canyon. Georgie ran white water expeditions on the Colorado River for 47 years and made her final run on the river in 1991 at 81 years of age. She died of cancer the following year on May 12, 1992.

—Carolyn Stull

SUGGESTED READING

Westwood, Richard E., *Woman of the River: Georgie White Clark: White Water Pioneer,* Logan: Utah State University Press, 1997.

CLEAVELAND, AGNES MORLEY
(1874-1958)

Agnes Morley Cleaveland grew up on the family ranch in western New Mexico, in the late 19th and early 20th centuries. She was the oldest daughter of the famous railroad builder William Raymond Morley. Born in 1874 in New Mexico, she wrote several stories and a history of Cimarron County, *Satan's Paradise: From Lucien Maxwell to Fred Lambert* (1952). But her most famous text is her autobiographical *No Life for a Lady* (1941), which describes ranch life in turn-of-the-century New Mexico. Here Cleaveland describes a vanishing way of life and rewrites the history of the Southwest by means of autobiography. *No Life for a Lady* consists of a collection of reminiscences and stories told her by family members, neighbors, ranch hands, and other locals. At the age of 64, the author looks back on her life and focuses on her time spent on the Morley family ranch. Her account begins when she is a little girl, before she can remember the events on her own. Her mother has told her of this time: when mother and father moved to Cimarron, New Mexico, 2 years before Agnes was born, and when her father was a local hero and famous engineer. Her account ends when she is an old woman, trying to recall what she was like as a girl.

But unlike her literary predecessors, these accounts of derring-do and wild adventure are interspersed with a revisionist message. For instance, in the midst of her excited description of the family's first day in Datil Canyon, Cleaveland pauses to explore her mother's reactions to their new home in the wilds of New Mexico:

> Did Mother think it was bully? Of course I never knew. My eleven and a half years were entirely too few to give me an understanding of grown-ups' problems. It was another year or two before Mother shared hers with me.
>
> The next morning witnessed Mother's first gesture toward the homemaking, which she was desperately resolved to achieve, but which was always to prove futile. She had Navajo blankets strung across the center of the larger room. Now at least the house had three rooms!

Here the narrative moves from the children's dialogue to an introspective discussion of adult problems. (Brother Ray has just proclaimed this place "bully" and young Agnes has agreed with him.) By shifting her attention from the uncomplicated and romantic child's view to the more complicated and mature perspective of her mother, Cleaveland represents two often contradictory visions of western life. She portrays, through the children's voices, the tourist's simplified and immature version of the frontier: a place of adventure, excitement, and risk-taking—a place for men. She also suggests that this experience is at odds with the "real" experience of people, particularly women, who actually lived in this place and feared the unknown, worried about their families, and attempted to keep house in the wild. Cleaveland thus revises, through the insertion of her mother's concerns, the outsider's view of the Southwest. By claiming ancestral ties, in this case her biological link to her mother, she adds greater credence to her revisionist project.

By combining her personal experience with the personal experiences of her family, friends, neighbors, and employees (Ray, among others) and the written evidence contained in such documents as her family letters, Cleaveland attempts to provide a more complete version of New Mexican history. Her desire to amend southwestern history to include women's roles embodies her nostalgia for the Southwest. Longing for a way of life that probably never existed, Cleaveland constructs a world based on her desire for an egalitarian existence. The nostalgic impulse thus organizes her compilation of as-told-to narratives,

family stories, regional legends, and miscellaneous memories, and drives the construction of one woman's identity through its interaction with place. Even as Cleaveland appears to alter popular (male) history, *No Life for a Lady* perpetuates the myths that shape the nation's perception of the Southwest and passes off these regional, and usually masculine, tales as the stories of one woman's life. The narrative incision of women into traditionally male roles is an important step in historical revision. In this case, Cleaveland's nostalgia for a democratic and egalitarian society that supposedly existed in the past serves an important purpose: it shows her readers that a society free from gender bias can exist, at least in narrative.

Although she went east for preparatory school, west to California for college, and returned to California when she married, according to her account in *No Life for a Lady,* the ranch continued to represent the most important place for her. She generally omits anything from her autobiography that happens outside her central place (the ranch). She summarizes her time apart from this place in brief sentences or paragraphs at the end of chapters filled with details about New Mexico life. She deemphasizes the outside world and her time away from the ranch because her "other" life "at Ann Arbor, as at Philadelphia, had very little reality" for her. The ranch assumes the central place in Cleaveland's narrative; it comes to represent the world. Thus her life story, as she tells it, comprises childhood memories of the time when she actually lived on the ranch and nostalgic renderings of life before the homesteader and the tourist destroyed the glorious frontier ways of New Mexico. By locating reality within the geographical space of her family ranch, Cleaveland is able to reconstruct a world that both retains the most appealing elements of the outsider's vision of turn-of-the-century southwestern life and reveals an insider's view of this life. In other words, she satisfies her readers' desire for adventure even as she revises history to include the role of women in the Southwest.

In her autobiography, Cleaveland provides a female perspective of ranch life. She dedicates *No Life for a Lady* to "all those Pioneer Women whose stories can never be adequately told but whose courage, endurance and determination to hold fast to their highest ideals contributed to the making of AMERICA." Clearly, she hopes to include women, especially those women like her mother who went west, in the story of

America—in the historical and popular construction of a nation. She also says that she writes her "record" because she wants "to put into some semblance of permanent form the story of the girl who had vanished, and her life, the life that was not for what the world calls a lady." The title of her autobiography describes a struggle between her prescribed gender role—her role as a lady—and the demands of ranching life. Although she claims that she led "no life for a lady," her text nevertheless proves her ability both to live the ranching life *and* to live like a lady. Through her autobiography, she proves that women could perform ranching duties as competently as men and that women could be equal to men without sacrificing their womanhood. For example, in her chapter titled "Cowpuncher on a Sidesaddle," she explains:

> Although I rode sidesaddle like a lady, the double standard did not exist on the ranch. Up to the point of my actual physical limitations, I worked side by side with the men, receiving the same praise or same censure for like undertakings.

Cleaveland appears to live both the life of a lady (the role encouraged by her mother and promoted by her eastern education) and the life of a woman who remains tied to the land (a role she admires but realizes she cannot be completely happy with). She occupies a position somewhere in between these disparate worlds, since her family was in a unique position: they lacked a father for much of their ranching life, and thus the women, especially Agnes and her sisters, were forced to help out with the men's work. She does not perceive this lack of menfolk as a hardship. Rather, she sympathizes with the women of the region who suffered isolation and loneliness because of their restrictive gender role.

But throughout her narrative, Cleaveland betrays an anxiety about her own gender role, and her autobiography's title reminds us that her textual mission is to resolve, or at least to explore, gender roles in the Southwest, and perhaps the nation in general. She reminds us that she is indeed a woman. She rides sidesaddle, she uses a parasol, she sews, she knits, and she has "some knowledge of the rudiments of household arts." And yet she is neither able nor is she willing to limit her life to such womanly concerns. Her discomfort with the label of "lady" emerges frequently in her text. For instance, in her chapter titled "Satan Didn't Like Parasols," she describes an

incident that exemplifies the contradictory nature of her two roles. While riding into town on a hot day, her male companion suggested that she put up her parasol. She explains to her readers, "Yes, I really carried a parasol when I masqueraded as a young lady." She obliges the man, raises her parasol, and spooks the horse (Satan), thus proving her recurring argument that ladies do not belong in her Southwest. Ultimately, her story of one woman's life becomes emblematic of the female struggle against the superficial constraints of society and the struggle for free expression and self-representation.

Although she claims the ranch as her reality, Cleaveland comes and goes from this place, inhabiting the world outside for the majority of her life. In her chapter titled "We Took It and Liked It," she states that "men walked in a sort of perpetual adventure, but women waited." Here she claims to belong to the category of women who "took it and liked it." This kind of woman is restricted to her role as ranch wife, housekeeper, and mother. Cleaveland, on the other hand, is not restricted to this role. She does not have to wait because she is herself involved in the adventures. She is both the woman who must wait and the man who has freedom. She occupies a position between prescribed gender roles; she can see the view from both vantage points. Her contemporary Erna Fergusson, in *New Mexico: A Pageant of Three Peoples*, praises Cleaveland's mother, Mrs. Ada McPherson Morley, who she says "succeeded in giving her children a sense of superiority that demanded superior standards without snobbery." In addition to being inside and outside southwestern life, Cleaveland is both inside and outside her gender role. She plays the lady, she says; she also plays the man, when she goes out on the range. In spite of her dress and her sidesaddle, she states that the men treat her as an equal. *No Life for a Lady* constructs a world that enables her, and presumably other women, to play both roles: she can be the waiting wife who suffers hardship and she can be the ranch hand who understands and experiences "real" life.

Cleaveland constructs a place where gender inequity does not exist; on her ranch a woman performs the work of men. In *No Life for a Lady*, she constructs a democracy where women are equal to men and everybody, from cowboy to ranch owner, enjoys and participates eagerly in the work. Without insiders like Cleaveland, the Southwest would lack a gender-inflected and a culture-oriented history. Cleaveland's autobiography reveals the progressive, integrative power of nostalgia to solidify the formation of identity and to advance the revisionist work of gender and cultural history.

—Becky Jo (Gesteland) McShane

SUGGESTED READINGS

Cleaveland, Norman. *The Morleys—Young Upstarts on the Southwest Frontier*. Albuquerque, NM: Calvin Horn, 1971.

Fergusson, Erna. *New Mexico: A Pageant of Three Peoples*. New York: Knopf, 1951.

Foote, Cheryl J. *Women of the New Mexico Frontier, 1846-1912*. Niwot: University Press of Colorado, 1990.

CLEGHORN, MILDRED IMACH
(1910-1997)

Mildred Imach Cleghorn, former tribal leader of the Fort Sill Chiricahua Apache, was born on December 11, 1910, at Fort Sill, Oklahoma. At the time of her birth, the Apache people were being held as prisoners of the U.S. government following the surrender of Geronimo in 1886. When she was 4 years old, the Apache people were released from U.S. custody after 27 years of imprisonment. Her parents, Amy Wratten and Richard Imach, had each been born into U.S. custody and had two daughters: Myrtle, who died in infancy, and Mildred. When the Imachs were released, they decided to remain at Fort Sill and each was given an allotment of land to start a new life. Mildred lived on these same allotments for the rest of her life. During the Depression, Mildred attended school at the Haskell Institute in Lawrence, Kansas, and later graduated from their business school. She also continued her education at a number of colleges and universities in the area, including Oklahoma University in Norman, Oklahoma State University in Stillwater, the University of Texas in Austin, and Cameron College in Lawton, Oklahoma. Following her graduation in 1941 with a degree in home economics, she began teaching at Riverside Indian School.

Mildred spent her early adult life teaching at Fort Sill and Riverside Indian schools, and after her retirement she returned to the classroom to be a teacher's aide in the Fort Sill School. The bulk of her adult life was spent serving as a home extension agent for several agencies, including the Mescalero Apache Reservation in New Mexico, the Cheyenne, Arapahoe, and Pawnee agencies in Oklahoma, and at the Potawatomi agency in Horton, Kansas. She retired from civil service in 1965. During her time as a home extension agent, she began making dolls that would represent the women of the tribes she served. Each doll was painstakingly researched and adorned to reflect the different styles of dress among women of the tribes. She started her dolls during her first job with the U.S. Indian Service and continued the practice through her time as a home extension agent. Her goal was to create a doll for each tribe she had worked with.

Mildred married Richard Cleghorn on the Mescalero Indian Reservation in a double wedding with her cousin. The couple had no children of their own, but did adopt one daughter, Penny. Mildred also served as an elder for the Reform Church of America and participated in several councils related to the church and Native Americans. In 1979 she began serving as chairperson for the Fort Sill Apache Tribe, a position she was to hold for over a decade. In 1989 she was named Indian of the Year. While driving one of her 10 grandchildren to school on April 15, 1997, she was hit by another car and killed. Her grandson survived the accident, but the Apache people mourned the loss of one of their most beloved leaders.

—Vanessa Anne Gunther

SUGGESTED READINGS

Carter Anon Museum, Anadarko, Oklahoma. *Dolls by Mildred Cleghorn: An Exhibition*. December 19, 1971-January 29, 1972.

Stockel, H. Henrietta. *Women of the Apache Nation: Voices of Truth*. Reno: University of Nevada Press, 1991.

CLUBS (WOMEN'S) IN THE WEST

Women's participation in voluntary associations is a major theme in American history. Denied equal involvement in political and economic affairs, women used volunteer work to contribute to their communities and to participate in American public life.

Volunteerism gave women autonomy and self-reliance, as well as a means of self-improvement, continuing education, and social interaction. At the same time, women's welfare work helped ameliorate many social problems accompanying industrialization, urbanization, and immigration. Clubwomen also contributed to their communities' cultural life by organizing museums, libraries, art exhibits, and musical events. These activities, in turn, helped define and legitimate new professions for women, including social work, public health, and librarianship. Finally, female volunteerism originated and sustained the woman's suffrage movement, which culminated with the passage in 1920 of the Nineteenth Amendment.

American women's clubs evolved over 2 centuries, expanding and contracting in response to the prevailing political climate and social conditions. Women first engaged in church-run charities in the 1790s to assist the needy and to raise funds for religious and missionary activities. Although modest, these original associations established a formal infrastructure—constitutions, by-laws, elected officers, and regular meetings—that thereafter continued. Often female charities served as auxiliaries to male associations, though some women's groups operated independently. Men's and women's organizations often cooperated, but gender segregation was the norm. After 1820 some women's groups, especially in New England and Upstate New York, added social reform such as temperance, abolition, moral reform, and even woman's rights to their organized activities. Such sweeping voluntarism waned during the Civil War, as women throughout the nation devoted themselves to relief work.

Between 1865 and 1920 women's clubs significantly enlarged their sphere of influence. Although some women remained committed to religious and missionary work, many others formed reading groups to discuss literature and the arts. Seeking self-improvement, literary circles provided advanced education for women whose access to college was limited. Soon clubs began studying current social and political topics in addition to the great authors. By 1900 clubwomen—under the umbrella of "municipal housekeeping"—were organizing kindergartens, playgrounds, and libraries, as well as partnering with men on civic improvement and municipal reform. In the ensuing decades, municipal housekeepers established settlement houses that operated day nurseries, offered language and other classes, and provided social services for the urban poor. This same organized womanhood lobbied government representatives to pass protective labor legislation, pure food acts, and environmental regulations. Clubwomen's political action eventually coalesced in the final battle to secure women the vote.

With the Nineteenth Amendment's passage, the club movement collapsed. Traditional female networks were undermined as women sought higher education, professional work, and positions on government boards and commissions. Moreover, as American culture became more consumer oriented, municipal housekeeping seemed outmoded. Women-only clubs did not disappear but became more conservative and narrowly defined. The Depression witnessed a resurgence of female charitable work, and during World War II many women engaged in war relief activities. During the 1960s voluntarism was reinvigorated as women joined various protest and civil rights movements. Indeed, historians have noted the commonalities between women's social activism in the 1830s and 1840s and the civil rights and feminist movements of the 1960s.

As a by-product of 1960s' politics, historians reconsidered standard historical narratives. The traditional history of women's clubs, for example, had largely chronicled the actions of elite eastern white women, without recognizing the experiences of women from other backgrounds and regions. Similarly, histories of western women had related how white pioneers re-created eastern organizations in their adopted communities. By contrast, the so-called new western history takes issue with this construct and attempts to show how women's clubs in the West were as much influenced by region, ethnicity, race, and class as by gender. Western clubs also had a different developmental cycle than their eastern counterparts, due, in part, to the fact that western states led the nation in granting women suffrage. Although historians note that suffrage did not significantly alter the club-based female political subculture, they have found that western women's clubs were more overtly political that those in the East. The history of clubs in the West was also influenced by the region's diversity. Ethnic and immigrant women were not simply recipients of white clubwomen's charity, but also participated in the club movement, albeit on their own terms. Finally, as Sandra Haarsager observes, pioneer women had their own "imagined" West, which emphasized shared community, family, and cultural values, not gun-slinging and gold-seeking. Through their volunteerism, western women helped shape the region's society and politics and establish its unique culture and values.

Women's clubs first appeared in the West in the 1830s, when Anglo missionaries' wives organized the Columbia Maternal Association for mutual support in child care. Prior to the Civil War, other female newcomers coalesced to organize community events and provide for each other during times of hardship and natural disaster. Pioneer churches also brought women together in the 1850s and 1860s as they participated in Hebrew women's associations, Catholic ladies aid societies, Mormon women's relief societies, and Protestant "mite societies."

By the late 1880s, two women's club movements were progressing throughout the West: one driven by established eastern associations, another emerging from exigencies of pioneer life. The Women's Christian Temperance Union (WCTU) was the most widespread of the eastern imports, capitalizing on preexisting Protestant networks and temperance sympathies. Pioneer women were part of the 1870s' grassroots temperance crusade, so when WCTU President Frances Willard toured western states and territories in the early 1880s, they responded enthusiastically by creating numerous local unions. By 1890 the WCTU was the largest women's organization not only in the West but nationwide. The national WCTU endorsed a broad social vision covering temperance, social purity, peace, labor rights, and suffrage. Western women implemented this agenda by creating kindergartens, Sunday schools, settlement houses, and libraries to push the WCTU's temperance and antivice message. Individual WCTU unions also developed programs to address their community's immediate needs. In Kansas, for example, the WCTU funded missionary projects among foreign-born miners, while the Los Angeles and Denver unions ran homes for unwed mothers. The Phoenix union (among many others) was involved in creating a public library. Nevada activists focused on legislative measures, including an antigambling campaign. After 1900 the WCTU's popularity diminished, as clubwomen became less concerned about moral control (though this did not altogether vanish) and more involved in personal and community advancement.

The secularized club movement began during the late 1870s simultaneously with but separate from the temperance crusade. In 1871 women in Lawrence, Kansas, formed one of the earliest study clubs called Friends in Council. California's club movement was officially inaugurated with the Oakland Ebell Society's founding in 1876. Utah women formed the pioneering Salt Lake City Ladies Literary Club in 1877, and clubs appeared in the Dakotas in 1879. Colorado, Washington, Nebraska, Texas, and Idaho developed dynamic organizations in the 1880s, and New Mexico, Montana, Wyoming, Arizona, Nevada, and Oregon's clubs commenced in the 1890s.

Many women credited earlier club experience back East with inspiring them to form parallel groups in the West. Caroline Severance, for instance, was active in Boston organizations before founding the Los Angeles Woman's Club in 1878. Adelia Wade, also familiar with eastern clubs, established the first women's group in Oregon in 1894. Delphine Squires was likewise involved in clubs prior to moving to Nevada in 1906. Las Vegas was still a tent city when she started organizing women there. As a Dakota clubwoman explained in J. C. Croly's 1898 commemorative *History of Woman's Club Movement in America*: "Our Western women are really Eastern women transplanted, and many of us look back to homes in dear old New York or New England. . . . [S]o, in your thought of us, do not feel as if we were anything strange or far off."

Despite eastern models, pioneer women confronted enormous challenges in creating their own clubs. Social conditions in the West were of a "very different character from that of older States," an Idaho clubwoman explained. "Lacking everything, environment had to be created." Montana was a land of "magnificent distances" and "sparse and scattered populations." It took some time, clubwomen there recalled, to develop the state's "gentler elements." The Lemoore Woman's Club (established in California in 1884) confronted the same obstacles. Residing in a county as large as Connecticut and Rhode Island combined, members traveled miles to attend meetings. Yet they persevered, frequently bringing "a baby with them, or their sewing or knitting."

Initially, pioneer women formed literary societies to encourage reading and to develop friendships. The Pioneer Reading Club of Grand Forks, North Dakota, was organized in 1884 by a small group of "thoughtful women, most of them absorbed in domestic cares, and finding in their club their principal intellectual aid and stimulus." Dallas women formed a Shakespeare Club in 1886 to examine the Bard's writings, while women in Helena, Montana, organized the Fortnightly Club in 1890, promising to devote at least 3 hours a week to study. Literary-minded Spokane women formed the Sorosis Club in 1891 in hopes of covering a different author each year. A member of the Tuesday Study Club of Lingle, Wyoming, who joined within a year of homesteading in a tarpaper shack, expressed the driving force behind these early clubs. "Membership in this small club," she wrote, "was all that kept me from rusticating completely."

Many study clubs had a broader agenda, taking up history, art, and philosophy in addition to literature. The Zetetic Club, established by women in Weeping Water, Nebraska, in 1884, met at members' homes to discuss books on history and literature. Wichita's Hypatia Club (established in 1886) considered varied topics including Egyptology, Russian literature, the race problem, and "cranks of all times and climes." The Fifteen Club of Santa Fe (established in 1891) initially studied Italian art and culture, but quickly moved on to political issues like Indian affairs, Chinese exclusion, anarchists, and the Cuban Question. Many western clubs followed this same evolution from literary topics to political and social concerns. As an Oregonian explained:

> The women's clubs here, as elsewhere, represent the thoughtful, earnest, educated women of the community; women not satisfied to lead lives given up to frivolity or drudgery, as the case may be, without interest in or knowledge of the great questions and movements of the day. . . . Nearly all the clubs began work from five to ten years ago as simple reading clubs, but most of them have grown into other work, have become classes for real study in various lines, including literature, art, civics, music, education, and household economics.

Although club membership was often limited to 15 or 20, some urban associations grew quite large, expanding their influence and range of interests along with their numbers. Over 150 women formed the Omaha Woman's Club in 1893. From the outset this impressive association had an elaborate infrastructure, with seven departments coordinating the study of art, literature, history, education, political economy, social science, and philosophy. Within a few years, club membership increased to 500, and departments in psychology, philanthropy, current issues, and music were added. Departments were responsible for hosting one program each year. The club also published the *Woman's Weekly,* which also served as the organ for the Nebraska Federation of Women's Clubs.

These urban clubs were extremely influential in their city's social life and politics. Established in 1883, the Woman's Club of Olympia, Washington, was the region's most prestigious club and hosted receptions for distinguished visitors. San Francisco's Century Club (established 1888), presided over by Phoebe Apperson Hearst, played a corresponding role in that city's society. According to J. C. Croly, "No man or woman of distinction visits San Francisco without the desire of being received by the Century Club." The Century Club, like many prominent women's organizations, built an impressive clubhouse to host meetings and large events. Often located proximate to city hall, these clubhouses served urban women as political bases to conduct business.

Large urban associations were often known for their elaborate social events. In fact, in many cities certain club memberships became a status symbol and entrée into local elite circles. Yet these clubs' primary objectives remained educational and civic-minded. Members researched, wrote, and presented scholarly treatises as well as organized expert lectures on pressing political and social issues. Club meetings were highly structured and conducted under parliamentary procedure, exposing women to forms of political discourse. As women's confidence grew, so did their ambitions, and soon these large associations were designing municipal improvement projects, drafting labor and public health legislation, and managing welfare programs and educational institutions.

Urban clubs aggressively sought places for women on civic boards and commissions, especially those that dealt directly with women and children. Los Angeles clubs were particularly successful in this endeavor. In the early 1900s, Los Angeles clubwomen convinced city officials to appoint female police officers, hire a matron at juvenile hall, and create a separate court to hear cases involving women and children. Between 1902 and 1912 women were also appointed to the playground commission, public art commission, housing commission, school and library boards, as well as the planning commission. In 1912 and 1913 clubwomen helped form the motion picture censor's board and the municipal charities commission. In 1915 Los Angeles elected its first female (a clubwoman) to the city council.

Small-town clubs were equally productive in the rural West as women endeavored to raise their towns' intellectual and moral climate and provide for the welfare of their communities. The Literary Teacups of Fargo, North Dakota, sponsored a local relief program, a kindergarten, and an orphanage. California's Lemoore Woman's Club organized a free reading room and relief committee, as well as planted trees along the city streets, maintained a public park, and investigated alleys and backyards to educate neighbors on sanitation and disease. The Woman's Club of Cripple Creek, Colorado, was equally ambitious. It formed a small chorus, put on the first art show, established a library association, organized a kindergarten, and ran a newsboys club. "Where there are no theatres, no lectures, and but little social life," one member explained, "the Woman's Club is an infinite blessing." Western women's clubs showed an early interest in conservation as well. Idaho clubwomen were active in preventing timber mining in national forests and in establishing some of the state's earliest national parks. Clubwomen in Colorado rallied support to save Mesa Verde, while Utah women were instrumental in preserving Monument Valley. In California, women's clubs lobbied to preserve ancient sequoia stands and protested the environmentally destructive Hetch Hetchy Dam.

Professional women often collaborated with clubwomen, contributing their expertise to projects involving conservation, free libraries, public health, and the like. Professionals also established separate associations, such as the National Woman's Press Club, that had chapters in California, Colorado, Oregon, Kansas, Washington, and Texas. Press clubs included journalists and illustrators, though some chapters allowed any woman writer to join. The Pacific Coast Woman's Press Association, established in San Francisco in 1890, was one of the most prominent professional women's groups and included among its members established authors like Charlotte Perkins Gilman and Ina Coolbrith.

Most women's clubs, however, were comprised of volunteers drawn from the white middle and upper classes, for dues, meeting schedules, and time commitments made working women's participation unfeasible. Often clubs based membership on "moral character," a 19th-century concept used to exclude women of different ethnic and religious backgrounds. A few clubs were integrated or formed affiliated ethnic chapters. The Denver YWCA accepted African Americans, while the San Francisco YWCA sponsored a successful Chinese branch. More often, white women's clubs considered ethnic and working-class women recipients of their patronage, not peers or colleagues in organized womanhood. Consequently, western women of color developed a parallel club movement, often adopting white organizational models, yet adapting them to their community's specialized needs.

This dynamic was particularly true for African American women in the West. By the 1880s western states had sizable African American populations, and black women quickly became the backbone of their churches and community life. One of the earliest secular clubs was the Colored Ladies Legal Rights Association, organized in Denver around 1885 to protest racial discrimination. Over the next decade and a half, black women's clubs were formed in Oakland, Los Angeles, Butte, Houston, Fort Worth, Tacoma, Cheyenne, Billings, Kalispell, Pueblo, and Colorado Springs, to name only a few. By the early 1900s African American women's clubs were numerous enough that Colorado, Washington, Texas, California, Montana, and Kansas organized state chapters of the National Association of Colored Women's Clubs. In 1907 the Colorado State Federation added Utah and Wyoming clubs to its membership. Oregon established its federation in 1917.

In Denver alone, at least 22 African American women's clubs were created between 1900 and 1925, sporting names like the Book Lovers Club, Taka Art Club, Camelia Art and Mothers Club, and the Narcissus Art, Literary, and Social Club. These organizations followed the procedural models of white clubs, with constitutions, by-laws, elected officers, and formal meetings. Black women, like their white counterparts, sought self-improvement and companionship, and together these women studied art, music, and needlework as well as prepared and delivered research papers. Unlike white women, they often read African American authors. Black clubwomen were not particularly involved in mass movements like suffrage and temperance. They were more concerned with poverty and discrimination and with countering negative stereotypes of black women.

Like whites, blacks broadened their activities from personal enlightenment to community improvement. In Los Angeles, African American women opened a Woman's Day Nursery Association in 1908 to care for the children of working black mothers, many of whom were live-in domestics. The city's black women also founded a Sojourner Truth Industrial (STI) Club to lobby for the rights of black workers and fund a residence for single girls. Many similar STI clubs were formed throughout the West to sponsor social events and educational programs and to generally uplift their community.

Jewish women were equally enthusiastic volunteers. In fact, they formed some of the earliest women's clubs in the West. As early as 1856, San Francisco's Jewish women were involved in two associations: the Hebrew Ladies' Benevolent Society and Der Israelitische Frauenverein. Portland women established the First Hebrew Ladies Benevolent Society in 1874 "to administer relief to the poor, the needy, the sick, and to prepare the dead for interment." They also raised money for Russian Jews and aided Jewish victims of the 1906 San Francisco earthquake. Although Portland's society did not support non-Jewish causes, other Jewish women's groups participated in the wider community. The Los Angeles Ladies' Hebrew Benevolent Society (established in 1870) contributed to various relief and civic improvement efforts, and in nearby San Bernardino, the Ladies' Hebrew Benevolent Society (established in 1886) promised "to render pecuniary assistance and otherwise alleviate the sufferings of the sick and distressed poor, regardless of religious denomination." Frances Jacobs, who formed the Denver Hebrew Ladies' Society in 1872, also ran the nonsectarian Denver Ladies' Relief Society. Indeed, Jacobs is lauded as Denver's "Mother of Charities," and her portrait hangs with other prominent citizens in the Colorado statehouse.

Native-born Catholic and Mormon women also retained ties to traditional church-based charities while participating in the secular club movement. In Utah, club work was generally segregated into Mormon and non-Mormon organizations, with Mormons preferring to channel their charitable efforts into Mormon relief societies. However, Mormon women also formed societies outside the church, such as the Salt Lake City Reaper's Club that Emmeline Wells founded in 1892. Mormon women's clubs participated in Utah's State Federation of Women's Clubs, successfully collaborating with non-Mormons on projects of mutual concern. Although traditionally the Sisters of Mercy and other religious orders oversaw Catholic charity, lay Catholic women also contributed to organized womanhood. The club work of Los Angeles's Mary Julia Workman provides a good case in point. From a notable Catholic family, Workman devoted her life to religious and social causes. She was a pioneering kindergarten teacher in the early 1900s and a volunteer in the College Settlement Association's home located in one of the city's poorest neighborhoods. At the same time, Workman was the moving spirit behind the Brownson House Settlement Association, which had been created in 1901 to provide religious instruction and social services to poor and foreign-born Catholics.

Women of other ethnic backgrounds, especially immigrants with limited English, had less opportunity to participate in the vibrant club life of American-born women. Yet, isolated as these women were, they still developed significant female networks through which they cared for one another and sustained their cultural traditions. For example, in 1889 women in Denver's Little Italy organized a benevolent society, which survived into the 1920s. Los Angeles's French women established the Ladies of Charity in 1904, and the Daughters of Norway flourished throughout Washington, especially in Seattle, Tacoma, Spokane, and other communities with sizable Norwegian enclaves. German immigrants in Kansas benefited from comparable ethnic societies, such as the Trinity Lutheran Ladies Aid of Block organized in 1912 to sew for orphanages and other charitable institutions. Irish women in Anaconda, Montana, participated in at least three ethnic organizations in the 1880s: the Ladies Auxiliary of the Ancient Order of Hibernians, the Daughters of Erin, and the Ladies of the Catholic Church. Typical of ethnic women's groups, Anaconda miners' wives coordinated social events and traditional Irish celebrations, provided for the community's poor, and raised funds for their parish and Irish causes.

Native and Mexican American women did not participate in the secular club movement in the manner of black and white women. For them, volunteerism was not so much a gendered activity but consolidated within family, community, and church networks. Mexico did have a well-established mutual aid tradition, which immigrants brought to the American West. Thus by the late 1800s, Laredo, Texas, supported no less than 14 Mexican mutual-aid societies, 4 of which were run by women. In contrast to Anglos, women of Mexican heritage were more likely to affiliate with fraternal organizations, either working with men or, more commonly, forming female auxiliaries. Founded in Tucson, Arizona, in 1894, the Alianza Hispano-Americana was the nation's largest Latino mutual aid society, with chapters in Arizona, New Mexico, and California. Though male-dominated, women's auxiliaries played a significant role in Alianza's fund-raising and charitable endeavors.

Asian women too participated in traditional mutual aid societies (usually revolving around family associations or prefectures), but they also experimented with white forms of collective action. First-generation Japanese women established *funjinkai,* or church-based associations, to conduct religious good works. At the same time, Japanese and Chinese Christian converts were quickly drawn into Protestant charities. In turn-of-the-century San Francisco, Chinese women were involved in several Protestant groups, including the Congregational Mothers and Daughters Society, the Presbyterian Circle of the Kings' Daughters, and the Methodist Missionary Society. As Asian communities settled and expanded, women became more involved in American public life. The Chinese Women's Jeleab [Self-Reliance] Association was among the earliest secular Asian groups, formed in 1913 by prosperous women in San Francisco and Oakland. Modeled on white women's clubs, the Jeleab Association fostered "social intercourse, benevolent work, educational advantages, and mutual assistance." A larger, more enduring Chinese group was the San Francisco Chinese Young Women's Christian Association, established in 1916. With 500 members by 1920, the Chinese YWCA provided the Chinese community with essential educational and social services, including language classes, health care, domestic problems, and interpreting services.

Immigrant clubs played an important role in easing women's transition into American society. They assisted immigrant women in maintaining cultural traditions and patterns of sociability, yet also helped them learn American forms of public discourse and action. Ultimately, though, immigrant women's involvement in the club movement was limited. As Carol Coburn writes of German immigrants in Block, Kansas, "[F]or busy rural women, reform societies such as suffrage or temperance organizations were a luxury when domestic work had to be done and families fed and clothed."

Reflecting national trends, women's clubs in the West declined during the 1920s. June Underwood found that by 1925, Kansas women had abandoned public activism in favor of apolitical benevolence that had characterized clubs in the 1870s. Jo Ann Ruckman observed the same phenomenon in Idaho:

It comes almost as a shock to read through Pocatello newspapers toward the end of the twenties and discover that middle-class Pocatello women, at least, were then almost totally absorbed in family, religious, and social life (especially card-playing). The high civic purpose that characterized women's public life before and during the war had almost disappeared, with the exception of a very few individuals and organizations.

Historians have attributed this backlash against female activism to various, interconnected factors: the rejection of Victorian gender ideals emphasizing female purity and moral authority; new employment options for women, especially in social work, where clubwomen once found "careers" in volunteering; the bureaucratization of social and charitable institutions, which diminished clubwomen's authority and responsibility; the appointment of women to government boards and commissions through which they exercised formal political power; and disillusion with progressive ideals within an increasingly conservative political climate.

In the West, surviving women's groups reverted to more recreational pursuits and single-issue causes. Established in 1920, the League of Women Voters was, arguably, the most important women's club to emerge at this time. The League continued clubwomen's traditions of studying public policy and lobbying for protective legislation targeting women and children. Other clubs focused their volunteerism on Americanization programs to help assimilate immigrant and nonwhite women into mainstream American society. Ethnic groups often absorbed this assimilation model and added Americanization programs to their clubs' agenda. For example, young Japanese American women attending the University of Washington organized a club in 1925 "to aid them in attaining a better understanding of the highest ideals of Japan and America." Accordingly, their activities ranged from traditional flower arranging to classes on American etiquette, manners, leadership, and dress. Similarly, San Francisco's Chinese YWCA promoted Americanization by offering classes in cooking, fashion, and homemaking. Reflecting a new generation's needs and interests, white ethnic associations also sponsored American-orientated classes and conducted meetings in English.

During the Depression, women's volunteerism rebounded, as clubs responded to their communities' distress. In Santa Fe, New Mexico, black and white clubwomen held food and clothing fairs, sewed garments, helped locate jobs, and established laundry and bathing facilities for transients. Other women eschewed these traditional benevolent activities to engage in labor organizing. Irish women in Butte, Montana, were leaders of the Women's Protective Union, and Mexican women had a strong presence in the Workers' Alliance of San Antonio, Texas. In 1938 the Alliance's charismatic organizer, Emma Tenayuca, led 10,000 female pecan-shellers, mostly of Mexican descent, in a major labor dispute and strike. Tenayuca and other 1930s' female activists also participated in numerous political groups, including the Communist Party.

While the Cold War was not conducive to women's activism, their interest in social causes was resuscitated after 1960. Women's renewed enthusiasm for collective action, however, differed from the earlier club movement in important ways. Contemporary groups downplayed municipal housekeeping in favor of gender equality. Moreover, instead of using club work to promote and expand their role as moral guardians, women's groups condemned prevailing gender stereotypes. So when feminists established the National Organization for Women in 1966, they emphasized that NOW was an association *for* women and not *of* women and granted men full membership. Likewise, women demanded full admittance into male-only clubs as well as leadership positions in organizations that previously limited them to supportive roles. Gaining a foothold in these former bastions of male power, women helped broaden these organizations' interests and activities. The once male-run Japanese American Citizens League has experienced a significant increase in elected female officers and has liberalized its platform to cover a wide range of civil and human rights issues. Finally admitting females in 1987, the Rotary Club had nearly 1,900 female chapter presidents by 2001. The Rotary Club now supports numerous female-oriented projects. A prime case in point is California's Los Altos Rotary Club, which in 2002 funded business loans to Guatemalan women and inaugurated in India a women's empowerment computer center.

At the community level, women's clubs regained their former momentum as a social and political force as women revived traditional female networks to fight domestic violence, job discrimination, and other issues confronting women. Like their Victorian predecessors, women volunteers also set up day-care centers, women's health clinics, and rape crisis centers to help their less fortunate sisters. In fact, during the late 1960s, the Office of Economic Opportunity estimated that 20 million women volunteers battled in the war of poverty.

Latino, African American, and other ethnic women were particularly effective in contemporary community organizing. Called "grassroots warriors," these women took the lead in fighting poor housing conditions, crime, substance abuse, and other problems that threatened their neighborhoods. A good example of this new activism is the Mothers of East Los Angeles (MELA). Formed in 1984, MELA mobilized 400 women to battle the construction of a prison and toxic waste plant in their Boyle Heights neighborhood. Still vital after nearly 2 decades, MELA currently sponsors public awareness programs, funds scholarships, and provides health and educational services for at-risk youth.

Despite new and more varied avenues for women to participate in public life, many of the pioneering women's clubs founded in the 1890s and early 1900s still exist today. The Omaha Woman's Club, Los Angeles Friday Morning Club, Prescott Woman's Club, Woman's Club of San Antonio, and numerous others continue to support educational and cultural events, fund scholarships, and contribute time and money to local charities and social service agencies. These venerable associations stand as monuments to the power and enduring value of organized womanhood and the role women's clubs once played—and continue to play—in the social, cultural, and political development of the American West.

—Debra L. Gold Hansen

SUGGESTED READINGS

Blair, Karen J. *The Clubwoman as Feminist: True Womanhood Redefined, 1868-1914.* New York: Holmes & Meier, 1980.

Brandenstein, Sherilyn. "The Colorado Cottage Home." *Colorado* magazine *53* (Summer 1976): 229-242.

Buck, Holly J. "'The Powerful Instrumentalities of Our Up-Building': The Woman's Study League of Pocatello, 1896-1916." *Pacific Northwest Quarterly 93* (1, 2001-02): 3-12.

Carver, Sharon Snow. *Club Women of the Three Intermountain Cities of Denver, Boise and Salt Lake City between 1893 and 1929.* Ph.D. dissertation. Brigham Young University, 2000.

Chan, Sucheng. "Race, Ethnic Culture, and Gender in the Construction of Identities Among Second Generation Chinese Americans, 1880s to 1930s," in K. Scott Wong and Sucheng Chan, eds., *Claiming America: Constructing Chinese American Identities During the*

Exclusion Era. Philadelphia, PA: Temple University Press, 1998.

Christman, Anastasia J. *The Best Laid Plans: Women's Clubs and City Planning in Los Angeles, 1890-1930*. Ph.D. dissertation. University of California, Los Angeles, 2000.

Coburn, Carol. "Ethnicity, Religion, and Gender: The Women of Block, Kansas, 1868-1940," in Frederick C. Luebke, ed., *European Immigrants in the American West: Community Histories*. Albuquerque: University of New Mexico Press, 1998.

Croly, J. C. *The History of the Woman's Club Movement in America*. New York: Harry G. Allen, 1898.

Cunningham, Mary S. *The Woman's Club of El Paso: Its First Thirty Years*. El Paso: Texas Western Press, 1978.

de Graaf, Lawrence B. "Race, Sex, and Region: Black Women in the American West, 1850-1920." *Pacific Historical Review* 49(2, 1980): 285-313.

Dickson, Lynda Faye. *The Early Club Movement Among Black Women in Denver, 1890-1925*. Ph.D. dissertation. University of Colorado, Boulder, 1982.

Engh, Michael E. "Mary Julia Workman, the Catholic Conscience of Los Angeles." *California History* 72(Spring 1993): 2-19.

Friday, Chris. "Recasting Identities: American-born Chinese and Nisei in the Era of the Pacific War," in Richard White and John M. Findlay, eds., *Power and Place in the North American West*. Seattle: University of Washington Press, 1999.

Gere, Anne Ruggles. *Intimate Practices: Literacy and Cultural Work in U.S. Women's Clubs, 1880-1920*. Urbana: University of Illinois, 1997.

Gullett, Gayle. "Women Progressives and the Politics of Americanization in California, 1915-1920." *Pacific Historical Review* 64(1, 1995): 71-94.

Haarsager, Sandra. *Organized Womanhood: Cultural Politics in the Pacific Northwest, 1840-1920*. Norman: University of Oklahoma Press, 1997.

Hornbein, Marjorie. "Frances Jacobs: Denver's Mother of Charities." *Western States Jewish Historical Quarterly* 15(2, 1983): 131-145.

Irwin, Mary Ann. "'Going About and Doing Good': The Politics of Benevolence, Welfare, and Gender in San Francisco, 1850-1880." *Pacific Historical Review* 68(3, 1999): 365-396.

Jackson, Hugh. "The History of Volunteering in Wyoming." *Annals of Wyoming* 59(1, 1987): 38-47.

James, Ronald M., and Elizabeth C. Raymond, eds. *Comstock Women: The Making of a Mining Community*. Reno: University of Nevada Press, 1997.

Jensen, Richard L. "Forgotten Relief Societies, 1844-67." *Dialogue* 16(1, 1983): 105-125.

Kreider, Marie L., and Michael R. Wells, eds. "White Ribbon Women: The Women's Christian Temperance Movement in Riverside, California." *Southern California Quarterly 81* (Spring 1999): 115-134.

Lothrop, Gloria Ricci. "Strength Made Stronger: The Role of Women in Southern California Philanthropy." *Southern California Quarterly 71*(2-3, 1989): 143-194.

Luckingham, Bradford. "Benevolence in Emergent San Francisco: A Note on Immigrant Life in the Urban Far West." *Southern California Quarterly 55*(Winter 1973): 431-443.

Lykes, Aimée de Potter. "Phoenix Women in the Development of Public Policy: Territorial Beginnings," in G. Wesley Johnson Jr., ed., *Phoenix in the Twentieth Century: Essays in Community History*. Norman: University of Oklahoma Press, 1993.

Matsumoto, Valerie J. "Japanese American Women and the Creation of Urban Nisei Culture in the 1930s," in Valerie J. Matsumoto and Blake Allmendinger, eds., *Over the Edge: Remapping the American West*. Berkeley: University of California Press, 1999.

McCarthy, Kathleen D., ed. *Lady Bountiful Revisited: Women, Philanthropy, and Power*. New Brunswick, NJ: Rutgers University Press, 1990.

Mercier, Laurie K. "We Are Women Irish: Gender, Class, and Ethnic Identity in Anaconda, Montana." *Montana: The Magazine of Western History 44* (1, 1994): 28-41.

Nakano, Mei. *Japanese American Women: Three Generations, 1890-1990*. Berkeley, CA: Mina Publishing; National Japanese Historical Society, 1990.

Naples, Nina A. *Grassroots Warriors: Activist Mothering, Community Work, and the War on Poverty*. New York: Routledge, 1998.

Orozco, Cynthia E. "Beyond Machismo, La Familia, and Ladies Auxiliaries: A Historiography of Mexican-Origin Women's Participation in Voluntary Associations and Politics in the United States, 1870-1990." *Perspectives in Mexican American Studies 5*(1995): 1-34.

Pardo, Mary. "Mexican American Women Grassroots Community Activists: Mothers of East Los Angeles." *Frontiers 11*(1, 1990): 1-7.

Pascoe, Peggy. *Relations of Rescue: The Search for Female Moral Authority in the American West, 1874-1939*. New York: Oxford University Press, 1990.

Pichardo, Nelson. "The Establishment and Development of Chicano Voluntary Associations in California, 1910-1930." *Aztlán 19*(2, 1988-1990): 93-155.

Raftery, Judith. "Los Angeles Clubwomen and Progressive Reform," in William Deverell and Tom Sitton, eds., *California Progressivism Revisited*. Berkeley: University of California Press, 1994.

Ruckman, Jo Ann. "'Knit, Knit, and Then Knit': The Women of Pocatello and the War Effort, 1917-1918." *Idaho Yesterdays 26* (Spring 1982): 26-36.

Sanchez, George. "'Go After the Women': Americanization and the Mexican Immigrant Woman, 1915-1929," in Vicki L. Ruiz and Ellen Carol DuBois, eds., *Unequal Sisters: A Multicultural Reader in U.S. Women's History* (2d ed.). New York: Rutledge, 1994.

Schackel, Sandra. *Social Housekeepers: Women Shaping Public Policy in New Mexico, 1920-1940*. Albuquerque: University of New Mexico Press, 1992.

Scott, Anne Firor. *Natural Allies: Women's Associations in American History*. Urbana: University of Illinois Press, 1991.

Stefanco, Carolyn J. *Pathways to Power: Women and Voluntary Associations in Denver, Colorado, 1876-1893*. Ph.D. dissertation. Duke University, 1987.

Tubbs, Stephenie Ambrose. "Montana Women's Clubs at the Turn of the Century." *Montana: The Magazine of the West 36* (Winter 1986): 26-35.

Underwood, June O. "Civilizing Kansas: Women's Organizations, 1880-1920." *Kansas History 7* (Winter 1984/85): 291-306.

Vargas, Zaragosa. "Tejana Radical: Emma Tenayuca and the San Antonio Labor Movement During the Great Depression." *Pacific Historical Review 66* (November 1997): 553-580.

Waite, Robert G. "The Woman's Club Movement in Idaho: A Document on the Early Years." *Idaho Yesterdays 36*(2, 1992): 19-23.

Watson, Anita Ernst. *Into Their Own: Nevada Women Emerging Into Public Life*. Reno: Nevada Humanities Committee, 2000.

Yung, Judy. *Unbound Feet: A Social History of Chinese Women in San Francisco*. Berkeley: University of California Press, 1995.

CLUBWOMEN OF BOISE

Attempting to develop familiar female networks that would help them fight frontier isolation and immorality, the women of Boise, Idaho, joined the surge of women's club organizations that occurred nationally in the last decade of the 19th century. Most Idaho women's clubs and organizations that were started in the 1890s were absorbed to some degree by both civic and cultural betterment issues. Many clubs were started by women who had belonged to women's clubs before moving to Idaho or who knew clubwomen from other states, and these clubs, while meeting in part for companionship and self-culture, did not go through the strictly literary stage of the national clubs with earlier beginnings. Idaho was a frontier state where the ratio of men to women in 1870 was 4 to 1, but by 1890 the number of men to women evened out, with 1½ men to every woman in the territory. As the proportion began to balance, women transplanted their cultures as well as themselves and their families. In diverse places where a few women settled, women's clubs, organized for personal and civic improvement, sprang up.

The Columbian Club, Boise's earliest, was first organized to work with the Board of Lady Managers at the Chicago World's Fair in 1893 (known as the Columbian Exposition in honor of Columbus's arrival in America 401 years earlier). The club's purpose was to sponsor a women's room in the Idaho building at the Exposition. The clubwomen raised money, furnished the room, and also provided for its upkeep during the fair. The successful completion of their first undertaking inspired the women to continue their association, so they turned their sights to activities of local interest. They established Boise's first lending library in two rooms of the city hall. The club paid the salary of a professional librarian and also provided new books when possible. Later, as the city took more responsibility for the library, the Columbian Club remained involved. Clubwomen applied for and secured funding from the Carnegie Foundation for the city's first library building and raised the matching funds that Carnegie required. Other early Columbian Club projects included placing waste cans along Main Street and campaigning against unsightly billboards. While clubwomen recognized the economic advantages of billboard advertising, they fought for city ordinances to control the size, location, and content of the increasingly enormous structures. The Columbian Club even suggested a boycott of products advertised on objectionable signs. Boise began as a frontier fort, and it wasn't until clubwomen campaigned for the creation of parks that the first land was set aside. They also recognized the value of playgrounds for the health of children. Clubwomen not only lobbied Boise to provide playgrounds, but they also arranged for some themselves by contacting the owners of vacant lots around the city.

Boise's Southside Improvement Club is a good example of a small, limited club (about 40 members). Organized in 1904 when the unincorporated village of South Boise was separate from Boise City, it successfully concentrated on school and park improvement in a small geographic area. In 1913, when Boise annexed South Boise, the club remained a viable advocate for improvement in the south part of Boise. The small club made sure their area got its share of parks, services, and general attention from the city.

Although the Idaho Federation of Women's Clubs was not organized until 1905, the General Federation of Women's Clubs (GFWC) allowed individual clubs to join the national federation before a state organization was in place. The 2-year-old Boise Columbian Club enrolled in 1894, and other clubs in the state also joined on an individual club basis. Although a state federation was still 7 years away, it was this national affiliation that seemed to trigger broader state and national interests and the organization of district federations. In December 1900 some of the Idaho clubs met to organize the Idaho Second District Federation that included Ada County, in which Boise was situated. In its first public action, the new Second District Federation endorsed a library bill that would be presented at the next session of Idaho's General Assembly. In the next 2 years, the first and third districts were officially formed, but still Idaho women had not organized a state federation. The districts generally addressed issues that were paramount in their own areas while loosely following the national GFWC agenda. When statewide concerns such as education, legislation, and historic preservation came up, however, the districts cooperated to achieve success.

On January 31, 1905, the three Idaho Federated Districts, along with non-Federated clubs, met to organize the Idaho Federation of Women's Clubs (IFWC). Idaho's size, unique topography, and scattered sparse population presented a variety of problems for the organization of a statewide federation; nevertheless, 17 clubs were represented at the organizational meeting, and when a snowstorm prevented attendance, another 7 sent dues and support. The new federation's first order of business was to affiliate with the General Federation. At this first meeting, the new IFWC appointed three standing committees—legislative, educational, and historical—that have been continuous throughout the history of the state

organization, while other committees were formed and abandoned as needed. The organizing convention decided that the new federation's first actions would be to propose three types of bills to the legislature. These were laws that dealt with a juvenile court system, child labor, and married women's property rights. Eventually, the clubwomen of Idaho were successful in each of these areas. The IFWC united women from across the Gem State, and in 1908, 3 years after its establishment, it boasted a membership of 34 clubs representing 1,400 club members. Four years later, in 1912, it had enlarged to include 52 clubs with 2,000 members.

Always interested in conservation, Idaho clubs proposed national and state parks to preserve nature for the next generation. They also worked to conserve the health of Boise's citizens. When the state health inspector asked for the assistance of women's clubs to enforce health laws, the women began inspecting and reporting abuses. On the national level, Idaho clubwomen supported the Heyburn Pure Food Law and then worked on similar laws for the state. Idaho, supported by its women's clubs, was the first western state to pass a slaughter house inspection law. Women's clubs attacked the widely used public drinking cup and succeeded in eliminating it in businesses, schools, and industry. In addition, they raised funds to provide public drinking fountains in the downtown. Clubwomen asked for and got a comfort station for women who worked downtown and visiting women from areas outside the city. Once the comfort station was provided in the basement of city hall, clubwomen hired a matron to staff the facility.

In 1897 the Columbian Club instituted the Idaho Traveling Library, which provided books to rural areas of the state. The IFWC and later the state eventually assumed the daily operation of the traveling library, but clubwomen stayed involved. They also worked to better the school systems by emphasizing patriotism and citizenship in the classrooms, and they provided visual aids to teachers. In addition, they supported vocational training and domestic education.

The Idaho Federation successfully sponsored protective legislation that regulated the hours, conditions, and wages of working women. After failing to convince Idaho legislators to pass state civil service reform, Boise women were able to pass city laws requiring the merit system for city employees. When city corruption came to light, the women worked to clean up city politics.

The IFWC was active in lobbying the legislature through their legislative committee. They encountered resistance and complaints from various legislators, but they remained firm. In 1913 one group of legislators publicly told women to stay out of "men's business" like taxes and property laws, and called the woman's efforts "nagging" and "unwomanly." Often the women's bills were stopped in committee or amended so as to become ineffective or even reverse the original intent of the bill. The women were not fooled by these tactics, and persisted to achieve success. A mother's pension law, various protective statutes, and the woman's equal property rights law were some of the successes of the legislative committee.

The juvenile court system was one of the first successful projects of the IFWC. The women also lobbied for the national Children's Bureau, and were proud that one of its sponsors was their own Senator W. E. Borah. Clubwomen also worked to eliminate or control child labor.

The Boise clubwomen engaged in a purity crusade that attacked gambling, drinking, prostitution, and other vices. Many of the programs not universally supported or successful were very progressive and included sex education in schools, a uniform divorce law, medical exams before marriage, and prohibition. The fight against prostitution targeted venereal diseases associated with the practice rather than the women. Clubwomen worked to provide aid and jobs to women who wanted to leave prostitution.

Like clubwomen across the nation, Idaho women were patriotic. When Idaho women gained the vote in 1896, clubwomen rushed to learn how to vote. They conducted classes and discussion groups on a variety of topics and endorsed candidates who supported club views. Clubwomen considered knowledgeable voting their patriotic duty. When the nation entered World War I, war work became the number one goal. Most clubs in the city organized their own chapters of the Red Cross, and clubwomen provided a variety of items and services to further the war effort. Clubwoman Gertrude Hays of Boise was chair of the Woman's Council of Defense in Idaho. Before and after the war, many Boise clubs conducted peace conferences and supported national peace organizations.

Idaho's unique history and settlement patterns, along with its wide open spaces, offered women interested in reform various opportunities. Their choice to use women's clubs provided women with the organization and backing to focus their efforts and be successful. Club leaders, local, state, and national, were remarkably consistent in their advice to women to thoroughly study issues before making decisions. They encouraged women to be aware of the needs of their local communities. The Idaho clubwomen were proud of the full citizenship rights that they exercised, and continually emphasized the need for women to prove themselves by being the best, most aware, patriotic, and active citizens.

—Sharon Snow Carver

SUGGESTED READINGS

Carver, Sharon Snow. *Club Women of the Three Intermountain Cities of Denver, Boise and Salt Lake City Between 1893 and 1929.* Ph.D. dissertation. Brigham Young University, 2000.

Croly, Jennie Cunningham (Jennie June). *The History of the Woman's Club Movement in America.* New York: Henry G. Allen, 1898.

Hogsett, Vernetta Murchison. *The Golden Years: A History of the Idaho Federation of Women's Clubs, 1905-1955.* Caldwell, ID: Caxton, 1955.

Waite, Robert G. "The Woman's Club Movement in Idaho: A Document on the Early Years." *Idaho Yesterdays 36* (Summer 1992):19.

Weimann, Jeanne Madeline. *The Fair Women.* Chicago: Academy Chicago, 1981.

CLUBWOMEN OF DENVER

Denver, Colorado, was established in 1860 as a mining town where men outnumbered women by 16 to 1. Businessmen and political bosses controlled Denver, a wide-open town flowing with vice and corruption. While the male business leaders of the city had little concern for charity or the plight of the poor that flooded Denver looking for a better or healthier life, some women—wives and daughters of these leaders—took steps to alleviate the distress in the city.

Denver's first women's philanthropic club, the Ladies Union Aid Society (later the Ladies Relief Society), was organized in 1860 to help the poor. The society raised funds to pursue a varied program of relief, including charity, a free clinic, a day nursery, and a home for the aged. As more women arrived in Denver, additional women's clubs were formed. The 1880s produced several study clubs, including the

Denver Fortnightly Club and the Monday Literary Club (originally the Pleasant Hours Club), which attracted members of Denver's elite. In 1889 the wives of businessmen organized the Round Table Club, which was interested in world events, literature, civic affairs, public education, and social improvement. Clubs designed for specific groups of women, such as the Denver Woman's Press Club (1898) and the Reviewers (1892), were created during the last decade of the 19th century. Other women's clubs based on different interests were formed in the last decade of the 19th century and the first 2 decades of the 20th century, but most had components of philanthropy, reform, and community service.

When Colorado women received full citizenship in 1893, they formed political and civic groups. The City League of Denver and the Twenty-Second Avenue Study Club had developed to push equal suffrage and continued for civic improvement. The Civic Federation of Denver got under way in 1895 as a nonpartisan club with three departments—public morals, education, and municipal philanthropy; however, the Civic Federation's main emphasis was cleaning up the corruption in Denver city government.

Shortly after gaining suffrage, Denver women established a branch of the Jane Jefferson Democratic Club and its counterparts, the Young Woman's League, the Woman's Populist League, and the Woman's Department of the State Republican Party. The Twentieth Century Discussion Club of Denver was organized in 1896 as the Woman's Populist Club. When the 1896 elections proved successful for the club's sponsored candidates, they decided to reorganize as a mutual improvement society, where religion and politics were taboo. In addition, Denver women joined societies that sponsored specific action such as the Civil Service Reform League and the City Improvement Society.

In 1894 over 200 women met to organize the Woman's Club of Denver, the city's first large, unlimited membership club with a variety of departments to address different interests. The initial departments were home, education, philanthropy, art and literature, science and philosophy, and reform. Women would join the department or departments that interested them and also participate in the programs sponsored by the whole club. Inspired by the success of the highly popular Chicago Woman's Club, the Woman's Club of Denver focused on reform and philanthropic work, but also studied literary subjects. Sarah Pratt

Decker, dynamic first president of the Woman's Club of Denver, emphasized in 1897 that the club's 638 members had "attained that standard where selfishness is subordinate to altruism, where the entertainment and self-culture of the individual is of less importance than a true spirit of practical helpfulness in the community."

In 1895, 166 women living on the north side of the city created Denver's second largest departmental club. While it never reached the size of the Woman's Club of Denver, the North Side Woman's Club became a large and influential group in the city. It originally had four departments—home and education, literature and science, reform and philanthropy, and social affairs—and participated in literary study, community reform, and philanthropy.

Several individual Colorado clubs joined the General Federation of Women's Clubs (GFWC) without first organizing a state federation. In 1895 five Federated clubs from Denver—the Denver Fortnightly, the Monday Literary Club, the Round Table Club, the Clio Club, and the Woman's Club of Denver—issued a call to all clubs in the state to organize a state federation. The convention call received enthusiastic response from all parts of the state. When the Colorado Federation of Women's Clubs was established, 70 delegates were present representing 37 known clubs. Just 3 years later in 1898, Denver clubwomen hosted the large and successful national convention of the GFWC.

While the GFWC encouraged service and reform after its formation in 1894, it wasn't until 1907 that Denver's own Sarah Pratt Decker became president of the national organization and service to the community became the major emphasis of the General Federation. Individual clubs, however, chose their own crusades and decided which of the many suggestions and programs from the General Federation they would adopt.

African American women's clubs were active in Denver and worked on many social problems, but their influence on actual city policy appears to be limited. In the white, middle-class clubs, race appears to have been a subject for study on occasion. An exception is the Civic Federation of Denver, which in 1895 attempted to enlist the aid of the African American woman's community for one of its reform projects. In addition, both an African American club and the Jewish Council of Women were included in the charter clubs for the organization of the state federation. In 1900, when a controversy arose in the GFWC regarding the admittance of African American clubs, Colorado supported allowing African American clubs into the General Federation. The controversy might have split the GFWC when the southern clubs threatened to withdraw; however, just before the 1902 biennial in Los Angeles, a compromise was reached. It was decided to leave the admittance of African American clubs to the individual states on a three-fifths vote of the member clubs.

Colorado women's clubs sponsored reform on local, state, and national levels with varying degrees of success. Civic housekeeping, or cleaning up their city, was usually successful, in part because men generally accepted women's involvement in clean-up efforts. The Civic Federation of Denver investigated garbage collection and tried to eliminate the corruption surrounding the awarding of city contracts. They provided the city's first downtown rubbish cans and participated in the health department's "clean-up week." In 1897 the Woman's Club of Denver sponsored "free baths" in the city and later opened a public bathhouse.

Health issues were always important to women, and their clubs campaigned for pure food and pure milk. Twice a year the Woman's Club clubhouse was turned into a well baby clinic. Demand by women's clubs helped Colorado pass laws requiring vital statistic registration as a health issue. Women's clubs in Denver tried, unsuccessfully, for several years to persuade the city government to fund a public tuberculosis hospital for the indigent sufferers.

Conservation and beautification were important to women's clubs. From 1895 to 1900 Denver clubs encouraged a program called Pingree Gardens, where weed-filled lots were converted to vegetable gardens, which provided produce to the neighborhood poor. Clubs always supported parks and playgrounds in the city and were especially interested in tree planting. In order to raise awareness of wildlife protection, Denver clubs sponsored the adoption of a Colorado state bird, flower, and tree.

Denver women's clubs always promoted education. They supported libraries from their beginnings, and in 1885 clubwomen from various city clubs organized the City Library Association, which oversaw the building and running of the Denver Carnegie Public Library. The Woman's Club of Denver began the free traveling library in 1896 in an attempt to take education and books to rural areas of the state. Large wooden boxes crisscrossed the state, stopping at small communities, schoolhouses, and post offices and bringing a wide variety of adult and carefully chosen children's books to the small towns and isolated areas of Colorado. Clubs also studied schools and their curriculum and made suggestions for improvement. One 1897 Woman's Club report took the very progressive stand that the religion and marital status of teachers was "beyond the prerogative of the school board." Women's clubs strongly supported vocational education, domestic science, and adult education programs.

While Denver did not have the huge problems with child labor that plagued other states, many children left school during the beet season to work as laborers in the fields. This was not just a problem of agricultural areas; in 1921 over 500 children in Denver also participated. These children often got behind and dropped out of school. Clubs worked with school boards offering alternate programs and with the state legislature to make the practice illegal. They met with some success with child labor laws, but found the most help was sponsoring and later insisting on the enforcement of mandatory school attendance laws. Another group of children who attracted clubwomen's concern was newsboys. They offered programs, schools, a clubhouse, and proposed laws for their protection.

Suffrage in 1893 brought the aggressive interest of Denver clubwomen to politics. Although Colorado women had gained suffrage, they strongly supported national women's suffrage. The Civic Federation of Denver actively served as a watchdog of city government. They investigated corruption, sponsored candidates, educated Denver women on how to vote, and even provided rides to the polls. The Legislative Committee of the Colorado Federation of Women's Clubs, begun in the 1890s, became one of the largest and most effective women's political committees in the nation. Representatives from throughout the state met in Denver and studied, discussed, and recommended action on state and national legislation. Colorado women saw new civil service legislation passed, but dishonesty, cheating, and general corruption on the part of city and state officials prevented it from being meaningful reform. In the 1920s the Colorado women supported the national Sheppard-Towner Infant and Maternity Act and were against the Equal Rights Amendment, which, they felt, would nullify their achievements in female protective legislation.

Patriotism was a major part of Denver women's club activities. They emphasized that voting was a patriotic duty and provided short citizenship lessons at most club meetings, and each club organized a department of American citizenship. When the United States entered World War I, club programs shifted to war-related efforts. Most clubs became chapters of the Red Cross. They provided visitors and supplies to Denver veteran's hospitals and soldiers stationed away from home and ran canteens or military hospitality centers. Clubs sold war bonds and stamps, donated jewelry and other scarce items, rolled bandages, and made items for the front in a general surge of patriotism.

After the war, women supported peace, disarmament, and the League of Nations. The Woman's Club of Denver, along with the Colorado WCTU, joined and were active in the national Woman's Peace Party. Denver clubs held a "Cause and Cure of War" conference and in 1925 actively supported the ratification of the Kellogg-Briand Treaty.

Denver women's clubs were an active part of progressive era reform. They investigated, studied, published, and acted for the betterment of society in general. At a time when women were not encouraged to step out of their homes, these upper-class and middle-class women challenged long-accepted habits of society and made changes in their community, state, and nation.

—Sharon Snow Carver

SUGGESTED READINGS

Beaton, Gail Marjorie. *The Literary Study and Philanthropic Work of Six Women's Clubs in Denver, 1881-1945.* Master's thesis. University of Colorado, 1987.

Carver, Sharon Snow. *Club Women of the Three Intermountain Cities of Denver, Boise and Salt Lake City Between 1893 and 1929.* Ph.D. dissertation. Brigham Young University, 2000.

Scott, Anne Firor. "Most Invisible of All: Black Women's Voluntary Association," *Journal of Southern History 56* (February 1990).

Sinton, May L. *A History of the Women's Clubs of Denver, 1894-1915.* Master's thesis. University of Colorado, Denver, 1987.

Stefano, Carolyn J. *Pathways to Power: Women and Voluntary Associations in Denver, 1876-93.* Ph.D. dissertation. Duke University, 1987.

Women's Clubs of Denver, Essays in Colorado History, No. 13. Denver, CO: Colorado Historical Society, 1993.

CLUBWOMEN OF HUNTINGTON BEACH

The women's club movement began in the 19th century, when women found themselves predominantly in charge of domestic concerns while men left home to carry out duties of work and politics in the public sphere. Now in charge of their own domain, women worked within the circumscribed definitions placed on them in order to create an identity that belonged solely to females. Although some women did attach themselves to radical feminist movements, the clubwomen preferred to use the stereotypes of domestication and moral leadership to push the boundaries that confined them to the household and, in doing so, forced their way into the public realm. One woman stated, "[It is] better to play possum, and wear a mask of submission. No use in rousing any unnecessary antagonism. . . . I shall reach my goal just as quick in my velvet shoes, as if I tramped on rough-shod as they do with their Woman's Rights brogans."

Women found ways to express their opinions through supporting moral reform movements such as abolition and temperance and, after the 1860s, through joining the women's club. This represented an expanding of the female sphere, which included the responsibility to take care of the children and provide a moral and decent society. Through the actions of J. C. Croly, the General Federation of Women's Clubs (GFWC) was established in 1894. Middle-class and upper-class women in America joined together to create an organization that could be used as an outlet for women's concerns. The Federation grew out of Croly's own women's club, which she established in 1868 after she was excluded from a New York Press Club dinner for Charles Dickens. The establishment of Croly's women's club, called Sorosis, was a result of women's dissatisfaction with being excluded from a male-dominated society.

Although some of the women who joined the club held radical opinions for their era, Croly insisted that their agenda was not to be actively voiced through the medium of the women's club, and discouraged heated topics such as the vote and religion in order to ensure a friendly, comfortable milieu where women could share their common experiences and struggles. The women's clubs differed from other 19th-century "radical" feminist movements, since they provided an alternative, engaging organization where women could organize, free from being criticized for unfeminine behavior.

The goal of Croly's women's club was to use domestic feminism to empower women to make changes within society. That is, Croly hoped that through collectively using their supposed "natural talents" of motherhood, morality, and domesticity, women would begin to reach out into the community and expand their role outside the household. Proclaiming these innocuous motivations, women could leave the confines of the home, create a place for themselves in the public sphere, and redefine the role of women without abandoning domestic values.

THE LOCAL CLUB

Eventually, women's clubs were organized in various states. Although the GFWC worked to address various domestic concerns in the United States, it was realized that the smaller, local clubs dealt with their own obstacles, especially when it came to the new clubs established in the western part of the United States. Because these new towns were largely unsettled, the women would have additional challenges to overcome. Croly stated that "[t]he club life of women in California presents many interesting features. It differs from the club life of the East in being almost wholly centered in towns and cities . . . the country neighborhoods having been for the most part unsettled, the populations widely scattered and extremely fluctuating."

The GFWC recognized that the needs of each state were different; thus the GFWC strongly supported the creation of independent state federations. The local clubs based in smaller towns and cities were loosely connected to the state federations. At both the state and local level, the women's clubs demonstrated much flexibility and autonomy. This is especially true of the women's clubs in the West.

The early communities in the West during the 1900s were comprised of small towns, which allowed women to exercise new roles in their communities and redefine themselves in the public sphere. They organized in clubs to accomplish a wide variety of tasks in their society.

THE HUNTINGTON BEACH CLUB

No community better illustrates the contributions clubwomen made within a growing western town than the example of the Woman's Club of Huntington Beach, California. This was a small, western community where the women used the local Woman's Club to fully participate in the shaping of their society. Through the Woman's Club, the women of Huntington Beach organized a vast array of projects for their community. These projects evolved from very basic contributions to the community, such as the beautification of the city, to tackling more modern issues, such as topics surrounding the world wars. Eventually, the Woman's Club in Huntington Beach would be used as a vehicle for women of that community to fully enter into the public sphere. By the end of the 1900s, it was a politically active organization, which sought to pass laws in order to create a society that was harmonious with the ideals of motherhood.

Huntington Beach was a small beach community located on the West Coast of California. By 1903 there were only 12 families living in Huntington Beach; however, by 1909 the population had reached just over 900. The Woman's Club was established in 1908 by the women of the community who expressed a need for civic improvements in the small city. The women stated that their mission did not simply involve improving the city, but also included the desire for self-improvement and community support. On their agenda the women stated their desires to develop skills involving household economics, to encourage the study of literary works, and to promote social activities within their community.

From 1910 to 1920, life in Huntington Beach was about the settling of a developing town, and the club's meetings reflected that. In its rudimentary beginnings, the Woman's Club of Huntington Beach mainly worked at the local level and was concerned with the immediate needs of civic improvements within their community. However, females also used the club as a medium to educate themselves about literature, domestic issues, and national concerns.

In the first decade, the Woman's Club pushed for civic improvements. The females of the club had a large influence on the development of the town through their efforts to beautify their surroundings. The women added flowers, cleaned up garbage, removed weeds from empty lots, and assisted local churches and schools to do the same. The women encouraged access to books and reading through supporting the building of the first library and reading rooms in the city.

In the first few years, the Woman's Club focused on self-improvement and issues concerning home economics. The women invited guest lecturers to give talks on how to improve the healthy environment within the home. At other meetings, papers were presented on Emerson, Shakespeare, and various European plays. The clubwomen sought inspiring female figures by leading discussions on the role of women in literature and famous female reformers in history. Furthermore, the club encouraged young women to expose their families to the outside world by instituting a "travel day," where the women would invite guests to relive their exciting journeys abroad. The Woman's Club organized functions in order to maintain the familiarity within the budding community by holding celebrations, such as the one in 1908 when a dinner was held in honor of Martha Washington.

Throughout the club's history, the women did engage in political discussions. This was especially true when an issue had a direct impact on the women's sphere. They conversed on the subjects of peace, domestic issues, community development, and consumer concerns. In June 1908 the club held a discussion on the peace movement, and in 1911 the women passed a resolution advocating the erection of a peace statue at the entrance to the Panama Canal.

During the 1890s Croly had steered away from heated topics such as female suffrage. However, in time, as such movements were gaining momentum throughout the nation, the Woman's Club of Huntington Beach expressed interest in some of the political issues of their day. By 1910 the issue of a woman's right to vote had gained impetus throughout the country, and the Woman's Club of Huntington Beach held discussions on the topic. Many of the club members expressed a desire for the vote; however, a few members refused to support the movement. In September 1911 a small number of clubwomen gathered in support of a rally advocating the vote. Later that year, the women from the Huntington Beach club attended the state federation meeting in Long Beach and voted in favor of women's suffrage.

In reaction to World War I, the Woman's Club held discussions on the changing tide of German politics. The clubwomen gave presentations on German industries and the role of German women in the workplace. They expressed a keen interest in German art and culture during the war years. In 1919 clubwomen dealt with topics that women in America were faced with, such as women's work in the factories during the war. As World War I droned on, the clubwomen grew weary of the topic of war, mirroring the national sentiment and America's isolationist stance. In 1919 the clubwomen agreed that the meetings of the last year were absorbed in war topics and that they should divert from the focus of war in future meetings. With Europe engaged in warfare again in 1939, the women of Huntington Beach invited guest speakers and held discussions on the war in Europe; however, their primary interests did not revolve around the political climate, and they maintained a distance from global concerns.

For the most part, the activities of the Woman's Club of Huntington Beach remained consistent until the late 1970s. As the community settled into a comfortable state of suburbia, the Woman's Club developed a routine system that pervades the board minutes of the 1960s and 1970s. The discussion topics generally involved community service, maintenance of the clubhouse, election of officers, community work, and networking with other clubs. The Woman's Club continued to develop and aid the community, achieve self-improvement, and provide entertainment for the locals.

In regard to community service, the women sponsored scholarships for the seven local high schools in Huntington Beach. They donated money to organizations such as the Girl Scouts of America and March of Dimes. The women continued their philanthropic activities through the 1960s with the Veterans Administration Voluntary Service Program and the care of the elderly. They received awards from the California Federation of Women's Clubs as well as certificates of appreciation from the Long Beach Veterans Administration hospital, honoring them for their help. The women were consistent in pursuing their interests in the arts and entertaining, and held art exhibits, fashion shows, and luncheons. They sponsored art students from Edison High School and also participated in travel discussions on a regular basis.

THE WOMAN'S CLUB GETS POLITICAL

Croly saw the potential of her club in fostering the development of female leaders: "It is an interesting thing to watch the career of a natural born leader in one of the [woman's] clubs. . . . [B]y some strange fate the right women are usually found occupying the prominent positions."

One of those women who found a prominent position in the Woman's Club of Huntington Beach was Shirlee Earley. In the late 1970s the Woman's Club entered into a new era of activity, partially due to the admittance of charismatic leaders such as the new president, Shirlee Earley. Under Earley's leadership, the club was used to pass legislation concerning women's issues. Although the GFWC displayed some activity in the legislative process, local clubs like the Woman's Club of Huntington Beach rarely rallied behind the passing of legislation. However, under the leadership of Earley, the Woman's Club found new momentum for the political process.

The club in Huntington Beach employed Croly's idea of domestic feminism to launch campaigns for legislation protecting matters that were clearly in a woman's domain. Earley's projects for the club grappled with concerns that were within the context of a woman's sphere and further demonstrated using a feminine agenda to create a female place in the political realm. Earley led the clubwomen from Huntington Beach in campaigns to pass legislation to address issues such as consumer concerns, the elderly, and child safety, all of which encompassed the duties and responsibilities of women in society. In one of her many speeches rallying the women of the club, Earley stated that "[a]s we begin to take our rightful place in governing this nation, the importance of the Women's Club and other organizations has become very clear. It is through organizations that we can make our voices heard. . . . Public officials are our employees. . . . [W]e, the people are the ones who must outline the programs they should follow . . . [I]t is up to us to see that they do it. We are the boss."

During the late 1970s and through the 1980s, the most notable change that occurred in the Woman's Club of Huntington Beach was the new drive to involve the organization in active campaigning for legislation. Members of the club became politically active wives, mothers, and citizens, attempting to sign up voters, initiate letter-writing campaigns, and even organize transportation to legislative meetings in San Diego to demonstrate to the politicians of California the collective force behind the Woman's Club. By the 1980s the Huntington Beach club took on a plethora of legislative campaigns.

Club meetings were used to organize the women into politically active citizens. The women circulated petitions and resolutions and worked in conjunction with sister clubs throughout the state of California to pass a vast array of laws. They collected signatures, mailed letters, appealed to city councils, and talked with assemblymen as well as state senators.

Women from the club packed chartered buses and were transported to San Diego to demonstrate to the state legislators their determination to get their laws passed. They sought support of the local community and placed ads in the local newspaper asking other concerned voters within Huntington Beach to join them in their fight. The Huntington Beach club had now transformed itself into a formidable group of female constituents that politicians were forced to reckon with.

In January 1982 the Huntington Beach club supported the Lemon Bill (AB 1787), which protected patrons from purchasing defective cars from dealerships. Women saw this as an obvious concern of women, being the representatives of the household. With the collective efforts of the Huntington Beach club and its sister clubs, the Lemon Auto Law was passed in California in 1983.

Harriet Wieder, the Orange County supervisor, saw the potential of these political activists and continued to present projects to Earley and the Huntington Beach clubwomen in the following years. All the laws supported by the Huntington Beach club were issues that concerned women. In 1982 the Huntington Beach club pursued the Long Term Care Bill (AB 2860), which sought to provide help for the care of the elderly in their homes and in institutions. In 1983 the clubwomen supported the Peace Academy Bill and contested escalating utility rates in the state Senate Bill 399. The women fought to protect children with the support of child care and prevention laws (SB 303, AB 225, AB 606), and supported the Nursing Home Patients' Protection Act of 1984. This latter bill was first vetoed by Governor George Deukmejian but was reversed after the clubwomen's continual persistence and letter-writing campaigns. The governor called Earley at her home to inform her of the reversal of his veto before the decision was made public. From 1990 to 1992, the women of the club contributed to passing laws that protected the interests of children. This is evident in the clubwomen's fight for gun control with their support of the Brady Bill, and the campaign for helmet and safety belt laws, as well as the "4 years or 40-pound child restraint" legislation. All of these sought to enact safety laws to protect children.

The women's club movement has been a vital organization where women have used domestic feminism in order to expand their roles outside the home and accomplish their goal of molding the society in which they lived. There is no better example of this than the Woman's Club of Huntington Beach. Initially, the club provided the women from this small western beach town with the ability to mold their budding community. However, under the auspices of domestic feminism, these women were eventually able to participate fully in the political sphere. This is seen in the role of the Huntington Beach club, which made a metamorphosis from the early 1900s, when the club sponsored the beautification projects of the small but growing western town, to the 1980s, which saw a more politically active club that sought to shape their society politically through the passing of legislation. Ultimately, through the club movement, the women of Huntington Beach expanded their role in society and established themselves in what would be considered a male domain.

—Mary Hardy

SUGGESTED READINGS

Blair, Karen J. *The Clubwoman as Feminist: True Womanhood Redefined, 1868-1914.* New York: Holmes & Meier, 1980.

Croly, J. C. *The History of the Woman's Club Movement in America.* New York: Henry G. Allen, 1889.

Wentworth, Alicia. *The Ultimate Challenge.* City of Huntington Beach Miscellaneous Data, Special Collections, California State University, Fullerton.

CLUBWOMEN OF LOS ANGELES

For more than a century, a group of women known as the Friday Morning Club (FMC) have met each week in Los Angeles. While few Southern Californians today have ever heard of this group, there was a time when households throughout Los Angeles would have instantly recognized its name and when some 1 million clubwomen nationwide would have known of its existence through newsletters and magazines. The FMC and similar organizations around the country, in fact, stood in the center sphere of Progressive era civic culture.

Founded in 1891, by the early 1920s the FMC had become the largest member within the nation's General Federation of Women's Clubs (GFWC). At its peak, close to 3,000 members supported the club, and thousands more attended its innumerable meetings, forums, and events. Political and cultural dignitaries visiting Southern California almost invariably appeared there and spoke to its members, who comprised a who's who of the region's prominent women reformers, artists, philanthropists, professionals, and business leaders. When in 1924 FMC members opened their new $600,000, six-story clubhouse near downtown Los Angeles, thousands attended the ceremony.

The contrast between the FMC's impressive place in early 20th-century Los Angeles and its more modest contemporary status alerts historians to some dramatic shifts in the experiences of urban women. Why and how did women's clubs grow to occupy such a prominent role in the lives of many Americans, and in urban civic life? When, why, and how did these clubs decline? The story of the once prestigious FMC illuminates an important historical moment in the history of Los Angeles and of America's urban female elite. At its founding, the FMC provided Los Angeles's most powerful women a springboard from which to pursue new social, cultural, intellectual, and political activities. The size, location, and breadth of its 1924 headquarters testifies to just how many had come to draw on its resources. Its steady decline shortly thereafter, however, points to major transformations in the social infrastructure of urban women's experience.

Large metropolitan women's clubs like the FMC grew and thrived throughout the nation beginning in the late 19th century through the 1920s. Involvement in expansive, corporate-structured, same-sex associations dominated daily life for affluent white women. Indeed, by 1914, 85% of noncareer women in the United States belonged to at least one woman's club; 79% of professional women and 80% of women in education were club members. Nowhere did women's clubs flourish more than in Los Angeles. In the early 1920s, the city housed the first (the FMC), second, and third largest members of the national GFWC, along with a nonfederated club of comparable size. In 1923 the Los Angeles District of the California Federation of Women's Clubs comprised 172 associations, with a total membership of more than 30,000. The smallest clubs numbered 60 or more members.

In the complex world of Progressive era club life, barriers of race and class defined club memberships.

The "color question"—whether or not African American women should be admitted—rocked the GFWC conventions at the turn of the century and sharply polarized its membership. In 1902, when the organization held its annual meeting in Los Angeles, members adopted the conservative "state's rights" position, allowing local societies to determine membership criteria and thus effectively excluding African American women from many clubs. Not only did many of Los Angeles's most prominent clubs, such as the FMC, refuse to admit women of color, but their leaders lobbied for exclusionary policies in state and national women's associations. In response, Southern California's women of color founded clubs of their own. The newspaper *The Crisis* reported in 1912 that "Los Angeles is perhaps the greatest center of colored-club activity in California." Local black women's clubs included the Sojourner Truth Industrial Club, the Day Nursery Association, the Progressive Woman's Club, the Married Ladies' Social and Art Club, and many others. There exist few published histories of Latina, Asian American, or African American women's clubs in Los Angeles, but a recent ethnologic photography project of Los Angeles's communities, called *Shades of L.A.*, turned up hundreds of pictures showing such clubs throughout the 20th century.

In the FMC's exclusionary membership requirements lay the catalyst for the club's growth and success, as well as its ultimate decline. The FMC and other elite women's clubs in Los Angeles and throughout the nation thrived because they presented a class of privately privileged, but publicly disempowered, women a place to educate themselves in multiple circles beyond their fashionable homes. At a time when women confronted severe barriers to their participation in business, politics, and other privileged public arenas, the FMC became an avenue for its members to venture into many otherwise restricted Los Angeles circles. It provided a setting in which women debated and defined public issues, engaged in political activism within the club, and gradually took their interests and skills into circles beyond the clubhouse.

The construction of the FMC's grand new headquarters in 1924 evidenced its members' commitment and enthusiasm. Ironically, however, its opening did not usher in a grand new chapter of club history, but instead, marked its apex. Several trends crippled the institution, and women's clubdom itself, just at its moment of greatest promise. Financial obligations proved increasingly strenuous for club members during the 1920s. The FMC's growing infrastructure, best seen in the construction of its massive new headquarters, required larger dues, which served to narrow its potential membership base. When the economy crashed in 1929, the FMC's already dwindling rosters plummeted. The real blow to the club's energy, however, came from larger transformations in women's culture. Urban middle-class and elite women in the 1920s were a more heterogeneous group than they had been only a generation or two earlier, and were less united by the material and cultural constraints of domesticity. Quite simply, they had many more options to participate in public life, including entering directly into the very political causes that they had earlier engaged in through the club. While the suffrage cause had allowed women of diverse politics to unite around a common goal, its victory served to fragment those women's associations rooted in public objectives and allowed women to directly enter political life. Women's access to graduate and professional schools also increased significantly during the 20th century's first 2 decades, and many American women pursued business and professional careers that offered little time or space for club life.

While in the 1890s the FMC had attracted many of Los Angeles's most ambitious and powerful women, by the late 1920s it beckoned a class of members better known as "society women," who were not always so bold or public-minded. Many women who wished to take advantage of the new opportunities society offered learned that women's clubs were not necessarily the best place from which to pursue their ambitions.

EARLY ENTHUSIASM, 1891-1901

Though established in 1891, the FMC's origins date back to the beginning of the women's club movement. Its founder, Caroline Severance, had been active in antislavery, women's rights, and benevolent associations during the 1840s and 1850s in Cleveland, Ohio, where she and her husband, a local banker, had raised their family. Severance nevertheless described Cleveland as a city "with few intellectual resources," and longed for some opportunity for intellectual enrichment, particularly with other women. She found such opportunities in Boston, where they moved in 1855. There she joined Susan B. Anthony in organizing the American Equal Rights Association in 1866 and Lucretia Mott in organizing the Free Religious

Association in 1867. In 1868, after speaking with Ralph Waldo Emerson about ways to gather the "interesting" women of Boston together, she founded the New England Woman's Club, hailed alongside New York's Sorosis, which emerged concurrently, as the nation's first major urban women's clubs.

In 1875 the presence of their two sons and the promise of improved health lured the Severances to Los Angeles. Severance quickly became an active player in civic life. The Severance home, located on a 10-acre lot in the fashionable West Adams district and named El Nido, became the initial meeting place for the city's first Unitarian Church and housed the city's first lending library. Severance also began Los Angeles's first kindergarten, and within several years persuaded the local public school system to make kindergartens a permanent part of the local public school system. Among her many civic causes, none mattered more to Severance than the women's club movement. In April of 1878, she gathered 25 women to form a club that she hoped would become "an organized social center for united thought and action." They met in the parlor of the local Unitarian Church she had helped to build, the only place where the gathering would be sheltered from public ire, according to an early member. Such meetings drew criticism from the *Los Angeles Herald*, which condemned the idea of women gathering publicly for intellectual debate, stating that "[v]irtue and intellect were incompatible in women."

Los Angeles's first women's club lasted only 5 years, disbanding in 1880 while Severance vacationed in Boston. In 1885 Severance reestablished the Los Angeles Woman's Club, but it again closed 3 years later when she moved to Boston for a short time. After two unsuccessful tries, Severance's third effort at building a permanent women's club in Los Angeles proved to be one of the most successful ventures in the movement's history. On April 16, 1891, she gathered 11 women together in the upstairs parlor of the Hollenbeck Hotel, where they wrote and agreed to the constitution and by-laws of the Friday Morning Club of Los Angeles. According to their declaration, the club's purpose would be to convene every Friday morning in order to "consider and discuss subjects of general interest, whether literary, social, or educational."

The FMC recruited Los Angeles's elite white women, who swelled its ranks from 87 in 1891 to 400 by century's close. Each week, the club would either invite speakers or ask its own members to present papers. Early meetings, indeed, covered a wide range of topics, including "Great Problems of the Unemployed with Jane Addams," "Psychological Research," "Judges and the School Board," and "The Gentiles' Misunderstanding of the Jew."

Early FMC records suggest a great deal of enthusiasm for club activities. Most programs ended with time for discussion, and extended and heated debates often resulted. On November 10, 1893, for instance, a "larger than normal" crowd gathered for a session titled "The Decadence of Marriage." Speakers noted with disapproval the declining percentage of marriages and frequent laudatory remarks made by men about bachelorhood. The addresses created considerable tumult, leading to the chair's announcement that the club would hold a special additional meeting to discuss the topic further. Two weeks later, leaders devoted an entire meeting to addressing "changing norms of marriage." Members expressed widely diverging opinions about the institution's significance and worth. Women, so long constrained, saw in the club an opportunity for logical debate, public speaking, and parliamentary practice leading to a new civic activism.

The role of women in society proved a hotly contested topic for many early FMC meetings. One week FMC members would be reminded that their real duty was to husband and children, only the next week to hear that women and men were now equal partners in the family and society. Whatever the level and nature of feminist thought among club members, the overwhelming majority were the wives of wealthy men who did not work outside the home. Club life provided an environment for them to talk about broadened roles and opportunities without necessarily engaging in such roles. Only in the next generation of FMC families would this rhetoric become a widespread reality, a fact that would alter the club's history.

In the meantime, the club served as sort of a safe zone where members could express new and even "radical" opinions and could seek to arrive at an informed judgment on hotly contested issues. The FMC avoided damaging internal political rifts by not taking stands on electoral measures. It instead emphasized its role as a place where members could learn about all positions on ballot measures and about all candidates. Suffrage provided one key exception. Members voted in March 1893 to endorse a suffrage bill under consideration in the California legislature, and the organization officially supported women's suffrage from that point on. Even on the issue of suffrage, however, officers retained a careful and balanced approach to public issues, as its frequent voting rights forums always included speakers opposing the franchise for women.

As the FMC's membership grew during the 1890s, divisions emerged over its purpose and mission. It had begun as a "program club," but members increasingly considered other roles and functions. There developed much pressure on club leadership to promote more social activities for members, though such responses often met with harsh criticism from those who mocked this lack of seriousness. Nevertheless, the club did begin to periodically break from its lectures and debates for social occasions. In 1898, for instance, the board voted to begin hosting "club teas."

In coping with the strains of expansion and an increasingly fragmented membership, the FMC drew on the organizational revolution occurring around it and bureaucratized in complex ways. President Sartori announced in 1899 that the club would reach a "happy medium" between programs and fellowship, its activities to be directed by committees on "books," "everyday topics," and "hospitality." In agreeing to "do it all," and in creating new committees and administrative structures to accomplish this, Sartori's presidency foreshadowed the organization's future.

GROWTH AND BUREAUCRATIZATION, 1900-1924

Between the years 1900 and 1924, the FMC's membership swelled from 400 to more than 2,400 (with literally thousands more in attendance as guests). Club rosters show that members lived as far away as Santa Monica, Long Beach, and Redlands, 70 miles from downtown Los Angeles. Its growing membership, furthermore, paralleled a shift in its function and activities. Expanding from its Friday morning programs on cultural and intellectual matters, its activities gradually grew to include political as well as social matters and to occur throughout the week.

Growth and bureaucratization characterized FMC life in the early 20th century. The organizational revolution sweeping American society washed over women's clubs as well. In 1900, for instance, the rapidly growing numbers of women's clubs led Los Angeles Ebell Club leader Clara Burdette to organize the California Federation of Women's Clubs. In

1920 Burdette helped to reorganize the national General Federation of Women's Clubs (GFWC) to deal with its enlarged membership, and that same year, FMC founder Caroline Severance helped to establish the International Federation of Women's Clubs.

The FMC's early 20th-century story centers around the emergence of a vast new roster of members and the development of a complex managerial structure to direct its increasingly broad spectrum of activities. The FMC opened the century by moving into a large new clubhouse on the outskirts of downtown. Having met in at least six different locations during its first 9 years, the acquisition of its own building in a fashionable district of the city provided the FMC with a material and no doubt enhanced psychological foundation for growth and optimism. Within 5 years of opening its new headquarters, membership had more than doubled to 900. The number of guests who attended surged to more than 2,700.

From the beginning, FMC leaders had continually reformed its administrative structure and operations to cope with membership's new needs and growing demands. At its founding, the club's management consisted of a board of directors and six officers, with biweekly meetings held to direct activities. In January 1892, less than a year after the club's founding, officers established a business committee to address the prospect of reorganizing the club into divisions. Members proposed five committees to plan and direct meetings on various topics: art and literature, reform and philanthropy, science and metaphysics, home and education, and magazines. From that point on, the club continually revised its administrative structure, forming new offices, committees, and divisions to better conduct and oversee enlarging operations.

By 1913 eight additional administrative positions in areas such as finance and printing, each structured around a separate committee, supported club directors. The Program Committee now operated over six subcommittees, some of which had as many as four separate committees under their direction. The club also ran four different public welfare projects, with an oversight committee for each. By 1925, 24 standing committees directed the club's operations, many of which had additional committees beneath them. The Public Affairs Committee, for example, comprised 11 subcommittees, including those on education, films, recreation, social services, city and county planning, disabled soldiers, industrial relations, public utilities, legislation, city council, and the board of supervisors.

By 1925, when the club boasted an income of more than $100,000 and assets of $784,000, it had become big business. The FMC's vast managerial apparatus orchestrated a broad agenda. While the club initially had formed to host Friday morning meetings, by the 1920s members could attend activities at the clubhouse nearly every weekday. Between the continual schedule of programs and events and the club's large administrative structure in which hundreds participated, FMC membership offered a career of sorts to affluent Los Angeles women. Club member Emma L. Reed herself described club life as employment for wealthy women: "What women refer to as their clubwork is rapidly taking on an important and a constructive definiteness that might justify us in naming it a new profession."

Clubwomen indeed seemed to take their involvement seriously. In 1906, of its approximately 900 members, only 32 members resigned, 9 were dropped for delinquent dues, and but 10 were regularly "missing" from meetings. Officers attended 37 board meetings during that year, and of the last 6 board meetings, only 1 woman was absent.

The FMC took its commitment to supporting women's place in public life seriously. In 1905, for instance, members expressed outrage when the City of Los Angeles selected Charles Lummis as city librarian rather than the incumbent, Mary Jones. The club passed a resolution condemning Lummis's appointment and declared: "A special phase of this matter most humiliating to us as women is that competence and special fitness are made of no account if one is a woman."

The national suffrage campaign particularly stirred the FMC's enthusiasm. The unsuccessful California suffrage effort in 1906 galvanized members to work even harder for its passage. Following its ultimate adoption by state voters in 1911, organizations throughout California refocused their attention toward preparing members for their new responsibilities. The FMC joined in the new politicization of California women, increasingly devoting its programs to matters of politics and reform and joining in nonpartisan political crusades, including support for juvenile courts, immigrant education, home teachers in schools, mothers' pensions, 8-hour law for women, salaries for probation officers, humane treatment of women prisoners, and separate buildings or wings for children in prisons and hospitals.

While the FMC's growth and increasing scope affirmed its members' burgeoning interests and opportunities during this time of massive social and political change, club members' class position and social and cultural expectations for their behavior limited their empowerment. While FMC members frequently heard positive comments about women attaining economic independence, most did not do so, and there were usually caveats to these assertions. Catherine Perce Wheat praised women for learning the "joy of work, of independence," for instance, but noted that while "there is hardly a vocation, a profession, or industry which woman has not entered, and found profitable and enjoyable, there are many, many who still feel the home is their rightful place."

As women's clubs became larger and more bureaucratic, they simultaneously served to both broaden and restrain the roles their members could play in society. This contradiction would prove significant for the fate of women's clubs in the 1920s.

ZENITH AND RETRENCHMENT, 1924-1931

By 1924 the FMC had secured its position as one of the city's leading social and civic institutions. Its members encompassed a large cohort of the region's female elite, including a host of women prominent throughout the city, state, and country. Club bulletins lauded the fact that only 4 years after the Nineteenth Amendment, 33 members had or were serving in city government, 17 worked at the state level, and 3 served in the federal government. Among these women were Mabel Walker Willebrandt, assistant attorney general of the United States, Mrs. Seward Simons, California State chair of Industrial Relations, Martha Nelson McCan, superintendent of the women's division of the Federal Labor Bureau, Grace Stoermer, assistant secretary for the California legislature, Mrs. Joseph Sartori, member of the University of California Board of Regents, and Mrs. John J. Abramson, president of the Los Angeles City Planning Commission. Spokeswomen also noted that both major national political parties had elected FMC members for their national committees and that FMC members had served as presidential electors in each election since 1912.

The 1924 opening of the organization's new clubhouse fittingly symbolized its prominent stature. By the mid 1920s, the FMC stood as a major manifestation of affluent women's dramatic gains during the Progressive era. The imposing clubhouse drew thousands of women every week to meetings ranging from academic lectures to political debates. FMC membership entailed the opportunity to become learned on matters of culture and politics and to form opinions and take stands on issues of public concern. Women so desiring could work their way up the complex ladders of committee positions and administrative posts, ultimately gaining the right to direct a significant organization that played a noted role in Los Angeles's social and political affairs.

While the FMC had arguably been the most significant women's organization in Los Angeles during its early history, the opening of its new headquarters ironically preceded a steady decline in both its visibility and activism. Throughout the 1920s, the FMC remained a major urban woman's organization committed to providing for its members a full array of lectures and forums on diverse matters of social, cultural, intellectual, and political significance, yet signs of decline abounded. FMC membership, which had increased every year since 1891, began to fall in 1925. The club lost 500 members by 1929 and another 700 in the 4 years following the stock market crash. Steady expansion had created an optimistic atmosphere of change and improvement for women through the club's early years. Membership declines in the late 1920s, however, placed limits on club activities and for the first time fostered an atmosphere of doubt and pessimism.

Part of the FMC's membership decline occurred as a simple fact of the city's urban sprawl. When the FMC opened in 1891, most members lived within a short distance from the city's central business district. During the 1920s, however, Los Angeles's swelling middle and upper classes began moving into more distant suburbs, particularly near Pasadena and westward from downtown along Wilshire Boulevard. As more and more members moved outside the central city, difficult commutes into downtown proved less appealing, and many women engaged in organizational activities closer to home.

But the FMC's decline reflected far more than a changing urban geography. During a very short period of time in the late 1920s, the FMC's stature and energy fizzled. Many FMC members seemed to direct less energy into club life. Club elections, for instance, no longer stirred such passion. Campaigns for FMC offices had historically entailed combative electioneering and attracted considerable local interest, but this diminished throughout the 1920s. In the spring of 1928, the *Times* noted that all major Los Angeles women's clubs were having difficulty securing candidates for club offices. Within weeks of the vote, in fact, the FMC did not yet have a single candidate declared for the office of presidency.

The apathy surrounding club elections increasingly pervaded other club activities. In February 1926, for instance, the president of Mills College, Dr. Aurelia Reinhardt, addressed Los Angeles clubwomen, asserting that they had become victims of the "lecture habit" and were unfortunately better listeners than workers. She chided Los Angeles clubwomen for increasing laziness. Local media also began noting a decreasing interest on the part of women in club meetings. In September 1928 the *Times* noted a "definite change" in the women's club movement, reporting that in previous times "the banquet hall was filled with women in eager anticipation of the discussion indicated." Now, however, many in the audience left during the reading of papers, and only "mild discussions" followed. The newspaper further reported that only "comparatively minor subjects" were presented for discussion. Even for those women who pursued clubwork as their "career," and there were still many, the nature of club life rapidly changed. The FMC transformed from an aggressive women's association dedicated to their public empowerment into a much smaller organization devoted to providing members with social and cultural opportunities.

More significantly, the barriers to women's entrance into the public sphere that had fueled the FMC's agenda for 30 years became significantly more permeable in the 1920s. Those who sought to observe or participate in public life no longer needed a women's club for entrance keys. In fact, club life became a distinct alternative, if not an impediment, to public roles. While FMC leaders boasted about the activities of members who enjoyed prominent public careers, the club became a minor part of these members' lives. Meetings were held primarily during the daytime and almost always on weekdays. Active club membership thus posed problems for working women or those involved in other public roles. The ranks of club members were thus increasingly comprised of women who rejected involvement in careers and other public roles.

Changing national political climates also marred club operations. The passage of suffrage had the ironic effect of problematizing political debate in women's associations. While the struggle for its passage provided a common rallying point for middle- and upper-class women, there existed less agreement on what to do with the vote, once gained. Those who agreed on the need for public participation disagreed on how exactly to participate, and political divisions between women became far more clear. During the 1920s, the FMC's political forums gradually became usurped by other club activities. As the FMC became less of a vehicle for women's entrance into the public sphere, purely social functions assumed a larger and more heralded place in its activities.

Such dramatic changes had occurred in women's experiences and culture that, by the 1920s, the purpose of women's clubs seemed suddenly unclear. In January 1928 a national journal asserted that women's clubs had reached the peak of their achievements and were now in a state of decline. The statement became a matter of significant national debate for club members. The FMC held a symposium on the subject, featuring the presidents of several major Los Angeles women's clubs. Rather than defending women's clubs or promising a bright future for them, however, the panelists generally pondered reasons for their decline and speculated on varying scenarios for their future. These responses revealed a lack of unity on the purpose and meaning of women's clubs. In contrast to the powerful emancipation rhetoric surrounding early club activity, few club activists now seemed able to articulate any compelling reason for their existence.

CONCLUSION

The FMC emerged in Progressive era Los Angeles as a monument to a unique time and place in women's history. Its founders had been inspired by the fervor of the abolitionist crusade and the Civil War, the suffrage campaign had sharpened their commitment to social reform and women's rights, and their place in a new and rapidly evolving urban center rife with needs and opportunities for civic betterment provided a ready outlet for their passions. The second and following generations of club leaders both came from a different social environment and worked in a new cultural milieu. Throughout the 1920s, the culture of club life for affluent Los Angeles women had shifted from aggressive optimism over women's broadening spheres to a more passive social-oriented elitism. Clubwomen showed increasing interest in social and entertainment activities and decreasing enthusiasm for the kinds of intellectual and political debate that had

characterized earlier club affairs. As American women gained entrance into the political sphere, increased opportunities to work in professional capacities, and were no longer considered unfit to take part in intellectual and cultural debates, women's clubs lost their original purpose. Women who wanted to pursue newly won opportunities decreased their participation in club life, leaving predominantly "society-minded" women to run the organizations.

For all its early empowering implications for women in American society, women's club life entailed a highly restrained ideology that quickly ran its course. The opportunities clubs provided in the late 19th century had challenged the boundaries of appropriate female behavior, but soon became commonplace. By the 1920s, few contested a woman's right to gather around, learn about, and take a stand on matters of intellectual and public affairs. Rather than evolving to address the changing role of women, women's clubs largely ignored the issues that surrounded women's struggles for equality following suffrage. The class position of most members restrained them from envisioning broader horizons beyond intellectual and cultural debate. Relatively secure in economic and social terms, at least, few sought further cultural transformations or greater opportunities for financial independence and professional life.

After 3 decades of tremendous social and political change for American women, the enthusiasm and activism of Progressive era club life dulled to a more society-oriented elitism. Just when the FMC emerged as a major social force in the city and the state's affairs, it hesitantly retreated from the bolder aspects of the Progressive era affluent women's culture it had kindled and nurtured. The FMC would remain a cherished organization for many Los Angeles women, but it never again occupied a prominent role in the city's public life, nor did it ever again serve as an entryway into the public sphere as it did for its early members.

—Clark Davis

SELECTED READINGS

Jensen, Joan M. "After Slavery: Caroline Severance in Los Angeles," *Southern California Quarterly 48* (June 1966): 175-186.

Lothrop, Gloria, and Thelma Lee Hubbell. "The Friday Morning Club: A Los Angeles Legacy," *Southern California Quarterly 50* (March 1968): 59-90.

Raftery, Judith. "Los Angeles Clubwomen and Progressive Reform," in William Deverell and Tom Sitton, eds., *California Progressivism Revisited*. Berkeley: University of California Press, 1994, 144-174.

CLUBWOMEN OF SALT LAKE CITY

Members of the Church of Jesus Christ of Latter-day Saints (also known as Mormons) established Salt Lake City, Utah, in 1847. In 1869 the transcontinental railroad brought a variety of settlers to Salt Lake City, and the flow of non-Mormon immigrants enabled various denominations—Protestant, Catholic, and Jewish—to establish themselves in the city. By 1870 there were about 87,000 Euro-Americans scattered along the western side of the Wasatch Mountains running north and south, with Salt Lake City in the center of the settlement.

Salt Lake City women recognized the effectiveness of joint action; however, new service and cultural clubs formed along religious lines with a Mormon/non-Mormon split. This type of split is common for cultural clubs, according to club historian Karen Blair, who demonstrates that women joined clubs with members whose interests, connections, backgrounds, or religion were congenial with their own. Although early service or literary clubs drew membership from specific interest groups, they did not officially limit their membership based on religion. The Reaper's Club organized in 1892, for instance, drew Mormon women (many of them practicing polygamy) who were the leaders or wives of the leaders of Salt Lake City and the Mormon Church. These women felt comfortable together, but there were no rules that prevented non-Mormon women from joining. One of the earliest clubs formed by non-Mormon women was the exclusive Blue Tea Club. The Salt Lake Ladies' Literary Club, with unlimited membership, was organized in 1877 by non-Mormon women and was the first large departmental club in the city. The Ladies' Literary Club boasted 368 members in 1913, 520 in 1921, and 499 in 1929. The primary purpose of the Ladies' Literary Club was self-culture, but it took an active interest in community welfare. In 1927, 11 of the 16 past presidents of the Utah Federation of Women's Clubs (UFWC) had been members of the Ladies' Literary Club.

In 1893, when the UFWC was organized, it became the second state federation to join the General Federation of Women's Clubs (GFWC). It was also the first major attempt to foster cooperation between Mormon and non-Mormon women's groups in the state. The UFWC offered resolutions on national affairs, education, public health, forestry, and cooperation with other organizations with similar objectives. As the various clubs' interests moved from self-education to civic improvement and as religious division in politics lessened, clubs and organizations cooperated to achieve community reform.

At the end of 1911, as social issues overshadowed diminishing literary interests, the GFWC recommended that federated clubs form small groups to "act together for local work." The Salt Lake Federation of Women's Clubs (SLF), organized on February 26, 1912, under the umbrella of the UFWC, successfully brought together both Mormon and non-Mormon delegates to work for civic improvement. The new organization wanted "the betterment of the social, civic, and moral conditions of the city." Member clubs could require neither political nor religious test of its members. After 2 years, 15 clubs representing almost 1,000 women had joined, and just 7 years later in 1921 there were over 3,000 Salt Lake women represented by the 29 member clubs of the SLF. The city Federation offered a group small enough to institute local reform, while being large enough to effectively influence government agencies.

Women of the Church of Jesus Christ of Latter-Day Saints organized as the Female Relief Society of Nauvoo in 1842 in the newly established city of Nauvoo, Illinois. Their purpose was benevolence and education, and they offered relief and charity to the community. As mobs attacked the Illinois city and church members fled, the fledgling organization was disbanded. After over 20 years of "unofficial" organization in Utah, the Mormon Relief Society was officially revived in 1867. Because religion was an essential part of the society, it did not meet the criteria for membership in the state or national federation.

While the Relief Society was not an official member of the SLF, its officers and members who resided in Salt Lake City were often Federation members. Emmeline B. Wells, general Relief Society resident from 1910 to 1921, represented the Cleofan Club in the SLF, and was appointed to the standing committee for public health in 1916. The Relief Society was an active participant in the Salt Lake progressive movement for moral, social, and civic reform. The Relief Society's community reform projects paralleled and complemented the work of the SLF. Working through the Relief Society, Mormon women became involved in an impressive array of state and national social welfare endeavors, including maternity and child care, the juvenile court, a minimum-wage law, a widowed mothers' pension law, equal guardianship for children, fund drives, defense efforts, Near East relief, and the Sheppard-Towner Maternity and Infant Protection Act. This list compares to a similar sampling of interests extrapolated from various local women's club minutes, and these same issues caught women's attention nationally. Extensive involvement in the same national and state issues by both the Relief Society and women's clubs suggests that these concerns were women-oriented rather than religiously driven.

Taking community reform seriously, the SLF in the first few months of its existence investigated fire protection in the Salt Lake theaters, sheep herds contaminating the city water supply, and unsightly billboards in residential sections of the city. In addition, the SLF instituted a citywide clean-up campaign and formed sanitation, legislative, health, humane, educational, and civic standing committees. The club systematically investigated, agitated, organized, and worked to improve the quality of life in Salt Lake City.

The SLF encouraged and endorsed female candidates as jurors, policewomen, health inspectors, and juvenile judges. The appointment of a woman food inspector to the city's exclusively male list of food and sanitation inspectors was a major accomplishment for the SLF. Mrs. Elizabeth Cook, an SLF member, was assigned to meat and food inspection overseeing city groceries, meat markets, and eating places. Improvement was noted under Cook as flies, mice, and roaches became less evident. In the fall, when she was assigned the inspection of Market Row, Cook went to the SLF for help in an education program that included several newspaper articles emphasizing the importance of covering fruits until fly season was over. When Cook informed the SLF that some merchants were reluctant to comply with the law requiring that meat be covered and that bread be wrapped, the women began a letter-writing campaign to merchants calling attention to the law and asking for compliance. The merchants were reminded that their refusal would be publicized so that women could determine where to shop. This grass-roots enforcement, paralleling the National Consumers League's "White List," was a success as merchants scrambled to comply.

In 1915 SLF women investigated the "injustice in the matter of salary as between women and men employees of [the] city," and agitated for an increase in women workers' salaries. Equal pay for equal work was their motto.

The welfare of the girls and boys of the city was a major concern of the SLF. The child labor law, a loan fund for university education, underage newsboys, minors smoking, punch boards, juvenile confinement in the state penitentiary, preschool nutrition, pure milk, and free milk to the poor were some of the child welfare issues that it was interested and involved in. Early in 1921 the SLF appointed a special committee to investigate the various girls' organizations to determine if they "meet the requirements of the young women of the city." As a result, the SLF gave substantial financial support as well as hours of volunteer labor to the success of the Girl Scout movement.

The SLF and its individual clubs promoted improved recreation facilities, including new parks and playgrounds. Playgrounds were not included in parks until women's clubs emphasized their necessity for the health of city children. Clubwomen sponsored specific playgrounds and provided supervision or the money to hire supervisors. Petitions to the City Commission brought the addition of new parks in areas of the city that had none. A lengthy campaign induced the city to purchase property and convert it to a neighborhood park. Because of lack of funds, the City Council first denied the SLF's request to purchase the property, so the women arranged for the city to lease it on very favorable terms until it could be purchased. The SLF supported improvements and sponsored tree planting parks and playgrounds throughout the city. They also instigated the installation of comfort stations and benches in parks and playgrounds. In addition to new parks, the SLF was vitally concerned with existing recreational facilities like Warm Springs when it opposed the lease of the city resort to private enterprise. The women also became concerned about the unhealthy and deteriorating conditions at Saltair Resort on the Great Salt Lake, and worked with the owners, the City Commission, and even called in the manager's wife to make improvements.

The matter of garbage disposal came to the attention of the SLF, and a year later in 1917, several ordinances were passed to control the garbage "evil" in Salt Lake City. Even after the passage of the ordinances, the SLF maintained a watchful eye on the situation, and in 1921 a committee investigated the garbage situation and convinced the city to try a short-lived venture in recycling.

One of the major negative effects of rapid industrialization that the SLF worked to eradicate was the constant problem of smoke caused by industry, railroads, and coal-burning home furnaces. The geography of Salt Lake City and its weather inversions made the problem especially dangerous to citizens' health. The SLF's efforts were aimed at the enforcement of the city's existing smoke ordinance. By 1919 the City Commission, aided by both men's and women's organizations, was involved in an aggressive smoke eradication campaign devised and aided by the U.S. Bureau of Mines and the University of Utah. Maintaining an active smokeless city committee, the SLF pushed the City Commission, when necessary, to continue a firm stand.

Patriotism to the state and the nation was a major emphasis of SLF clubs. This patriotic fervor took several avenues, including citizenship education, war work, Red Cross membership, and conservation of all resources, including food, land, and citizens. One of the main manifestations of patriotism for clubwomen was their involvement in Americanizing foreign women and children.

The Utah Federated Legislative Council organized in 1911 effectively screened, sponsored, and arranged to have bills introduced and supported by clubwomen of the state. When the council sponsored a bill, clubwomen wrote letters, signed petitions, phoned legislators, and showed up en masse at relevant meetings. The voting percentage of Utah clubwomen was consistently higher than women in the rest of the nation. Some of the bills the clubwomen saw passed involved married women's property rights, mothers' pensions, divorce reform, health exams, child labor, mandatory school attendance, and a host of bills designed to do away with vices such as drinking, smoking, gambling, and prostitution.

Organized women worked as coparticipants in civic betterment through their participation in women's associations—clubs, federations, and the Relief Society—as they contributed substantially to community reform.

—Sharon Snow Carver

SUGGESTED READINGS

Alexander, Thomas G. "An Experiment in Progressive Legislation: The Granting of Woman Suffrage in Utah in 1870." *Utah Historical Quarterly* 38 (Winter, 1970): 20.

Alexander, Thomas G. *Utah, The Right Place.* Salt Lake City, UT: Gibbs-Smith, 1995.

Blair, Karen. *The Clubwoman as Feminist: True Womanhood Redefined, 1868-1914.* New York: Holmes & Meier, 1980.

Carver, Sharon Snow. "Salt Lake City's Reapers' Club," *Utah Historical Quarterly* 64 (Spring 1996): 108.

Carver, Sharon Snow. *Club Women of the Three Intermountain Cities of Denver, Boise and Salt Lake City Between 1893 and 1929.* Ph.D. dissertation. Brigham Young University, 2000.

Croly, Jennie Cunningham (Jennie June). *The History of the Woman's Club Movement in America.* New York: Henry G. Allen, 1898.

Derr, Jill Mulvay, Janath Russell Cannon, and Maureen Ursenbach Beecher. *Women of Covenant: The Story of Relief Society.* Salt Lake City, UT: Deseret Book Company, 1992.

Madsen, Carol Cornwall. "Decade of Detente: Mormon/ Gentile Female Relationship in Nineteenth Century Utah." *Utah Historical Quarterly* 63 (Fall 1995): 298.

Parsons, Katherine B. *History of Fifty Years, Utah Federation of Women's Clubs.* Salt Lake City, UT: Arrow Press, 1927.

COEL, MARGARET (1937-)

Margaret Coel was born in Denver, Colorado. She received her undergraduate education at Marquette University and went on to graduate studies at the University of Colorado and Oxford University. Her early career was in the newspaper business. She was a reporter for the *Westminster Journal* and wrote features for the *Boulder Daily Camera*.

Coel's literary career began in 1981 with the publication of her first nonfiction work, *Chief Left Hand: Southern Arapaho.* Four other nonfiction books, including the story of Colorado's state capitol, followed. The daughter of a railroad engineer, she published *Goin' Railroading: A Century of the Colorado High Iron* in 1986.

Coel's study of the Arapaho Nation influenced her fiction writing. Her first novel, *The Eagle Catcher,* was published in 1995 and was based largely on her research for *Chief Left Hand.* In it she introduced her main characters: Father John O'Malley, S.J., and Arapaho attorney Vicky Holden. Her other titles include *The Ghost Walker, Dead End,* and *The Story Teller.*

Coel is the winner of the Best Nonfiction Book of the Year Award presented by the National Association of Press Women and the Top Hand Award for Best Nonfiction Book by a Colorado Author presented by the Colorado Authors League. She was a Fellow at the Bread Loaf Writers' Conference in 1981 and is a member of the Board of Directors for Historic Boulder.

In addition to her books and novels, Coel continues to write for newspapers and magazines, including articles for the *New York Times* and *American Heritage,* as well as book reviews for the *Denver Post.* She married George Coel in 1961 and had three children. Her leisure activities are spent mostly out of doors traveling.

—Neal Lynch

SUGGESTED READINGS

Mystery News. Retrieved from www.blackravenpress.com.

Mystery Writers of America, Rocky Mountain Chapter. Retrieved from www.mystery-tales.com/AuthorPages/AuthorsC.htm#MargaretCoel.

COLLINS, AUDREY B. (1945-)

Audrey B. Collins was born in Chester, Pennsylvania, the daughter of a dentist and an English teacher. She earned her B.A. in 1967 from Howard University and her M.A. from American University in 1969. She began her career as a high school teacher after earning her master's degree, teaching in 1969-1970 and in 1972. In 1970 and 1971, she worked for the Model Cities Project, and was a student affairs counselor at the University of Southern California from 1971 to 1973.

Her husband, Dr. Tim Collins, encouraged her to pursue further educational opportunities, and Audrey did so, earning her law degree from the University of California, Los Angeles, in 1977. In 1978 she joined the Los Angeles County District Attorney's Office. She was the first African American to become a head deputy in the Los Angeles County District Attorney's Office and, following a subsequent promotion, the first African American assistant director, the third highest position in the office. She was also the first black to be elected president of the Association of Deputy District Attorneys.

Collins did not originally intend to pursue a federal judgeship when she entered law school, but did so after several years as a prosecutor, feeling that it was a better way to make a difference.

President Bill Clinton appointed her to the U.S. District Court for the Central District of California in 1994. This was also the year in which she received the Distinguished Service Award from the National Black Prosecutors Association, and she also received the 1997 UCLA Alumni Association Award.

—Scott Kesilis

SUGGESTED READINGS

Just the Beginning Foundation, "Audrey B. Collins." Retrieved from www.jtbf.org/article_iii_judges/collins_a.htm.

"The National Law Review Tenth Anniversary: Assistant District Attorneys," *National Law Review* (September 26, 1988).

CONSERVATION MOVEMENT, 1870-1940

The involvement of western women in all types of conservation activities is often overlooked or even ignored. Yet women in the trans-Mississippi West, including Alaska and Hawaii, began to participate in the early conservation movement shortly after the end of the Civil War in 1864. Although these women numbered in the thousands, they are largely invisible in environmental history because they were not active in the same ways as men, that is, in holding political office, voting, lobbying, and speech-making. Often excluded from the political realm, women used such socially acceptable "female" interests as writing, drawing, and joining reform organizations to put their conservation ideas into effect. Looking at women's proclivities reveals a huge number of women dedicated to some aspect of conservation.

Because middle- and upper-class white women had the education and leisure to pursue such undertakings as botanizing, painting watercolors, and joining women's clubs, they dominated women's conservation efforts until the mid-20th century. At the same time that women of color expressed their environmental concerns by campaigning for garbage pickup or playgrounds for their children, white women of the upper classes exerted themselves on behalf of western canyons, forests, and giant redwoods.

These are the same Victorians who are stereotyped as passive, domestic, and definitely not outdoors people. In truth, however, a huge proportion of these women loved nature. White European women, especially English, had already established a long-standing tradition of outdoor ventures that encouraged American women to inquire into nature. In addition, American women who were told that females feared nature responded by gradually feminizing the "wild" West. For example, women's poetry and painting offered a softer, less threatening view of nature that seemed to welcome women. Meanwhile, women mountain climbers and other athletes imposed a female presence on the West—in the form of "ladies" campgrounds or by developing outdoor clothing that was still within the realm of "proper."

Typically, women approached western landscapes with different assumptions than men. In settling the West, white societal values prompted men to exploit western resources in the name of progress. At the same time, women were urged to save and protect their families, cultures, and surroundings, which, to women, clearly included the physical environment. As "social conservators," women also believed it was their God-given, moral duty to safeguard western landscapes. Gradually, women who also argued that environmentalism was a high form of patriotism identified the environmental ethic with such enduring American values as Mom, God, and flag waving.

In turn, women learned a great deal from their participation in the emerging conservation movement. In seizing upon the salvation of the West as a good cause, women gained an appreciation of networking, organizing, lobbying, and using the political structure. Many of them spoke in public, pursued advanced degrees, and changed their clothing styles. Some saw the West as a feminist Eden where they could climb mountains, revel in nature's beauty, and, driving their own automobiles, experience the independence of the open road. Whether consciously or not, women environmentalists widened their own sphere of activity and action. At the same time that women's rights and so-called "new women" raised hackles on the necks of many Americans, however, women conservationists received kudos for their work. That these women were subtle feminists went unremarked. Although their more strident sisters were labeled "strong-minded" women, they endured no such name calling.

Examples of specific cases are numerous. In the area of botanizers, birders, and other female naturalists, enough illustrations exist to fill a small encyclopedia. Throughout the late 19th and early 20th century, the American environment, especially the West, attracted millions of women—as botanizers, birders, collectors, geologists, and more. One of the best known was Alice Eastwood, a leading American botanist and a conservation advocate between the early 1890s and the late 1940s. Born in Canada, Eastwood at the age of 14 moved with her family to Denver. After graduating as valedictorian from East Denver High School in 1879, she taught there for the next 10 years. During that decade, she set out to explore the Rocky Mountains. Traveling by railroad, horseback, buggy, and on foot, she found specimens of plants to be identified, named, and protected. In 1892 she moved to San Francisco to join herbarium curator Katharine Brandegee at the California Academy of Sciences. The employment of the two women was due to the exceptional foresight of academy founder Albert Kellogg, who ensured that the Academy's minutes of August 1, 1853, read, "[W]e highly approve the aid of females in every department of natural history, and that we earnestly invite their cooperation."

Eastwood had many accomplishments to her credit. She found a shrubby daisy subsequently named *Eastwoodia* and, in 1905, published *A Handbook of the Trees of California*, which included her own line drawings. She also joined the Sierra Club and, in 1903, climbed Mount Whitney. Throughout her career, she urged Californians to preserve native species, ranging from stumpy salt marsh plants to enormous redwoods. Her advocacy of environmental preservation earned her honors ranging from local garden club awards to inclusion in every edition of *American Men of Science*. By her retirement in 1949 at age 90, she had written over 300 leaflets, articles, and books, including essays that gained her a reputation as an early environmentalist.

Clearly, Eastwood helped develop a 19th-century botanical tradition for American women. By the latter decades of the 19th century, botany had become a must for educated American women. One scholar has identified 1,185 active female botanists working during the 19th century. During the latter half of the century, 23% of these women prepared specimen collections, over half taught school, and a large number wrote books and articles.

In addition to botanizers, female birders not only studied birds but fought for their preservation. Florence Merriam Bailey established her reputation in these areas. Although Bailey lived in Washington, D.C., she did her field work primarily in New Mexico. After Bailey's first western jaunt in 1891, she returned to the West many times, sometimes alone, other times with her biologist husband, Vernon Bailey, whom she married in 1899. As early as her Smith College days during 1882-1886, she had tried to protect birds from being butchered by commercial suppliers of feathers and stuffed birds for decorations on women's hats. Protection of birds became a theme in Bailey's life. She wrote articles for the *Audubon* magazine and protested what she called "bird murder" in such newspapers as the Washington, D.C., *Evening Star* and *Watertown* (New York) *Times*. In 1923 she received an honorary degree from the University of New Mexico and in 1929 became the first woman elected a fellow of the American Ornithologists' Union.

Bailey's efforts inspired thousands of other women. For example, farther west in Hawaii, Mary Dorothea Rice Isenberg, born on Kauai, campaigned to bring bird population back to the islands. She also served as a leader of the Hui Manu, organized in 1930 to reestablish the Hawaiian bird population.

Numerous women also ventured into the field, enduring everything from inclement weather to mosquitoes, spiders, and other insects that besieged field collectors. Bailey wrote of difficult trips by wagon and pack outfit across western prairies, mountains, and deserts, as well as 12- to 15-hour days in the field. California collector Annie Alexander recorded wind, sleet storms, thunder showers, rain, cold, and frozen specimens. With her friend Louise Kellogg, Alexander camped in tents, crawled under barbed wire fences, set traps in the dark and rain, hiked and climbed miles carrying steel traps, and walked over lava beds. And when California botanist Sara Allen Plummer Lemmon and her husband made what she called "a botanical wedding trip" in 1880 into the Santa Catalina Mountains, she reported that they slept in a cave on a bed of dried grass, where they fought off pack rats and other small animals.

In spite of such obstacles, female naturalists pushed ahead, conquering the West in their own way. They impressed their female personalities on the region, creating decorum and safety where none had existed before. They also faced issues that did not exist for their male counterparts, especially cumbersome clothing. During the last 3 decades of the 19th century, most American women still aspired to be "ladies." Consequently, early female naturalists attempted to wear acceptable clothing that was also appropriate to their endeavors. In 1880 Sara Lemmon donned "a short suit of strong material, the best of firm calfskin shoes . . . substantial leather leggings . . . a broad-brimmed hat with a buckskin mask, and heavy gloves." Despite her eccentric appearance, Lemmon became an excellent botanist, speaker, and flower painter. With her botanist husband, she discovered 3% of California's vascular plants. One colleague remarked that "she may have been responsible for much of the work that made her husband famous."

During the 1890s Alice Eastwood adopted a full skirt that reached to her shoe tops, but such skirts hindered her in the field. In 1893 she dragged with her up the slope of Mount Shasta a skirt made of yards of corduroy, which quickly became soaked with snow. After that experience, she created a blue denim outfit using a cotton nightgown as a bustle. Its skirt, open in front and back, could be fastened by buttons concealed inside a flap or, when riding horseback, could be unbuttoned. Other women simply wore leggings and breeches, or trousers. By the late 1930s, when the Nevada botanist Edith Van Allen Murphey began government field work on Indian reservations, she favored knee-high boots, breeches, a long-sleeved shirt, and a floppy brimmed hat.

In addition to clothing, women faced other problems. For instance, because sidesaddles were ineffective in rough terrain, women naturalists learned to ride astride. During the 1890s Californian Kate Brandegee not only wore trousers but rode into the mountains near San Jose del Cabo astride a mule. Equipment constituted another predicament. Women carried everything from canteens and lunch sacks to collecting cases, plant presses, and sketch pads. In some of their pockets could be found handguns. On pack mules, and later in automobiles, they transported water, suitcases, tents, cooking equipment and stoves, scientific instruments, field glasses, cameras and tripods, and food supplies.

Some female collectors also packed rifles, with which they shot specimens, thus incurring public censure. After the taxidermist Martha Maxwell founded the Rocky Mountain Museum in 1874, she became adept at presenting specimens in natural poses and habitats, often in diorama form. In her exhibit at the Philadelphia Centennial Exposition in 1876, she further supported the cause of preservation, claiming that it was "woman's work." Maxwell, however, obtained her animals and birds by bringing them down with a rifle. This under 5-foot woman, described as a "modest, tenderhearted" female, frequently posed for photographs with her rifle by her side. Fortunately, by the end of the 19th century, technological change provided cameras as a humane alternative for many collectors.

Scores of other women, perhaps with a less scientific bent, engaged nature through the medium of words. Female writers and poets made important and often neglected contributions to the early conservation movement. Through nature essays, books, and poems, these women, who often became conservation proponents, helped shape public attitudes toward landscapes. After the Civil War, women writers—a growing number of them westerners—rejected male themes of conquest and domination of landscapes. Instead, they focused on the beauty and spirituality of nature, as well as employing female images to describe the environment. These writers portrayed the West as accommodating and welcoming, especially of assertive women willing to meet nature's challenges. They also ignored the widespread belief that people had hegemony over nature, stressing instead that humans would only survive by living in harmony with their environment.

As early as the 1860s, writer Helen Hunt Jackson probed such ideas. After Jackson moved to Colorado Springs in 1873, she wrote essays, poems, and travel sketches about the Colorado landscape. She thought the Colorado scenery beautiful, spiritual, and accessible to women. She also described landscapes by using women's metaphors, including family and birth. In the December 1876 issue of the *Atlantic Monthly*, she concluded that the wilderness had a special silence, one "like that in which the world lay pregnant before time again." She also saw death in nature. In her *Bits of Travel at Home* (1879), her images of dead trees, their bodies "stiffened straight in death and its myriad limbs convulsed and cramped in agony," reminded readers that even though landscapes were not always bucolic, they were still dramatic and meaningful.

During the early 20th century, the New Mexican writer Mary Hunter Austin enlarged on these themes. A transplanted easterner who loved New Mexico and the Southwest, Austin celebrated the region and its

peoples in everything from essays and articles to some 30 books. In 1903 her first book, *The Land of Little Rain*, rejoiced in the desert's pleasures, which she called "strange things" in the area's "tumultuous privacy." She explained, "I like the smother of sound among the dunes, and finding small coiled snakes in open places." For those who wished to live in the desert, she suggested as models American Indian and Hispanic peoples, who knew how to live harmoniously with nature rather than destroying it.

After Austin attained stature as a literary figure, she proclaimed in her 1932 autobiography, *Earth Horizon*, that she also viewed herself as a nature writer and environmentalist. "All places were beautiful and interesting" to her, she wrote, "so long as they were outdoors." She committed herself "to the idea that she was to write of the West," as well as to work for its conservation. Her environmentalism had a feminist bent, notably her determination to revitalize women's relationships to western wilderness. Throughout her work, her white men were materialistic and exploitative, sacrificing their very souls to the desert, while her white women understood and sympathized with the land. Moreover, she regarded the West as a place where women could "walk off" the societal dictates that hampered them. Her personal life also demonstrated her enduring allegiance to an ethic of stewardship of the West. In 1905, for example, she protested the Bureau of Reclamation's scheme to divert water from the Owens Valley to Los Angeles. Over a decade later, she opposed Boulder (Hoover) Dam, saying it was a "debacle" demonstrating the avarice of its backers.

Despite her writings and personal activism, Austin became less well known as the 20th century progressed. After her death in 1934, her short stories and many of her books went out of print. Although *The Land of Little Rain* remained available, it failed to receive the attention deserved by a classic of early 20th-century nature writing. Fortunately, the contemporary feminist movement that began in the 1960s revived Austin's reputation and work, giving *The Land of Little Rain* its due.

Following the lead of Jackson and Austin, by the late 19th and early 20th centuries, women writers developed a form called a woman's pastoral, which placed female characters at its center. Moreover, women's symbols dominated, so that the western environment became *Mother* Earth, who was hospitable to women. During the early 20th century, such novelists as Willa Cather and Ellen Glasgow added a decided feminist overtone to the women's pastoral format. In Cather's *O Pioneers!* (1913) and Glasgow's *Barren Ground* (1925), women agriculturalists rescue the land from harsh or uninformed usage. By rejuvenating the land, these female characters establish a spiritual bond with nature, which gives them satisfaction and autonomy.

Another well-known 20th-century writer to argue for the necessity of living in harmony with nature was the Nebraskan Mari Sandoz. Although known primarily as a novelist and a historian of the Great Plains, Sandoz expressed environmentalism in many of her books, articles, speeches, and dinner addresses. In fact, her major focus was people's impact on western lands and resources. In *Old Jules* (1935), she even listed as a character "The Region. The upper Niobrara country," and used the environmental cycle as a unifying motif. In *Slogum House* (1937), she blamed male politicians, financiers, and land-grabbers as the major forces in defiling western lands. In later years, she wrote entire novels about men's senseless exploitation of buffalo and beaver.

Scores of other women writers took different tacks, some writing to newspapers. The issue that inflamed popular author Caroline Lockhart of Cody, Wyoming, was the Montana Fish and Game Department's policies. Lockhart opposed the agency's plan to exterminate such species as the bobcat. She also editorialized in the Cody *Enterprise* against recreational hunting. A staunch outdoor enthusiast, in 1924 she bought the L Slash Heart ranch west of the Big Horn River Canyon, where she put her conservation principles into practice.

Still other women expressed themselves in verse. Mid-20th-century poets frequently reminded readers that the western landscape was God's creation. One commented that the "patient hand of God" had chiseled the cliffs and chasms of Mesa Verde, now being marred by invading white civilization. During the 1910s and early 1920s, Arizona poet Phoebe Bogan spoke for deserts, saying that rather than "wastelands" they were places of "untamed beauty." Although Bogan admitted that she sometimes longed to go east where she could "surrender" to "spring moods," she always chose the desert, which offered her a sense of peace and fulfillment.

It is more difficult to pinpoint the contributions of female visual image-makers to the early conservation movement. Unlike naturalists and nature writers, female illustrators, artists, photographers, gardeners, and landscape architects seldom hoped to convey explicit environmental tenets in their work. On a subtle level, however, visual image-makers put western landscapes in such appealing format that viewers came to believe that the environment *could* be shaped, managed, and conserved for human use, at present and in the future. In the hands of female image-makers, nature appeared tractable and in balance with its surroundings, totally "female" in its beauty and lushness. These women demonstrated that for recreation, wildlife habitats, or reforestation, humankind had the ability to pattern nature as it chose.

Between the 1890s and 1940, women artists were numerous and enjoyed social acceptance. Most Americans approved of women dabbling in art and believed it acceptable for women to depict nature, especially if done in a family setting. For instance, in 1864 Helen Tanner Brodt accompanied her husband on a military expedition to California's Mount Lassen and brought back many sketches, which she translated into finished works. Later, she added other California landscapes and ranch scenes to her growing repertoire. During the 1870s and 1880s, "flower artists" prospered. Alice Stewart, who studied at New York's Cooper Institute, the New York Academy of Design, and with a Chicago floral portrait painter, on her pony investigated the Colorado Springs area for floral specimens, which she painted or used in instructing her many students.

Women's interpretations of western nature reached more and more Americans every year. During the early 1900s, Louise Keeler of Berkeley, California, illustrated her husband's nature books, took photographs for him, and lectured about his ideas. Professionally, her artistic interpretations of nature influenced scientific thought; personally, her work encouraged her to initiate a "save-the-trees" campaign.

Other women's work appeared as illustrations in books, journals, and newspapers; on greeting cards and in garden books; in art and craft exhibits; in lectures and stage shows; and in railroad company advertising material. The work of women artists for railway companies appeared on illustrated posters, as well as in guidebooks, brochures, and calendars. During the summers of 1925 and 1926, for the Great Northern Railway Company, Minnesota artist Elsa Jemne painted in Glacier National Park. She created top-quality landscapes and portraits of the Blackfeet people, featured in Great Northern leaflets and guides. During the 1930s, when the New Deal's Works

Progress Administration programs supported artists, women painted murals and landscapes on post office walls and in other public buildings so that their interpretations of rolling hillsides to verdant prairies greeted visitors all over the nation.

Female photographers were also important, bringing a new dimension and firsthand feeling to viewers' perceptions of the outdoors. Also, they often became committed environmentalists. Beginning in the 1890s, Alice Hare photographed California scenes, including parks and gardens, to preserve their beauty forever. Soon such magazines as *Sunset* published Hare's nature photographs. By the early 1900s, she also participated in the restoration and renovation of Santa Clara's oldest plaza and helped found a park. After she moved to Merced in 1911, she initiated a tree-planting campaign.

Similarly, women gardeners and landscape architects reshaped people's ideas regarding physical environments and advocated the care of native species. A San Diego horticulturalist, Kate Olivia Sessions, collected the Matilija poppy, San Diego lilac, aloe, bougainvillea, and eucalyptus. Sessions, who in 1881 earned a doctorate from the University of California, Berkeley, planted each year a hundred trees in Balboa Park. Other female gardeners also took responsibility for public green spaces, applying their skills to community, state, and national parks, roadsides, public gardens, recreation areas, and forests.

In 1913, when the Garden Club of America organized in New York City, its mission statement included environmental concerns. Under the leadership of Margaret McKenny of Olympia, Washington, the celebration of Arbor Day and tree planting were observed. After returning to Washington state, she chaired the Conservation Committee of Washington Garden Clubs and was president of the Audubon Society. Eventually, under the leadership of Minnerva Hamilton Hoyt, garden club members spoke, wrote, and lobbied for national parks and monuments, especially Joshua Tree National Monument (1936) in Southern California. Hoyt also hoped to interest the public in desert conservation by creating special garden club exhibits.

Between 1870 and 1940 nature-oriented architects also contributed to the social construction of nature. The architect Mary Elizabeth Jane Colter, who had studied at the California School of Design in San Francisco (now the San Francisco Art Institute), is known for developing National Park Service "rustic style" design buildings, consistent with their natural environments. One of Colter's most famous buildings is the Hopi House built in 1904 in Grand Canyon National Park. In 1914 she planned a refreshment center known as Hermit's Rest in the park made of stone and crude posts and furnished with pieces crafted from twisted tree stumps. She was an environmental reformer in other ways as well. In 1916, when Grand Canyon was about to become a national park, she contributed conservation ideas to the park plan. Later, during the 1930s, she consulted with officials from Grand Canyon National Park superintendents to those from Secretary of the Interior Harold Ickes's office.

Clearly, Colter assisted conservation in many ways. She helped in the early 20th-century construction of western nature and its aesthetics. She gave millions of visitors as authentic an experience of the western environment and its peoples as they were likely to get. While providing visitors with a gentle, "female" view of the West, Colter's work helped Americans understand why the West needed preserving. And she attracted thousands of female park visitors to hike, ride muleback, and climb.

Not surprisingly, female mountain climbers and other athletes often enlarged the ranks of the early conservation movement. Especially in such western states as Colorado, California, Oregon, and Washington, 19th-century women scaled every summit in sight and became environmentalists. As early as 1858, for example, 20-year-old feminist Julia Anna Archibald Holmes ascended Colorado's Pikes Peak wearing what she called the "American Costume"—bloomers. Thirty-two years later, another bloomer girl made a similar incredible climb. Schoolteacher Fay Fuller hoped to excite interest in the sport of climbing and to publicize the Pacific Northwest's highest peak, Mount Rainier. Fuller climbed with four men, including a photographer whose shots were later crucial in the creation of Mount Rainier National Park. Fuller advised anyone who wanted "to begin life anew" and "to fall in love with the world again" to spend a few days on Rainier's slopes. Subsequently, her reputation and frequent writings helped popularize climbing as well as the creation of Mount Rainier National Park.

Women climbers hoped to show others the glory of nature and to teach its judicious use. For instance, during the 1910s and 1920s, "girl" guides Anne and Isabel Pifer led male and female hikers up Longs Peak and other slopes, instructing them to "look while you're hiking" and to "enjoy" nature as they climbed.

In 1918, as men left for service in World War I, Helen Wagen landed a job, previously held by men, as a guide in Mount Rainier National Park. Wagen also led men and women on climbs, instilling a love of nature in them and helping them appreciate what she called "life on the world's top side."

Female climbers interested in the environment often found expression in the projects of such climbing clubs as the Sierra Club in California that organized in 1892; the Mazamas in Portland, Oregon, in 1895; the Mountaineers in Washington State in 1907; and the Colorado Mountain Club (CMC) in 1912. All of these groups welcomed women. Although the main purpose of climbing clubs was to climb mountains, members also hoped to preserve the natural environment. In 1916, for example, Mountaineers' members discussed the Permanent Wildlife Protection Fund, the National Parks Conference in Washington, D.C., and the preservation of the Chinook language and culture. Subsequently, they considered the establishment of public camps, studied the wisdom of allowing sheep-grazing on public lands, and erected markers along trails. In addition, Mountaineers' organizations cooperated with local units of the Federation of Women's Clubs to promote environmental programs and establish national parks. A charter member of the Fort Collins CMC, Laura Makepeace, pointed out that members were also committed to the preservation of nature. CMC members saved endangered trees, established nature trails and bird sanctuaries, and supported the founding of Rocky Mountain National Park and Dinosaur National Park.

Other female outdoor athletes were also conservationists. In Montana during the early 1900s, rancher and rodeo performer Fannie Sperry Steele worked in the Blackfoot Valley as a hunter, outfitter, and guide. Although she declared that "I think like an elk so I know where to find game," she opposed people who misused the environment, especially trophy hunters seeking animal heads for their walls. At age 74, Steel proclaimed, "I will prosecute them every chance I get."

Nor were young women forgotten. They were introduced to conservationists through the Girl Scouts of America, founded in 1912 by Juliette Gordon Low in Washington, D.C. Girl Scout groups rapidly spread westward, where their emphasis on outdoor activities attracted a wide membership. By 1919 Girl Scout troops existed in every state except Utah and extended across the Pacific Ocean to the territory of Hawaii. Through nature study, hikes, girl's camps, and other activities, the Girl Scouts taught both white women and women of color the advantages of outdoor exercise and the necessity to preserve the environment. Recently, a Low biographer explained that because Juliette threw her own cloak of respectability around outdoor ventures, thousands of girls had the opportunity to develop environmental awareness.

Obviously, all Victorian women were not passive, domestic, and indoors beings. Much like Juliette Low, huge numbers of them busily widened their spheres of activity, increasingly turning to reform and charitable activities. Between 1870 and 1940 such reforming and benevolent women worked on their own, or supported through membership in a group, environmental causes, including the salvation of birds, the establishment of parks, and the preservation of everything from bison to waterfalls and streams, mountains and forests. In so doing, they not only reshaped people's visions of the environment but enlarged women's roles and impact on American society.

As early as the 1870s, for example, Mary Ann Dyer Goodnight of the Texas Panhandle, who had a lifelong interest in the outdoors, began rescuing orphaned baby buffaloes, more properly called bisons. Goodnight's husband and brothers brought to her helpless buffalo calves that she intended to raise by hand to preserve the breed. Not until 1886 did the Smithsonian Institution first warn westerners regarding the imminent disappearance of the species. By then, Mary Ann's first orphans produced the Goodnight Buffalo and Cattalo Park. After her husband's death in 1929, the herd—which numbered approximately 200 animals that each summer produced between 16 and 20 calves—eventually became the Colonel Charles A. Goodnight Herd (rather than the Mary Ann Goodnight Herd). Although the Colonel always gave his wife credit for rescuing the Texas bison herd from extinction, her name disappeared.

Mary Ann Dyer Goodnight was not alone in her environmental concerns. Much of this work was carried on by the women's clubs that emerged in the United States after the Civil War. Prohibited from joining male clubs, women founded groups of their own. These groups usually had strong religious and patriotic overtones, which soon rubbed off on women's environmental projects. Members of one club asked God to "guide and inspire" the assembled women and their conservation projects. Clubs also dedicated special undertakings, including parks and forests, with prayers and invocations seeking God's protection for club gifts to communities. Others stressed patriotism, as did the Utah group who founded a George Washington Memorial Park. Thus did clubwomen associate Mom, God, and Americanism with the conservation ethic. Women's club philosophy specifically touched upon conservation, decreeing that any aspect of the environment affecting women and their families fell under the purview of women's clubs, which included virtually all aspects of the outdoors. In addition, a club's conservation policies had to be meaningful to the group's members, fulfill an important need of the times, and be relevant to an organization's locale. In Nevada, for example, the Mesquite Club of Las Vegas, formed in 1911, undertook tree planting, reportedly planting more than 2,000 trees in 1 day through its Town Beautiful project. In 1919 the U-Wah-Un Study Club, also of Las Vegas, soon engaged in studying Indian baskets and the desert and in donating nature books to the local library. In 1928 the Goldfield Woman's Club stated that its goals included the betterment of its community, especially improvement of the physical environment.

By the 1910s and 1920s most women's clubs had environmental agendas. Even in Hawaii, the clubwoman and philanthropist Ethel Frances Smith Baldwin initiated beautification programs on the island of Maui. During the 1910s and 1920s Baldwin sponsored public parks and the planting of trees along Baldwin Avenue from Paia to Makawao.

The women's club movement became so pervasive that local clubs organized on a state level and state clubs joined on a national level. The state and national groups were quick to develop environmental policies and pass them on to lower echelon clubs. During the 1880s, for example, Virginia Donaghe McClurg explored Colorado's Mesa Verde cliff dwellings and lectured about the need for preservation of the area. When in 1900 she approached the Colorado Federation of Women's Clubs, the group appointed her head of a committee "to save the Cliff Dwellings." Six years later, after much campaigning and vacillating, the U.S. Congress created Mesa Verde National Park.

The women's club movement marshaled tremendous numbers of members and nationwide organizations on behalf of environmental issues. Its leaders often pinpointed problems before anyone else. As early as 1896, Amy P. S. Stacy, the first president of the Washington Federation of Women's Clubs, urged forest preservation and opposition to the incursions of the logging industry. Moreover, women's clubs

established a network that intensified the effectiveness of environmental programs. In a circular movement across the West, local and state groups fed ideas upward to the national federation, while the national organization sent initiatives downward to other local and state groups. In 1905, for example, a Topeka clubwoman founded the West Side Forestry Club, a concept that had its roots in the forestry program of the national federation and the forestry committee of the Kansas State federation.

In 1912 the clubwoman and philanthropist Marion Crocker addressed the General Federation of Women's Clubs, making clear women's position on the issue. She spoke for the preservation of plant life, animals, and birds, pleading with women "to choose some other decoration" than birds for their hats. Crocker also urged environmental education among children to lay "the foundation of things for the next generation." She warned that if misuse of natural resources continued, "the time will come when the world will not be able to support life; then we shall have no need of conservation of health, strength or vital force."

In addition to being active in the extensive women's club network, some women pursued other avenues of reform. Some supported the lecture, education, and lobbying efforts of such conservation organizations as the Save-the-Redwoods League, founded in 1918 in San Francisco's Palace Hotel. Those who were bolder gave speeches, wrote articles, and authored books. Because public speakers played a critical role in the growth of any social movement, American women took the platform, asking Americans to preserve the fragile western environment.

Another example of a woman combining club work and other activities was the Californian Josephine Clifford McCrackin, who joined such environmental groups as the Sempervirens Club to save the giant redwoods and, during the early 1900s, wrote letters, founded the Ladies' Forest and Song Birds Protective Association, and became the first woman member of the California Game and Protective Association. During the 1920s and 1930s a Nebraska cattle rancher in the Sand Hills, Maud Ham Schooler-Briggs-Nelson, fought for city parks and cemetery beautification. At the same time, Essie Buchan Davis, owner and operator of a huge ranch north of Hyannis, was an energetic conservationist who, in 1939, was the first woman to receive the Nebraska Master Farmer award.

Even though this overview touches on only a few of the conservation-oriented women between 1870 and 1940, it reveals the huge numbers of women and depth of information available if investigators look in the right places. Especially in the early decades of this era, women were seldom found in the male-dominated political arena. Rather, they botanized in their homes, using the dining room table as a workplace, or organized women's clubs that met in members' homes or in local churches or schools. Because they had the education and leisure time, white women of the middle and upper classes predominated during the early years. Counter to the usual stereotype, they were not afraid of nature and the physical environment. Unlike men, they focused upon the spirituality and aesthetic side of western nature rather than insisting on the exploitation of western resources, thus feminizing public images of the West. Women also believed that God intended them to conserve a family's larger home, the outdoors.

From their conservation efforts, women learned a great deal, including how to network, speak in public, and become effective politically. After women received the right to vote in 1920, increasing numbers of them could be found not only voting but holding political office. Thus female conservationists demonstrated that they had feminist agendas, although environmentalism usually came first. Female conservationists also proved they could still be ladies. One even posed for a photograph while perched on a hilltop with a china teacup and saucer in her hands. For all their energy, finesse, and impact, women deserve a central place in environmental history.

—Glenda L. Riley

SUGGESTED READING

Riley, Glenda. *Women and Nature: Saving the Wild West.* Lincoln: University of Nebraska Press, 1999.

COWGIRLS

Cowgirls: were they a reality in the West or just one of Hollywood's inventions for the silver screen? Much focus has been placed on cowboys, but until just recently historians have largely ignored "cowboy girls," as they were referred to during the 19th century. Cowboy girls worked as cowhands on ranches and trails, including the famous Chisholm Trail. If they were fortunate, they owned their own ranches and had their own brands. According to the 1900 census, there were 800,000 women west of the Mississippi. While most women did not leave written records behind, there is enough information to make clear that there were women in the American West that made their living by herding cattle.

In reality, the heyday of the cowboy lasted only 25 years. In 1866 the first cowboys were hired to drive longhorn cattle from the plains of southwest Texas to the rail lines in Kansas. By the late 1880s, the trail drives came to an end. During that time, about 9 million Texas longhorns had either made it to the rail terminus or had been sent farther north as the cattle business expanded across the prairie and the Canadian West. Cowboys were still required to do the lonely, dirty, poorly paid job of herding cattle. In the legends of the old West, women were either wearing a sun bonnet and looking after the hearth while their husbands tended to all outside labors or they were prostitutes working in brothels.

One of Texas's most famous and successful cattle dealers was a woman named Lizzie Johnson Williams. She was not a native of Texas; she moved there to become a schoolteacher and writer. It was through her writing success that she was able to establish herself in the cattle business. By 1871 she had her own land, cattle, and cattle brand. In 1879 she married Hezekiah Williams. She insisted on what today would be called a prenuptial agreement. Williams signed a document that allowed his wife to remain in sole possession of her property, including any that she might acquire during their marriage. Lizzie was a successful rancher, whereas her husband never really prospered. On numerous occasions, she was known to help him out of financial difficulties but always insisted on repayment. During the 1880s, she took to the cattle trail. Riding in a buggy, she followed her cattle up the Chisholm Trail to the market in Kansas. She carefully kept all of her cows accounted for and was always quick to know what her profit would be.

There are stories of women tricking men into believing that they were men. Consider the story of Willie Matthews, who hired on as a cowhand. The trail boss was very happy with Matthews and the way "he" handled the cows. One evening a young woman showed up at camp and all the cowhands were shocked. No one recognized Willie as the now transformed Wilhelmina, who had grown up listening to her father tell stories of the cow trails and decided to disguise herself so she could experience this lifestyle firsthand. Cowboy Jo was another woman who fooled everyone. Jo Monaghan had been in Idaho for 30 years and was known for ranching and for riding roundups. Jo had voted and served on juries, which at the time were male privileges. No one worried because Jo was believed to be a male. However, upon her death, it was discovered that she was really a Josephine. Monaghan moved to Idaho after her parents disowned her due to a pregnancy out of wedlock. She tried mining and sheep herding but decided to ranch on her own. At her death, she owned several hundred head of cattle as well as horses and had her own brand, "JO." Another interesting story is of Fanny Seabride, a governess from Chicago who came to Texas to work. According to this story, a fence rider had been thrown from his horse and someone was needed to go and fix the fence. Seabride herself took on the job and performed so well at her new tasks that she was hired as a cowhand. Eventually, she leased some land, purchased cattle, and established herself as a rancher with the money she saved from bounty hunting (animals such as bears, coyotes, and wolves).

Not all women who were successful out on the range had an easy time of it. Ellen Watson from Wyoming is famous because she is the only woman in the American West to be lynched. In 1889 she had a successful ranch and became the object of other cattle barons envious of the location of her ranch. Newspaper accounts proclaimed Watson to have been very unwomanly. She was called a cattle rustler and a whore and known to ride straddle instead of sidesaddle as would become a lady. Apparently these "crimes" were sufficient to lynch her.

Watson and other cowgirls like her had to deal with making decisions about how to ride and what to wear. During this time period, women were expected to ride sidesaddle and wear long cumbersome skirts. Both of these made life for a cowgirl difficult. Practical clothing was a must, so some cowgirls turned to the "California riding costume," which was a divided skirt made of leather. Unfortunately, these skirts were huge and were very hot, but they allowed women to mount a horse and ride a man's saddle. By the turn of the century, riding sidesaddle was no longer in vogue.

Many women became cowgirls because of family necessity. If a wife or daughter were needed to help with ranching duties, then they would do whatever was necessary, such as herding cows and wild horses, helping with branding, or breaking horses. It can be argued that daughters had an easier time accepting this new role of a woman with many masculine traits than a newly settled wife from the East who might still subscribe to the rigorous rules of the cult of domesticity. A famous woman who took to the male way of living was Martha Jane Canary, better known as Calamity Jane. She was orphaned as a young teen and became a scout for the U.S. Army. She wore men's clothes and was known to be a hard drinker. She got her name when, in Goose Creek, Wyoming, the Army was ordered to stop an Indian uprising. On the way back to their post, the Army was ambushed. She managed to save her captain, who had been shot by the Indians. She took the captain safely back to the fort and he said, "I name you Calamity Jane, the heroine of the plains." Canary was also a successful pony express rider. She was given one of the roughest and most dangerous routes between Deadwood and Custer in Black Hills country.

Some women became ranchers due to their husbands' deaths, not wanting to sell out but to continue what they had helped their husbands build. One such woman was Helen Wiser Stewart. The Stewart family established a ranch in Nevada, which was successful enough for her husband to have created enemies. A ranch hand murdered her husband, who left behind no will. Stewart immediately engaged a lawyer to help her protect her interest in the ranch. She was able to manage the land and turn the ranch into one of the largest in Lincoln County, Nevada, with over 2,000 acres. She also bought and sold cattle and raised crops, including fruits. She became a successful rancher not by setting out to be one but because of family circumstances.

Performers with the traveling Wild West shows brought the cowgirl image east. Perhaps the most famous of these was Buffalo Bill's Wild West, owned by Buffalo Bill Cody (William Frederick Cody). Cody employed Annie Oakley as sharpshooter. Oakley had earned her living with a gun since she was a young woman, when she shot game for restaurants. She married Frank Butler, who was a professional marksman, and joined him on stage as a marksman. The crowd loved Oakley, and soon Butler became her assistant. Oakley was always behind the gun, shooting a dime out of her husband's hand or splitting an apple from atop a dog's head. She also rode a bicycle around the ring and shot moving targets. Her most famous stunt was having her target behind her, her rifle on top of her head, and finding her aim by looking in a mirror. Oakley became world famous, performing before royalty, and the biggest box office draw the Wild West show had. She was very successful in her cowgirl role. She was able to take a very masculine job and do it well and receive praise instead of criticism.

Rodeos were also a place to find cowgirls. The first rodeo was in 1897 in Cheyenne, Wyoming, during the Cheyenne Frontier Days. This event focused on horseback races, calf riding, bronco busting and riding, and steer roping. All of these things had long been practiced in the West. However, there were no events for women to compete in. It was not until 1902, when Bertha Kapernick entered in the bronco riding contest and the wild horse race, that the way was paved for other women to enter. Luckily, none of the rules kept women out of these events, so she was allowed to participate. Soon women became famous on the rodeo scene for roping and hog tying steers as well as the Roman race, in which riders stand astride two horses and race them for half a mile. They also entered the dangerous bulldogging event, where the performer leaped from a running horse onto the back of a steer and grabbed its horns and tried to bring it down by wrenching its neck.

With the advent of moving pictures, it didn't take Hollywood long to get in on the cowgirl act. Perhaps the most famous of the silent movies was the Texas Guinan series. Texas was the star of her movies as well as the hero; she made it perfectly clear that a cowboy would not upstage her. Among her movies were *The Girl Sheriff, The She Wolf* and *I Am the Woman*. While promoting these movies, it was always made clear that Texas Guinan was a "real woman." In a film called *Little Miss Deputy,* Texas had to decide whether to hang the man she loved—the right thing for a sheriff to do, but anathema for a woman to disown her man in this time. However, she was able to prove he was framed, and thus they all lived happily ever after within the confines of society.

The 1950s brought a whole new load of cowgirl films. Movies like *Cattle Queen* and Barbara Stanwyk's *The Maverick Queen* showed cowgirls in action riding to stop the bad guy and succeeding. Perhaps the most recognizable cowgirl name from Hollywood is Dale Evans. She brought the cowgirl into the home every week and became a role model for little girls. Evans was paired off with Roy Rogers in the movies and a television series. Her character would eventually have comics, books, and View-Master stories.

In the end, it doesn't matter whether cowgirls arose out of necessity in order for families to survive or because women liked the independence that the role of a cowhand gave them. What is important to remember is that women took on roles and work that society did not prescribe for them, and they loved it and made a living from it and have given us some heroines to remember.

—Michelle A. Stretch

SUGGESTED READINGS

Jordan, Teresa. *Cowgirls: Women of the American West.* Lincoln: University of Nebraska Press, 1992.

LeCompte, Mary Lou. *Cowgirls of the Rodeo.* Urbana: University of Illinois Press, 1993.

CROW DOG, MARY (1953-)

Mary Crow Dog, nee Brave Bird, was born in He Dog on the South Dakota Rosebud Reservation as a member of the Sichangu Lakota. She is a self-described "half breed," having Irish ancestors. When she was around 6 years old, she was taken from her grandparents by her mother and placed in a Catholic school. The school, and her mother, suppressed American Indian culture, and she grew to resent it.

The suppression and cruelty she experienced in the Catholic school motivated her, in 1971, to participate in the American Indian Movement as a political activist. She also authored two books, *Lakota Woman,* for which she earned the American Book Award in 1991, and *Ohitika Woman*. She participated in the occupation of the BIA building in Washington, D.C., and the second Wounded Knee battle in 1973. During the fight, she had her first child by her husband, Leonard Crow Dog.

She and Leonard participated in the crusades against the U.S. government's treatment of American Indians. She eventually left Leonard and lived in extreme poverty with her children. She met and married Rudi Olguin in 1991. Today, she has five children in all, and they all live together on the Rosebud Reservation.

—Lori S. Iacovelli

SUGGESTED READING

Brave Bird, Mary. *Ohitika Woman*. New York: Grove Press, 1993.

DARDEN, FANNIE BAKER
(1829-1890)

Fannie Amelia Dickson Baker Darden was born in Autauga County, Alabama. She was the daughter of General Moseley Baker and his wife, Eliza. Her family moved to Texas during her childhood. She married William John Darden in 1847 and had two sons.

She was an accomplished painter and taught art at Colorado College before the Civil War. She was also a distinguished poet and known as the Poet Laureate of Columbus, Texas. She wrote poetry for newspapers in Columbus, Galveston, Houston, and New Orleans. One of her poems reflected her love and fierce pride for Texas, as shown in *Loved Texas*: "When the red Rio Grande flows swiftly and proud, where the mountains stand wrapped in their tissuey clouds, thou art mine! For my father his willing sword drew when to save thee from tyrants he stood with the few who gave thee to freedom, the Texian band; and for these do I love thee, oh glorious land!" She continued her writing career even after undergoing surgery for breast cancer in 1882 when she wrote a series of love stories known as *Romances of the Texas Revolution* for the magazine *Texas Prairie Flower*.

She was known to be a "pious Christian" and devoted Confederate. She died in Columbus, Texas, in 1890.

Photograph courtesy of Nesbitt Memorial Library, Columbus, Texas.

—Lori S. Iacovelli

SUGGESTED READINGS

Knight, Lucian Lamar, ed. *Biographical Dictionary of Southern Authors*. Detroit, MI: Gale Research, 1978.

Stein, Bill, and Easterling, Jayne, eds. "The Writings of Fannie Amelia Dickson Darden." *Nesbitt Memorial Library Journal: A Journal of Colorado County History* 9(3) (1999): 131-194.

Texas Settlement Region. Retrieved on March 9, 2002, from www.tsir.org.

DAVIS, MOLLIE EVELYN MOORE (1844-1909)

Born Mary Evalina Moore on April 12, 1844, in Talladega, Alabama, she changed her name to Mollie Evelyn Moore at age 14. In 1855 her family moved to Texas, and she was educated at home with her brother. When she was 16, she began writing for newspapers, and soon after, her poetry became well known. In 1867 her family moved to Galveston, Texas, and *Minding the Gap*, her first book of verse, was published.

Mollie married Thomas E. Davis, a former Confederate major, in 1874. In 1879 Thomas was made associate editor of the *New Orleans Times*, so they moved to New Orleans. There Mollie continued to have her poems and sketches published in *Harper's* and the *Saturday Evening Post*, and she wrote novels. She became a leader in New Orleans's literary society and presided over a literary circle called Graphics and a literary club called Quarante. In 1889 she became editor of *Picayune*, which had previously printed several of her essays.

Titles of her books include *In War Times at La Rose Blanche* (1888), *Under the Man-Fig* (1895), *A Christmas Masque of Saint Roch* (1896), *Under Six Flags* (1897), *An Elephant's Track and Other Stories* (1897), *The Wire-Cutters* (1899), *The Queen's Garden* (1900), *Jaconetta: Her Loves* (1901), *A Bunch of Roses and Other Parlor Plays* (1903), *The Little Chevalier* (1903), *The Price of Silence* (1907), and *The Moons of Balbanca* (1908). Another anthology of her poetry, *Selected Poems* (1927), was printed posthumously by friends. Mollie died on January 1, 1909.

—Carolyn Stull

SUGGESTED READINGS

Encyclopedia Louisiana. "Louisiana Timeline, 1879." Retrieved from www.enlou.com/time/year1879.htm.

Gray, Janet, ed. *She Wields a Pen: American Women Poets of the Nineteenth Century.* Iowa City: University of Iowa Press, 1997.

The Handbook of Texas Online. "Davis, Mollie Evelyn Moore." Retrieved from www.tsha.utexas.edu/handbook/online/articles/view/DD/fda44.html.

DELORIA, ELLA CARA (1889-1971)

Ella Cara Deloria was born on the Yankton Sioux Reservation into a prominent Lakota family. Her grandfather was a tribal leader and her father a deacon in the reservation's Episcopal Church. In 1890 the family moved to the Standing Rock Reservation when her father became a deacon at the St. Elizabeth's Mission Church. Two years later, he became a priest of the church. Ella's childhood instruction and her formal education were in the Episcopal faith and in its schools until she attended the University of Chicago, Oberlin College of Ohio, and Columbia University.

At Columbia, she started a long association with prominent anthropologist Franz Boas. After graduation from Columbia, she taught at All Saints School in Sioux Falls, South Dakota, and won fame for her physical education program. In 1927 she started on a 15-year research and writing program with Boas that resulted in a number of significant publications. Her "Sun Dance of the Oglala Sioux" saw print in the 1929 edition of the *Journal of American Folklore*. There soon followed *Dakota Texts* (1932), *Dakota Grammar* (1941), and *Speaking of Indians* (1944). This body of work stands today as a foundation for the study of Sioux dialects, myths, and ethnography.

Her *Waterlily* (1988) was published posthumously and is a novel about a Teton Sioux woman's life and lifeways.

—Gordon Morris Bakken

SUGGESTED READINGS

Miller, Carol. "Mediation and Authority: The Native American Voices of Mourning Dove and Ella Deloria." In James A. Banks, ed., *Multicultural Education,*

Transformative Knowledge, and Action. New York: Teachers College Press, 1996, 141-155.

Rice, Julian. *Deer Women and Elk Men: The Lakota Narratives of Ella Deloria.* Albuquerque: University of New Mexico Press, 1992.

DOHENY, ESTELLE (1875-1958)

Carrie Estelle Betzold married Edward Laurence Doheny on October 25, 1918. She became the wife of a wealthy oil tycoon and spent her busy life accompanying her husband by traveling, entertaining, and assisting his enterprises. The couple built magnificent homes on their Beverly Hills Ranch and Ferndale Ranch near Santa Paula, California. Her Chester Place home contained a private deer park containing tame deer, monkeys, and a spectacular steel conservatory housing a collection of rare palm trees, tropical trees, and orchids. Mrs. Doheny's orchid collection exceeded 5,000 specimens.

Estelle was a philanthropist. She funded many charitable organizations and was generous to Southern California churches. Her donations helped build the Los Angeles Orphanage, the Orthopedic and Children's Hospital, and the St. Vincent's Seminary. In Washington, D.C., She funded the construction of the Vincentian House of Studies. She was afflicted by glaucoma and hoped to help other victims of this eye disease. In 1936 she expanded the Estelle Doheny Eye Foundation of St. Vincent's Hospital with a five-story building. In 1932 the Dohenys bestowed a memorial library at the University of Southern California in honor of their son. The beautifully built library was made of marble, brick, and stone. Special attention was paid to the maximization of air and light within its hallways and reading rooms.

In honor of her late husband, she established a world-renowned library in Camarillo, California. The library contained the famous Estelle Doheny Collection of rare books, manuscripts, and works of art acquired during her lifetime. Her collection represented one of the rarest book libraries in the United States. Within the collection, 4,000 volumes were rare books and first editions. Fifteen hundred of the volumes were comprised of autograph letters and important historical and literary manuscripts. Early vellum manuscripts such as bibles, gospels, commentaries, liturgical works, and ornamented books revealed the prominence of the collection. In 1949 the Carrie Estelle Doheny Foundation was established to promote the advancement of education, medicine, religion, and science. On June 29, 1939, Pope Pius XII conferred on Doheny the title of papal countess in recognition of her charitable deeds. This was the first bestowal of this kind granted in Southern California. The seminary system in the Archdiocese of Los Angeles is financed by an endowment fund established in her honor.

The Sisters of Charity operate the Los Angeles Orphanage Guild known as Maryvale. The Estelle Doheny Eye Foundation relocated its research facility in 1961 from the Los Angeles St. Vincent's Hospital to a newly constructed facility affiliated with the University of Southern California and Los Angeles County Medical Complex. The new organization hoped to ensure expanded exposure for people seeking its healing services. In 1975 the Estelle Doheny Eye Foundation moved completely away from St. Vincent's Hospital, which is under the care of the Los Angeles Sisters of Charity. Foundation teams operated throughout local hospitals until the new Estelle Doheny Eye Hospital was built in the mid-1980s. Her continuing support for the eye foundation helped many people afflicted with eye diseases. The Estelle Doheny Foundation continues its present-day charitable activities of advancing education, aiding the needy, improving health and welfare, medical improvements, and furthering religion.

—Henry Fay Cheung

SUGGESTED READINGS

Brenton, Thaddeus Reamy. *An Exhibition of Rare Manuscripts and Books From the Library of Mrs. Edward Laurence Doheny.* Los Angeles: College Press, 1936.

Gayle, Mary Redus. *Glass Paperweights From the Estelle Doheny Collection at St. John's Seminary, Camarillo, California and St. Mary's of the Barrens Seminary, Perryville, Missouri.* Ephrata, PA: Science Press, 1971.

La Botz, Dan. *Edward L. Doheny: Petroleum, Power, and Politics in the United States and Mexico.* New York: Praeger, 1991.

Miller, Lucille V. *The Book as a Work of Art.* Los Angeles: Ward Ritchie, 1935.

Ritchie, Ward. *The Dohenys of Los Angeles.* Los Angeles: Dawson's Book Shop, 1974.

Starr, Kevin. *Material Dreams: Southern California Through the 1920s.* New York: Oxford University Press, 1990.

Webber, Carl J. *A Thousand and One Fore-Edge Paintings.* Waterville, ME: Colby College Press, 1949.

Weber, Francis J. *Southern California's First Family.* Fullerton, CA: Lorson's Books and Prints, 1993.

DONNER, TAMSEN (1801-1847)

Tamsen Eustis was born in Newburyport, Massachusetts, in 1801. She married Tully Dozier and bore him two children, but her happiness was short lived. In a letter to her sister, she revealed that her son died very young of disease, her premature daughter died in infancy, and she lost her husband, all between September and December 1831. She settled in Sangamon County, Illinois, with her brother, William, caring for his children.

Tamsen met George Donner in Illinois where she taught school at Sugar Creek. She married Donner, a well-to-do Illinois farmer, in 1839. It was her second marriage and his third. George brought with him seven children from his two previous marriages. Together they had three daughters—Frances Eustis, Georgia Ann, and Eliza Poor—the youngest named for Tamsen's sister.

Tamsen was a small woman, barely 5 feet tall and weighing less than 100 pounds. She was a teacher by profession and wrote poetry, some published in the *Sangamon Journal* of Springfield, Illinois.

In 1846 George decided to move to California. Tamsen looked forward to the journey and planned to open a ladies seminary on the West Coast. The wagons and provisions packed, they set off. Legend has it that Tamsen stitched the family's money, $10,000, into a quilt for the journey.

She was kind hearted and affectionate. With the wagons of over 90 travelers fully loaded with food and supplies, she agreed to take in an unknown young man named Luke Halloran, who was suffering from what is today known as tuberculosis. He died along the route and left the Donner family $1,500.

Ever mindful of her children, she packed books and painting supplies for the journey. When the heat of the desert weighed on them, she gave them peppermint-flavored sugar to ease their discomfort. When water was in short supply, she gave them bullets to suck on, the lead generating saliva to soothe a dry throat. Further on when trapped in snow, in an effort to save her children the fate of so many others, she paid two members of a rescue party $500 to take her children to Sutter's Fort. She insisted on staying with her dying husband.

The ultimate reality of the Donner expedition was suffering, hunger, tragedy, cannibalism, and intrigue. Tamsen met her end in the snow of the Sierra Nevada. The circumstances surrounding her brutal death are a mystery to this day. Strong evidence suggests that she was murdered by fellow traveler, Lewis Keseberg. A rescue party found her mutilated body in Keseberg's cabin.

—Neal Lynch

SUGGESTED READINGS

Bryant, Edwin. *What I Saw in California: Being the Journal of a Tour, by the Emigrant Route and South Pass of the Rocky Mountains, Across the Continent of North America, the Great Desert Basin, and Through California, in the Years 1846-1847.* Minneapolis, MN: Ross & Haines, 1967.

Holmes, Kenneth L., and David Duniway. *Covered Wagon Women: Diaries & Letters from the Western Trails, 1840-1849.* Glendale, CA: Arthur H. Clark, 1983.

Houghton, Eliza P. Donner. *The Expedition of the Donner Party and Its Tragic Fate.* Chicago: A. C. McClurg, 1911.

Johnson, Kristin. *Donner Party Bulletin, Issue No.1, September/October, 1997.* Retrieved from www.utahcrossroads.org/DonnerParty/Bulletin1.htm.

Johnson, Kristin. *Donner Party Bulletin, Issue No. 3, January/February, 1998.* Retrieved from www.utahcrossroads.org/DonnerParty/Bulletin1.htm.

Lewis, Daniel. Forensics II, *"The Donner Party."* Retrieved from raiboy.tripod.com/Donner/id16.html.

McGlashan, Charles Fayette. *History of the Donner Party: A Tragedy of the Sierra.* Stanford, CA: Stanford University Press, 1968.

Monaghan, Jay. *The Overland Trail.* Indianapolis, IN: Bobbs-Merrill, 1947.

Powell, John Carroll. "Early Settlers of Sangamon County—1876." Retrieved from www.rootsweb.com/~ilsangam/1876/donnerg.htm.

Stewart, George Rippey. *Ordeal by Hunger: The Story of the Donner Party.* Boston, MA: Houghton Mifflin, 1960.

Whitman, Ruth. *Tamsen Donner: A Woman's Journey.* Cambridge, MA: Alice James Books, 1977.

DORSEY, REBECCA LEE (1859-1954)

Rebecca Lee Dorsey was born in 1859 in Maryland and, according to her unpublished memoirs, was self-sufficient from the age of 9. She moved to Philadelphia and became a servant, using the money to put herself through grammar school. She attended Wellesley College by earning money doing menial jobs for other students. While pursuing another degree at Boston University, she cared for sick people in order to provide herself with an income. She graduated in June 1882. She spent several years in Europe pursuing her studies before deciding to settle in Los Angeles, California.

In 1886 Dorsey began her own medical practice in Los Angeles and worked out of St. Vincent's Medical Center. She drove a horse and buggy to the various homes and ranches that required her services. She had a very large obstetrics practice; she was the attending physician at over 4,000 births. Perhaps her most famous delivery was Earl Warren, a governor of California and Chief Justice of the U.S. Supreme Court. She boasted that she never lost a baby or mother during delivery because she adhered to four rules: (1) she had a perfect understanding of the measurement of a mother's pelvis as well as the size and weight of the child, (2) she advocated good prenatal care, (3) she had a strictly aseptic technique, and (4) she made sure that the afterbirth was completely delivered. She was also boastful of the claim that she never had one case of septicemia, otherwise known as childbed fever, due to her knowledge of sterilization, which she learned from Joseph Lister during her time in Europe. She also used forceps without serious injury to any of the babies she delivered.

Dorsey claims to have performed the first three successful appendectomies in Los Angeles County and administered the first diphtheria inoculation in Los Angeles around 1893. She helped establish the first training school for nurses in Los Angeles. During World War I, she consulted for the Secretary of War regarding the number of women nurses available in the United States, and offered suggestions for a rapid multiplication of trained women available in a time of emergency. After 60 years of practice, she retired and invested her money in dates at her Big Four Ranch near Indio, California, in the Coachella Valley. In fact, she is credited with

bringing the date industry to California. She died at 95 years of age.

—Michelle A. Stretch

DREXEL, KATHARINE (1858-1955)

Katharine Drexel was an American philanthropist, business figure, and religious leader who had a significant impact on the education of children of color in the American West and South. Her early life did not point to her future as an influential figure in the women's West. Born to a family of great wealth, Drexel, her sister, Elizabeth, and half-sister, Louise, were raised amid the plush trappings of Philadelphia society. Her parents—father Francis and stepmother Emma—surrounded their daughters with gracious living and the rhythms of the Roman Catholic faith. Emma Drexel in particular molded her three daughters with a moral philosophy that emphasized that the privilege of wealth included responsibility to others. Social engagements, intellectual interests, religious fervor, and business dealings were woven through the fabric of the young sisters' lives and bonded the siblings into an unusually close threesome, whose personal vision matched that of their parents. The five traveled abroad, and their visits to Italy included private audiences with the pope. In the United States, the Drexel family moved comfortably through the highest levels of Catholic society, entertained members of the church hierarchy, worshiped in a private chapel, and established a legacy of philanthropy that enriched various religious institutions in the Philadelphia area.

Following the premature deaths of their parents—Emma in 1883 and Francis in 1885—the three sisters, heirs to a banking fortune of approximately $14 million dollars, while a separate $1.5 million was awarded to Catholic institutions around Philadelphia, found themselves the subjects of widespread reports in the secular and religious press. The sisters quickly became the targets for many charities that looked to the trio with hopes that the Drexel history of supporting Catholic needs would continue uninterrupted. The Drexel daughters, each now with an annual income from the estate's interest of about $350,000 in an era that predated personal income taxation, did not disappoint their many supplicants.

Mother Mary Katharine Drexel oversaw a vast philanthropy directed to the education of children of color in the West.

Photograph courtesy of Archives, Sisters of the Blessed Sacrament, Bensalem, Pennsylvania.

Father Joseph Stephan, director of the Bureau of Catholic Indian Missions, and Bishop James O'Connor of Omaha, Nebraska, both known for some years to the Drexel family, invited the young women to make an exploratory social service trip into the American West. These clergymen, with their firsthand knowledge of the West and its peoples, fueled

Katharine's vision that increasingly looked beyond the urban centers of the East to land once known as the frontier. With assertions that hundreds of thousands of Native Americans lacked spiritual care, because too few missionaries could tolerate the extreme conditions of the West, the bishops begged Katharine to shore up mission efforts. Through this tour, O'Connor and Stephan hoped to convince all the Drexel daughters to contribute to western Catholic mission schools, staffed by members of a number of struggling religious congregations.

In 1887 the three young women made the first of their western expeditions to the Rosebud Indian reservation in South Dakota. The young heiresses mingled with some ease in the Native communities, supped with Indian people and, although accustomed to a life of opulence in the East, accepted the rough accommodations of the West with equanimity. All three responded with gentle humor to the physical inconveniences, more interested in their cultural surroundings and the quality of life for those they met. This tour had a profound impact on Katharine Drexel, drawing her into the dynamics of the West for the remainder of her long life. Her visit to South Dakota ignited her sense of personal mission, soon to be cast in the language of the West. When she returned to her Philadelphia home, she brought with her an attachment for the American West that anchored her social justice actions for the next 7 decades.

Katharine had not been blinded by the welcoming hospitality of the Indians and missionaries. She looked beyond the friendly dinners and evening dances to the long-range implications of what she had seen. The extreme poverty for Native people and their few missionaries convinced Drexel that Catholic educational goals, as well as Indian cultures, in the Far

West were doomed to collapse. She agreed with Stephan and O'Connor that the mission initiative would never attract a sufficient number of workers, as the rigors of outpost living were too debilitating. Shortly, she felt Native people would not be able to fend off the "civilizing" forces of Anglo society, losing land and culture with each passing year.

In Katharine's view, shaped by her commitment to Catholic ideals, personnel and funding were spread so thinly across vast western regions that it was impossible to effect positive change for Native people. True, some Indians gravitated toward these missions, little more than outposts of white paupers, as possible sources of sustenance. However, good example, proselytism, and a few material items created only meager links between the missionary and the Indian. Rather, biting cold, crippling hunger, and deadly isolation overtook missionary and Native alike. In Katharine's view, the reservation system offered no viable future to Native people, leaving them mired in poverty and early death. Without Anglo schooling, the Indians had no chance to extricate themselves from the dreary arrangements imposed by a distant white society or to be brought into the circle of Christianity. She believed these disastrous conditions could only be reversed with a systematic infusion of funding that would support Catholic education for Native people, in a mission system designed to protect Indian children and families from the encroachment of the white population. She determined to construct an infrastructure that would sustain Catholic schools at Native American missions, with the hope of providing economic, intellectual, and spiritual tools for people caught in an avalanche of cultural destruction. In this move, she expanded an existing family philanthropy to African American children in the South, embracing a broader personal commitment to the education of all children of color in the United States.

For the next several years, Katharine bought western land, consulted with architects, hired Native workers as farmers and carpenters, built schools, and negotiated teaching agreements with religious congregations. Although the Bureau for Catholic Indian Missions might have been willing to assume oversight for these projects, she intended to stay engaged with every phase of the operation. She was aware that disagreements among the managers of the Bureau had dragged on for at least a decade, resulting in a torturously slow distribution of funds to the West. Anxious to bring about rapid change, she had no interest in watching a cumbersome bureaucracy cloud her

progress. In addition, she always supervised to the smallest detail the use of her funds and kept a militant watch for any misdirection of her dollars.

Drawing on entrepreneurial skills learned from her father, Katharine used several strategies to sustain the mission initiatives of various Catholic groups. She diversified her allocations, avoiding the risk of channeling the money through a single account that could be corrupted. Instead, she relied on a loan here or a stipend there, salaries for four nuns or insurance for one mission, to keep the sums manageable and easy to track. While perhaps not every decision reflected the most appropriate ideas for a western environment or for Indian people, the sheer magnitude of the undertaking reflected the scope of her thinking. The result of this multilayered activity was that Drexel money began to flow directly to educational, cultural, and economic centers for Native people.

In 1888 Katharine and her two sisters returned to the West to visit the Red Lake and White Earth Indian reservations in Minnesota, where two Benedictine nuns operated a small school. This second Drexel trip mirrored and reinforced the earlier trek. Long John, White Cloud, Little Feather, Hole in the Sky, Clouds Drifting Along, Leading Thunder—these were among the Chippewa men greeting the sisters, who did not overlook the work, weddings, and parenting of the Indian women they saw moving about the mission grounds. Katharine was not pleased to learn that at the Red Lake station there had been no resident priest for 5 years. She offered to provide transportation and building funds immediately if the Benedictine priests from St. John's Abbey and the nuns from St. Benedict's Priory, both in Minnesota, would send personnel. The following year, with the backing of Drexel money, the two monasteries sent a small staff to the remote mission at Red Lake.

Upon her return to Philadelphia, Katharine again focused on the school building plan. Fresh from the Minnesota missions, she decided to award $40,000 to the two Benedictine nuns who had maintained the poor little establishment at White Earth for 10 years. This money gave new life to the school and resulted in internal and external strengthening of the mission. The two nuns, Philomena and Lioba, alone had managed day students, boarders, orphans, and an annex school miles distant. Now they found the staff expanded to seven, allowing a greater division of daily labors and a closer adherence to their personal spiritual duties. A new brick schoolhouse for 150 children opened in 1890. In an apparent fulfillment of

Katharine's pronouncement of the ineffectiveness of poor mission stations, Native families showed themselves much more enthusiastic about enrolling their children in a greatly improved facility, where eventually the staff numbered 18. Of these, Sisters Philomena and Lioba served together at White Earth for 50 years, retiring to their St. Benedict's Priory in 1928.

In the meantime, Katharine spent the next 5 years planting her school and mission organization across the West. Her largesse, distributed under rigid regulations of accountability, established and supported western schools for, among others, Arapaho, Sioux, Nez Perce, Osage, Cheyenne, Blackfeet, and Pueblo Indians. At the same time, she underwrote the mission activities of several different Roman Catholic congregations of women and men, including Franciscans, Jesuits, Dominicans, and Benedictines, who, without her financial encouragement, endorsed through regular letters and checks, confronted overwhelming frontier poverty and the likely faltering of their missionary efforts.

In this manner, Katharine designed and implemented a regional program of education under a Catholic umbrella. Her business arrangements, almost exclusively managed by herself, influenced the economic development of local western areas. Entire Native families drew from the mission schools—the children in classrooms and the parents as the paid staff that maintained the operation through agriculture, construction, and animal husbandry. Although these were rural occupations whereby white society generally expected to tie Native people to the land, in several locations Indian families sought the economic stimulation gained from this employment.

In these monetary arrangements, Drexel held to an inflexible rule that her funds must be spent to the benefit of full-blood Indian children. This could include direct tuition and board payments, wages for Native employees, grocery bills, and insurance. She would not tolerate, however, any other use of the funds, as she constantly worried about the ways that Indian people were facing economic, cultural, and political disenfranchisement. If it came to her attention that funding went for expenses she thought inappropriate, she did not hesitate to recall the money and reduce her future contributions. She tracked her gifts and loans through a complex system of letter writing, eventually amassing a collection of more than 20,000 letters.

Despite her great wealth, Katharine sought personal fulfillment through her commitment to Catholic religious ideals. Almost immediately following the demise of her parents, she expressed a desire to devote herself to religious life as a Roman Catholic sister. She felt herself drawn to a congregation that stressed an active ministry rather than a contemplative order that would be bound by the rule of enclosure. For some time, she had admired two religious groups in the Philadelphia area—the Sisters of Mercy and the Sisters of St. Francis of Glen Riddle, Pennsylvania, both of whom took their charities to the needy of the community and had well-established missions in western areas.

Her confidantes in the Catholic clergy, concerned about access to the Drexel money, which would go to the treasury of her chosen religious order, opposed her wishes, insisting that Katharine remain in the secular world and manage her estate. Finally, in 1889 Katharine refused to be deterred any longer and entered the convent of the Sisters of Mercy of Philadelphia. Thirty years of age, she undertook the prescribed routines for the formation of a sister of the Roman Catholic religion and as a postulant with the Mercy Sisters, exploring the rigors of the convent. Katharine spent the summer months learning the tenets of religious life, and in November received the habit of the Mercy Sisters as a novice in that order. Not all the routines proved agreeable to her. Although she felt comfortable with the spiritual rituals of daily life, she appeared to recognize that her talents lay not in the classroom, but where she had already proven her skills—in administration. Throughout her stay with the Mercy Sisters, Katharine continued to oversee her vast western organization, keeping abreast of her correspondence, consulting with professional advisers, and making the sharp business decisions for which she was so well known.

In a concession to her clergy advisers, she had agreed to stay with the Mercy Sisters only for a period of spiritual training, after which she would establish a separate congregation of sisters. During this period, despite this understanding with Philadelphia Archbishop P. J. Ryan, she thought about remaining permanently with the Mercy Sisters. She knew and respected these women and felt a lingering reluctance about the challenges of forming a new congregation of sisters.

Finally resolving this personal dilemma, by 1891 Katharine had, with her exceptional financial resources, the support of her biological sisters, and the forceful encouragement of the Roman Catholic clergy, including the pope, organized her own religious community of women, the Sisters of the Blessed Sacrament for Colored and Indian People. After this date, she was known as Mother Mary Katharine Drexel, founder and leader of a community of women with an explicit commitment to persons of color in the United States. Following the pronouncement of her religious vows, she withdrew from the Mercy convent and moved her original group of 13 nuns to the Drexel summer home near Philadelphia. There, under the continued guidance of Sister Inez of the Mercy order and the supervision of Archbishop Ryan, the recently professed devoted themselves to shaping the identity of the new order.

One crucial decision concerned selecting a location for a mother house for the new congregation. Western bishops appealed for places near them, especially a California or South Dakota spot. Drexel declined these invitations, choosing to remain close to the environment of her youth. In September 1890 her older sister, Elizabeth, had died unexpectedly in childbirth, a blow to Katharine that bonded her even more closely with her younger sibling, Louise. A mother house in the West would have meant yet another family separation, a move clearly unattractive to both Mother Katharine and Louise. Furthermore, Archbishop Ryan, involved with the Drexel family's practice of Catholicism for many years, wanted to keep Katharine within his own arena of authority, reluctant to allow bishops in other jurisdictions to have too much influence over her disbursements. Thus events led Katharine to organize a community with a distinctly western orientation around a fixed eastern base.

Only a short time after her arrival at the summer house, Katharine left on a trip to St. Stephen's in Wyoming, an Arapaho/Shoshone mission that she had tried to sustain through several years of funding to the Sisters of Charity of Leavenworth. When these sisters, overwhelmed by the rugged conditions and administrative problems not of their making, withdrew, Drexel decided to refurbish the school and convent, so that Blessed Sacrament sisters could staff the struggling facility. With a companion, she set out for the remote mission in a western trip that included meals in public eating houses and odd hours for stage travel.

Traveling under the escort of the bishop of Cheyenne, Mother Katharine and Sister Patrick recaptured the zest of the 1888 western trip of the Drexel sisters. Full of enthusiasm for the landscape, the adventure, and the needs of the school, Drexel wrote effusive descriptions of her travels to Sister Inez. Accustomed to charting her own course at the missions, she now looked forward to sending her own sisters into the West.

Apparently, both Archbishop Ryan and Sister Inez considered these circumstances to be inappropriate, given the youthfulness of the little sisterhood, and they squelched Drexel's ambitious plans for St. Stephen's. It was an episode that pointed to the complexity of Katharine's position in church politics and how convent life altered her status. On the one hand, she continued to be perhaps the most powerful woman in the American church, armed with a lifetime of unique financial power and forcefully overseeing a vast fortune on behalf of her religion. On the other hand, the superiors of that church now negotiated with her in the context of her status as a nun, a role that gave them the advantage and placed her under a vow of obedience. Once she had become a sister, the archbishop could add "command" to his directives, and he did. Ryan ordered Katharine to see to the formation of her new sisterhood in a location where he could personally watch her progress. The selection of members, organization of policies, construction of the novitiate and mother house, and the Catholic church requirements for official approbation were expected to be the priorities.

Although she experienced considerable disappointment when Ryan checked her immediate goals for St. Stephen's, Drexel accepted the constraints with grace. St. Stephen's went to the care of Drexel's highly regarded friends, the Sisters of St. Francis of Glen Riddle, who stabilized the school and served there from 1892 to 1984.

In 1894 Drexel received permission to send her sisters to the West, where they began their work in Santa Fe, New Mexico, at St. Catherine's Convent and Boarding School. Katharine expected her sisters to establish a public ministry and to do so promptly. In response to her wishes, the Sisters of the Blessed Sacrament immersed themselves in the environment of New Mexico. They took on a range of community activities that many would not associate with convent living. They journeyed by wagon into the mountains to recruit students, stayed in the homes of local families, taught school, attended festivals, sang at weddings, volunteered at the penitentiary, nursed victims of epidemics, and opened a hospice program for traveling Indians.

Drexel, from her mother house at Cornwells Heights, Pennsylvania, kept close watch over the routines of the sisters. At last she knew that sisters entirely accountable to her and loyal to her vision for children of color were in place. Those at the mission wrote long and descriptive letters, which Drexel shared with the growing congregation. In this way, she introduced the images of the mission work to the new candidates for her order, bonding the West of Native people to the East of her young sisters.

These sisters had accepted a substantial challenge when they joined Drexel's order. The congregation was never destined to be very large, and many scorned its commitment to educate people of color. Concerns about personal safety for the sisters were a reality. On more than one occasion, including the day of the dedication ceremony, anonymous threats were made against the mother house. Drexel gave scant attention to such episodes, focusing instead on preparing young women to live and work in locations quite unlike eastern Pennsylvania.

At the same time, these young women had aligned themselves with arguably the most influential woman in the American Catholic church. Drexel was a force in a church administered by a totally male hierarchy. Through their association with her, young sisters had the opportunity to circumvent that male authority, implement strategies for social action, travel to the American West, interact with persons of differing cultures, and assume positions of power more quickly than would be the case in a more established religious community, where the important posts went to members with the greatest seniority.

Personally, Drexel derived great pleasure in annual trips to the West, where she could witness her educational programs on behalf of people of color and enjoy contact with Native people. Occasionally, she blundered in these relationships. For example, she seemed to overlook that fact that asking Indian families to send their children many miles to a mission school was too much of a parental wrench, even though she expressed great admiration for the strength of the Native families she met. On one occasion, despite warnings to stay at the convent, she tried to force her way into an Indian home where a virulent illness was raging. Overcome by her desire to be directly involved in nursing the sick, she misjudged the feeling about outsiders within that particular Native family. Yet despite these few missteps, overall she established solid connections within western communities, and

Native people welcomed her warmly each time she visited.

In 1902 Drexel fulfilled a personal interest, traveling to the Oklahoma Territory to assess the progress in the schools she had supported for many years. As usual, she wrote lengthy letters to the sisters at the mother house, describing in great detail each of the missions. The trip left her disheartened, for in all the classrooms she found mixed-blood and white children to be the majority of the students. The argument that white families brought tuition dollars to the schools did not impress her. In her observations, the few full-blood children were pushed aside by the others, not only in the school but in local political and economic endeavors. She felt particularly uneasy about the relationships between full-blood and mixed-blood children, the latter, she observed, asserting themselves in a number of ways over the former. She continued to insist that in the schools she controlled, the Sisters of the Blessed Sacrament should travel to the hinterlands, searching out and enrolling only "true" Indian children.

It was not, however, the practice of the Sisters of the Blessed Sacrament to accept Native American or African American women into the congregation. Given Drexel's forceful conviction that only through intermarriage of races could human society come to commonality, this decision appeared discordant. According to the oral history of the Sisters of the Blessed Sacrament, the mother superior of the Sisters of the Holy Family, an African American congregation in New Orleans, had personally asked Drexel not to admit women of color to the novitiate at Cornwells Heights. This Holy Family sister reasoned that if such were permitted, the congregations founded by women of color, already struggling with few members and small funding, would never be able to recruit sufficient sisters. Whether this is accurate or not, the 19th-century admission ban did not mesh with the history of Drexel's sweeping initiatives for people of color.

She was enthusiastic about the efforts of a priest in South Dakota to establish a religious congregation of Sioux women, and offered to lend personnel for that venture. She also applauded the work of Mother Margaret Mary Healy Murphy, a well-to-do Texas widow, who organized a sisterhood for the education of people of color. Katharine traveled deep into the Lone Star State to visit the schools of these Sisters of the Holy Ghost, whose foundress from the outset had

Mother Mary Katharine Drexel (right) and Mother Francis Xavier visited with Arizona Navajo families in 1920.

Photograph courtesy of Sisters of the Blessed Sacrament, Bensalem, Pennsylvania.

expected Mexican American women to be part of her convent.

In 1935 Drexel suffered a severe heart attack and retired to the infirmary of the convent in Pennsylvania. She had suffered from fragile health since 1911, but this second illness ended her chances to visit with her religious sisters in New Mexico and Arizona. Never again well enough to travel to the West, which she loved, she spent her remaining years as an administrator.

Through all her convent years, she remained extremely close to her sister Louise and her brother-in-law, Edward Morrell. Edward and Louise Morrell devoted themselves to philanthropy as thoroughly as did Mother Katharine. They were well informed about her western activities, conferred with her about plans, and worried about the exhausting schedule that had led to her ill health. Together the couple focused their charities on schools for African Americans, as had the deceased older sister, Elizabeth.

While Drexel had always worked closely with the Catholic Bureau for Indians, she remained reluctant to

be totally forthcoming about her finances. She watched her investments and was unwilling that anyone should know exactly how much money she had or how it was dispersed. In addition, she was hesitant to turn over the administration of the congregation to others, only gradually releasing various matters to other sisters.

Drexel died in 1955, at the age of 98. By the terms of her father's will, with no living grandchildren to Francis Drexel, the remainder of the fortune reverted to Catholic institutions in the Philadelphia area. Although the injustice of this arrangement was negotiated to a more equitable settlement, the Sisters of the Blessed Sacrament continued their work among people of color under conditions more closely associated with the spirit of poverty exhibited by their foundress than the familial wealth from which she came.

Drexel's activities as a social reformer aligned with the emergence of the Progressive era. Like many American women of the late 19th and early 20th centuries, she sought direct and specific ways in which to contribute to the improvement of society. She approached her work with a sense of optimism and an expectation of success, underscored by her religious convictions. Using her business acumen, great wealth, forceful character, and personal moral compass, she forged the direction of Catholic education for children of color. These same qualities allowed her to reach out to young Catholic women through a religious congregation, giving them a legitimate way in which to find meaningful employment, define their personal social activism, travel into the far reaches of the West, and participate in the progressive reforms of the day.

Those communities served by the sisters also drew from her contact. From their first chances for work and schooling at Drexel schools, Native people initiated relationships that would prove to have far-reaching results. Together with the sisters, Indians in many locations engaged in culture exchanges that have been little understood. They knew clearly what they hoped to gain from the mission schools. Although that perception may have been overlooked by some of their nun patrons in the 19th century, Native people had an institutional setting from which to articulate their cultural views, as minority people of the 20th century reformulated their sense of community identity and their expectations as citizens.

In the 1960s, in part inspired by the reforms of Vatican II, the Sisters of the Blessed Sacrament also reexamined their social mission, making changes that reflected the emergence of a new style of Catholic action by nuns. In the 20th century, some women of color entered the Sisters of the Blessed Sacrament, and in the 1980s an African American woman, Sister Juliana Haynes, led the congregation.

In 1988 Drexel was beatified in ceremonies at the Vatican, where American Indians danced on the altar of St. Peter's Basilica and the Navajo language echoed through the ancient edifice for the first time. In 2000 Mother Mary Katharine Drexel, an adopted daughter of the American West, was declared a saint by the Roman Catholic church.

—Anne M. Butler

SUGGESTED READINGS

Baldwin, Lou. *A Call to Sanctity: The Formation and Life of Mother Katherine Drexel.* Philadelphia, PA: Catholic Standard and Times, 1987.

Butler, Anne M. "Mother Katharine Drexel: Spiritual Visionary for the West," in Glenda Riley and Richard W. Etulain, eds., *By Grit and Grace: Eleven Women Who Shaped the American West.* Golden, CO: Fulcrum, 1997, 198-220.

Duffey, Sister Consuela Marie. *Katherine Drexel: A Biography.* Bensalem, PA: Mother Katharine Drexel Guild, 1987.

DRIVERS, WOMEN

The automobile made its first appearance in the United States in 1893. Karl Benz and Gottlieb Daimler exhibited the Duryea model at the Chicago World's Fair along with European makes. There were many different types of automobiles built during this early time period, from electric to steam, but it was the ability to be personally transported without benefit of animal power that characterized them all. The year 1897 marked the effective start of the automobile industry in the United States. By 1900 there were already 8,000 cars registered in the United States, although that same year the Census Bureau lumped automobile manufacturing in a miscellaneous category, with the production output being only 4,192. By 1908 production rose to 65,000, due in part to Henry Ford and the birth of his Model T. The increase in automobile availability at a reasonable price contributed to its widespread acceptance among both men and women.

Only 1 year after the effective start of the automobile industry in the United States, the first licenses to drive were required. Among the first people to become licensed was a woman. The name of that first licensed driver has been lost to history, and it was likely not a woman, but fortunately, licensed or not, we do know the name of the first woman motorist: Genevra Delphine Mudge. Genevra drove a Waverly Electric automobile in New York in 1898. There is some dispute as to who the actual first woman motorist was, since there are other accounts listing Daisy Post, a niece of Mrs. Frederick Vanderbilt, as being the first woman driver to appear in public, but the year was 1900, 2 years after Genevra. With the likely honor of being the first woman motorist, it is of little surprise that Genevra also holds the titles, or has achieved recognition, for being the first woman race driver and the first woman to have an automobile accident. As for the first women on record to have received a license to drive in the United States, the list is short: Anna

Rainsford French, of Washington, D.C., was awarded a Steam Engineer's License, Locomobile Class, on March 22, 1900; Mrs. John Howell Phillips received her license some 2 months earlier in Chicago; and also in Chicago, 13-year-old Jeanette Lindstrom, who indicated she had been driving since she was 12, received her license. It did not take too many more years for the first Woman's Motoring Club to be founded and for women to take to the road in a grand manner.

TOURING

Women began touring as early as 1905, when Mrs. Newton J. Cuneo of New York appeared as the only female driver in the first Glidden Tour. A few years later, in 1909, Alice Ramsey, president of the Woman's Motoring Club, and three companions, Nettie Powell, Margaret Atwood, and Hermine Jones, drove a Maxwell touring car from New York west to San Francisco in less than 60 days. These four women proved themselves to be quite capable as they managed to keep their car running, change tires along the way, and perhaps most notably, find their way on unmarked roads. An article titled "What a Woman Can Do With an Auto," written by Robert Sloss in 1910, noted that the women demonstrated "completely their ability to manage and care for their own machines 'en route' without any assistance from the stronger sex."

Alice Ramsey remained an active driver after her historic trip, including in later years organizing the Red Cross Motor Corps for Camp Merritt in DuMont, New Jersey, during World War I. After moving west to Covina, California, she took many trips to national parks in the United States, taking her children and grandchildren along. Alice made at least 30 more trips across the country, never sharing the driving responsibilities with her husband, John, since John, a congressman, never learned to drive.

In 1960 Alice Ramsey received the titles of Woman Motorist of the Century from the American Automobile Association and First Lady of Automobile Travel from the Automobile Manufacturers Association.

RACING

From touring, the next logical step was into racing, and women were no strangers in this endeavor either. Mrs. Andrew Cuneo had already won several races between 1905 and 1908 and was being urged to drive cars with which men had earned recognition on the racing circuit. "Racing with such experts as DePalma, Robertson, Strang, Bruman, Ryall, and others, she beat the last named three in every event she entered, and beat Robertson in all but one. She thus won the national amateur championship and five other valuable prizes. This would never have been the end of Mrs. Cuneo's racing victories over male competitors had not the American Automobile Association shortly afterward adopted a rule that no woman should in the future be allowed to drive, or even ride, in a car in any of their contests.

Among other notable women racers of the early years is silent film actress Anita King, who may hold the distinction of being the first woman race driver on the West Coast. King gained celebrity status for her daring exploits behind the wheel of an automobile, giving up the sport only after she was almost killed while driving at high speeds at a race in Phoenix.

In addition to her race car driving, King also holds the distinction of being the first person, man or woman, to complete a transcontinental journey alone, driving from Los Angeles, north to San Francisco, and across the country to New York. Her travels were well recorded and reported in the *New York Dramatic Mirror*, beginning with an article in August titled "Lone Girl to Cross Continent" and ending in October with "Anita King Arrives: Paramount Girl Completes Daring Cross Country Trip in Auto."

HOLLYWOOD AND THE WOMAN DRIVER

Anita King was not the only silent film actress to take to the roads both on and off screen. As early as 1908, Hollywood produced a film titled *An Auto Heroine*, in which a young woman takes the place of her kidnapped father and drives his automobile to victory. Although history did not record the name of the actress in that film, only a few years later, Mary Pickford, America's Sweetheart, would earn the distinction of being the driver in what would be the first of many great Hollywood movie car chases for her role in *A Beast at Bay*.

Mary Pickford played an important role on screen and off when it came to encouraging women to get behind the wheel. In 1915, in response to a question submitted to her Daily Talks column, she wrote, "I see no reason why a woman shouldn't drive her own car. I drive mine, and I drive through the crowded streets of New York. You know the men say that women shouldn't drive cars because they can't keep their heads in time of accident. I don't believe that. If a woman has poise and is not nervous she is ready for any emergency." Other Hollywood actresses to take to the road included Mabel Normand (who wrote, directed, and starred in *Mabel at the Wheel),* Bessie Eyton, Pearl White, and Gloria Swanson. Pearl White was described as "an ardent suffragette, warm-hearted, high-spirited and very independent," and characterized the kind of woman who reveled in and embraced the automobile, but it was Gloria Swanson who provided us with the most vivid description of what it was like for a woman to learn how to drive in those early years when she wrote, "I loved the feeling of all that power, frightening though it was. No wonder Wally [Beery] was happy-go-lucky. He'd found the secret of how to escape. And now he was sharing it with me. I had lots more to learn before I could drive by myself, but I would always remember that first thrilling Sunday. It was almost as exciting as being engaged."

SOCIAL IMPACT OF WOMEN DRIVERS

It did not require status as an actress or a racer to be able to drive an automobile and experience its impact firsthand. Whenever women got behind the wheel, their lives changed. Young women soon discovered that the automobile offered more comfort and privacy for them and their dates than the front porch of their parent's home. That may not represent the greatest social impact that women experienced as a result of the automobile, but it is certainly among the most enduring.

The numbers of women taking to the road increased, and by 1926 so many women were driving cars that the topic became a monthly feature called The Woman at the Wheel by George W. Sutton in *Pictorial Review.* The very first column discussed the importance of motoring to the professional woman, declaring that it meant "more to her than to almost any other type of person." In addition, the article offered her assistance in choosing a car to suit her needs, but it also concluded, "The designing of cars for the modern business woman is an important consideration in the motor world."

A later column focused on the introduction of the small car and how "ideal they are for the everyday activities of the American woman, be she housewife or professional woman—or both." The article highlighted the features of the new automobiles and explained that "these were all-important considerations with the woman who is managing a family budget, who does the family marketing, takes the children to school, and wants to do her personal social calling with the minimum amount of effort, traffic difficulty and cost."

The final article in the series focused on the importance of the automobile to the homemaker of 1926. "The home-maker today without personal automotive transportation is not living and working real efficiency. She is missing the freedom of action, the labor-saving, money-saving mobility, the broadening of her social mental horizon, and the harmless, but psychologically important uplift to her price—all of which come with the ownership or sponsorship of a car."

Women taking to the streets to drive their automobiles was not simply an urban phenomenon. The automobile allowed farm communities to send their children to town schools where they had better schools and more choices. In addition, it allowed farm families to shop more frequently and with greater variety at the same time it provided access for the urban housewife to fresh milk, dairy, and produce purchased directly from the farmers.

In addition to the greater social impact of the automobile on women, there are several articles providing anecdotal evidence of the positive impact learning how to drive had on women. One such article, published in June 1925, provides great detail about how learning how to drive enabled a young woman to rise "from almost complete physical wreckage to perfect health through the aid of an automobile." The author concludes that after years of living on pills and medication, "the combination of an automobile and outdoor exercise in the country which the car enables one to get, is more beneficial to the promotion of good health than all the possible mental and physical remedies that you buy in a box."

BUSES AND TRUCKS

Pioneer women of the road were not just those who took to the automobile for touring, racing, or even to thrill the movie-going audiences of the early 1900s. With all the concern over women behind the wheel of an automobile, it is understandable that Helen Schultz, founder of the first woman-owned bus line, was greeted with protests when she opened Red Ball Transportation Company in 1922. Surprisingly, the protests were not about her ability to drive a bus but came instead from railroad corporations fearing competition. Like many of her contemporaries, Helen capitalized on her newsworthy image as an attractive young woman and was named Iowa Bus Queen by the local paper. She sold the company in 1930 for $200,000 and retired.

Further south, and a few years later, Lillie Elizabeth McGee Drennan became the first woman truck driver when she received her commercial truck driver's license in Texas in 1929. Lillie drove and operated the Drennan Truck Company for more than 23 years. Not unlike some of the other early women drivers, Lillie had a colorful personality and achieved some fame or notoriety as a result. Dressed in khaki pants, work boots, and a 10-gallon hat, she sported a loaded revolver by her side whenever she drove. She never let anyone become one of her drivers without training them herself, often kicking them in the seat of their pants threatening to pistol-whip them if they violated her rules. In spite of or perhaps because of her strong personality, Lillie was able to successfully recruit women truck drivers to the quartermaster corps in World War II, for which she received praise from the Army.

CONCLUSION

By 1939 there were 40 million licensed drivers in America, but only one fourth of them were women, in spite of the fact that in the same year, the Automobile Association of America encouraged women to learn to drive well so that they "gain confidence, quickness, and speed." Young women, as well as young men, still see a license to drive as being one step closer to freedom, so in one sense, not much has changed from the way Gloria Swanson felt about it when she wrote, "I'd never had such a thrill. Nothing existed in the whole world but the power of that car. The tiniest turn of the wheel and the whole thing responded. I had the feeling I could go anywhere and nothing could stop me."

—Mary Adams

SUGGESTED READINGS

Autoshop Online. "Automotive 101, Automotive History." Retrieved from www.autoshop-online.com/auto101/histtext.html.

Drew, William M. "Speeding Sweethearts, Part VI." *New York Dramatic Mirror*, September 1, 1915, 29.

Drew, William M. "Speeding Sweethearts, Part VII." Mary Pickford, Answers to Correspondents, Daily Talks. *Detroit News*, December 11, 1915.

Drew, William M. "Speeding Sweethearts, Part I." Gloria Swanson, *Swanson on Swanson*. New York: Random House, 1980, 56-57.

Drivers.com. Retrieved from www.drivers.com/Top_Driving_Women.html.

Ferrar, Ann. *Hear Me Roar: Women, Motorcycles, and the Rapture of the Road* (2d ed.). North Conway, NH: Whitehorse Press, 2001.

Lady Truck Drivers.com. "The First Lady Truck Driver." Retrieved from www.ladytruckdrivers.com/firstladytrckdriver.htm.

Lane, Rose Wilder. "Drive Like a Woman!" *Good Housekeeping*, January 1939.

McConnell, Curt. *A Reliable Car and a Woman Who Knows It: The First Coast-To-Coast Auto Trips by Women, 1899-1916*. Jefferson, NC: McFarland, 2000.

McFerren, Martha. *Women in Cars*. Kansas City, MO: Helicon Nine Editions, 1992.

Moline, Norman T. *Mobility and the Small Town 1900-1930*. Chicago: University of Chicago, 1971.

Nauen, Elinor. *Ladies, Start Your Engines*. New York: Faber & Faber, 1996.

Root, Marilyn. *Women at the Wheel: 42 Stories of Freedom, Fanbelts and the Lure of the Open Road*. Naperville, IL: Sourcebooks Trade, 1999.

Scharff, Virginia. *Taking the Wheel: Women and the Coming of the Motor Age*. Albuquerque: University of New Mexico Press, 1992.

Sloss, Robert Sloss. "What a Woman Can Do With an Auto," *Outing* (April, 1910).

U.S. Department of Transportation, Women in Transportation. "Bus Operators." Retrieved from www.fhwa.dot.gov/wit/bus.htm.

Your Car: A Magazine of Romance, Fact and Fiction, 1925

DUNIWAY, ABIGAIL SCOTT (1834-1915)

Born and raised in the farm town of Groveland, Illinois, Abigail Jane Scott, called Jenny by her family, traveled the Oregon Trail in 1852. Her journal told of the spectacular scenery and horrible tragedy. Along the way her mother and younger brother died of cholera.

custody, and equal pay for equal work. This attracted the attention of Susan B. Anthony, whose speaking tour in the Northwest she managed. In 1873 Abigail helped found the Oregon Equal Suffrage Association and became its president.

Her work was a family affair, both pro and con. With the help of her five sons, she published the *New Northwest* until 1887. Not everyone supported her, however. Harvey Scott, her brother and editor of *The Oregonian,* opposed her views on woman suffrage and published editorials contrary to her.

Abigail did not limit herself to Oregon. She worked tirelessly on behalf of women throughout Washington and Idaho as well. Remembered as the Mother of Woman Suffrage she died on October 11, 1915, in Portland.

—Neal Lynch

Abigail married Benjamin Duniway in 1853 and started a family that would grow to include six children. The early years were spent as a homesteader and a schoolteacher. When her husband suffered a debilitating accident on their farm, Abigail ran a boarding school and opened a millinery (hats and accessories) store to support the family.

In 1859 Abigail published *Captain Gray's Company,* chronicling her journey across country. It was not only her first novel, but it was the first novel published in Oregon. In 1871 she began publishing her own weekly newspaper, the *New Northwest,* dedicated to a wide range of women's topics. In it she serialized her many novels. She also published responses to letters written to government officials addressing woman suffrage. Her writings and public appearances addressed civil disabilities, including property rights, the right to engage in contracts, child

SUGGESTED READINGS

Morrison, Dorothy. *Ladies Were Not Expected: Abigail Scott Duniway and Women's Rights*. New York: Antheneum, 1977.

Moynihan, Ruth Baines. *Rebel for Rights: Abigail Scott Duniway*. New Haven, CT: Yale University Press, 1983.

Oregon Blue Book. "Notable Oregonians: Abigail Scott Duniway, Women's Rights Pioneer." Retrieved from bluebook.state.or.us/notable/notduniway.htm.

Shein, Debra. *Feminist Voices and Visions*, "Abigail Scott Duniway Exhibit Text." Retrieved from libweb.uoregon.edu/exhibits/feminist-voices/duntext.html.

Smith, Bridget E., ed. "Women Win the Right to Vote." *Historical Gazette (3)*5, August 20, 1925. Retrieved from www.aracnet.com/~histgaz/abigail.htm.

E

EAGLE WOMAN (1820-1888)

Born along the banks of the Missouri River in 1820, Eagle Woman That All Look At grew to be one of the greatest chiefs and peacemakers of the western Sioux people. With her parents, Two Lance and Rosy Light of Dawn, Eagle Woman spent her early years growing up on the western plains of modern-day South Dakota far from contact with white civilization. However, the influx of whites into the Plains during the 1830s and 1840s had a profound effect on Eagle Woman and her people. Following the death of her parents, she married Honore Picotte, a general agent for the American Fur Company. They had two daughters, Lulu and Louise. In 1850 she married a second time to Charles Galpin, an employee of the Northwest Fur Company, who used his connections to the Sioux people to become a prominent trader at the Grand River Agency. Her second marriage resulted in two more daughters, Annie and Alma, and four sons. Galpin's death on November 30, 1869, allowed Eagle Woman to blossom as a leader among her people.

Following her husband's death, Eagle Woman assumed her husband's role as a trader on the Sioux reservation, the first woman to assume this position. While noted for her generosity, she was also committed to seeing her people sustain themselves independently of the white man. Above all she believed that the Sioux must live peacefully with the whites or face annihilation. Her commitment to peace caused her to shun trade in arms and ammunition. In 1872 she was instrumental in getting tribal leaders to leave nonreservation lands and tour the East Coast. The purpose of the tour was to demonstrate the military might of the U.S. Army and to encourage the Sioux to accept white ways and uphold the territorial boundaries that had been set with the Treaty of Fort Laramie in 1868.

When gold was discovered in the Black Hills in 1874, the influx of prospectors threatened the fragile peace that existed between the Sioux and the whites. Eagle Woman worked tirelessly to maintain peace between her people and the invading whites. When the Sioux War broke out in 1876, the government refused to provide provisions for the Sioux reservation until the tribe had agreed to cede the Black Hills. Government commissioners attempted to force the Sioux to accept a new treaty that would have ceded the disputed lands to the United States. While Eagle Woman played a role as a translator for her people during these negotiations, she did not support the Standing Rock treaty. This treaty was later deemed fraudulent because it did not contain the required signatures of three fourths of the adult male Indians of the tribe. When the Sioux War ended in the early 1880s, Eagle Woman again played an instrumental role in easing the transition to reservation living for her people. On December 18, 1888, she died peacefully at the home of her daughter.

—Vanessa Anne Gunther

SUGGESTED READING

Gray, John S. "The Story of Mrs. Picotte-Galpin, a Sioux Heroine." *Montana: The Magazine of Western History 36* (Summer 1986): 2-21.

EDUCATION

Women have been closely connected to the rise of education in all areas and eras of western history. Erratic patterns, however, frequently marked the process of building educational institutions. Uneven distribution of the population, lack of public funding, discrimination against people of color, and conflicting cultural values often interfered with the steady rise of pedagogy. Women, nonetheless, as teachers and students, remained central to the emergence of the western educational system.

Anxiety about frontier education emerged almost as quickly as 18th-century pioneers turned their backs on the eastern seaboard. Trappers, explorers, traders, and families ignored the ineffective English attempt to block western migration through the Proclamation Line of 1763 and crossed the Appalachian Mountains, heading west in search of good fortune. They moved into areas with few, if any, institutions in place to meet the needs of a new population. Those who remained in the Atlantic communities fretted about what they perceived as a weakened hold over the social and political behaviors of this rapidly growing collection of frontiersmen and frontierswomen.

Concerns in this time of the New Republic centered on a fear that the western settlers would detach themselves from their earlier allegiance to eastern institutions and the men who administered them. Great distances, lack of communication, backwoods malcontents, and foreign influences were all viewed as threats to the national loyalty of frontier people. Thus disconnected, easterners could only imagine the lawlessness and Godlessness that would result. With fear of political upheaval and social debauchery of every kind, it was not surprising that the proposed solution to this impending doom took shape in widespread advocacy for Christian education. With access to biblical teachings through universal literacy as a linchpin, easterners could envision a means for reinforcing the political and cultural standards of the era, despite the many miles between themselves and western communities.

On the other side of this dilemma, the frontier residents, especially those clearing land and building family farms, perhaps blanched at descriptions of their "wildness." Their own vision of a life sustained by family working together with common cultural values jarred with eastern depictions of radical social and political behaviors. With that aside, in small communities they welcomed educational opportunities for the growing numbers of white children born in the West. It is likely that they quite appreciated the spirit of the Land Ordinance of 1785, which provided that proceeds from one section of a newly surveyed township be set aside for public education. Although the implementation of that requirement varied, its codification set in place an official acknowledgment that schooling should be central to western life. Furthermore, the Protestant campaign of the early 19th century that promised a Bible for every home in the Ohio Valley added to the attempt to spread education more evenly across the frontier, as did a plan to send eastern women teachers into the Old Northwest. A workforce of women educators, unlike the largely male corps of an earlier era, suggested that teachers could be treated as short-time workers, forced from the classroom at marriage, given limited compensation, and subsequently never expect or receive the status of trained professionals.

In the West beyond the Mississippi River, education, like all its social and political counterparts, was shaped by eastern-generated attitudes, as well as a multitude of regional and local factors. These kept education something of a controversial subject, particularly in matters of religious disagreement within communities. Invariably, pedagogy involved issues of race, class, and gender, making the growth of education part of the fabric of the women's West.

Unlike the East, with its collection of private academies and colleges, in the West public school systems eventually prevailed. This does not suggest that the West was devoid of private education, only that in the main, public institutions, especially at the college and university level, became the norm. In terms of women's education, the West did not produce counterparts to the famous Seven Sisters colleges of the East.

In the West, public schools became the responsibility of the community, guaranteeing a tradition of local control by local school boards and local citizens. This led frontier people to a number of educational questions, including how to finance local schooling, who should be taxed to do so, how to build the curriculum, and how to agree on its philosophical underpinnings. None of these questions was ever given systematic and sufficient consideration in a broad regional context, leaving the development of education to be based on the expedient and often least costly choice of the moment.

A 19th-century Idaho teacher with her students and dog.

Source: A-1235, Special Collection and Archives, Utah State University, Logan, Utah.

In general, Americans were content to think of education and teachers in a stereotypical framework that sidestepped serious and challenging intellectual concerns. Rather, Americans relied on the image of the western schoolhouse—a crude one-room shack, where pupils of all ages gathered under the supervision of an idealistic young woman—as the way to understand frontier education. In this rough environment, with her often unruly pupils, the teacher brought the qualities of the "gentle tamer" to a frontier world. Winslow Homer, in his 1871 painting *The Country School,* captured the flavor of America's one-room schoolhouses, at least as Americans liked to believe they existed. In many ways, Homer's stereotype was not so far off the mark, at least in physical setting, and examples of such institutions can be found in many western locales, including Montana, Idaho, and Utah, where one-room schoolhouses operated into the 20th century.

There has been slight attention paid to the professional training of the teachers in these schools, training that for many years remained haphazard, without overarching regional standards and regulations. Rather, the "frontier teacher" has survived as an American icon, suggesting that young, unmarried easterners descended on "wild West" towns not only to teach reading and arithmetic but also to inculcate children and their ill-behaved elders with "civilizing" graces. This womanly personification of eastern cultural values has been consistently reinforced by American literature and film. For example, Owen Wister's *The Virginian* relied heavily on the importance of the graceful eastern teacher, in the character of Molly Wood, who left Vermont for a classroom and ultimately a cowboy in Wyoming.

The credentials of the teacher, her career goals, and her motivations remained hazy in the fictional and cinematic treatments. Yet these elements illuminate much about western education, the women who stood at the front of primitive classrooms, and those who promoted the importance of women teachers for the West.

Catharine Beecher (1800-1878), of the prominent social activist Beecher family, played a major part in designing a teacher preparatory program for the West. In 1846 her brother Edward Beecher, in an address to the Ladies Society for the Promotion of Education at the West, had warned that the Roman Catholic church intended to convert the West by "the power of the female mind." Catharine Beecher, in agreement with her brother's fears, determined that a well-formulated procedure for sending women educators to frontier regions should be introduced. Drawing on her interest in women's education, her belief in the moral superiority of women, and her own anti-Catholic sentiments, Beecher envisioned a program that would direct teachers away from the limited eastern job openings to western employment opportunities. Fearful that Catholic schools would overtake western education, and convinced of the importance of Protestant dominance under the rubric of an evangelical tradition, Beecher organized the National Popular Board of Education, which sought to recruit and train young women, steeped in Protestant values, for teaching careers in the West.

The board of education, minus Beecher, who had moved on to other projects, established a 6-week training institute at Hartford, Connecticut. There, under the supervision of a widely respected teacher, Nancy Swift (1801-1884), volunteers, mainly from New England, passed through a tuition-free session designed to prepare them for western living and find them an appropriate match for employment. While the number of women who relocated to the West was never great, hovering around the 200 mark, the teachers' experiences suggested that western living could offer a solid future for single women in the 19th century. For example, most of the women teachers undertook their journey—from train to steamer to stagecoach—to the West entirely alone, turning on its head the notion that in Victorian America no "respectable" woman would make an overnight trip unescorted by a companion.

Single women who accepted the challenge to relocate by themselves in distant western regions did so for a variety of reasons. Unmarried women, assessing the discouraging marriage possibilities about them, especially those from families of limited means, needed to be self-supporting—for them, employment

was a necessity, rather than a luxury. Some of these young women expected to be major contributors to the well-being of their families and intended to send monetary contributions back to elderly or infirm parents. Others wished to remove themselves from a place where unpleasant memories lingered—family frictions, broken relationships, and deceased loved ones. Undergirding all their motivations, convictions about the importance of teaching, the value of a "correct" education, the special role of women as moral guardians of children, or the chance to live out in practical ways one's religious belief fueled most who headed into the West.

The western conditions that greeted the teachers were often quite harsh, and the 2-year teaching requirement written into most contracts must have seemed daunting at the outset. Some towns had not actually built the schoolhouse, so that the first classes took place with makeshift arrangements—under the shelter of a grape arbor or by the river. Women teachers who had a school building discovered they were to furnish the classroom, gather the children's supplies, and serve as the janitor—hauling water, sweeping out bugs, and stoking the pot-bellied stove. Indoor plumbing was nonexistent. Winter meant cold classes in the poorly insulated buildings, while summer brought sweltering heat. Harassment from itinerant passersby was common, and an occasional teacher kept a loaded weapon as protection for herself and the students or as defense against those overly exuberant frontier pupils who brought their guns to class.

The youngest students in the schoolhouse might only be 5 years of age, while the oldest could be in their early 20s. Student skills were as uneven as their ages, as was their deportment. These teachers could use corporal punishment, as was the style of school discipline in the 19th century. Permitted to use a rod and being able to do so with some of the older and rambunctious students could be two different issues. Accordingly, young teachers were encouraged to maintain a strict demeanor from the outset of the school session if they were to avoid humiliating showdowns with their larger charges.

Confronted with so many grade levels and possibly 25 to 50 scholars in one room, teachers had to prepare all academic subjects across a broad spectrum. With textbooks and tablets in short supply, western teachers depended on their wit and ingenuity to provide materials to be used in daily lessons. A chalkboard, the Bible, and *McGuffey's Reader* were standard equipment, supplemented by mail order catalogs, magazines, and an occasional map. The classroom routines were rigid—patriotic and religious opening exercises, followed by silent seat work for those at their desks while the teacher guided another group through its oral recitations.

By the 1890s, in return for this wide sweeping set of responsibilities, a teacher might earn $40 a month. Some districts paid only a per head/per diem rate, so the compensation dropped during those weeks farm families kept children at home for agricultural chores or because the winter roads were impassable. When trained teachers were not available, local girls, 16 or 17 years of age, could secure teaching employment with little academic preparation, and their poor wages reflected that lack of professional education. Some rural counties, for example in Texas, could only afford to pay salaries for 4 months, placing an unmarried teacher in economic jeopardy for the greater part of the year. All teachers knew that in times of extreme fiscal hardship, already poor counties might suspend wages or offer them in the form of local agricultural products.

Women teachers faced constraints outside the classroom, as well. Many districts required the teacher to board with a local family. Presented as a safety factor for the teacher and a money-saving strategy for the town, forced residence in a family struck many young women as an excuse to monitor their personal conduct. Furthermore, they were inconvenienced by frequent moves, when individual families chose to limit these domestic arrangements to 3 or 4 months at a time. Some teaching contracts spelled out a number of prohibited behaviors for teachers. For example, a teacher could not smoke, drink alcoholic beverages, be out alone after dark, or accept unchaperoned social invitations from men.

While teachers were watched over, they were not necessarily cared for in their living arrangements. Some suffered from ill health brought on by adverse physical conditions. As single women, they lacked the concerned attention they might have enjoyed if living with their own families or a spouse. Some withdrew early from their assignments or returned to the East at the completion of the contract.

Frontier teaching, however, was not all a negative experience. In fact, it energized women in their pursuit of independence and professional advancement, as evidenced by the steady increase in women schoolteachers by the 1890s. Those women who had come to

the West in part because of a desire for adventure were not disappointed. The travel, the environment, the new cultural atmosphere, and the diverse responsibilities all offered young women a way in which to test their abilities and to accumulate impressive personal accomplishments. In some climates, the out-of-doors, fresh air lifestyle far outweighed the medical hazards of the tuberculosis-ridden East. If they cared to marry and have families, teachers found at least an interesting pool of bachelors in the West and could wed quickly, shifting from a marginal unmarried status into positions of social influence. Although most teaching contracts called for the dismissal of a teacher once she married, many communities found this to be impractical, and immediately rehired the teacher/bride so that the local school could continue. The cumulative effects were positive for those teachers who gained in self-confidence, improved their health, came to appreciate their own economic power, contributed to society as community builders, and set professional goals for themselves, as well as for the daughters they raised to become the next generation of achieving western women.

These Protestant teachers had counterparts among Roman Catholic sisters who came to the West in the 19th century. By 1890 possibly 6,000 to 9,000 professed sisters lived in the lands west of the Mississippi River. Most worked in social service areas, covering for the public institutions not yet well established by state and territorial governments.

Since the 1700s Catholic priests and bishops had begged various religious congregations of women to send sisters for missions among a scattered Catholic flock. Catholic immigrants added their voices to the requests, insisting that their children needed religious schools run by sisters. Especially after 1850, nuns from France emigrated to Texas, from Ireland to the Dakotas, from Belgium to California, and from Canada to the Pacific Northwest. Sisters of the Holy Names, Daughters of Charity, Sisters of Mercy, Benedictines, Dominicans, Ursulines, and Franciscans spread to the far reaches of the West, carrying with them the curriculum and values of Catholic education.

These female educators also changed the face of western womanhood. Living outside the structures of traditional family relationships, unmarried, and traveling in tiny groups of four and five, Catholic nuns over time brought schools, hospitals, day-care homes, orphanages, and colleges to the American West. The early western life of these women, who in many cases

Surrounded by secular and religious symbols of education, Sister Antonina Hayden, OP, reads in her classroom in Eagle Grove, Iowa.

Source: Archives, Sinisinawa Dominicans, Sinisinawa, Wisconsin.

became regional heroines, was marked by great physical hardship. Such a heroine was Mother Joseph Pariseau (1823-1902), pioneer teacher and administrator, a member of the Sisters of Providence from Montreal, Canada. Mother Joseph's impact on the Pacific Northwest was so extensive and widely recognized that the State of Washington chose her image to be one of its two sent to Statuary Hall in the U.S. House of Representatives of the Capitol Building in Washington, D.C.

Like secular teachers, nuns often found that the small school, promised by the clergy during the mission negotiations with a mother superior, was more abstract than real. In a number of frontier regions,

missioned sisters moved into abandoned shacks, muddy basements, or old chicken coops until suitable housing could be constructed. The sisters had accepted the missions, confident they would be able to earn a living from their various enterprises, all based on social service. The town's promised financial support did not always materialize, and sisters, expected to be self-sufficient in their mission houses, hurried to establish a way to make a living. A small school required little overhead to open, and brought the sisters income, although as for the secular teachers, that payment sometimes took the form of vegetables or chickens.

Most congregations were enjoined from teaching boys past the age of 10, permitting the sisters to maintain a mixed gender elementary school. Tuition receipts were negligible in these grammar schools, so the sisters drew in wealthier families by opening a secondary academy for girls, one that might also be a boarding facility. These female academies proved to be extremely popular, especially before western governments had built a satisfactory network of public schools. Families, both Catholic and non-Catholic, sought out these "young ladies' seminaries." In Utah, Brigham Young, leader of the Church of Jesus Christ of Latter-Day Saints, sent several of his daughters to be educated by the Sisters of the Holy Cross at St. Mary's of the Wasatch Academy, as did a number of other Mormon families.

In these schools, parents expected their daughters to be educated in social graces, but also with a suitable academic curriculum. The courses of study included several foreign languages, literature, science, mathematics, composition, declamation, religious training, and classical music, both vocal and instrumental. The content of each discipline was more intellectually weighty than might appear by a reading of the school catalog. The academies were noted for their musical performances, dramatic presentations, and poetry recitations, which were widely attended by the community and described in detail by the local press.

In 1893, a Texas widow, Mother Margaret Mary Healy Murphy (1833-1907), established a religious congregation solely dedicated to the education of African American and Mexican American children. In a political and cultural environment dangerously hostile to the advancement of black Americans and where it proved impossible to retain white teachers, Murphy staffed her schools by recruiting young women from Ireland for her religious order. It was also Murphy's practice to look for Mexican and Mexican American women to join her religious congregation and teaching staff, and she had some success in this area.

Few women of color entered congregations with an Anglo-European grounding, perhaps because of cultural discomfort or direct discrimination. Convent-bound African American women educated as school girls in the West joined the Holy Family Sisters in New Orleans, Louisiana, or the Oblate Sisters of Providence in Baltimore, Maryland. After the Civil War, these African American sister/teachers accepted missions in the West, opening orphanages and schools and expanding the educational opportunities of disadvantaged children.

Schools for Native American children were sustained largely through government contracts and by the direct philanthropy of Mother Mary Katharine Drexel (1858-1955), a Philadelphia heiress who used her fortune to build Catholic schools for children of color in the South and the West. Beginning in 1888 and until her death in 1955, Drexel supported the educational efforts of nuns teaching among many different Native people, including the Cheyennes, Arapaho, Osage, Chippewa, Nez Perce, Cherokees, Blackfeet, Navajo, Sioux, and Pueblo Indians. She articulated a strong respect for the dynamics within Native families, although she remained concerned that the early age of marriage for Indian girls ended their formal education. As the founder of her own religious congregation, the Sisters of the Blessed Sacrament for Colored and Indian People, she sent young white women into the centers of Native culture, where learning flowed in two directions. Two of her most famous and enduring schools were St. Michael's Mission in Arizona and St. Catherine's Convent and Boarding School in New Mexico.

Like African American women, only an occasional Native woman was drawn to a white religious community. In 1885 Father Francis Craft, a missionary at Standing Rock Reservation in the Dakotas, organized a dozen or so Native women into a congregation devoted to teaching, especially English, and rescue work among the Sioux. In less than a decade, several of the sisters had died, others had withdrawn, the venture was near collapse, and the prospects for a flourishing convent of Native women teachers for Native people had dimmed. Some of the former Sioux nuns continued to devote themselves to social service and educational work on the reservation well into the 20th century.

In all areas of the West, reservation schools did not always run smoothly. There were inevitable conflicts between white teachers and Native students over various religious and cultural questions. Catholic sisters often had to answer to Protestant government supervisors, and on occasion those interactions were fractious. Also, when the U.S. government arbitrarily divided the care of reservation schools between Catholic and Protestant missionaries, ill will flared across religious lines, a detriment to the education of Native children.

Some of the problems reflected the early 19th-century anti-Catholic Nativist sentiment that swept through the United States but also the growing pains for all schools that came with greater state regulation and oversight. For example, the Texas Radical School

Law of 1871 instituted a three-part system that graded schools by curriculum content, introduced a graduated salary schedule, and required certification for faculty. When Texas counties hired nuns to teach in public schools, the sisters, like secular teachers, were required to pass these certifying examinations. At the same time, the general trend toward more uniform quality within a school district and the impetus for refining teaching methods that emerged at the end of the 19th century brought many public administrators and nun teachers into a closer alliance.

Teaching orders recognized that the sisters needed to complete university degrees, secure state certificates, and meet curriculum requirements that would lead to accreditation for their schools. Sisters who came to religious life with a university degree and teaching experience immersed themselves in tutoring younger members of the order. During summer vacations, sisters lacking certification prepared for state examinations through study packets and tests sent from the mother house and returned there for grading. In the West, sisters associated themselves with the emerging extension programs of state universities. Mother superiors hired professors from local colleges, priests from nearby seminaries, or lay women from the community to teach evening courses inside the convent. After 1911 many congregations tried to send one or two sisters to summer school at the Catholic University of America in Washington, D.C. Overall, the system was unwieldy, required repeated permissions from the local bishop, and took sisters many years to complete the undergraduate degree.

In part, this circumstance led religious orders to establish their own institutions of higher learning to expedite the education of sisters. An example of this was to be found in the development of health care education through schools of nursing that sisters attached to their frontier hospitals. In South Dakota by 1912 the Presentation Sisters from Ireland operated four hospitals with 3-year nursing programs. As in the elementary and high schools of the West, nuns strove to upgrade curriculum standards of these nursing programs to meet the increasing state and national professionalization of health care. Presentation Sisters, as well as nun-students from other congregations in South Dakota, benefited from the accessibility of a Catholic-sponsored program of nursing instruction. In a larger context, however, the beneficiaries proved to be the young women of South Dakota who wished to pursue careers in medicine. Graduates of the 3-year

program frequently went on to universities for a bachelor of science and/or master's degree in nursing. The outreach planning of the sister educators and the importance of the nursing schools for young women were evident in the Presentations' successful 1942 application to the Cadet Nurse Corps, a federally sponsored World War II project to address the critical shortage of nurses during a time of military crisis. This wartime initiative and the Presentation Sisters' response to growing professionalization brought the medical education of western women into the national arena and elevated the reputation of nursing education in South Dakota.

Given the great distances, rural populations, and various forms of gender discrimination, persevering to secure a formal education gave western women a mark of distinction in American history. Young girls and young women could find educational opportunities in the West, but getting to them and staying in the programs could be quite another matter. Farm families looked to their daughters as domestic workers; schooling had its place, but only if it reinforced cultural values concerning traditional womanhood and not if it drew daughters too far from home or away from their "true future" as wives and mothers. In the urban clusters of the West, more regular elementary education could be found for girls, who even had the chance to complete a secondary program, especially if admitted to one of the private academies. As the public education system of the West took shape, more and more secondary schools routinely admitted young women.

At the same time, the schools largely retained barriers of racial discrimination. Mexican American, Asian American, and African American students, by official policy, attended separate schoolhouses of an inferior level, weakened by lesser funding and fewer resources. Native Americans continued to be educated in a reservation environment or at the Carlisle School for Indians in Pennsylvania. None of these circumstances inherently advanced the education of young women of color from any community. Their greatest relief came from individual teachers, often driven by personal Protestant or Catholic conviction, who saw education to be of importance for both male and female students.

The biggest hurdle for young women, of course, was admission to colleges and universities. In the West, the state institutions more or less moved ahead without objection to the enrollment of women. The

Western women took advantage of classes taught through extension services of local land-grant colleges.

Source: C-0135, Special Collection and Archives, Utah State University, Logan, Utah.

University of Minnesota opened as a coeducational institution in 1851, and by the turn of the century more than half a dozen western state schools had followed.

Yet admission alone did not define the totality of a woman's educational experience. The actual numbers of enrolled women remained slight during the 1800s, and the treatment of female students on western campuses was hardly edifying. Male trustees, male administrators, male faculty, male-centered curriculum, male student body, male athletics, and male clubs all combined to create, at the best, a challenging, at the worst, a defeating, academic life for women. In this environment, the women who persevered, despite special regulations, gender-slanted restrictions, lack of teacher and/or family encouragement, and limited curriculum offerings, truly proved their western mettle.

In this arena of mixed chance, some western women made a significant mark as students and subsequently as educators of other women. For example, the early schooling of Jeannette Rankin (1880-1973) replicated the experiences of many western women. Born into a country family, Rankin attended the public schools of Missoula, Montana. Unlike women who lived hundreds of miles from an institution of higher learning, Rankin benefited from the proximity of the University of Montana at Missoula and graduated from there in 1902. She turned to teaching in the rural schools of Montana, but moved on to other professional employment as a social worker in New York. She returned to the West to attend the University of Washington, Seattle, where she developed a commitment to American politics, especially on issues that concerned women. The first woman elected in her own right to the U.S. House of Representatives, Rankin spent the remainder of her long life as an advocate of several important causes, most of which are linked to the importance of educating American women.

In the 20th century, Barbara Jordan (1936-1996) duplicated the Rankin story, with the added dimensions experienced by a woman of color. Born into the racially segregated society of Houston, Texas, Jordan overcame the long-standing elements of discrimination that had plagued the education of children of color through the history of the Lone Star State. She graduated from Phillis Wheatley Public High School and Texas Southern University, compiling impressive academic and extracurricular records in both institutions. When she graduated from the Boston University School of Law, she might have chosen to remain in the somewhat more racially cordial Northeast. Instead, she returned to her home state and embarked on a political career that saw her elected to the Texas Senate, the first woman ever and first African American since 1883 to do so. She followed her many Texas political successes with election to the U.S. House of Representatives. Upon completion of a highly visible and dramatic national political career, she brought the educational story of western women, Anglo and of color, full cycle by returning to the West and assuming a teaching post at the University of Texas at Austin. There she advanced the respect for education learned as a child in her family, mentoring minority students until her death in 1996.

Clearly, western girls and women carved out remarkable educational experiences in the West, which both helped and hindered their academic progress. The account includes the narratives of hundreds of teachers—Protestant and Catholic—who persisted in the face of physical and intellectual adversity to bring learning to western children of many hues and cultures. It also touches the lives of young women from every culture who found an educational base from which to launch their personal and professional achievements. Out of their lives as educators and students and from their example, in many capacities, rose a new generation of western scholars—young women, who in modern America accept as natural the varied educational selections, public and private, they find in the West.

—Anne M. Butler

SUGGESTED READINGS

Hackett, Sheila. *Dominican Women in Texas: From Ohio to Galveston and Beyond.* Houston, TX: D. Armstrong, 1986.

Hine, Robert V. *The American West: An Interpretive History.* New York: Little, Brown, 1975.

Kaufman, Polly Welts. *Women Teachers on the Frontier.* New Haven, CT: Yale University Press, 1984.

Passet, Joanne E. *Cultural Crusaders: Women Librarians in the American West, 1900-1917.* Albuquerque: University of New Mexico Press, 1994.

Sklar, Kathryn Kish. *Catherine Beecher: A Study in American Domesticity.* New Haven, CT: Yale University Press, 1973.

EHMANN, FREDA (1839-1932)

Born in Germany in 1839, Freda (Loeber) Ehmann became known as the Mother of the California Olive Industry. She made her mark late in life. At age 56 she was poor and had recently buried her husband and 19-year-old daughter. Her only asset was a 20-acre orchard of olive trees she owned with her son, Edwin, near Oroville, California.

Olives were first brought to California by the Franciscan missionaries in the mid-1700s and had flourished in the Mediterranean-like climate of California's great Central Valley. No one in the olive business had been successful in generating a product that would not spoil in a short period of time. Working with Professor Eugene Hilgard at the University of California, Berkeley, she developed the process of curing ripe olives to effectively preserve them.

Ehmann traveled throughout Canada and the United States, particularly Philadelphia and New York, obtaining contracts for her product. In 1898 she started the Ehmann Olive Company in Oroville. It was a family affair, with Edwin marketing and selling and her son-in-law, Charles Bolles, helping her with production.

Ehmann was a fair and generous employer. During a time when foreign workers were violently discriminated against, she provided work for many Asian immigrants and paid them the same wage as their American counterparts. Women were also looked after and provided with special amenities. Active in woman suffrage, she was admired by Susan B. Anthony and Carrie Chapman Catt.

Ehmann died in 1932. Her efforts helped the California olive industry prosper into over 35,000 acres of orchards producing in excess of 100,000 tons of olives tended by some 1,200 growers. The Ehmann home, known as the House the Olives Built, was constructed in 1911 and is currently maintained by the Butte County Historical Society in Oroville.

—Neal Lynch

SUGGESTED READINGS

Guide to Butte County. "Paradise in Northern California." Retrieved from www.paradisedirect.com/paradise/butte.html.

Ireland, Norma Olin. *Index to Women of the World from Ancient to Modern Times: A Supplement.* Westwood, MA: F. W. Faxon, 1970.

Lodestar Olive Oil. "Tradition." Retrieved from www.lodestarfarms.com/tradition/index.html.

Olive Heritage. Retrieved from www.calolive.org/foodservice/heritage.html. Copyright 2003 California Olive Industry.

Oppedisano, Jeannette M. *Historical Encyclopedia of American Women Entrepreneurs: 1776 to the Present.* Westport, CN: Greenwood Press, 2000.

Oroville, California, Attractions. "Butte County Historical Society Ehmann Home." Retrieved from oroville.com/orovilleattractions.shtml.

FARENTHOLD, FRANCES "SISSY" TARLTON (1926-)

Frances "Sissy" Tarlton Farenthold, legislator and activist, daughter of Benjamin Dudley and Catherine Bluntzer Tarlton, was born on October 2, 1926. She graduated from Vassar College in 1946 and received her J.D. from the University of Texas Law School in 1949, one of 3 female students in a class of 800. Her years of working in the legal profession gave her a close-up view of poverty and other social problems. These experiences shaped her beliefs and compelled her to enter politics.

In 1968 Farenthold was elected to the Texas legislature despite taking a bold pro-choice stance on abortion in the conservative climate of Texas. She served until 1972, when she unsuccessfully ran for governor of Texas. She was a forceful advocate for the attainment of gender equality. She continued to promote her views even when they did not necessarily guarantee votes and public popularity. She served as a delegate to the 1972 Democratic National Convention in Miami. While there, Gloria Steinem, among others, nominated her for vice president. She came in second to Missouri Senator Thomas Eagleton.

Farenthold served as the 13th president of Wells College from 1976 to 1980, the first woman to be named president since the college's founding in 1868. She believes that women's colleges have a special responsibility to educate women for leadership roles, and she sought to ensure that that was accomplished during her tenure.

She has been involved in public affairs at the local, state, national, and international levels. In 1984 she served as a delegate to the Democratic National Convention. In 1985 she met with Soviet leader Mikhail Gorbachev. In 1988 she was a delegate to the Platform Committee of the Democratic National Committee. In 1991 she met with the president of the United Nations Security Council. Over 3 decades, she has acted as a human rights observer in numerous countries, including Cuba, El Salvador, Guatemala, Honduras, Iraq, Nicaragua, South Korea, and the former Soviet Union. She has testified before four congressional committees on topics such as day care, campaign finance reform, and the situation of migrant workers.

Farenthold was the cofounder and first chair of the National Women's Political Caucus. She received the Lyndon B. Johnson Woman of the Year award in 1973 and the Lifetime Service award from the Democratic Party of Texas in 1988. Today, Farenthold travels, speaks, writes, and serves in order to continue her advocacy for equality and democracy.

—Tiffany E. Dalpe

SUGGESTED READINGS

Dallas Morning News, July 14, 1988; April 9, 1991.

Wells College News & Events. "Human Rights Advocate Will Give Wells Commencement Address." May 2002. Retrieved from www.wells.edu/whatsnew/wnnwar31. htm.

Who's Who of American Women 2000-2001. New Providence, NJ: Marquis Who's Who, 2000.

FARNHAM, ELIZA WOOD BURHANS (1815-1864)

Eliza W. Farnham was born in Rensselaerville, New York. Orphaned at an early age, she went to live with an aunt and uncle in Maple Springs, New York. Her early life was filled with neglect, but her aunt's atheism provided Eliza with distrust for religion, which was evident throughout her life.

In 1836 she moved to Illinois with one of her brothers to join her sister. Also in 1836 she married Thomas Jefferson Farnham, an author of travel books. She lived on the Illinois prairie until 1841. During that time she bore three children, only one of whom survived.

In 1841 she and her husband moved to Washington Hollow, New York. In 1844, when her husband was in California, Farnham took work as a matron at Sing Sing Prison. While there, she instituted prison reforms, particularly in living conditions and humane treatment of inmates.

In 1846 she wrote a book, *Life in Prairie Land,* about her experiences in Illinois.

In 1848, after a conflict regarding her reforms, Farnham moved to Boston to work briefly with reformer Samuel Gridley Howe at the New England Asylum for the blind. However, her husband died in California, so in 1848 she went to California to deal with his estate. For this venture, she first tried to raise a group of young women to go to California to be brides. Unfortunately, opposition to this plan, in the form of rumors regarding the purpose of the expedition, made the project unsuccessful.

Her friend and assistant at Sing Sing, Georgiana Bruce, joined her in California at the ranch her husband had left her in Santa Cruz. (She would later dedicate her semifictional autobiography, *My Early Days,* to Georgiana.) In 1852 she married William Fitzpatrick, with whom she had one child, who died in infancy. The marriage was abusive, however, and they divorced in 1856.

Farnham's book *California, In-doors and Out* (1856) was a product of her observations of California culture, and included a call to women to mitigate the ills of the overwhelmingly male California society. (In 1850 over 90% of California's population were male.)

After her divorce, she returned to New York, where she stayed the rest of her life, save for 3 years from 1859 to 1862 when she served as a matron at the Stockton Insane Asylum.

Farnham's most influential book was *Woman and Her Era* (1864), in which she argued that women's ability to bear children was the basis of a biological superiority to men, and denounced women's rights movements that sought only equality with men. She had previously argued the supremacy of women at the National Women's Rights Convention in 1858.

Farnham contracted tuberculosis at Gettysburg while serving as a nurse for the Union Army. She returned to New York City, where she died the next year.

—Scott Kesilis

SUGGESTED READINGS

Herr, Pamela. "Reformer," in *Western Writers of America: Women Who Made the West.* Garden City, NY: Doubleday, 1980, 205-219.

Hicks, Jack. *Literature of California.* Berkeley: University of California Press, 2000.

FEINSTEIN, DIANNE (1933-)

Dianne Feinstein is California's senior U.S. Senator. She was born in San Francisco, earned her B.A. in history at Stanford University in 1955, served as student body vice president while at Stanford, was a member of the San Francisco Board of Supervisors, and served as mayor of San Francisco from 1978 until 1988. In 1987 the *City and State* magazine named her our nation's "most effective mayor." Feinstein was the first woman president of the San Francisco Board of Supervisors and mayor of the city.

The people of California sent her to the Senate in 1992, filling the remaining 2 years of Senator Pete Wilson's term. In 1994 she won her first 6-year term and was elected in 2000 for a second 6-year term. In the Senate she was the first woman to serve on the Judiciary Committee. She is the ranking Democrat and member of the Technology and Terrorism Subcommittee. She also serves on the Senate Appropriations Committee and the Rules and Administration Committee. She is a member of the Select Committee on Intelligence and the Energy and Natural Resources Committee.

Feinstein has sponsored numerous pieces of national legislation, including the Assault Weapons

Ban, the California Desert Protection Act, the Comprehensive Methamphetamine Control Act, the Lake Tahoe Restoration Act, the Gun-Free Schools Act, the Foreign Kingpins Designation Act, and the Headwaters Forest Agreement. In addition, she cochairs the Senate Cancer Coalition and is vice chair of the National Dialogue on Cancer. Most significantly, she was instrumental in the issuance of the Breast Cancer Research Stamp.

She is married to Richard C. Blum, has a daughter, Katherine, three stepdaughters, Annette, Heidi, and Eileen, and three grandchildren.

—Gordon Morris Bakken

SUGGESTED READING

Whitney, Catherine. *Nine and Counting: The Women of the Senate.* New York: HarperCollins, 2001.

FERGUSON, MIRIAM "MA" AMANDA WALLACE (1875-1961)

Miriam Amanda Wallace Ferguson, the first female governor of Texas, was born on June 13, 1875, in Bell County, Texas. She was the eldest of three daughters and the third of six children of Joseph Lapsley and Eliza Garrison Wallace. She received her early education by private tutor at home and at the preparatory school Salado College. Next she attended Baylor Female College (later Mary Hardin-Baylor College). On December 31, 1899, she married James Edward Ferguson, her cousin by marriage. In 1914 Jim Ferguson was elected governor of Texas. There was little criticism of Miriam as First Lady. During Jim's first term, there was much criticism of his handling of the state finances, yet he was reelected to a second term in 1916. The next year, he was impeached, convicted, and removed from office. With his conviction, Jim was banned from holding office in Texas, so Miriam began her political career. From 1917 to 1924 Jim fought the ban, but the Texas Supreme Court upheld it, so he announced Miriam's candidacy for governor. The Ferguson campaign never tried to hide the fact that Miriam was just a stand-in for her husband. Her campaign slogan was "Two Governors for the Price of One." During the campaign, a newspaper reporter substituted the initials "MA" for "Miriam Amanda." From then on she was known as Ma Ferguson.

Ferguson disliked the nickname, but the matronly image had great appeal in the rural and small-town areas. In her platform, Ferguson was anti-Ku Klux Klan, publicly supported tolerance of Catholics and Jews, promised better economy in government, better administration of state penitentiaries, and easing of the prohibition laws. This last subject was one on which the Fergusons publicly disagreed. Once in office, Ferguson called for the strengthening of the laws preventing the sale of alcohol. Elected in November 1924, she became the nation's second female governor (Nellie Tayloe Rose of Wyoming was inaugurated 15 days before Ferguson) and Texas's first. Her first term in office was unsuccessful. She failed to lower state expenditures and failed to raise taxes to build highways and aid education; she was successful in gaining passage of an antimask law, specifically aimed at the K.K.K, but it was overturned by the courts. There was great controversy over her liberal use of her pardon and parole power. Critics of her administration charged that pardons were for sale and that construction contracts were awarded to friends of Jim, whom Miriam had appointed highway commissioner. She was defeated in the primaries for reelection in 1926 and 1930. She won a second term in 1932, though her victory was challenged.

Ferguson's second administration was dominated by the problems of the Depression. She did not seek reelection in 1934, but ran again in 1940 and was defeated. Ferguson felt that the key to her political success was her ability to identify with the common people and to capitalize on timely issues. She died of heart failure on June 25, 1961, in Austin.

—Tiffany E. Dalpe

SUGGESTED READINGS

Brown, Norman D. *Hood, Bonnet, and Little Brown Jug: Texas Politics, 1921-1928.* College Station: Texas A&M University Press, 1984.

The Handbook of Texas Online. "Ferguson, Miriam Amanda Wallace (MA)." Retrieved from www.tsha. utexas.edu/handbook/online/articles/view/FF/ffe6.html.

James Edward Ferguson Collection, Barker Texas History Center, University of Texas, Austin.

Nalle, Ouida Ferguson. *The Fergusons of Texas, or "Two Governors for the Price of One": A Biography of James*

Edward Ferguson and His Wife. San Antonio, TX: Naylor, 1946.

Sicherman, Barbara, and Carol Hurd Green, eds. *Notable American Women: A Biographical Dictionary.* 4 vols. Cambridge, MA: Belknap, 1980.

FLANNER, HILDEGARDE (1899-1987)

Hildegarde Flanner was born in Indianapolis, Indiana, and was the youngest daughter of Francis William and Mary Ellen Hockett Flanner. Her parents instilled in her at an early age a sense of respect, fairness, and equality in regard to all humans. Her mother as a child was in a production of *Uncle Tom's Cabin*, and both her parents created a house to aid the poor situation for Africans in Indianapolis. She was also raised with a religious background, which created in her a moral foundation.

Flanner recalled her childhood as one that created pleasure and ease for her mother. She attended an all-girls' school in Indianapolis called Tudor Hall. Her family traveled internationally to educate their daughter Marie in the arts of the piano from the finest teachers in the world. They traveled to Berlin, Munich, England, and Scotland before they returned to Indiana. After her father's death, she changed schools and attended Short Ridge High School. Upon graduation, she briefly attended Briar College and then moved on to the University of California, Berkeley, where she studied poetry.

Flanner's poetry represented a response to the world around her. While in school at Berkeley, she wrote "Young Girl" and received the Emily Chamberlain Cook Prize. The poem described the path of a woman who was trying to make sense of the world around her through her own and God's eyes. She wrote and described her and her family's experience in the great Berkeley fire of 1923 in "Wildfire: Berkeley, 1923" and "To My Books Who Perished by Fire." Her Altadena garden was the source of works such as "Pacific Winter," "White Magnolia Blossom," "The Owl," and "The Snail." Her poems "Hawk Is a Woman," "Flight," "Never Ask Why," and "Rattlesnake" represented an anticipated fear of the devastating power that humans exhibited in killing one another. These were published shortly before World War II.

Porter Garnett was reported as saying that the poems of Flanner represented a type of honesty and

brought out her real feelings, which painted a real picture of Flanner's life. She avoided the jaded representation that befell other writers.

—Kevin Christy

SUGGESTED READINGS

Flanner, Hildegarde. *Mansions: A Play in One Act.* Cincinnati, OH: Stewart & Kidd, 1920.

Flanner, Hildegarde. *Younger Girl and Other Poems.* San Francisco: Crocker, 1920.

Flanner, Hildegarde. *A Tree in Bloom and Other Verses.* San Francisco: Lantern Press, 1924.

Flanner, Hildegarde. *Time's Profile.* New York: Macmillan, 1929.

Flanner, Hildegarde. *The White Bridge: A Play in One Act.* New York: Appleton, 1938.

Flanner, Hildegarde. *A Vanishing Land.* Portola Valley, CA: No Dead Lines, 1980.

Flanner, Hildegarde. *Brief Cherishing: A Napa Valley Harvest.* Santa Barbara, CA: John Daniel, 1985.

Mainiero, Lisa. *American Women Writers: A Critical Reference Guide from Colonial Times to the Present.* New York: Ungar, 1979-1994.

Rood, Karen L., ed. *American Literary Almanac.* New York: Facts on File, 1988.

FOLTZ, CLARA SHORTRIDGE (1849-1934)

In 1878 Clara Shortridge Foltz was the first woman admitted to the California bar. She was the first woman to attend the Hastings Law School in San Francisco, the first to practice in San Jose, San Francisco, and San Diego, the first to serve on the Board of Charities and Corrections, the first to argue for a public defender's office, and the first to be a deputy district attorney in Los Angeles.

Foltz was an astute politician in the cause of women's rights and access to employment. Finding that women could not practice law in California because of a statutory limitation, she conducted a personal lobbying campaign to amend California Civil Code, section 275, by deleting the word "male." With the legislation in hand, she made a personal visit to Governor William Irwin's office to make sure that he signed the bill. The bill became known as the Foltz

Woman Lawyer's Act, and she took advantage of it by passing the California bar examination. She then applied to law schools, and Hastings Law School promptly informed her that women were not admitted to study. She immediately sued the law school and won a California Supreme Court decision allowing women into law school.

In addition to private practice, Foltz continued her reform efforts. She was one of the creators of the California parole system in 1893 and the author of the Foltz Defender Bill that created a state system of public defenders for the criminally accused. This latter reform gained great national notoriety because Foltz presented the concept at the 1893 World's Fair.

On February 8, 2002, the Clara Shortridge Foltz Criminal Justice Center at the corner of Temple and Broadway in Los Angeles was rededicated in her name. The 19-story building housing 60 courtrooms, the offices of the Public Defender and the District Attorney, and numerous other departments sits on the site of the old Red Sandstone Courthouse, the early home of the Los Angeles Superior Court. Foltz practiced at the old Red Sandstone Courthouse, both as defense attorney and a deputy district attorney for Los Angeles.

—Gordon Morris Bakken

SUGGESTED READINGS

Babcock, Barbara Allen. "Clara Shortridge Foltz. 'First Woman.'" *Arizona Law Review 30* (1988): 673-717.

Bakken, Gordon Morris. *Practicing Law in Frontier California*. Lincoln: University of Nebraska Press, 1991.

Stanford Law School. "Clara Shortridge Foltz." Retrieved from www.law.stanford.edu/library/wlhbp/clara.

FOOTE, MARY "MOLLY" HALLOCK (1847-1938)

Mary "Molly" Hallock Foote was America's leading literary and artistic figure from the 1880s until the 1920s. Combining a gift for pen-and-ink illustration with a dedicated and disciplined literary pen, she authored 16 books, 20 short stories, 7 sketches, 16 children's stories, and numerous published illustrations. Much of her work depicts life in the American West.

Raised in a Quaker home in the East, she married Arthur Foote, a mining engineer, on February 9, 1876, and moved to the West. Already an accomplished artist, Molly boarded the Overland Limited bound for San Francisco and then the New Almaden Mine in California. New Almaden was a well-ordered company town with an ethnically diverse population. This setting provided her with material for "A California Mining Camp," which appeared in the February 1878 issue of *Scribner's*. The story depicted a mining camp in passing seasons with its "curious mixture of races." The reading public in the East now had a realistic view of part of the West. A visit to Santa Cruz, California, resulted in "A Sea-Port on the Pacific" in the August issue, telling readers of the "heterogeneous mass of transplanted life growing and blooming together." In 1881 her first work of mature fiction appeared as "In Exile." This work placed her squarely within the local color movement that dominated the literature of her times. *The Led-Horse Claim* (1883) was the first of three Leadville, Colorado, novels that established her as a western writer.

Other short stories and novels of the mining West followed. *John Bodewin's Testimony*, published as a serial in *Century* starting in November 1885 and later in book form in 1886, focused on a boundary claim dispute between mining companies. Molly's descriptions and characterizations were realistic and artistically constructed, further establishing her reputation as a leading western writer. "The Fate of a Voice" appeared in *Century* in 1886, accurately describing the Boise Canyon of Idaho and the work of mining engineers. These men were bright, attractive, and loving men given personas with her well-crafted prose. *The Last Assembly Ball,* another Leadville novel, appeared in *Century* in 1889 and as a book from Houghton Mifflin & Company the same year. In this work, Molly described the rigid class structure of western mining communities. *The Chosen Valley* saw print in *Century* in 1892 and book form from Houghton Mifflin the same year. The stark realism of Idaho landscapes, the human costs of exploitation, and the degradation of the environment resonate throughout the novel.

Molly and Arthur moved to Grass Valley, California, in 1895 and took up residence at North Star Cottage for over 3 decades. Her short stories and novels draw upon her experiences in Grass Valley. Her emphasis was on real families and ordinary events like the failure of a mine pump bringing personal and economic disaster to a community. She described local color with great detail and realism, a day-to-day realism unavailable in many of the contemporary novels about the West in her day.

Mary Hallock Foote, throughout her artistic and literary career, put family first, voiced compassion for the working class while criticizing labor unionism, and allowed reading Americans to visualize the West from the kitchen window, within a household, and with a verbal acuity seldom matched.

—Gordon Morris Bakken

SUGGESTED READING

Miller, Darlis A. *Mary Hallock Foote, Author-Illustrator of the American West.* Norman: University of Oklahoma Press, 2002.

G

GATES, SUSA YOUNG
(1856-1933)

Susa Young was born in Salt Lake City, Utah, the daughter of Brigham Young and Lucy Bigelow Young. Lucy was one of Brigham's 19 wives and Susa was one of 56 children fathered by Brigham. The Youngs were members of the Church of Jesus Christ of Latter-Day Saints. All accepted the principle of plural marriage for male members. This led to an interesting early childhood for Susa.

Susa recalls her early years as being of "a carefree childhood and a happy joyous youth." All of Brigham's wives and children lived together in a large house, and it was here that Susa received her early education. In addition, she learned "domestic arts" such as knitting, weaving, spinning, cooking, and cleaning.

While a college education for most women during this period was unheard of, Brigham encouraged all of his children to further their education. Susa entered the University of Deseret at age 13. Later she founded the Department of Music and was coeditor of the college newspaper while enrolled at the Brigham Young Academy. She later used her education to write and publish several novels and biographies as well as pamphlets in defense of her religion.

At the age of 16, Susa married Dr. Alma Bailey Dunford and had two children with him, Leah and Alma. The marriage ended in divorce after only a few years. Susa remarried in 1880 to Jacob F. Gates and the couple had 11 children, though only 4 survived to adulthood.

Susa was a tireless advocate for women's rights. She was a representative to women's congresses in Denver, London, Toronto, and Washington, D.C. She was most concerned with the topic of equal moral standards for men and women. In addition, she served as press chairman of the National Council of Women.

Growing up as a member of the Mormon Church, which believed in education for women, as well as one of Brigham Young's daughters afforded Susa many opportunities most women did not have at the time. She embraced these opportunities and during her life worked as a writer, publisher, teacher, missionary, genealogist, and temple worker.

Susa died on May 27, 1933. She was a very accomplished and talented woman, not only for her era but also by modern standards.

—Brenda Bitgood

SELECTED READINGS

Gates, Susa Young. *History of Young Ladie's Mutual Improvement Association of the Church of Jesus Christ of Latter Day Saints.* Salt Lake City, UT: Deseret News, 1911.

Gates, Susa Young. *The Life Story of Brigham Young.* New York: Macmillan, 1930.

Plummer, Louise. "Susa Young Gates," *Encyclopedia of Mormonism: Vol. 2.* New York: Macmillan, 1992.

GONZALEZ, IRMA ELSA (1948-)

Irma Elsa Gonzalez was born in Palo Alto, California. She received a bachelor of arts degree from Stanford University in 1970 and her J.D. from the University of Arizona College of Law in 1973. She went on to an extensive and successful law career.

She began her career in 1973 as law clerk for William C. Frey, U.S. District Court, District of Arizona. She moved on to become an Assistant U.S. Attorney in the criminal division of the U.S. Attorney's Office in 1975. In 1979 she worked as a trial attorney for the U.S. Department of Justice Anti-Trust division in Los Angeles. She returned to Assistant U.S. Attorney in the criminal division of the Central District of California in the same year. From 1981 to 1984 she was in private practice. She then became the U.S. magistrate for the U.S. District Court for the Southern District of California. She became a superior court judge for San Diego County in 1991, and in 1992 President George H. W. Bush appointed her to a federal judgeship. She now sits on the bench for the Southern District of California and is one of the first Hispanic women appointed to a federal judgeship.

—Lori S. Iacovelli

SUGGESTED READINGS

Irma Elsa Gonzalez. Retrieved March 23, 2002, from air.fjc.gov/newweb/jnetweb.nsf/fjc_bio. Source: History of the Federal Judiciary. http://www.fjc.gov. Web site of the Federal Judicial Center, Washington, D.C.

Martin, Mart. *The Almanac of Women and Minorities in American Politics 2002*. Boulder, CO: Westview Press, 2001.

GORDON, LAURA DE FORCE
(1838-1907)

Laura de Force Gordon was born in Pennsylvania in 1838 and attended public schools in Erie County and Chautauqua County. Her father suffered rheumatism and was unable to work.

Following the death of one of her brothers in 1855, Laura and much of her family became devout Christian Spiritualists. She traveled through New York and Pennsylvania as a trance speaker. In fact, her first visit to California in 1867 was prompted by an invitation from the Friends of Progress, a spiritualist group based in San Francisco. She spoke in Denver, Salt Lake City, Virginia City, and others on the West Coast, sharing her beliefs about spiritualism. She was praised as an outstanding

spokesperson and a fine orator. On February 18, 1868, she delivered the first public speech on woman suffrage in California at Platt's Hall in San Francisco.

She married Charles H. Gordon, a medical doctor from Scotland, in 1862, whom she would divorce on grounds of adultery in 1877. She bore no children from this union. Laura and Charles relocated to Treasure City, Nevada, where her husband was searching for mineral wealth. Charles contracted a near-fatal case of pneumonia, and they relocated to the San Joaquin Valley to aid in Charles's recovery.

Her political life was closely tied to the issue of suffrage. In 1870 the first meeting of the California State Woman Suffrage Society met, and Laura was in attendance. The San Joaquin Independent Party nominated her for a seat in the California State Senate in 1871, and she used the exposure garnered by her nomination to advance her views about universal suffrage. The year 1872 saw her as part of a delegation to a conference on national women's suffrage in Washington, D.C. In 1874 she led a successful lobbying campaign to give women the right to run for some educational offices.

From 1884 until 1894 she was the president of the California State Woman Suffrage Society.

In 1879 she worked with Clara Shortridge Foltz to pass an amendment to the California State Constitution guaranteeing women the right to work in the profession of their choice. The amendment, known as the Woman Lawyer's Bill, passed the legislature, despite heated debate. The California Supreme Court heard her case when she and Foltz sued Hastings School of Law for admission to the law program. In 1880 she became the second woman, after Foltz, admitted to the California bar. Laura was the first woman in California to defend a murder suspect. Throughout the 1880s she had a thriving law practice, specializing in family and criminal law. In 1885, she was one of the first women lawyers admitted to practice before the U.S. Supreme Court.

Laura died in Lodi, California, at the age of 69.

—Scott Kesilis

SUGGESTED READINGS

Downey, Lynn. "Laura de Force Gordon," *American National Biography*. New York: Oxford University Press, 1999.

Hawkins, Renee Frances. "Laura de Force Gordon: Fragments of a Feminist Pioneer." Retrieved from www.stanford.edu/group/WLHP/papers/gordon.html.

H

HALE, JANET CAMPBELL (1946-)

Janet Campbell Hale was born to Nicholas Patrick and Margaret Sullivan Campbell on January 11, 1946. Although members of the Coeur d'Alene tribe in northern Idaho, the Campbells traveled to visit family in Southern California when Margaret was pregnant with Janet to ensure that her baby was born in a hospital. Janet's father, a veteran of the Great War and a carpenter by trade, was a full-blooded Coeur d'Alene Indian. The family name was derived from her great-great-grandfather, Colemannee. Her mother was Irish/ Kootenay and was descended from John McLoughlin, a doctor for the Northwest Fur Company. He is credited with the founding of Oregon.

Janet was a product of an abusive home. Her father was an alcoholic who physically and verbally abused her mother. Her mother was equally abusive, telling Janet she was a failure and would never amount to anything and disavowing her Indian heritage. The abuse carried forward into her young adult life with her marriage to Arthur Dudley in 1984. They had a son and divorced the following year.

Janet began writing poetry at age 15, this after moving from school to school and finally dropping out after the eighth grade. Her poems reflected the dream of some day becoming a real writer. At age 18 she went back to school at San Francisco City College and from there to the University of California, Berkeley, where she graduated in 1972. She received her master's degree from the University of California, Davis, in 1984.

Her writings are largely autobiographical, focusing on her tumultuous childhood and an abusive husband. She was first published in 1972 in an anthology of poems by young Native American writers. She then published her first novel, *The Owl's Song,* a book of poems titled *Custer Lives in Humboldt County and Other Poems,* and her master's thesis, *The Jailing of Cecelia Capture,* which was nominated for a Pulitzer Prize in 1985.

Janet's writing also embraces a sense of her historical past. *Bloodlines: Odyssey of a Native Daughter,* published in 1993, is a collection of autobiographical essays that reflect on her past and her heritage, with accounts of her paternal grandmother, who was a follower of Chief Joseph, and of a U.S. government destined to destroy them.

In addition to the Pulitzer nomination, Janet's honors include the New York Poetry Day award in 1964, the American Book award in 1994, and the Creative Writing Grant from the National Endowment for the Arts in 1995. She also received an appointment as a Visiting Professor of Native American Literature at the University of California, Santa Cruz, in 1998.

—Neal Lynch

SUGGESTED READINGS

Directory of American Poets and Fiction Writers. New York: Poets & Writers, 2001.

Hale, Janet Campbell, and Karen M. Strom. "Janet Campbell Hale." Retrieved from www.hanksville.org/storytellers/jchale.

Malinowski, Sharon, and George H. J. Abrams. *Notable Native Americans.* New York: Gale Research, 1995.

Native American Authors Project. "Janet Campbell Hale." Retrieved from www.ipl.org/cgi/ref/native/browse.pl/A36.

Sonneborn, Liz. *A to Z of Native American Women*. New York: Facts on File, 1998.

University of Minnesota Voices from the Gaps: Women Writers of Color. "Janet Campbell Hale." Retrieved from voices.cla.umn.edu/authors/HALEjanetcampbell.html.

Welch, Linda M. "Janet Campbell Hale Visit." Retrieved from nativenet.uthscsa.edu/archive/nn-dialogue/9911/0002.html.

Westfall, Connie. "Janet Campbell Hale—1946." Retrieved from www.ncteamericancollection.org/litmap/hale_janet_campbell_id.htm.

HALL, CYNTHIA HOLCOMB (1929-)

Cynthia Holcomb Hall was born in Los Angeles in 1929. She received her A.B. from Stanford University in 1951, after which she entered the U.S. Naval Reserve and served in the Korean Conflict as a lieutenant in the JAG Corps. She earned her LL.B. from Stanford in 1954. Also in 1954 she became the first law clerk to serve on the U.S. Court of Appeals for the Ninth Circuit, serving under Judge Richard H. Chambers. She earned her LL.M. in taxation from New York University in 1960. From 1960 to 1964 she worked as a lawyer for the U.S. Department of Justice, after which she worked for the Department of the Treasury from 1964 until 1966. From 1966 until 1972, she was a partner in the firm of Brawerman & Holcomb. She served as a judge in the U.S. Tax Court from 1972, when President Richard Nixon appointed her, until 1981, when she was appointed as a U.S. District Court judge for the Central District of California. She served in the District Court until she was appointed by Ronald Reagan in 1984 to serve on the Ninth Circuit Court of Appeals, where she served until 1997. In 1997 she took senior status on the court, after 13 years on the court. She has served as the chair of the Committee on International Judicial Affairs for the Judicial Conference of the United States and as a visiting judge to the Second, Fourth, Fifth, and Eleventh Circuit Courts.

—Scott Kesilis

SUGGESTED READINGS

"Ninth Circuit Judge to Take Senior Status." *Metropolitan News-Enterprise*. Capitol News Service, August 29, 1997.

Stanford Lawyer, No. 58 (Summer 2000).

HAMILTON, PHYLLIS J. (1952-)

In 1952 Phyllis J. Hamilton was born in Jacksonville, Illinois. She moved to California to study for her bachelor's degree at Stanford University. Upon her graduation in 1974, she began her postgraduate work at Santa Clara University School of Law. After receiving her J.D. in 1976, she became the deputy public defender for California's Office of the Public Defender. After a brief stint as the Manager of E.E.O. Programs at Farinon Electric Corporation in 1980, she became an administrative judge for the U.S. Merit Systems Protection Board in the San Francisco Regional Office. From 1985 to 1991 she was the court commissioner for the municipal court in the Oakland-Piedmont-Emeryville Judicial District. From there she moved on to become the U.S. Magistrate Judge for the Northern District of California, and remained there until 2000. When a new seat was created in the U.S. District Court for the Northern District of California by 104 Stat. 5089, 5105, President Bill Clinton nominated her for it. She received her commission on May 25, 2000, after the Senate had confirmed her nomination the day before.

—Marcus J. Schwoerer

SUGGESTED READING

Phyllis J. Hamilton. Retrieved from air.fjc.gov/servlet/tGetInfo?jid=2863. Source: History of the Federal Judiciary, http://www.fjc.gov. Web site of the Federal Judicial Center, Washington, D.C.

HANDLER, RUTH (1916-2002)

Ruth Handler was the motive force behind the creation of Mattel Inc., a producer of America's most enduring toys of the 20th century. She was the 10th and last child of the Mosko family. Her mother gave birth at age 40, and due to her mother's poor health, Ruth's Aunt Sarah and her husband raised Ruth. Sarah, an accomplished businesswoman, always worked outside the home and became the role model for Ruth. By age 10, Ruth was working in her aunt's drugstore. She developed a preference for working instead of playing with other children and toys.

Ruth met her future husband and business partner, Elliott Handler, in 1932 when she was16. Their relationship was on again/off again, particularly due to her aunt's animus toward Elliott. Ruth attended Denver University with an aspiration for a career in law, but on summer break, a chance meeting with a girl named Jenny Cohen landed Ruth on a trip to Los Angeles. There she visited a family friend, Evelyn Lee, who worked at Paramount Studios. At lunch in the Paramount cafeteria, Evelyn told Ruth that it was impossible to get a job there, but within an hour, Ruth had a job in the stenographic pool for $25 per week. Aunt Sarah was thrilled. Elliott arrived in Los Angeles 1 month later, quickly found work as a lighting fixture designer, and soon began to formally study industrial design. Their relationship matured and they were married in Denver on June 26, 1938.

Back in Los Angeles, their dream apartment sans furniture was more space than meaning. Elliott turned to designing coffee tables, lamps, and accessories. Convinced that Ruth could sell these items, the couple purchased equipment and established a shop in the garage. Neighbor complaints forced a move to a small Chinese laundry building. There they produced consumer goods and Ruth honed her sales talents.

In 1944 this cottage industry became Mattel, originally Mattel Creations of Hawthorne, California, producing picture frames and doll furniture. They soon turned their attention to the production of the Uke-A-Doodle (a ukulele), but intense competition plagued Matt Mattson, a business partner, fearing the loss of his initial $10,000 investment. Under the circumstances, Ruth and Elliott convinced Aunt Sarah and her husband to buy out Mattson's interest. Soon other music-making toys such as the baby grand piano, pop goes the weasel jack-in-the-box, and realistic toy guns followed. The Handlers used the media to promote these products. They agreed in 1955 to sponsor Walt Disney's new television program *The Mickey Mouse Club*. Their innovative products in the new media created year-round demand. From 1948 to 1957 Ruth was executive vice president of Mattel. In 1967 she became company president. In 1973 she was chair of the board of directors, sharing duties with Elliott as cochair of the board.

With financial foundations laid, the Handlers turned to further innovation. In 1959 Barbie, named for their daughter, Barbara, and in 1961, Ken, named for their son, swept the nation. Ruth was instrumental in convincing a reluctant sales force that a doll with breasts would sell. Sell it did, contributing with other products to $100 million in 1966. Mattel was a national player in the toy business. For example, over 1 billion Barbies have been sold in over 100 countries since 1959.

In 1970 tragedy struck. Ruth was diagnosed with breast cancer and had her left breast removed. She lost her confidence at the same time Mattel was in business trouble. The federal government accused Ruth of violations of federal securities law by the issuance of false financial statements between 1969 and 1974. It was argued that these false statements were used to influence the market price of Mattel stock, enabling the company to acquire other companies and bank loans. Ruth entered a plea of no contest to the 10 counts and paid a fine of $57,000. The court also required that she serve an unprecedented 500 hours of community service for 5 years. She left Mattel in 1975 and Elliott followed her 6 months later.

Ruth, never able to sit still, created Nearly Me, a breast prosthesis company. Her own dissatisfaction with the current state of the art moved her to improve on it for the sake of women similarly situated. She later sold the company to a subsidiary of Kimberly Clark.

On April 27, 2002, Ruth passed away due to complications from colon surgery. Her legacy will live in the heart of every child who ever played with a Mattel toy. In November 2002 her daughter, Barbara Handler Segal, placed the hand and footprints of a Barbie doll outside the Egyptian Theatre on Hollywood Boulevard to commemorate the film *Barbie as Rapunzel*.

—Brenda Farrington

SUGGESTED READING

Handler, Ruth, with Jacqueline Shannon. *Dream Doll: The Ruth Handler Story.* Stamford, CT: Longmeadow Press, 1994.

HASSELSTROM, LINDA M. (1943-)

Linda Hasselstrom is a writer, rancher, educator, and environmentalist. She is known for her poetry and nonfiction work, primarily focused upon the lives of western women and her life on a South Dakota cattle ranch. In addition to writing, she has also been a reporter, educator, and public speaker, and currently performs readings for elementary school teachers and offers writing workshops from her ranch for other women authors. She received a B.A. in English and Journalism from the University of South Dakota in 1965 and an M.A. in English from the University of Missouri, Columbia, in 1969. She began teaching in different Missouri colleges such as Columbia College and Black Hills State College in Columbia, moved back to South Dakota, and became a writer-in-schools for the South Dakota Arts Council, teaching poetry and fiction. She also taught freshman English at South Dakota School of Mines and Technology.

Throughout the years 1971 to 1985, Hasselstrom founded Lame Johnny Press and edited 23 books as well as a literary magazine called *Sunday Clothes: A Magazine of the Arts*. When she was awarded a National Endowment for the Arts fellowship for poetry in 1984, she closed the press and magazine to pursue writing full time. She has received numerous awards, including Author of the Year by the South Dakota Hall of Fame in 1989, the Western American Writer award in 1990, the first woman to receive it, and the Governor's Award in Arts for Distinction in Creative Achievement. Her books include *Windbreak*, *Going Over East*, *Road Kill*, *Caught by One Wing*, *Dakota Bones*, and *Lad Circle: Writings Collected From the Land*.

Hasselstrom's writing is unique in that it portrays the everyday realities of living and growing up on a cattle ranch. Her nonfiction works are autobiographical and reflect the natural cycles of life and women's roles in relation to the people in their lives. Her poetry reflects her growing up on the ranch of her stepfather and the impact both he and the ranch had on her life. When she returned to South Dakota, after starting her writing career, her second husband, George Snell, also worked on the ranch with her until his death in 1988. The success of her writing has allowed her to maintain the ranch after the passing of her parents and husband. Her contributions to the role of women ranchers and to the environment continue through her writing and public speaking.

—Michelle Bean

SUGGESTED READINGS

Hasselstrom, Linda M. *Going Over East: Reflections of a Woman Rancher*. Golden, CO: Fulcrum, 1987.

La Rocca, Linda. Review of *Bitter Creek Junction* by Linda M. Hasselstrom. Retrieved from www.cozine.com/archive/cc2000/00780448.htm.

Linda M. Hasselstrom. Retrieved from www.netwalk.com/~vireo/hasselstrom.html.

Paregien, Stan, ed. *Directory of Western Writers and Entertainers*. "Linda M. Hasselstrom." Retrieved from www.texmexx.net/H/h-as.html.

Windbreak House. "Writing Retreats for Women with Author Linda M. Hasselstrom." Retrieved from www.windbreakhouse.com.

HEARST, PHOEBE APPERSON (1842-1919)

Phoebe Apperson was born in Franklin County, Missouri. She worked as a teacher in various local schools until she married George Hearst at the age of 19. George was 22 years her senior at the time of their marriage.

Shortly after marriage, the Hearsts moved to San Francisco, California. Phoebe gave birth to their only child, William Randolph Hearst, in 1863. When William was only 10 years old, Phoebe took him on a tour of Europe for more than a year to expose him to art, architecture, and culture. This trip was the inspiration for the later construction of the famous Hearst Castle in Southern California.

In 1887 George was elected to the U.S. Senate and the couple moved to Washington, D.C., where Phoebe spent her time entertaining statesmen and dignitaries. In 1891 George passed away and Phoebe returned to California as sole heir to the Hearst fortune.

Armed with her new fortune, Phoebe commissioned architect Julia Morgan to finish construction on an extravagant residence in Pleasanton, California. Later, Julia was also the architect for the Hearst Castle.

In addition to lavish homes, Phoebe used her fortune as a generous contributor to various educational accomplishments. She created several scholarships for women students at the University of California, Berkeley. She also funded an international architectural competition for the university and presented the campus with the Hearst Memorial Mining Building and Hearst Hall.

Later, Phoebe financed a school for the education of kindergarten teachers and founded the first free kindergarten in the United States. In 1897 she founded the national Congress of Mothers, a forerunner to the National Council of Parents and Teachers, known today as the PTA. She remained dedicated to the furthering of education until her death, a victim of the influenza epidemic of 1918-1919.

—Brenda Bitgood

SUGGESTED READINGS

Chaney, Lindsay. *The Hearsts: Family and Empire.* New York: Simon & Schuster, 1981.

Davies, Marion. *The Time We Had.* New York: Ballantine Books, 1975.

Hearst Castle. "Phoebe Apperson Hearst." Retrieved from www.hearstcastle.org/history/phoebe_hearst.asp.

Robinson, Judith. *The Hearsts: An American Dynasty.* New York: Acon Books, 1991.

HECOX, MARGARET M. (1815-1908)

Schoolteacher Margaret Hamer of Northumberland County, Pennsylvania, married Adna Hecox in February 1829. Adna Hecox is known for preaching possibly the first Protestant religious services in California and serving other civil responsibilities in early California, which included judge, justice of the peace, county treasurer, and even lighthouse keeper of Santa Cruz. Margaret is especially known for writing one of three known accounts of the Imus Party's journey on the Overland Trail into California, hers being the only female perspective.

The Hecox family started their journey from Illinois on March 23, 1846, which lasted until October 1 of that same year when they reached Sutter's Fort. They were quickly urged on to Mission Santa Clara, where they survived a siege by the Mexican army during the Mexican-American War. Margaret traveled with three girls and an infant son in a covered wagon pulled by oxen, as many pioneers did. In her reminiscences she recalls her encounters with several tribes of American Indians and various hardships along the trail. She also describes how they caught up with the Donner Party and just barely missed suffering the same fate due to mountain man Caleb Greenwood's wise decision of keeping to the Fort Hall road instead of taking Lansford Hasting's cut-off. After crossing

the Sierra Nevada mountain range, their party rested at Sutter's Fort and moved on to the Mission of Santa Clara, where they were besieged by Mexicans during the Mexican-American War. After their release, they moved to Santa Cruz, where they lived out the remainder of their days as distinguished citizens performing various civil services.

Margaret's *Overland Trail Memoir* was dictated many years later to her daughter, Maria, who became a magazine writer. Margaret died in Santa Cruz on November 18, 1908.

—Carolyn Stull

SUGGESTED READINGS

Dillon, Richard. *California Caravan: The 1846 Overland Trail Memoir of Margaret M. Hecox.* San Jose, CA: Harlan-Young Press, 1966.

Hecox Family Miscellany. "Adna A. Hecox Family" Retrieved from home.earthlink.net/~butlers/hecox-misc.html.

HOGAN, LINDA (1947-)

Chickasaw novelist and poet Linda Hogan was born in Denver, Colorado. Her father was in the army and the family moved constantly during her childhood. Therefore, she considers Oklahoma, where her father's family now resides, to be her true home. Her first compilation of poetry, *Calling Myself Home,* reflects the background and traditions of the Chickasaw relocation land in Gene Autry, Oklahoma.

Linda did not plan to become a writer, and actually had very little experience writing when she started work on her first collection of poetry. At the time, she worked with handicapped children but devoted her lunch hours to reading and writing. She followed her call to writing by entering the University of Colorado, Colorado Springs, in her late 20s. After completing her undergraduate degree in Colorado Springs, she went on to receive her master's degree in English at the University of Colorado, Boulder, in 1978.

The following year, Linda adopted two girls of Oglala Lakota heritage. Her new daughters, Sandra Dawn Protector and Tanya Thunder Horse, influenced her next two collected works of poetry, *Daughters, I Love You,* written in 1981, and *Eclipse,* written in 1983. These works demonstrate a blend of her familiar topics of the need for environmental protection and the importance of preserving one's heritage.

Several of Linda's following books, *Seeing Through the Sun, Savings,* and her novel *Mean Spirit,* infuse ecological issues with the problems Native Americans faced due to the settlement of the frontier. Linda confronts the issues of oppression, poverty, racism, urban relocation, and land allotment experienced by her people under U.S. government control. Remarkably, she deals with these problems in a manner that reflects the strength and dignity of her people rather than as negative political criticism. Her work is an affirmation of the vitality of the human spirit and reflects a connectedness between this spirit and the land that all humans must share.

Linda has received many honors and awards. In 1980 she received a D'Arcy McNickle Memorial Fellowship at the Newberry Library. Two years later she received a Yaddo Colony Fellowship. She was also the recipient of a national endowment grant in fiction in 1986 and a Lannan award in 1994. Her novel *Mean Spirit* earned her a distinction as a finalist for a Pulitzer Prize in writing.

Perhaps her greatest achievement is the writing of her own memoir, *The Woman Who Watches Over the World.* In writing this memoir, she was forced to confront her own difficult past as well as the troubled and painful history of her people. Once more, her powerful spirit triumphs over the pain of times gone by. When commenting on the experience of writing her memoir, she writes, "I sat down to write a book about pain and ended up writing about love."

—Brenda Bitgood

SELECTED READINGS

amazon.com. "Endangered Wisdom." Retrieved from www. amazon.com/exec/obidos/tg/feature/-/5195.

Hogan, Linda. *Calling Myself Home.* Greenfield Center, NY: Greenfield Review Press, 1978.

Hogan, Linda. *Mean Spirit.* New York: Atheneum. 1990.

Hogan, Linda. *Power.* New York: Norton. 1998.

Hogan, Linda. *The Woman Who Watches Over the World.* New York: Norton. 2001.

Native American Authors Project. "Linda Hogan." Retrieved from www.ipl.org/cgi/ref/native/browse. pl/A40.

HOMESTEADERS

The Homestead Act of 1862 was relatively, and remarkably, free of gender bias. Given its 19th-century context, this is surprising. At a time when women could neither vote nor hold elective office, Congress granted women the same opportunity for potential economic gain as men. The Act allowed women to apply for land under the same conditions, requiring only that they be at least 21 years old, single, widowed, divorced, or the head of a household. In other words, any woman—except for a currently married woman who, it was assumed, acknowledged her husband as the head of their household—could file for her own stake on the public domain. The government's offer was this: the homesteader paid a nominal filing fee (approximately $12-$15), selected up to 160 acres of public domain, lived on that parcel for 5 consecutive years, and made some improvements. Applicants also had to swear that the homestead was for their exclusive right and that they were not applying on behalf of someone else trying to acquire vast tracts of public lands through "dummy" entries. At the end of 5 years, the homesteader would acquire title to, or "prove up" on, the property. Other homestead-related legislation that followed, including the Enlarged Homestead Act, maintained similar gender-free restrictions. Women qualified along with their brothers, fathers, or former husbands. The Desert Land Act of 1878 guidelines allowed even married women to file for land.

Of course, the vast majority of women who took up the government's homesteading challenge did so as wives of the official entrants. Their names, however, do not appear in the land office records. Although, one presumes, in most cases these women served as partners in the family enterprise, they tend to vanish from historical accounts because they do not exist in the General Land Office (GLO) entry books or county courthouse property ledgers. The more visible women, then, were those who filed for homesteads as single, divorced, widowed, or heads of households. Ascertaining their numbers requires painstaking research in local courthouse records, scrutinizing the names of homesteaders, and counting the number of women among them. Fortunately, some scholars have done just that and produced a collection of studies that provide precise data on the numbers of women homestead entrants in specific regions of the West. One study of 43 townships in North Dakota, for example, revealed that between the 1870s and 1910, the number of women land registrants ranged from 1% to 22%, averaging out to about 10%. Another study revealed that before 1900, women made up 12% of the entrants in Logan County and 10% in Washington County, Colorado. After 1900, the percentages reached nearly 18 in both counties. A third study indicated that nearly 12% of homestead patents issued in Wyoming counties between 1888 and 1943 went to women. These numbers are significant, if not overwhelming. Clearly, then, between the wives of official entrants and the "single" women who took advantage of access to public lands, women represented an important percentage of homesteaders.

If scholars can estimate accurately the number of women homesteaders, they find that identifying their motives more elusive. Did they file with the intention of securing independently earned and managed homesteads for themselves? Were they speculating? Or were they operating in the context of family interests? To what extent could one see feminist impulses at stake here? To what extent, traditional, domestic ones? The answer is complicated, representing the whole spectrum of possibilities—not surprising, given the wide range of people involved. Still, research to date suggests that the majority of women homesteaders operated within the context of family. Of course, the same could be said of men. Homesteading, particularly in the arid or semiarid West, was difficult, and most people discovered that their chances for success improved considerably if undertaken in concert and cooperation with other family members.

Elinore Pruitt Stewart's example suggests the complexity of women's motives. Stewart, author of *Letters of a Woman Homesteader* and subject of the film *Heartland,* is perhaps the best known woman homesteader. Her case is interesting and somewhat perplexing because her public explanation of why she homesteaded, as articulated in her book, and her private motives, as revealed in official land office and marriage documents, reveal motives at seeming cross-purposes. In the book, Stewart presents women homesteading as a panacea for wage-working, urban women such as herself, offering a path out of poverty. In addition, she suggests it is a way for women to prove, to themselves and others, their abilities to manage independently. In her words: "Any woman who can stand her own company, can see the beauty of the sunset, loves growing things, and is willing to put in as much time and careful labor as she does over the washtub, will certainly succeed; will have independence, plenty to eat all the time, and a home of her own in the end." By independence, Stewart meant doing it alone—without the help of a man. There is, in the book then, an undeniably feminist message: women can do it on their own. Stewart intended to prove it, by "proving up" by herself.

An examination of official documents, however, reveals an alternative scenario. In 1909 Stewart moved to Wyoming to work as housekeeper on Clyde Stewart's ranch. Five weeks after her arrival in Wyoming, she filed on a 147-acre homestead as a single woman. One week after that, she married Clyde Stewart. Clearly, her days as a "single" woman homesteader were limited. Moreover, her homestead adjoined Clyde's, and rather than building a new home on Elinore's entry, the couple lived in Clyde's house. Eventually, Elinore relinquished her homestead—she gave up her rights to her widowed mother-in-law, probably fearing she had violated the conditions of the Homestead Act by virtue of the marriage and residency, and thus forfeited her right to prove up. Eventually, her mother-in-law acquired title and sold the acreage to the Stewarts. What we have here, then, is a family working together to acquire sufficient property under the government's land laws to make a living at ranching. Husband, wife, mother-in-law—all did what they could to enhance the family's land holdings and possibilities for success in a challenging environment. Actually, this legal version of her story demonstrates the way many homesteaders used the land laws to their own advantage. Success required not only back-breaking work from the entire family but also a willingness to press the land laws to their limits, sometimes creatively, sometimes fraudulently, in order to survive. Although Elinore did not prove up on her own homestead, the property did remain in the family's hands, thanks to another woman, and that was the most crucial goal for the Stewarts. True, she did not succeed as an "independent woman homesteader," in her own narrowly defined sense of that term. However, if "independent" also means individualistic and self-reliant, the term applies here. She was free-spirited. She worked alongside, not under the domination of, her husband. In the end, her case represents a blend of individualist ideology and family strategy, and suggests how many men and women blended these two in the course of homesteading.

Other women homesteaders remained single, contributed to family strategies, and simultaneously created an economic stake for themselves. They relied upon, and in turn helped, their relatives, yet maintained a measure of independence and economic power. In South Dakota, for instance, Erikka Hansen, a schoolteacher, filed a claim adjoining her brother's. Another brother filed on a third homestead and the siblings helped each other. Hansen, who made her actual living by teaching, eventually proved up and sold her homestead for $500, having succeeded, with the help of family members, to acquire a personal nest egg. In the Dakotas and many other places strewn across the West, GLO tract books reveal this commonplace strategy of husbands, wives, brothers, sisters, aunts, uncles, and cousins taking up blocks of land in adjoining claims. Family and kinship ties, in sum, offered a better chance to survive, whether the goal was long-term land acquisition or short-term (personal) economic gain.

It is difficult to overemphasize the importance of this fact: homesteading offered single women the possibility of land ownership—an opportunity that was far from commonplace in 19th-century America. It was, actually, quite astounding that the federal government allowed these women the same economic chances as men. Moreover, this had repercussions beyond property rights. It allowed, even encouraged, women to expand the scope of their activities within their communities as well as blur some gender-determined roles within families. This, in turn, increased their responsibilities and their decision-making powers in many families and communities. Of course, such generalizations have their limits. In Mormon Utah, for instance, religious doctrine and recent European immigrants' beliefs reinforced patriarchal authority. Before 1900 the percentage of women entrants approximated that of other western places; in the 20th century, the numbers remained static in Utah while rising elsewhere. Whereas economic opportunity coupled with relatively egalitarian homestead families allowed women in places such as Colorado to engage in land speculation and ownership, Mormon women exhibited no such entrepreneurial impulses. Their religious responsibilities as wives and mothers allowed no room for personal gain. They homesteaded either to add land to the family operation or, in the case of polygamous wives, to support themselves and their children. The economic advantages that accrued to other women homesteaders did not materialize among Mormon women.

Of course, not all homesteaders—whether men or women—succeeded. In northeast Colorado, for example, nearly half of all entrants did not prove up or patent the land they originally claimed. It is difficult to ascertain how many of these should be figured "failures," however. Some profited by selling their relinquishments to other homesteaders, for instance. Still, many others did abandon their claims and suffered net losses as a consequence. So far there is no evidence that such failures affected women more than men. In fact, most historians conclude that the benefits outweighed the penalties for women. They gained more than they lost.

Homesteading in the Plains and mountain West essentially ended by the early 1920s. An agricultural depression devastated the region's farming and ranching economies. Drought and the 1930s' Depression only compounded these hardships, which together ended the opportunity homestead legislation had provided women to become land owners, in their own right. Many families lost their land altogether and migrated to cities. The momentum homesteading had provided women in expanding their economic options in the agricultural sector was lost.

—Sherry L. Smith

SUGGESTED READINGS

Gould, Florence C., and Patricia N. Pando. *Claiming Their Land: Women Homesteaders in Texas.* El Paso: Texas Western Press, 1991.

Harris, Katherine. *Long Vistas: Women and Families on Colorado Homesteads.* Niwot: University Press of Colorado, 1993.

Lindgren, H. Elaine. *Land in Her Own Name: Women Homesteaders in North Dakota.* Fargo: North Dakota Institute for Regional Studies, 1991.

Smith, Sherry L. "Single Women Homesteaders: The Perplexing Case of Elinore Pruitt Stewart," *Western Historical Quarterly 22* (May 1991): 163-183.

HUBBLE, GRACE LILLIAN BURKE (1889-1981)

Grace Burke Hubble, wife of famed astronomer Edwin Powell Hubble, lived most of her life in California, traveled to Europe, vacationed in Colorado, loved nature, read rapaciously, enjoyed intellectual conversation, and entertained some of the world's most prominent scientists and Hollywood celebrities in her San Marino home. Although described in her obituary as a writer, Grace was not a writer or journalist in the traditional sense; her work remains unpublished. She wrote daily in journals and letters, gathering her observations, analysis, and opinions of people, politics, nature, and art. She wrote of the ordinary and extraordinary, the ridiculous and sublime. Whether writing of flora and fauna during a vacation in the Colorado wilderness or political debates after dinner by the fire, Grace Hubble's writing reveals an observant eye, sagacious ear, and cultivated pen. Her journals and correspondence define the years of her marriage to Edwin, 1924 until his death in 1953, after which personal anecdotes disappeared as she devoted her time to writing Edwin's memoir, preserving his accomplishments. Grace's journals are part of the Edwin Powell Hubble Papers at the Huntington Library in San Marino, California. The collection she donated in 1954 and expanded in subsequent years includes Edwin's scientific papers, correspondence of both Hubbles, photographs, and the memoir of Edwin's life. The archive is open to scholars; however, access was restricted during the first 20 years to those she authorized.

Grace Hubble, a brilliant woman with a keen wit, led an extraordinary life at the center of the intellectual community of the California Institute of Technology in Pasadena with members of the British émigré community in Los Angeles and among Hollywood's elite. During her lifetime, she enjoyed access to the ears and minds of many influential people. A childhood friend described Grace as "a small girl with hazel eyes and a face of charming vivacity. Friendly, clever, and athletic." Born to John Patrick and Luella Kepford Burke in Walnut, Iowa, in 1889, Grace was the eldest of two girls. In 1891 the family moved to California, living first in San Jose and settling in Los Angeles, where John Burke, as vice president of the First National Bank, became a prominent member of the community. The family lived comfortably in upscale Hancock Park. Grace and her younger sister, "Max," attended the prestigious Marlborough School for Girls, and Grace continued her education at Stanford University, graduating Phi Beta Kappa in 1912 with a degree in English. This serious student maintained an active social life as a member of the English Club and Alpha Phi sorority. While at Stanford, she sustained her fondness for horses and nature, taking advantage of the nearby stables and riding often in the open countryside surrounding the campus.

Grace married twice, first in 1912 to Earl Warren Russell Leib, whom she met at Stanford. In 1921 Leib's work as a geologist for the Southern Pacific Company took him to Amador County near Sacramento, where he met with a fatal accident in the shaft of an idle coal mine. Shortly before his death, Grace traveled with Earl's sister to the Mount Wilson Observatory, where she met the young astronomer Edwin Hubble. Years later, writing Edwin's memoir, Grace recalled her thoughts as she, unobserved, watched him for the first time: "The astronomer looked an Olympian, tall, strong, and beautiful, with the shoulders of the Hermes of Praxiteles, and the benign serenity. . . . There was a sense of power, channeled and directed in an adventure that had nothing to do with personal ambition and its anxieties." She neglected to mention her marital status at the time.

Within a year of Leib's death, Edwin and Grace began a discreet courtship. In Edwin she saw a "finely tempered will, in the face of the blind forces of nature, . . . as decent a way to follow as any that life offers. It was this and much more than this, a choice and a balance of spirit, that I was looking for and recognized for the first time when I saw it, in Edwin." On February 26, 1924, the two married in a private ceremony at the Burke home, enjoyed a week at the Burke cottage in Pebble Beach, then left for England aboard the *Montlaurier* for an extended honeymoon. In England they renewed friendships from Edwin's years as a Rhodes scholar, he spoke to the Royal Astronomical Society, and Grace was awed by everything English. Several people she met remained lifelong friends she would visit on future trips, entertain in California, and corresponded with faithfully. During World War II, Grace feared for her friends' safety and sent parcels of food and clothing, items made scarce by war. Her first experience in England, her honeymoon trip, allowed her to see firsthand much that she had studied and read.

This was the beginning of many years in the limelight. As she thrived in her role as hostess and Los Angeles tour guide for friends and colleagues, the Hubble home on Woodstock Road became an enclave for a select circle of friends. In 1931 Robert Millikan, president of Cal Tech, asked Grace to serve as unofficial hostess to Albert Einstein on his first visit to Pasadena, driving him to meetings, assisting with personal needs (such as lining up a dentist for Frau Einstein), and entertaining the Einsteins in her home. The famous people Grace met in her lifetime

Grace Hubble, 1931.

Source: This item is reproduced by permission of *The Huntington Library, San Marino, California.*

were not limited to academics and scientists, however.

From his post at the observatory, Edwin Hubble proved the universe is constantly expanding, the first evidence of the Big Bang theory, and became an

instant celebrity. In 1990 the National Aeronautics and Space Administration placed in orbit a space telescope named for him. His fame and the proximity of the Mount Wilson Observatory to Hollywood brought notable personalities to peer through the telescope and talk with the astronomer. As Edwin worked at the telescope, Grace pondered the surrounding landscape and nature. She enthusiastically embraced the outdoors, felt deeply about her surroundings, cared for the wildlife around her, and wrote with clarity of her observations. Edwin made his observations with the help of a telescope; Grace made hers with eyes alone, observations destined to be a part of her legacy. Grace frequented the mountaintop, and here in 1937 her lifelong friendship developed with Anita Loos, the screenwriter and author of *Gentlemen Prefer Blondes.* The Hubbles regularly dined at the Loos home on the "Gold Coast" of Santa Monica. She and Grace were close confidantes and their correspondence is illuminating. Anita's admiration for Edwin's work prompted her to arrange for other entertainment personalities to visit Mount Wilson.

British writer Aldous Huxley and wife, Maria, were among those introduced by Loos, and quickly entered the circle of friends. Anita Loos once wrote, "The few successful marriages I have known were between intellectuals, . . . married pairs like Aldous and Maria Huxley, and Edwin and Grace Hubble." The relationship with the Huxleys meant intellectual companionship for both Hubbles and provided Grace with an opportunity to hone her editing and proofreading skills. Aldous, plagued with poor eyesight, relied on Grace to edit manuscripts, a task she accepted enthusiastically. One of the first books she assisted him with was *Many a Summer Dies the Swan*. She did not stop at proofreading, but offered opinions and made suggestions. In 1943 Grace joined Edwin at the Aberdeen Proving Grounds in Maryland, where he headed the army's wartime ballistic testing program. Maria Huxley wrote Grace of the selfish regret Aldous felt at "the departure of his most trusted proofreader." Aldous regretted the loss; nevertheless, he continued to send Grace copies to proofread. This friendship lasted until the mid-1950s, when both Edwin and Maria passed away and Aldous pursued other interests with his new wife. Grace did not accept her dear friend's new adventure into the world of mind-altering drug experimentation, and they no longer spoke.

In her journals, Grace detailed their daily lives, their dinners, walks, and conversations with colleagues and neighbors. She wrote of sitting at Frank Capra's table during the 1937 Academy Awards and later of her place beside William Randolph Hearst at the Hearst Ranch. On vacations in the Sierra Nevadas or fishing and horseback riding in Colorado, the journals became the master's canvas as Grace painted pictures with her words. The incredibly detailed knowledge of plant and animal life she recorded in her journals reflected both her education and her lifelong affection for nature. In 1936 Grace's words became more intent, more purposeful; she understood she was recording history. Cross-country train trips to conferences where Edwin presented scientific findings are laid out in careful detail, including the topics presented, people in attendance, reviews of his presentation by others, and, of course, her incomparable praise. She was never too timid to come to his defense, never hesitated to offer her help. When the scriptwriter for a 1940 radio broadcast failed to produce acceptable copy on historical scientific personalities for Edwin, Grace stepped in to do a quick revision of content and grammar. According to Edwin, Grace was his first line of defense. "The only purpose of the journals was to recapture the clues of memory," wrote Grace. Edwin kept them by his bed, rereading them, making corrections. Grace wrote little when separated, and once reunited at the Proving Ground, she thought it "wiser not to write." Following the war, she continued to record trips to the mountains and Europe, but worried that the journals had begun to resemble 18th-century English diarists and travel writers.

It is fitting that Grace's journals now reside at the Huntington, a place that held special meaning to the Hubbles, their choice for regular Sunday walks with neighbors. Although closed to the public on Sundays during those years, their connections with library staff allowed them entrance to the grounds. In 1938 the Huntington trustees elected Edwin Hubble to succeed George Ellery Hale on the board, a position he maintained with pride until his death. Edwin and Grace enjoyed the friendship of Max Farrand, the Huntington's first director of research, as well as other staff members. As a result, visitors from abroad arriving with Grace received an exceptionally warm welcome. During the war years, in Edwin's absence, Grace obtained a reader's card, and her tremendous intellectual curiosity and ability to peruse the stacks of this great institution offered a stimulating way to fill otherwise empty hours.

Grace Hubble on horseback.

Source: This item is reproduced by permission of *The Huntington Library, San Marino, California.*

After Edwin's death, Grace returned to the Huntington's collections to occupy her time. She read literature, history, science, and books on travel, continued her walks in the gardens, and admired art in the gallery.

The years between Edwin's death in 1953 and Grace's death in 1981 are elusive. During Edwin's lifetime, Grace rarely wrote in his absence unless recording his activities or his calls home, and after his death saw no need to continue. With the journals closed, she turned to the task of producing his memoir, writing mostly by hand, and relying on her journals and correspondence as the primary source. She later destroyed many letters and Edwin's personal papers. Why is a question that looms large. Grace took great care, however, to see that all the scientific papers and the library from their home were safely placed at the Huntington.

The journals and memoir are not without problems. Gaps in the narrative of Edwin's life, particularly his early years, have prompted some scholars to suggest Grace manipulated the historical record. The foremost critic is Professor Kip S. Thorne of Cal Tech, whose criticism, while essentially limited to Edwin Hubble's early years, clouds the remaining entries with a shadow of doubt. A second critic and recent biographer of Edwin Hubble, Gale Christianson, wrote that Grace not only refused information offered by Edwin's relatives, but also destroyed accounts not meeting her objective. Edwin never introduced Grace to his family and may have embellished his past while they courted, perhaps in an attempt to impress a young woman and her family that he was their social equal; regardless, Grace chose to believe him. Grace showed bias when she wrote of the man she loved, but any deviations of his record were personal, not professional.

"We say it has been a perfect trip, no regrets, no omissions, not much that we would have had happen differently. And we should be grateful for having had it so." Grace wrote these words the day they returned from their last trip to Europe. She could as easily have been referring to the life she shared with Edwin. In her remaining years, Grace quietly read and wrote, never complaining. She continued her walks in the Huntington gardens every Sunday, entertained visitors from England and colleagues of Edwin. She did not travel, though she corresponded with friends. When she could read no longer, close friends like Ida Crotty, her longtime friend and neighbor, visited and read to her. According to Ida, "many people in the journals were just as much interested in conversation with Grace as they were with Edwin." Her desire for intellectual stimulation remained up to the end. Grace's death certificate listed her occupation as housewife; her obituary called her a writer. Grace Burke Hubble, the writer, crafted the legacy to her husband that now resides in the archives of the Huntington Library. Alongside that archive is another legacy, the legacy of Grace Burke Hubble, as represented by her writing. In her heart, Grace Burke Hubble was a writer, a writer to the stars.

—Linda Frances Mollno

SUGGESTED READING

Christianson, Gale E. *Edwin Hubble: Mariner of the Nebulae.* New York: Farrar, Straus & Giroux, 1995, 228.

HUFF, MARILYN M. (1951-)

Born in Ann Arbor, Michigan, in 1951, Marilyn M. Huff studied for her bachelor's degree at Calvin College. Following her graduation in 1972, she pursued her J.D. at the University of Michigan Law School. Upon receiving her law degree in 1976, she moved to San Diego, California, to open her private law practice. On March 12, 1991, President George H. W. Bush nominated her to fill William B. Enright's vacated seat on the U.S. District Court for the Southern District of California. The Senate confirmed her nomination on May 9, 1991, and she received her commission on May 14 of that year. In 1998 she began serving as chief judge and remains there to this day.

—Marcus J. Schwoerer

SUGGESTED READING

Marilyn M. Huff. Retrieved from air.fjc.gov/servlet/tGetInfopjid=1110. Source: History of the Federal Judiciary. http://www.fjc.gov. Web site of the Federal Judicial Center, Washington, D.C.

HUFSTEDLER, SHIRLEY ANN MOUNT (1925-)

Shirley Hufstedler was among the generation of women who first went to law school after World

War II. She received her B.A. from the University of New Mexico and her J.D. from Stanford in 1949. She was the first woman elected to the *Stanford Law Review*. She worked as a practicing lawyer from 1950 through 1960. She was appointed a judge in the Los Angeles County Superior Court in 1961 and was elected to the position in 1962. She worked on the California Court of Appeals for 2 years, beginning in 1966. She was one of the first women appointed to the federal bench in 1968, when President Lyndon Johnson appointed her to the U.S. Court of Appeals for the Ninth Circuit. She served there until President Jimmy Carter, in a newly reorganized Cabinet, appointed her the first Secretary of Education, a post she served in from 1980 to 1981. The most important controversy during her tenure was a fierce debate over the implementation of bilingual education in American schools. She has taught at the University of California at Irvine and Santa Cruz, the University of Iowa, the University of Vermont, Stanford Law School, and the University of Oregon. She has also served the American Bar Association (ABA) and the State Department on a delegation to negotiate exchanges of legal scholars between the United States and the Soviet Union, Poland, and Hungary. She was the first woman awarded the ABA Medal in 1995. She chaired the U.S. Commission on Immigration Reform from 1994, after the untimely death of the first chair, until 1997. She is regularly called upon to analyze judicial systems and recommend ways to improve their efficiency. She is presently a partner at Morrison & Foerster in Los Angeles.

—Scott Kesilis

SUGGESTED READING

Wharton, Joseph. "ABA Honors Shirley Hufstedler: Former Federal Judge Is First Woman to Be Awarded ABA Medal." *ABA Journal,* August 1995.

HUGHES, SARAH TILGHMAN
(1896-1985)

Sarah Tilghman Hughes was one of Texas's most important jurists, politicians, and feminists of the 20th century. She was born on August 1, 1896, in Baltimore, Maryland. Her parents, James Cooke and Elizabeth Haughton Tilghman, were descendents of colonial families who had immigrated to North America in the 1660s. She attended public school in Baltimore. In 1917 Tilghman graduated from Goucher College with an A.B. in biology. Following graduation, she taught science at Winston Salem Academy in North Carolina. She enrolled in the George Washington University Law School in 1919. While attending law school at night, she worked as a police officer in Washington, D.C., during the day. She graduated from George Washington with an LL.B. in 1922; the same year, on March 13, she married George Ernest Hughes, who had been her classmate at law school.

In 1923 Hughes joined the firm of Priest, Herndon, and Ledbetter, where she practiced until 1935. She served three consecutive terms in the Texas House of Representatives, beginning in 1930. In 1933 Austin newspaper reporters named her the most effective representative in the state. In 1935 she became the first woman to serve as a Texas district judge when Governor James Allred appointed her to the 14th District Court in Dallas. In 1936 she was elected to the bench in her own right and was reelected on six subsequent occasions, the last time being 1960.

In 1946 Hughes ran for a U.S. Senate seat, but lost in the Democratic primary. She believed that her liberal views were to blame for her defeat. In 1958 she ran unsuccessfully for the Texas Supreme Court. In 1961 she asked Senator Ralph Yarborough and Vice President Lyndon B. Johnson to recommend her to the federal judgeship of the Northern District of Texas. President John F. Kennedy denied her appointment, based on the recommendations of Attorney General Robert Kennedy and the American Bar Association, both of which claimed that her age was of concern. At the time she was 65. Women's organizations such as the Business and Professional Women's Club staged a letter-writing campaign in support of her candidacy. Yarborough, Johnson, and Speaker of the House Samuel T. Rayburn continued to lobby on her behalf. After an effective letter-writing and lobbying campaign, in October 1961 President Kennedy gave Hughes the appointment. She became the first woman to serve as a federal judge in Texas.

Hughes was involved in many important legal decisions, including *Schultz v. Brookhaven General Hospital* (1969), *Roe v. Wade* (1970), and *Taylor v. Sterrett* (1972). She became a national figure with the assassination of President John F. Kennedy because she administered the oath of office to Lyndon Johnson aboard Air Force One at Love Field on November 22, 1963. Hughes was a founding member of the Hoblitzelle Foundation and served as national president of the Business and Professional Women's Clubs. In 1975 Hughes retired from the active federal bench. She died on April 23, 1985, at the age of 88 after several years of illness.

—Tiffany E. Dalpe

SUGGESTED READINGS

Dallas Morning News, April 25, 1985.

The Handbook of Texas Online. Retrieved from www.tsha.utexas.edu/handbook/online.

Riddlesperger, James W. *Sarah T. Hughes.* M.A. thesis. North Texas University, 1980.

Sarah T. Hughes Papers, University of North Texas Archives.

Sarah T. Hughes, Oral History Interviews, University of North Texas Archives.

HUTCHISON, KAY BAILEY (1944-)

U.S. Senator Kay Bailey Hutchison was the first woman to represent Texas in the U.S. Senate. She grew up in La Marque, Texas, graduated from the University of Texas and the University of Texas Law School, served in the Texas House of Representatives and as Texas State Treasurer. In the Senate, she serves on the Senate Commerce Committee and chairs the Subcommittee on Surface Transportation and Merchant Marine. She drafted and passed the Ocean Shipping Reform Act of 1998. Other significant duties include chair of the Board of Visitors of the U.S. Military Academy at West Point and as U.S. Delegate to the Commission on Security and Cooperation in Europe. She also is cochair of the Congressional Oil and Gas Caucus.

Hutchison has won numerous awards. including the Border Texan of the Year in 2000, the Clare Booth Luce Policy Institute Conservative Leadership award in 1999, the Texan of the Year award from the Texas Legislative Conference in 1997, and the Republican Woman of the Year award from the National Federation of Republican Women in 1995.

Hutchison lives in Dallas with her husband, Ray, a partner in the law firm of Vinson & Elkins.

—Gordon Morris Bakken

SUGGESTED READING

Whitney, Catherine. *Nine and Counting: The Women of the Senate.* New York: HarperCollins, 2001.

I

ILLSTON, SUSAN YVONNE (1948-)

Born in Tokyo, Japan, in 1948, Susan Yvonne Illston moved to the United States and began attending Duke University. She graduated in 1970 with a bachelor of arts degree, and moved to California to attend Stanford Law School. She received her J.D. in 1973 and promptly opened her private practice in Burlingame, California. She remained there for the next 22 years, until January 23, 1995, when President Bill Clinton nominated her for a seat on the U.S. District Court for the Northern District of California. The seat had been vacated by Barbara A. Caulfield. Illston was confirmed by the Senate on May 25, 1995, and she received her commission on the following day.

—Marcus J. Schwoerer

SUGGESTED READING

Illston, Susan Yvonne. Retrieved from air.fjc.gov/servlet/tGetInfo?jid=1143. Source: *History of the Federal Judiciary*. http://www.fjc.gov. Web site of the Federal Judicial Center, Washington, D.C.

IN PENITENTIARIES

The history of crime and punishment in the American West seldom includes substantive detail about the incarceration of women, leaving the inaccurate impression that only western men spent time behind bars. In part, the lack of information points to the slight interest in prison history, with the exception of a few sensational accounts that deal with the unhappy fate of the Jesse James Gang or the Younger Brothers. The paucity of well-ordered and accessible research documents also has been an inhibitor of scholarship concerning the western penitentiary.

Prison inmates in the West, as in other locales, tended to be ethnic and minority people, less powerful and easy targets for arrest and conviction by the dominant and dominating Anglo community. Many 19th-century inmates were illiterate and generated few records by which to document their experiences. Also, many died at a young age, the narratives of their short lives slipping away with them. Each of these factors intensified for women inmates, making incarceration of western females difficult, but not impossible, to trace. The growing attention to the regional importance of race and class has added to the potential for reclaiming the history of criminal and imprisoned western women.

In the frontier West, the principal house of detention was the local jail, overseen by a federal marshal or a county sheriff. In many towns, the jail was little more than one or two cells inside the law office. In others, it was a free-standing cage-like structure placed out of doors. Jails were not intended for long-term residence. In the 19th-century West, they provided a temporary lockup until adjudication had been reached concerning criminal behavior. In the criminal process, one charged with breaking the law was arrested, placed in a cell, brought before the court, and returned to the cell until execution or internment at the state penitentiary, all these events taking place within

145

a matter of days. As early western women were not commonly associated with crimes that resulted in execution or long prison sentences, they had slight connection to these first jails, which had no separate women's section.

With growing western populations and the attendant increase in crime, the use of the jail inflated to make it the place for punishing those convicted of misdemeanors but unable to pay their fines, as well as lawbreakers waiting to be hanged or transported to the state prison. Small towns began to feel the necessity of better constructed jails to accommodate the rising local inmate population. The additional convictions for misdemeanors and the more permanent facilities opened local jails to women offenders, whose crimes were of a minor sort. Typically, women in frontier towns were arrested for prostitution, disturbing the peace, public fighting, or drunk and disorderly conduct.

The environment of the jails was not pleasant, but at least local law officers were responsible for those in the lockup. The procedures lacked the institutional aloofness of law enforcement in large urban centers, as all the participants lived in the same community, knew each other according to their public roles, and had, if not a personal relationship, at least a slight acquaintanceship. For example, a sheriff probably arrested a woman, almost certain to be a repeat offender, in the saloon district, in or close to her place of employment. The officer escorted her through the justice of the peace court, took her to the jail for confinement, and expected to arrest her again in a short time.

It was not unheard of for a magistrate to release an indigent prostitute to the streets to continue her trade so that she could earn her court costs. When a woman could not pay the fine imposed by the court, her jail sentence, depending on the number of her arrests, usually ranged from 10 to 30 days. During her incarceration, she might be required to do some cleaning or cooking, but in most situations no clear assignments occupied the time of women prisoners, who spent their days locked in the small cells. In more than one frontier town, women were released before expiration of the sentence because the jailer, operating on a small budget, did not wish to continue the expenses of room and board.

The circumstances for western criminal women shifted when the American penal system underwent changes that called for fewer executions and longer incarcerations in better built, more formal, and seriously imposing institutions of punishment. This policy shifted inmates—male and female—away from local people and local control, placing them under the jurisdiction of distant state legislators, who never saw them, and under the daily supervision of strangers, who directed their lives over long periods of time. Gone were those arrangements, although marked by uneven power relationships, that gave poor women access to the movers of local government and a chance for helpful intervention. Women sent from jails to state and territorial prisons entered into an entirely new prison world.

Western penitentiaries were planned, built, and maintained by men for other men, without concern for possible gender implications in any part of the prison process. Although prison commissions were usually charged to select healthful and conveniently located building sites for prisons, such did not result. For example, Huntsville, Texas, chosen in the mid-1800s for the new state penitentiary, was more than 60 difficult miles from Houston.

Such isolation was true for most western prisons, built in remote locations, ensuring that what happened inside the walls would be little known or cared about by the so-called free people of a community. The designing, financing, and constructing of the prison had almost certainly involved fraud and thievery at every level. Once the prison opened, the warden was typically a political appointee with little or no formal training in penology, and the same was true for his staff. Poorly trained personnel, participants in a policy of institutionalized corruption, had little incentive to look on themselves as guardians of good government or of "bad" inmates, and allowed their facilities to be overrun with scandal. This disorder was further compounded because there was so little agreement concerning the purpose of incarceration, whether it should be punitive or rehabilitative. In these circumstances of confusion about policy, materials, and humans, women faced a number of disadvantages.

First, those responsible for prison management did not consider women a significant part of their concern. Women sent to state and territorial prisons remained few in number. How frequently would a woman—especially an Anglo—be convicted of homicide or arson? The authorities were inclined to believe the occasion would always be rare. For example, in 1915 Governor Moses Alexander of Idaho vetoed an allocation to enlarge the female ward at the penitentiary because he declared the state would not have any increase in women inmates, a statement disproven with each succeeding year.

Idaho officials tried to segregate women prisoners by housing them in this walled compound (foreground).

Source: Idaho Historical Society.

For example, in Missouri's pre-Civil War days, a random one or two women were incarcerated at the men's penitentiary, but after 1865 the state saw its female inmate number leap from the teens to nearly 50 and continue to ascend. During the post-Civil War era, most prisons witnessed some increase, perhaps of one or two women inmates per year. Administrators allowed the slight annual increases to distract them, overlooking the persistent and steadily rising numbers of women inmates. Furthermore, they failed to ask themselves about the changing postwar demographics or to explore the reasons, including a national tendency to arrest and imprison more persons for longer periods, for the increased numbers.

This misreading of a climbing inmate index resulted in systemic failures to address the growing needs of women prisoners. Throughout the 19th century, women entered penitentiaries that had no segregated women's wing, so female inmates were crowded together into one or two old storage rooms. Wardens showed little interest in the problem, beyond complaining to the legislature about the inconvenience of dealing with women inmates. In 1890 the warden of the Arizona Territorial Prison at Yuma constructed a shack in the center of the prison yard for the only woman inmate. He permitted her to wander through the prison, making herself available for intimacy with both guards and prisoners. When an inquiring journalist discovered the situation and reported that the young woman had given birth to one child and was pregnant with another, the prison administration blamed the inmate for "corrupting the morals" of the men and quickly released her. Similar accounts appear in the records of Missouri, Idaho, Texas, and Montana.

The poor housing arrangements inevitably led to other problems for women inmates. Their overall health and well-being declined quickly inside the penitentiary. While it had been estimated by one warden that no prisoner could survive more than 10 years in any western penitentiary, women particularly suffered because of the unfit sanitation and poor nutrition.

A steady supply of clean water was a rarity, yet one more outcome of the poor features of the sites chosen for prison buildings. In Arizona and Idaho, the poor soil and faulty drainage around the prison led to noxious odors and undrinkable water. One prisoner conceded inmates took one bath a week, but all used the same tub of filthy water.

The prison diet was notoriously bad for all inmates. Those purchasing food materials did not hesitate to appropriate for themselves the better supplies or buy spoiled goods for a fraction of the allotted costs, pocketing the difference. A steady and meager menu of stale bread, lard, moldy potatoes, and coffee with sugar did not contribute to the health of women, especially those pregnant or nursing infants, who required fresh milk, cheese, rice, eggs, vegetables, and unspoiled meats.

Women with chronic illnesses fared badly as well. Medical care was substandard, a fact that particularly angered Kate Richards O'Hare, a political activist who served in the Missouri penitentiary for protesting World War I. If a woman entered prison in ill health—suffering from asthma, heart disease, or arthritis—her condition was certain to worsen quickly. Fluctuating temperatures in drafty cells, broken sleep, and lack of proper bathing and toileting all contributed to illness. Furthermore, prison doctors were expected to keep inmate laborers at their jobs and not "pamper" them with time off for illness. Physicians who insisted that the unsanitary health conditions be corrected were quickly silenced or fired.

Pregnant women could count on little medical assistance. No appropriate facilities existed for childbirth. In Texas, an African American woman gave birth under a tree next to the field where she had been working. In Missouri, a warden suggested to the governor a child should not be born in December in a prison that had no heat. In New Mexico, a pregnant African American woman was confined to solitary on a diet of bread and water. In Texas, a foreman publicly shaved the head of a postpartum woman before he took away the newborn and placed the inmate mother in the dark cell.

Few administrators wanted the difficulties of providing for an infant in a penal institution. Because of that sentiment, pregnancy nearly guaranteed that an Anglo woman would receive a pardon, regardless of the seriousness of the crime for which she was serving

time. While difficult to prove, apparently some women tried to become pregnant, using their condition to attract unfavorable media attention that could result in a gubernatorial pardon. Such seemed to be the strategy of Pearl Hart, released from the Arizona prison in 1902, and Josie Kensler, who left the Idaho penitentiary in 1909 after successfully exploiting a scandal about her pregnancy and abortion.

In addition to poor health conditions, the prison work environment for women was often debilitating. Penitentiaries in the West frequently negotiated labor contracts with private manufacturers. By these, a businessman came into the prison and used inmate labor for a twine or shoe or shingle-making enterprise. Although these businesses did not have skilled jobs for women inmates, females provided free domestic support, doing laundry, cooking meals, scrubbing floors, washing windows, and cleaning offices. This "housekeeping" work was critical to the management of the prison, where the goal of the business owner was to shape the penitentiary into a self-sufficient, enclosed community, where profits could be maximized and expenses reduced as much as possible.

In Minnesota, the prison company of Seymour and Sabin became so successful that it employed inmates as well as nonprison citizens inside the walls. In Missouri, in the early 20th century, women prisoners worked in 9-hour unbroken shifts sewing men's pants, shirts, and jackets. The conditions in these factories were extreme—sweltering in the summer, freezing in the winter. In all work situations, prisoners, whether male or female, looked for opportunities to sabotage the undertaking. Broken tools, lost supplies, and "accidental" fires were common ways to undermine the profits extracted from the work of unpaid laborers.

In some areas of the West, especially those with close ties to the South, the lease system became a popular form of using inmate labor for private gain. In this arrangement, the warden leased out the work of prisoners to a private business located outside the walls of the prison. Typically, these prisoners were sent to agricultural camps, working at heavy farm labor in fields of rice, cotton, and tobacco. Women prisoners were also "leased out" to participate in the field work at the farm camps. Without exception, these inmate laborers were African American women. This system led to even greater abuse, as it removed prisoners from state supervision, left them with a private individual who was subjected to little or no regulation, and eliminated any chance for protest or grievance to public officials.

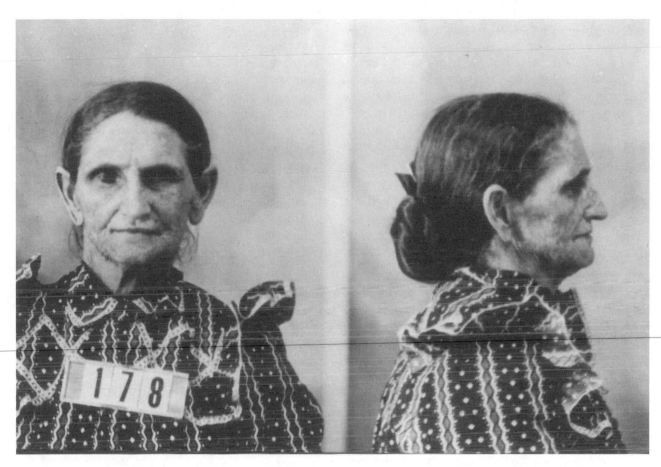

After 1 year in the Kansas penitentiary, this blind prisoner was transferred back to the authorities in the Oklahoma Territory.

Source: Kansas State Historical Society, Topeka, Kansas

Furthermore, some women of color were leased to private homes, where they were to give domestic service. The practice was widely condemned, but continued unabated into the 20th century. Although such an arrangement gave a woman inmate a chance to live in a cleaner environment with better food, she remained a "prisoner" of the family for whom she worked and could be returned to the penitentiary at a moment's notice for the slightest transgression—real or imagined. Some families did actively seek a pardon for the inmate, with the understanding that she would remain as their servant. This type of lease was fueled by race, class, and gender imperatives, with white women directly petitioning the warden for the lease of an indigent African American female inmate.

While some prison work actually gave male inmates industrial training that could be useful upon release, such was not true for women prisoners.

Women prisoners were closed out from learning trades. When Progressive era reformers began to call for more educational programs for inmates, women were excluded from full participation. Women attended separate classes and were not permitted the privilege on class nights of dining together at tables where conversation was permitted. Most of women's prison labor concentrated on traditional domestic chores, rather than preparing female inmates for trade that would mean better-paying occupations on release.

All the elements in the prison experience of women led to an inevitable result. Extraordinary violence underscored their prison lives. On the day that a woman entered the penitentiary, she was required to submit to the Bertillon examinations, named after its originator, who thought body types revealed inherited criminality. The new inmate was required to stand naked while men measured and examined every part of her body, recording breast size, head diameter, burn and bullet scars. The new prisoner's head was not shaved unless she balked at the exam conducted by male guards and trustee inmates. This initiation to prison life set the tone for the unmitigated violence that women found inside western prisons.

Every aspect of prison life added to the physical and mental assaults on women inmates. The makeshift accommodations that awaited them foreshadowed the way they would be treated as part of the prison population. Just as they had no decent quarters, they only occasionally received decent clothing. Women inmates in Texas worked at the farm camps barefoot and wearing only a skimpy tunic-like shift.

In this setting, emotional and physical abuse were common as prison males—guards and inmates alike—saw the women as available sexual partners. No system of protection was in place to help the woman who objected to rape. Guards, whose power was unchallenged, could "report" a woman inmate for breeches of discipline, when in fact she had rebuffed sexual advances. The ensuing punishment included one or all of the following: a diet of bread and water, confinement to solitary, or public whippings and torture. In Kansas, as late as 1913, matrons reported that women inmates were chained to the wall, with their feet barely touching the floor. In other prisons, women were hung in the stocks and gagged, whipped by one or more guards, or locked to a ball and chain. Perhaps most destructive to a woman's mental well-being was the power the guards possessed to arbitrarily subtract from an inmate's accumulated "good time" points, the effect of which was to delay the prisoner's expected date of release.

The path that had brought many women to prison had been littered with personal violence, frequently involving a spouse or partner. Women were moved through the court system in but a few days and then found themselves sent to a state penitentiary. Given the nature of the process, they had little time to organize a defense, get help from their families, or even understand the charges against them. Courts were reluctant to accept a plea of self-defense, even when witnesses insisted that a woman was in danger of immediate death from a drunken and vicious attacker.

There seemed to be little concern for matters of self-incrimination, and all manner of "confessions" were used against the women, and juries were, of course, made up exclusively of white males. In 1887 in Texas, a woman of color was arrested, taken directly to court, given no access to legal assistance, and immediately convicted through her own "confession" that a dog she had tethered broke loose and attacked a hog. While this Texas woman was not actually sent to the penitentiary, she had to apply for a gubernatorial pardon to secure a remission of fines she had paid. Sixteen years later, in Montana, an illiterate deaf African American woman was sent to the penitentiary for stealing a $10 gold piece, although there was no evidence she understood the charges she faced or what transpired in the courtroom.

In all western penitentiaries, women of color were incarcerated in greater numbers, for lesser crimes, and served longer sentences than Anglo women. Between 1865 and 1906, at least 150 of the 200 women who were sent to the Kansas penitentiary were African Americans. Other western states replicated this trend, as reported by the 1910 U.S. Census. Its statistics showed that the percentage of African American women incarcerated in all regions, including the West, was greater than any other defined group, including African American men. Along with African American women, Mexican American women were at risk in Texas, California, New Mexico, and Arizona. Yet local forms of discrimination varied their "race" designations. In the 1880s Anglo women were favored over Latinas in the New Mexico penitentiary. The latter were housed in a single crowded room and given the most demanding work assignments, while a single white inmate had her own private room, complete with a piano. In Texas, however, Mexican American women were classified as "white," lived in separate housing with Anglo prisoners, and like them did not join the African American women in doing field labor.

Many women of color found themselves incarcerated at the state penitentiary for crimes that might more correctly have sent them to the local jail. For example, their infractions included stealing a shirtwaist, a pair of curtains, a sleeping robe, or a hat. Frequently, the charges did not match the definition of grand larceny, which indicated that the stolen property should be valued at $20 or more. The penitentiary sentence might be as long as 2 to 10 years at hard labor for crimes that saw white men and women serving their time in the local jail.

Once at the penitentiary, women of color could not rely on the pardon and parole system to be of great benefit to them. In Arkansas, over a 25-year period, 252 of the 270 women sent to the penitentiary were African American. Of the 18 white women, prison files

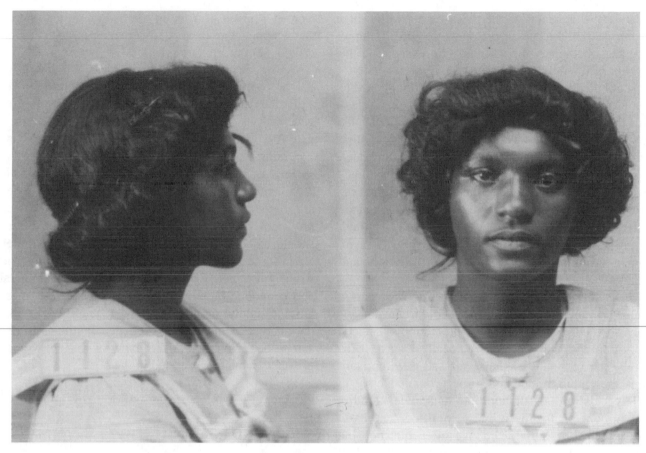

African American domestic workers, such as Cora Thomas, often served lengthy prison terms for minor offenses.

Source: Kansas State Historical Society, Topeka, Kansas.

showed that early pardons were routine, one only 3 weeks after the inmate came to the prison. In contrast, African American women generally served at least half of a sentence before a chance of pardon, and those receiving amnesty numbered fewer than a dozen.

Women convicted of violent crime—homicide or manslaughter—were more likely to serve out the bulk of the sentence. Exceptions to this could be found in Arkansas, Texas, and Louisiana, where Anglo women were quickly pardoned. Regardless of race, prostitutes found guilty of murder rarely filed successful petitions for pardon or parole. These women won early release from the penitentiary if they were diagnosed with a terminal disease, became a subject in a highly publicized prison scandal, committed suicide, or died.

Although the prison world was slanted against women, denying them personal dignity, educational opportunities, or freedom from violence, female inmates found ways to push back against the forces that weighed them down. It was clear that women inmates needed strategies inside the prison if they were to survive or be released. Some found their survival by striking a posture of accommodation, "willingly" seeking out intimate relationships with wardens or guards in return for personal protection, better food, clothing, and the possibility that a pregnancy could mean release. Some responded with aggression, both verbal and physical, willing to do so even though their actions brought swift and brutal punishment. Some banded together with other inmates, both male and female, to create a relentless string of guerilla-like attacks on the prison routines. They destroyed property, smuggled contraband to each other, warned one another of pending disciplines or cell searches, and entered into forbidden sexual liaisons. Some cooperated with outside contacts, especially the press, to bring attention to prison abuses. Some hoped for their families to organize legal assistance or appealed to the governor for relief. In a system designed to break prisoners, to force compliance and obedience, the various actions speak to the courage of the human spirit in the face of adversity.

That human spirit undergirded all that happened to women prisoners. From the outset of the initial clash with the law, from the first public denunciation of a woman, those charged with crime learned quickly that their heaviest burden concerned the way in which their actions were seen as "immoral." Male criminals never faced anything equal to the power of public censure heaped on women perceived as having broken the societal covenants of correct womanhood. Through the press, community response, and the legal system, women criminals were castigated as "aberrant and unnatural."

Once she lost her status as a "true woman," a female criminal faced a daunting set of circumstances. Since she no longer deserved the protection of society, a criminal woman became a social outcast. Ultimately, the judgments against her and the imprisonment she endured appeared to be grounded more in society's definitions of appropriate female morality than in concern for the crime committed. The haste with which the courts acted, the often questionable acceptance of circumstantial evidence, the slight crimes treated with the same gravity as serious felonies, the severity of the sentences, and the inhumane conditions of the penitentiaries all suggested that something more grievous than the theft of curtains had occurred.

Women prisoners paid a double price, one whose components included crime breaking and gender offenses. Although this was the case for women prisoners everywhere in the United States, in the 19th-century American West, with its self-conscious attempts to create solid communities based on eastern and Anglo values, female inmates represented a group especially in need of societal control. In a sense, the West succeeded in creating a fearsome image of how women who strayed from society's expectations would be handled.

Through women inmates, society honed the mechanisms of gender control but never developed a strategy for the balanced treatment of female criminals and prisoners. The frontier West disappeared, but the conditions of women inmates slipped into the 20th century with as many negatives as from an earlier era. States finally hired trained matrons and built separate facilities for women, but not quickly—Nebraska opened its

women's prison at York in 1930. Punishment stocks and whipping bats disappeared. In their place, however, came other unfortunate practices.

Fewer educational opportunities for women prisoners, as compared to the offerings for men, a slower and more uneven pardon and parole system, less generous visiting rights, more limited access to mail delivery, greater censure as failed parents but few programs to address mother/child needs—these and variations on them became the markers of the 20th-century western prison system for women. They are based on long-held assumptions that women prisoners will remain few in number, their futures should be domestically oriented, as lawbreakers they are in some way deficient in their gender identity, and women of minority cultures are unworthy of political and economic attention. In the modern West, these attitudes inhibit an informed response to the fact that the number of incarcerated females continues to rise across the region, but the treatment of western women prisoners remains grounded in the past.

—Anne M. Butler

SUGGESTED READING

Butler, Anne M. *Gendered Justice in the American West: Women Prisoners in Men's Penitentiaries*. Urbana: University of Illinois Press, 1997.

IVINS, MOLLY (1944-)

Molly Tyler Ivins was born in Monterey, California, in 1944. Her father was a military man who served in World War II, her mother coming from an affluent society family on the East Coast. She followed both her mother and grandmother to Smith College, where she graduated in 1966. She went on to Columbia University, earning her master's degree in journalism.

A rebel in her youth, Ivins was active in the 1960s' anti-Vietnam protests and the civil rights movement. Other causes throughout her career include her service as a board member of the National News Council, her writings on behalf of the American Civil Liberties Union, and her participation in the Journalism Network of Amnesty International.

Her early career included employment with the *Houston Chronicle*, where she worked in the

Complaint Department and as sewer editor. At the *Minneapolis Tribune*, she reported on police activities and an assignment called Movements for Social Change, giving her a first taste of conflict dealing with the radical and militant elements.

At the so-called alternative publication *Texas Observer,* where she was coeditor, Ivins was exposed to a more political and social atmosphere that fed her passion for politics Texas style, especially the Texas legislature. This, combined with her sense of humor and her satirical wit, provided for a very entertaining viewpoint of the political world.

In 1976 Ivins became a political reporter for the *New York Times*, covering New York City Hall, the state house in Albany, and eventually becoming the Rocky Mountain Bureau Chief. Her style not being conservative enough for the *Times,* Ivins went back to Texas in 1982 to write for the *Dallas Times Herald* and ultimately the *Fort Worth Star-Telegram.* In addition to the many newspapers she has written for, she has also freelanced with notables such as *Esquire, Atlantic, The Nation, Time,* and *Mother Jones Magazine.*

Ivins's book publications include *Molly Ivins Can't Say That, Can She?, Nothin' but Good Times Ahead, You Got to Dance With Them What Brung You* (speaking of former President Bill Clinton: "he's weaker than bus-station chili"), and her latest jab, *Shrub: The Short but Happy Political Life of George W. Bush.* Her career awards include the Smith Gold Medal,

Outstanding Alumna by Columbia University School of Journalism, National Society of Newspaper Columnists' Lifetime Achievement award, and three-time finalist for the Pulitzer Prize.

A breast cancer survivor, Ivins currently writes for Creators Syndicate in Los Angeles and is syndicated in over 200 newspapers throughout the country.

—Neal Lynch

SUGGESTED READINGS

Celeste, Eric. "Molly Ivins Leaves the *Star-Telegram's Staff,* but Not Its Pages." Retrieved from www.dallasob-server.com/issues/2001-04-19/filler.html.

Davidson, Cathy N., and Linda Wagner-Martin. *The Oxford Companion to Women's Writing in the United States.* New York: Oxford University Press, 1995.

Ferrar, Miranda H. *The Writers Directory 2001.* Detroit, MI: St. James Press, 2001.

Ivins, Molly. "'Dissent' Is Not a Dirty Word." Retrieved from www.dfw.com/mld/startelegram/news/columnists/molly_ivins/3056069.ht . . . /printstory.js.

Molly Ivins to Speak at Smith College as One of Four Outstanding Alumnae to Be Honored. Retrieved from www.smith.edu/newsoffice/Releases/00-053.html.

The Quotable Ivins. Retrieved from www.salon.com/people/feature/2000/12/12/ivins_quotes/print.html.

Rubien, David. "Molly Ivins." Retrieved from www.salon.com/people/bc/2000/12/12/ivins/print.html.

J

JACKSON, HELEN HUNT (1831-1885)

In the late 19th century, Helen Hunt Jackson became synonymous with the struggle for Native American rights in America. Despite this renown, this remarkable woman had achieved recognition for her writing talents prior to the publication of her two most enduring works, *A Century of Dishonor* and *Ramona*. Born Helen Maria Fiske in Amherst, Massachusetts, on October 15, 1831, to Nathan Welby and Deborah Fiske, Jackson was the beneficiary of her parents' intellectual and literary talents. Her mother was a writer and her father a professor at Amherst College. Unfortunately, her mother died of tuberculosis when Jackson was 12, and her father died 3 years later. For the remainder of her adolescence, she was educated at the Ipswich Female Academy. While at the Academy, she met Emily Dickinson, and the two maintained a lifelong friendship.

In 1852 Jackson married Edward Bissell Hunt, an engineer for the U.S. Army. The couple had two sons, Murray, born in 1854, who died in infancy, and Rennie, born in 1855. In 1863, at the height of the Civil War, Edward was suffocated to death in an accident with a submarine of his design. This tragedy was compounded 2 years later when Rennie contracted diphtheria and suddenly died. In order to support herself, Jackson moved to Newport, Rhode Island, and with the help of friends launched her literary career. For the next several years, she focused her attention on children's stories, poems, and novels. Her work was well received and eventually resulted in over 30 books. However, her literary success was contrasted with declining health, and in 1872, on the advice of her physician, she traveled to the West in an attempt to cure a persistent respiratory ailment. In 1873-1874 she was in Colorado Springs, Colorado, where she met William Sharpless Jackson, a prominent businessman. In 1875 they were married.

By 1879 Jackson had heard a lecture by Chief Standing Bear on the government's forcible removal of the Ponca Indians from their home in Nebraska to Indian Territory. Standing Bear's plight so moved Jackson that she devoted the remainder of her life to vigorously defending the rights of Native Americans. In 1881 she published *A Century of Dishonor*. Her work exposed the systematic disregard for Native American rights that had characterized U.S. government treatment of Indians and led to public outcry. In an attempt to sway the options of Congress, she sent a copy of the book to every member of the legislature. Her publishing success, however, resulted in little change for the Indians whose cause she championed. In 1882 she was designated as a special commissioner of Indian Affairs and journeyed to California to investigate the conditions of the Mission Indians. Sadly, her report to the Indian Commission again bore little fruit, but in 1884 she was inspired to write *Ramona,* a semifictionalized account of the murder of a native man by a prominent white rancher. In June 1884 she was diagnosed with cancer and died on August 12, 1885.

—Vanessa Anne Gunther

SUGGESTED READINGS

Mathes, Valerie Sherer. *Helen Hunt Jackson and Her Indian Reform Legacy.* Austin: University of Texas Press, 1990;

Reprint with new preface, Norman: University of Oklahoma Press, 1997.

Mathes, Valerie Sherer. "Helen Hunt Jackson: Official Agent to the California Mission Indians," in Doyce B. Nunis Jr., ed., *Women in the Life of Southern California.* Los Angeles: Historical Society of Southern California, 1996.

Mathes, Valerie Sherer. *The Indian Reform Letters of Helen Hunt Jackson, 1879-1885.* Norman: University of Oklahoma Press, 1998.

Senier, Siobhan. *Voices of American Indian Assimilation and Resistance: Helen Hunt Jackson, Sarah Winnemucca and Victoria Howard.* Norman: University of Oklahoma Press, 2001.

JAIL MATRONS IN LOS ANGELES

On May 5, 1923, Mrs. George W. Shehi wrote a humble letter to Los Angeles County Sheriff William Traeger. In the letter, Mrs. Shehi requested the sheriff's support, as she sought a retirement from the county for her 16 years of service as jail matron "with one half my salary as pension." She went on to state that

I feel justified in making this request. . . . For nearly seven years I was the only matron appointed by law; consequently during all that time my only opportunity for leaving the department to obtain fresh air and outdoor exercise was when my daughter relieved me, which she did at no expense to the County.

On July 10 Sheriff Traeger forwarded Mrs. Shehi's letter to the Civil Service Commission, who sent it to the Board of Supervisors. There is no indication that they took any action on this request. Defeated in her effort to secure an early retirement, Mrs. Shehi continued to work as a matron until October 1927, when her health finally forced her departure.

Los Angeles Sheriff's Department historian F. W. Emerson called Mrs. Shehi the "first matron of the Los Angeles County Jail." This is not correct, but her status as the only matron for over 6 years is not in doubt. There were female prisoners in the Los Angeles County Jail at various times from the county's earliest days, but like so many jails and prisons across the nation, women did not always supervise women. Just how women arrived in a supervising role in the first place is a murkier story.

The problem of men supervising women prisoners appears obvious, but remedying this problem was anything but obvious early in the 19th century. Like many reforms in this country, the roots of the movement leading to the participation of women in penal institutions can be traced to England. In 1815 Elizabeth Gurney Fry "rapped at the prison doors in England . . . [and] sounded a call to women in other lands to enter upon a most Christ-like mission." Fry, a Quaker minister, began her interest in helping women in prison after her first visit to Newgate Gaol in 1813. Fry encountered women in deplorable conditions and determined to do something. By 1816 she helped create the Ladies Association for the Improvement of Female Prisoners. This group organized workshops, conducted Bible classes, and developed a system of internal discipline. It also helped hire the first jail matron.

Fry and her followers believed that wayward women could be reformed and rehabilitated. The prejudice of the day was willing to accept that men could stumble and, like the prodigal son, be saved, but wayward women were Jezebels. Fry and her followers' strict adherence to the contrary, coupled with her continued insistence upon "women's superintendence of female inmates," eventually caused her to fall into disfavor with the male hierarchy that ran British prisons, and most of her reforms were gone by 1835.

By the 1820s American women from many denominations were visiting incarcerated women. Institutions in New York and Philadelphia were among the first to meet their acquaintance. They were often the daughters of upper middle-class or wealthy families, and the eternal salvation of the women prisoners was of as great an interest to them as was their physical condition and that of their surroundings. Historian Estelle Freedman noted that most of them "were married, had large families and were active in benevolent associations"; indeed "their lives conformed . . . to the cultural ideals of true womanhood." Like Fry in England, these reformers often were frustrated with the treatment of female prisoners by male guards and of themselves by males in the reform movement.

The arrival of matrons in eastern jails and prisons progressed slowly. Rachel Perijo was hired at the Baltimore prison in 1822 and may very well have been the nation's first matron. Others were hired in Pennsylvania, New York, and Massachusetts. Still, the practice was inconsistent. But it was often not what was proper that drove the administration of jails and prisons, but rather what was practical and economical.

In many places there simply were not that many female prisoners. There were certainly not enough inmates to justify a "Woman's Department," as was often demanded in larger cities. It was not until the number of women prisoners began to increase in the 1870s that women began supervising women in larger numbers.

The sentiment for women's reform in jails and prisons may have existed in the West after 1850, but there were simply not enough women on either side of the bars for the situation to merit any kind of serious attention. This was certainly true in early Los Angeles. During the period of Mexican control of California, women rarely appear in the records of the time as suspects of crimes.

When Americans took control in Los Angeles, they inherited the local jail. They also inherited a similar breakdown in the demographics of lawbreakers. Women's names are again rarely found. The question of just where female lawbreakers could be incarcerated in the early 1850s was a valid one. The Los Angeles County Jail from 1850 to 1853 was a grossly inadequate structure even for male prisoners. It was essentially a one-room adobe building, "one long room, built of logs, and without cells." Housing female prisoners in this configuration was obviously not practical. The jail constructed in 1853 addressed this concern. It was a two-story brick structure. "The first floor is . . . divided into two apartments, for males and females." This building would serve as the county jail until December 1886.

During all those years, there is no evidence that women played any role in the supervision of their incarcerated sisters. The sheriff held the overall responsibility for the jail, but the jailer managed its day-to-day operation. The jailer hired assistant jailers to help him as necessary. The character of some early jailers was questionable, but no accusation of abuse against a female prisoner was ever made.

No Los Angeles jail records survive between the early 1850s and early 1880s. The first jail register listing the comings and goings of inmates in the county jail is dated from August 1, 1884. There were only 1.17 women in jail on the first of each month in 1885. The number was 2.58 in 1886 and 2.67 in 1887. During the later months of 1887 and into 1888, however, there was rarely a day when there was not at least one female in jail. The average count for June 1887 through February 1888 was 3.77. The number of women in the county jail at any time pales by

comparison to men. By February 1888 there were 213 men in jail and only 3 women, but a constant female presence behind bars meant that the need for a matron was justified. There were only 32 women in jail for all of 1887, but by 1889 the total was 73 and the following year it jumped to 145.

Grand juries gave some attention to the condition of women in jail but never mentioned a need for matrons or noted their performance once they arrived. S. W. Burke, chair of the 1890 Grand Jury Jail Committee, found the housing of female prisoners cramped and inadequate for "women of high moral sensibility and lady-like delicacy and decency." Burke went on to suggest that "a partition be run subdividing the department."

Jail costs were always an issue and entered into the decision-making process on whether a matron would be hired. The price of feeding and caring for inmates was of paramount concern. In 1850 the county officials created an allowance of 50¢ each day for feeding inmates. By 1905 that amount dropped to 11¢ a day. The hiring of a matron was a decision that the sheriff could not make on his own if he had any intention of paying for the position.

The 1880s was the decade when women's groups, nationwide, led by the Women's Christian Temperance Union (WCTU), began to agitate for the addition of jail matrons in jails and prisons. WCTU groups were instrumental in hiring matrons in a number of cities. In Los Angeles, the Women's Benevolent Society played an important role. One woman who was outspoken in this area and in the condition of wayward children was Helen A. Watson. She was a tireless reformer and her actions did not go unnoticed.

In 1888 a growing controversy about the location of brothels and the frequency of arrests of prostitutes led to a call for the restriction of this prominent business. This situation was an ongoing problem in the early 1880s. The indifference and alleged complicity of law enforcement officials in this wayward occupation did not help matters. Finally, in one response to this controversy, Mayor William Workman appointed Helen Watson as the city's first matron. Here, it was no doubt hoped that she would apply her skills as a social reformer on the community's fallen women. She was to be paid $60 a month. Her tenure was brief, however, and by the end of the year, Lucy Thompson Gray, a mother of 10, was working as matron.

The name of the county jail's first matron is unknown, but when Sheriff Gibson took office on

January 1, 1891, there was one in place. The Board of Supervisors informed the sheriff that upon taking control of his office, he was authorized to hire a number of positions including "1 Matron [at] $50 [per month]."

The matron was paid $25 less each month than the two assistant jailers were, although their jobs were essentially the same. Sheriff Gibson later asked the supervisors for a third assistant jailer at $50 a month. This request was granted. One can only wonder what the third assistant jailer thought about being paid the same as the matron.

Like the jailer, jail matrons toiled in obscurity. While they often took exception to the condition of either the county or city jail, there is no complaint from the 1890s' grand juries about the performance of either jailers or matrons. The 1898 grand jury did use the term "Women's Department" for the first time in its report, suggesting that females in the Los Angeles County Jail finally achieved a status similar to their eastern counterparts.

The new 1903 Los Angeles County Jail included better quarters for the matron. By this time, the matron was expected to live at the jail full time. In a little over a decade, the county jail went from having no matron to having one assigned on a permanent basis who was literally living with the inmates. Sometimes this was actually the case, as women of a "better class" shared quarters with the matron. The construction of the new jail provided relief from this predicament, but a return look at Mrs. Shehi's letter confirms that her alleged plight of not being able to escape the jail was no exaggeration.

An assistant for Mrs. Shehi was not hired until November 1913, when Sheriff Hammel received permission from the Board of Supervisors to add one. Elizabeth Bartoo was hired as assistant matron. Sheriff Hammel did add another woman to the payroll the year before Mrs. Bartoo, however. On February 16, 1912, Margaret Q. Adams was sworn in as the department's first female deputy sheriff. She arrived at the department 18 months after Alice Stebbins Wells was hired as the first female police officer in the Los Angeles Police Department. With the arrival of women as police officers, the place of matrons in law enforcement began to diminish. This is not to say that their role declined, but once women started becoming sworn officers, the focus changed. Matrons in many cities attempted to be recognized as police officers. In other cities, policewomen began to distance themselves from matrons because they were seen as untrained and unskilled and diminished the place of policewomen. There is no evidence that Margaret Adams ever spent a shift in the county jail. She was assigned to the civil division, where she spent her entire career. While the debate over the arrival of policewomen raged throughout the country, and Mrs. Adams was settling into her position in the civil division, Mrs. Shehi was all too happy to welcome the arrival of Elizabeth Bartoo. It meant she would finally receive a day off. The Women's Department of the jail truly became a department with the hiring of Mrs. Bartoo.

The inmate population continued to rise during the 1910s. By 1920 the jail designed to house 150 prisoners often housed over 400. The number of women prisoners increased as well. In 1919 Sheriff Cline requested that additional matrons be hired. In a 1925 photograph of jail personnel, four matrons are seen. The condition of the jail was unbearable for staff as well as for prisoners. A major riot in 1921 hastened the construction of a new jail. In 1926, 875 inmates crossed the street and entered the new jail that was located on the 9th through 15th floors of the new Hall of Justice. The lower floors housed offices and courtrooms.

By June 1927 the female inmate population outgrew their accommodations on the 13th floor, and the roof chapel was converted to a dormitory to house some of the 181 female prisoners. The female population continued to rise. By 1932 Vada C. Sullivan was head matron over a Women's Department with a staff of 17.

In late 1923 Sheriff William Traeger attempted to fire jail matron Rose Ruff for showing favoritism to certain inmates and being a disruptive presence among the matrons. She was eventually fined for her actions but retained as a matron. This event is significant. It demonstrates that matrons were being held to the same standards as men. By 1923 they were clearly seen as employees, not social workers.

Today, social workers, counselors, and special education personnel continue to work with female prisoners, but the female staff that supervises them long ago transitioned from social worker to security officer. This began when women started to become sworn peace officers in large numbers and demanded to be taken more seriously in their role in law enforcement.

Matrons decreased in importance in the 20th century as the role of policewomen increased. Still, it was this occupation that provided the entry point for women into law enforcement. In Los Angeles, the introduction of women into jails went smoothly and with little fanfare. Indeed, there was so little attention paid to it that the name of the sheriff's department's first matron is unknown. Yet without the trailblazing efforts of these women, Margaret Q. Adams is unlikely to have become the department's first deputy sheriff as early as 1912.

—John Joseph Stanley

SUGGESTED READINGS

Bookspan, Shelley. *A Germ of Goodness: The California State Prison System, 1851-1944.* Lincoln: University of Nebraska Press, 1991.

Butler, Anna M. *Gendered Justice in the American West: Women Prisoners in Men's Penitentiaries.* Chicago: University of Illinois Press, 1997.

Emerson, F. W. *History of the Los Angeles Sheriff's Department, 1850-1940.* Pasadena, CA: Federal Writer's Project, 1940.

Freedman, Estelle B. *Their Sister's Keepers: Women's Prison Reform in America, 1830-1930.* Ann Arbor: University of Michigan Press, 1981.

Langum, David J. *Law and Community of the Mexican California Frontier: Anglo-American Expatriates and the Clash of Legal Traditions, 1821-1846.* Norman: University of Oklahoma Press, 1987.

Rothman, David J. *The Discovery of the Asylum: Social Order and Disorder in the New Republic.* Boston, MA: Little, Brown, 1971.

Schultz, Dorothy Moses. *From Social Worker to Crimefighter: Women in United States Municipal Policing.* Westport, CT: Greenwood Press, 1995.

Stanley, John Joseph. "L.A. Behind Bars, 1847 to 1886: Establishing a Secure Institution," in Gordon Morris Bakken, ed., *California History: A Topical Approach.* Wheeling, IL: Harlan Davidson, 2003.

JARAMILLO, CLEOFAS MARTÍNEZ (1878-1956)

Cleofas Martínez Jaramillo was born in Arroyo Hondo, New Mexico, on December 6, 1878. Her parents, Marina Lucero Martínez and Julían Antonio Martínez, were prosperous descendents of traders and landowners. Thus Jaramillo received a good education at the Loretto Convent School in Taos and the Loretto Academy in Santa Fe. When she was 20 years old, she married a cousin, Venceslao (Ven) Jaramillo, a successful businessman and politician. But her life was not all romance and luxury.

Early in their marriage, the Jaramillos lost two infants, and in 1920, when their third child was only 4 years old, Ven died of a lifelong illness. Faced with a young daughter and no significant source of income—her husband did not leave the estate in her name—Jaramillo was forced to manage the family's finances. Then, 11 years later, further tragedy struck: her daughter, Angelina, was murdered. So in 1931, when women in upper-class Hispanic society were expected to stay home and be quiet, Jaramillo found herself thrust into the public sphere. As she conquered her personal reticence and her culture's silence, she propelled herself into the role of cultural authority and found her voice. She became an expert on and spokesperson for Hispanic culture and thus gained the narrative authority to speak in the dominant discourse.

Like many southwestern women writers during the early part of the 20th century, Jaramillo wrote and published cultural histories and culinary collections that sought to rectify misconceptions about southwestern life. Upon publication of Erna Fergusson's *Mexican Cookbook* in 1934, some Hispanic women felt that they, rather than Anglo women, should be the purveyors of their culture's culinary history. In 1935 Jaramillo founded La Sociedad Folklórica de Santa Fe in order to reclaim her people's past and preserve a dying way of life. She also published a cookbook and folklore collection of her own. In 1939 she published two books: *Cuentos del hogar/Spanish Fairy Tales* and *The Genuine New Mexico Tasty Recipes: Old and Quaint Formulas for the Preparation of Seventy-Five Delicious Spanish Dishes.* Both collections served as correctives to the popular folktales and recipes collected in Fergusson's book. While Fergusson acquired her recipes from an informant, Doña Lola Chaves de Armijo, Jaramillo claimed ancestral access to "genuine" Spanish recipes. In 1941 Jaramillo published another folklore collection, *Sombras del Pasado/Shadows of the Past,* which also revised Anglo versions of southwestern life. In 1955 she published her autobiography, *Romance of a Little Village Girl,* which reveals how Hispanic women, such as Jaramillo, have resisted the colonization of Hispanic recipes, rituals, and history in Anglo discourse by women such as Erna Fergusson. But her autobiography also demonstrates how an individual woman employs her cultural experience and ancestral roots to construct a new national and cultural identity for herself and her people.

In *Romance of a Little Village Girl,* Jaramillo foregrounds her desire to re-create the more pleasing aspects of her memory of the past and, in the process, elides the less pleasing aspects. Her preface lays bare the nostalgic desire that shapes her narrative:

> It is not unnatural for one who lived a harmonious, happy young life to desire to revive those years, to people the melting ruins of a once-happy home, to live again in memory the girlhood years that were enriched with comfort and love, innocent of any wickedness, sheltered from all care and grief, and to live again among those kind, humble people, loyal to their God's religion, respectful and honest.

In this passage, Jaramillo not only reveals her nostalgia, she celebrates it. She describes a past that is colored by the presumably disharmonious and unhappy circumstances of the present: her home is in ruins, ruins that are melting away from memory. Her desire to "revive," to "people," to "live again" the innocent years suggests that now, in her present world of New Mexico, these conditions are gone, ruined, tainted by some unmentioned transformation, such as the passage of time, an influx of new people into New Mexico, or sociopolitical movements within or without that affect the people who inhabit the region. Although Jaramillo avoids any overt explanation of this transformation, her nostalgic desire reflects a sense of cultural displacement that generates her need for tradition, community, and stability in order to stave off the effects of this displacement.

After explaining her nostalgic desire "to people the melting ruins of a once-happy home," Jaramillo situates her narrative in a geographic place:

> In this little valley of the Arroyo Hondo River, situated in the northern part of the state of New Mexico, hemmed in by high mountains and hills, sheltered from the contamination of the outside world, the inhabitants lived peacefully, preserving the customs and traditions of their ancestors.

In this passage, Jaramillo combines region with the cultural history of her people. The landscape mirrors the position of Hispanos before the Americanos took over their land and lives: they are "hemmed in" and "sheltered from the contamination of the outside world" by the protective mountains and hills. They are isolated from the rest of the world but they are safe from it as well. This passage describes geographic influences and their cultural manifestations; region determines the human characteristic of cultural silence and protects people from the influences of extraregional events. But in the end, even the land cannot shield Jaramillo or her people from the outside world. Cupid's arrow makes its way into the "verdant little nook," and the activities of the outer world begin to affect the once-insulated life of Arroyo Hondo. Jaramillo thus blends the region's influence on Hispanos with her personal and cultural nostalgia for a pre-Anglo-American existence. The result of her combination is a depiction of southwestern landscape and culture that maintains connections with place and past. She grounds her text in a regional space even as she generates a new but not unfamiliar world out of her encounter with the past. *Romance of a Little Village Girl* is situated in an apparently real place that, through the application of memory and the nostalgic impulse, becomes a better place—a world that satisfies the human need for a sense of self and a place to be at home.

Jaramillo's decision to write her autobiography marks a break from her culture's silence with regard to Anglo society. In her Preface, she indicates her desire to disrupt this silence:

> Under the apparent deadness of our New Mexico villages there runs a romantic current invisible to the stranger and understood only by their inhabitants. This quiet romance I will try to describe in the following pages of my autobiography, although I feel an appaling [sic] shortage of words, not being a writer, and writing in a language almost foreign to me.

The romantic qualities here include a depth beneath the surface, a life under the deadness, an unseen current that nourishes the inhabitants. This "romantic current" is an imaginary construct that is nevertheless very real to the people who know of its existence. Jaramillo wants to reveal this current to outsiders, to show them the source that sustains the inhabitants. In her society, she argues, silence about Hispanic culture and life allows Americans to speak for Hispanos; it lets the outsiders tell and retell the wrong tortilla recipe. She feels that she and her people must speak the as yet unspeakable and uncover the now hidden truths about their ways of life in order to revise the national story about Hispanos.

As Jaramillo constructs her autobiographical self, in *Romance of a Little Village Girl* she also demonstrates her ability to speak as a regional/cultural authority by providing elaborate culinary descriptions and instructions. Throughout her narrative, she uses her culinary details to rewrite the cultural record as Anglos such as Erna Fergusson wrote it. These detailed cooking accounts—in her cookbook, *The Genuine New Mexico Tasty Recipes: Old and Quaint Formulas for the Preparation of Seventy-Five Delicious Spanish Dishes*, and in her autobiography—thus perpetuate, for instance, her culture's recipe for "real" tortillas. While these cooking details function as validations of her cultural expertise, they also function as strategic bridges across the gap between past and present. Like writing, cooking is both a personal and a collective cultural act: a woman tells and retells a recipe as she makes it her own. Cooking, like writing and storytelling, keeps the recipe/story alive.

In her own story, Cleofas Jaramillo charts her personal development from a silent and complicit girl living an isolated life in Arroyo Hondo to a vocal and confident woman living an active social life in Santa Fe. This development parallels the thematic progression of the narrative from her culture's quiet stillness, "the apparent deadness of our New Mexico villages" to its lively activity in the Santa Fe Fiesta, where the women wear their ancestors' restored gowns, "all ready to leap out of old trunks from the past to the present and have their wrinkles shaken out in the air, to portray the styles of by-gone days." These gowns renew the past; they innovate and interrupt the present by bringing the past into play again. These gowns are objects recontextualized in the present; they re-create a sense of the past in the present. By wearing the gowns in the fiesta's parade, the women of Jaramillo's folklore society transform their present reality into a world that incorporates elements of both the past and present.

The final two chapters of Jaramillo's autobiography revisit "the Dear Village" of Taos, which has been changed by the automobile and the atomic bomb, and return her to, as she says, her rightful home in Santa Fe. Here in the ancient city she finds herself alone but doing her part to further the cause of cultural preservation: "I must contribute my bit. I must try to put this little work on the market." Through the course of her narrative we see a quiet little village girl evolve into a vocal cultural spokeswoman. We see a culture, a

woman, and a landscape move from the silence and isolation of the past to the noise and commerce of the present.

After a life dedicated to preserving her culture's past for future generations, Cleofas Jaramillo died in 1956, at the age of 78.

—Becky Jo (Gesteland) McShane

SUGGESTED READINGS

Fergusson, Erna. *Mexican Cookbook*. Santa Fe, NM: Rydall, 1934.

Ponce, Mary Helen. "The Lives and Works of Five Hispanic New Mexican Writers, 1878-1991." *Southwest Hispanic Research Institute Working Paper No. 119*. Albuquerque: University of New Mexico Press, 1992.

Rebolledo, Tey Diana. Introduction. *Romance of a Little Village Girl*. By Cleofas Jaramillo. Albuquerque: University of New Mexico Press, 2000 (reprint of 1955 edition), xv-xxvii.

JORDAN, BARBARA (1936-1996)

Barbara Jordan, the first black woman to be elected to the Texas legislature, was born in Houston, Texas, on February 21, 1936. She was the youngest daughter of Benjamin and Arlyne Patten Jordan. She grew up in the Fourth Ward of Houston in one of the city's largest black ghettos. She attended Texas Southern University, a school created for blacks, who were not allowed to attend the University of Texas, where she excelled at debate and graduated magna cum laude in 1956. In 1959 she graduated with a law degree from Boston University and passed the bar exam in both Massachusetts and Texas that same year. She taught at the Tuskegee Institute for 1 year before returning home. Once home, she set up a private law practice from her parents' home. She worked out of their home for 3 years while saving enough money to open an office. In 1960 she first became involved in politics when she registered black voters for the presidential campaign. She ran unsuccessfully for the Texas House of Representatives in 1962 and 1964 because she could not attract white voters. In 1966, thanks to redistricting and an increase in black voter registration, she was able to secure a seat in the Texas Senate. She won the election by a 2 to 1 margin. Her win made national news because she was the first black Texas senator since 1883 and the first black woman to be elected to the Texas legislature. President Lyndon B. Johnson endorsed and helped facilitate her career.

Jordan gained the respect of her white male colleagues by being a master of detail and an effective pragmatist who was willing to work with both sides of the aisle to accomplish her objectives. During her 6-year tenure as state senator, she saw half of the bills she submitted enacted into law. Her peers elected her an outstanding freshman senator. While in the legislature, she fought to secure minimum wage laws and chaired the Labor and Management Relations Committee. In 1972 she was unanimously elected president pro tempore of the Texas Senate. That same year, she was given the honor of Governor for a Day. In 1972 she was also elected to the U.S. House of Representatives, where she served three consecutive terms. She was the first black woman elected to Congress from the South. While serving, she was known for her independence. She was willing to forge alliances with conservatives and even cross party lines to work closely with Republicans, always following conscience over party politics. She worked to push through legislation that expanded voting rights to non-English-speaking residents and prohibited discrimination in publicly funded industries. She championed women's causes. She fought to pass the Equal Rights Amendment to the Constitution. She also fought for abortion rights and sought entitlement of homemakers to Social Security benefits. While in the House of Representatives, she served on the Judiciary Committee.

She was a prominent figure in the Nixon impeachment hearings. She delivered a 15-minute televised speech regarding the Watergate scandal, where she asserted, "My faith in the Constitution is whole, it is complete, it is total. I am not going to sit here and be an idle spectator to the diminution, the subversion, the destruction of the Constitution." Impressed by her eloquence, the Democratic Party chose her to deliver the keynote address at the 1976 Democratic National Convention. She was the first African American to have this honor. In 1979, after three terms in office, Jordan retired from politics and accepted the Lyndon Baines Johnson Public Service Professorship at the LBJ School of Public Affairs at the University of Texas, Austin, where she taught courses on ethics, intergovernmental relations, and political values. That same year, she published her autobiography, *Barbara Jordan: A Self-Portrait.* During the early 1990s she served as ethics adviser to Governor Ann Richards. Jordan once again delivered the keynote address at the Democratic National Convention in 1992. In 1994 she served as chairwoman of the U.S. Commission on Immigration Reform. She received numerous honors, including induction into the National Women's Hall of Fame in 1990 and a Presidential Medal of Freedom in 1994. She suffered from a number of health problems in her later years, including a form of multiple sclerosis, and was confined to a wheelchair. She never married. Jordan succumbed to leukemia and pneumonia in Austin, Texas, on January 17, 1996. Her papers are housed at the Barbara Jordan Archives at Texas Southern University.

—Tiffany E. Dalpe

SUGGESTED READINGS

The Handbook of Texas Online. Retrieved from www.tsha.utexas.edu/handbook/online.

Jordan, Barbara, and Shelby Hearon. *Barbara Jordan: A Self-Portrait.* Garden City, NY: Doubleday, 1979.

Rogers, Mary Beth. *Barbara Jordan: American Hero.* New York: Bantam, 1998.

Barker Texas History Center, Vertical Files, University of Texas, Austin.

K

KANSAS

Women in Kansas have demonstrated many of the same daring attributes as their counterparts in other western states. During the 19th century Kansas women led the nation in the female suffrage movement and were the first to vote in municipal elections. In the 20th century women like Amelia Earhart and Olive Beech paved the way for female prominence in the nation's aviation industry.

Some of the first women came to Kansas to pursue the traditional role of teacher, first among the native peoples and later among fellow white settlers. Rose Philippine Duchesne pursued her lifelong goal of working with the Indians when she came to southeast Kansas in 1841 at the age of 72. Despite her own ill health, she led a group of Sacred Heart nuns to an area about 70 miles southwest of Kansas City to work in a Jesuit mission. She impressed the Indians, who called her The Woman Who Prays Always. She lived there only a year, but for her cumulative life's work she was beatified in 1940.

Mary Bridget Hayden came to southeast Kansas in 1847 as part of a group of nuns who were going to work with Indian girls at the government school in Osage Mission, near present St. Paul. Most of her life was dedicated to this school and the Catholic girls' school that succeeded it. Sister Mary Bridget journeyed by boat and lumber wagon along with two other nuns to southeast Kansas. When she took over as mother superior in 1859, they had 73 girls and taught academic subjects such as reading, writing, and arithmetic along with sewing and housekeeping skills.

Civil war-era violence forced the nuns from the school in 1863. They were able to return in 1867, but the Indians had moved south to Indian Territory. Two Catholic schools replaced the Indian school in 1870, and Mother Mary Bridget was put in charge of St. Ann's Academy for girls. The school earned a widespread reputation, with students coming from as far away as Texas to study art and music. A few Indians still attended the school, and the Sisters of Loretto sometimes used some of their own funds to send them on for further education. Mother Mary Bridget worked until her death in 1890. After fire destroyed all the school buildings, the sisters left the Osage Mission in 1895.

Eliza McCoy may not have been the first Protestant missionary in Kansas, but she was one of the first to leave a detailed accounting of her experiences on the Kansas prairie. McCoy's uncle was one of the organizers of the American Indian Mission Association, and in 1844 McCoy and her long-time companion, Sarah Ann Osgood, applied to become missionaries. Osgood would work her entire life with the Wea Tribe near Paola. McCoy went to work with the Potawatomie Indians approximately 50 miles southeast of Kansas City. Barely surviving a tornado before her departure, McCoy was appalled at the horrible living conditions and drinking she found when she arrived in Kansas. The Indians were moved to another location 60 miles west of Kansas City and the missionaries followed, only to be greeted by a run-down house and a snowstorm. After her uncle's death, she experienced a decline in funding and greater competition from nearby Jesuit missionaries. McCoy gave up her work with the Indians within a year of her partner's death and went to teach in Indiana and died in Dallas in 1891.

Sarah Griffin Boone married the son of Kentucky frontiersman Daniel Boone, and she and their children accompanied him to present-day Jefferson County, Kansas, when the government appointed him to teach farming methods to Kansas Indians. Sarah gave birth to the first white child born in Kansas when she bore her 12th child in 1828.

Elizabeth Custer was never far behind her famous military husband, George Custer, and followed him to Kansas when he was assigned to scout the stage route from Fort Hayes to Fort McPherson. One of the few military wives to follow their husbands on such dangerous duty assignments, Elizabeth was extremely loyal and spent almost 6 decades of widowhood making sure her husband was immortalized despite his famous defeat at Little Big Horn.

Sara Robinson, known as the first First Lady of Kansas, came to Lawrence in 1855. Her husband, Charles Robinson, had arrived a year earlier with the Emigrant Aid Society of New England to found the town. He became governor in February 1861 as a result of his dedicated antislavery work in the state during the era of Bleeding Kansas. A dedicated wife, Sara had undertaken a speaking tour in favor of free-state efforts that took her throughout the East Coast while her husband was imprisoned by the proslavery territorial government at LeCompton. Sara also wrote one of the first histories of Kansas, published in 1856. The book, however, was most important as a propaganda tool to popularize her husband's work as a free-state advocate during the state's territorial days.

Mary Tenney Gray not only followed her husband to Kansas in 1859 when he founded the city of Wyandotte but also earned the title of Mother of the Woman's Club Movement and was known for her work in support of women's rights. As the Kansas/ Wyandotte Constitution was being written, Gray led a group of women who promoted the inclusion of women's equal rights to hold property and control their own children, which included voting in local school board elections. This group also pushed for the guarantee that everyone in Kansas would have equal educational rights. Two decades later, Gray organized what would become the predecessor of the Kansas Federation of Women's Clubs during a Leavenworth meeting that organized a Social Science Club for Kansas and nearby Missouri.

Margaret Greever is credited with being the Mother of Prohibition in Kansas. Along with being a prohibitionist, Greever was a schoolteacher in Wyandotte, and accompanied her husband to the state legislature in Topeka in 1879. When he voted no on the amendment that would outlaw open saloons, she rushed to her husband's side and reportedly spoke rapidly while the roll call continued. The prohibition amendment was one vote short of the required two-thirds majority, but Greever surprised the chambers when he stood up and announced that he wanted to change his vote to aye. In the final vote, two other representatives also changed their votes and the prohibition amendment passed.

Radical Carrie Nation earned a national reputation by destroying saloons across Kansas. Her statewide rampage began in December 1900 at the luxurious Cary Hotel barroom in Wichita. Her husband was reportedly out of town. Wearing mostly black and white, Nation's 6-foot-tall frame created an imposing presence, especially when she was swinging an ax. She claimed that what she was doing was not illegal, because Kansas had a prohibition amendment that made saloons illegal.

After serving 2 weeks in jail, she returned to her crusade and destroyed two more Wichita saloons but was run out of Enterprise after she destroyed a saloon there. In January 1901 she visited Topeka and was eventually hit over the head as she made her way through a mob to the *Topeka Daily Capital* to tell her story. When she leaned over to retrieve her bonnet, it is reported that the bar owner's wife "smote her upon the portion of the anatomy which chanced to be uppermost."

As the state capital where the legislature had just returned to session and the meeting site of the Kansas State Temperance Union, Topeka was a natural target for Nation's hatchetations, as her smashings had become known. She knew that heading toward the Senate Saloon, a well-known legislative watering hole, would generate publicity, since these same legislators had supposedly supported prohibition. When she met with the governor, he paid little heed to her calls for enforcements of the state's prohibition laws, and simply referred her to the state's attorney general. She pointed to the black eye she had received a few days earlier in Enterprise and asserted, "Governor, *you* gave me that black eye." Then, on January 31, Nation and her supporters marched to visit an area in which the bars had thrown up barricades in her path.

When Nation arrived, she found the owners peering out from behind the barricades and called to them, "Aren't you going to let your mother in, boys? She wants to talk with you." Surprisingly enough, Nation spoke to them in a quiet tone and the bar owners gradually emerged to hear what she had to say about the damage alcohol caused to families and that they should close down their establishments. No hatchetations took place that day.

In February of that year, Nation led her group, the Home Defenders, before the legislature and organized another saloon-smashing mission in Holton. On February 10, 3,000 people attended a Topeka temperance meeting, and 2 days later, the Kansas State Temperance Union and the WCTU urged a general uprising.

Turning away from saloon-smashing, Nation joined with Nick Childs from Topeka on February 22 to publish *The Smasher's Mail*, the first of several temperance newspapers. When she was divorced by her husband, who charged her with desertion, in 1901, Nation changed the official spelling of her name from Carrie to Carry; she claimed that a family Bible indicated the latter as the correct spelling. This name change just happened to provide a catchy slogan for her prohibitionist crusade. When she registered in a Chicago hotel in 1940, she wrote her name as "Carry A. Nation, your loving home defender," and reportedly told the hotel clerk that she planned to "carry a nation to prohibition and glory."

Nation organized public-speaking engagements through the United States and donated most of the money she earned to support her home for drunkards' wives and mothers in Kansas City. She also spoke out against smoking and gambling and in favor of women's health issues along with suffrage. The home was open from 1903 until 1910, when it closed due to a lack of occupants. She chose the epitaph "She hath done what she could."

Although instrumental groups such as the WCTU never endorsed Nation or her earlier saloon-smashing tactics, thousands of people supported her with their small contributions. She collapsed on stage in early 1911 and died later that year in a Leavenworth sanitarium.

Credited with the famous statement that farmers needed to "raise less corn and more hell," Mary Elizabeth Lease became a prominent Populist leader advocating woman suffrage and temperance by the turn of the century. Lease arrived in Kansas in 1870 to teach at the Catholic girls' school at Osage Mission. She married a local pharmacist and had four children. After spending some time in Texas, Lease and her family returned to the Wichita area in 1883. Bored with her traditional life, she studied law, was admitted to the Kansas bar in 1885, and became active in civic affairs. She traveled through Kansas in 1890 and made over 160 speeches in favor of Populist causes and was named to the group's national committee in 1892. She gave the seconding speech nominating James B. Weaver at the party's convention that year. Even noted Kansas editor William Allen White, who did not share her political views, wrote that "she could recite the multiplication table and set a crowd hooting and hur-rahing at her will." Her fiery nature, however, led to trouble within the party, and she was exiled from the party when she refused to support William Jennings Bryan in 1894. She also left Kansas and later divorced her husband. She died in 1933 in New York.

Another Kansas woman active in the Populist era was Annie Diggs. Arriving in Lawrence in 1873, she soon became active in the temperance and suffrage movements, including writing a regular column for the *Lawrence Journal*. Her first position was to serve in 1877 as a poll watcher for a local prohibitionist election (Lawrence). Then in 1881 she helped found the Kansas Liberal Union and, after a trip to the East Coast, decided that reforms were necessary. She became active in the Farmer's Alliance, as one way to spread the word about the Populist cause most important to her. In stark contrast to Mary Elizabeth Lease, her soft-spoken nature and smaller stature stood out and won her many friends and supporters throughout and outside the state. Apparently, Diggs and Lease never did get along, but any association they maintained suffered a permanent blow in 1894 when Diggs called Lease "an enemy of the Populist party and a traitor to the cause of equal suffrage." As Lease's influence in the Populist party decreased, that of Diggs increased. At the peak of the Populist movement in 1898, Diggs was appointed as the state librarian and was thus the first woman to hold a state office. Diggs was also president of the Kansas Free Silver League and the Kansas Equal Suffrage Association.

In the suffrage arena, Kansas led the nation by being the first state to consider giving women the right to vote. It was the seventh state to actually pass a female suffrage law. Earlier, Kansas women had been allowed to vote in municipal and school elections and, in some cases, even have equal property rights with their spouses. Kansas was also the first state to elect a female sheriff and the first to elect a woman mayor.

Debate over the women's rights issue in Kansas first appeared in 1859 at the Wyandotte constitutional convention. Three feminists representing Shawnee and Douglas County women's groups, Clarina Nichols, Mother Armstrong, and Mary Tenney Gray, attended the meeting held in present-day Kansas City. Although the men did not allow them to speak during the convention, their presence did help secure the unprecedented right of women to acquire and own property, and allowed them equal custody of their children. According to reports of the proceedings, Clarina Nichols urged women to revolt and even refuse to marry a man if he did not grant them equal rights. Despite her best efforts, however, Nichols did not convince the writers to include female suffrage in the Wyandotte Constitution, but did make some progress by securing equal property rights and equal power in raising their children. The latter included the right to vote in school elections.

In 1861 Kansas became the 34th state in the Union, and women in the new state were partially responsible for it entering as a free state. Women, however, were not given the vote except in school elections, and women's issues soon took a back seat to the Civil War.

One of the most bizarre stories of the Civil War was about the woman who served as a man in the Union Army. She sometimes "disguised" herself as a woman to serve as a spy during the war. Her story came to light after the war when she was living in Fort Scott, Kansas. She originally left home to escape her abusive father and disguised herself as a man and landed a job selling Bibles in Canada. She was apparently successful in this career but soon grew restless and signed up with a volunteer company to join the Union Army. Her disguise worked, since no physical exams were required. By June 1861 Seelye had participated in several campaigns, including the first battle of Bull Run. She worked in the camp hospitals, as a mail carrier, and as a colonel's aide. At least one fellow soldier noted in his diary that he knew "Frank" was a woman. Seelye deserted in 1863, probably to follow a fellow deserter. She wrote a fictionalized account of her adventures, *Nurse and Spy in the Union Army*, and married in 1867. While living out her last years in Fort Scott, Seelye tried to clear her name and obtain an army pension from the U.S. government. Her fellow soldiers rallied to her cause and confirmed her participation in the war. Finally, in 1884 the U.S. Congress authorized the Secretary of the Interior to place Seelye's name on the pension roles. In addition, she became the only woman to be regularly mustered into the Grand Army of the Republic. She died in Texas in 1898.

Details are sketchy about Kate Bender, one of the most infamous women in Kansas. During the 1870s, she had her family murder travelers who passed through their southeast Kansas roadhouse, located approximately 10 miles west of Galesburg on the old trail from Independence to Osage Mission. Kate's reported beauty, including her red hair and ample figure, probably attracted many travelers. Some local residents even credited her with psychic and healing abilities, which only added to the air of mystery at the Bender roadhouse. However, as several travelers disappeared, rumors began to fly about what had happened to them after their stay at the Bender roadhouse. In March 1873 local residents became concerned enough to send out a search party of 50 men and even stopped at the Bender house to ask Kate to use her clairvoyant powers to assist them. Only a few days later, the locals found the Bender house abandoned, and in a nearby orchard they found the bodies of several travelers. One victim had a smashed head and his throat had been cut from ear to ear. Inside the house, the search party found a blood-stained hammer and a trap door. According to reports, the Benders would ask their guests to sit down to dinner in front of a curtain that separated the two rooms of the roadhouse. When they were eating, another family member would hit the guest from behind with a hammer and then stuff them through the trap door once they had collected any valuables they had with them. After it was dark, the family would bury their victims outside. As with other legends, no one knows exactly what happened, and no member of the Bender family was ever located.

Reconstruction era equality efforts brought woman suffrage back to the forefront, and Kansas became the first state to consider full suffrage for women in 1867. As with other suffrage movements throughout the country, women believed that if black men were going to get equal suffrage with white males, they should be accorded the same rights. A resolution was submitted to the Kansas legislature proposing a constitutional amendment to be ratified by the voters that would strike the word "white" from the phrase "white male citizens the right to vote." Another legislator then proposed that the word "male" also be stricken from the resolution. This was only a hint at the controversy over women's equality in Kansas that would be stirred during the Populist and Progressive eras. In 1866 the newly founded University of Kansas became the first state university in the nation to invite women to enter on equal terms with men, according to Glenda Riley.

Nationally known women suffragists, including Susan B. Anthony, Elizabeth Cady Stanton, and Lucy Stone, all came to the state to promote equality for women. Among the first to arrive were Lucy Stone and her husband, Henry Blackwell, who led meetings in a newly built Methodist church in Salina. Soon thereafter, Susan B. Anthony and Elizabeth Cady Stanton worked tirelessly toward female equality with the support of former Kansas governor Charles Robinson. Reports indicate that 14 of Kansas's 20 newspapers supported this endeavor, but on the whole, national newspapers still stacked up against such efforts for woman suffrage.

Prominent Republicans, however, did not appreciate the "Eastern emissaries," and threatened to leave the party that dominated state politics in Kansas. Some observers even assert that this premature push for suffrage may have contributed to the defeat of any type of proposal for either blacks or women in Kansas during that time period.

In 1869 a women's convention was held in Topeka in a failed attempt to revise the cause. But progress was gradually made and the state's Prohibition Party endorsed woman suffrage in 1874. Several more years passed before Anna C. Wait formed a local suffrage association in Lincoln, Kansas, in 1879. Then, in June 1884, the Kansas Equal Suffrage Association began holding annual meetings as it became a truly statewide organization. The movement was revived as suffragists' efforts to create a standing committee on the political rights of women were successful.

Bills granting women the right to vote in city elections were introduced in both the Senate and the House of Representatives in a special legislative session held in 1886. Again, these particular legislative proposals were ahead of their time, and the bills did not become law. However, women were more effectively mobilized, and the American Woman Suffrage Association gathered for its annual meeting in Topeka in October of 1886. Lucy Stone and Susan B. Anthony both returned to Kansas to help promote this vital issue.

In addition to the Kansas Woman Suffrage Association, the WCTU canvassed the state to promote female equality. This time their efforts were more fruitful. A bill giving women the right to vote in municipal elections was introduced in the Senate again later that same year and, after a long debate, was passed and forwarded to the governor, who signed it into law on February 15, 1887. Kansas thus became the first state in the nation to grant municipal voting rights to women, including the right to hold municipal office. Women suffragists continued to cover the state both in person and through the distribution of an estimated 50,000 pamphlets to help ensure that women exercised this newly acquired right.

The WCTU was originally founded as an organization in favor of prohibition, but later expanded its interests to address the wider issues concerning women. In 1875 a Lawrence woman, Amanda Way, attended the WCTU's national meeting and was appointed to plan the group's Kansas chapter that was officially organized by 1878. The group's first president was Mrs. M. B. Smith.

Despite these successful efforts, controversy continued to cloud the issue of women's rights, and the 1887 municipal elections were no exception. Newspapers throughout the nation commented on the events as Argonia elected the first woman mayor anywhere in the United States, and Syracuse voters elected five women to the city council. The Kansas Supreme Court ruled that a January 1887 law permitting female municipal suffrage was valid. But this ruling came a mere 3 weeks before the election. It is relevant to note that Syracuse later became the county seat of Hamilton County.

Women had been allowed to run for county school superintendent in Kansas since 1872 but could still not vote for any candidates who ran for that position. In 1877 Hamilton County in far southwestern Kansas elected its first female superintendent, Elizabeth "Lizzie" Culver. This was seen as a more "acceptable" political position for a woman than serving on the city council, since education was "women's work."

Kate Warthen was the next female who won the title of county school superintendent. She vowed not to repeat the mistakes of her predecessor, and she made sure that her brother accompanied her on the campaign trail in order to negate any appearances of impropriety. Her winning margin was not as large as Culver's, but her victory still solidified women's gains. Traditional expectations still ruled the day, however, and she left the state after her marriage in 1894.

Kansas elected the first woman mayor in the United States when it chose Susanna Madora Salter to lead city government in Argonia. Her father had been mayor 2 years earlier and her father-in-law was the former lieutenant governor of Kansas, but the ballots with her name on it began as a joke intended to disgrace both her and the WCTU, of which she was an officer. This attempt to embarrass Salter backfired and she earned a two-thirds majority of the vote only weeks after women had gained the right to vote in city elections. Only 27 years old, Salter let the city commission members know that it was their responsibility to actually govern the city and that she would help them to the best of her ability. She later claimed the year was uneventful. Salter made headlines as a speaker at the Kansas Equal Suffrage Association in Newton in fall of 1887.

Approximately a year later, Oskaloosa elected six women to the city council. In fact, each woman received more than 100 votes each, while their male opponents garnered less than 50. The women in Oskaloosa, however, reported having a more difficult time partly due to inheriting only 85¢ in the treasury along with outstanding bills. They asked the citizens of their town if they wanted any improvements and, as a result, raised taxes from 5 mills to 7 mills to fund road and sidewalk improvements. They also promoted strict enforcement of both curfew laws for minor boys to help curtail vandalism and laws prohibiting merchants from being open for trade on Sundays.

The Oskaloosa women were elected to a second term but declined to run for a third. It would take decades to repeat this accomplishment when, in 1935, New Albany, Kansas, also elected an all-female city council.

In the years 1888-1889, other towns, including Cottonwood Falls, Rossville, Elk Falls, and Baldwin, followed Argonia's lead and elected female mayors. The next decade witnessed many more women mayors.

As they made forward strides toward full suffrage, Kansas women began aligning themselves with the mainstream Republican and Democratic parties. The head of the Kansas State Suffrage Association, Laura M. Johns, for example, became president of the Republican Woman's Association. Johns, however, was forced to concede to the party's wishes and wait to endorse female suffrage. National woman suffrage leaders were livid at these concessions, but some Kansas women saw the traditional party route as the only possible way to eventually attain equality with men as political players in the state.

Kansas was one of four states to vote in favor of suffrage in 1912; all of its counterparts lay geographically to its west. Later, Kansas was one of the first three states to ratify the Nineteenth Amendment to the U.S. Constitution granting women the right to vote.

Ella Wilson had a much more difficult time than Salter as mayor after she was elected the top official of Hunnewell in 1911. One of her first official acts was to appoint another woman, Rosie Osburne, as the town's chief of police. With two women in such prominent positions in the city, the male council members immediately rebelled by refusing to meet at the times and places established by Wilson. Instead, they attempted to embarrass her by meeting in a bedroom located in a local hotel, somewhere the two women would not go. Securing help from the state attorney general, the mayor eventually threw the male council members out of office. The Kansas Supreme Court heard the case and fined the men and upheld their dismissal. Wilson then appointed a council and chose not to run for reelection.

Expanding the power base of women in Kansas, Minnie Grinstead became the state's first female legislator in 1918. She had been a successful teacher and was a judge's wife. Grinstead also was a leading suffragist and had served for 15 years as a national lecturer for the WCTU. During the 1912 election, she was president of the 7th Congressional District suffrage campaign and delivered the votes of all but 4 of the 32 counties in her district. She was elected to the state legislature for two terms beginning in 1919. Grinstead paved the way for three other women to join the legislature the next year.

Lorraine "Lizzie" Wooster was the first woman to serve as the elected state superintendent of public instruction from 1919 to 1923. Besides being a teacher, she had a law degree and had been a practicing lawyer along with writing several textbooks that were used throughout the state. She led a moral crusade that forbade teachers from wearing cosmetics, dancing, or playing cards. Furthermore, they were not allowed to drink or smoke, even in their own homes. After leaving office, she continued to write textbooks and ran for attorney general as a Republican in 1932. She died in poverty in 1953.

The first woman sheriff was Mable Chase, who began her service by running for the office her husband had held but was not allowed to hold for three consecutive terms. She had served as a deputy sheriff during his tenure and won the 1926 election, appointing her husband as undersheriff.

Kathryn O'Loughlin first served in the Kansas House of Representatives and then was elected to Congress in 1932, defeating eight male opponents. She returned to her law practice when she was defeated in a bid for a second term.

Washburn University graduate Georgia Neese Clark Gray was appointed the first woman U.S. Treasurer in 1949. She later recalled that when President Harry Truman pointed out the low pay that came along with the job and asked her if she could afford to take the job, Gray replied, "Can I afford not to?" She started out life as an actress but returned to Kansas when the Depression struck and worked at her father's Richland State Bank. In addition, Gray became active in Democratic politics when she began speaking in support of Franklin Roosevelt. She served as the state's Democratic National Committeewoman for 28 years beginning in 1936. She became president of the bank when her father died in 1937.

Not only was Hayes native Kathryn O'Laughlin McCarthy single and Catholic, she was also a Democrat in a primarily Republican district when she ran for the U.S. House of Representatives in 1932. Despite these challenges, she became the first woman from Kansas to serve in the U.S. Congress. Her father had been a state representative, and in 1921 she began her political career as a clerk for the House Judiciary Committee after passing the Kansas bar exam. She then moved to Illinois to practice law and worked for legal aid services in Chicago. She returned to Kansas in 1929 and earned a spot in the state legislature in 1930. As a Washington legislator, she was defeated in 1934 by Frank Carlson as the state lost faith in the Democrats' New Deal agricultural policy.

Maize native Nancy Landon Kassebaum is one of the most famous living Kansas women. She was the first woman elected to the U.S. Senate who was not the widow of a Congressman and was the only woman senator for her first 2 years in the Senate. She emphasized that she was a "fresh face" in politics and a housewife who could understand the concerns of the average person. Her father had been a two-term governor of Kansas who lost a presidential bid to Franklin D. Roosevelt in 1936. Kassebaum earned a political science degree from the University of Kansas in 1954 and a master's degree from the University of Michigan 2 years later. While raising her four children, she kept her hand in Kansas politics by serving on the Kansas Government Ethics Commission and the Kansas Council for the Humanities. She served on the Maize School Board from 1972 to 1975. When she divorced her husband in 1975, Kassebaum moved to Washington, D.C., to work as an aide for Kansas Senator Jim Pearson. Kassebaum was elected to the U.S. Senate in 1978 but began her service early when the governor appointed her on December 23 to fill the seat vacated by her predecessor's early retirement. She defeated eight other Republican candidates to secure the party's nomination before she won the general election. While in the Senate, Kassebaum served on the Foreign Relations, Budget, and Labor and Human Resources committees and took a strong interest in welfare and health care reform. She represented Kansas in the nation's capital until 1996, when she declined to run for reelection and married fellow former senator Howard Baker. She currently lives in Japan during his service as the U.S. Ambassador.

The first woman to serve on the Kansas Supreme Court was Kay McFarland in 1977. She graduated from the law school at Washburn University and passed the bar exam in 1964. She became a probate and juvenile court judge in Shawnee County in 1971 and served as the state's first woman district judge beginning in 1973.

Lutie Lytle was the first black woman in the United States to be admitted to the practice of law. Lytle grew up in Topeka but left when she was 21 to teach school and go to law school in Tennessee. In another professional arena, Lucy Hobbes Taylor was the first woman in the world who was professionally trained in dentistry.

Kansas also takes credit for leaders in the entertainment industry. Bennington native Peggy Hull Deuell worked for several Kansas newspapers before heading to Colorado when she was 18. She later wrote for papers in San Francisco and Hawaii before returning to the continental United States when World War II erupted. She then began work for the *Cleveland Plain Dealer* and followed the Ohio National Guard when it was mobilized to go to the Mexican border near El Paso, Texas. Although not sanctioned by the government, she was eventually able to cover the campaign conducted by General John J. Pershing. Most newspapers balked at the idea of a female war correspondent, but Deuell persisted until a Texas newspaper sent her to Europe. Shortly thereafter, she decided instead to follow an expedition to Siberia in

1918. She still needed military credentials, however, but finally succeeded in obtaining them and became the first accredited woman war correspondent from the United States. Next, she ended up in China covering the nation's war with Japan in the early 1930s for the *New York Daily News*. She later married her managing editor.

There were also several more adventuresome females among the ranks of Kansas women. In 1858 Lawrence native Julia Archibald Holmes became the first woman to climb Pike's Peak. Holmes and her husband initially traveled to Colorado to prospect for gold in the Rocky Mountains, but when they found none, they quickly turned their sights on Pike's Peak. Holmes was an active participant in the era's controversial "bloomer movement." Long cumbersome skirts often made it difficult for women to participate in traditionally male activities, and Holmes was one of the many women who wore bloomers—loose pants worn underneath their skirts that enhanced ease of movement. The *Lawrence Daily Republican* newspaper published a letter Holmes wrote to her mother and further publicized her heroic efforts. It is worth noting that Holmes's mother was a friend of Susan B. Anthony and herself was active in the women's rights movement. The young Julia met many leading political figures of the day in her own home. Later, when her husband was made secretary of New Mexico, Holmes wrote for the *New York Herald*. She returned to Washington, D.C., after she divorced her husband and remained active in the woman suffrage movement. Along with her mother, Holmes was a delegate at the first woman suffrage convention held in D.C. in January 1869. In addition, before her death in 1887, Holmes worked for the U.S. Bureau of Education.

Amelia Earhart is perhaps the state's most famous woman. Born in Atchison in 1897, she grew up in Kansas City but visited Atchison frequently. After moving to several midwestern cities because of her father's alcoholism and financial problems, Amelia returned to Kansas City for a brief period before her mother moved her and her sister to Chicago, where Earhart graduated from high school in 1916. After visiting her sister in Canada, Earhart became involved in the war effort by volunteering as an aide for the Red Cross. Here she watched the Royal Flying Corps. Although regulations kept her from hopping aboard one of the airplanes, she remained enthralled with aviation. After exploring various interests over the course of the next year, Earhart moved to California. Here she took her first airplane ride and embarked on flying lessons. By June 1921 she had taken her first solo flight and purchased an airplane on her 25th birthday.

Aviation, however, remained only a hobby, as she continued to teach and do social work. Her life changed dramatically when another woman chosen by publisher George Palmer Putnam to be the first to fly across the Atlantic backed out. Putnam had heard of Earhart's aviation interest and asked her to join the trip as a passenger charged with keeping a log of the flight. She wrote a book about the adventure, *20 Hours, 40 Minutes*, and subsequently this 1928 journey put her in the public eye. Earhart soon became known as Lady Lindy. The aviator took part in the first Women's Air Derby from California to Cleveland, and then in 1929 became one of the founding members of an international organization for women pilots called the Ninety-Nines. Her 1931 marriage to Putnam only enhanced her popularity as he supervised her business interests and the publication of her two later books.

In May 1932 Earhart became the first woman to make a solo flight across the Atlantic. She made several other transoceanic flights before attempting "just one more flight" in 1935. While working at Purdue University as a consultant in the department for the study of careers for women, Earhart was given a Lockheed Electra that she thought capable of making a trip around the world. She wasn't interested in a speed record but in the encouragement of global air travel. She could accomplish this goal by observing factors like human reaction to high altitudes and extreme temperatures as she was flying.

She also wanted a new challenge as she neared her 40th birthday. Numerous mishaps and problems did not deter her as she finally began the journey on June 1, 1937, from Miami, Florida. In the hop from New Guinea to Howland Island in the Pacific, Earhart and her navigator, Fred Noonan, became lost and were never heard from again. The U.S. government sponsored a rescue attempt that scoured 250,000 square miles of ocean and spent $4 million but found nothing. Numerous rumors still abound about Earhart's actual fate, including that she may still be alive on a deserted island. Some also believe that she might have been a spy during this pre-World War II era. The most likely scenario is that her plane was never able to find the tiny island and crashed into the ocean, killing all aboard. Earhart's pioneering spirit helped build the aviation industry in the United States.

Kansas was also the setting for another pioneering effort in the aviation field as Olive Ann Beech, along with her husband, established Beech Aircraft Corporation. Beech worked for a Wichita travel agency and became secretary to the president and the office manager. She later married her boss, Walter Beech, in 1930. The couple, partners in marriage and in business, founded Beech Aircraft in 1932. She served as her husband's right-hand person in addition to fulfilling the duties of secretary-treasurer and holding a seat on the board of directors.

Beech first suggested to her husband that he hire female pilots to demonstrate the ease with which their aircraft could be flown. The resulting publicity greatly enhanced the company's reputation in the aviation industry During World War II, Beech Aircraft became one of the leading manufacturers of military aircraft. When her husband died in 1950, Beech soon became president and the chief executive officer of the company.

Chanute native Osa Johnson, along with her husband, Martin, traveled the world and conducted lecture tours about their adventures. Osa was formally introduced to her husband-to-be in 1910 during his 2-year vaudeville stint showing the photographs he had taken during his South Seas voyages with Jack London. Married 3 weeks after they met, the Johnsons continued on the lecture circuit and collected money for their next adventure. Osa took charge of the travel arrangements and financial affairs of the adventuresome couple and often piloted her own plane alongside her husband's. They took some of the first aerial shots of African wildlife and native peoples. Osa was often right by her husband's side as he photographed previously unrecorded exotic scenes, most of which were not staged. One time she even shot a charging rhinoceros as Martin captured every moment on film. On one trip, she oversaw the 235 porters who carried their supplies where vehicles could not travel.

The couple published nine books and made eight feature movies of their travels. Their pictures of head-hunting cannibals were quite controversial. The couple made five trips to Africa along with numerous other trips to Borneo and the Solomon Islands. They made several motion pictures about life in the remote jungles of the world, including the first sound picture made in Africa, *Congorilla*. A commercial airplane crash in California in 1937 killed her husband and left Osa in a wheelchair. Osa, however, continued her adventures, wrote several books, and led a large

expedition back to Africa for the filming of the motion picture *Stanley and Livingstone*. She died in New York in 1953 while planning a return visit to East Africa.

Wichita native Lynette Woodward exhibited an early interest in basketball as she played sockball with the neighborhood boys. She claimed that her brother invented the game and that they named themselves after players from Wichita State and later the NBA. As a player for Wichita North High School, Lynette led the team to two state championships and was named an All-American High School Team Member as a junior. Woodward spent her collegiate career at the University of Kansas, where she led the Lady Jayhawks to three straight Big Eight Championship wins and scored half the entire team's points during her 4-year tenure. Woodward was part of the U.S. team for the Pan American Games and also a member of the 1980 and 1984 Olympic teams. The Moscow boycott prevented her team from participating in 1980, but the U.S. team, led by Woodward, won the gold medal in the next Olympic contest. This was the first gold medal for the U.S. women's basketball team. When the Harlem Globetrotters were seeking their first female member, they asked Woodward to try out in 1985; she was chosen from a field of 30. She later returned to the Midwest and served as the first athletics director for the Kansas City, Missouri, School District and as head of the Women's National Basketball Association. She recently joined the Kansas University Athletics Department as special assistant for internal relations and women's basketball.

Among women who made a name for themselves in the entertainment industry, Louise Brooks was a dancer and silent-film star who appeared in over 20 films during the 1920s and 1930s. She left the United States for Paris at age 24 and starred in classic films like *Pandora's Box* and *Diary of a Lost Girl*.

Coffeyville native Eva Jessye demonstrated an early interest in singing spirituals, leading singing ensembles, and later in writing poetry. Born in 1895, she became the first chorale director of stage shows such as *Porgy and Bess* and of *Hallelujah*, the first black musical motion picture. Jessye believed that the "Negro" spirituals were a distinct component of the African American heritage. She taught school and wrote for an African American newspaper in New York City prior to her work in the musical theater. In the late 1920s she published *My Spirituals*, a collection of traditional songs intended partly to remind fellow African Americans of their other musical heritage besides the increasingly popular jazz. Jessye participated in the 1963 March on Washington, and her group was the official choir for the event. The "grand dame of black music in America" later returned to Kansas and died in 1992.

For her work in the movie *Gone With the Wind,* Wichita native Hattie McDaniel was the first African American woman to win an Academy Award.

Margaret Hill McCarter wrote novels in which the Kansas prairies often served as the backdrop. Her work *The Price of the Prairie* dealt with settlers in post-Civil War Kansas, and *A Wall of Man* portrayed the territory's struggles during the era of Bleeding Kansas. She was a dedicated civic participant and, in 1920, became the first woman to address the Republican National Convention.

Two Kansas women have served as Miss America: Overland Park's Deborah Bryant was chosen in 1965 and Moran native Debra Barnes was crowned in 1967.

—Kelly A. Woestman

SUGGESTED READINGS

Armitage, Susan, and Elizabeth Jamison, eds. *The Women's West.* Norman: University of Oklahoma Press, 1987.

Gardner, Ann L. *Kansas Women.* Lawrence: Kansas Key Press, 1986.

Goldberg, Michael Lewis. *An Army of Women: Gender and Politics in Gilded Age Kansas.* Baltimore, MD: Johns Hopkins University Press, 1997.

Kansas State Historical Society, "People in Kansas History." Retrieved December 2002 from www. kshs.org.

Riley, Glenda. *The Female Frontier: A Comparative View of Women on the Prairie and the Plains.* Lawrence: University Press of Kansas, 1988.

KEEP, JUDITH N. (1944-)

Born in Omaha, Nebraska, in 1944, Judith N. Keep moved to California to attend Scripps College in Claremont. After graduating with her B.A. in 1966, she studied law at the University of San Diego School of Law, where she received her J.D. in 1970. That same year she served briefly as a law clerk for Westgate-California Inc. before taking a position as an attorney with Defenders Inc. in San Diego, California.

She remained in San Diego to open her private practice there in 1973, where she stayed for 3 years. In 1976 she served as an assistant U.S. attorney before becoming a municipal court judge in San Diego. On May 9, 1980, President Jimmy Carter nominated her for the new seat on the U.S. District Court for the Southern District of California, created by 92 Stat. 1629. She received her commission on June 30, 1980, after her Senate confirmation 4 days earlier. From 1991 to 1998, she served as the chief judge on that court.

—Marcus J. Schwoerer

SUGGESTED READING

Judith N. Keep. Retrieved from air.fjc.gov/servlet/tGetInfo?jid=1241. Source: History of the Federal Judiciary. http://www.fjc.gov. Web site of the Federal Judicial Center, Washington, D.C.

KELSEY, NANCY (1823-1896)

Nancy Kelsey was the first white woman to cross the Sierra Nevada and arrive in California with an overland party. She was only 18 when she, her husband, Benjamin, and his brothers, Andrew and Samuel, left from Missouri in 1841 to travel to California as members of the Bartleson-Bidwell Company. Kelsey was one of five women in the party who traveled together, under the guide of Thomas Fitzpatrick, to Soda Springs, Idaho. Here the party separated, with a majority deciding to travel the better-known route to Oregon instead of the unknown way to California. Her husband decided to continue on to California with Nancy and their baby daughter, Martha Ann. The trip was perilous and the group encountered Indians, some helpful and some hostile. They lost oxen and wagons and were forced to go on horseback for the last portion of the journey, many times leading the packed horses on foot. They reached California in November 1841.

Kelsey later witnessed the birth of California as a state in her time at Sutter's Fort and later in Sonoma during the Bear Flag Revolt. The American settlers, whose numbers were growing, wanted California to become a protectorate of the United States rather than a part of Mexico. Emboldened by U.S. soldiers led by

Lt. John C. Fremont, the settlers decided to attack the unprotected headquarters of Mexico's military commander in Northern California, General M. G. Vallejo. The attack occurred during the night of June 14, 1846, and Vallejo surrendered Sonoma without a fight. The settlers then declared California a republic and raised a flag of their own creation. Some accounts claim that it was a piece of cloth from the red petticoat of Nancy Kelsey that formed the border of the hand-sewn flag. The flag flew for less than 30 days, until word finally reached the settlers that the United States was already at war with Mexico and U.S. forces occupied Monterey on July 7, 1846.

The Kelseys had further years of success and hardship. They raised three daughters and moved in and out of California, traveling to Oregon, Texas, and even Mexico. They tried gold mining, cattle and sheep ranching, and operating a sawmill. After the death of her husband in 1888, Nancy retired to a cabin in the Cuyama Mountains and became a midwife and herbalist to the local residents. Though she was illiterate, friends and local newspapers preserved her adventures through interviews in her later years. She is buried in a marked grave in Cottonwood Canyon, California.

—Michelle Bean

SUGGESTED READINGS

The Bear Flag Revolt. Retrieved from www.colusi.org/linked/html/bear_flag_revolt.htm.

Carter, Lyndia. "Nancy Kelsey, the First Woman to Cross Utah." Retrieved from www.utahhistorytogo.org/kelsey.html. June 14.

Levy, Joann. *They Saw the Elephant: Women in the California Gold Rush.* Hamden, CT: Archon Books, 1990.

Nancy Kelsey. Retrieved from gcclearn.gcc.cc.va.us/adams/pw2-kelsn.htm.

Nunis, Doyce B., ed. *The Bidwell-Bartleson Party: 1841 California Emigrant Adventure.* Santa Cruz, CA: Western Tanager Press, 1991.

KENNARD, JOYCE (1941-)

Joyce Kennard has a celebrated judicial career that has pinnacled with her appointment to the California

Supreme Court in 1989. On the road to that great achievement, she started out as a secretary for Occidental Life Insurance after she immigrated to the United States in 1961. While at this job, her mother, who lived in Holland, died and left her an inheritance of $5,000. With that money, she wisely funded her education, which eventually led her to her high-ranking position on the California bench. She started out at Pasadena City College and then transferred to the University of Southern California. After 3 years, she graduated with a bachelor's degree in German. In 1974 she graduated from Gould School of Law at the University of Southern California, and was among the 15% of her graduating class who were women. In 1975 she was accepted to work in the criminal division of the attorney general's office. She moved on to the Court of Appeals and stayed there for 7 years. She became deputy attorney general and remained in that position from 1975 to 1979. Governor Jerry Brown turned her down for a judgeship, but she found new life under Governor George Deukmejian. In 1986 the governor appointed her to the municipal court in San Francisco, and she moved to a superior court judge position the following year. The next year she was the associate judge to the Second District Court of Appeals. Finally, in 1989, the governor appointed her to the California Supreme Court.

Kennard was born in Bandung, West Java, in Indonesia. Her mother, Wilhelmine, was Chinese Indonesian and part Dutch and Belgian. Her father, Johan, was Dutch, Indonesian, and German. This varied cultural background made it hard for her to associate with any particular racial group. Kennard lived a very modest childhood due to the death of her father in a Japanese concentration camp and the ill treatment of her and her mother while living in Southeast Asia. After fleeing to Java, they were forced into citizenship in 1949 when Java declared its independence. They moved to Dutch New Guinea in hopes of a better life. Even though enduring an oil drum bathtub and a makeshift toilet, she educated herself through library reading, a missionary school, and listening to the radio. At the age of 14, she and her mother moved to Holland, and she was exposed to some of the conveniences of life that had been denied her in Java. Tragedy struck at the age of 14, when she developed cancer on her right leg. The leg was amputated, yet she moves freely even today, due to her determination and quality prosthetic leg.

Her many awards include the Margaret Brent Woman Lawyer Achievement award, the Women of the Nineties award, Justice of the Year award, and the 1st Annual Netherlands-American Heritage award, to name a few. Her difficult life and severe living conditions as a child have instilled in her a sense of humility and have greater prepared her for judgeship.

—Kevin Christy

SUGGESTED READING

Gall, Susan B., and Helen Zia. "Joyce Kennard." *Notable Asian Americans.* New York: Gale Research, 1995.

KING, CHARLOTTE WINTER
(1898-1969)

Charlotte Winter King (born Charlotte Lucille Winter) was active in community affairs in the Southern California community of South Pasadena from the late 1930s until her death in 1969. In 1942 she became the first woman to be elected to that city's council and subsequently also chaired the landmark Monterey Hills Redevelopment Project. Her political career is of interest because it demonstrates that one did not have to be a clubwoman or a Democrat to enjoy political success in the 1930s and 1940s.

Charlotte was born in Colville, Washington, on October 7, 1898, the second child of Thaddeus Winter and Maude Jacobs. Her mother's family was among the pioneer settlers of Pasadena, California, in 1888. Her father was a businessman and capitalist, the founder-president of the Bank of Latah in Colville and subsequently one of the founding partners of the Richfield Oil Company (later ARCO) in Los Angeles. Charlotte's mother died in 1908, after which Charlotte moved, with her older brother, Arthur, and her younger sister, Marion, to live with her maternal grandparents in Pasadena, California. Her father died in 1917 when Charlotte was in her second year at the University of Washington, but she continued with her education and was awarded a B.A. in business administration and economics in 1919.

While at the university, Charlotte met William Gregory King Jr., son of a prominent Seattle businessman. They were married in 1921 and had two children, Charlotte and William III. For the next 17 years, Charlotte followed her husband as he pursued a business career on the Pacific Coast, moving her family from Seattle to British Columbia's Queen Charlotte Islands, then back to Seattle, then to San Francisco, and finally to Pasadena. The Kings finally purchased a home in the small San Gabriel Valley community of South Pasadena in 1939.

After settling into her new home, Charlotte became involved in community activities. At first her activities were typical of middle-class parents across America: the P.T.A. and Scouting. Between 1938 and 1941 she cochaired fund-raising activities for the Pasadena San Gabriel Valley Boy Scouts of America, enjoying noteworthy results. Before long, however, her horizon widened, probably under the influence of her next-door neighbor, Charlotte McGaughey, who was active in local Republican politics.

Concerned that the lack of zoning ordinances in South Pasadena threatened that city's continued existence as a small-town bedroom community in the face of Southern California's ongoing growth, Charlotte joined South Pasadenans Inc. to oppose unzoned development and to deal with rising traffic problems caused by the opening of the Arroyo Seco Parkway (today's Pasadena Freeway) and the slow death of the regional electric railway network. Soon she was appointed as a member of the Committee on City Planning of the Los Angeles County Regional Planning Commission. In 1940 she led a recall campaign against then Mayor John C. Jacobs (no relation), which, although unsuccessful, brought her to the attention of South Pasadena voters for the first time.

In March 1942, just 24 hours before the filing deadline, Charlotte King entered the race for a seat on the South Pasadena City Council. Her candidacy made news; it was only the second time a woman had run for a council seat in the city (the first was the unsuccessful try by Dorothy A. Matson in 1934). The only woman in a field of seven candidates, she appealed to women voters "to take a more sincere and active part in government." During her campaign, she pointed out that needed economies in the city's wartime budget "could be effected by increasing efficiency rather than by reducing services," and consistently demonstrated a thorough knowledge of the organization and operations of every aspect of the city's government, as well as the impact the war was having upon its functioning.

At the municipal election on April 14, 1942, King won a seat on the South Pasadena City Council, the first woman ever elected to a municipal office in California. As one columnist observed, "Mrs. King was elected not through . . . holding meetings in which the discussions get exactly nowhere, but because a few friends and supporters rallied around her, and these supporters weren't civic leaders, nor successful club women, they were just plain citizens willing to work."

As a councilwoman, King worked toward formation of the city's first youth recreation program and was active in the organization and implementation of civil defense efforts during the war. Her daughter recalls with pride how her mother even personally planted, tended, and harvested a large victory garden on a vacant lot near her home each year of the war. Her wartime activities also included service as a director of the Citizens' Service Corps and chairing the regional War Bond Drive.

Charlotte was reelected to a second term on the city council in 1946; during this term she was elected by her fellow councilmen to the honorary position of mayor. She bitterly opposed the pending abandonment of the Pacific Electric Railway's electric rail lines, two of which ran through South Pasadena and enhanced its status as a bedroom community. She viewed replacement of the trains with diesel buses as a tragic error that would lead to more street traffic and smellier air (the term "smog" had yet to come into common use), but she was unable to prevent this change from taking place. More successful was her continuing support for recreation programs, which resulted in lighted playing fields, swimming lessons, sponsored dances, bowling, and opening school gyms for weekend and summer use. By 1950, when she decided not to run for a third term on the city council, South Pasadena's outstanding parks and recreation system drew attention from small towns across the United States.

In mid-1948, a new concern appeared in South Pasadena: what to do with the undeveloped lands in the hilly southeast corner of the city. This issue would be central to King's political activities for the remainder of her life. The Monterey Hills area had originally been subdivided in 1900-1902 by a private speculator, who, following the often careless practices of turn-of-the-century "boomers," arbitrarily laid out rectangular plots with no reference to the actual topography of the land. Although many of these plots had been sold to investors all over the United States, no construction of homes had ever taken place due to the absence of streets, water, sewers, and other utilities. As a result, for decades this isolated corner of the city had been home to rabbits, coyotes, trash piles, and sagebrush. Eventually, the City of South Pasadena declared the area "blighted," and began buying back plots in tax delinquency sales. But not until passage of the Community Redevelopment Act of California in 1945 did the city receive the powers it needed to undertake a major project. Debate over the future of the Monterey Hills was triggered in 1948 by a proposal to convert the city-owned land to a municipal golf course. Although this plan was quickly abandoned (the city already owned land in the nearby Arroyo Seco earmarked for that use), the city was forced to confront the issue of development. In January 1953 King was appointed a charter member of the South Pasadena Community Redevelopment Agency, to which was assigned the task of redeveloping the Monterey Hills district. In September she became chairman (the term she always preferred) of the group, a position she held until her death.

Under her tutelage, the agency considered the complex questions of land use and extent of development. The project area encompassed over 300 acres, representing one fifth of the entire land area of the city, so its value to the city's future was unquestionable. A plan for home development and open land preservation was formulated, and the federal Housing and Home Finance Agency was approached for a loan of $4.5 million to undertake grading of the site to prepare it for home construction. Unfortunately, the federal government seemed disinterested, claiming that federal funds were for the rehabilitation of built-up areas, and the project appeared doomed when, in October 1956, word was leaked that the loan would not be approved. Undismayed, King went off to Washington, D.C., and spent 38 days in intense discussions with the appropriate federal officials to convince them of the soundness of the city's proposal. On November 19, 1956, the federal loan was approved, and the Monterey Hills project could go ahead. The final contract was signed in July 1959 and grading work began. By the spring of 1962, the area had been graded, roads built, and utilities installed; the project lay ready for the construction of 631 new homes.

The agency decided to auction the home sites in small blocks over several months, and carefully prevented any one developer from purchasing too many of them. The intent was to keep home construction in the hands of small contractors or individual homeowners. Also, in a decision that was viewed with trepidation by some in the community, King insisted that no racial covenants be imposed on home buyers; the home sites in the newly christened Altos de Monterey were to be available to any and all—assuming, of course, that they could afford the approximately $20,000 price of a lot (in 1964).

King's management of the Monterey Hills project was kept true to her long-held vision of preserving the status of South Pasadena as a small town, despite its being surrounded by the urban sprawl of Southern California. Although some of the project's decisions may seem inappropriate to our later era, notably the lack of low-income housing and insufficient environmental intervention, for its time and place it was a very successful attempt to permit controlled development while preserving the cultural values of its sponsoring city. King was very pleased by the success of this crowning civic duty of her long career. Not only was it the first open-land urban renewal project, but it was the only redevelopment project in the United States to fully repay all of its federal loans with interest (in November 1965).

Although King's civic career as an activist, council member, and agency chair spanned some 30 years, she found time to undertake other activities as well. She was a member of the Pasadena Community Chest (a forerunner of United Way) from 1942 to 1958. In 1944 she began an 11-year term on the Women's Hospital Board in Pasadena, including several years as its president. In 1954 she began a 6-year term as a member of the Pasadena Dispensary, a health-care outreach program affiliated with the Huntington Memorial Hospital in Pasadena in those long-ago days before federal and state health care. She served as the dispensary's president in 1959. She also served on the South Pasadena Library Board from 1947 to 1951, and its chair in 1950. In 1948 she was cofounder of the South Pasadena Chapter of the League of Women Voters. When her husband, himself a noted businessman and outdoorsman, retired in 1965, Charlotte found time in her busy schedule to join him in a 2-month, four-wheel-drive tour of then nearly roadless Baja California.

King fought a losing battle with cancer in the late 1960s, while never once slowing from her many civic and family activities. She passed away on April 22, 1969, greatly missed by family, friends, and citizens alike. The City of South Pasadena honored her memory by naming the main street in the Monterey Hills project Via Del Rey (King Way). That road, the development through which it runs, and indeed the continuing small-town status of South Pasadena are Charlotte King's enduring monuments. One columnist called her "one of the San Gabriel Valley's most illustrious and dedicated citizens," and noted that she "will be sorely missed." Now, decades later, American society is fortunate to have many women as dedicated and as politically skilled as was Charlotte King, but she remains a pioneer deserving of acknowledgment.

—William Allan Myers

KINGSOLVER, BARBARA (1955-)

Born in Maryland in 1955 and raised in eastern Kentucky, Barbara Kingsolver's fiction is nonetheless firmly rooted in the American West. Her highly acclaimed first novel, *The Bean Trees* (1988), introduced readers not only to her authorial voice and political concerns but also to her love of the landscape and inhabitants of her adopted home, Tucson, Arizona. In this novel, the central character, Taylor

Greer, embarks on a journey from Kentucky to Tucson that mirrors Kingsolver's own adult relocation. Along the way, Taylor becomes the caretaker to an abused and abandoned Cherokee child. As Taylor forges a new life among a community of women and children in Tucson, she confronts single motherhood, the reality of child abuse, poverty, and the plight of Guatemalan refugees escaping political persecution. Taylor's eventual decision to adopt the child signifies a commitment to both her new role and her new home. Kingsolver herself seems equally committed to her adopted southwestern home, for while her subsequent novels and short stories explore a variety of locales and themes, her narratives often return to the landscape and people of the American West.

Kingsolver's upbringing in the rural South provided the roots for the committed social conscience evident in all of her work. Her father was a doctor who treated many working-class patients in her home state of Kentucky. He also took his practice to the Congo (now Zaire) in 1963 and to the island of St. Lucia in 1967, both times taking his family with him. Through these experiences, Kingsolver was made vividly aware of the distinctions between rich and poor and the divisions and inequalities perpetuated by racism. She came to identify with those on the outside of the power structure and to sense an "obligation to do the right thing rather than . . . the thing that rewards you financially." In her novels, Kingsolver often explores the effects of poverty and racism on the indigenous peoples of the southwestern reservations. Her interest in her own Cherokee great-grandmother further influenced her identification with the plight of Native Americans.

All these themes are obvious in her second novel, *Animal Dreams* (1990), and in the sequel to *The Bean Trees, Pigs in Heaven* (1993). In both texts, Native American characters confront historical and contemporary oppression by the dominant Anglo culture. These and other novels also rely on strong, insightful female characters, which reveal Kingsolver's feminist sensibilities. The women of her novels embrace the ideals of community and connectedness, which Kingsolver feels are essential for healing society and the environment. As she stated in one interview, "Independence is stupidity. . . . I celebrate dependency."

Her 1998 novel, *The Poisonwood Bible,* marks an even deeper involvement with these ideals. In this narrative, Kingsolver achieves a thematic and stylistic complexity beyond any of her earlier work. The novel focuses on the fate of the Price family, who have been led by the fiercely patriarchal and fundamentalist Nathan Price into the jungles of the Belgian Congo in 1959. The story covers nearly 30 years and is told from multiple perspectives, with Nathan's wife, Orleanna, and their four daughters each telling her own version of the family's experience and its lasting impact on their lives. Through this family's eventual collapse, Kingsolver explores the damaging effects of sexist oppression, racist/colonialist ideology, and U.S. complicity in the continued turmoil in this African nation. In *The Poisonwood Bible*, the idea of "the West" takes on a global and negative connotation, as Nathan Price's arrogant attempts to impose western Christianity on the African villagers mirrors the U.S. imposition in postcolonial Zaire's political development.

In her latest novel, *Prodigal Summer* (2000), Kingsolver returns to her familial roots of southern Appalachia. She interweaves the story of Deanna Wolfe, a solitary National Forest game warden and trail keeper; Lusa Widener, a newly transplanted Jewish city girl; and Garnett Walker, a cantankerous and self-righteous old man. Through each of these interconnected tales, Kingsolver explores themes of isolation, community, and growth. She also draws extensively on her knowledge of ecology and plant and animal life (she received her master's degree in ecology and evolutionary biology from the University of Arizona, Tucson), providing her reader with a detailed education in the mating habits and survival skills of various insects and mammals. Again, the female characters provide an understanding of tolerance and biological interdependencies that counter the masculine impulse toward dominance and destruction.

Although this novel does not seem to fit in with her earlier southwestern pieces, it continues to address issues of environmental destruction and responsibility, themes that are clearly present in all of her writing. As her vision as an author/activist becomes wider and more universal, one can reread her earlier "western" novels as themselves intertwined with her later work that moves beyond that specific landscape. The problems and potential solutions she examines in the former are echoed in those of the latter.

Kingsolver's Marxist/eco-feminist approach to these and her other texts provides an important counter-voice to the typically masculinist constructions of Western literature. She joins other women writers such as Leslie Marmon Silko and Louise

Erdrich who challenge the traditional wilderness myth in which the heroic (male) individual leaves his community to confront and subdue the natural world. Instead, Kingsolver's writing celebrates friendship, family, and gentle coexistence with the land. These potentially sentimental values have occasionally led to criticism that her writing reinforces idealistic stereotypes of the West and Native Americans or that she provides "easy" conventional answers to complex social problems. Nonetheless, her narratives manage to steer clear of sentimentalism and instead educate and challenge readers to question the dominant myth of the isolated and self-sufficient western hero.

—Maureen Woodard Dana

SUGGESTED READINGS

Comer, Krista. "Sidestepping Environmental Justice: 'Natural' Landscapes and the Wilderness Plot," in Sherrie Innes and Diana Royer, eds., *Breaking Boundaries: New Perspectives on Women's Regional Writing, 1997*. Iowa City: University of Iowa Press, 1997.

DeMarr, Mary Jean. *Barbara Kingsolver: A Critical Companion*. Westport, CT: Greenwood Press, 1999.

Kingsolver, Barbara. *The Bean Trees*. New York: Harper & Row, 1988.

Kingsolver, Barbara. *Homeland and Other Stories*. New York: Harper & Row, 1989.

Kingsolver, Barbara. *Animal Dreams*. New York: HarperCollins, 1990.

Kingsolver, Barbara. *Pigs in Heaven*. New York: HarperCollins, 1993.

Kingsolver, Barbara. *The Poisonwood Bible*. New York: HarperCollins, 1998.

Kingsolver, Barbara. *Prodigal Summer*. New York: HarperCollins, 2000.

Perry, Donna. *Backtalk: Women Writers Speak Out*. New Brunswick, NJ: Rutgers University Press, 1993.

Ryan, Maureen. "Barbara Kingsolver's Lowfat Fiction," *Journal of American Culture 18*(4, Winter 1995): 77-82.

KINGSTON, MAXINE HONG (1940-)

Maxine Hong Kingston, author of *The Woman Warrior, China Men,* and *Tripmaster Monkey: His Fake Book,* is one of the foremost American writers and most prominent Asian American authors. Her first book, *The Woman Warrior* (1976), is the most widely assigned 20th-century literary text on high school and college campuses and is lauded as a "literary masterpiece." Moreover, it is required reading for sociology, anthropology, history, and political science courses. Kingston won the National Book Critics Circle award for nonfiction for *The Woman Warrior* and the National Book award for *China Men*. *China Men* was also named to the American Library Association Notable Books List in 1980 and nominated for the National Book Critics Circle award and a finalist for the Pulitzer Prize in nonfiction.

Kingston was born on October 27, 1940, the year of the dragon, in Stockton, California, to parents Ying Lan Chew (Brave Orchid) and Tom Hong. She was the first of six children born in the United States. Two older siblings born in China had died before they immigrated to America. Her parents named her Maxine Ting Ting Hong. Her parents were highly educated; her father was trained in China as a scholar, and Kingston describes him as a poet, and her mother had extensive medical training and practiced as a physician.

Tom went to America in 1925 and Ying Lan Chew joined him 15 years later. In New York City, Tom worked in a laundry and then moved to Stockton, where he managed a gambling house, naming Maxine after a lucky blond gambler. When the gambling house closed, the Hongs opened their own laundry in Stockton. It was here that Kingston heard the talk-story of her family and relatives that became the basis for her books.

Kingston earned her B.A. in English from the University of California, Berkeley, in 1962 and married Earl Kingston, an actor, later that year. Joseph Lawrence Chung Mei, their only son, was born the following year. Kingston has her teaching certificate and taught English and math at Sunset High School in Hayward, California; her husband also taught high school. They moved to Hawaii in 1967 to escape the violence of the antiwar movement and the counterculture of the drug world and stayed for the next 17 years.

Nationally recognized for her contribution to American literature, Kingston received the Award in Literature from the American Academy and Institute of Arts and Letters in 1990. She won the Stockton Arts Commission award and the Asian-Pacific Women's Network Woman of the Year award in 1981. She also received awards from Hawaii and California: the Hawaii Award for Literature (1983) and the California Governor's Award for the Arts (1985). She holds honorary doctoral degrees from Eastern Michigan University, Colby College, Brandeis University, and the University of Massachusetts. President Bill Clinton awarded her the National Humanities Medal in 1997.

THE WOMAN WARRIOR: MEMOIRS OF A GIRLHOOD AMONG GHOSTS (1967)

The Woman Warrior is mostly classified as an autobiography, but it includes fiction, history, and poetry. It can also be classified as "indigenous ethnography," as the works of Toni Morrison and Leslie Marmon Silko are. Kingston's work falls in line with other women of color as she addresses issues of two cultures, femininity and self-identity. She deals with issues of racism and sexism both within the Chinese culture as well as part of the immigrant experience. She employs "talk-story," a form of storytelling that incorporates myth, legend, family history, and ghost tales. She inherited this oral tradition, an ancient folk art form of storytelling, from her family. Her use of talk-story allows her to translate her family's oral tradition and sense of community into a written record.

The Warrior Woman is the story of Kingston's coming of age—a common story of the Chinese woman who is young, insecure, and confused; yet her story is uncommon in the sense that she transcends her powerlessness by finding a voice and discovering an identity that reconciles the cultural tensions between East and West.

"No Name Woman"

The book begins with Kingston learning from her mother, Brave Orchid, the story of her unknown aunt, whose sexual infidelity caused the family's humiliation and her suicide. Brave Orchid tells Maxine this secret at the onset of menstruation as a warning about life, but this only serves to confuse the young Maxine as she struggles to reconcile her American life and Chinese culture. The evening the baby was due to be delivered, the villagers ransacked the house, slaughtered the stock, and destroyed their harvest. The next morning, Brave Orchid discovers her sister-in-law and baby drowned in the well. In an effort to understand, the narrator (Maxine) reinvents her aunt's life and

motives, asking questions about her death. Was it rape or seduction? Did she fall in love with someone else? These questions allow Kingston to explore the boundaries of Chinese culture and the roles of women. Moreover, in telling the story of No Name Woman, she breaks the silence and establishes an identity for her forgotten aunt.

"White Tigers"

This story introduces the warrior woman, a blend of Chinese legends of Fa Mu Lan and General Yue Fei (1103-1141). *White Tigers* recollects Kingston's mother's stories, her dreams, and the Chinese movies she watched growing up. The warrior is a role model—it is the story of Fa Mu Lan, who took her father's place in battle and avenged the people of her village. Kingston imagines her training and her leadership in battle. Before she goes into battle, she returns home to her parents, who perform a ceremonial ritual carving the grievances of her village onto her back with small blades. The mother catches the blood in a bowl and dresses the wounds. This engraving ritual comes from the story of Yue Fei, who writes "jing zhong bao guo," or "serve one's country with loyalty" on his back.

The legend of the warrior woman allows Kingston to imagine herself in a role of power with a voice. She explores the cultural injustices of racism and sexism that the woman warrior fights against. The woman warrior does not kill and destroy after she defeats the enemy; in contrast, she brings peace and order. Moreover, Kingston's Fa Mu Lan marries and bears a son during her time of military service—even sending her husband and son home for safety while she continues fighting. Kingston creates an epic heroine who is able to remain intensely filial yet has a career and fulfills cultural expectations by bearing a son. Fa Mu Lan achieves revenge for her village by taking action and using her voice and mind to determine her own fate. Likewise, Kingston attempts to obtain revenge and finds a voice through her stories challenging the patriarchal gender roles.

"Shaman"

Kingston tells her mother's story of her life in China while her husband was in America. Brave Orchid trains as a doctor and obstetrician. During her studies, she must confront a ghost, Sitting Ghost, that haunts one of the rooms. She spends the night in the haunted room and does battle with the ghost. By confronting fear and evil, Brave Orchid becomes a shaman or another heroine. A shaman cured others and warded off death usually through being possessed by the souls of dead children. Brave Orchid returns to her village to become a renowned doctor. Her determination and perseverance parallels that of Fa Mu Lan. Kingston says of Brave Orchid that she "has gone away ordinary and come back miraculous." Brave Orchid also returns to her family a heroine.

Juxtaposed to the story of Brave Orchid, Kingston grapples with her mother's practice of enslaving women, because Brave Orchid purchases a slave girl upon graduation. Once again she asks questions in an attempt to discover her ancestors as well as the woman within herself. However, Brave Orchid finds many similarities between herself and the slave girl, and by training the slave to assist her, she has actually elevated her status. Brave Orchid remains loyal to her husband and demonstrates her determination and bravery by working alongside him in the laundry.

"At the Western Palace"

This is the story of Kingston's aunt, Moon Orchid, a small, thin, silent woman. Brave Orchid convinces her to come to America to join her lost husband. Upon arrival, however, she learns her husband has become completely Americanized, a doctor with an English-speaking wife and, according to Brave Orchid, a ghost. Her husband is dumbfounded as to why Moon Orchid would even come. Moon Orchid believes in the Chinese culture and follows the traditions of women—she is pampered and passive. When her husband refuses her, she loses her identity and this ghost drives her mad. She dies in a mental asylum.

Interestingly, this story is told in the third-person narrative and was told to Kingston by her sister, who heard it from her brother. Essentially, Moon Orchid has no voice; this silence evidences her inability to conform to American culture and the tragedy of embracing the Chinese culture. Moon Orchid embodies the female Chinese image of the Moon Goddess who lives separated from her husband on the moon. Throughout the story, Moon Orchid is compared to Brave Orchid as Kingston reveals a warrior identity and, in contrast, the female identity of Moon Orchid that she hopes to avoid.

"A Song for a Barbarian Reed Pipe"

The last story tells of Maxine's finding her identity through a brief descent into madness and a final discovery manifest through the story of Ts'ai Yen, a woman captured by the Huns and enslaved as a concubine. She bears two sons but is later ransomed, and they are left behind. Ts'ai Yen becomes China's first renowned female poet. Her poetry and song spoke of the shared sadness and pain that both the Chinese and barbarians experienced during the political chaos. Kingston creates a new heroine whose power rests in her words. She tells the story of young Maxine, who attacks another Chinese girl because she embodies the Chinese cultural norms for women and will not speak. These attacks throw Maxine into psychological and physical turmoil, leaving her in bed for months. In the end, Maxine forges a new identity for herself in terms of both her Chinese and American worlds.

The Woman Warrior evokes images of feminine heroines—women who create their own code of bravery and power in order to transform their world. Kingston explores three themes in *The Woman Warrior:* the idea of silence and its opposite, voice, as well as the issue of identity and then the idea of rebellion. Voice and identity are integral to overcoming the barriers of racial and gender oppression. Kingston has created a voice for herself with identity in both the Chinese and American cultures, yet it is forged as her book, in a new mode or new vision.

CHINA MEN (1980)

Like *The Woman Warrior, China Men* is a collection of memoirs that combines autobiography, myth, and history, and is viewed as a companion to *The Warrior Woman.* Here Kingston tells the story of her father and his family—it is the story of the oppression and discrimination of the Chinese men in America. Each of the six stories ends with a retelling of a Chinese myth. Kingston focuses on portraying her ancestors as heroes and the rightful heirs of American history that they fought for and sacrificed for. Kingston, inspired by William Carlos Williams, continues his narrative, telling the story of her ancestors who broke ground for the transcontinental railroad and cleared mountains for the Hawaiian sugar cane plantations. *China Men* won the American Book award and the National Book Critics Circle award.

The six sections of *China Men*—"The Father from China," "The Great Grandfather of the Sandalwood Mountains," "The Grandfather of the Sierra Nevada Mountains," "The Making of More Americans," "The American Father," and "The Brother in Vietnam"—span over 100 years of history and tell stories of Imperial China as well as life in Stockton, California. The principal story is that of Tom Hong and his son and the stories of her other ancestral immigrants—great-grandfathers, grandfathers, and uncles. The focus of the story is life in the Gold Mountain during the late 19th and early 20th centuries. Kingston creates a new American history that illustrates the emasculation of the Chinese male immigrants while trying to include the contributions of her ancestors. Equally at the forefront of her examination is the continual oppression of women; she examines the oppression of Chinese men in America juxtaposed to the continued sexism practiced by Chinese men toward women.

The central story is that of BaBa, Kingston's father, who became an honored scholar and then a failed schoolmaster and laundryman. BaBa travels across the ocean to America, facing adversity and discrimination, eventually establishing his own laundry and sending for his wife.

The heroic tales of Kingston's great-grandfather (Bak Goong) and grandfather (Ah Goong) illustrate the Chinese immigrant's contribution to the settling of the American West. They, too, travel across the waters—Bak Goong to the plantations of Hawaii and Ah Goong to labor on the railroad. In the middle of the book, Kingston records the anti-immigration legislation from 1868 until 1978 in list form. This inclusion brought harsh criticism for disrupting her narrative, but it is yet another piece of American history.

Kingston returns to her theme of silence in *China Men*. Foremost, she explores the ways discrimination and racial oppression silenced Chinese immigrants. BaBa chooses to be silent about his story and does not talk-story his life to his children; moreover, this silence is a form of forgotten memories, like the aunt in *No Name Woman*. Like herself in *The Warrior Woman*, her male protagonists also discover a voice and a new American identity. Her last chapter, "The Brother in Vietnam," epitomizes the ultimate clash of cultural identities when he enlists with the U.S. Army to fight in Vietnam. Fearful that he will be thought of as a traitor by the Vietnamese and seen as the "other" by Americans, the brother must find a means to protect himself during the war and returns home a war veteran with legal American status—he has found himself in both his Chinese identity and with his homeland, America.

TRIPMASTER MONKEY: HIS FAKE BOOK (1989)

Kingston's fictional book, *Tripmaster Monkey*, is often referred to as a postmodern novel. Like her previous publications, the story focuses on Wittman Ah Sing's search for his identity in 1963 San Francisco. Wittman is a Chinese poet and beatnik, his character inspired by Walt Whitman and his poem *Song of Myself*. *Tripmaster Monkey* details the almost epic escapades of Wittman during only a 2-month period in which he gets married, loses his job, visits many relatives, and writes and performs in his own theater production. Kuan Yin, the Chinese goddess of mercy, narrates the story and controls both Wittman and the reader. Kingston models Wittman's character after the mythic Monkey King. The Monkey manifests as Wittman's mischievous side as well as revealing many of the cultural stereotypes that confuse identity. Monkey is a traditional troublemaker in Chinese mythology and the contemporary American trickster.

Tripmaster Monkey explores the theme of transcendence as well as alienation and assimilation. Kingston once again evokes the question of identity: what is an American? Wittman is continually confronted with the identity of the Other and suffers alienation because of confusion about his own place of origin. Although he is a fifth-generation American, he is continually the object of discrimination based upon his Asian features. His ability to claim his identity, like other characters of Kingston, rests in his incorporation of ancestral histories, including Chinese myth and legends.

Like Brave Orchid, Wittman becomes a code hero or postmodern hero, who in the face of social and political chaos, when change is constant, scripts for himself his own identity based upon an intertwining of the moral codes of his Chinese culture and his American life. He is ever mindful of the "I" that defines him but must always relate to the world that encodes him as the Other. Wittman creates his own community in the theater and discovers himself as the voices of diversity and multiculturalism.

Kingston's literary masterpiece, *The Woman Warrior*, brought popular success and critical acclaim like no other Asian American writer has received.

Other writings include *Hawaii One Summer* (1978) and *Through the Black Curtain* (1987). Her work is most commonly discussed among feminists and post-modernists emphasizing her themes of race and gender. She is the most influential woman of color of the 20th century.

—Angela E. Henderson

SUGGESTED READINGS

Huntley, E. D. *Maxine Hong Kingston: A Critical Companion.* Westport, CT: Greenwood Press, 2001.

Ling, Amy. "Maxine Hong Kingston and the Dialogic Dilemma of Asian American Writers." *Bucknell Review* *39*(1, 1995): 151-166.

Madsen, Deborah. *Literary Masters: Maxine Hong Kingston.* Vol. 9. Detroit, MI: Gale Group, 2000.

Simmons, Diane. *Maxine Hong Kingston.* New York: Twayne, 1999.

Skandera-Trombley, Laura E., ed. *Critical Essays on Maxine Hong Kingston.* New York: G. K. Hall, 1998.

Skenazy, Paul, and Tera Martin, eds. *Conversations with Maxine Hong Kingston.* Jackson: University of Mississippi Press, 1998.

Wong, Sau-Ling Cynthia. *Maxine Hong Kingston's The Woman Warrior: A Casebook.* New York: Oxford University Press, 1999.

LAPORTE, ELIZABETH D. (1953-)

Elizabeth D. Laporte grew up in the 1960s during a time when African Americans were struggling for civil rights. She admired Martin Luther King Jr. and was inspired to do something with her life to defend civil rights. In 1977 Elizabeth graduated from Princeton University and worked for the Federal Trade Commission. In 1979 she graduated from Yale Law School. She moved to the San Francisco Bay Area and clerked for Judge Marilyn Hall Patel from 1982 to 1983. In 1983 she joined the litigation firm of Turner & Brorby, where she focused on civil rights, employment, consumer, First Amendment, and environmental law. From 1991 to 1996 she was employed by the State Department of Insurance, where she decided to become a jurist. Finally, on April 14, 1998, Elizabeth was made a magistrate judge for the U.S. District Court for the Northern District of California.

—Carolyn Stull

SUGGESTED READING

Wolf, Michele. "U.S. District Judge Elizabeth D. Laporte." *San Francisco Attorney Magazine*, April/May 1998.

LIBRARIANSHIP IN CALIFORNIA: THE IRREPRESSIBLE EXPANSIONISTS

Between 1880 and 1920 middle-class women chose to enter the workforce as teachers, nurses, social workers, and librarians. In effect, these professions became feminized, which on one hand provided women with untold opportunities to influence policy and shape the early development of these occupations. On the other hand, these pioneering professionals, limited by their gender and social constructions of femininity, confronted the sexual double standard head on; few women reached the top of their fields as administrators, and all women faced wage inequities.

There are numerous studies that explore the role of women in the fields of social work, nursing, and education, and though there are a growing number of studies on librarianship, library women have been largely overlooked by women historians and remain to be integrated into mainstream library history. The invisibility of women librarians' contributions to the profession and society is partially linked to our political culture; libraries lack a high profile in the larger political scheme compared to other professions such as teaching and nursing, and are even less likely to receive attention when it comes to policy making and funding.

Given the low profile of the profession, it is even less surprising that women librarians have been largely ignored. In *Reclaiming the American Past: Writing Women In,* Suzanne Hildenbrand writes: "Library women's history is merely an add-on and this is an intolerable situation in an occupation where women are 80% of the workforce. A way must be found to make the experiences of women central to library history." Hildenbrand rightfully identifies the marginalization of women librarians as historical subjects, and she has successfully challenged scholars to "write women in." She also argues that the feminization of the profession resulted in a "golden age" where women "transformed passive repositories into dynamic cultural institutions."

Historian Joanne Passet's work documenting the golden age of early female librarians is a good example of the growing interest to write women in. Indeed, there is a growing body of work documenting the contributions of these early pioneers, and they tell the story of women "as active agents, choosing their work and making valuable contributions in the face of enormous obstacles." In *Cultural Crusaders: Women Librarians in the American West 1900-1917* (1994), Passet not only documents the golden age of pioneer librarians but also connects their professionalization to the rise of the clubwomen's movement, the "new woman," and Progressive era reform.

This entry explores the state of scholarship documenting the contributions of professional and paraprofessional women in building the Los Angeles Public Library during the Progressive era. Middle-class women had a unique opportunity to create a female dominion locally and nationally. Historian Robyn Muncy, looking at Progressive era female reform, used the term "female dominion" to represent the variety of female reform organizations in the "mostly male empire of policymaking." The notion of a female dominion fits into the larger construction of gender that relied heavily on the belief of female moral authority. This authority allowed women new opportunities to push for political, social, and economic rights. Library women formed similar organizational networks to advance library work, entered the public arena delivering speeches, participated in community politics, and used their influence and power to increase library services; their work as librarians was intimately tied to clubwomen activities and a shared belief in the idea of the new woman.

Women librarians and teachers came from similar backgrounds and were active participants in the clubwomen's movement. They believed in the Progressive theory of cultural uplift, and used librarianship and education as a means to instill civic intelligence and responsibility. For example, Cornelia Marvin, secretary of the Oregon State Library Commission, "believed that libraries had the power to eradicate ignorance, foster good government, and create responsible, intelligent citizens." Marvin's belief mirrored other Progressive educators' views, and by World War I, cultural uplift took on new meaning as reform-minded librarians and educators expanded

their domain to Americanize the growing immigrant population.

The golden age of librarianship flowered under the leadership of Melvil Dewey, when he formed his School of Library Economy at Columbia University. A dozen or more schools formed in the East, and by the 1930s the West followed suit. From the start, Dewey believed that college-educated women were well suited for the vocation of librarianship. The expansion of colleges and universities provided new opportunities for women to pursue professional careers. Popular literature further promoted librarianship as an ideal profession for women. Katharine L. Sharp, writing in 1898, described the profession as a "new world to conquer, a new profession to enter. It appeals to legal, medical, domestic, and above all philanthropic instincts. . . . The library is a laboratory, a workshop, a school, a university of the people, from which the students are never graduated." In a similar vein, Herbert Putnam, Librarian of the Library of Congress, wrote "What It Means to Be a Librarian" in the February 1901 issue of the *Ladies Home Journal*. These articles helped to promote female entry into the profession and reinforced the teaching role of librarians and the importance of lifelong learning. Tying librarianship to Progressive moral and social reform secured a strong female workforce as they flocked to library schools. Indeed, matriculation records indicate that 94% of the graduates between 1888 and 1921 were women, many of whom headed west to cultivate the "library spirit."

PROGRESSIVISM

The expansion of public and academic libraries coincided with the Progressive movement, which took place between 1880 and 1927. In 1951 George Mowry narrowly defined California progressivism as a political movement designed to take control of urban politics and end the corruption and dominance of the Southern Pacific Railroad in state politics. According to this view, the typical Progressive was Republican, a lawyer or businessman, middle-aged, Protestant, and class- and reform-minded. Most of these individuals could trace their ancestry to New England. Unfortunately, this model completely ignored the role of Progressive women. Both male and female Progressives shared some of these qualities, although historians have offered a variety of definitions. In *Cultural Crusaders*, Joanne Passet relies on

Robert N. Cruden's definition, which focused on Protestant moral values and education. Both Progressive era men and women "sought careers that provided an outlet for service," and they embraced the new professions of "social work, journalism, and librarianship as outlets for their reforming zeal." This reforming zeal took on a variety of negative tones but especially an antiforeigner, nationalistic one after World War I. As a result, a strong assimilation program known as the "100 Per Cent American Movement" became part of the educational curriculum in California. California clubwomen, teachers, and librarians developed a variety of programs designed to educate and "culturally uplift" the growing immigrant population; home teachers, traveling libraries, and branch libraries offered courses and resources to rural communities and to the growing immigrant population.

WESTERN EXPANSION

In 1905 the American Library Association (ALA) President, Ernest C. Richardson, described librarians as "irrepressible expansionists," and advanced the mission of the association to extend the boundaries of the field to the West. This description took on new meaning as the field witnessed tremendous expansion between 1887 and 1917.

The establishment of professional training programs did not immediately translate into employment opportunities for new graduates. Most libraries were controlled by a local board; whether a one-person shop or a larger institution, mostly untrained male directors were reticent to hire trained nonlocal women when they could hire local women at a lower salary and avoid paying traveling expenses. As professionalization took root, however, library boards recognized the importance of hiring temporary librarians to help organize collections and train local women. Itinerant librarians traveled across the United States to organize library collections with the hope of finding permanent work. These same women traveled west, expecting higher wages and new opportunities for professional appointments. Despite the fact that librarians on average earned higher salaries then did teachers and nurses between 1892 and 1913, the western environment did not initially meet these women's expectations for salaries or professional appointments.

The West urbanized slowly and in many areas remained rural. Many communities focused on developing basic services, and while they desired churches, schools, and libraries, the economic climate limited the development of these institutions. W. P. Kimball described the library situation in California in 1902 as "meagerly sustained" and one of "blank, gaunt poverty of all mental resources." He argued that a competent state commission was needed to establish public libraries and a traveling library system to meet the needs of the population. Although the state library in Sacramento boasted a collection of 120,000 volumes, Californians had limited access to library resources. The formation and funding of public libraries and traveling libraries became the key to improving literacy and civic participation, and library women met the challenge by venturing west and promoting library programs and general civic literacy.

CLUBWOMEN, NEW WOMEN—LIBRARY WOMEN

The growth of the West opened doors for new library school graduates. Women were active participants in the development of western communities. These early pioneers, taking the lead from Eastern reform organizations, pressed the boundaries of "separate spheres," formed clubs and societies, took on public roles, and entered politics. Women's clubs provided women a forum from which they could develop skills in public speaking, organizing, and leadership. These experiences eventually led to social and education reform and secured California women with the right to vote. Sophonisba Breckenridge, in her landmark study *Women in the Twentieth Century,* believed that the General Federation of Women's Clubs (GFWC) played a major role in the developing professions of social work, teaching, and librarianship. She wrote: "The American Library Association is reported to credit women's clubs with the responsibility for initiating 75% of the public libraries now in existence in the United States." It is hard to say whether these clubs had this level of influence, yet it is clear that clubwomen were active in the formation of early public libraries.

Women's clubs flourished during the Progressive era. Historian Judith Raftery noted that women's clubs were organized to provide women with opportunities for self-betterment and to form collective agencies for social reform. Modernization, industrialization, and immigration shaped clubwomen's social reform efforts. Fearing the corruption of the modern world, they hoped to reform social, moral, and civic behavior while enforcing the hegemony of middle-class American values; immigrants became the primary target group to reform and educate. On the other hand, these women hoped to create a political niche for themselves as "municipal housekeepers." In this capacity, women served their families, the community, and the nation; as moral guardians they extended their responsibilities beyond the home, influenced policy making, and eventually opened civic and political doors for all women.

In 1890 women formed the GFWC, a national organization, to facilitate political access. State and local chapters soon followed; the California Federation of Women's Clubs (CFWC) was formed in 1900 and was instrumental in pursuing political recognition. They were highly organized, promoted pure milk laws, established kindergartens in public schools, founded public libraries, and provided English classes to the immigrant population. Indeed, throughout the United States, clubwomen interested in self-improvement supported the development of libraries for their own betterment but soon promoted public and traveling libraries. They also promoted legislation to establish public libraries and to form state library commissions.

Caroline Severance organized the first women's club in Los Angles, the Friday Morning Club (FMC). The founder of the New England Women's Club, she brought experience and leadership and helped to form one of the most successful clubs in the state. Her efforts primarily focused on suffrage, but her Progressive legacy was in the establishment of kindergartens, summer school, after-school playgrounds, and teacher training programs. Many of these services mostly benefited poor and immigrant children and became an important tool in the Americanization process. In the same vein, Mary Simons Gibson, the first woman to be appointed to the California Commission of Immigration and Housing (1913-1921) and the architect of the Home Teachers Act, used her fundraising skills to raise money for the Los Angeles Public Library (LAPL). As a member of the FMC, she focused her reform efforts on suffrage and education. Both Caroline Severance and Mary Gibson helped to lay the groundwork for clubwomen reform. Their reform activities varied, but their connection to the FMC and the GFWC reveals a keen interest in creating a female dominion as civic housekeepers, particularly in the arena of education of immigrant women and children.

There has been a great deal of documentation on the role of California women in the budding Americanization programs, particularly in relationship to Mary Gibson's work in building the home teachers movement through the passage of the Home Teachers Act in 1915. Teachers and librarians could be placed in a similar category as clubwomen and active reformers. The library literature clearly indicates that library women were part of the clubwomen movement and purveyors of cultural literacy. Despite the centrality of library work to clubwomen activities and to education, there is a paucity of literature tying library women to the municipal housekeepers movement.

LOS ANGELES PUBLIC LIBRARY

The Los Angeles Library Association (LALA), the precursor to the LAPL, was formed in 1872 when Los Angeles was nothing more than a frontier outpost. Historian William Spalding characterized Los Angeles as an amalgam of "old Spanish-American, early California pioneers, and more modern east-of-the-Rockies manners and customs." The early American population transformed itself from an economy dependent on cattle ranching and agriculture to an urban city by the 1880s. During these early years, the native California population still dominated and did not have a tradition for public libraries; Los Angeles lacked basic cultural institutions such as art galleries, museums, concert halls, and libraries, not to mention government services and public education.

Prior to 1878 California had no government-funded public libraries. Some school districts had libraries, but the public library movement grew out of local voluntary associations that formed libraries for their members. In keeping with the early Progressive goals, these libraries formed to provide moral uplift and self-improvement to their members. The elite men of the city founded the LALA, which evolved into the LAPL. The library consisted of two small rooms: the Gentleman's Sitting Room, consisting of board games, and the Book Room. The first library board appointed as librarian Warner Littlefield, a New Englander and editor of the *Weekly Express,* a local newspaper, who apparently had a high moral character, one of the primary requirements for the job. Moral uplift not surprisingly became one of the primary goals of the library, next to cultural enrichment. On March 1, 1878, the *Evening Express* reported: "The library rooms are filled every night with a crowd of thoughtful, earnest young men, intent on improving their minds and increasing their stock of knowledge."

Women had little to do with the founding of the LALA and the LAPL. As noted in "At the Pleasure of the Board: Women Librarians and the Founding of the Los Angeles Public Library, 1880-1905," women were denied access to the library until 1876, when a Ladies Room was added. In 1878, when the LALA became a tax-supported institution, the gendered use of the library permanently shifted, but unfortunately for aspiring librarians, the position of librarian was a yearly political appointment and a tenuous one at that. As women became dominant library users, a movement to replace the incumbent librarian, Patrick Connolly, with a female surfaced. The library board recognized the patronage of female users and appointed Mary E. Foy as the first city librarian (1880-1884).

LADY LIBRARIANS

Mary Foy's appointment reflected the patronage-based system present in Los Angeles politics. The daughter of businessman Samuel Foy, Mary, a graduate of Los Angeles High School, became the first woman appointed to the post of city librarian. Foy's appointment represents the local librarian mentality of early library boards; she lacked professional library training, and as a young, unemployed 18-year-old, she needed a job—reinforcing Joanne Passet's view that library appointments were often based on charity. Sheri D. Irvin has further suggested that salary may have been one of the defining factors in promoting lady librarians. Foy earned $75 per month, which included payment for performing janitorial services in addition to her work as librarian.

Despite her lack of training, Foy agreed to study librarianship as a condition of her appointment, and consulted with Ina Coolbirth of the Oakland Library and Frederick Perkins of the San Francisco Public Library. She also advanced the library holdings from 2,550 to 3,237. A good portion of the added volumes came from donations from women's literary organizations. In 1884 the board voted to appoint Jessie Gavitt, largely on her financial need rather than her experience. Mary Foy left librarianship for education, but future city librarians reviewed her tenure favorably. Charles Fletcher Lummis later commented that "Ms. Foy was the first person to grasp the privileges and responsibilities of librarianship." Lummis, best know as a historian, joined the ranks of city librarians

under less than desirable circumstances during a period of crisis.

During Jessie Gavitt's (1884-1889) tenure, the city experienced greater prosperity and in turn provided the funds needed to increase the collection from 3,237 volumes to 6,247. Despite the growth of the collection, she did not succeed in increasing circulation, one of the primary measures used by the board to evaluate librarian performance. Gavitt experienced the same fate as Mary Foy and lost the election based on financial need, but her lack of success in building the patron base clearly hurt her election; she later served as assistant librarian under a different library board. In 1889 the library board appointed Lydia A. Prescott, but her 1-year term reflected some of the political changes facing the new charter and reorganization of city government. At the end of 1889, one of the local newspapers described the library collection as nothing more than old donated books of little interest to the general population. No doubt the quality of the collection depended on donations, but it also appeared that the paltry library budget failed to meet the needs of the growing population.

Real expansion and use of the library took place under the leadership of Tessa Kelso (1889-1895). Kelso, an experienced newspaperwoman and publicist, possessed the leadership skills needed to transform the LAPL from a small library to an impressive civic institution. She represented the classic Progressive era female. She melded politics and reform into her agenda as city librarian and as an active suffragist. In 1892 she spoke out against an ALA proposal to establish a separate women's section. In the November volume of the *Library Journal*, she wrote: "For years woman has worked, talked, and accepted all sorts of compromises to prove her fitness to hold the position of librarian, and to demonstrate that sex should have no weight where ability is equal. . . . In all these years the accomplishment is seen in the table of wages paid woman librarians in comparison with those paid men for like work. For women to now come forward with the argument that a woman librarian has a point of view and such limitation that they must be discussed apart from the open court of library affairs is a serious mistake."

Kelso proved her skills as an administrator and library innovator during her tenure. She introduced the Dewey Decimal Classification Scheme, interlibrary loan services, and library training classes, founded the Southern California Library Club, instituted a civil service program for all new librarian hires, and opened free access to students and teachers. As a member of the Friday Morning Club, she established art programs sponsored by the club. Adelaide Hasse served as her right arm, first as a library attendant and later as the assistant librarian. Hasse quickly became an expert in government documents and later developed a classification scheme for government documents, still in use today. Together Tessa Kelso and Adelaide Hasse helped turn the LAPL into a modern progressive library. Kelso's days were numbered, however, as controversy arose over her attendance at the World's Congress of Librarians and the ALA in Chicago in 1893. On the approval of the library board, Kelso attended the conference and submitted her bills to the city auditor, Fred H. Teale, for reimbursement. Teale challenged her request and Kelso later sued. When all was said and done, accusations of misappropriation of funds led to a separate slander suit and a petition to the California Supreme Court. Despite her success and popularity, her days were numbered. Kelso and Hasse tendered their resignations, despite support from part of the library board and the superintendent of schools.

Kelso's tenure clearly marked a turning point in the status and size of the LAPL. The collection increased from 6,356 to 42,313 volumes, library card holders increased dramatically from 132 in 1889 to 18,057 in 1894, and circulation likewise increased from 19,565 to 329,405. She had a clear understanding of the issues affecting libraries, and as a woman she understood too well the obstacles of gender. She held fast to the notions of the new woman. According to one description, she was "forceful . . . rather than distinctive or femininely attractive. She wore low heeled, broad-toed shoes, often went without a hat, wore short hair, smoked cigarettes occasionally, and often acted with that unconventional freedom."

Notwithstanding the board's decision, the local community, members of the library board, and her ALA colleagues praised her work. Marion Horton, acting principal of the Los Angeles Library School, remarked that her views on library training, government documents, and community relations were 25 years ahead of her time. Charles Lummis later credited Kelso for laying the foundation for expansion and modernization of the LAPL. Both Kelso and Hasse left Los Angeles to pursue very successful careers in the East. Kelso left librarianship for publishing work but kept a foot in the door as the head of the library department of Baker and Taylor. Hasse continued down her chosen career path as a librarian of government documents.

Her career took her to Washington, D.C., where she worked as a specialist with the U.S. Department of Agriculture, and later to the New York Public Library.

By 1895 education became the primary mission of the LAPL, and according to annual reports, collection development efforts focused on "local history, local pride, moral guidance and uplift, preparation for citizenship, and wholesome entertainment." The influence of women librarians continued with Clara Fowler (1895-1897) and Harriet Child Wadleigh (1897-1900). Both administrations felt the pinch of city generosity; the collection leveled off, as did circulation. Fowler had no library training or experience, but as an accountant and the first woman bank teller in Los Angeles, the board had high hopes that she would be a strong fiscal leader. Indeed, she managed to end both years of her service with a budget surplus and created an efficient file management program; unfortunately, she proved to be a better accountant than librarian, and the board asked her to resign. Ironically, they cited her lack of knowledge and training in library science, her lack of general knowledge of literature, and her inability to manage personnel.

Harriet Child Wadleigh lacked library training as well but had some exposure as a teacher and later as an assistant librarian in Massachusetts. Prior to her appointment, she was active in the Friday Morning Club and served as vice president of the South California Library Club. To her credit, she opened the general stacks of the library but continued to have personnel problems, largely related to the enforcement of a civil service examination and raising questions over favoritism. The board asked her to resign, and when she refused, they dismissed her for failing to "maintain proper discipline among the library attendants and executive incompetency"; she was reminded that she served "at the "pleasure of the board." The situation was not entirely resolved until a new board took over in April of 1900; Wadleigh tendered her resignation but stayed on until the board appointed a new librarian.

Mary L. Jones (1900-1905) accepted the board's nomination with the blessing of Wadleigh. She too "served at the pleasure of the board." Her incumbency, however, was mired by personnel problems and a power struggle between her and the members of the board. According to historian Debra Hansen, Jones's administration "culminated a generation of feminization and professionalization" within the LAPL; the board determined that a male librarian would better suit the goals of the library board, and as suggested by

Hansen, the board hoped to turn the LAPL into a major research institution that would rival the New York Public Library and Boston Public Library. In contrast, Jones focused on building a library with "strong recreational and social-service features."

Prior to her appointment in Los Angeles, Jones experienced similar problems while serving as the first librarian to head the University of Nebraska's library. Despite her success in building the library program, she confronted hostility from the male faculty and faced an uphill battle with the chancellor, who told her that he would "secure a man for librarian as soon as the University could pay a fitting salary." She managed to hold on to her position for 2 years, but she entered into a long drawn-out tug-of-war for control over the collection development, funding, personnel, and salaries, which she eventually lost, and quietly resigned.

Los Angeles presented a new set of problems, again focused on gender, but this time Jones gathered strength and publicity from sister suffragists Susan B. Anthony and Anna B. Shaw, Melvil Dewey, clubwomen, and ALA members. Between June and July of 1905, several hearings took place to evaluate the board's actions, during which time Jones refused to tender her resignation and continued to occupy the librarian's office. The press provided plenty of editorials to satisfy the curious public. On June 23, 1905, one headline read, "Club Women Rally Round Deposed Librarian." The press reported that some 999 clubwomen signed a petition asking the mayor to remove all the "offending" board members. They were particularly galled to learn that Lummis was offered one third more in salary than Jones. In another example, clubwomen crowded the librarian's office, bringing her flowers and moral support. The board quickly squelched a female uprising and ruled "that the librarian's office was not to be used by women to 'congregate and gossip.'" Several days later, close to a thousand women gathered to hear Susan B. Anthony and Anna B. Shaw speak on the situation. The mayor, pressured by these women, fired the entire library board. The city council reviewed the case but determined that the librarian served at the pleasure of the board, and appointed Charles Lummis. Jones left Los Angles for Berkeley, where she accepted the directorship of the summer library program at the University of California, Berkeley.

Mary Jones, nonetheless, brought strong Progressive goals to the job and succeeded in strengthening local ties with schools, settlement houses, and other clubwomen reforms. She modernized the library, established children's services and branch libraries, eliminated monetary guarantees for lending, established a "new book" shelf, and developed a popular fiction collection, increasing circulation from 392,000 in 1900 to 751,000 in 1904.

Historian Hansen concluded that Jones's focus on women and children—less serious library users—in contrast to the "serious" male researcher, led the board to reevaluate the role of women librarians. Personnel problems also plagued her administration, but gender played a significant role and her difficulties served to reinforce the growing position of the board that a male librarian would better suit their goals. Indeed, the director of the library board, Isadore Dockweiler, hoped to fire Jones as early as 1902 in order to hire local historian Lummis. No doubt Jones's emphasis on building a children's collection countered the board's goal to turn LAPL into a research institution, but the sexual double standard dominated the discourse. On June 21, 1905, Jones attended the library board meeting and read a prepared statement that justified her refusal to resign based on gender:

> At first it was my inclination to yield to the request. . . . But upon reflection, I have concluded that it would not be fitting for me to tender my resignation as the head of a department in which women only are employed when such resignation is requested solely on the ground that the best interests of the department demand that its affairs no longer be administered by a woman.

Clearly, the termination hearings became both political and personal. Helen Haines later commented that Jones was ousted based on "shameless political jobbery," and the subsequent incumbency of the "brilliant, eccentric historian," Charles Lummis, "enriched the library's Californiana, but his vagaries and eccentricities as a librarian dominated . . . the next six years . . . and made the Los Angeles Public Library appear to the library world as a cross between a comic opera and a tragedy. This has always seemed to me one of the disgraceful episodes in our profession's history" and poorly reflects on the capabilities of the leaders of the day.

CONCLUSION

California provides one view of the challenges and obstacles early women librarians faced as they pursued their careers. The golden age provided women with new opportunities to develop library collections, and they were instrumental in the expansion of the profession. Joanne Passet in *Cultural Crusaders* provides scholars with a foundation for understanding the challenges and obstacles women faced as they moved west and brought the library gospel to growing rural and urban populations. Clubwomen clearly played an important role in the founding of western libraries and influenced the development of policies and educational curriculum designed to improve the literacy of Americans and new immigrants.

The Progressive era provided a unique opportunity for women to pursue political, social, and moral reform. The experiences of Mary Foy, Tessa Kelso, and Mary Jones testify to the strength of women's clubs in local and state politics and reinforces the role that these women took seriously—their role as purveyors of cultural literacy and as municipal housekeepers. These early librarians faced daunting sexual discrimination, as is evident in the firing of Mary Jones. Notwithstanding the obstacles and the sexual double standard, women librarians faced the challenges and adapted to their social environments. They were not introverted or passive in dealing with all-male library boards, but were confident, articulate, and sometimes aggressive to a fault. While these new women served at the pleasure of the library board, they served the local community and created a modern progressive public library.

Women's history has come a long way in the last 30 years, and library women's experiences are beginning to take shape as more scholars focus on the role of women in this profession. The history of California library women's experiences continues to grow as scholars make a concerted effort to write women in. There are a number of studies documenting the role of progressive women as educators, suffragists, and social reformers, but library women's experiences remain untapped, and what work as been done lives outside the general history. Furthermore, the connection between clubwomen's roles in shepherding the library movement and the professionalization of librarians needs further exploration. The cultural, political, and social landscape of California during the Progressive era, particularly with the rise of the Americanization movement, is another area that could be explored. Librarians as cultural crusaders developed collections and services designed to support the needs of the state and were committed to the same ideologies of cultural uplift as clubwomen and as educators.

—Danelle Moon

SUGGESTED READINGS

Cao, Jerry Finely. "The Los Angeles Public Library: Origins and Development." Ph.D. dissertation. University of Southern California, 1977.

Gordon, Lynn D. *Gender and Higher Education in the Progressive Era*. New Haven, CT: Yale University Press, 1990.

Gullett, Gayle. *Becoming Citizens: The Emergence and Development of the California Women's Movement, 1880-1911*. Urbana: University of Illinois Press, 2000.

Hansen, Debra, Karen F. Gracy, and Sheri D. Irvin. "At the Pleasure of the Board: Women Librarians and the Los Angeles Public Library, 1880-1905." *Libraries and Culture 34* (1999): 311-347.

Hildenbrand, Suzanne. "A Historical Perspective on Gender Issues in American Librarianship." *Canadian Journal of Information Science 17* (September 1992): 18-28.

Hildenbrand, Suzanne. *Reclaiming the Library Past: Writing the Women in*. Norwood, NJ: Ablex, 1996.

Moon, Danelle. "Educational Housekeepers: Female Reformers and the California Americanization Program, 1900-1927," in Gordon Morris Bakken, ed., *California History: A Topical Approach*. Wheeling, IL: Harlan Davidson, 2002, 108-124.

Mowry, George E. *The California Progressives*. Berkeley: University of California Press, 1951.

Muncy, Robyn. *Creating a Female Dominion in American Reform, 1890-1935*. New York: Oxford University Press, 1991.

Passet, Joanne E. *Cultural Crusaders: Women Librarians in the American West 1900-1917*. Albuquerque: University of New Mexico Press, 1994.

Raftery, Judith Rosenberg. *Land of Fair Promise: Politics and Reform in Los Angeles Schools, 1885-1941*. Stanford, CA: Stanford University Press, 1992.

LOCKWOOD, LORNA C.
(1903-1977)

Politics and law have often been family traditions in Arizona. Children of prominent figures are even more likely to be successful, so it might seem likely that progeny of a state Supreme Court judge would achieve important positions in Phoenix's legal and judicial system. Lorna Lockwood's political success in Phoenix and then as an Arizona Supreme Court justice (1960-1975) clearly echoed the judicial attainments of her father, Alfred Lockwood (Arizona Supreme Court, 1925-1942). But although Lorna's goals were early shaped by interaction with her father, significant aspects of her career and the reasons for her success reflect her own choices and interaction with the political and legal environment.

Lorna was born to Alfred C. and Daisy Maude Lockwood in the mining town of Douglas, Arizona. Alfred had come to the territory as a young man, and after farming, teaching school, and reading law in the border town of Nogales, he was admitted to the Arizona bar in 1902. Moving in 1903 to practice law in the larger city of Douglas, where he later served as city attorney, Alfred early developed a close relationship with his daughter. Lorna later remembered her father's promise that if he became city attorney, she could have whatever she wanted. After his election, she asked for a gun, which he gave her. In 1913 the new state's governor appointed her father circuit court judge of Cochise County, and the family moved to Tombstone. During that period, Lorna visited her father's law office and used to think how wonderful it would be if she could some day practice law with him. Lorna graduated from the town's small high school in 1920, where she participated in various sports and musical activities.

Although some family members had gone to Pomona College in California, Lorna decided to attend the University of Arizona because it had a law school. Majoring in Spanish, writing for the student newspaper, and active in athletic and musical groups, Lorna took an overload and graduated in 3 years. Although skeptical about her becoming a lawyer, her father went with her to visit the law school dean. As an undergraduate, she had been permitted to take some law classes, and upon graduating she was accepted into the law school. Only the second female student to attend the school (Nellie Trent Bush had been the first), Lorna graduated in 1925 near the top of her class and as president of the Student Bar Association.

Unable to practice with her father, since he had just been elected to the state Supreme Court, Lorna could not find another partnership, despite her law school success. She therefore began working for her father

as a clerk and secretary. Later, after suffering a somewhat lengthy illness, she worked as a legal secretary for a large Phoenix law firm, an experience she later described as a useful, practical education. Finally, in 1939 she began practicing law, first with Loretta Savage Whitney (1939-1942) and then (1945-1948) with her brother-in-law, Z. Simpson Cox, and her father, who lost a bid for reelection to the Arizona Supreme Court.

But while her legal career began slowly, Lorna experienced more rapid success in politics. Starting as a precinct committee woman in the 1920s, she soon became president of the Democratic Women's Club, and in 1929 she moved into high party councils as a member of the executive committee of the Democratic State Committee. An active member in the influential Business and Professional Women's Club, in 1938 the club recruited her to run for the state legislature. Continuing a pattern of Arizona—and especially Phoenix—women holding legislative office and with substantial party support, she won election to the state House of Representatives and was reelected in 1940. Going beyond the traditional female legislative role that focused on social and educational issues, she chaired the powerful Judiciary Committee.

Eschewing further reelection, in 1942 she went to Washington, D.C., to work as an assistant to Arizona Congressman John Murdock. Desiring to participate in war-related work, in 1944 she returned to Phoenix to serve as district price attorney in the Office of Price Administration, where she served until the war ended in 1945. The following year, Lockwood returned for another term in the state legislature, where she continued to redefine women's legislative roles: she again chaired the Judiciary Committee and won a seat on the important Rules Committee. As further indication of her increasing local prominence, Phoenix Mayor Ray Busey appointed her to the very important Charter Revision Committee in 1947. In 1949 she left private practice with her father and brother-in-law to accept appointment as assistant attorney general, serving as attorney for Arizona's welfare department.

Building on her record and contacts, in 1950 Lockwood expanded her list of accomplishments by winning election to the Maricopa Superior Court bench. As the first woman serving as an Arizona Superior Court judge, she encountered skepticism from some attorneys, and she received additional public attention the first time she pronounced a death sentence on a prisoner. In general, however, the bar quickly accepted her, and she faced little public criticism about her pathbreaking position. As a superior court judge, she had normal judicial duties, but during her service as the county's juvenile court judge from 1954 through 1957, she achieved more notice and established her reputation as a thoughtful and sensitive jurist. She sought greater attention for the court's activities by inviting representatives of churches, clubs, and the press to attend juvenile hearings. She promoted arts and crafts for youths in detention, helped start the Delinquency Control Institute of Arizona to study crime and delinquency, and advocated neighborhood councils to improve conditions for juveniles. Reflecting her experience within her own close family, her close relationship with her nephews and nieces, and her membership in the Congregational Church, Lockwood argued that church and family were crucial elements in preventing delinquency. She emphasized that children bore some responsibility for their actions, and she recommended that those who were chronic offenders or who committed serious traffic offenses be tried as adults, but she also believed that juveniles should receive more opportunities for rehabilitation than adults. After holding this position for 3 years, Lockwood decided that the great emotional and mental strain of the job was adversely affecting her health, and she returned to the general county bench for the next 3 years.

In 1960 Lockwood aspired to break another barrier, seeking to become the first woman on the Arizona Supreme Court and one of the first women Supreme Court justices in the United States. Contesting the seat of an incumbent, she persuaded a fellow attorney and pilot, Virginia Hash, to fly her around the state to campaign (borrowing this tactic from Barry Goldwater). Following her election, she moved into the suite her father had occupied and even used his former desk. "I cannot fill my father's shoes," she claimed modestly. "I hope I can follow in his footsteps." Her prominence rose further in 1965 when she became the first woman to serve as a state's chief justice (an honor she repeated in 1970). Although the significance was slightly lessened because this post rotated regularly between all justices, the general importance was symbolized by a note from President Lyndon Johnson.

Lockwood was an activist judge, seeking to dispense with outdated precedents and to defend the reasonable expansion of judicial authority. A notable instance was her decision that permitted injured citizens to sue the state without needing its prior permission, claiming that when the reason for a certain rule no longer exists, the rule itself should be abandoned. She advocated equal treatment under the law, ruling that a wife could ask for damages if a husband were injured, and that Indians were eligible to hold public office. She sided with consumers in arguing that no duty rests upon the ultimate consumer or user to search for or guard against the possibility of product defects. She defended decisions by the U.S. Supreme Court during the mid-1960s, explaining that it was merely extending protections of the U.S. Constitution equally as prohibitions against state interference with individual rights. Finally, she was a vigorous advocate of a uniform code for criminal procedure and criticized pretrial detention, confinement without parole, and consecutive sentencing. When vacancies occurred on the U.S. Supreme Court in 1965 and 1967, Senator Carl Hayden recommended her nomination. Despite enthusiastic support, especially from the National Professional and Business Women's Club, she did not became the first Arizonan and first woman to be named to that court, and Lockwood remained on the Arizona bench until her retirement in 1975. Her influence on the court was substantial, and a tribute to her service emphasized her strong support of the rights of the poor, the uneducated, and the indigent.

Throughout her career, Lockwood vigorously supported advancing opportunities for women. One aspect of this effort was her active membership in numerous women's service clubs, sororities, and legal clubs. Her most important association was with the Business and Professional Women's Club, which she served as state president (1956-1957), western regional director (1957-1958), and national board chair for public affairs (1959-1960). During the 1950s, she helped form the Plus 60 Personnel (and continued later to serve as a board member), an organization that assisted senior women who needed help in retraining and finding work. Lockwood cherished her role as a judge but she also advocated political action. In 1968, under sponsorship of the U.S. Chamber of Commerce, she taught a class at the YWCA in practical politics for women. And she repeated this effort throughout the state a few years later. (One apparent consequence of this was the candidacy in the 1969 Phoenix City Council election of Lockwood's sister, Charlotte Cox.) Finally, Lockwood was a determined and articulate defender during the 1970s of the Equal Rights Amendment.

Throughout her career, Lockwood remained active in various social groups and presented herself with some awareness of traditional public expectations. She maintained her love of music, and she professed an interest in reading mysteries and cooking, even offering two cooking recipes in the newspaper. Such stories did not, however, detract from her obvious strengths as a judicial and public figure, as evidenced by her numerous public awards. When she died in 1977, she had succeeded not only in ably following her father but also in establishing new expectations for women.

SOURCES

Although Lockwood's judicial decisions are published, she left no private papers. A brief but useful interview is included in Abe Chanin, with Mildred Chanin, comp., *This Land, These Voices: A Different View of Arizona History in the Words of Those Who Lived It.* Tucson, AZ: Midbar Press, 1988, 217-221. There are collections of newspaper clippings at the Arizona Room, Burton Barr Public Library, Phoenix, Arizona; Hayden Arizona Collection, Arizona State University, Biography of Lorna E. Lockwood; and Arizona Historical Foundation, Arizona State University, Biography of Lorna E. Lockwood. The Arizona Historical Society, Central Division, Arizona Women's Hall of Fame Collection, Box 1, Folder 19, contains clippings and a few miscellaneous items.

The only published biographical work on Lockwood is a brief, unfootnoted discussion in James W. Johnson, *Arizona Politicians: The Noble and the Notorious.* Tucson: University of Arizona Press, 2002, 141-148. Unpublished works include Thomas A. Jacobs, *Justice Was a Lady: A Biography of the Public Life of Lorna E. Lockwood* (typed manuscript). Tucson, AZ: Arizona Historical Society, 1998, and David M. Quantz, *A Legal Biography of Lorna E. Lockwood* (unpublished paper, 1978, University of Arizona, Law Library Special Collections).

A useful context for Lockwood's career in the legislature and politics is Heidi J. Osselaer, *A Woman for a Woman's Job: Arizona Women in Politics, 1900-1950.* Ph.D. dissertation. Arizona State University, 2001.

—Philip R. VanderMeer

M

MAGOFFIN, SUSAN SHELBY
(1827-1855)

Susan Shelby was born into a wealthy Kentucky family on June 30, 1827. As Howard R. Lamar noted in the Foreword to her diary, Susan came from a long line of pioneers and war heroes. She was raised at Arcadia, her father's home near Danville. She lived a privileged life, which included private tutors.

Eighteen-year-old Susan married Santa Fe trader Samuel Magoffin, a man much older than she, on November 25, 1845. The young bride was soon to accompany her husband on a trip down the Santa Fe Trail and begin the diary that would ensure her mark in history.

The newly married couple honeymooned for 6 months in New York and Philadelphia before starting their trip down the Santa Fe Trail into Mexico. The trip began in June 1846, a few months after war with Mexico had been officially declared.

Susan decided to keep a written journal of her experiences along the Santa Fe Trail. Her diary is considered the first written record of travel along the trail kept by a woman. The journal contains information on the Santa Fe Trail trade during its high point, the customs and culture of the Mexican people, and Gen. Kearny's conquest of New Mexico, not to mention the progress of the war with Mexico. Her diary also reads as a list of prominent (non-American) men and women in New Mexico and also of army men like Zachary Taylor and Stephen Kearny.

As Kelley Pounds observed, Susan traveled in relative comfort in a Rockaway carriage complete with driver, her personal maid, Jane, and three other servants hired by her husband. She was even able to bring her dog. Despite the ease of her life on the trail, this "wandering princess" liked to compare herself to her pioneering grandmother, and hoped to make her proud.

Susan's party traveled to Bent's Fort. It was here that she celebrated her 19th birthday, and it was here that she suffered a miscarriage. Howard Lamar noted that she treated this sad event candidly in her journal. Her words showed a change in her character toward religious piousness that stayed with her for the rest of her journey. They traveled on to Santa Fe and from there to El Paso del Norte, Chihuahua, and other points in Mexico. Susan's party followed in the wake of the U.S. Army troops under Col. Alexander Doniphan, thus U.S. Army movements in the border areas were noted in her journal. The dangers the Magoffins and their party were exposed to were very real. She faced them all stoically, her religious faith becoming stronger and stronger amid all the rumors, both of war and of her brother-in-law's death. She was no shrinking violet, however, and she had a thirst for knowledge. She taught herself Spanish, helped her husband run his store, and became adept at dealing with shopkeepers, beating them at their own bargaining games.

Susan's diary is important, too, because it shows how she grew as an individual along the trail. At first she was naïve and saw this journey as a lark, but as she experienced hardship on the trail and the fear of being in what was then enemy territory, fear for herself, her husband, and her other family members, she came to understand the realities of her life. As

Kelly Pounds noted, her adoration for her husband gave way to the reality of womanhood and marriage. Her life on the trail was not all fun and games, and they helped her grow as a person.

The trail took its toll on Susan, and after a little over a year of travel, she was ready to go home. She was tired of being a curiosity (since she was one of the only white women around). She no longer took an active interest in recording her experiences, and her diary ended on September 8, 1847, just before she and her husband boarded a ship to Camargo.

Susan contracted yellow fever in Matamoras. While she was sick, she gave birth to a second child, a son who died shortly after his birth. After she had recovered from her illness, she and her husband boarded a ship that took them to New Orleans, and from there they returned to Kentucky.

Susan's husband gave up trade on the Santa Fe Trail to deal in real estate. In 1851 Susan gave birth to her third child, a daughter she named after her maid, Jane. The Magoffins moved to Barrett's Station near Kirkwood, Missouri. Shortly after the birth of her fourth child, another daughter in 1855, Susan died. She was buried in Bellefontaine Cemetery in St. Louis, Missouri.

—Shannon Orr

SUGGESTED READINGS

Dary, David. *The Santa Fe Trail*. New York: Alfred P. Knopf, 2001.

Drum, Stella M., ed. *Down the Santa Fe Trail and Into Mexico: The Diary of Susan Shelby Magoffin*. New Haven, CT: Yale University Press, 1926.

Pounds, Kelley. "The Manifest Destiny of Susan Shelby Magoffin." *Calico Trails*, July 1997. Retrieved from kclleypounds.tripod.com/magoffin.htm.

MANELLA, NORA MARGARET (1951-)

In 1951 Nora Margaret Manella was born in Los Angeles. She earned her bachelor's degree from Wellesley College in Massachusetts in 1972. She pursued her J.D. at the University of Southern California, where she graduated in 1975. After receiving her degree, she was a clerk for the Hon. John Minor

Wisdom in the U.S. Court of Appeals for the Fifth circuit. From 1976 to 1978 she served as legal counsel on the U.S. Senate Judiciary Committee's Subcommittee on the Constitution. After a brief stint in her own private practice, she became the assistant U.S. attorney for the Central District of California in 1982. After 8 years, she moved on to become a judge in the Los Angeles Municipal Court, and then in 1992 she became a judge on the Superior Court of California. In 1992 she served as justice pro tem for the California Court of Appeal. From 1994 to 1998 she was a U.S. attorney for the Central District of California. When Mariana R. Pfaelzer vacated her seat on the U.S. District Court for the Central District of California, President Bill Clinton nominated her for it on March 31, 1998. She received her commission on October 22, 1998, one day after her Senate confirmation.

—Marcus J. Schwoerer

SUGGESTED READING

Nora Margaret Manella. Retrieved from air.fjc.gov/servlet/tGetInfo?jid=2798. Source: History of the Federal Judiciary. http://www.fjc.gov. Web site of the Federal Judicial Center, Washington, D.C.

MARION, FRANCES (1888-1973)

At the turn of the 20th century, talented women seeking a place to demonstrate their capabilities as professional artists flocked to young Hollywood, which welcomed them with open arms. Still a young industry, Hollywood had not been infiltrated with the male prejudices these women found in other fields. Because the public at that time did not view film making as a serious business, the women who came here found an abundance of career opportunities. Not only could they work as actresses in front of the camera, but they also found work and success as directors, writers, and producers. One such woman, who contributed much to the success of the rising industry, was Frances Marion, actress, writer, director, and producer.

Frances was born on November 18, 1888, in San Francisco into a well-to-do Jewish family. As a young girl she dreamed of becoming a painter. She also demonstrated a gift for writing short stories and poems. After the devastating earthquake of 1906, her family lost their wealth as well as all hopes of sending their talented daughter to an eastern college. The only logical thing for Frances to do, at least in her mind, was to get married. At 17 years of age, she married Wesley de Lappe, a 19-year-old artist. The teenage marriage was doomed to fail, and in 1910 the two artists divorced. The following year she married Robert Pike, who offered her economic security and social acceptance. In 1917 Pike sued Frances for divorce on the grounds of desertion. She was to marry twice more in the years to come.

After working as a cub reporter for the *San Francisco Chronicle,* Frances became a commercial artist and set out to Los Angeles to work on theatrical posters for Oliver Morosco. She was disappointed with the growing city, and vowed to return quickly to her native San Francisco as soon as her job was finished. She never made good on her promise, but rather stayed and began a successful career, both in front and in back of the camera, which lasted half a century.

When her chance to return to San Francisco came, the Hollywood bug had already bit her. She saw in young Hollywood a growing industry, one that she wanted to be a part of. However, she did not see herself as an actress, so she set out to find a way to get into the business through other means. Her chance came when Owen Moore offered to introduce her to his wife, Mary Pickford, America's Sweetheart. Moore had seen Frances's posters and was sure Mary would like to have one made for her. Frances was nervous yet excited about meeting the famous actress with the golden curls. She traveled to the set and met with Mary. The two became instant friends, forming a bond that endured career highs and lows, marriage, and divorce. The two women became inseparable, leaning on and supporting one another throughout their lives.

Frances's itch to get into the movie business continued, even after she was made head of the art department at her advertising firm. Adela Rogers recommended that she speak to Lois Weber, the only female director at the time. Frances explained that she had no desire to act in front of the camera. However, after 2 hours, and at the age of 24, she had signed a contract with the Bosworth studio as "Frances Marion. Actress. Refined type. Age 19."

Frances was eager to learn every aspect of the business. She helped wherever she could, from costume and set designing to working in the cutting room. She was even willing to act in front of the camera after her initial self-doubt about her acting skills wore away. However, she became famous for her scenario writing, and turned out to be the highest paid writer in Hollywood.

At the time, the highest paid scenario writer earned $75 per week. Frances hoped to prove her talent as a writer with her original story "The Foundling," which she submitted to Mary Pickford. Mary filmed the movie, but before the studio released it, a fire destroyed all copies. With no success to point to on the screen, Frances made a bold move. She wrote to several studio bosses, asking for an unheard of salary of $200 per week, with an option of working 2 weeks for free in order to prove her worth as a writer. William A. Brady, head of the World Film Company, hired her after Frances saved a shelved film, starring his daughter, Alice Brady. She added a prologue and epilogue, turning the failed melodrama into a successful comedy. When her contract with the World Film Company was up, Mary hired Frances as her scenario writer with a starting salary of $500 per week, which would increase to $1,000 at the end of a year.

The United States's entrance into World War I sent Hollywood into a frenzy as it tried to produce enough patriotic films to satisfy a demanding public. Frances was set to leave for Washington to request a job as a war correspondent when she met Fred Thomson, who was on his way to France. The two made plans to marry after the war, and once at the capitol, Frances begged for permission to go to France, on the chance that she might see Fred. She obtained the job and became the first woman to cross the Rhine into Germany.

After the war, Robert Hearst offered Frances a contract as a writer and director for the Cosmopolitan Studio with a salary of $2,000 per week. Although she experienced several successes with the company, she decided that as soon as her contract was up, she would become a freelance writer. She enjoyed her freedom and was able to negotiate higher salaries from studios that competed for her. She even survived the death of the silent movie as she smoothly transitioned from writing scenarios to writing actual dialogue. She proved her talent with her original story, The Big House, a movie about a prison riot in San Quentin.

After a long and rewarding career in the movie industry, doctors diagnosed Frances with cancer in early 1973. She died of an aneurysm later that year on

May 11 at the age of 84. She had lived a full life, witnessing and participating in the rise of Hollywood.

—Michelle L. Oropeza

SUGGESTED READING

Beauchamp, Cari. *Without Lying Down: Frances Marion and the Powerful Women of Early Hollywood.* New York: Simon & Schuster, 1997.

MARSHALL, CONSUELO BLAND (1936-)

Born in Knoxville, Tennessee, Federal Judge Consuelo Bland Marshall grew up in Los Angeles, California. She attended Los Angeles City College and received her associate of arts degree in 1956 and went on to receive a bachelor of arts degree from Howard University in 1958 as well as her LL.B. in 1961. During this time, the lawyers and activists of the civil rights movement heavily influenced her. Her mentors included Albert Matthews and George Jones.

Marshall's career in law began when she became deputy city attorney for the Los Angeles City Attorney's Office in 1962. She stayed there until 1967, when she moved on to her own private practice. In 1971 she became the commissioner for the juvenile court and in 1976 a judge for the civil and criminal divisions of the Inglewood Municipal Court. In 1977 she became a Los Angeles Superior Court judge. President Jimmy Carter appointed her to a federal judgeship for the Central District of California in 1980, and she has been chief judge since 2001. She was the first African American woman to be appointed as a federal judge to that district.

Throughout her career, Marshall received numerous awards. She received one of her first awards from the Black Women Lawyers Association in 1976. In 1978 she won the award for the National Business and Professional Women's Club of Los Angeles. Howard University named her Graduate of the Year in 1981. The Los Angeles Sentinel named her Woman of the Year in 1983. In 1984 she garnered the Presidential Award in Recognition for Services and Contributions in Improving the Quality of Life for Mankind. She continues to work as a federal judge.

—Lori S. Iacovelli

SUGGESTED READINGS

Bliss, Mary Lee, ed. *The American Bench: Judges of the Nation 1999-2000* (10th ed.). Sacramento, CA: Forster-Long, 1999.

Consuelo Bland Marshall. Retrieved from air.fjc.gov/servlet/tGetInfo?jid=1485. Source: History of the Federal Judiciary. http://www.fjc.gov. Web site of the Federal Judicial Center, Washington, D.C.

Just the Beginning Foundation: From Slavery to the Supreme Court. Retrieved on March 9, 2002, from www.jtbf.org.

MCDONALD, JUANITA MILLENDER (1938-)

Juanita Millender was born in Birmingham, Alabama, and started on the road to a successful political career, earning her B.S. at the University of Redlands in 1981 and M.A. at California State University of Los Angeles. She is currently pursuing her doctorate at the University of Southern California.

She has been a teacher, administrator, and editor-writer. She was the director of gender equity programs for the Los Angeles Unified School District, a member of the Carson (California) City Council (1990-1992), and a member of the Carson Assembly (1993-1996). In 1996 the people elected her a member of the House of Representatives as a Democrat from the 37th Congressional District. She serves on the Transportation and Infrastructure and Small Business Committees.

Throughout her political career, she has supported women's wellness and women's achievements. She had distinguished herself as the founder of the League of African-American Women and of the Young Advocates of Southern California. She achieved the Watts Walk of Fame in 1998, and was the first African American woman to give the Democratic Radio Response to the Nation. Her topic was aid to Afghan women.

She is married to James McDonald Jr. They have five children and five grandchildren. She and her husband now reside in Carson, California.

—Lori S. Iacovelli

SUGGESTED READINGS

Schultz, Jeffrey D., and Laura van Assendelft, eds. *Encyclopedia of Women in American Politics.* Phoenix, AZ: Oryx Press, 1999.

Treese, Joel D., ed. *2001/Fall Congressional Staff Directory: 107th Congress, First Session* (62d ed.). Washington, DC: CQ Press, 2001.

United States House of Representatives. Retrieved from www.house.gov.

MCGLADREY, DONNA JOY
(1935-1959)

Donna Joy McGladrey and her twin Dorothy were born to Rev. Leslie David and Verna McGladrey on April 19, 1935, in Mora, Minnesota. Together with their older sister, Joan, the twins grew up in Methodist parsonages throughout Minnesota and Illinois. They participated in Methodist Youth Fellowship, sang in choirs, helped clean the church, and tabulated offerings. Even though they always had a home, the family suffered with the rest of the nation during the Depression. The girls acquired clothing as hand-me-downs, from church rummage sales, or they made their own. They tended victory gardens during World War II and picked their grandmother's strawberries to sell to the grocer. But financial gaps still existed, so their father got a second job at the Railway Express in the 1930s and as a traveling insurance adjuster in the 1940s. When he was traveling, rather than leave his family in Chicago for weeks at a time or have them stay in hotels with him, he dropped them off at a Wisconsin YMCA family camp. At the camp they stayed in primitive cabins for a pittance. They had to haul their own water and use a community latrine, yet they loved the clean air, trees, lakes, sandy beaches, and the pristine wilderness. They swam, canoed, played softball and volleyball, and hung out with their friends. Each year they returned to rekindle friendships.

Back home in smoggy Chicago, Donna attended the University of Chicago Laboratory School until financial strains forced the girls to attend Parker High School instead. She then majored in music education at MacMurray College in Jacksonville, Illinois. She became an accomplished organist and vocalist, participating in numerous musical performances.

After graduating in May 1957, she took a job as a music teacher at Meadowbrook School in an affluent Chicago-area neighborhood. She was not used to wealthy children's attitudes and dominating school boards, and began her search for a new job in the spring of 1958. That summer, her mother and father were camping in Alaska. They wrote about beautiful mountains, pristine forests and lakes, and clear air. Donna begged them to find her a teaching job. They found her one in Dillingham, a small fishing village on the Nushagak River in Bristol Bay (southwestern Alaska). In August 1958 Donna packed 44 pounds of belongings and headed west for the adventure of a lifetime.

She dreaded taking planes and desperately feared flying, yet she knew the only way to get to Dillingham was by plane. She wrote to her family when she arrived in Anchorage, "I was lonely, scared and homesick and ready to give it all up and go home." Donna had heard of Dillingham, approximately 350 miles west of Anchorage: "It's terribly primitive." Then, "I SAW A GLACIER! WOW!" Although the prospect of living so austerely and remotely frightened her, the natural beauty reassured her and instilled in her a sense of self-confidence.

In Dillingham she shared a room with Ann Carr, a grandmother, talker, smoker, and drinker. Ann and Donna had their differences. Donna quickly learned that "the only way I can get along with her is to do exactly as she wants. . . . At least she's somebody to talk to." She learned to adapt to frustrating circumstances. Their apartment had no heat other than that which entered from the hallway, and a chemical bucket for a toilet. Unfortunately, by the end of October, they were evicted. For weeks she had no permanent home, for awhile living with a family or sleeping behind the kitchen of the Green Front Cafe, the only restaurant in town.

She described Dillingham as a "typical Eskimo fishing village," the largest one in the area, "but as barbarian, primitive, uncultured, remote, dirty, shacky, miserable, etc. . . . For me + those like me, it's bad, but the people don't know any better." Donna quickly recognized that she could not judge the local population by her traditional family standards.

She described her first school day:

My 5th is fine; 6th boys are dreadful; 7th need help; 8th boys need a whip; 9th all girls—just fabulous—best group; 10th & 11th scared to sing. . . . They have had little or no music + know NOTHING of instruments. . . . However, they are all enthusiastic about starting a band.

Donna understood that teaching them would be a challenge. She wrote, "IF I live through it." Her fears of death and sense of insecurity diminished over time as she became more independent and self-confident.

Donna started an instrumental program and band but found the lack of instruments frustrating. The school had no music supplies and the children reacted to discipline as if they never received any at home. She wrote that the lack of full-time employment by their parents caused the children's problems. The only employer in Dillingham consisted of a cannery that operated only during the salmon harvest.

She believed that these larger social problems inhibited the children's ability to concentrate or maintain self-control. Crimes occurred in the community, many of them serious and startling. She explained how parents commonly drank to get drunk, a reflection of the economy. Therefore, the kids ran wild and remained undisciplined. Many young women dropped out of school to have illegitimate children. Smoking started as early as sixth grade. Regardless, Donna found herself defending the students. When Ann disparaged the students, claiming that "a child's background is no excuse for his behavior at school," Donna retorted, "The heck it isn't. When kids have to

go home and fend for themselves while their folks go off on a binge, never have clean clothes—proper food, discipline or attention, I don't doubt they are as they are. Their background makes such a big difference on their behavior."

By the end of her first semester, she began to defend the children's behavior, blaming it on their upbringing, which in turn she blamed on the economy.

Disciplining the children and keeping their attention caused Donna consternation. "My 6th grade is composed of 'holy terrors.'" Yet by the end of October she wrote, "I'm beginning to get the brats in line. . . . Owoo do they drive me insane." The kids loved her and she wrote of her pride in their performances and instrumental progress.

Donna loved teaching. She had instrument classes before class, during lunch, and after school. She even started a faculty band. Her programs ranged from traditional classical music to African folk songs and Japanese costume dancing. The biggest constraint on her time was copying music, for Dillingham had no music stores. Therefore, she begged her family to send her music, which she then copied by hand, orchestrating each piece for the entire band and choir. When music was not available, she composed her own scores. Donna often worked until 2:00 a.m.

Regardless of her busy schedule, she always set aside time to participate in Sunday church, Wednesday Bible study, and to perform in trios and quartets. At church, she developed two very strong friendships with Roberta Tews and Martha Jay, young Church of Christ missionaries. Together they went cross-country skiing, participated in church activities, and had long conversations at the Green Front Cafe. She also met Guy Vander Hoek and his wife, Tressie, her best friend. She began dating Richard Newton, who owned a plumbing company with his brother. Richard was Baptist and "a very fine, kind, thoughtful Christian young man. . . . He's good looking . . . but I don't know if I'll ever love him." Donna was cautious about men, since she had never dated, especially men like Richard, who had already been divorced. She allowed him to pursue her but found herself in turmoil over him as the year progressed. He loved her but, Donna wrote, "This makes me very unhappy because I'm not in love with him." Donna had to reconcile her newfound freedom with the entanglement of a man and society's demands that a woman her age get married and have a family.

Demands on her time by Richard and her work schedule caused her health to decline. She often became ill, suffered weight loss, and occasionally fainted. Perhaps the lack of fresh fruits and vegetables made her sick, or maybe it was the heavy mineral concentration in the well water that she hauled daily. Also, the E. coli bacteria existed in the small sewage trench that ran down Main Street and trash pits behind homes that overflowed during rainstorms and spring melt. Or perhaps it was nerves from having to deal with an overbearing boyfriend.

But Donna remained resilient in her love of Alaska: "I love it here!" She enjoyed her many adventures in nature. For example, Donna, Roberta, and Martha borrowed cross-country skis and explored the surrounding areas. They acquired bloody blisters and fell down numerous times. Her toes were "like ice," her cheeks windblown, her body ached, hunger overtook her, and she was thoroughly exhausted. But she wrote of her excitement to go again.

Donna also confronted nature alone. Feeling lonely and depressed without her family at Christmas, she got an ax, trudged into the woods, chopped down a tree, and dragged it back to her place to decorate it. She needed to create a sense of home, and Christian tradition insisted that she have symbols of the season. A Christmas tree meant a lot to a minister's daughter who seemed half a world away from her family.

Alaska truly called to Donna:

There's a spirit in Alaska that can't be found anywhere else in the world. . . . I wouldn't go back to Chicago for all the gold in Alaska. The scenery is spectacular everywhere up here. . . . I find life among these people a very interesting experience. . . . Alaska is indeed the "last frontier" and I'm thankful for the opportunity to be here and see things first hand.

She understood the significance of her experience and planned to write a book some day. By January 1959 she told her family that she belonged in the newest state: "I have no fear of death now—I did before. I can see a purpose to life." She had finally begun to feel at home, not just in Alaska, but also in herself.

After spending the summer of 1959 taking music education master's courses at Northern Illinois University, she returned to Alaska, but this time to Chugiak. When she arrived in Anchorage, she purchased a beige Volkswagen Beetle that gave her mobility. She explored Peter's Creek, Thunderbird Falls, and Anchorage. She moved into a trailer close to school and enjoyed settling in to her new teaching schedule, which did not seem as demanding. She relished the camaraderie of her new colleagues, sharing stories and coffee, and enjoying the occasional square dance. She particularly loved her new kitten, Chena. But her illnesses returned.

Richard's unrelenting pursuit made Donna nervous. She wavered in her feelings toward him. She wrote that differences between her and Richard could not be resolved, due to his jealous and controlling nature. Yet she continued to spend time with him. On one occasion, they visited Richard's mother, Stella Eva Newton, at her homestead less than a mile north of Susitna River Station. For days they worked on her cabin, cut down trees, put in plank flooring, and lived off the land. At the end of the trip, she wrote again about the possibility of wedding bells.

When a truck hit Chena just before Christmas, Richard invited Donna to go with him to Dillingham to visit Roberta and Martha. Earlier that fall, the plumbing company bought a new Cessna 175. While she still feared flying, she wrote, "We'll fly in it! He's even going to let me fly. I'm scared of the trip—over uninhabited territory, mtns lakes etc—esp in the winter."

On December 30, 1959, Richard and Donna waited for hours at Merrill Air Field in Anchorage for the all clear. Finally, in the afternoon, they boarded his Cessna for Dillingham. But they never arrived. The plane went down in a storm southeast of Dillingham, and after a couple of months of desperate searching by her father and dozens of friends, the authorities called off the search. The following June, pilot Orin Seybert discovered the wreckage. Donna and Richard had died instantly.

Although Donna lived in Alaska a short time, she defended Alaska Native children against other teachers who lambasted their culture, behavior, and motivation. And within months of her arrival, Donna knew she would spend the rest of her life in Alaska. Even more, she recognized the importance of this critical juncture in Alaskan history and her own life, and kept diligent records through personal letters, still photographs, and moving pictures. Donna's life exemplified the "pioneer spirit" that many assumed had died with the end of the "frontier" in 1890.

—Sandra K. Mathews-Lamb

SUGGESTED READINGS

Jacobs, Jane, ed. *A Schoolteacher in Old Alaska: The Story of Hanna Breece*. New York: Vintage Books, 1997.

Specht, Robert. *Tisha: The Story of a Young Teacher in the Alaska Wilderness*. New York: Bantam Doubleday Dell, 1977.

MCLAUGHLIN, LINDA HODGE (1942-1999)

Born in Los Angeles, California, on February 13, 1942, Linda Hodge McLaughlin received her bachelor of arts degree from Stanford University in 1963. Three years later, she received her LL.B. from Boalt School of Law at the University of California, Berkeley. She opened her first private practice in Los Angeles in 1966 but moved it to Newport Beach and Costa Mesa, California, in 1970. After 10 years she became a judge for the California Municipal Court in the North Orange County Judicial District. In 1982 she became a judge of the Superior Court in Orange County. In 1984 she served as the associate justice pro tem for the California Supreme Court, and in 1985 she was again the associate justice pro tem, this time for the California Court of Appeals, Fourth Appellate District, Division 3. When 104 Stat. 5089 created a seat on the U.S. District Court for the Central District of California, President George H. W. Bush nominated her for it on March 20, 1992. On August 12, 1992, she was confirmed by the Senate and received her commission on August 17, 1992. Her service was terminated due to her death on March 7, 1999.

—Marcus J. Schwoerer

SUGGESTED READING

Linda Hodge McLaughlin. Retrieved from air.fjc.gov/servlet/tGetInfo?jid=1578. Source: History of the Federal Judiciary. http://www.fjc.gov. Web site of the Federal Judicial Center, Washington, D.C.

MCPHERSON, AIMEE SEMPLE (1890-1944)

Aimee Semple McPherson, or "Sister" Aimee, as she was known, was arguably the most famous Pentecostal evangelist of the early 20th century. She was born in Canada in October 1890 to Robert and Minnie Kennedy. Her father was a Methodist farmer and her mother belonged to the Salvation Army. Her mother decided Aimee would be brought up with the Salvation Army beliefs, which meant that she was not baptized, because they did not believe that this sacrament is necessary for salvation. Aimee was brought up in a strong evangelical and charitable environment. She and her mother constantly went to prayer meetings, holiness meetings, street meetings, and Band of Love gatherings. This early religious training and the fact that the Salvation Army believed that men and women were equal in the sight of the Lord helped Aimee become such a strong evangelist.

Aimee was a good student, and by the time she was a young woman, she was known for her public speaking abilities, winning prizes in school and at competitions. Activities that she chose to engage in outside the Army meetings also helped prepare her in the path she chose as an adult. She was a member of Loyal Temperance, the children's branch of the Women's Christian Temperance Union. Here she gave speeches on the evils of alcohol. She loved drama and became involved in town productions. When she was in high school, her religious convictions were tested in class by her introduction to the theories of Darwin. She struggled with the theory of evolution and its contradictions to the Bible, but ultimately chose religion over science; this greatly strengthened her faith.

In 1907 Aimee first heard about Pentecostalism, which was a relatively new denomination, perhaps founded in Kansas in 1901 by Charles Parham. Parham taught that all Christians should be baptized in the Holy Spirit, which always led to speaking in tongues; he also warned that Christ might come at any time, so it was best to be prepared. The Pentecostals arrived in the farming area of Ontario, Canada, and Aimee was drawn to the revivals, where it was said the people jumped, danced, and spoke in tongues. On her first visit, the young, handsome evangelist Robert Semple spoke of repenting your sins and being baptized by the Holy Spirit. Aimee was captivated when he spoke in tongues. She began to skip school and go to meetings, her grades slipped, and the Salvation Army people complained that such a prominent young woman should not be at these meetings. Her parents threatened to withdraw her from school. But Aimee, after an inner struggle, decided to convert to Pentecostalism. Her mother was aghast when she found this out, but Aimee challenged her mother to find something in the Bible to prove the Pentecostals wrong. Minnie pored over the Bible, but in the end concluded that the Bible was on the Pentecostals' side. Six months after her conversion, Aimee married Robert Semple, the man who had spoken at the first meeting she had attended. She followed Robert in his preaching, and they soon found themselves called to China. Their mission to China was cut short by the death of Robert after a few months there. Aimee, also seriously ill, found herself alone with a newborn daughter and no money. Her parents cabled the money to bring her and their new granddaughter, Roberta Star Semple, home.

Aimee decided to stay in New York, where her mother was raising funds for the Salvation Army. In New York she met and married her second husband, Harold Stewart McPherson. Her son, Rolf Potter McPherson, was born, and Aimee tried to settle down to motherhood. But she believed that she had been called to the ministry and wanted to evangelize full time. She left her husband to become an itinerant minister, and when he realized she would not come back, he joined her. Aimee bought a tent and took her family on the road preaching the Pentecostal message. Six years after their marriage, Harold McPherson divorced Aimee. He knew that he could no longer be part of the life she chose, and there was no point in remaining married.

In 1919 Aimee headed west to Los Angeles. At this time she was also gaining a steady reputation and people thronged to hear her speak. In 1923, in Echo Park, Los Angeles, she opened the doors to the Angelus Temple that seated over 5,000. She designed the temple, and the furnishings alone cost over $1 million. At one point, her congregation swelled to over 10,000 members. She gave three services on Sunday as well as a service every night of the week, and people still had to be turned away. She soon became a religious, political, and financial power in Los Angeles. Commentators of the time described her meetings as shows that competed with nearby Hollywood. There was no denying that she had a dramatic flair with her illustrated sermons that were short stage plays to illuminate stories from the Bible. She founded her own radio station (the third in Los Angeles) to broadcast to the rest of her followers in the West. She was the first woman to ever preach a sermon over the radio. Her messages were practical, with no formal theology, but used everyday situations

and her own experience to relay the message to her followers.

In 1926 Aimee disappeared from Ocean Park Beach in broad daylight and remained missing for over one month. She claimed to have been kidnapped and held for ransom in Mexico before she made her escape. She never fully explained her disappearance, but it only slightly slowed things down at the Temple and her followers remained loyal. In 1931 she married her third husband, David Hutton, going against the principles that she preached of divorced persons remarrying while the other spouse was still alive. This marriage, however, soon ended in divorce, which created problems within her organization. At this point, Aimee began her slide from the top. While troubles within the temple cannot be blamed fully for this, the United States was in the midst of the Great Depression, and the message that Sister Aimee preached no longer seemed as relevant.

In 1944 McPherson passed away and her death too was shrouded in mystery. Some believe she may have committed suicide, because an autopsy revealed a drug overdose as well as kidney disease. However, the death was ruled as accidental.

—Michelle A. Stretch

SUGGESTED READINGS

Blumhoffer, Edith L. *Aimee Semple McPherson: Everybody's Sister*. Grand Rapids, MI: William B. Eerdman's, 1993.

Mark, Daniel. *Sister Aimee: The Life of Aimee Semple McPherson*. New York: Epstein Harcourt Brace Jovanovich, 1993.

Thomas, Lately. *The Vanishing Evangelist: The Aimee Semple McPherson Kidnapping Affair*. New York: Viking Press, 1959.

Thomas, Lately. *Storming Heaven: The Lives and Turmoils of Minnie Kennedy and Aimee Semple McPherson*. New York: William Morrow, 1970.

MEHARG, EMMA GRIGSBY (1873-1937)

Emma Grigsby Meharg, the first female Texas secretary of state, was born on August 1, 1873, at Lynnville, Tennessee. In 1883 her parents, Jasper N.

and Mary Amanda Calvert Grigsby, moved the family to Italy, Texas, where Emma attended public school. She graduated from Southwestern Normal College in 1895 and married Samuel W. Meharg on June 24, 1902. The couple had two children. Emma worked as a schoolteacher. Governor Miriam "Ma" Ferguson appointed her secretary of state, serving during 1925 and 1926. During her tenure, she recommended many changes regarding corporations, securities, administration of the office of the secretary of state, the institution of a civil service system for state employees, and others. Subsequent legislatures enacted many of her changes. One of her most important recommendations was that the office of secretary of state be changed to an elected position, because the duties were of a more public nature than they had been at the time the office was instituted under the 1876 constitution. During her term, she took many historical records out of storage, restored them, and processed them for easy reference and exhibit. She was a leader in church, cultural, civic, and political affairs. She served on the Plainview, Texas, board of trustees and on the board of regents for Texas Technological College (now Texas Tech University) from 1932 to 1937. She died in Plainview, Texas, on September 4, 1937.

—Tiffany E. Dalpe

SUGGESTED READINGS

Acheson, Sam Hanna, Herbert P. Gambrell, Mary Carter Toomey, and Alex M. Acheson Jr., eds. *Texian Who's Who: Vol. 1*. Dallas, TX: Texian, 1937.

Dallas Morning News, December 26, 1926.

The Handbook of Texas Online. Retrieved from www.tsha.utexas.edu/handbook/online.

MILITARY/WIVES/OUTPOSTS

The presence of women on 19th-century western military posts might strike modern readers as surprising. After all, these were days long before the U.S. Army offered women positions within the nation's military academies, officer corps, or enlisted ranks. Yet women were there, most often in the roles of wife and mother. Some officers, and less often enlisted men, brought spouses along on frontier duty. Interestingly, the army only officially recognized those women who worked as laundresses. Officers' wives consequently existed in a rather ambiguous position, neither officially recognized nor totally overlooked. All of these women, along with the occasional single woman who worked as a laundress for enlisted men or as a servant in an officer's home, shared the challenges of western travel and domestic life in isolated posts. But much also separated them, particularly the military caste system, which stressed hierarchy and stratification. Victorian class and racial attitudes further underscored the gulf between officers' wives and soldiers' spouses.

The army needed laundresses and usually found willing workers among soldiers' wives. Regulations provided enough rations, housing, and medical care to allow 1 laundress for every 17 men, with a limit of 4 laundresses per company (usually about 100 men). The post commander retained tremendous power over a laundress's life and work, with a board of senior officers setting wages that ranged from $2 per month per "gentleman" at one post to 50¢ per soldier per month at others, in the pre-Civil War era. By the 1870s, 1,316 women worked as army laundresses. At that point, Congress reconsidered the wisdom of the policy as it listened to testimony ranging from complaints about the women as nuisances to praise for the various duties they performed beyond the laundry. In 1878 the army banned further enrollment of laundresses, although they allowed those already employed to retain their positions.

Living conditions for these women were often primitive, sometimes quite horrible. A few senior noncommissioned officers and laundress wives received government-provided quarters, but many others took up residency in abandoned structures (in one case, a former cavalry stable that still retained the odors of its previous occupants) or thrown-together shanties. Still, life was not always grim. Picnics, dances, band concerts, and other post social events offered pleasant diversions from daily drudgery. The isolation that homesteaders experienced was not shared by military wives, who, whatever their circumstances, never found themselves alone. The post community could always provide companionship of one sort or another. In truth, however, we know little about these women's lives other than what comes through official post commander records or officers' and their wives' accounts. Typically, these documents emphasize the more troublesome, even sordid, aspects of their existence, while the day-to-day, common events and experiences remain largely unrecorded. Domestic quarrels sometimes escalated into violence and required official intervention. Occasionally, commanders dismissed laundresses for theft, lewdness, and drunkenness. In one most dramatic case, a laundress, upon her death, was discovered to be a man, whereupon her widower (who happened to be her third husband) committed suicide. Nevertheless, the majority of laundress/military wives toiled in obscurity and caused little or no trouble to authorities.

Women who found work within an officer's household as servant or cook or nanny had things a bit better. She could eat from the officer's larder and received housing that was a cut above her colleagues'. Occasionally, the women who took up such positions came west as single women. They usually retained that status for only a short time, however, finding many suitors among the ranks. In a place that offered little competition for marital companionship, even less attractive women found themselves in demand. Officers' wives complained about the difficulties of keeping such women in their employ, and usually solved the dilemma by hiring men servants, including "strikers" or soldiers who served within an officer's household—a practice that Congress declared unlawful but which continued well into the 1880s nonetheless.

The lot of officers' wives was not only much more comfortable, but better documented. Many of these wives derived from the middle class were literate and aware of the historical significance of their situation. Consequently, some wrote letters, diaries, and even books about their experiences that, in turn, provide historians with much of what they know about army dependents in the West. Sometimes wives took up the pen out of personal inclination to express themselves. Several who lived in posts along the Bozeman Trail during the so-called Red Cloud War of 1866-1868 responded to Gen. Phil Sheridan's encouragement to record their relatively unique experiences in the war zone. And still others wrote to explain and justify their husbands' careers. Elizabeth Custer, widow of Lt. Col. George Armstrong Custer and author of several books, is the primary example of this last type. Of course, not all officers' spouses shared the impulse to write. Particularly during the Civil War, when laundresses' husbands received commissions, working-class women moved up the military hierarchy, too. Such women, however, did not write books. Moreover, they found themselves snubbed by their more literate, educated "sisters."

Life as an officer's wife usually began with travel immediately following an eastern wedding. Before the Civil War, moving to a western post taxed even the most adventurous of these women, entailing either crossing the plains by wagon or traveling to Texas or the West Coast by sea voyage. Postings in California or the Pacific Northwest might entail travel across Panama (before the Canal) or around Cape Horn. Completion of the transcontinental railroad in 1869 reduced travel times considerably and improved conditions as well. Still, movement from post to post, particularly in the desert Southwest, proved daunting through much of the 19th century. Most who wrote about these hardships did not dwell on them, however. Enthusiasm and good spirits prevailed over grousing (at least in print). Once settled into their new post, officers' wives found that the quality of their housing varied from tents, dugouts, or adobe houses in the more remote locations to log cabins, frame, or brick dwellings in more established places. The Presidio in San Francisco, for example, offered some of the finest lodgings; a post in Arizona, with much less comfortable and luxurious homes, offered the worst.

Officers' wives understood they retained no official status. But neither did the army entirely ignore them, providing for them through assignment of housing and other privileges to their husbands, commensurate with their rank. The hierarchical nature of military society posed problems for families, particularly when a higher ranking officer displaced a lower ranking one by literally forcing him to evacuate housing the former coveted. Occasionally, a generous bachelor officer would defer to a subordinate's needs, if he had a family. But army wives could not, and did not, count on that. Most of the wives' days and duties revolved around domestic life. Cooking, sewing, child bearing, and child rearing occupied their time, and for newlyweds, in particular, the challenges of keeping house in isolated posts, away from family and friends who might provide guidance, was often stressful. Yet servants could offset some of the strain. Anglo-American, European immigrant, African American, Native American, and Chinese men and women served in this capacity, bringing an element of the multicultural West into the very heart of military homes. Wives expressed a uniform need for such help but also demonstrated a range of opinions about the usefulness of particular servants. For every officer's wife who expressed frustration and even anger with "the help," one can find another who was grateful.

Nevertheless, racism played a key role in these domestic relationships. Even more open-minded women retained 19th-century assumptions about the supposed inherent inferiority of black, Indian, and Asian employees. The one experience that offered opportunities to transcend racial and ethnic differences came in the context of childbirth and child rearing. Examples of Indian women serving as wet nurses for officers' infants or officers' wives entertaining Native American children with stories and sweets were not unusual. Children, in other words, could bridge the gap, however fleeting the connection might be.

Officers' wives did more than provide homes for their husbands. They also enhanced social and cultural life on posts by organizing dances, band concerts, picnics, card games, and parties. These middle-class women also organized lectures, hosted notable guests that passed through, such as author Mark Twain and artist Frederic Remington, and started Sunday schools. To be sure, close quarters and consequent friction also bred gossip and unpleasantness. Officer Charles King's novels about army life tended to underscore the fissures in post communities. And whether a military post exhibited a tranquil or a turbulent atmosphere depended mostly on the collection of personalities in residence. Incidents of adultery and, in at least one case, incest revealed that military life was not immune from human frailties and faults.

Issues of policy, or politics, rarely appear in officers' wives accounts. They would not hesitate to defend their husbands or the army, however, from attack, closing ranks when it came to answering critics and insisting that the army's work was honorable. They expressed little patience with those who would carp from safe distances. The most sensitive issue, of course, revolved around the conquest of Native Americans. Officers' wives responded to charges that the army resorted to force too often and sometimes abused its powers, brooking no such claims. Particularly during war itself, their primary concern rested with their husbands' well being. Yet their personal opinions revealed, in some cases, genuine sympathy for the position of Native Americans, particularly once the fighting ceased and the defeated Indians faced imprisonment or the limitations of reservation life. As for personal safety, they expressed fears in times of conflict but often put them aside when tensions eased. Their curiosity about Indian people, as well as a consciousness that their position allowed them unusual opportunities for observation

and contact, often proved sufficient to overcome fear and engage with the Indians, although usually on superficial levels. Officers' wives revealed a greater willingness to admit initial fear than their husbands did, but they also demonstrated the same complicated and ambiguous responses to Indians and Indian policy one finds in military men's accounts.

—Sherry L. Smith

SUGGESTED READINGS

Coffman, Edward M. *The Old Army: A Portrait of the American Army in Peacetime, 1784-1898.* New York: Oxford University Press, 1986.

Knight, Oliver. *Life and Manners in the Frontier Army.* Norman: University of Oklahoma Press, 1978.

Leckie, William H., and Shirley A. Leckie. *Unlikely Warriors: General Benjamin H. Grierson and His Family.* Norman: University of Oklahoma Press, 1984.

Smith, Sherry Lynn. *The View From Officers' Row: Army Perceptions of Western Indians.* Tucson: University of Arizona Press,1990.

Stallard, Patricia. *Glittering Misery: Dependents of the Indian Fighting Army.* Norman: University of Oklahoma Press, 1978, 1992.

MISSION INDIAN FEDERATION

In the last decades of the 19th century, federal Indian policy evolved from one of containment to one of assimilation. The passage of the Dawes Act in 1887 determined to divide Indian lands into individual allotments in an attempt to destroy the communal nature of tribal life and to make more lands available for white settlement. While much of land allotment in Southern California was not started until the 1920s, the allotment process, when coupled with the paternalistic policies of the government, served as the catalyst for the birth of the Mission Indian Federation, a Native American protest movement that operated in Southern California from 1919 until 1960.

Created in 1919 at the behest of Jonathan Tibbet, a wealthy white land developer in Riverside, California, the Federation set about to prevent the further destruction of tribal culture. With Tibbet as the "chief counselor" and Adan Castillo as the group's first president, the Federation focused its attention on preventing the further allotment of native lands, increased educational opportunities for native children, and the preservation of tribal integrity. Despite the all-male listing of Federation officers, many women played a dominant role behind the scenes in the direction of the group.

The importance of women to the success of the Mission Indian Federation cannot be understated. Whole families such as the Bellardes, Lobos, and Castillos supported the organization's goal for Indian self-rule. Women such as Celia Macado McGee and Juanita Ortega, among many others, were active in the decision-making process of the group, which included everything from fund-raising to making decisions about the group's position toward government assistance for roadways, housing, and allotment. While many of the women's names do not survive, their very presence can be seen in the photographs of the Federation's annual gathering. In 1924 a picture at the Tibbett residence in Riverside, California, shows 52 individuals—10 of whom are women.

Initially, the white community lauded the efforts of the Federation as a noble attempt to maintain tribal integrity. However, as Federation members began asserting themselves by establishing a tribal government, police force, and judiciary, they came into conflict with government authority and non-Federation tribal members. As a self-appointed authority on tribal lands, the Federation denounced the further allotment of native lands and attempted to block individual tribal members from accepting their allotments. Many of these attempts turned violent and served to polarize public and tribal opinion against Federation members.

By 1930 the Federation entered another phase of its existence. Jonathan Tibbet had died and Purl Willis assumed the position of chief counselor. The direct action that had been encouraged by Tibbet was replaced by Willis's attempts to manipulate public and legislative opinion in order to support the goals of the Federation. Despite this change in tactics, the Federation did not gain many adherents. The adoption of the Indian Reorganization Act (IRA) in 1934 removed the central issue that had been fought against by the Federation—the allotment of tribal lands. Following the passage of the IRA, the Federation focused its attention on the discriminatory practices in the local school system that had denied many Indian people an education.

By the 1950s, the government's decision to do away with federal oversight of tribes through the policy of termination found ardent supporters among the Federation members. The passage of termination legislation, however, left many tribes mired in poverty without the potential for assistance from the government. The dire poverty faced by most tribal members and the death of Adan Castillo in 1953 essentially ended the life of the Federation. Purl Willis continued to serve as the nominal mouthpiece of the defunct organization until his death in 1960.

—Vanessa Anne Gunther

SUGGESTED READINGS

Castillo, Edward. "The Impact of Euro-American Exploration and Settlement," in Robert F. Heizer, ed., *Handbook of North American Indians: Vol. 8.* Washington, DC: Smithsonian Institution, 1978, 119-120.

Haas, Lisbeth. *Conquests and Historical Identities in California, 1769-1936.* Berkeley: University of California Press, 1995.

Shipek, Florence Connolly. *Pushed Into the Rocks: Southern California Indian Land Tenure, 1769-1986.* Lincoln: University of Nebraska Press, 1987.

MORENO, LUISA (1907-1992)

Born to an upper-class family in Guatemala, Blanca Rosa Lopez Rodrigues changed her name to Luisa Moreno after she became active in organized labor. She went to school in Oakland, California, and upon completion returned to Guatemala and worked for various newspapers. In 1928 she moved to New York City and supported her unemployed husband and infant daughter by working in a garment factory. She became a radical activist for workers' rights and a labor organizer in reaction to that industry's deplorable working conditions. Moreno believed that unions could greatly benefit the poorly educated worker.

In the 1930s she became a professional labor organizer and reportedly joined the Communist Party. She became a champion for Mexican American women and other minorities against oppressive employers. Her bilingual ability enabled her to mediate between employers and employees, and she was very successful at organizing women and minority workers with the help of her political shrewdness and charismatic personality.

She joined the Congress of Industrial Organizations (CIO) in 1934 and was soon elected the first woman and Latino member of the CIO council. In 1935 the American Federation of Labor (AFL) hired her as a professional organizer and the next year assigned her to organize Florida tobacco workers. Later that year she attended the AFL's annual convention in Tampa and took part in the formation of the Unified Cannery, Agricultural, Packing, and Allied Workers of America (UCAPAWA, also called the FTA, or Food, Tobacco, Agricultural, and Allied Workers of America). She became the international vice president of the UCA-PAWA in 1941 and came to Southern California to organize labor at food-processing plants. During that time, she helped organize numerous labor affiliates of the UCAPAWA, including unionizing Local 2 of Fullerton, the largest cannery in Southern California at the time. In 1943 she and Dixie Tiller founded the Citrus Workers Organizing Committee in Riverside and Redlands, California. During the Great Northern Cannery Struggle of 1945-1946, Moreno assembled the largest group of organizers ever for a single campaign.

During the late 1930s and 1940s, Moreno became a champion for Hispanic civil rights. She was the organizer and founder of the National Congress of Spanish Speaking Peoples in 1938. In response to the Sleepy Lagoon Case in Los Angeles in 1942-1943, she helped assemble a defense committee to fight for Mexican Americans wrongfully arrested and detained during that incident. She was alarmed by the violence against Hispanic Americans that erupted in the 1943 Zoot Suit Riots, and campaigned against racism hostile to the Mexican American community. She retired from public life in 1947 and was deported due to her affiliation with the Communist Party in 1950. She resided in Guatemala until her death on November 4, 1992.

—Carolyn Stull

SUGGESTED READINGS

Larralde, Carlos, and Richard Griswold del Castillo. "Luisa Moreno: A Hispanic Civil Rights Leader in San Diego." *Journal of San Diego History 41*(4, Fall 1995): 284-311.

Larralde, Carlos, and Richard Griswold del Castillo. "Luisa Moreno and the Beginnings of the Mexican American Civil Rights Movement." *Journal of San Diego History 43*(3, Summer 1997): 158-175.

Ruiz, Vicky L. *Cannery Women: Cannery Lives: Mexican, Women, Unionization, and the California Food Processing Industry, 1930-1950.* Albuquerque: University of New Mexico, 1987.

N

NARANJO-MORSE, NORA (1953-)

Nora Naranjo-Morse was born in Espanola, New Mexico, and spent most of her adolescence in Taos. She was the ninth of a family of ten children. She graduated from high school with no long-lasting career aspirations and took several menial jobs, such as sorting mail and selling fireworks, while she decided what to do with her life. After she returned to her native New Mexico, she met her husband, Greg, and they had twins named Eliza and Zakary. During this time of motherhood, she managed to earn a bachelor's degree in social welfare by the year 1980.

In the presence of her mother and sisters, she developed her love and passion for pottery. As a little child she had learned some basic techniques by watching her mother create pottery similar to other Pueblo women. As she became more familiar and expert with her skill, she developed a style separate from her families and more traditional to her culture. She created small figures that were images of people and of animals. She also was influenced by the work of modern artists Henry Moore and Helen Cordero.

Examples of her work include sculptures in her Pearlene sequence. By using the same character, she was able to represent her own life experiences and show how modern Tewa Indians responded to the changing world around them. She also showed how these Indians reconciled their Indian and current lifestyles. One such work was titled *Pearlene Teaching Her Cousins Poker*. After her popularity soared, she began speaking and having galleries that she supported solely with her own work. She has spoken in New York, Denmark, Germany, and San Francisco. She also was the principal focus in a venture put on by the Museum of Northern Arizona called Separate Visions. Her current accomplishments include attempts to mix adobe clay with metal in order to create larger and sturdier sculptures.

Her greatest work, called *Mud Women*, is a look into the mixture of art and poetry and the struggle between culture and social evolution. Through this work, she was able to convey her idea that she is taking part in something far beyond herself.

—Kevin Christy

SUGGESTED READINGS

Abbott, Lawrence. "Nora Naranjo-Morse." *I Stand in the Center of the Good: Interviews of Contemporary North American Artists.* Lincoln: University of Nebraska Press, 1994, 197-203.

Berner, Robert L. "Book Review of Mud Women: Poems from the Clay." *World Literature Today* 67(2, Spring 1993): 422.

Kelly, Brendan. "Inspirations." *Variety 368*(10, October 13, 1997): 100.

Lichtenstein, Grace. "The Evolution of a Craft Tradition: Three Generations of Navajo Women." *Ms. 11* (April 1983): 59-60, 92.

Naranjo-Morse. *Mud Women: Poems from the Clay.* Tucson: University of Arizona Press, 1992.

Trimble, Steven. "Brown Earth and Laughter: The Clay People of Nora Naranjo Morse." *American Indian Art 12* (Autumn 1987): 58-65.

NATIVE AMERICAN PROTEST MOVEMENTS IN THE 20TH CENTURY

Since the inception of native-white contact, Indian protest has largely been recorded as a violent struggle between men of both races. Women, when they appear, are relegated to the role of victim or helpmate. However, native women have a long history of serving their people as warriors (Buffalo Calf Road), political leaders (Molly Brant), and religious leaders (Mary Slocum). Modern native women have continued to follow in the footsteps of these remarkable women.

The assimilation and allotment policies of the late 19th century served as a catalyst for many of the pan-Indian movements that characterized the 20th century. Prior to the 20th century, Indian protest movements were largely led by reform-minded whites who made little attempt to discover what native people wanted or needed. The most prominent among these groups was the Indian Rights Association (IRA). Despite being shut out from groups that purportedly represented their interests, individual Indians, such as Sarah Winnemucca, protested government policies but lacked the strength of a pan-Indian group in effecting significant change by the turn of the century.

In 1911 members of 19 tribes gathered in Ohio to form what became known as the Society of American Indians (SAI). The focus of the SAI was to promote the acculturation and assimilation of Native Americans. Many women, including Laura Cornelius of the Oneida and Gertrude Bonnin of the Yankton Sioux, participated in the formation of the group. While popular with whites, the SAI had few tribal adherents, and disbanded in the 1920s. Another organization, the Mission Indian Federation, served as the antithesis of the SAI. Founded in 1919, the Federation included tribes throughout Southern California and Arizona. Together they were organized to protest government involvement in tribal affairs, including allotment and the imposition of federal authority over tribal government. The focus of the Federation changed significantly after the passage of the Indian Reorganization Act in 1934, but it remained a force in Indian affairs for the next several decades.

As the focus of the Federation changed, many of the Indians who had supported the group changed their allegiance to the National Congress of American Indians (NCAI), formed in 1944 to protest federal incursions of tribal sovereignty. When the federal government adopted a policy of termination in 1953, the NCAI zealously attacked the policy. Aside from the NCAI, individuals such as Lucy Covington of the Colville Confederated Tribes and Ada Deer of the Menominee were both instrumental in either preventing termination or restoring lost native rights, and accentuated the efforts of the NCAI. In the 1950s, several national protests were staged to protest the encroachment of individual states on the fishing rights of native peoples. Through the 1950s and 1960s, native people throughout the United States and Canada staged what became known as "fish-ins" to preserve traditional fishing rights. In 1966 the U.S. Supreme Court decision in *Puyallup Tribe v. Department of Game* (1968) confirmed native preemptive fishing rights.

In the 1960s the radicalization of politics spread to all racial groups. For Native Americans, self-determination under the rubric of Red Power became the focus of continued protest. Native Americans were no longer content to watch as treaty rights were abrogated and tribal religious customs came under attack. The idea of self-determination resulted in the creation of several groups, including the Alaska Federated Natives, which formed in 1965 to protect native lands from further incursion by whites. In 1961 the National Indian Youth Council (NIYC) was formed to promote self-determination, and counted among its members Shirley Hill Witt of the Akwesasne Mohawk. The NIYC would find itself embroiled in a number of other national protests that characterized the Red Power movement. As the 1960s progressed, other Red Power groups emerged, including the National Indian Education Association, the National Council on Indian Opportunity, the National Tribal Chairman's Association, and the American Indian Movement (AIM).

The AIM gained notoriety after seizing Alcatraz in 1969. Initially, several remarkable women, including Wilma Mankiller, Stella Leach, and Grace Thorpe, led the group. In 1972 AIM joined with other native protesters in the seizure and occupation of the offices of the Bureau of Indian Affairs in an attempt to change paternalistic federal policy toward native people. In 1973 AIM took over the Pine Ridge Reservation at Wounded Knee, South Dakota, to protest the corrupt policies of the tribal chair, Richard Wilson, and to seek the reestablishment of treaty relations between the United States and the tribe. During the conflict, two Native Americans were killed and one federal agent shot and paralyzed. In 1975 a second armed incident occurred on the Pine Ridge Reservation, and three government agents were killed.

Despite the popularity of such national organizations, native protest was not limited to native groups. Individuals such as Janet McCloud of the Puyallup, who led a group of Indians to protest the federal encroachment of native fishing rights in 1970, were active in the movement. As the Red Power movement expanded, tribal groups began to demand improvements in housing, health, and education. From February to July 1978, a group of Native Americans marched from San Francisco to Washington, D.C., in what became known as the Longest Walk. The purpose of the demonstration was to draw national attention to the plight of Native Americans and to expose the duplicity that characterized federal dealings with Indian people. Native protest led to the passage of the Indian Education Act of 1972, the Indian Self-Determination and Education Assistance Act of 1975, and the American Indian Religious Freedom Act of 1978.

Many of the women who actively participated in the Red Power movement of the 1960-1970s continued to serve their people in the closing years of the century. Wilma Mankiller became the tribal leader of the Cherokee and Ada Deer was appointed to head the Bureau of Indian Affairs during the Clinton administration. Despite these gains, native people have continued to fight to preserve their sacred places and tribal customs. The burden of this struggle will continue to be equally shouldered by native women.

—Vanessa Anne Gunther

SUGGESTED READINGS

Nagel, Joane. *American Indian Ethnic Renewal: Red Power and the Resurgence of Identity and Culture.* New York: Oxford University Press, 1996.

Trafzer, Clifford E. *As Long as the Grass Shall Grow and Rivers Flow: A History of Native Americans.* New York: Harcourt, 2000.

NEAL, MARGIE ELIZABETH
(1875-1971)

Margie Elizabeth Neal, the first woman elected to the Texas Senate, was born on April 20, 1875, near Clayton, Texas. She was the second of four children of William Lafayette and Martha Gholston Neal. She lived in Carthage, Texas, most of her life. She attended but did not graduate from the Sam Houston State Teachers College. She had a short teaching career. In 1903 her father purchased *The Texas Mule,* a weekly paper. Neal became the editor and publisher. She renamed the paper the *East Texas Register* and continued its publication until she sold it in 1911. Neal was the first woman to register to vote in Panola County. She was appointed the first female member of the board of regents of the State Teachers Colleges (1921-1927). She was the first woman to serve as a member of the Texas State Democratic Committee.

In 1920 she was a delegate to the National Democratic Convention in San Francisco. In 1926 she was elected to the Texas Senate, representing Panola County. She served four consecutive terms. While in the Senate, she oversaw a variety of legislation dealing with education within Texas. She introduced the bill that established the State Board of Education, sponsored a bill that introduced public school physical education classes, actively supported a bill that made the study of state and national constitutions mandatory, and was instrumental in the passage of legislation to appropriate the largest amount of money to that time used to fund rural education in Texas. She also helped secure legislation for the rehabilitation of disabled persons.

In 1935 she moved to Washington, D.C., where she worked with the National Recovery Administration and the federal Social Security Administration. She soon transferred back to Texas and worked in San Antonio and Dallas as a facilities analyst. She resigned in 1945 and moved back to Carthage. Neal never married. She died on December 19, 1971, in Carthage, Texas.

—Tiffany E. Dalpe

SUGGESTED READINGS

Barker Texas History Center, Vertical Files, University of Texas at Austin.

The Handbook of Texas Online. Retrieved from www.tsha. utexas.edu/handbook/online.

Harris, Walter. "Margie E. Neal: First Woman Senator in Texas." *East Texas Historical Journal 11* (Spring 1973).

Margie E. Neal Papers, Barker Texas History Center, University of Texas at Austin.

Miss Margie Neal. Retrieved from www.carthagetexas. com/neal.htm.

NELSON, DOROTHY WRIGHT
(1928-)

Dorothy Jean Wright was born to Harry and Lorna Wright on September 30, 1928. She earned her bachelor's degree from the University of California, Los Angeles, in 1950, and shortly thereafter married James Nelson, a lawyer and state court judge in Los Angeles. She continued her education, earning her J.D. from UCLA in 1953 and her LL.M. from the University of Southern California in 1956.

Nelson was in private practice in Los Angeles starting in 1954 until she joined the faculty at USC in 1957. There she advanced through the ranks of instructor, assistant professor, and associate professor to the post of interim dean in 1967. Then as a full professor, and barely 40 years of age, she became dean of the USC Law Center in 1969, a post she held until 1980. In 1979 President Jimmy Carter appointed her to the U.S. Court of Appeals for the Ninth Circuit.

Nelson has received many honors throughout her career, among them the Bernard E. Witkin Medal for extraordinary service and contribution to legal scholarship in California, awarded by the California State Bar in 2000. The Board of Councilors at the USC Law School established an award in Nelson's honor. The Judge Dorothy W. Nelson Justice Award is presented annually to the student who has made a significant contribution toward the administration of justice.

Nelson has worked under four U.S. presidents, contributing to the Board of Visitors of the U.S. Air Force Academy, the Board of Trustees of the James Madison Memorial Fellowship Foundation, and the White House Conference on Children.

A mother of two children, Nelson has emphasized collaboration and teamwork in her duties throughout her career by showing interest in student matters. She is active in the Baha'i faith, a Middle Eastern religion that proclaims unity among all religions and people. She currently resides in Southern California.

—Neal Lynch

SUGGESTED READINGS

California Bar Journal. Retrieved from www.calbar.org/2cbj/00nov.

Dorothy Wright Nelson. Retrieved from air.fjc.gov/servlet/uGetInfo?jid=1742. Source: History of the Federal Judiciary. http://www.fjc.gov. Web site of the Federal Judicial Center, Washington, D.C.

Kloppenberg, Lisa A. "A Mentor of Her Own." Retrieved from law.utoledo.edu/lawreview/publication_archives/v33_n1_fall2001/koppenberg.htm.

San Francisco Chronicle, December 31, 1998.

San Francisco Chronicle, May 5, 1999.

San Francisco Chronicle, March 30, 2001.

OAKLEY, ANNIE (1860-1926)

Annie Oakley was one of America's most accomplished shooters and a Wild West show star. Born Annie Moses to Jacob and Susan Moses in Darke County, Ohio, she learned to shoot at the age of 8, providing her family with needed revenue as a meat hunter selling to Charles Leopold Katzenberger, who shipped her dressed game to Cincinnati hotels. Annie's abilities as a sharpshooter, in fact, saved the family farm from the bank, paying with nickels and dimes when the mortgage came due. Annie turned to the more lucrative business of circus shooting after defeating Frank Butler, a professional stage shooter, in an 1876 match. Annie married Frank on August 23, 1876, and began touring with him. Her big break into national fame began in 1884 when Sitting Bull saw her perform and adopted her as Little Sure Shot. Frank and Annie toured with the Sells Brothers Circus in 1884 and joined Buffalo Bill Cody's Wild West Show the next year.

In her Wild West Show performances, Annie demonstrated her sharpshooter talent with numerous trick shots. Accomplished with a shotgun and a rifle, she amazed crowds by shooting cigarettes out of and coins from the hand of Frank, now her manager and show assistant. In 1889 she toured Europe and performed outside the gates of the World's Colombian Exposition in 1893. In addition to performances at shows, Annie shot in competition and won numerous contests. On one occasion, she demonstrated extraordinary ability with a rifle, hitting 943 out of 1,000 glass balls tossed in the air. With a shotgun, she was able to hit 4,772 out of 5,000 balls over a 9-hour period.

Injured in a train accident in 1901, she left the Wild West Show, but continued shooting. A decade later she toured with Vernon Seavers's Young Buffalo Show for three seasons. In 1913 she and Frank retired to the Carolina Hotel in Pinehurst, North Carolina, where they passed time giving shooting lessons. During World War I they joined the war effort by raising funds for the Red Cross and demonstrating shooting in army camps.

Her legend lives on in books, magazine articles, Irving Berlin's musical *Annie Get Your Gun*, and movies. Her public image as western heroine is ageless, but she was in life a modest Quaker woman, who did needlework between shows.

—Gordon Morris Bakken

SUGGESTED READING

Riley, Glenda. *The Life and Legacy of Annie Oakley.* Norman: University of Oklahoma Press, 1994.

OKLAHOMA'S DAUGHTERS: A NEGLECTED GENDER

Women's ethnicity, frontier experiences, and political genesis played a central role in the development of Oklahoma's cultural, economic, political, and social affairs from 1800 to 2000.

OKLAHOMA PREHISTORY

Any study of Oklahoma must begin with a brief examination of the region's topographical environment to understand its effects on human settlement and trade. Oklahoma is situated between the 34th to 37th degree northern latitude and 94th to 103rd degree west of Greenwich and occupies approximately 69,903 square miles, making it nearly centered in the United States. This geophysical area, formed some 300 million years ago during the Paleozoic era, gave rise to the Arbuckle Mountains in southern and central Oklahoma, the Quachita to the southeast, and lesser elevations: the Ozarks, Glass, Poteau, San Bois, and Rattlesnake. Oklahoma's Red River borders northern Texas, its northeastern boundary is the Arkansas River, and together these mountains and rivers formed broad valleys, hills, and plains.

This dry ecological belt created the southern prairies and plains, making the territory suitable to savannahs, grasslands, and swamps in which were found deer, fish, wild turkeys, and nut-bearing trees. To the west abounded buffalo, pronghorns, prairie chickens, and grassland tubers. In addition, Oklahoma's southern plains are rich in archaeological ruins, with earthwork complexes of Hopewell of southern Ohio extended far south into Oklahoma. Traces of human life, possibly 10,000 to 15,000 years old, support mankind's cultural evolution, ranging from crude stone implements to pottery, and marked primordial Oklahomans as a pre-Columbian Caddo Spiro entrepreneurial culture, trading between the buffalo-hunting tribes of the plains and the urban, corn-growing Cahokia.

Oklahoma's recorded history began in 1541 when Spanish explorer Francisco Vasquez de Coronado ventured into the area on his quest for the Lost City of Gold and discovered instead the Caddo culture in eastern Oklahoma. Among these intrepid adventurers, early reports indicated that explorers traveled with women and one "Ana Mendez, a servant . . . hired to perform household duties for conquistadors," thus ensuring this one female her place in Spain's New World conquest.

The French, contesting Spanish territorial rights, explored the Mississippi basin in the late seventeenth century under Chevalier Robert de La Salle in 1685, and on occasion French explorers traveled with young, marriageable women to establish a mixed French and Indian community. Moreover, in 1719 Jean-Baptiste Benard, Sieur de La Harpe, led an expedition into Oklahoma that authorized contraband trade with the Spanish on the Red River to further France's commercial interests in the region.

All this changed when the United States purchased from France the Louisiana Territory on April 30, 1803, and Thomas Jefferson commissioned Meriwether Lewis and William Clark to explore the valleys of the Upper Missouri, the Yellowstone, and the Columbia. By 1812 America had claimed all the region west of the Mississippi, established trading centers, and as early as 1820, establishment of an Indian Territory had been proposed and Congress passed an act in 1830 that systematically moved Indians into Oklahoma. Following the Civil War, several events occurred in which America's need for beef expanded the territory for ranching and white settlement. In 1885 Congress gave President Hayes permission to open vacant land, and on April 22, 1889, the first land run essentially ended Oklahoma as a territory.

In order to understand Oklahoma's unconventional women, it is important to provide an overview of the diverse ethnic cultures that built settlements, structured change, shaped, and made pivotal inroads in Oklahoma's state politics and social reforms.

WOMEN OF THE WEST: RACIAL IDENTITY

Foremost among the citizens in the region were Oklahoma's aboriginal populations. Archaeological evidence showed that the most important groups during the historic period were the Caddo, who ranged over the valley of the Red River, and the Wichita, who occupied the southwestern part of the state. The French found that Caddos were prosperous agriculturalists who subsisted on a diet of maize, legumes, and wild game. Moreover, agricultural fields were located in the center of villages and managed by both men and women. Where women controlled production in the fields, matrilineal systems were common and enabled Caddo society to permit women's participation in village governance.

The Wichita, also of the Caddo linguistic family, maintained both an agricultural and nomadic existence in which they relied upon buffalo hunting more than their sedentary cousins. However, from 1805 to 1811, adventurous men explored the Red and Arkansas Rivers along the western shores of the Mississippi and increased America's cultivable landscape for agriculture and husbandry that destined the area to a rugged individualism that made Oklahoma known to 19th-century America. Herds of buffalo, elk, deer, and the region's agricultural wealth in corn and grains reinforced the importance of trade with the Indians in Oklahoma and ensured that the southern plains became trade centers.

In this convoluted but effective Indian trading network, Indian women lived harsh lives, but such images were deceptive, because the single most important factor in village society was the surplus of corn that women produced. Corn crops caused great changes in material cultures, and with the Caddo organization divided into a multileveled political structure, it deeply depended upon the support of the matrilineal clan to broker all lucrative trade agreements. Also, in clan politics, the familiar, private social and family dynamics gave meaning to their lives, and Indian women's status within their own culture reveals they fulfilled valuable economic and social roles that maintained stability in an erratic existence.

No less striking in historical study were the Spanish-speaking women in Oklahoma. The Spanish in Florida had migrated into the West long years before blending the cultures of Spain and Native America into a new community of North Americans. As they conquered indigenous populations, Spaniards became a complicated cultural encounter that followed gold and silver mines northward to incorporate provinces into an economic backwater during the colonial period.

Moreover, the presence of Spanish-speaking peoples in the region is further documented by the fact that women participated in the northward migration streams that augmented Spanish and Mexican settlements throughout the Southwest. Though communities of Spanish origin were isolated in the late 18th century, families thrived on the frontier because Hispanic women brought a kinship system critical to the family's economic stability, contracted shrewd marriages for themselves and their children, extended Catholicism and Iberian culture, and ensured Spain's dominion in Oklahoma from other European explorers.

Though Lewis and Clark in 1804, and later Zebulon Pike in 1805, had explored portions of the land contiguous to the Mississippi following America's acquisition of the Louisiana Purchase from France, very few English-speaking Americans penetrated this remote interior until after the close of the War of 1812. Disputes over boundaries between Spain and the United States prevented early settlement, and the period of 19th-century industrialization

found the area teeming with adventurers, investors, and missionaries.

By 1817 a military post, Fort Smith, was established on the eastern border of Oklahoma, and by 1824 Fort Gibson and Fort Towson were founded to preserve order among the Indians and the unruly white element. As the United States expanded westward, Oklahoma became a stronghold for ranchmen with their flocks and herds eager for the excellent pasturage left vacant by the slaughter of the buffalo. However, agricultural settlement increased as waves of emigration swept over the prairies and plains and into unsettled areas between the Mississippi and the Pacific. The opening of lands to white settlement encompassed the outward behavior of language, dress, cultural patterns, and religious beliefs to the migrants' perception that the West was indeed a land of freedom.

Families sought new farmlands and voluntarily joined others to create rural communities constructed around common pasts. Moreover, migration westward was dependent upon farmers that relied on a boom-bust economy, national growth, and the anticipated continued unfolding of the American republic. The period 1841 to 1867 witnessed the greatest growth of white American migration across the overland western frontier in which many young, married white women and their children traveled from homes in the East to the prairies, as attested in their diaries and letters.

One diarist recalled her departure from Massachusetts in 1822 in a wagon train as consisting of single rigs, six-mule teams, and parties on horseback that left a plethora of views of the frontier and acknowledged the emotional impact of emigration, the feeling of isolation and loneliness as it reduced the monotony of travel, fear, and uncertainty. Moreover, apprehension about prairie life only magnified women's anxieties about becoming desiccated, old before their time, and losing the capacity for feminine coquetry associated with westward emigration. Scant information exists about black women on the frontier prior to the Civil War because most were enslaved on farms and plantations in the southern United States. Inauguration of the infamous Trail of Tears, the federal government's relocation policy, forced Native Americans and African Americans, who were often slave property of Indians, to move westward. Though this brought black women into Indian Territory, the text *Racial Encounters in the Multi-Cultural West* suggested that blacks were invisible in the founding of the frontier because, western historians claimed, "Negroes did not participate in the settlement of the west," with little or no research proving the contrary.

The presence of blacks on the prairies does not describe the composition of the black population, but a sufficient number of black cowboys were in the area as part of the western cattle-raising business. These brought families, since advertisements in newspapers requested black female servants to work in white households.

Asian migration into Oklahoma occurred slowly, since their appearance was tied to the development of the transcontinental railroad. Steamboats, used to assist with the fur trade, to move troops and supplies to military posts, and to facilitate colonization were outdated, and an urgent need for improved land transportation was desired because of the booming cattle and agriculture industry and growth in settlers.

The Civil War halted the development of a progressive transportation system, though late in Oklahoma, railroads made articles available that previously had been home manufactured, and brought supplies that eased chores. In fact, the railroad industry brought itinerant peddlers such as the Chinese vegetable man to the frontier, and despite reports that the Chinese were nonassimilative and had no social interaction with whites, they augmented the mercantile needs of western families.

SHAPING THE FRONTIER, TERRITORY, AND STATE

The plains and prairies were a rugged environment waiting for women's intervention and gentling. To change Oklahoma from a raw wilderness into a refined civilization, the area required the nurturing values of the female consciousness. It would take the work of women to mold the frontier into cohesive cultural communities that reflected the social order of human relations and still provide its occupants a fertile economic base. American Indian women represented the earliest architects, affecting change on the Oklahoma frontier with their baskets and grinding tools and beadwork, materials taken directly from the earth that offered the landscape a sense of décor and style. And though not expected or wanted, Indian women shaped the frontier with their bodies through purchase, prostitution, or intermarriage with Europeans.

Caucasian women's migration to Oklahoma further stabilized frontier identities, experiences, and encounters. White settlement officially began in 1889 with the opening of unclaimed lands, and the white female was the backbone of pioneer efforts in shaping attitudes toward education, culture, materialism, and national ideals and problems. Germans, Russian-Orthodox, Irish, Greek-Catholic, Italian, and Scots white women lived on farms, worked in small businesses, or sold agricultural implements, built churches, and organized civic groups. By the end of the 19th century, the daughters of these earlier immigrants eventually impacted 20th-century Oklahoma and statehood.

Women effected change in Oklahoma because of their overall development and involvement in education, politics, the frontier community, and public service. Once settlement concerns were satisfied, the lives of pioneer heroines were drawn to new vistas. Lack of female companionship was the overwhelming cause for women's interests in frontier and territorial politics because they sought to create an active social community through public service as a buffer to isolated farm life.

Through their small family cottage industries, the sale of homespun garments and dairy products, pioneer women gained access to political forums that aided not only women in taming the frontier but added to its economic development. Women's avid interests in education and politics marked many as social activists as they overcame a sense of loneliness and the frontier's lack of social amenities.

Women's civic responsibilities transcended individual needs and encompassed a world outside their own. These late 19th-century pioneer women used their maternal instincts to sophisticate a frontier life that inevitably inflamed the prairies with democratic values, acculturation, and pride. In fact, during the last decade of the 19th century and the first two decades of the 20th century, two separate situations galvanized Oklahoma's prairie people. The growth of Populism and the Green Corn Rebellion were political movements destined to determine the political direction of the territory.

The years 1887 to 1897 represented a watershed in American history; it was the era of Populism. This period pitted the tenets of federal politics against agrarian philosophy. One could argue that farmers and politicians were hostile toward one another because the federal government had supported western expansion and settlement and urban bank speculation.

Politically, the Republicans of the 1890 era had legislated scores of internal improvement projects, pension legislation, and tariff and antitrust bills, but these public services were both costly to the consumer and to implement.

Western and southern farmers, incensed with overproduction, farm debts, and a national interest in industrialization, found that cotton, wheat, corn, and meat products flooded home markets and that inflexible marketing arrangement profited middlemen and left farmers overproduced and underpaid. Though these were the immediate concerns of rural America, women's needs were not far behind, and the latter two decades of the 19th century found females defiant and active in their role as family supporters. If farms were going to waste, this impacted wives and children, whose interests in temperance, prohibition, and suffragette organizations represented counterbalances to government's excesses.

The Populist professed a need for political change in the nation because big business was siphoning funds into even greater governmental projects while poor Americans were subjected to the whims of trade embargoes and regulations. This was the period of political divestment with cumulating social resentments poured into the great Populist revolt in which women exercised their party participation to bring about gender equality.

Tired of misrepresentation, inertia, and the standard political party platform, the exclusion of women's rights from national concerns increasingly mimicked the exclusion of farmers from agrarian policies. With the development of gas lighting and municipal water systems, women were no longer tied to the homestead and more women were educated and in teaching, medical, and professional positions. These women's organizations were not simply social sewing circles, but viable and influential reform caucuses. The benchmark for these females was a political consciousness that broadened their social and educational interests in the disenfranchisement of their gender. And though rural women were not activists, they were nonetheless knowledgeable about scientific advances in agriculture and the diversification of programs that influenced the isolated farm family.

Populism developed because farmers and laborers believed they were in the midst of a nation brought to the verge of moral, political, and material ruin. Essentially, the Populist movement revolved around social constructs arising from the growth and expansion of America. The nation was no longer an untamed wilderness with dirt roads and isolated communities, but a conglomerate of states accountable to its citizenry. Populists sought diversification of resources to benefit the national economic boom, Oklahoma farm families embraced Populism to diffuse government and private monopolies, and women joined as part of a national interest in party politics.

In researching Oklahoma's participation in the Green Corn Movement, one is reminded of the 1968 Vietnam protests, the 1992 Ruby Ridge assault, the 1993 Branch Davidian conflagration, and the 1996 Montana Freemen antitax protests. These groups sought to reject all governmental controls as a right to civil liberties expressly sanctioned in the First, Second, and Fourth Amendments to the U.S. Constitution.

The Green Corn Movement is important to Oklahoma because it represented one of the few genuine popular uprisings in American history that portrayed the 1917 draft rebellion in which U.S. troops shot it out with farmers who refused to be drafted to fight in Europe in what they considered to be a rich man's war. Moreover, it chronicled a politically embarrassing and neglected skirmish in the conflict between labor and government, galvanized home defense organizations like the Oklahoma State Federation of Women's Clubs, and cultivated a civic activism that rallied industry, school boards, churches, and city councils. In 1917 Oklahoma women disavowed this bad national publicity following the draft resistance movement known as the Green Corn Rebellion.

Furthermore, Oklahoma's current state of affairs arose from the ashes of such past histories of government disapproval, racial hatred, and gender neglect. On June 1, 1921, a white mob marched across the railroad tracks dividing black from white in Tulsa and obliterated a black community, then celebrated as one of America's most prosperous. Why, one would argue, begin with this ancient story? The Tulsa Race Riots of 1921, by modern necessity, an embarrassment as one of the nation's worst racial atrocities, is a salient reminder of failed human relationships. Oklahoma, when faced with two cruel adversaries, bigotry and harassment, has had to seek western principles of fairness and equal justice, and this change is most evident in its legislature with 159 members in the House and Senate; 15 are women, making them 10% of elected officials. Moreover, women account for 50.9% of the population, with women entrepreneurs representing 24% of private sector businesses, and 3.8% of the state are foreign born.

Essentially, this rugged environment produced equally tough women who gave identity, shape, and refinement to Oklahoma's path to modernity. They were intrepid females whose destinies defied convention as they trailblazed throughout Oklahoma.

WHO'S WHO OF OKLAHOMA WOMEN

Viewed as an unobtrusive state in the middle of the United States, Oklahoma belied the experiences of its women, despite obstacles and adversity; women residents had much to do with the development and responsible endorsement of Oklahoma public opinion. It is only fitting to recognize the prolific historical achievements of women of the state. The following Oklahoma profiles is a select list of individuals who participated in the establishment and evolution of a woman's presence in the state's history:

- *Sanapia*—Comanche, Medicine Woman
- *Nancy "Nan'yehi" Ward*—Cherokee, Tribal Spokeswoman, 1820
- *Hannah E. M. Chapman*—Teacher, Union Mission Society, 1820
- *Rosina Gambold*—Teacher/Botanist, Cherokee Nation, 1820
- *Arsenath Viall*—Teacher, Osage Nation, 1820
- *Anna Eliza Worchester*—Teacher, Union Mission Society, 1821
- *Harriet Bunce Wright*—Teacher/Founder, Wheelock Mission, 1832
- *Anna Burnham*—Teacher, Choctaws, 1833
- *Eunice Clough*—Teacher, Choctaws, 1838
- *Mary Avery*—Teacher, Koweta Mission, 1839
- *Maria James*—Osage, Dwight Mission, 1841
- *Nancy Thompson*—Teacher, Creek Nation, 1849
- *Sarah Worchester*—Cherokee, Assistant Teacher, Cherokee Female Seminary, 1851
- *Ellen Whitmore*—Principal Teacher, Cherokee Female Seminary, Park Hill, 1851
- *Clara W. Eddy*—Teacher, Creek and Choctaw Nations, 1852-1867
- *Angelina H. Carr*—Teacher, Chickasaws, 1856
- *Isabel Crawford*—Missionary and Educator of Comanche and Kiowa children
- *Elizabeth Fulton Hester*—Teacher/Founder, Muskogee Day Nursery, 1857

- *Harriet Newell Mitchell Wright*—Teacher, Choctaws, 1859
- *Cynthia A. Parker*—Mother of Quanah Parker, Chief of Comanches
- *Belle Starr*—Outlaw
- *Eliza M. Bushyhead*—Cherokee, Student, Cherokee Female Seminary, 1861
- *Ann Florence Wilson*—Principal Teacher, Cherokee Female Seminary, 1875-1901
- *Laura E. Harsha*—Teacher, Indian Public School, Okmulgee, 1878
- *Myrtle Archer Crawford*—Founder/President, Sapulpa Social Club, 1891
- *Kate E. May*—Oklahoma Homestead & Land Rush, 1893
- *Jane McCurtain*—Superintendent, Jones Academy, 1894-1898
- *Julia S. Douglas*—Director, Oklahoma & Indian Territory Federation, 1898
- *Luretta Rainey*—Federation Historian, Federation of Women's Clubs
- *Mary Harris*—Teacher, Free Kindergarten, Oklahoma City
- *Kate Barnard*—Politician/Labor Activist, Child Labor & Compulsory Education
- *Frances F. Threadgill*—Chair, Federation of Women's Clubs Legislative Committee
- *Lola S. Scott*—President, Federation of Women's Clubs, 1904-1906
- *Charlotte Mayes Sanders*—Cherokee, Student, Cherokee Female Seminary, 1906
- *Martha M. Starr*—Chair, Federation's of Women's Clubs Civil & Forestry Department, 1907
- *Letitia Riddle*—Chickasaw, Chair, Legislative Committee, Federation of Women's Clubs, 1907
- *Rachel Caroline Eaton*—Organizer, Sequoyah Historical Society, 1908
- *Lucia Caroline Loomis Ferguson*—Journalist, *Oklahoma News*, 1910
- *Ethel Brewer McMillan*—Chair, Pioneer Women Delta Kappa Gamma, 1910
- *Zoe Agnes Tilghman*—Author, 1910
- *Alice Ross Howard*—Cherokee, Superintendent, Five Civilized Tribes, 1913
- *Mabel P. Little*—African American, Businesswoman, Tulsa, 1913
- *Edith Cherry Johnson*—Journalist, *Daily Oklahoman*, 1915
- *Drusilla Dunjee Houston*—African American, Journalist, *Black Dispatch*, 1915

- *Bessie Marie Huff*—Educator, 1915-1950
- *Ellen Howard Miller*—Cherokee, Naturalist, Oklahoma Historical Society, 1917
- *Lillian Delly*—Poet/Writer
- *Margaret McVean*—Oklahoma City Attorney, 1918
- *Edith Force Kassing*—Ornithologist/Educator, 1918-1956
- *Elva Shartel Ferguson*—Journalist, *Watonga Republican*, 1920
- *Lucia Caroline Loomis Ferguson*—Journalist, *Oklahoma News*, 1920
- *Alice Mary Robertson*—First Oklahoma Congressional Representative, 1921
- *Loula Williams*—African American, Williams Dreamland Theater, Tulsa, 1921
- *Lola Clark Pearson* Spokeswoman, *Oklahoma Farmer-Stockman*, 1925
- *Norma Smallwood*—Miss America 1926
- *Augusta Robertson Moore*—Teacher, Tullahassee Indian School, Nuyaka Mission
- *Willa Allegra Strong*—African American, Educator, 1928-1969
- *Emma Estill-Harbour*—Educator, 1929-1955
- *Edith Taubman*—Jewish Quiltmaker, 1930
- *Muriel H. Wright*—Historian, 1930-1955
- *Zelia Breaux*—African American, Educator/Musician, 1930-1960
- *Eula E. Fullerton*—Journalist, 1934
- *Anna Lewis*—Teacher/Author/Historian
- *Agnes "Sis" Cunningham*—Folk Singer/Songwriter, 1938
- *Carolyn Thomas Foreman*—Writer/Historian, *Chronicles of Oklahoma*, 1938-1953
- *Pearl C. Moyer*—Artist/Ceramist, Oklahoma Blood Plasma Fund, 1941-1945
- *Elizabeth Maria Tallchief*—Osage, American Prima Ballerina, 1942
- *Jessie Thatcher Bost*—American Indian, World War II WAC, 1942
- *Hannah Atkins*—World War II WAVE, 1942
- *Jane Heard Clinton*—Civic/Cultural Organizer, Tulsa, 1942
- *Jennie Harris Oliver*—Writer/Poet, 1942
- *Ethel McMillan*—Contributor, *Chronicles of Oklahoma*, 1949
- *Ada Lois Sipuel Fisher*—African American, Graduate of Oklahoma University School of Law, 1951
- *Ruth Brown*—Librarian/Civil Rights Activist, 1960
- *La Donna Harris*—Comanche, Political Activist

- *Wilma Mankiller*—First Woman Principal Chief of the Cherokee Nation, 1985
- *Wally Funk*—Pilot/Flight Instructor
- *Marilyn Murrell*—Mayor, Arcadia, Oklahoma, 1988
- *Reba McEntire*—Country Western Vocalist
- *Shannon Miller*—Gymnast, U.S. Olympics
- *Karen Silkwood*—Whistleblower, Chemical Waste
- *Angie Debo*—Historian/University Professor
- *Jeane Kirkpatrick*—Diplomat/Educator
- *Le Anne Howe*—Choctaw, Writer
- *Christine A. Lawrence*—Manager/Pilot, Transportation Safety Institute
- *Joy Harjo*—Creek, Writer
- *Barbara Lawrence Sloane*—Pilot, Member, Ninety-Nines Women's Flying Group
- *Daneka Allen*—African American, Community Relations Coordinator
- *Shannon Lucid*—NASA Astronaut
- *Vera Miles*—Actress
- *Clara Luper*—African American, Educator/Civil Rights Activist
- *Juanita Kidd Stout*—African American, Judge/Attorney/Educator
- *Maxine Horner*—African American, State Senator, Personnel Management
- *Angela Zoe Monson*—African American, State Senator, Business Consultant
- *Nilda Reyes*—Hispanic, Educator/High School Administrator
- *Carmen Pettie*—African American, Program Director, Tulsa YWCA
- *Joan Hill*—American Indian, Artist, Muskogee
- *Rebecca Fenster*—Collector/Founder, Sherwin Miller Museum of Jewish Art, 1966
- *Jane Joyroe*—Miss America 1967
- *Cathy Martin*—Ceramic Artist
- *Rilla Askew*—Author
- *Ann Simank*—Ward 6 Councilwoman, 1995
- *Lu Hollander*—Pilot/Communications Professional, Member, Ninety-Nines Women's Flying Group
- *Jerrie Cobb*—Pilot/Aviation Pioneer/Astronaut/Mercury 13/Missionary
- *Susan Powell*—Miss America 1981
- *Anita Hill*—Attorney/Law Professor/Author, testified before the U.S. Senate, 1991
- *Willa Johnson*—African American, Ward 7 Councilwoman, 1993
- *Regina Bonney*—Officer, Midwest City Police Department, 1995

- *Samina Quraeshi*—East Indian, Architect, Oklahoma City Bombing Memorial
- *Shawntel Smith*—Miss America 1996
- *Londa Cox*—Cherokee, Manager, Cherokee Education & Human Services, 1998
- *Dana Eversole*—Cherokee, Assistant Professor, Northeastern State University, 1998
- *Julie Deerinwater*—Cherokee, Health Educator, Cherokee Nation, 1998
- *Lisa Trice*—Cherokee, Manager Housing Authority, Cherokee Nation, 1998
- *Amy U. Brooks*—Ward 2 Councilwoman, 1999
- *Priti Patel*—Asian American, Board Member AAHOA, 1999
- *Carol Miller*—Cherokee, Educator, University of Minnesota
- *Julia Lookout*—Osage, Vice President, Greenwood Performance Systems, 2000
- *Anna Gregory*—Genealogist, Wilburton, 2001
- *Rebecca Marks-Jimerson*—African American, Instructor, Tulsa Community College
- *Lucinda Poahway*—Kiowa, Woman of the Year, Oklahoma Federation of Indian Women, 2001
- *Brenda Horton*—African American, Minority Businesswoman, 2001
- *Sheri Horner-Tisdale*—African American, Editor/Publisher, *ExcellStyle* Magazine
- *Karin Woodruff*—Mayor, Wilburton, elected 2002
- *Margaret L. Hill*—African American, Genealogist, Hartshorne, 2002

CONCLUSION

In an effort to piece together a compelling history of Oklahoma's invisible heroines, our journey took on many facets, tracing Oklahoma's history from its archaeological beginnings, early primordial inhabitants, the traumatic changes European society made on Native Americans, the impact of western culture, race, Populism, the Green Corn Movement, and most significantly, the diversity of gender that coalesced, formed, and nurtured a heritage that is still evolving.

Oklahoma men have eclipsed the biographies of women who have contributed to the character of Oklahoma through its nation-building process and as a state in the union. The story of Oklahoma women demonstrates that they were of the same caliber as their men and that their lives were the precursor to a legacy of sophistication and hope at times when none ventured to break racial or gender barriers. Oklahoma

women's contributions, both past and present, are an ever present mandate to challenge, effectuate change, and define the woman's presence in the state of Oklahoma.

—Jayne Sinegal

SUGGESTED READINGS

"1958-1964." *Chronicles of Oklahoma* 59(2, Summer 1981): 152-163.

Abbott, Devon. "Ann Florence Wilson: Matriarch of the Cherokee Female Seminary." *Chronicles of Oklahoma* 67(4, Winter 1989-1990): 426-435.

Agnew, Brad. "A Legacy of Education: The History of the Cherokee Seminaries." *Chronicles of Oklahoma* 63(2, Summer 1985): 128-145.

Allen, Susan L. "Progressive Spirit: The Oklahoma and Indian Territory Federation of Women's Clubs." *Chronicles of Oklahoma* 66(1, Spring 1988): 4-19.

American Police Hall of Fame. "Officer of the Year 1996: Corporal Regina Bonny." Retrieved August 26, 2002, from www.aphf.org.

Belcher, Dixie. "A Democratic School for Democratic Women." *Chronicles of Oklahoma* 61(4, Winter 1983-1984): 414.

Bertram, Peggy Brooks. "Rescuing Drusilla: Drusilla Dunjee Houston." Retrieved October 14, 2002, from wings.buffalo.edu/dunjeehouston/history/bio.htm.

Blackburn, Bob L. "Zelia Breaux and Bricktown: Crossroads of Commerce, Crossroads of Diversity, Crossroads of Renewal." Bricktown History. Retrieved October 2, 2001, from www.bricktownokc.com.

Blossom, Debbie. "African-American Businesswomen in Tulsa, Oklahoma, Head to Conference." *Tulsa World,* August 25, 2001. Retrieved October 22, 2001, from www.web.lexis-nexis.com/universe/doc.

Bostic, E. McCurdy. "Elizabeth Fulton Hester." *Chronicles of Oklahoma* 6(4, December 1928): 449-452.

Casey, Naomi Taylor. "Miss Edith Johnson, Pioneer Newspaper Woman." *Chronicles of Oklahoma* 60(1, Spring 1982): 71.

"Cathy Martin: Functional Ceramic Art." Retrieved October 25, 2001, from members.aol.com/cmartin27.

Clark, J. Stanley. "Carolyn Thomas Foreman." *Chronicles of Oklahoma* 45(4, Winter 1967-1968): 368-375.

Costello, David F. *The Prairie World.* Minneapolis: University of Minnesota Press, 1980.

Crockett, Bernice Norman. "No Job for a Woman." *Chronicles of Oklahoma* 61(2, Summer 1983): 156.

Debo, Angie. "Jane Heard Clinton." *Chronicles of Oklahoma 24*(1, Spring 1946): 20-25.

Delly, Lillian. "Ellen Howard Miller." *Chronicles of Oklahoma 26*(2, Summer 1948): 174-177.

Eversole, Dana. "She Has Surely Done Her Share: Miss Bessie Huff and the Muskogee Junior College." *Chronicles of Oklahoma 79*(4, Winter 2001-2002): 430-438.

"First Female Astronaut Still Hoping to Go Up: Jerrie Cobb." *CNN Science-Technology.* Retrieved August 27, 2002, from www.cnn.com/TECH/space/9810/28/first.woman.astronaut.

Fisher-Sipuel, Ada Lois. *A Matter of Black & White: The Autobiography of Ada Lois Sipuel Fisher.* Norman: University of Oklahoma Press, 1996.

Foreman, Carolyn Thomas. "Aunt Eliza of Tahlequah." *Chronicles of Oklahoma 9*(1, March 1931): 43-55.

Foreman, Carolyn Thomas. "Augusta Robertson Moore: A Sketch of Her Life and Times." *Chronicles of Oklahoma 13*(4, December 1935): 398-420.

Foreman, Carolyn Thomas. "Mrs. Laura E. Harsha." *Chronicles of Oklahoma 18*(2, June 1940): 182-184.

Foreman, Carolyn Thomas. "Alice Ross Howard." *Chronicles of Oklahoma 23*(3, Autumn 1945): 249-253.

Foreman, Grant. "The Honorable Alice M. Robertson." *Chronicles of Oklahoma 10*(1, March 1932): 12-17.

Funk, Wally. "The Ninety-Nines: Wally Funk, Air Safety Investigator." Retrieved October 20, 2001, from www.ninety-nines.org/funk.htm.

Gale Group UXL Biographies. "Nancy Ward: Cherokee Tribal Leader 1738-1824," Celebrating Women's History Month 1996. Retrieved October 12, 2001, from www.roup.com/freresrc/womenhst/bio/ward.htm.

Gibson, A. M. "Prehistory of Oklahoma." *Chronicles of Oklahoma 43*(1, Spring 1965): 2-8.

Goetz, Henry Kilian. "Kate's Quarter Section: A Woman in the Cherokee Strip." *Chronicles of Oklahoma 61*(3, Fall 1983): 246-265.

Graves, Carl R. "The Right to be Served: Oklahoma City's Lunch Counter Sit-Ins, 1958-1964." *Chronicles of Oklahoma 59*(2, Summer 1981): 152-163.

Gravitt, Winnie Lewis. "Anna Lewis: A Great Woman of Oklahoma." *Chronicles of Oklahoma 40*(4, Winter 1962-1963): 326-329.

Hamburg, Jill. "Raising Oklahoma: A Devastated City Gets a New Look." *Working Woman* (October 1998): 11.

Hamilton, Anne M. "A Daring Young Girl on the Flying Trapeze of Life." *Hartford Courant,* September 30, 2001, p. H2. Retrieved October 6, 2001, from www.web.lexis-nexis.com/universe/doc.

Harries, Keith D., and H. Wayne Morgan, eds. "Land and Climate." *World Book Encyclopedia,* 1999.

Herring, Rebecca. "Their Work Was Never Done: Women Missionaries on the Kiowa-Comanche Reservation." *Chronicles of Oklahoma 64*(1, Spring 1986): 68-83.

Hildenbrand, Kathleen. "Big Trouble in Little Tulsa: It Was One of the Nation's Worst Outbreaks of Racial Violence." *Alice 1*(1, January 31, 2000): 48. Retrieved October 22, 2001, from www.enw.softlineweb.com.

Hill, Anita. "Anita Hill," in Brian Lamb, ed., *Booknotes Life Stories: Notable Biographers on the People Who Shaped America.* New York: Times Books, 1992.

Hoder-Salmon, Marilyn. "Myrtle Archer McDougal: Leader of Oklahoma's Timid Sisters." *Chronicles of Oklahoma 60*(3, Fall 1982): 332-343.

Hoig, Stan. *Tribal Wars of the Southern Plains.* Norman: University of Oklahoma Press, 1993.

Jackson, Joe. "Dr. Emma Estill-Harbour, 1884-1967." *Chronicles of Oklahoma 45*(2, Summer 1967): 230-233.

Jaffe, A. J. *The First Immigrants from Asia: A Population History of the North American Indians.* New York: Plenum, 1992.

James, Louise Boyd. "The Woman Suffrage Issue in Oklahoma's Constitutional Convention." *Chronicles of Oklahoma 64*(4, Winter 1978-1979): 379.

James, Parthena Louise. "Reconstruction in the Chickasaw Nation: The Freedmen Problem." *Chronicles of Oklahoma 45*(1, Spring 1967): 44-57.

Lewis, Anna. "Jane McCurtain." *Chronicles of Oklahoma 11*(4, December 1933): 1024-1033.

"Local Women Named Outstanding Young Oklahomans." *Cherokee Advocate 22*(3-4, April 30, 1998): 10. Retrieved October 22, 2001, from www.enw.softlineweb.com.

"Lookout Named Vice President of Greenwood Systems." *Oklahoma Indian Times 6*(7, July 31, 2000): 8. Retrieved October 22, 2001, from www.enw.softlineweb.com.

Mabry, Russ. "Woodruff Elected New Mayor of Wilburton." *Latimer County News 106*(2, January 10, 2002): 1-3.

Malinowski, Sharon, and Simon Glickman, eds. *Native North American Biography.* New York: Gale Research, 1996.

"Mayors Convene in Denver," *Sacramento Observer.* May 12, 1999, p. A12. Retrieved October 22, 2001, from www.enw.softlineweb.com.

McMillan, Ethel. "Women Teachers in Oklahoma, 1820-1860." *Chronicles of Oklahoma 27*(1, Spring 1949): 2-32.

Mills, Kenneth, and William B. Taylor, eds. *Colonial Spanish America: A Documentary History.* Wilmington, DE: Scholarly Books, 1998.

"Miss America Pageant." Retrieved August 27, 2002, from www.pressplus.com/missam/pastwinners.

Morgan, H. Wayne, and Anne Hodges Morgan. *Oklahoma: A History.* Nashville, TN: Norton, 1977.

Myers, Sandra L. *Westering Women and the Frontier Experience, 1800-1915.* Albuquerque: University of New Mexico Press, 1982.

National Aeronautics and Space Administration. "Shannon W. Lucid: Astronaut," Lyndon B. Johnson Space Center. Retrieved August 27, 2002, from www.jsc.nasa.gov/Bios/htmlbios/lucid.html.

Oklahoma City Hall. "Biographies of City Council Members." Retrieved October 2, 2001, from www.okc-cityhall.org/Mayor-Council.

Oklahoma State University. "Chief Wilma P. Mankiller: Principal Chief, Cherokee Nation," Henry G. Bennett Distinguished Service Award Winners. Retrieved October 12, 2001, from www.library.okstate.edu.

Oklahoma State University. "Judge Juanita Kidd Stout: Judge of the Common Pleas Court, Philadelphia, Pennsylvania," Henry G. Bennett Distinguished Service Award Winners. Retrieved August 27, 2002, from www.library.okstate.edu.

Rader, Brian F. *The Political Outsiders: Blacks and Indians in a Rural Oklahoma County.* San Francisco, CA: R&E Research, 1978.

Reese, Linda W. "Dear Oklahoma Lady: Women Journalists Speak Out." *Chronicles of Oklahoma 67*(3, Fall 1989): 264-291.

Reese, Linda. *Women of Oklahoma, 1890-1920.* Norman: University of Oklahoma Press, 1997.

Riley, Glenda. *The Female Frontier: A Comparative View of Women on the Prairie and the Plains.* Lawrence: University Press of Kansas, 1988.

Risjord, Norman J. *Jefferson's America, 1760-1815.* Madison, WI: Madison House, 1991.

Robbins, Louise S. *The Dismissal of Miss Ruth Brown: Civil Rights, Censorship, and the American Library.* Norman: University of Oklahoma Press, 2000.

Schafer, Delbert F. "French Explorers in Oklahoma." *Chronicles of Oklahoma 55*(4, Winter 1977-1978): 392-402.

Schrems, Suzanne H. "Radicalism and Song." *Chronicles of Oklahoma 62*(2, Summer 1984): 190-205.

Scott-Smith, Daniel. "Female Householding in Late Eighteenth Century America and the Problem of Poverty." *Journal of Southern History 28* (Fall 1994): 83-108.

Searcy, Howard. "Mrs. Howard Searcy: Pearl C. Moyer, 1875-1945." *Chronicles of Oklahoma 24*(1, Spring 1946): 15-19.

"Sherwin Miller Museum of Jewish History." Retrieved October 2, 2001, from www.jewishmuseum.net/Museum/history.htm.

Sonneborn, Liz. *Encyclopedia of Women: A to Z of Native American Women.* New York: Facts on File, 1998.

Sprague, William Forrest. *Women and the West: A Short Social History.* New York: Arno Press, 1972.

Stanley, Ruth Moore. "Alice M. Robertson: Oklahoma's First Congresswoman." *Chronicles of Oklahoma 45*(3, Autumn 1969): 278-288.

Steele, James, and Stephen Shennan, eds. *The Archaeology of Human Ancestry: Power, Sex and Tradition.* New York: Routledge, 1996.

Strickland, Rennard. "Oklahoma Indians." *The Native North American Almanac.* Detroit, MI: Gale Research, 1994.

Sullivan, James. "Country Sweetheart: Reba McEntire," *San Francisco Chronicle.* Retrieved October 6, 2001, from web.lexis-nexis.com/universe/doc.

Swanton, John R. *The Indian Tribes of North America.* Washington, DC: Scholarly Press, 1978.

Tallchief, Maria, and Larry Kaplan. "Maria Tallchief: America's Prima Ballerina," *Washington Post.* Retrieved May 14, 2001, from www.washingtonpost.com.

Tomer, John S. "Edith Force Kassing: Scientist With a Gift for Teaching." *Chronicles of Oklahoma 63*(4, Winter 1985-1986): 396-408.

Tran, Quin. "KFOR-TV News Channel 4 People: Quin Tran." Retrieved May 17, 2001, from www.kfor.com.

Truitt, Bess. "Jennie Harris Oliver." *Chronicles of Oklahoma 22*(2, Summer 1944): 137-141.

University of Minnesota, American Indian Studies Department. "Carol Miller: Associate Professor American Studies and American Indian Studies." Retrieved September 25, 2002, from www.cla.umn.edu/amerind/staff/cmiller.html.

Vehik, Susan C. "Cultural Continuity and Discontinuity in the Southern Prairies and Cross Timbers," in Karl H. Schlesier, ed., *Plains Indians, A.D. 500-1500: The Archaeological Past of Historical Groups.* Norman: University of Oklahoma Press, 1994.

Webber, David J. *The Spanish Frontier in North America.* New Haven, CT: Yale University Press, 1992.

Wellman, Paul I. "Cynthia Ann Parker." *Chronicles of Oklahoma 12*(2, June 1934): 163-171.

Wenke, Robert J. *Patterns in Prehistory: Mankind's First Three Million Years.* New York: Oxford University Press, 1980.

"Women's Advancement New AAHOA Initiative for 1999," *India West*. September 4, 1998, p. A40. Retrieved October 22, 2001, from enw.softlineweb.com.

Wright, Muriel H. "Choctaws and Chickasaws Were Allied With Confederacy," in Mattie Lloyd Wooten, ed., *Women Tell the Story of the Southwest*. San Antonio, TX: Naylor, 1940.

O'LEARY, KATHLEEN E. (1951-)

Kathleen O'Leary's interest in law began while she was a student at Loyola Marymount University. After earning her B.A. in Political Science, she went on to Southwestern University, where she graduated in 1975. After graduation she spent several years as a public defender and credits her success as a jurist to her experience as a litigator. When asked why she opted for a career in public service law, she responded that it was the best opportunity for women "because most women in private practice were researchers."

Governor Jerry Brown first appointed O'Leary a judge of the West Orange County Municipal Court in 1981. In 1986 Governor George Deukmejian appointed her to the superior court. It was here that Justice O'Leary gained recognition as the first woman in Orange County history to be elected as the presiding judge. In 2000 Governor Gray Davis appointed her to the California Court of Appeal.

O'Leary is an active teacher and considers education a continual process for the entire judiciary.

She is a member of the California Judicial Education and Research Governing Board. In addition, she is a teacher conducting courses and seminars at many judicial colleges and institutes throughout the United States. She is active in keeping the judiciary and the courts current in law-related education, including the areas of science and technology.

Many organizations have recognized O'Leary, including the League of Women Voters, the Orange County Women Lawyers, the American Legion, and the Hispanic Bar Association. She has received many awards, such as the Judicial Council's Jurist of the Year award in 1999 and the California Consumer Attorney's Outstanding Judicial Achievement award.

O'Leary is an example not only to women but also to all people who choose a career in public service. She demonstrates the importance of education for all jurists to ensure fairness and justice for all citizens of California as well as our nation.

—Brenda Bitgood

SUGGESTED READINGS

Kathleen E. O'Leary, Associate Justice. Retrieved from www.courtinfo.ca.gov/courts/courtsofappeal/4thDistrict Div3/justices/oleary.htm.

Southwestern University School of Law. "Hon. Kathleen O'Leary." Retrieved from www.swlaw.edu/alumni/oleary.html

P

PARSONS, ELSIE CLEWS (1874-1941)

Elsie Worthington Clews Parsons was born in 1874 at Grosvenor House on Fifth Avenue in New York City to a family of great wealth and privilege. Her parents, Henry Clews and Lucy Worthington, were part of the moneyed class of New York in the late 19th century and were deeply involved with the political powers of the day, friends of Presidents Lincoln and Grant. While Elsie was an eastern aristocrat by birth and lived in New York and Rhode Island for most of her life, her most influential fieldwork was conducted in the Southwest.

Elsie graduated from Barnard College in 1896 and Columbia University in 1897 in sociology. In 1899 she received a Ph.D. in sociology from Columbia, becoming one of the few women to study and complete advanced graduate work at the time. While at Columbia, she was first introduced to French sociologist Gabriel de Tarde's theories of social processes. "Tarde's notions of imitation, invention, and conversation gave Parsons the basis for her life's work." Tarde argued that the process of conversation enabled individuals to shift ideological perspectives and form coalitions; through spontaneous personal relationships, broader structural effects could be mitigated.

In 1901 Elsie married Herbert Parsons and began her "experimental" life as wife and mother. Elsie, the first daughter, was born that year, John in 1903, Herbert in 1909, and Henry McIlvaine in 1911. Several later pregnancies were unsuccessful. In 1904 Herbert, a close friend of Theodore Roosevelt, was elected to Congress. This relationship with Roosevelt,

as well as the Parsons's friendship with Taft, opened the doors for Elsie's first forays into ethnography on a political trip to the Philippines and then her later work in the Southwest. She also did extensive fieldwork in Ecuador, Mexico, and the Caribbean later in her career. An unconventional woman for her time, her career as wife and mother was often second to her professional life as an ethnographer, public intellectual, social activist, and writer.

By the time Parsons had made her first trip to the Southwest on a 1910 political jaunt with her congressman husband Herbert, her sociological thinking regarding culture, change, and social processes was undergoing a decided transformation. Her first professional trip to the Southwest in 1912 was to study archeological sites in the area of Parajito Ranch outside Santa Fe for the museum of natural history. But in keeping with her appreciation of Tarde's theories of social transformation through face-to-face talk and mass communication as the most important way of encouraging and spreading innovation, Parsons became interested in the life and social practices of her guide.

For the next 25 years, Parsons returned to northwest New Mexico and the Pueblos nearly 20 times to study and record the indigenous cultures of the Southwest. She met pioneering anthropologist Franz Boas in 1915, and the relationship became a lifelong professional collaboration. Her work was directly influenced by Boas, and in turn she influenced the scope and direction of Boasian anthropology and ethnography through her writing, as well as through her financial and personal support of a number of the most recognizable members of the Boasian anthropological tradition and the professional organizations that gave shape to the emerging discipline. The Boasian school in general, but Parsons in particular, looked to the western indigenous groups as the place to gain insights into acculturation, personality, and social conventions. Parsons was devoted to "an exacting study of the historical processes of imitation and invention in the making of the Pueblo communities of America's Southwest, a study that fulfilled all Tarde's methodological tenets in its attention to detail, personality, and wide-ranging comparison."

The year 1919 was a key year for Parsons professionally. She was a major player in the founding of The New School for Social Research, she was elected president of the American Folklore Society, she made the *Who's Who in Pacifism and Radicalism* list, Herbert returned from World War I, and the American Southwest was awash with rich writers, artists, and tourists along with Parsons. During this year of incredible activity, she published a major ethnographic study on women's lives, *Mothers and Children at Laguna*, as well as 15 other articles, essays, and reviews. In 1923 her father died and she became independently wealthy.

Parsons was a prolific writer. Her early sociological writings like *The Family* (1906) and *Social Rule* (1916) are less well known than her ethnographic studies of the Pueblo Indians of the American Southwest. "Laguna Genealogies" (1923), "Notes on Laguna Ceremonialism" (1920), and "Spanish Tales From Laguna and Zuni" (1920) were part of the large number of essays she published in the major anthropological journals like the *Journal of American Folklore* and *American Anthropologist,* journals that also benefited from her ongoing financial support. In 1939 she published her most complete collection of ethnographic material, *Pueblo Indian Religion.* It was her primary preoccupation between 1934 and 1937, addressing the question of "the magnitude, velocity, and direction of culture change"—or acculturation among Pueblo tribal groups. The book was first planned in 1918 as an encyclopedia of Pueblo culture. Ultimately, it covered the 25 years of her fieldwork and conversations in the pueblos, published just before Germany invaded Poland as the world was poised for World War II. *Pueblo Indian Religion* is at first glance a regional study of indigenous people of the Southwest. On closer examination, it is clearly Parsons' contribution to the ethnographic conversation as she shares her conclusions about cultural dynamics, acculturation, cultural variants, the Southwest, and the possibilities for social change through conversations.

Parsons made numerous contributions to western anthropology and culture studies. Her work influenced generations of women living, working, and writing in the West, from Esther Goldfrank, Ruth Bunzel, Gladys Reichard, Erna Gunther, Helen Roberts, Ruth Benedict, and Ruth Underhill, to Barbara Babcock, Nancy Parezo, and subsequent generations of women anthropologists. It is clear that there has been some historical repression of her contributions to ethnography, but there are a number of new projects that highlight her importance as an iconoclast, individualist, scientist, innovator, and feminist. Deasley Deacon, Pauline Strong, and Barbara Babcock have done much to advance scholarship on Parsons. Her work has had considerable influence on the ethnographic enterprise through her financial support, as a powerful role model, and by breaking the sexual taboo of unmarried men and women working together in the field. Parsons transformed the study of anthropology and helped to make visible the study of the southwestern Pueblos. Her work influenced ideas about race, ethnicity, and identity, and as a prolific writer and public intellectual, she was able to connect her work in the Southwest to eastern intellectual circles. By 1919 she was one of the best-known anthropologists in the United States.

In 1941 Parsons returned from a fieldwork trip to Peguche, Ecuador, to address the American Anthropological Association (AAA) meeting in New York. She had recently been elected president of this organization that had been an integral part of her professional life and had relied heavily on her financial and intellectual support as well. She was hospitalized on December 11 with uremia, and died at age 67. Gladys Reichard read her undelivered address to the AAA meeting. As anthropologist Alfred Kroeber wrote after her death, "She studied the science of society the better to fight back against society." She was an unconventional woman, indefatigable, always resisting social conventions that would limit individual free expression.

—Renae Moore Bredin

SUGGESTED READINGS

Deacon, Desley. *Elsie Clews Parsons: Inventing Modern Life.* Chicago: University of Chicago Press, 1997.

Parsons, Elsie Clews. "Mothers and Children at Laguna." *Man 19* (1919): 34-38.

Parsons, Elsie Clews. *Pueblo Indian Religion*. Chicago: University of Chicago Press, 1939.

PATEL, MARILYN HALL (1938-)

Marilyn Hall Patel was born in Amsterdam, New York, in 1938. She graduated from Wheaton College in 1959 and went on to study at Fordham University School of Law. After receiving her J.D. from Fordham in 1963, she opened her private law practice in New York City. After 4 years, she moved to San Francisco to take a position as an attorney for the Immigration and Naturalization Service, a branch of the U.S. Department of Justice. Remaining in the Bay Area, she opened her private practice in San Francisco in 1971 and remained in practice until 1976. During this time, she served as an adjunct professor of law for the Hastings College of Law at the University of California, San Francisco, from 1974 to 1976. She became a judge in the municipal court in the Oakland-Piedmont Judicial District for the State of California in 1976 and remained there for 4 years. President Jimmy Carter nominated her for the seat on the U.S. District Court for the Northern District of California vacated by Lloyd Hudson Burke on May 9, 1980. After being confirmed by the Senate on June 26, 1980, she was given her commission on June 30, 1980. She has served as the chief judge on that court since 1997.

—Marcus J. Schwoerer

SUGGESTED READING

Marilyn Hall Patel. Retrieved from air.fjc.gov/servlet/tGetInfo?jid=1846. Source: History of the Federal Judiciary. http://www.fjc.gov. Web site of the Federal Judicial Center, Washington, D.C.

PFAELZER, MARIANA R. (1926-)

Native Californian Judge Mariana R. Pfaelzer was well established in a teaching career in the Los Angeles school system when she decided to make a career change. With a bachelor's degree from the University of California, Santa Barbara, and a graduate degree from the University of California, Los Angeles, in political science, the field of law was an understandable choice.

After graduating from law school at UCLA in 1957, Pfaelzer went to work for Wyman, Bautzer, Rothman & Kuchel and helped the firm grow from only 5 attorneys to nearly 60 by the time of her departure as senior partner in 1978. She credits her long tenure with the firm to the fact that they hired her when jobs were scarce for both men and women fresh out of law school. Although there have been many obstacles for women in the field of law, she firmly believes that excellence will always win in the end, whether by a man or a woman. This attitude toward excellence certainly was the driving force behind her successful career.

President Jimmy Carter appointed Pfaelzer to the U.S. District Court for the Central District of California in 1978. Although she was first recommended by President Gerald Ford in 1975, she declined the nomination because two partners in her firm had recently passed away. With her appointment in 1978, she became the first woman appointed to the U.S. District Court in California. She took senior status in 1997.

During her extensive and accomplished career, Pfaelzer has held several other significant positions. She served on the Los Angeles Police Commission from 1974 until she took the bench in 1978 and served as president of the Board of Police Commissioners during her last year there. She maintains a position on the boards of both Loyola Law School and the Claremont Colleges. In addition, she serves as chair of the Women's Rights Subcommittee of the Human Rights Section of the Los Angeles County Bar Association, chair of the State Bar of California's Committee on Professional Ethics, chair of the State Bar of California's Special Committee on Juvenile Justice, and as president of the Ninth Circuit District Judges Association.

Pfaelzer has received many honors, including the UCLA Alumnus award for Professional Achievement, the UCLA School of Law Alumnus of the Year award, the Beverly Hills Bar Association's Federal Trial Judge of the Year award, and the University of California, Santa Barbara, Distinguished Alumnus award.

In an interview shortly before she was sworn in back in 1978, Pfaelzer stated, "I strongly favor breaking down artificial barriers for women and for minorities, too." Her incredible career has proven that no barriers are insurmountable for someone who is committed to hard work and excellence.

—Brenda Bitgood

SUGGESTED READING

Stineman, Esther. *American Political Women: Contemporary and Historical Profiles.* Littleton, CO: Libraries Unlimited, 1980.

PHILANTHROPY IN THE AMERICAN WEST

Until recently, the history of the American West has been depicted as a progression of Anglo male conquests over a raw land and its native inhabitants. Nineteenth-century images of dust-covered cowboys corralling Longhorn steers, fearless lawmen enforcing frontier justice, and U.S. cavalrymen waging ethnic wars against Native Americans have dominated the literature—even assuming almost mythical proportions. A narrow concentration on the 19th-century frontier of mountain men, cowboys, and miners has fostered such stereotypes, eclipsing a more inclusionary approach. Only occasionally did the experiences and perspectives of women and minorities intrude as marginal figures in these much-celebrated narratives. As a result, such one-dimensional depictions have denied the complexity and diversity of the western experience.

As scholars now acknowledge, there was another West. Inhabiting these "other frontiers" were women who were members of families, communities, and a variety of ethnic and social groups. While a few western females fit the earlier stereotypes of gentle civilizers, uncomplaining helpmates, and "fallen women," they were not all isolated, submissive members of pioneering societies. Many were also civic-minded organizers, active marital partners, and charitable public servants. As such, they became a major force for social, educational, and cultural reform in the American West.

Confined in part to a private sphere of housekeeping and child raising, western women initially joined together to establish friendships and alleviate loneliness. But in the wilderness, devoid of government structures, they also united to build a social infrastructure through which a rural society could address its myriad problems. Consequently, as women moved west, they brought with them their ideas about charitable work and community building to their new homes. They formed voluntary associations such as the Ladies Library Association of Seattle, benevolent organizations such as the Ladies Protection and Relief Society of San Francisco, and missionary societies such as the Christian Refuge Home for Women to improve local conditions. Such activities provided women an avenue of expressing their concerns, performing community service, and pursuing meaningful work.

By the post-1890 West, however, industrialization and urban growth revolutionized civic stewardship and gave rise to modern, organized philanthropy. To meet the needs of a less isolated, less rural, and more diverse population, charitable-minded philanthropists established a broader, more permanent vehicle—the private foundation—to address better their diverse problems. Pioneered by industrialist Andrew Carnegie, this new form of "wholesale philanthropy" advocated innovative approaches to long-standing traditions of private charity. Unlike temporary palliative aid, charitable handouts, or individual almsgiving, philanthropic organizations sought long-term solutions to the improvement in the quality of life. Rather than simply providing immediate aid to the sick and needy, a few wealthy donors began asking questions about the underlying causes of poverty, illness, and ignorance. For example, they believed that a cure for a disease was a better goal than another hospital for the sick. And they prized research to improve crop yields more than supporting settlement houses or soup kitchens.

Foundation philanthropy, or organized giving for the public good, was largely a product of the late 19th century with its laissez-faire economics, rapid urbanization, and Progressive era "search for order." Its development generally followed the pattern of economic growth and westward expansion. Beginning in the East with the Carnegie Foundation for Advancement of Teaching (1905) and the Russell Sage Foundation (1907), established by heiress Margaret Olivia Sage, the new movement quickly proceeded west. The unparalleled upsurge in railroad building, mining bonanzas, ranching expansion, and oil discoveries created a nouveau riche class of westerners with considerable surplus wealth. As a few millionaires amassed their colossal fortunes from the new transportation and extractive industries, they also secured the necessary seed money to sponsor philanthropic endeavors. But like their more recognizable eastern peers, they too yearned for a more systematic approach to the allocation of their charitable dollars. During the early decades of the 20th century, several wealthy individuals and families therefore established private foundations for scientific, religious, educational, and cultural purposes.

Like the omissions of the older western history, writers and scholars alike have characterized philanthropy, especially the founding and managing of grant-making organizations, as essentially a male preserve. Histories of well-known philanthropists such as Andrew Carnegie and John D. Rockefeller Sr. and their public gifts have been abundant. But similar to their 19th-century sisters, elite white women who practiced organized philanthropy have been virtually absent from traditional accounts. They seldom gained credit for their use of capital as a tool to leverage important social changes. Raised with a sharp sense of noblesse oblige, the typical "lady bountiful" was recognized more for her charitable service than for her institutional giving. She organized fund-raisers, volunteered in schools, and attended charity balls. Constrained by law, custom, and economic status, she encountered numerous disabilities that restricted her full participation in the public sector. Women therefore rarely were seen as donors, that is, creators of foundations.

Gradually, however, as early 20th-century women gained control over their estates, a few established charitable foundations as repositories for their surplus wealth. But female philanthropy remained the province of white, Anglo-Saxon, Protestant donors, at least until after mid-century. Few women of color such as Mexican Americans or blacks had amassed large holdings or controlled sufficient assets to establish grant-making organizations. Low wages, few opportunities, and inadequate education consigned them to positions of recipients rather than grant-makers. In addition, alternative patterns of giving, as well as discrimination, segregation, and poverty, precluded their participation in organized philanthropy. Rather than utilizing institutional tools such as foundations and endowments, Hispanics traditionally donated funds through their *mutualistas* and churches. African American women, legally separated from mainstream institutions since 1896, also adopted a more traditional, personal approach; they supported local religious groups and created black self-help organizations. Thus, philanthropic foundations created by women in the American West remained largely white, elitist institutions.

As women of wealth began to exercise their newfound independence, they also acquired a wide range of opportunities to dispose of their surplus income, including the creation of philanthropic organizations. Like their male counterparts, female donors possessed a highly developed concept of effective philanthropy that targeted the underlying causes of major social problems. As Margaret Sage, the foremost female philanthropist of her time, observed in 1905: "Women are bound by every law of morality to find a beneficent outlet for their powers." Furthermore, she advised that they should devote their talents "to the amelioration of the condition of her laboring sisters." As a result, women of the American West began to leverage their financial resources, whether through marriage, careers, or inheritance, to attain specific social goals. Many elites accomplished this task by independently establishing general-purpose foundations. For example, in 1935 Ellen Browning Scripps, a wealthy California newspaper heiress, supported scientific initiatives through the creation of a private foundation. As both a grant-making and operating organization, it helped finance the Scripps Institute of Oceanography and the Scripps Clinic and Research Foundation for Bio-Medical Research. In 1940 Ima Hogg, the wealthy daughter of Texas Governor Jim Hogg, concentrated on the prevention rather than the treatment of mental illness with the creation of the Hogg Foundation for Mental Health. And Grayce B. Kerr created the Kerr Foundation in 1964 to support the needs of farm and ranch families in Oklahoma.

Western women also formed philanthropic partnerships with their spouses to establish foundations. Sometimes their designation as codonor was in name only or to honor their memory. But many times wives and daughters played central roles as active founders or behind-the-scenes participants. For instance, in 1937 Mary Gibbs Jones, the quiet, retiring wife of New Deal administrator Jesse H. Jones, helped create the Houston Endowment to provide scholarships to worthy men and women of all races to complete their education. Her greatest joys, she later explained, "came from the charities they planned together," especially those benefiting education, health care, and children. From the revenues of one of the nation's most successful independent oil and gas production companies, Virginia and Algur Meadows formed their foundation in 1948. Defined broadly, its purpose was to assist the people and institutions of Texas. That same year, Lottie J. Mabee also aided her husband, John, a prosperous businessman who had struck it rich in the oil fields, in organizing their philanthropy—the Mabee Foundation. Created to support brick-and-mortar construction for established institutions such as colleges, hospitals, and social service organizations, it provided grants to benefit those states from which their millions came—namely, Oklahoma, Texas, Kansas, Arkansas, Missouri, and New Mexico.

In some cases, women supported organized philanthropy through the establishment of a second, subsidiary fund to an established foundation. Margarett Brown, a prominent patron of the arts and music in Houston, left her residual assets to the Brown Foundation, established by her husband in 1951. Ima Hogg set up an independent fund from her sizeable estate upon her death in 1975 to benefit the children of Houston and Harris County. And Lottie Mabee also bequeathed the remainder of her financial holdings following her death to the Mabee Foundation.

In collective philanthropic organizations, women also played an active role. Most noteworthy was the creation in 1948 of the Conference of Southwest Foundations (CSF), dedicated to the collaboration, interaction, and fellowship among its membership. Composed initially of donors from grant-making institutions in Texas, the organization later expanded to include regional representation from Arkansas, Oklahoma, Arizona, and New Mexico. Pioneered by Mary Elizabeth Holdsworth Butt, Margaret Scarbrough, and Robert Sutherland, director of the Hogg Foundation, the CSF was the first formal, cooperative community of philanthropists in the United States. Mary Butt, a member of a devout Baptist tithing family, was an unusual social activist of her day, who lobbied as an advocate for the health and educational needs of South Texas families. Margaret Scarbrough, also an energetic civic volunteer, helped establish with her husband an early Texas foundation. Together, they spearheaded a unique and powerful force for organized philanthropy, serving the needs of the people of the Southwest.

The feminization and professionalization of foundation management served as an additional avenue for women to exert their philanthropic influence. Often they shaped the scope and focus of mission statements by promoting traditional values of female giving such as education, children, health care, and the arts. At the same time, women pursued careers as philanthropic professionals, taking roles as program directors, board members, and executive officers. Many female family members, such as Mary Northen Moody, chair of the Moody Foundation (1942) of Galveston, and Ruth Carter Johnson, trustee and president of the Amon Carter Foundation (1945) in Fort Worth, assumed leadership positions within private foundations following the death of the founder. Others served board terms along with their spouses, such as Flora Hewlett of the Hewlett Foundation (1966), which concentrated its grant-making on projects in the western United States and the San Francisco Bay Area. Still others fashioned careers for themselves in the foundation world. Janice Kreamer and Mary Jalonick headed community foundations in Kansas City and Dallas. Anne Morgan, once head of the Kerr Foundation, served as an adviser to prospective donors and their families. And Maud Keeling, executive secretary-director of the Conference of Southwest Foundations, provided 47 years of uninterrupted service to that regional association.

More recently, several "women's funds" have evolved in many western states. Their purpose has been to sponsor innovative programs for women and girls that have been neglected by traditional funding sources. Usually, multiple donors, particularly professionals and females with inherited wealth, have contributed to such initiatives. One such outgrowth of efforts to improve the personal, economic, and professional status of women has been the Foundation for Women's Resources headquartered in Austin, Texas. Two of its largest projects have been Leadership Texas—a training ground for future female state leaders—and the Women's Museum, which opened in Dallas in 2002.

In the last 20 years, women, as members of family foundations, have created some of the largest philanthropic endowments with assets in the millions. In fact, western private foundations have accounted for the largest proportion of independent funding resources by region. Much of the wealth has stemmed from a new Gilded Age, resulting from advances in technology, media, and retailing. For example, Helen and Sam Walton launched the Walton Family Foundation in 1987 from Arkansas to support K-12 education and child development.

From their numerous successful business ventures, Bessie Mae and Albert Kronkosky organized in 1991 their charitable foundation to benefit several counties in south central Texas. Then in 1994 Melinda and Bill Gates established their charitable fund—the largest in the nation by assets. Located in Washington State, the Gates Foundation sponsors national educational initiatives and global health projects derived from their enormous profits in the Silicon Valley.

Female giving, however, has not been without rancor, especially when their estates have been sizeable. Their magnanimity has been subject to the same challenges, criticisms, and allegations directed at some male-sponsored institutions. One of the most famous cases in modern philanthropic history was the Buck Trust, established in 1975 by Beryl Buck for "non-profit, charitable, religious or educational purposes" in Marin County, California. Bequeathed to the San Francisco Foundation, a community trust, the fund dramatically increased in value, surpassing the needs of one of the nation's richest counties. As a result, a long court battle ensued, led by neighboring areas seeking to alter the founder's original intent and share in the donor's largess. Although the legal impasse was eventually broken when the foundation agreed to spend some of the Buck Trust income outside the county, the case revealed that female beneficence was not immune to political and legal wrangling. At the same time, the ruling reinforced one of the basic tenets of organized philanthropy—the right of wealthy patrons to designate the recipients of their wealth, in this case, the native community of the founder.

Although donors and their circumstances vary as much as the region itself, female philanthropy in the American West did not differ substantially from elsewhere in the nation. The activities and experiences of western women typified national development. Like their eastern sisters, they too utilized organized philanthropy to fashion an alternative sphere for social change. By conceiving, guiding, and helping fund philanthropic organizations, women were able to assume a rare autonomy at a time when socially constructed roles for the sexes prevailed. At the same time, they identified critical problems, acquired important public skills, and exercised a modicum of power and influence. Furthermore, once engaged in philanthropy, they usually were active donors, bringing an enlarged social consciousness and a unique set of values to their commitments, such as female education, child care, and health issues. Motivated by altruism and devotion to their community, women also turned to large-scale philanthropy as a sound financial investment—one that would protect their assets and reduce their tax burden. Thus, elite women in the American West modeled earlier national trends, utilizing their philanthropic vision, financial resources, and business acumen to promote social, cultural, and educational reform through private foundations.

So as the new millennium commences, as more and more women accumulate wealth from the emerging information and computer technology age, and as many baby boomers prepare for the largest generational transfer of wealth, the western United States is uniquely positioned to create unprecedented philanthropic capital. Moreover, many of the same issues and values articulated by female philanthropy—child welfare, health care, and environmental concerns—are once again at the center of public debate—as is the very nature of the American West. Recognition of the active and significant role of women in the development of institutional philanthropy helps broaden the stereotypical images of western women. Whether and how they leverage their private wealth for the public good is one of the major questions for the 21st century.

—Mary L. Kelley

SUGGESTED READINGS

Kelley, Mary L. *Private Wealth, Public Good: The Origins and Legacy of Foundation Philanthropy in Texas, 1920-1970.* Ph.D. dissertation. Texas Christian University, Fort Worth, Texas, 2000.

McCarthy, Kathleen D., ed. *Lady Bountiful Revisited: Women, Philanthropy, and Power.* New Brunswick, NJ: Rutgers University Press, 1990.

Nielsen, Waldemar. *Inside American Philanthropy: The Dramas of Donorship.* Norman: University of Oklahoma Press, 1972.

Nielsen, Waldemar. *The Golden Donors: A New Anatomy of the Great Foundations.* New York: Columbia University Press, 1972.

Odendahl, Teresa. *Charity Begins at Home: Generosity and Self-Interest Among the Philanthropic Elite.* New York: Basic Books, 1990.

Philanthropy in the Southwest. Austin, TX: The Hogg Foundation for Mental Health, 1965.

Sage, Margaret Olivia. "Opportunities and Responsibilities of Leisured Women." *North American Review 181* (April 1913): 103-108.

Schlegell, Abbie J. von, and Joan M. Fisher. *Women as Donors, Women as Philanthropists (New Directions for Philanthropic Fundraising, Series No. 2)*. New York: Jossey-Bass, 1993.

Schlissel, Lillian, Vicki L. Ruiz, and Janice Monk, eds. *Western Women: Their Land, Their Lives*. Albuquerque: University of New Mexico Press, 1988.

PHILLIPS, VIRGINIA A. (1957-)

Judge Virginia Phillips was born in Orange, California. She received her bachelor's degree from the University of California, Riverside, in 1979. Later Virginia attended the University of California, Berkeley, and Boalt Hall School of Law, graduating in 1982.

After graduation, Phillips returned to Riverside and went into private practice there from 1982 until 1991. She held the position of commissioner of the Riverside Superior Court from 1991 until 1995. From 1995 until 1999, she held the position of U.S. magistrate of the U.S. District Court for the Central District of California.

On January 26, 1999, President Bill Clinton nominated Phillips to a seat on the U.S. District Court for the Central District of California. She was confirmed by the Senate on November 10, 1999, and received her commission on November 15, 1999. She continues her work in the same district today.

—Brenda Bitgood

SUGGESTED READINGS

Kennedy, Ruth A. ed. *The American Bench: Judges of the Nation, 1997/1998* (9th ed.). Sacramento, CA: Forster-Long, 1997.

Virginia A. Phillips. Retrieved from air.fjc.gov/newweb/jnetweb.nsf/fjc_bio. Source: History of the Federal Judiciary. http://www.fjc.gov. Web site of the Federal Judicial Center, Washington, D.C.

PLEASANT, MARY ELLEN (1814-1904)

Mary Ellen Pleasant is one of the most colorful characters of California history. A determined woman who valued education and freedom, Mary Ellen, born into slavery, dreamed of equality for her people. She used her wits and her strikingly good looks to achieve her goal, as well as further herself financially and socially. Mary Ellen's story is full of mystery and deceit, as well as accomplishment and generosity.

Mary was born a slave in a plantation near Augusta, Georgia. She was the product of an illegitimate affair between her light-skinned slave mother and a Virginia planter. When she was 10, the plantation owner had decided to send Mary's rebellious mother away. Before her departure, she told Mary her father's name and that she was part of a long line of voodoo queens from Santo Domingo. Her mother instructed Mary to carry herself with pride and to keep a lookout for all visitors. If she could catch the eye of a white gentleman, perhaps he would be willing to buy the beautiful girl and save her from a hard life in the fields. Mary's mother told her that light-skinned girls such as herself could be sent to the quadroon balls in New Orleans, where she would be chosen as a mistress for a planter's son.

Armed with this information, Mary set a constant vigilance on the country road, waiting for the chance to catch the eye of a visitor. One day, she spied a rider and ran out on the chance that the man might need directions. Americus Price stared at the slave who held her head up with confidence as she gave him detailed directions. A few days after the encounter, Mary learned that her owner had sold her to Price for $600 and that she was to meet him in New Orleans.

Once in New Orleans, Mary learned from Price that she was not to go to his plantation. He had decided that a bright girl like Mary needed to be educated. Since it was illegal to educate a slave, Price made arrangements for Mary to enter a convent where the nuns there would tutor her in private. After a year, he sent Mary to Cincinnati to live with his friends Mr. and Mrs. Louis Alexander Williams. There she would attend an endowed school to continue her studies as well as wait on Mrs. Williams. Because Mary could easily pose as a Creole with her light skin, Price instructed her not to let anyone know of her colored blood.

The day after Mary arrived in Cincinnati, Williams, a wealthy silk importer, went off on a trip. Mary remained behind with the childless Ellen Williams, who treated the girl as her daughter. When Williams returned from his trip, Mary was harshly sent to live with the servants, where she learned that Price had died.

Furthermore, Williams had pocketed the money Price had provided for Mary's education. Mrs. Williams did not dare interfere with her husband's actions, although she cried as if separated from her own child when Mary was taken to New England. There Williams sold her as a bond servant to a Quaker woman named Mary Hussey. Here on Nantucket Island Mary took on the name of Mary Ellen Williams in honor of the woman who had treated her as her own child. Mary Ellen stayed on the island until the age of 24, when the aged Mrs. Hussey died.

Mary Ellen then traveled to Boston, where she took a job as a seamstress in a tailor shop. Here she first saw James W. Smith, part Cuban, who owned a tobacco plantation in West Virginia and whom she would eventually marry. He owned a profitable plantation where all the workers were paid former slaves. Smith was an abolitionist, and together with Mary Ellen they worked tirelessly, helping slaves escape to Canada through the underground railroad. James Smith died in 1844 after asking Mary Ellen to use a part of his fortune to carry on their abolitionist work.

Even before Smith's death, Mary Ellen had been planning to marry the almost white freedman, John James Plaissance. He took his former owner's name of Pleasants as his own. Mary Ellen, knowing the Virginian planter to be her father, had married John in order to obtain the name that was rightly hers. After the marriage, John took his wife to meet Marie Laveau, voodoo queen of New Orleans. Mary Ellen's intentions were to learn as much as she could from Laveau, who had all of New Orleans at her feet through an intricate network of blackmail and fear, which spread through both the black and white populations. While studying the art of manipulation, as well as of cooking, Mary Ellen sent John to California. She did not follow him until her abolitionist activities had drawn too much attention and she needed to escape capture.

Once in San Francisco in the early 1850s, Mary Ellen continued her role as a white housekeeper. She found a growing city perfect for her plans. The city was where thieves, gamblers, and murderers came looking for a fresh start, a city where these men of once questionable reputations would rise to the top and become tomorrow's social and financial elite. Mary Ellen intended to learn every skeleton hidden in every closet of San Francisco in order to ensure her own rise to the top. Looking around at the young city, she envisioned a status of equality for her people,

which she alone would give. All of San Francisco would either fear her or be eternally grateful to her. She would own the city as well as a house on the hill.

Right away Mary Ellen began to weave her web. She obtained a job as a housekeeper where she gained access to several men of prestige. Using her connections, she placed grateful former slaves into critical positions where they could serve as her operatives. She found her white protégés, whom she had a strong hold over, wealthy husbands. She also invested her money in profitable stables, saloons, and three laundries. She played the stock market through information she gathered around the dining table as she served her employers. Although it would take years, Mary Ellen was slowly tightening her grip around San Francisco.

Once she felt the time was right, Mary Ellen revealed her black heritage. She took this opportunity to establish herself as the voodoo queen of San Francisco. From Laveau, she had learned that voodoo could be used to control not only the black population but the white as well. Mary Ellen promised prominent white men an exotic night in a remote cottage. The men would participate, along with Mary Ellen's quadroons, in the final rites of the voodoo ceremony that ended in an orgy. These men paid their hostess to keep their adventures quiet.

Mary Ellen created her network of blackmail through elaborate schemes, many of which only she understood. Although she manipulated a number of people, her two favorite puppets were Thomas Bell, who with her help became one of the wealthiest men in San Francisco, and her protégé, Theresa Percy, who later became Mrs. Bell. The often-deranged triangle these three formed caused the city to wonder about the true nature of their relationships. Even though Mary Ellen had a relentless hold on both Bell and Percy, her manipulation of their lives eventually caused her economic and social downfall.

As cunning and ruthless as Mary Ellen was, she was still generous and giving of her money. She could have easily been the wealthiest person in all of California if not for the fact that she continuously gave it away to help her race gain a status of equality. The ruthless woman continued her abolitionist activities. She even traveled to Canada to meet with John Brown and helped rally slaves throughout the South, although she felt his plan was doomed to fail.

Perhaps one of the most important acts of civil rights heroism of the 19th century belonged to Mary

Ellen. She was the plaintiff in the 1868 Trolley Car case that resulted in the desegregation of the trolley car system in the Bay Area. Not willing to accept the humiliation of being thrown off a car because she was black, she filed, funded, and persisted in a lawsuit that changed the lives of African Americans in the Bay Area.

On January 11, 1904, Mary Ellen Pleasant, or "Mammy," as she was also known, died of old age. Behind her she left a legacy of mystery and suspicion that critics remember more often than her generosity and efforts toward the equalization of her people.

—Michelle L. Oropeza

SUGGESTED READINGS

Bibbs, Susheel. *The Legacies of Mary Ellen Pleasant— Mother of Human Rights in California*. San Francisco: MEP Productions, 1998.

Holdredge, Helen. *Mammy Pleasant*. New York: Putnam, 1953.

Holdredge, Helen. *Mammy Pleasant's Partner*. New York: Putnam, 1954.

Holdredge, Helen. *Mammy Pleasant's Cookbook*. San Francisco: 101 Productions, 1970.

Riley, Glenda, and Richard Etulain. *By Grit and Grace: Eleven Women Who Shaped the American West*. Golden, CO: Fulcrum Press, 1997.

PRIEST, IVY BAKER (1905-1975)

Ivy Baker was born in Kimberly, Utah, in 1905 into a poor mining family. Her father, Orange Baker, mined gold and copper. When his mine petered out, they moved to Coalville, then to Bingham Canyon. Her mother, Clara Baker nee Fernley, opened their home in Bingham as a boarding house.

Ivy's mother provided the impetus to her daughter's future political aspirations. Ivy witnessed her mother's successful efforts in the election of their family physician, Dr. Straupp, to the office of mayor of Bingham. Her mother had become frustrated with the poor condition of the streets in their Utah town and traded her support for Dr. Straupp for his promise to improve them upon his election.

Ivy began pursuing leadership roles in high school. Her first foray into politics occurred in 1932 when she was a delegate to the Republican Convention. She continued her political career throughout her marriage to Roy F. Priest in 1935 and the birth of their three children.

Priest began serving as a Republican National Committeewoman in 1944 and continued doing so until 1950. In 1952 she was in charge of the women's division of the Republican National Committee and successfully helped to acquire women voters for Dwight Eisenhower. These voters accounted for over half of President Eisenhower's victory margin. In 1953 she became the second woman appointed to the office of U.S. Treasurer. She served the Eisenhower administration through 1961.

In 1966 she and her family moved to California. She pursued her career there by becoming the first woman to hold the office of California State treasurer. Governor Ronald Reagan reappointed her to the position in 1970. Her long-lived political career ended when she succumbed to cancer in 1975.

—Lori S. Iacovelli

SUGGESTED READINGS

Papers of Ivy Baker Priest and Orange Decatur, University of Utah, Special Collections.

Utah State Historical Society. "Utah History to Go." Retrieved on March 25, 2002, from www.utahhistory-togo.org.

Whitney, Colleen. *Worth Their Salt: Notable but Often Unnoted Women of Utah*. Logan: Utah State University Press, 1996.

PROSTITUTION

The 19th-century American West proved a hospitable, if tumultuous, environment for women seeking employment as prostitutes. Yet traditionally such women have been relegated to the margins of western history, considered to be either unimportant or too difficult to find in the historical record. More recent assessments that explore the patterns of the women's West suggest that prostitutes, workers in the emergence of western America, should be more central to the narrative.

Definitions of prostitution tend to focus on its commercial nature. Prostitution is typically described as an action by which one or more persons, for a monetary sum or material goods, engage in sexual activity with a customer or a series of customers. To be a prostitute one does not need to work exclusively at this trade, may hold some other job, and may drift in and out of prostitution over a period of several years. Although the occupation is not gender specific, women are usually considered the principal employees. This definition avoids moral judgments, transcends time and place, and is applicable in a nearly universal fashion.

In the American West, although the institution did not differ dramatically from other locations, regional circumstances, particularly in the 19th century, made this a useful region for study of the institution. In each of its distinct regions, particularly after 1800, the West, with its shallow social, economic, and political infrastructure, harbored conditions conducive to prostitution. These conditions included volatile and destructive cultural contacts, lopsided power relations and population demographics between men and women, fiscal instability in western industries, and poor management of military personnel at both urban and rural garrisons. In this scenario, prostitutes, as women who lived beyond acceptable gender roles, wielded little authority; their personal power was highly individualized and largely dependent on how well they could negotiate their local western circumstances.

During these years, widely labeled as the Frontier era, western "types" appear easy to identify. Western towns, thrown up in haste, were not very large. The locals easily demarcated the residential neighborhoods, saloon districts, and business areas, as well as the inhabitants of each. Miners, cowboys, soldiers—all could be spotted on city streets. This also proved true for prostitutes, usually noticeable for their unconventional attire and employment along the vice corridor. Town residents felt comfortable labeling prostitutes with a number of popular sobriquets: "daughters of the night," "soiled doves," "old blisters," "fille de Joie," "lewd women," "denizens of the demimonde," and the areas they lived as "the Bottoms," "Gunnell Hill," or "the Line."

Despite these unilateral terms, within prostitution all women were not ranked equally, and, as in all professions, some workers secured the better positions. Those who lived inside a brothel, overseen by a madam and possibly protected by the local law officers, were considered to hold the more desirable jobs. Residence in a brothel could mean decent living

accommodations, improved diet, more reliable salary, and safer surroundings. At the same time, the house overhead cut into profits if the owner employed domestics, musicians, and maintenance staff. Customers paid their fees directly to the madam, who doled out prostitute wages after subtracting the tariff for the payroll. A second tier of prostitutes worked in saloons as dance hall girls. They might live above the bar, but they often rented rooms or small houses away from the saloon district and reported for work, as would an employee in any job. Their duties included dancing with customers, pushing drinks, and accepting sexual clients. Streetwalkers and cribs residents, tenants in back-alley shanties, were usually the older or more unhealthy women, working under the least stable circumstances, where they made a small wage and enjoyed little or no safety.

The boundaries between these categories were quite flexible, and an individual woman might drift in and out of each, depending on where she was working at a particular time. There were other variations on the sociogram as well. For example, a woman might operate by herself out of a single hotel room, dependent on local hack drivers or desk clerks to send her customers. However, unlike most occupations, where longevity suggested greater prestige and remuneration, in prostitution the opposite was true, as an older woman, unless the owner of brothel property or employed as an abortionist, generally moved down in status, rather than up.

In all parts of the West, women of color endured added problems. In the mid-1800s, many Chinese women were duped into leaving their homeland for the San Francisco brothels, where a powerful hierarchy controlled prostitution. Seclusion within the Chinese community, scorn from the Anglo citizenry, and nearly insurmountable language barriers made it exceedingly difficult for these women to break away from prostitution or the agents who had arranged their transport. By the 1870s, a fairly small number of Chinese prostitutes could be found in Colorado, Wyoming, Utah, and Nevada. When the Chinese community began to spread into the Rocky Mountain West, journalistic and political attacks on these prostitutes, said to be a danger to the health of white American males, intensified, the vilification peaking with passage of the Chinese Exclusion Act in 1882. As the patterns of Chinese immigration shifted to a family model, prostitution lessened in all areas of the West.

Squirrel Tooth Alice, a prostitute in Dodge City, Kansas, reflected the young age of many brothel employees.

Source: Kansas State Historical Society, Topeka, Kansas.

In Texas, New Mexico, Arizona, and California, some Mexican and Mexican American women worked as prostitutes. Whether by virtue of poverty or personal choice, Mexican American prostitutes did not move to other western locations in great numbers. They generally remained around the centers of Mexican American life in the Southwest. The dynamics of their lives in these areas were shaded by a sharp division between the poor and the rich, a split hardly recognized by an advancing community of Anglos. The result was a triangle of cultural tensions, further aggravated by the Anglos' highly unflattering assessments of Hispanic women, often labeling all as prostitutes. That cultural phenomenon, shaped by various forms of racism and sexism, concerns issues outside prostitution.

Native American women also had a long history of negative stereotyping by Anglo men. With little regard for the sexual customs of Native people, men from outsider societies looked on all Indian women as "promiscuous." In fact, the earliest histories of Native people suggest there was little evidence of prostitution within indigenous groups. A population of Native prostitutes, which congregated around military garrisons, developed with the building of rural military camps and the rise of the reservation system. As Indian people faced ever-increasing economic constraints and exclusion from work or educational opportunities within white society, some women were encouraged to add to family earnings through prostitution with soldiers and traders.

African American women, especially after the Civil War, also worked as prostitutes in the American West. Most of these were very young and illiterate. It is possible that jobbers, much like the Chinese agents, transported black women in large groups to serve as prostitutes to the military. The initial targets to be clients were the famed Buffalo Soldiers, an African American cavalry unit, making it possible for black men to buy sex from black women. It appears, however, that African American women, although often at the "hog ranches" near an army fort, also moved into western urban areas. Black men exercised some caution as to which brothels they frequented, but white customers appeared to have no hesitation about patronizing a house with variety in its racial composition.

Perhaps most interesting, racial segregation among the women in the brothels and on the hog ranches blurred in several locations. Nineteenth-century Denver, Laramie, and Cheyenne all had racially mixed brothels. Some of the young black women may have been hired as domestic help, but were expected to provide the sexual service to African American patrons. In 1881 Laramie there was at least one case of a black prostitute nursing her white companion through a terminal illness.

In this mixed society, the profession was crowded and the competition keen. Although an exact tally remains elusive, it is possible that as many as 50,000 women worked as prostitutes in the 19th-century West. Among them could be found foreign immigrants, American-born migrants, and indigenous women, all from groups that contributed to the annals of the West. Thus, western prostitution cannot be separated from the economic and social history of the region.

The bonanza patterns associated with various male-dominated industrial booms—mining, herding, railroading, and lumbering—all had an impact on prostitution. Western employment opportunities were distinctly masculine, but prostitution gave women a way to infiltrate the boom towns as "auxiliary" workers, indirectly seeking to benefit from the regional industrial ventures. Prostitutes gravitated quickly toward any of these bachelor communities, where men living outside traditional family circles represented an accessible and accommodating supply of customers. The women seldom put down deep roots, always ready to depart quickly for the next rumored gold strike or to avoid an unpleasant encounter with the local law enforcement agency. In general, the life was shabby, unpredictable, and expensive, in both financial and personal terms.

Unlike the stereotypical view of the lonely young woman living by herself in an opulent "house of ill repute," prostitutes quite commonly married and had children. Turbulence marked many of these domestic relationships. Men and women married in haste. The families relocated on a regular basis, often moving several times inside one town. Husbands and wives were frequently apart for long periods, chasing employment hopes about the West. While husbands, perhaps a barkeep or a miner, expected their prostitute wives to contribute to the family income, volatile emotions often overtook the relationship. A spouse supervising a wife at work in a saloon might be stricken with a sudden burst of jealousy, especially when fueled by generous amounts of alcohol.

In any case, it was the woman who was most at risk, as an angry husband turned violent. Beatings were common, as was death. For example, in Deadwood, South Dakota, an enraged Curley LeRoy, after pummeling his wife, shot and killed her and himself over her supposed affections for another man. The following day, Curley and Kitty LeRoy, husband and wife, were laid out side by side in the saloon bedroom where the violence had occurred.

Wives were also known to attack their partners. They often lived in an environment, whether at home or at work, where both verbal and physical abuse were common. Sooner or later, domestic violence engulfed both partners. Such was the case for Irene Kent, a seamstress and prostitute, who with her husband operated a brothel in Tucumcari, New Mexico. After a long day that started with a picnic but evolved into unbroken drinking and fighting, the two, wrestling in a narrow hallway of their home, struggled over his gun, which discharged, killing him instantly. Western courts were not inclined to look on such episodes in a lenient manner for prostitutes, and Irene Kent served several years in the New Mexico penitentiary.

Although communities often expressed horror over these accounts of marital discord, they did little to recognize those marriages grounded in devotion. Newspapers were given to scoffing at a surviving spouse, grief-stricken and desperately seeking burial funds. If that survivor was a prostitute, the public seemed to assume that, just as she, by her occupation, had abandoned the standards of "true womanhood," it was impossible for her to feel the sentiments of a widow.

The children of prostitutes typically stayed with their mothers in prostitution. Girls of 12 or 13 were

Bell Warden operated a Denver brothel and a hairdressing business.

Source: Colorado Historical Society, Denver, Colorado.

Wyoming, with her 9-year-old daughter, Hattie. Eight years later, Mollie was still being arrested for prostitution and drunk and disorderly behavior, as was her daughter, now 17 years of age.

Opportunities for women to extricate themselves from prostitution were limited. Poor women with minimal education found jobs as milliners, seamstresses, waitresses, and laundresses. Long hours of work resulted in meager wages, encouraging some to engage in prostitution on a part-time basis. In this way, prostitutes structured a dual role as wage earners—on the one hand, supporting themselves through their "legitimate" skills, on the other, supplementing their scant income through vice. The chances to retrain or to move up the occupational ladder were few, as the social services that would have provided that type of education did not exist to any significant degree.

Clearly, some women succeeded in maintaining themselves financially, at least for a time, in prostitution. Regardless of the wages they secured, however, all prostitutes contended with an unending list of spiraling fees. Landlords were known to charge a prostitute double rent for a dingy dwelling in the poorest section of town. In addition to overpriced housing expenses, women paid regular fines in justice of the peace courts for a variety of offenses—maintaining a house of ill fame, residing in such a place, drunk and disorderly, public intoxication. If not faced with these charges on a weekly basis, a woman was slipping regular bribe money to the sheriff or constable in exchange for escaping the

known to inhabit brothels, encouraged by their prostitute/madam parent to do so. In this world, young women encountered a home life shaped by transient customers, a lack of nutritional diet, and irregular work hours. For example, in 1880 Mollie Severe, an African American prostitute, settled in Cheyenne,

Saturday night dragnet. Some towns arrested women, convicted them, and then turned them back to the streets to earn their court fine.

Customers were usually out of the same working class and had little cash to offer in exchange for sex, nor were they particularly interested in doing so. Arrangements for payment were negotiated typically after both parties had consumed considerable alcohol and each wanted to "best" the other on the price. In this economic environment, it is not surprising that many of the women turned to thievery to increment their meager salaries, and as a result, many spent time in the local jail or state penitentiary.

Western prostitutes also had a well-developed relationship with the frontier army. Although the designation "camp follower" suggests that women pursued the troops on their own initiative, such was not necessarily the case. Prostitutes traveled about the frontier with military protection, and daily orders often included the warning that only the official military laundresses could be given food. Once the troops arrived at the fort location, the women moved into a rough dwelling at the edge of the military reservation. These hog ranches thrown up by the soldiers became magnets for off-duty personnel. In addition, given their proximity to the post, prostitutes slipped on and off the garrison property with ease. The post trader, a civilian who ran the sutler's store, often housed one or two prostitutes at his establishment. The sutler, an army appointee, lived on the military grounds, making it difficult for officers to deny they had any knowledge of prostitution at their command.

It was common for small towns to spring up 3 or 4 miles from a post. Soldiers and officers were known to frequent these, despite directives that they were off limits. At Fort Union, New Mexico, Mexican farmers came to the post each week to sell fruit and vegetables, bringing along prostitutes and gamblers, according to the post surgeon. These activities, like similar ones at Fort Randall in the Dakota Territory and Fort Fauntleroy, also in New Mexico, showed the way that indigenous women were drawn into prostitution, when U.S. troops came into an area. The uneven economic and political situation encouraged soldiers and Native people alike to exploit each other through human sexuality. These garrison situations illuminated the patterns of rural prostitution, where isolation and gender imbalance became the catalysts for organizing prostitution.

Regardless of the type of working situation, all prostitutes—even the few well-to-do madams—lived under a shadow of violence. The women passed their years pushed to the margins of society. Even when their lives became more public than private, they rarely held a solid place in a community. They were not well positioned for life-saving intervention by the authorities when danger erupted. In the most "prestigious" bordellos, physical attack was as swift and surprising as in the poorest back-alley crib. Even the prominent Mattie Silks of Denver, reputed to be wealthy and elegant, experienced considerable violence in her personal and professional life. She was said to carry a gun at all times, and some of the most colorful stories about her center on her public inebriation. Within the vice district, regardless of occupational status, danger was sudden, multifaceted, and of interest to the town after the fact.

Prostitutes and madams faced violence, both personal and accidental, from customers. Fights broke out in brothels and saloons, men produced weapons, and mayhem followed. More than one young woman happened to be in the line of fire, killed by chance. On other occasions, the violence was personal and directed unexpectedly at a woman, such as Kitty LeRoy. Prostitutes also participated in the violence of their customers against other men, helping to lure a victim to an attack.

Prostitutes encountered violence from each other. While some prostitutes spent their work years as friends, looking out for one another, the opposite was also true. Friendships could be transitory, as women moved from one locale to another. Some were not averse to stealing from a companion, taking a few clothing items or a satchel, and heading for the train out of town. More seriously, the women did turn on each other in physical fights. Some of these were public brawls, where saloon patrons cheered on the combatants. Others occurred in "party" situations, but again alcohol consumption clouded the exchange, arguments began, and one woman shot, stabbed, or beat another to death.

Perhaps the most disastrous violence came from what the women inflicted on themselves. Alcoholism and drug addiction pervaded the vice district. Women only in their 20s were identified in local newspapers as "hopeless drunks." More than one woman combined the use of beer and the narcotic laudanum, a deadly concoction. Some deaths were accidental, but deliberate suicide also took the lives of many young women.

Convicted of murdering a brothel customer, Bell Warden was sentenced to 10 years in the Colorado penitentiary.

Source: Division of State Archives and Public Records, Denver, Colorado.

Given these various circumstances, as well as their employment in an "outlawed" profession, prostitutes had frequent contact with law enforcement officers. In some locations, these officers straddled the legal line, ignoring prostitution activities one day and apprehending prostitutes the next. The duty of the sheriff to collect town taxes from saloons and gambling halls put residents of the vice district at a disadvantage. Few checks existed to track the collection process, allowing an officer to demand one fee for the civic treasury and one fee for himself. Most citizens ignored these practices, content to leave regulation of local vice to the sheriff and the courts. With so little accountability, those charged with municipal oversight manipulated prostitution and gambling as they wished. Some acquired a shady reputation for their behavior, such as John Behan in Tombstone, Arizona. Some, like Wyatt Earp of Dodge City, Kansas, and Jim Clark of Telluride, Colorado, lived on both sides of the law, their attitudes about prostitution difficult to unravel. Others, such as the legendary Sam Howe of Denver, Colorado, compiled an impressive record in building law and order for a western municipality.

Western courts also built complex relationships with prostitutes. Most prostitutes came before the local justice of the peace, an individual with limited legal training. Charged with the responsibility to manage the implementation of local laws, most western justices of the peace developed complementary relationships with the arresting officers. In the area of vice, the justice and the officer enjoyed considerable latitude in towns that wanted vice controlled, not eliminated. The officials decided at will which violators would be arrested and which would be ignored. This broad authority encouraged madams and prostitutes with some dollars to pay their regular protection money, while those with fewer resources, especially women of color, faced a routine of weekly or bimonthly arrest. For example, Sophie Rickard, a prostitute in Laramie, Wyoming, was arrested at least 35 times in approximately a 5-year period, during which she was trying to maintain a "legitimate" seamstress business, conducted out of her shack by the railroad tracks.

Although experiences in the courts could be disheartening—women turned over fines or spent a month in the city jail—prostitutes were able to carve some presence for themselves before the bar. The usual space of civic conduct—schools, businesses, churches—were not welcoming to prostitutes. The courts, however, represented an arena in which they were experienced. They knew the personnel, the routines, and they learned some of the procedures. The women were not hesitant about coming to the courts. On occasion, they came seeking protection or complaining about a neighbor or threatening to sue a madam for back wages.

The courts also showed themselves ready to exploit the relationship with prostitutes. The criminal charges the women faced helped communities to build their infrastructure and convince themselves of the burgeoning strength of their institutions. The "respectable" could feel that law was suppressing the most "wild" elements of the West. On the other hand, the courts used prostitutes as players in the evolving record of law. The women gave important testimony in cases of homicide or suicide. Eyewitnesses to murderous events, prostitutes found that their illegal behaviors could be ignored in exchange for contributing to the legal process. In this way, just as the women created dual employment roles for themselves—one legal and one illegal—so too did the courts define them as citizens or criminals in matters of investigation or prosecution.

In general, western towns had little desire to eliminate houses of prostitution. Saloons, gambling houses, theaters, and brothels were seen as the necessary ingredients for attracting the male workforce of the West. Cowboys after a long drive, railroad crews fresh from the rails, miners in from the claim—all came with money for the town coffers. Providing them these vice inducements made good business sense to frontier competitors. Ironically, like the prostitutes who greeted them, these western working-class men found their welcome had worn thin once their money had been spent.

As urban centers settled into the routines of a more regulated society, prostitutes found that the "wide open" policy of the bonanza days had faded away. City leaders and boosters became more interested in town image. Although they were still willing to host a vice community, politicians and business owners began to demand that it be less visible on the city streets. Prostitutes found they were the target of various reform efforts. Reformers wanted prostitution and its practitioners forced away from the main arteries of town, while prostitutes resisted regulations that would make their employment even more constrained.

The reformers included the wives of the "respectable" male citizens, women who wanted to see the spread of schools, libraries, and churches through the West. Although there might have been a chance for the two disparate groups of women to bridge to each other, such did not occur, as there was little conversation across class lines. When women proposed organizing a system by which prostitutes might participate in family life, as in Denver in 1871, civic leaders expressed outrage and squelched the plan. In a somewhat different atmosphere—the environment created in houses of rescue—an activist group of women reformers made an effort to redirect the lives of fallen women. Even here in an intimate domestic setting the effort faltered, as the two groups had difficulty agreeing on common values.

In modern times, many western cities point with some pride to the prostitutes who lived in the West, embellishing their personal histories as a part of an authentic frontier past. Denver, Cheyenne, Austin, Santa Fe, Dodge City, Los Angeles, El Paso, Portland, Grand Junction, Tombstone—all hosted communities of prostitutes, as did many other municipalities. From among the brothels and newspapers emerged a few "celebrity" women—Laura Evans, Frenchy, Chicago Joe, Squirrel Tooth Alice—who have served in the present day to advertise western attractions for tourists. In this celebratory look into the past, the prostitute is often portrayed as a glamorous symbol of the wild West. Although their stories have been recounted in a merry fashion, the famous madams distract Americans from the thousands of nameless, poor women who worked in a demanding profession that slipped over into the 20th-century West, where it found new venues in a modern world.

—Anne M. Butler

SUGGESTED READING

Butler, Anne. *Daughters of Joy, Sisters of Misery: Prostitutes in the American West, 1865-90.* Urbana: University of Illinois Press, 1985.

PROSTITUTION IN 19TH-CENTURY TEXAS

Much like today, 19th-century Texas formed a mosaic of areas that could easily be compared and contrasted. The parched landscape of West Texas seemed the complete opposite of the lush piney woods found near her eastern border. There were ranchers and there were oilmen, and the interests of each routinely collided. Texas was a place of city and country folk, and the two groups ritualistically debated issues of religion, politics, or the finer aspects of high culture such as whether a bowl of Texas red chili should be served with beans or without. But the Lone Star State was also divided into areas of morality and conduct, and the values of these groups often clashed in profound, public ways. In practically any given city, one could find a number of God-fearing, traditional houses of worship, while not far off, perhaps on the other side of the tracks, a smattering of parlors or brothels opened their doors for parishioners of a different sort. In most locales, more churches automatically translated into more working women, and these two groups often found themselves at odds over defining the morals and public reputation of the area they called home.

Texas in the 19th century contained all the necessary features to ensure the success of prostitution. Because of the great migration westward, hundreds of thousands of young men left their homes in search of gold, land, employment, and adventure. The West was a place where men were expected to openly demonstrate their masculinity, and many eagerly did so through heavy drinking, gambling, fighting, or sexual exploits. Women were virtually nonexistent on the plains until 1900, and it was indeed a rare opportunity to be in the company of a lady, respectable or not. Young men who worked the cattle trails and rail lines often found few places where they could spend a paycheck, so an occasional trip to the city would provide all the desired opportunities to customers who would regularly be inclined to spend an entire paycheck on a single evening of wine and women.

In a land of extremes, settlers in Texas had to endure a number of hardships in their pursuit of land and wealth. Men were physically put to the test with scorching summer heat, devastating ice storms during the long winters, and pounding rain and hail throughout the entire year. Most men lived in the crudest of shelters, making the best of their transient lifestyle by finding cover in a tent, a barn, and sometimes even a small cave cut from canyon rock. But despite these many obstacles that parched the skin and left the mind dazed from a lack of sound sleep and any extended periods of relaxation, men suffered most from the profound loneliness brought about by an almost total lack of female contact and companionship. Where women were found, one would not have to look far to find whatever they wanted, whether it be whiskey, dancing, gambling, or even sex. All of these vices came, however, with a price.

Prostitutes usually possessed two traits: they were young and uneducated. Also motivated by wealth and adventure, women often turned to prostitution as a way to earn more money while gaining more stability in their lives. When unable to find suitable employment in the male-dominated West, some turned to sex as a way of dealing with their desperate situation. The profession was filled with women who possessed certain liabilities; many had unsavory reputations before entering prostitution and were already shunned by society, and others were nonwhite or did not speak English. While some clearly enjoyed the sex and living life as a seductress, prostitution was for the most part a profession of unwilling participants who, once painted with the brush of ill repute, were forced to spend the majority of their best years entertaining male customers.

During the heyday of prostitution in the American West, a distinct hierarchy quickly developed throughout Texas. At the top of the ladder were mistresses or courtesans, usually well-educated women who offered their services exclusively to a single customer in exchange for relatively large amounts of compensation and the privilege of being shielded from the routine hardships of the day. The amount of compensation would be greatly influenced by a man's social or political status within a given society, and it was generally acknowledged by most that having one or two exclusive mistresses on the side was simply a privilege reserved for the rich and powerful. Although truly romantic relationships did occasionally occur between those involved, it was much more common for wealthy men to dispose of unwanted companions at their leisure in search of younger, more interesting, or more sexually adventurous women when they grew tired of their current mistresses.

Just below the exclusive relationships enjoyed by a relatively few number of prostitutes were parlor houses that could be found in virtually any Texas city situated near a major route of transportation or commerce. The goal of a successful parlor house was to convey a feeling to the customer that he was an honored guest in the home of a close friend. Men deemed worthy enough to be allowed in received a warm welcome by the house madam or mom, and they would be led into a common area of the house to engage in light conversation while being given an opportunity to meet some of her "girls" or "boarders" who lived there much as her own daughters. If the man did not have a particular girl already in mind, it was customary for the madam to select a woman for him, and after initial introductions and nervous conversation, all present would sit down to a hearty meal that included wine or other spirits.

Once the money had been paid and the couple entered an upstairs bedroom, the man had a reasonable expectation of complete control with regard to the type and length of sex that evening. In many cases, a man would spend the entire night with a single girl, and this could easily cost him $50, an amount that included the price of the room and the cost of additional beverages or food. The women were expected to endure whatever the customers desired, regardless of how painful or humiliating the experience. But in exchange for any sexual or emotional hardships the girls had to endure, they were generally well fed and clothed, and were provided opportunities when not working in the evenings to sleep late, do needlepoint, or perhaps work in the parlor's garden.

Similar though not quite as exclusive as the parlor houses were brothels. Although normally concentrated together in a common area of downtown, they were usually situated near rail stations or other transportation hubs. Like those in Fort Worth, rail workers would usually leave their red lanterns on the front porch so they could be located in case of an emergency, and it was from this ritual that the term "red light" district is said to have come. Although not quite as opulent as a parlor, these brothels did provide similar amenities such as alcohol and food. Sexual encounters here were usually not all-night affairs, since the girls were expected to entertain a number of men in a single evening so that the madam would also earn a good profit while keeping the rates substantially lower than high-class parlors. Occasionally, these brothels operated as bars or dance halls, and a number of the girls working there doubled as dancers, bartenders, waitresses, or simply as inviting females sitting at the bar wanting to talk while their

companions were expected to purchase overpriced drinks for the two of them. In some cases, these madams took their girls on summer field trips to areas where large numbers of customers could be found, and for a month or so conducted their business from a series of tents or other temporary structures. Madams who took girls on such treks were generally held in high regard, since granting girls a rare opportunity to travel outside the boundaries of the brothel house was considered a treat in spite of the purpose of their journey.

Women who were unacceptable to well-established madams who owned brothels often found themselves working as cribs, women loosely organized together who might be working from a single shack, room, or sometimes even an alley. A girl might find herself in such a group for a number of reasons—age, race, lack of desirability, or an inability to provide male customers with an experience memorable enough to ensure repeat business. When times were bad, the ranks of crib women swelled as parlors and brothels cleaned house to keep costs down and to make room for new recruits who were brought in once times improved. Like house girls, these women spent much of their day out of sight from the public and local authorities, and most of their business was conducted away from the public for fear of public ridicule or entanglements with the law.

At the bottom of the prostitution chain were common prostitutes who spent most of their time walking streets in cow towns, mining areas, or army posts. These women were exposed to a number of occupational dangers that were largely absent from house girls, including nonpayment, disease, pregnancy, and being beaten or killed. They were also much more likely to draw the attention of local authorities, which viewed them as a nuisance and believed prostitutes should remain out of sight from the rest of the respectable society. In an 1881 sweep through the red light district of Fort Worth, 22 girls were taken into custody, spent the night in lockup, and forced to pay a $5 fine plus court costs. While the parlors and brothels largely avoided trouble with the law by faithfully paying taxes and making generous contributions to local charities and churches, those who worked in the streets were often viewed with public scorn and humiliation. Street prostitutes were also by far the most likely to turn to suicide as a way of ending their lonely, desperate existence.

At each level, the preferred customer was the businessman or worker who just happened to be passing through. Towns like Houston, San Antonio, and Austin were geared toward catering to the visitors' every need while methodically separating as much money from men as possible within a 24-hour period. Affectionately called "the Paris of the Plains," Fort Worth was to the cowboy what the seaport town of Galveston was to the sailor. An active Chisholm Trial and the busy railroad ensured the success of their Hell's Half Acre with a fresh load of visitors each day who were eager to spend money and mingle with the cowboys and buffalo hunters already there. Though not as renowned as their geographical counterpart, the red light district inhabitants of Deep Elm in Dallas constantly competed with Fort Worth patrons, and the two cities engaged in a continuous struggle to see which place could offer the most outrageous experience to those eager to spend.

Though prostitution in Texas had many supporters, not all of society approved of their crude practices. Groups like the Women's Christian Temperance Union (WCTU) spoke against the scourge of alcohol, pointing out the connection between drinking and spousal abuse. Working under the umbrella of improved social welfare, they pushed for total abstinence from alcohol in an attempt to put liquor dealers out of business as a way of reducing crime, poverty, and general immorality. The WCTU was also instrumental in gaining woman suffrage in Texas, and their later activities included the establishment of reformatories for youth and alcohol education in the public schools. Ordinary citizens also took issue with the proliferation of bawdy houses in their beloved towns. In 1874 a group of Fort Worth citizens led by J. G. Bishop petitioned the city council to rid Belknap Street of any houses of prostitution. Although the council accepted their petition, they indefinitely delayed any action on it. In the end, most parlors were forced to relocate to obscure corners of downtown districts, where local law authorities unofficially agreed to leave the madams and their girls alone in exchange for keeping their affairs out of sight of the general public.

Organized religious groups also publicly expressed their scorn to those who unashamedly pedaled sin. In Dallas, Baptists and Methodists often had churches in close proximity to brothels, not because they were on a crusade to save the wayward, but to take advantage of the relatively low rents and the availability of properties. In most cases, churches sought a more permanent home away from the wicked, and once they could afford higher rents, they left without looking back.

Notable exceptions to these were Catholics. Many permanent parishes were established very close to the red light districts, although this may have been more the result of their typical parishioners in the West during the 19th century: poor, recently arrived immigrants and Irish railroad men who never strayed far from the central area of towns and cities.

Like other states, prostitutes in 19th-century Texas carried the stigma of having sex for money while most of society accepted the idea of a man's right to visit a brothel. Those women who worked for sex had the most unstable of lives, and were expected to routinely move from one place to another to avoid the label of "old timer" and to maintain a fresh, young image. At each level of prostitution, women faced a number of occupational hazards, some of which would prove to be fatal. Most girls turned to prostitution not out of conscious choice but because it represented their only option to survive in the West without marriage or indentured servitude. But despite the many risks and the fact that they were universally shunned by respectable communities, many of these women turned the business of selling sex into a way to share in the prosperity and adventure that the new territories had to offer.

—Dale H. Sawyers

SUGGESTED READINGS

Abernethy, Francis Edward, ed. *Legendary Ladies of Texas.* Denton: University of North Texas Press, 1994.

Butler, Anne M. *Daughters of Joy, Sisters of Misery: Prostitutes in the American West, 1865-1890.* Urbana: University of Illinois Press, 1987.

Goldman, Marion S. *Gold Diggers and Silver Miners: Prostitution and Social Life on the Comstock Lode.* Ann Arbor: University of Michigan Press, 1981.

Hutson, Jan. *The Chicken Ranch: The True Story of the Best Little Whorehouse in Texas.* Cranbury, NJ: Barnes, 1980.

Seagraves, Anne. *Soiled Doves: Prostitution in the Early West.* Hayden, ID: Wesanne Publications, 1994.

Selcer, Richard F. *Hell's Half Acre.* Fort Worth: Texas Christian University Press, 1991.

PROSTITUTION IN SALT LAKE CITY

Prostitution in Salt Lake City has been shaped by its larger history. Unlike other "instant cities" like

San Francisco or Denver, which began as rowdy mining towns with open prostitution and later became "respectable," Salt Lake began in 1847 as an orderly, family-dominated Latter-Day Saints (or Mormon) settlement that became somewhat wilder 2 decades later with the advent of mining and railroads. The early Mormon pioneers condemned extramarital sex and evidently kept the city almost completely free of prostitutes. The transcontinental railroad, completed in 1869, brought non-Mormons (or gentiles) to the territory for mining, railroad, and other job opportunities, and prostitutes followed.

The first well-known madam, Kate Flint, began managing a brothel in 1872 on Commercial Street, just two blocks from the Latter-Day Saints' Temple Square. The city authorities, all Mormon, directed the all-Mormon police force to destroy Flint's and another woman's brothels. Flint sued the authorities and won a settlement that allowed her to continue in business for years, becoming a minor legend in the process. As the city grew and became more involved in capitalist markets, some businessmen and city authorities, Mormon and non-Mormon, saw the advantages of regulated prostitution and adopted that policy from the mid-1870s through 1911. Prostitutes worked under a typical regulationist regime: they worked within a limited geographical area and paid a set fine on a monthly or quarterly basis that constituted a de facto license. Flint and women who followed her built a network of downtown brothels that flourished for decades. At least one, Emma DeMarr, earned a small fortune. Most women who resorted to prostitution, however, did it because of economic necessity, and they often suffered violence and degradation.

Prostitution also played a role in the long struggle between Mormons and non-Mormons for political and economic power in the city. Some non-Mormons condemned Mormon polygamy and compared it to prostitution. Mormons responded that their marital system protected and elevated women, and that sinful non-Mormons had polluted Utah's pure communities with commercial sex. Activists on both sides used prostitution as a rhetorical weapon in the fight over polygamy, which quieted (temporarily) after the Woodruff Manifesto of 1890 counseled Mormons not to contract plural marriages. In 1908 the "American" political party, which revived local anti-Mormon politics, decided to create a new restricted prostitution district, the Stockade. They hired Belle London (Dora B. Topham) to manage the district, and protected it with the city police force. Most prostitutes and madams either moved to the Stockade or left the city, although a few continued to work in the traditional district. In 1911 Topham was convicted of pandering and closed the Stockade, although she was acquitted on appeal. The notoriety of Topham and the Stockade helped to defeat the "Americans," which helped quiet Mormon-gentile antagonisms.

After 1911 self-styled progressive reformers cracked down on regulated prostitution. Although some subsequent city administrations quietly allowed prostitutes to work in the traditional district, the era of regulation was over. Prostitutes moved to hotels, rooming houses, and the streets. In the decades since, women have sometimes worked in traditional brothels, but more often as call girls or street walkers.

—Jeffrey Nichols

SUGGESTED READING

Nichols, Jeffrey. *Prostitution, Polygamy, and Power: Salt Lake City, 1847-1918.* Urbana and Chicago: University of Illinois Press, 2002.

R

RANKIN, JEANNETTE (1880-1973)

Jeannette Rankin was the first woman to serve in the U.S. Congress. She spent her life in unwavering dedication to pacifism and social reforms. She never married, but enjoyed a long and distinguished career, maintaining an exhausting work and travel schedule that few have matched before or since. Although she is perhaps best known for her lone dissenting vote against World War II, she was also a staunch advocate of women's, children's, and labor issues.

She was the first child of John and Olive Pickering, and raised in Grant Creek, Montana. Her father was an industrious builder and rancher and away much of the time. Her mother placed on Jeannette much of the responsibility of the other six children at a young age. This seems to have suited young Jeannette, who earned a lifelong reputation for being capable of organizing and overseeing the tasks before her. Her father did not allow guns on the ranch, and this has been one reason put forth by historians to explain the origin of Jeannette's later abhorrence of weapons and war. Even as a child, she was both compassionate and mechanical, constructing a sidewalk for one of the houses her father built, sewing a leather shoe for the family dog's injured foot, and insisting on stitching up a badly injured horse. Her father worked his children hard with chores on the ranch but did not closely oversee their work, a fact that likely gave rise to Jeannette's independent, confident, and resourceful leadership qualities.

She suffered most of her life from tic douloureux, a condition in which unexpected sharp, racking pains occur in the cheeks. She kept this secret, however, and most people, even those closest to her, never knew it. Despite this malady, she did not let it slow her down. She remained constantly busy, always concerned with the pliht of others. Indeed, throughout her life she traveled extensively, attending to the needy and promoting peace wherever she went, even up into her 90s

She attended Montana State University, majoring in biology and graduating in June 1902. For a woman who would become a public agitator and make thousands of speeches, she was ironically known at this early stage as an extremely quiet and timid student. Yet she was also known as being stubborn and having a temper. Once when an instructor asked her to recite a piece of Tennyson's poetry that glorified war, she angrily refused.

She taught school in Grant Creek and Whitehall, Montana, but did not enjoy it. She left Whitehall and learned to be a seamstress, a profession she relied on many times. Thanks to her father's sound business dealings and her brother, Wellington's, competency as a young lawyer, when her father died she and her siblings received a monthly financial allowance. With that, Jeannette traveled to Washington, D.C., where she first encountered social deprivation. The sights of homelessness and poverty moved her. Witnessing the inauguration of Theodore Roosevelt impressed her, and she and her brother Wellington were swept up with the progressive idealism of the time.

In 1907, while visiting relatives in San Francisco, she went to work in a settlement house, teaching immigrant slum children to read while making sure they were fed and bathed. The following year she went to the New York School of Philanthropy, a school for social workers, from which she graduated in spring 1909. Here she was taught the philosophy that stayed with her the rest of her life, that it was up to society to reach out to the needy. This contrasted with other philosophies of the time such as Social Darwinism, which held that helping the poor would only be tampering with the natural process of nature.

In New York she first became interested in woman suffrage, which she learned about while doing research on a school project. She was shocked to find out that only few women had the right to vote. At about this time, Benjamin Kidd's *The Science of Power* also fascinated her. Kidd strongly believed that it was a woman's place to improve society for the benefit of the children of the nation. Rankin referred to this concept many times in her career while agitating and lobbying for labor laws and social reforms. Florence Kelley, a supremely confident and articulate lawyer and director of the National Consumers' League, a group that pursued reform through consumer involvement, also influenced her. The tactic of winning reforms through personal action and active recruitment at the grassroots level, and not by merely holding meetings, became Rankin's lifelong motto. She quit organizations whenever they relegated her to organizing meetings for members and when they refused to be proactive in the community.

After graduation in New York, she went back to Missoula to work on jail reform. But the local judge laughed at her and the people balked at her solo attempt at improving conditions at the county jail. She was a little cocky, having just graduated from social reform school, but here she learned not to talk down to people and to recruit people's assistance at the local level. Restless, she moved to Washington state, where she performed more social work, this time for the Washington Children's Home Society.

In Washington, she became dissatisfied with social work because she felt it was not accomplishing enough. She saw that legal reform was needed to prevent the sad situations that social work was trying, with only marginal success, to fix. She was also disturbed by the monopolization of management by men, and saw the potential of empowering women to have a hand in making rules. In 1910 she decided on her own to agitate for suffrage at the University of Washington. Impressed, the College Equal Suffrage League recruited her. Later that year, women won the right to vote in Washington.

In Seattle, Rankin worked with Minnie J. Reynolds, a woman who became a close friend and whose devotion to pacifism captivated Rankin. Reynolds also impressed upon Rankin a strategy for suffrage campaigning: remove the threat of prohibition and men would be more inclined to support suffrage. It was a tactic that Rankin employed successfully, but not without a price.

Rankin organized for suffrage in 15 states as well as lobbying the U.S. Congress. Some states proved extremely difficult, such as Florida, whose residents believed it unbecoming of a woman to seek public voice. Montana was not easy. One reason for the difficulty in Montana was the resistance of the powerful Anaconda Mining Company; another was the vast terrain of the state, making grassroots traveling difficult; still another was the diversity of immigrants and groups to convince. One of the biggest issues was prohibition. On this subject Rankin followed her friend Minnie's advice and took a neutral stand, setting up her own organization with no connection to groups in favor of prohibition. She upset members of the Women's Christian Temperance Union (WCTU), an organization strongly in favor of prohibition, by not allowing them to march with suffragists. She also refused affiliation with the National American Women Suffrage Association (NAWSA), the organization pioneered by Susan B. Anthony, which remained committed to prohibition, and ultimately won the state in large part because of her careful courting of the male vote. Ironically, she did this and worked for NAWSA as a field secretary around the same time.

After Montana women received the vote, Rankin was extremely popular. She had a falling out with the leadership at NAWSA and left to work in New Zealand, a country ahead of the United States in terms of social programs and national suffrage. Encouraged, she returned to Montana to campaign for Congress on the Republican ticket. She campaigned much as she had for suffrage, building on the organization she had founded, and now holding the advantage of the fact that Montana women could now vote for her.

Not all women approved, however. Some women from NAWSA, including Carrie Chapman Catt, were afraid she would embarrass them and hurt the woman's movement if she got defeated. This in part reflects the division of the women's movement in terms of East versus West. Catt wanted someone with more distinction and better credentials, such as a lawyer. Rankin even had to fight some Republican leaders who deliberately tried to impede her grassroots speaking strategy. In November 1916 she won, to the disbelief of many.

The biggest issue to grab the nation's attention at that time was the war in Europe. Rankin, in the national spotlight, was caught in the middle of a division between two prominent national women's organizations over sending America to war. Alice Paul of the Congressional Union, a personal friend of Rankin's and a devout pacifist, differed greatly with Catt, of NAWSA, who favored war. Rankin walked the line between the two groups, trying to maintain the appearance of unity. But she could not vote for war. When the time came, she voted no along with 49 other congressmen.

She was soundly criticized for her vote, and some women, such as Catt, disowned her. There was a big debate over whether or not she cried after declaring her vote. She supported the war effort after the country began prosecuting the war; she was patriotic, after all, and even managed to regain popularity. While in Congress, she befriended Fiorello LaGuardia, who was impressed with her and would later ask her to marry him. They remained lifelong friends. As a congresswoman, Rankin lobbied on behalf of women laborers against compulsory overtime and introduced many social and labor reform bills. The country was at war, however, and there was not much interest in domestic issues. Rankin was ahead of her time; these bills became law much after her tenure yet still during her lifetime.

Of these bills, the one Rankin cared about the most was the Rankin-Robinson bill, which later passed as the Shepard-Towner bill. Disturbed by the mother and infant mortality rate, she proposed federal funding for health education for pregnant mothers. The bill stalled, but in the meantime, after the war, the biggest national issue was national suffrage. Rankin spoke and debated opposing congressmen to enthusiastic applause. Women picketed the White House. Some women, including Rankin, feared that such militancy might hurt the cause, but neither the marching nor Rankin's pacifist vote prevented the Nineteenth Amendment from passing. Rankin had played a huge part in getting it passed.

In 1918 Rankin lost the bid for reelection as candidate of the socialist, progressive National Party, in large part due to the opposition of the Anaconda Mining Company, which was hostile to her for her support of miners who had struck in 1917. During the 1920s and 1930s, Rankin traveled the world, agitated

for peace, spoke against military buildup, and worked toward legislative reform for women and children. She lobbied Congress incessantly, and some believe she was more effective as a lobbyist in Congress than as a congresswoman. She went to Europe with Jane Addams and Florence Kelley to attend the Second International Congress of Women for Permanent Peace (later the Women's International League for Peace and Freedom). She worked as field secretary for the National Consumer's League, worked and stayed at Jane Addams's Hull House in Chicago, and helped her brother, Wellington, campaign for senator. In 1925 she bought 64 acres in Georgia, where she had a modest house built in 1925 and lived much of the rest of her life.

Rankin again ran for Congress as Montana's representative as a Republican and won in 1940, largely due to Wellington's support. Her term this time was short-lived, however, when Japan attacked Pearl Harbor. The nation was incensed. This time no one was voting against a declaration of war. People close to Rankin urged her not to vote against it. But she could not go against her principles. Despite an overwhelming tide of disapproval, she cast the lone dissenting vote. Scathing criticism harangued her this time. She had to have police escort her out of the building. She received hate mail, and her brother made it publicly clear that he disagreed with her. She did not begrudge him that, however, and they stayed close until his death in 1967.

Rankin's political career was ruined by that vote. After her term, for a long time she was too controversial to be an effective campaigner or even a spokeswoman for organizations. Yet she continued to speak of reform, becoming interested in electoral reform because she believed people could be better represented and peace would stand a better chance if there were more direct representation. She spent her time touring the world, often to India, with which she was fascinated because of their commitment to peace. She lived in Georgia and summered in Montana. She never ceased to speak and organize for peace and social reform, however, and everywhere she went she was active toward these ends. Her last public speaking engagement was just a few months before her death in May 1973, just a few weeks short of her 93rd birthday.

Rankin was one of the most traveled and persistently hard-working women of her time. Despite her tenuous relationship with some feminists, a later generation of feminists saw her as an inspiration.

In 1968 women marched on Washington to protest the Vietnam War and called themselves the Jeannette Rankin Brigade.

As an organizing political agitator, Rankin was brilliant. By avoiding excessive entanglements in political parties and women's organizations, she was able to organize more freely and win victories as a result. As a crusader, she was tireless. She worked much of the time without pay and believed extra effort was essential: she was known for having said, "A 40 hour a week job isn't worth doing." She traveled extensively, braved heavy criticism, and represented women with competence and dignity. She is revered for her pioneering work on behalf of women and children, and admired for her unwavering devotion to peace.

—Christopher Small

SUGGESTED READINGS

Block, Judy Rachel. *The First Woman in Congress: Jeannette Rankin.* New York: C.P.I., 1978.

Davidson, Sue. *A Heart in Politics: Jeannette Rankin and Patsy T. Mink.* Seattle, WA: Seal Press, 1994.

Giles, Kevin S. *Flight of the Dove: The Story of Jeannette Rankin.* Beaverton, OR: Lochsa Experience Publishers, 1980.

Harris, Ted Carlton. *Jeannette Rankin: Suffragist, First Woman Elected to Congress, and Pacifist.* New York: Arno Press, 1982.

Josephson, Hannah Geffen. *Jeannette Rankin, First Lady in Congress: A Biography.* Indianapolis, IN: Bobbs-Merrill, 1974.

Smith, Norma. *Jeannette Rankin: America's Conscience.* Helena: Montana Historical Society Press, 2002.

White, Florence Meiman. *First Woman in Congress, Jeannette Rankin.* New York: J. Messner, 1980.

RED SHIRT, DELPHINE (1957-)

Delphine Red Shirt is a member of the Lakota Indian tribe and is the best-known writer from that particular group. Her ability to bring out the cultural heritage and beliefs of her people enable readers to glance into the life of a Lakota Indian. Her best known work is *Bead on an Anthill: A Lakota Childhood.* In this work, she cleverly mixes Lakota language with English to bring out the greatest and most authentic representation of the Lakota way of life. She tells of how her grandmother teaches her to string beads together, and describes her part in a ceremonial dance where she dresses in buckskins and beads. Both stories give readers insight into the cultural norms that the Lakota basked in during their time on earth.

Red Shirt grew up in Nebraska and also spent time on the Pine Ridge Indian Reservation in South Dakota. Her writings showed her growth during the 1960s and the 1970s as she reconciled her ancient culture with the one that she was forced to live in. Her mother had 11 children and 3 who were lost at birth. Her father left them and had an irregular influence on her and her siblings' lives. Red Shirt saw her mother as strong and deeply rooted in her culture. Her desire to represent her people to the world also was due to her mother's influence. Her father preferred to use English rather than Lakota, and had words that he would regularly speak in English (like "daughter"). Her life on the reservation, life as an Indian, and influence from her parents enabled her to create a window to which the practices of her heritage could be clearly seen.

Red Shirt served in the U.S. Marine Corps from January 1977 until January 1978. She was the second woman trained as a field radio operator. In 1980 she earned a B.S. degree from Regis College in Denver and an M.A. from Wesleyan University in Middletown, Connecticut, in 1995. She was chair of the United Nations nongovernment organization Committee on the International Decade of the World's Indigenous People, 1995-1996.

Red Shirt is a lecturer at Yale University, and her most recent book is *Turtle Lung Woman's Granddaughter,* published by the University of Nebraska Press (2002).

—Kevin Christy

SUGGESTED READINGS

Bangs, Pat. "Red Shirt, Delphine." *School Library Journal* (November 1998): 162.

Batalle, Gretchen, and Laurie Lisa, eds. *Native American Women: A Biographical Dictionary* (2d ed.). New York: Routledge, 2001.

Indian Country Today. Retrieved from www.indiancountry.com/?author=44.

Red Shirt, Delphine. *Bead on an Anthill: A Lakota Childhood.* Lincoln: University of Nebraska Press, 1998.

REICHARD, GLADYS AMANDA (1893-1955)

Gladys Amanda Reichard was one of the first women anthropologists to study the Navajo. She worked with the Navajo for over 30 years, and in that time she developed and refined innovative fieldwork methods, such as the genealogical method and the participant-observation technique, that are now common features of ethnological research. She also taught anthropology at Barnard College for over 30 years, from 1923 to 1955. Over the course of her career as teacher and scholar, she wrote a variety of texts about her research into Navajo social organization, religion, linguistics, and aesthetics. Her most significant southwestern texts include her anthropological studies *Social Life of the Navajo Indians* (a description of Navajo society by means of the genealogical method), *Navajo Shepherd and Weaver* (a scientific/technical guide to Navajo weaving), and *Navajo Religion: A Study in Symbolism* (a compilation and explanation of religious symbols); her novel, *Dezba: Woman of the Desert*, which fictionalizes the people who taught her to weave; and her fieldwork account, *Spider Woman: A Story of Navajo Weavers and Chanters*, which is explicitly an autobiographical text.

Reichard was born in 1893 in Bangor, Pennsylvania, to a Quaker family. After high school she taught elementary school until 1915, when she enrolled in Swarthmore College. In 1919 she graduated with an A.B. in classics and then enrolled in Columbia University to study anthropology. She received her M.A. in 1920. In 1923 she was appointed Instructor at Barnard College, where she founded the Department of Anthropology. For many years, this was the only department of anthropology at an undergraduate women's college in the United States.

At Columbia, Reichard came under the influence of Franz Boas, who taught her salvage ethnology: the detailed accounting of every cultural belief, custom, way of life, and so on. Boas encouraged her to go into the field and learn about the cultural role of women. So, during the summers of 1923, 1924, and 1925, she went to the Navajo reservation with Pliny Goddard. The result of this fieldwork was her anthropological study of clan size and grouping, *Social Life of the Navajo Indians: With Some Attention to Minor Ceremonies* (1928). Here Reichard begins to show an interest in Navajo weaving. In her subsequent research, her dilemma becomes finding the most traditional weavers, the women who carry the knowledge of precontact techniques. This interest in the "old" ways brings Reichard back to the reservation in 1930 to learn the traditional weaving techniques and thus to perpetuate, through anthropological research, the form that predated the incursions of modern life.

In the 1930s, living with a native family was still an unusual fieldwork practice, and yet Reichard chose to live with a Navajo family for several summers in order to understand their culture better. For Reichard, placing herself inside a hogan, inside the web of female activity, was essential to understanding Navajo culture. Thus she employs the participant-observation technique: she finds a contact (an informant) to introduce her to a family and then spends a substantial amount of time living with, or alongside, this family. In an unpublished book, *Another Look at the Navajo*, probably written in 1950, she explains that she chose the craft of weaving because it afforded her entry into women's society and thus inside Navajo life:

> I was interested in crafts and decided that leaning [sic] to weave would be a way of developing the trust of the women, as well as of learning to weave and to speak the language. By this attempt I would put myself under the family aegis; my work would at first deal primarily with women, and I could observe the daily round as a participant, rather than as a mere onlooker.

From her stance inside a Navajo family, Reichard hoped to describe women's work accurately. She would learn the craft, she would discuss the craft with other women weavers, and she would come to know the intimacies, the daily round, of Navajo life.

Spider Woman: A Story of Navajo Weavers and Chanters (1934) emerged after her four summers with the Navajo. In her preface, she called the book "an informal personal account . . . a tale of digressions." Although she studies Navajo chanting in addition to weaving, her narrative focuses on weaving, because in Navajo society women are the weavers and men the chanters. She forms connections with the women in the Red-Point family—Marie, Atlnaba, and Maria Antonia—who then teach her to weave. She describes, in detail, the many hours she suffered in the cramped weaving position and her first frustrating attempts at a simple pattern. These trials teach her the intricacies of weaving, the subtle movements, and the mental processes necessary to weave successfully.

During her first summer, she works from sunup to sundown until weaving becomes instinctual:

> About this time in my career another marvel happens. I find myself no longer counting the rows or the warps which are or should be forward to make my triangles. Suddenly I *know* which ones they are. It seems so simple, the way they look, different on four rows, and the differences regularly repeated. How could I ever have been so confused as I was in those first days, after we had put in the design? It seems incredible that anyone could be so stupid.

After she learns the basic techniques of weaving, Reichard moves on to the "rare" and difficult double-faced blanket. She also learns to spin and dye wool, relishing the resurgence of interest in vegetal dyes, the "original" dyes used by Navajo women and also the most difficult to make. In the end, she demonstrates her skill when she acquires a "degree in weaving." She receives this reward when she is asked to teach another Navajo woman, Hastin-Gani's-Wife, how to make the diamond saddle blanket. When Hastin-Gani's-Wife asks her to demonstrate the weave, Reichard says, "This innocent remark is more precious to me than my degree from college. She, acknowledged among the best weavers of the tribe because of her skill and dexterity, asking *me* to show *her* how to make a saddle blanket!"

Contemporary and current readers of *Spider Woman* praise the book for its inside look at Navajo life and its innovative method: an autobiographical account of learning to weave while living with a Navajo family. Reichard's thorough accounting of her four summers of participatory/observational experience, combined with her literary skills, produced a narrative that somehow captures what many of her readers consider the essence of southwestern life. The book remains popular today.

Her next book was a kind of how-to guide to Navajo weaving: *Navajo Shepherd and Weaver* (1936). In her Foreword, she explains:

> My purpose in discussing the technique of Navajo weaving in this form has been twofold: first, to present the weaver's viewpoint; and second, to enable anyone with the will, to learn to weave a Navajo blanket.

Elsewhere, in her Preface, she discusses the difficulties she had learning to weave, for the Navajo method of teaching is "showing." She must learn a process by watching someone else perform it; she is not told how or why a process is performed. Without these explanations and generalizations, she must fend for herself by counting the rows, taking notes, reading books, and repeating the techniques Marie shows her. Reichard practiced and practiced and asked question after question until she gathered the knowledge necessary to explain how to weave a Navajo blanket. In a 1941 interview for *Books From a Shelf,* she boasts, "From this description at least three persons who have never seen a Navajo weave have made rugs much superior to my first one made under the direction of the Navajo women." Moreover, the republication of *Navajo Shepherd* as *Weaving a Navajo Blanket* in 1974 attests to the book's continued success.

From 1940 on, Reichard spent most of her summers and two sabbaticals in Flagstaff, Arizona. For the remainder of her life, she dedicated her energies to describing, explaining, and defending the Navajo people. In 1955 she died of a stroke while living and working at the Museum of Northern Arizona in Flagstaff.

—Becky Jo (Gesteland) McShane

SUGGESTED READINGS

Leacock, Eleanor. "Gladys Amanda Reichard," in Ute Gacs, Aisha Khan, Jerrie McIntyre, and Ruth Weinberg, eds., *Women Anthropologists: Selected Biographies.* Urbana: University of Illinois Press, 1989, 303-309.

Reichard, Gladys. *Another Look at the Navaho.* Ms. 29-37. Flagstaff: Museum of Northern Arizona.

Reichard, Gladys. *Books from a Shelf.* KTAR, KVOA, KYUM, Arizona. July 15, 1941. Ms 29-23-4. Flagstaff: Museum of Northern Arizona.

RICHARDS, ANN (1933-)

Ann Richards, former governor of Texas, was born Dorothy Ann Willis on September 1, 1933, in Waco, Texas. She attended Waco High School, where she met her future husband, David Richards. The couple eventually had four children. She attended Baylor University on a debate scholarship. She took graduate courses in education and earned her teaching certificate.

In 1962, while in Dallas, David joined a labor law firm in Texas. Ann and David soon became involved in Dallas politics. Ann and her friends were disappointed to discover that men who considered women to be inferior controlled the Democratic Party organization. In 1962 Ann and her friends founded the North Dallas Democratic Party to strengthen party loyalty and get like-minded people to run for party precinct positions and public office. In the late 1970s, feminism finally took a strong hold in Ann. Her first public action as a feminist came in 1977, when she introduced the Equal Rights Amendment plank at the International Women's Convention in Houston. Later that year, she and Mary Beth Rogers put together a political slide show with which they traveled all over Texas teaching women the fundamentals of politics and the basics of running for office.

Richards served on President Jimmy Carter's Commission on Women. In 1979 she instigated what turned into a 4-year project on historical accounts of Texas women. In 1981 the exhibition was displayed at the Institute of Texas Cultures in San Antonio. When she decided to run for office, many considered her feminism a liability. They were afraid that if she were portrayed as a feminist, the electorate would equate that to a shrill, narrow, and off-center woman. In 1975 David was asked to run for Travis County Commissioner. He declined. Ann was then approached in his stead. She initially declined, but then decided to run. She won her bid for office.

In 1981 Richards decided to run for state treasurer. People doubted that she could be a competitive candidate. In 1982 she was elected state treasurer, becoming the first woman to hold statewide office in 50 years. In 1984 she and David divorced. She ran unopposed in 1986. While treasurer, Richards changed the hiring policies at the Treasury Department, so that 55% of its employees were female, 27% were Hispanic, and 14% were African Americans. By the end of her term, she had made Texas more than $2 billion in nontax revenues.

In 1988 she gave the keynote address at the Democratic National Convention, where she caused much controversy by mocking Vice President George H. W. Bush for "being born with a silver foot in his mouth." In 1989 her autobiography, *Straight From the Heart: My Life in Politics and Other Places,* was published.

On June 10, 1989, on the capital grounds, Richards officially announced her candidacy for governor of Texas. She and her staff knew that she would have to appear both less liberal and less of a feminist than she was in fact in order to win the campaign. This would prove to be a great obstacle. Richards endured one of the most challenging campaigns in Texas history. Her struggle with alcoholism was revealed early on; she was even accused of being an abusive mother. Her opponents painted Richards as an "honorary lesbian" because of the number of gay women who worked in her campaign. In retaliation, Richards launched a negative campaign that disillusioned much of the electorate. She did manage to win the primary and runoff, but she emerged battered. After the 1988 Democratic National Convention, her positive rankings were high among Democrats and her negative rankings were high among Republicans. After the 1989 runoff, her negative rankings among Democrats were as high as her positives. The actual campaign would get even nastier. For a while, her campaign floundered against the success of Republican Clayton "Claytie" Williams, but she finally focused on the three most important issues that worked for her—experience, education, and ethics—and stayed with them to the end. On November 6, 1990, Ann Richards was elected governor of Texas. She carried 49.9% of the vote. Fewer than 100,000 votes gave her the victory over Williams. On January 15, 1991, she was inaugurated.

Though technically the second female governor of Texas, the first being Miriam "Ma" Ferguson, Richards was the first woman to hold the office in her own right and not as a mere figurehead. She appointed Barbara Jordan to be her special counsel on ethics. In a move that would have been unthinkable at any other time in history, Richards made her first appointment to the Railroad Commission, the three-member board that for years had set the world price of oil: a 32-year-old Hispanic woman, Lena Guerrero. Richards served as chairperson of the Democratic National Convention in 1992. As governor, she set a progressive agenda for a conservative state and appointed unprecedented numbers of women, Latinos, and African Americans to state offices. She served as governor until January 17, 1995, when George W. Bush was inaugurated as governor. Many credit her defeat with her controversial and unpopular veto of a bill that would have allowed every Texan to carry a concealed weapon.

Richards is now a business consultant who divides her time between Austin and New York. After being diagnosed with osteoporosis in 1994, she has gone public with her own battle against the disease in an effort to help women prevent the disease that crippled her mother and is changing her own life.

—Tiffany E. Dalpe

SUGGESTED READINGS

Morris, Celia. *Storming the Statehouse: Running for Governor with Ann Richards and Dianne Feinstein.* New York: Charles Scribner's Sons, 1992.

Richards, Ann, and Peter Knobler. *Straight From the Heart: My Life in Politics and Other Places.* New York: Simon & Schuster, 1989.

Shropshire, Mike, and Frank Schaefer. *The Thorny Rose of Texas: An Intimate Portrait of Governor Ann Richards.* Secaucus, NJ: Carol Publishing Group, 1994.

Tolleson-Rinehart, Sue, and Jeanie R. Stanley. *Claytie and the Lady: Ann Richards, Gender, and Politics in Texas.* Austin: University of Texas Press, 1994.

RINDGE, RHODA MAY KNIGHT (1864-1941)

"May" Knight Rindge was a schoolteacher from Trenton, Michigan, who came to California after marrying Fredrick Hastings Rindge in 1887. Her husband's dream was to have a "farm near the ocean," and they found Malibu, California, where he started a ranch. They had three children before he died in 1905, and as a widow, May took on her husband's business interests.

In her attempts to keep her land from being broken up, May earned the title Queen of the Malibu from the press as she vigorously fought legal battles for a quarter of a century. She defended Malibu Ranch's privacy all the way to the U.S. Supreme Court in the 1923 case *Rindge Co. v. Los Angeles County.* Los Angeles won by right of eminent domain. The Coast Highway was finally built through her ranch in 1928. By this time, she was a 65-year-old grandmother.

In an attempt to financially sustain her properties in 1926, May established Malibu Potteries. The business made decoratively painted ceramic tiles from the red clay and water readily available on her ranch. The tiles became renowned for their excellent quality and craftsmanship, and are found in several well-known landmarks such as Los Angeles City Hall and the Watts Towers.

They also are found extensively in the 50-room mansion known as the Rindge Castle, which she began construction on at Laudamus Hill in Malibu Canyon in 1928. It was to be a home for herself and all three of her children's families in each of the three wings. The mansion was never finished and was sold, due to financial difficulties. May died on February 8, 1941, at the age of 76, with her land in insolvency and little money to show for the struggles she endured in attempts to keep her "kingdom" intact.

—Carolyn Stull

SUGGESTED READINGS

Adamson House, California State Parks. Retrieved from www.parks.ca.gov/default.asp?page_id=672.

History, the Official Web site of the City of Malibu. Retrieved from ci.malibu.ca.us/index.cfm?fuseaction= Detail&CID=427&NavID=9.

RYMER, PAMELA ANN (1941-)

Vassar College graduated 20-year-old Pamela Ann Rymer in 1961. The Knoxville, Tennessee, native then moved on to Stanford Law School and received her LL.B. in 1964. After graduation, she became the director of Political Research and Analysis for the Goldwater for President Committee. In 1965 she became the vice president of Rus Walton and Associates in Los Altos, California. From 1966 to 1983 she owned her own practice in Los Angeles. Beginning in 1974 she was a member and chair of the California Post-Secondary Education Commission, and held that post until 1983. When William P. Gray stepped down, President Ronald Reagan nominated Rymer to his seat on the U.S. District Court for the Central District of California on January 31, 1984. The Senate confirmed her nomination on February 23, 1983, and she was given her commission on February 24, 1983. President George H. W. Bush called on Rymer to fill the seat vacated by Anthony McLeod Kennedy on the U.S. Court of Appeals for the Ninth Circuit. Officially nominated on February 28, 1989, she was confirmed by the Senate on May 18, 1989, and received her commission on May 22, 1989.

—Marcus J. Schwoerer

SUGGESTED READING

Pamela Ann Rymer. Retrieved from air.fjc.gov/servlet/ tGetInfo?jid=2083. Source: History of the Federal Judiciary. http://www.fjc.gov. Web site of the Federal Judicial Center, Washington, D.C.

S

SANDOZ, MARI
(MARIE SUSETTE) (1896-1966)

Mari Sandoz was the first of six children born to Swiss immigrants Mary and Jules Sandoz in Sheridan County, Nebraska. As a young girl, Mari spent most of her time cooking, gardening, and caring for her younger siblings. She did not begin attending school until the age of 9. However, this led to a "wonderful discovery" that school was the key to writing down her stories.

Mari proved a quick study and wrote her first story 1 year after starting school. She entered it in a local newspaper contest where it was published but did not win a prize. Her father was outraged and punished Mari by locking her in the cellar. After that, she continued to write but under a pen name.

By the age of 16, and with only 4½ years of education, Mari passed the rural teacher's examination and became a teacher. She taught in country schools for 7 years, finally deciding that she should pursue a college education in 1922. Although she did not have the necessary high school education, she was determined to get a college education. She sat in on conferences and waited around the deans' offices for weeks until they finally agreed to register her on June 5, 1922.

For the next 10 years, Mari attended college as much as possible while also working different afternoon jobs that helped her sharpen her writing skills. One job was as an English assistant and another was at the Nebraska State Historical Society. During these years, Mari wrote 78 short stories. Her break finally came in 1927 when her short story "The Vine" appeared in the first issue of the *Prairie Schooner*. This led to a position as associate editor of *School Executives* magazine, a position she held from 1927 to 1929.

Mari spent the next 30 years working on her Great Plains series, six books that became the core of her life's work. These books reflect the harsh environment she faced growing up on the American frontier. *The Beaver Man* is the story of the relationship of the early fur traders and Plains Indians. *The Buffalo Hunters* details the obliteration of the American bison. *The Cattlemen* traces the struggle between cattlemen and grangers. *Old Jules*, a story about her father, tells the personal struggles of immigrant homesteaders. *Cheyenne Autumn* and *Crazy Horse* give a heartfelt view of the abuse of Native Americans and the devastation of their culture by white men. Her controversial work portrayed some of the first unromantic images of the frontier.

Mari was the recipient of many awards and honors, including an honorary doctorate of literature from the University of Nebraska in 1950. In 1954 she received the Distinguished Achievement award of the Native Sons and Daughters of Nebraska for her "sincere and realistic presentation of Nebraska as it was."

Mari died of cancer on March 10, 1966, leaving an accurate and powerful vision of life in the American West.

—Brenda Bitgood

SELECTED READINGS

Sandoz, Mari. *Old Jules*. New York: Blue Ribbon Press, 1935.

Sandoz, Mari. *Crazy Horse: The Strange Man of the Oglalas*. Lincoln: University of Nebraska Press, 1942.

Sandoz, Mari. *Cheyenne Autumn.* New York: McGraw-Hill, 1953.

Sandoz, Mari. *The Buffalo Hunters: The Story of the Hide Men.* New York: Hastings House, 1954.

Sandoz, Mari. *The Cattlemen From the Rio Grande Across the Far Marias.* New York: Hastings House, 1958.

Sandoz, Mari. *The Beaver Men: Spearheads of Empire.* New York: Hastings House, 1964.

Sandoz, Mari. *Sandhill Sundays and Other Recollections.* Lincoln: University of Nebraska Press, 1970.

Stauffer, Helen Winter. *Mari Sandoz: Story Catcher of the Plains.* Lincoln: University of Nebraska Press, 1982.

SCUDDER, LAURA (1881-1959)

Laura Clough was born in Philadelphia in 1881. Her mother died when she was 2, and her father remarried. After graduation from high school, she worked at John Wanamaker's department store and learned a great deal about the power of advertising. She attended Temple University with the objective of becoming a doctor, but was unable to save enough money to go to medical school. In the alternative, she entered Mercer Hospital School of Nursing (Trenton, N.J.) in 1904, and after 3 years of 15-hour days, she earned her diploma.

While working at Mercer Hospital, she cared for Charles Scudder, a widower with three children and 21 years her senior. Charles grew increasingly fond of her and asked her to marry him. She said "sure," but waited through a season of courting until their marriage in 1908. Laura moved to Charles's farm on the Delaware River in New Jersey and there she bore her first child in January 1910. Trouble with her numerous in-laws living on the farm forced her to tell Charles that she was moving west. He consented and they moved to Seattle.

In Seattle, Charles became a produce salesman but continued to work on inventions. He patented a blind stitch sewing machine and invented food cartons such as an egg box. Unfortunately, Charles spent money without plan or budget; but fortunately, Laura's grandmother's estate brought her enough money to pay his bills and to start a business. Laura developed respiratory problems and the family moved to San Francisco in 1913 in hopes that the weather would improve her health. They subsequently moved to Ukiah, a small inland community without the coastal fog, and there bought the Little Davenport, a local cafe. Laura's food and service as well as Charles's demonstration of flapjacks flipping in the cafe's front window brought plenty of customers. Farmers, lawyers, and judges mingled in the cafe, enjoying the Scudder fare. Laura inquired of the members of the bar how one became a lawyer in California and, so informed, started to read law. She passed the California bar in March 1918 at the Fourth District Court in Sacramento and became Ukiah's first female lawyer. She did not practice but used the knowledge to her advantage in future business ventures.

A fire that wiped out a city block also took the cafe and enabled a move south with insurance money in hand. In Monterey Park, the Scudder family put down roots with a new home and a full-service gasoline station at the corner of Garvey and Wilson (now Atlantic). It was one of the first in the San Gabriel Valley. Charles and his eldest son from his first marriage, Charles A. Scudder, worked repairing vehicles, and Laura pumped gas. The profits went into a large brick building on the property, but when the renter defaulted, Laura looked for a more profitable use. Laura's action was typical of her search for a higher and better use for her property and ideas.

Turning to a friend in the potato chip business in San Diego, Laura quickly innovated in this stable and profitable enterprise. In 1926 she opened the business but refused to sell in bulk in favor of wax paper bag packaging. This innovation kept the product fresh, provided employment for housewives working at home, and vastly expanded the popularity of the product. Her Mayflower Chips became well known throughout Los Angeles County, and she soon expanded to Northern California with Blue Bird Chips in the Bay Area. Other business innovations included setting cash aside in lieu of depreciating her delivery trucks, reducing the costs of business financing and paying all invoices on the day of receipt, increasing vendor confidence, and encouraging fair dealing. Perhaps the most important innovation was advertising on outdoor billboards for the benefit of consumers and grocers, the retailers Laura was dependent upon for sales.

Laura's media savvy was significant. She held regular media meetings with her sales personnel. She controlled advertising content and kept it simple. For example, her Laura Scudder Peanut Butter billboard simply said "PURE," with an arrow pointing to the jar. This purity image was backed by her insistence that only the highest grade of ingredients be used in the products. For example, her peanut butter contained only the highest grade Virginia peanuts, with the bitter core removed before manufacture, resulting in a naturally sweet taste rather than the sugar-added flavor of the competition. Amidst the company's success and the building of an Oakland plant for Blue Bird Chips, Charles died at age 68. As a result, his son, Charles A., took a greater role in business management and grew closer to Laura. They married in 1929. In 1935 they built a new home in La Habra Heights.

The business continued to grow with California. Laura moved into the market for mayonnaise and bought a chicken ranch to ensure the quality of the eggs for the product. She used freshness-dating to further convince the consuming public of her commitment to quality.

World War II brought product shortages, but they were able to maintain the flow of their product, and the late 1940s saw a fantastic increase in demand. Laura moved further into media to make sure the public knew that her products were of the highest quality. She put a cooking program on the radio, demonstrated products and cooking in department stores, put advertising in Spanish on the radio in the 1950s, and moved into television in its infancy. She sponsored the *Lawrence Welk* program, *Engineer Bill's Cartoon Express* for kids, and the *Annie Oakley* show for western fans. Early commercials even featured animation and reached out to a wide audience watching black-and-white tubes. The mid-1950s produced the first $20 million gross year, a plant in Fresno, and trucks now numbering 350, but Laura's health failed. In 1957 she decided to sell and turned down an $11 million deal with Sunshine Biscuit because it lacked a guarantee of employment for her hundreds of loyal employees. She took $6 million from Signal Oil for the company to guarantee employment. She passed away in 1959, leaving a legacy in her employees and her products still on store shelves today.

—Brenda Farrington

SUGGESTED READING

Blackstock, Joseph R. *Report on Laura Scudder.* Monterey Park, CA: Historical Society of Monterey Park, 1974.

SEVERANCE, CAROLINE M. (1820-1914)

The women's movement in the United States has continually been one of struggle and perseverance. Many women have been extremely influential and have received much attention, based upon the far-reaching effects of the history-making movements that began in the 19th century. While famous women's movement supporters such as Susan B. Anthony and Elizabeth Cady Stanton deserve much of the recognition, many remain unknown. Perhaps the most overlooked woman to encourage the woman suffrage movement was Caroline Severance, who was responsible for the foundation of the movement's organization. Through Severance's active role in the basic operations of the woman suffrage movement, a newfound exuberance began that allowed women across the United States to expand their influence and continue the fight for equal opportunity and treatment.

Caroline M. Seymour Severance was born in Canadaigua, New York, in 1820 to a conservative banker, Orson Seymour, and a pioneering activist for women's rights, Caroline Clarke. After graduating with honors from the Female Seminary in Geneva, New York, in 1835 at the age of 15, she taught at Mrs. Luther Halsey's boarding school for girls on the Ohio River below Pittsburgh until 1840, when she married Theodoric Severance, an abolitionist Cleveland banker. At the time of her marriage, Severance claimed that her husband had "freed her from bondage to authority, dogmas and conservative ideas and for making a reformer of her." Perhaps this was the moment that Caroline decided to become an advocate for women's rights, as her household became a shining light for liberal causes. Not unlike other influential women in the 19th century, Severance believed in the woman's role as wife and mother, but began to add an emphasis on a woman's ability to shape and mold public policy.

In 1853, after settling in Cleveland, Severance attended several conventions on behalf of women's rights issues and made her first indelible mark on the lecture circuit with a speech at Boston's Mercantile Library concerning "humanity: a definition and a plea." In October of that same year, at the Women's Rights Convention in Cleveland, Horace Greeley, editor and influential political figure who crusaded against the oppression of women, pushed Caroline

Caroline M. Seymour Severance, circa 1910.

Severance into the true limelight of woman suffrage. Before the convention began, Greeley stated to Severance:

> I think the present state of our laws respecting property and inheritance, as respects married women, show very clearly that women OUGHT NOT to be satisfied with her present position; yet it may be that she is so. If all those who have never given this matter a serious thought are to be considered on the side of conservatism, of course, that side must preponderate. Be this as it may, woman alone can, in the present state of controversy, speak effectively for woman, since none others can speak with authority or from the depths of a personal experience.

From this point on, the fire had been lit. Caroline Severance, with the support of Greeley, realized that without the voice of women concerning women's rights, the message would not be as effective and, as a result, it would stagnate.

At this time, Severance became acquainted with Elizabeth Cady Stanton and Susan B. Anthony, but eventually split with them and supported a more conservative view of full integration of African Americans after the Civil War. She felt that unqualified integration into white society and women's clubs should be a state decision, rather than one made by the federal government. As the movement increased in fervor and strength, she aided Susan B. Anthony in founding the American Equal Rights Association in

1866, and in 1867, with Lucretia Mott and others, founded the Free Religious Association.

With the true foundation of the women's movement in place, organizations began to take hold of the movement's strength and determination and take it to new heights. In 1868 Severance was instrumental in founding the New England Women's Club (NEWC) in Boston. This club met the needs of women who "sought to exert their influence outside the home." As the club movement gathered steam, Severance insisted upon the importance of the society as an organized force to be reckoned with by women and men alike. This would be more than the typical good-works societies and homey associations in which women had been used to being involved. Severance felt that the term "club" was chosen to escape the "old special titles used for women's unions, in church and other activities, and this will be a new departure in fellowship and effort." It was evident that the women's movement was moving in a new direction. These newfound organizations differed from their predecessors in the depth and breadth of their interests, adding to the women's concern for continual "self-improvement."

As this movement spread, ideas and methods were incorporated into a multitude of advancements for women across the country. Through Severance's leadership, the women's club movement took on a number of diverse forms. Included in the foci of these groups were investigations into self-improvement, culture, and social problems. Social events were planned, moral reform societies organized, and charitable societies established to deal with the all-important problems facing women in the 19th century. As various clubs took hold around the nation, Severance found herself en route to the other coast and to the city of Los Angeles. Because of the poor health of her husband's mother, the Severances relocated to the West Coast in 1875, and immediately the infant metropolis felt the tenacity of Caroline Severance. In 1878, battling the city's newspapers and male leadership, she began to organize Angelino women and founded the Los Angeles Women's Club, which was dedicated to improving the lives of homeless children, and the Orphan's Home Society was quickly established immediately after.

As Severance advanced in years, her love for organizing women did not wane. After the death of her husband in 1892, she continued to toil in the areas of "Christian Socialism, Progressivism, anti-imperialism, and peace." A completely new radical persona had developed to complement her wide-ranging crusade for woman suffrage and other issues. With the advent of her death in 1914 at the tender age of 94, Severance left a brilliant legacy of stoic leadership throughout the women's movement, from the initial club movement on the eastern seaboard to the betterment of women's rights on the West Coast. Perhaps her life can best be described in her own words, relating the experience of women to a continued fight against those forces that suppressed them. She claimed:

> The woman's clubs and the members of the churches, the world over, might with one united stroke, overthrow the strongholds of vice, of selfish greed and oppression which stand entrenched in law and custom and defiant of human welfare.

The experiences and influential career of Severance might not receive top billing in the overall investigation of the women's movement, but her contributions must not be overlooked as an instrumental factor in paving the way for many organizations that followed her groundbreaking leads.

Charles Joseph Sedey

SUGGESTED READINGS

Blair, Karen J. *The Clubwoman as Feminist: True Womanhood Redefined, 1868-1914.* New York: Holmes & Meier, 1980.

Flexner, Eleanor, and Ellen Fitzpatrick. *Century of Struggle: The Woman's Rights Movement in the United States.* London: Belknap Press, 1959.

Gere, Anne Ruggles. *Intimate Practices: Literacy and Cultural Work in U.S. Women's Clubs, 1880-1920.* Urbana: University of Illinois Press, 1997.

Greeley, Horace. *Proceedings of the Women's Rights Convention, Cleveland, Ohio, 1853.* Cleveland, OH: Gray, Beardsley, Spear, 1854.

Haarsager, Sandra. *Organized Womanhood: Cultural Politics in the Pacific Northwest, 1840-1920.* Norman: University of Oklahoma Press, 1997.

SEWELL, HELEN MOORE (1896-1957)

Helen Moore Sewell was born at Mare Island Navy Yard, across the Napa River from Vallejo in California, on June 27, 1896. Her father, William, a Navy commander, soon moved the family to Guam, where he was appointed governor. Her mother died when she was a very young girl, and by age 7 Sewell had traveled the world with her father and two sisters. Her father died shortly before her 8th birthday, and she and her sisters grew up in Brooklyn in the home of her aunt and uncle.

Sewell began painting and drawing at an early age. At the age of 12, she became the youngest person ever to be admitted to the Pratt Institute, founded in New York by oil mogul and philanthropist Charles Pratt. She also studied under the Russian artist Alexander Archipenko, who dramatically influenced her style.

Sewell's early work was both as an author and an illustrator. She soon began drawing Christmas and greeting cards, and in 1924 illustrated her first book, *The Cruise of the Little Dipper and Other Fairy Tales.* Her many years of travel provided a variety of subjects to draw upon, including stories of a Japanese sailor on Guam *(Ming and Mehitable)* to her experiences with her sisters in England and France *(Peggy and the Pony).* She illustrated her own book, *ABC for Everyday,* in 1930, and a year later collaborated with her sister on a book titled *Building a House in Sweden.*

Though Sewell's written work was never recognized as significant, her artistry drew national attention. Her characters were primarily drawn from her imagination; she rarely used real people as subjects. In 1932 she illustrated *Little House in the Big Woods,* the first work of Laura Ingalls Wilder. Others followed in the Little House series. She went on to illustrate for such notables as Emily Dickinson, Jane Austen, Charlotte Bronte, and A. A. Milne. Sewell drawings also appeared in the *New Yorker* magazine.

Sewell branched out into new and different styles with the publication of *Three Tall Tales* in 1947. She employed a comic book style to put some "fun" into the stories. She listened to the advice of children who told her that her animals were too true to life and not exaggerated enough. The types of books she was illustrating were humorous, and in her words, "nonsense lends itself readily to this form."

In all, Sewell illustrated 72 books. She died after a long illness on February 24, 1957, in New York.

—Neal Lynch

SUGGESTED READINGS

Commire, Anne. *Something About the Author.* Detroit, MI: Gale Research, 1971.

Helen Sewell. Retrieved from webpages.marshall.edu/~irby1/laura/sewell.html.

Miller, Bertha E. Mahony. *Illustrators of Children's Books 1744-1945*. Boston, MA: Horn Book, 1947.

Silvey, Anita. *Children's Books and Their Creators*. Boston: Houghton Mifflin, 1995.

Women Children's Book Illustrators. "Helen Moore Sewell." Retrieved from www.ortakales.com/illustrators/Sewell.html.

SILKO, LESLIE MARMON (1948-)

Leslie Marmon Silko was born in Albuquerque, New Mexico, in 1948, and grew up on the Laguna Pueblo reservation near her birthplace. She claims a mixed heritage of Pueblo, Laguna, Mexican, and white blood. Her great-grandfather, Robert G. Marmon, was a white man who came to the reservation in the late 19th century, married a Pueblo woman, and became deeply involved in tribal politics. Over several generations, the Marmons have become an established part of the tribe, yet their position has always been complex, at once insiders and outsiders. Silko's own life has been rooted in the culture of the Laguna Pueblo, although she left the reservation to attend school, and later college, in Albuquerque. With the exception of a 2-year stay in Alaska, she has written, taught, and made her home in the Southwest. Married and divorced twice, with a son by each marriage, she currently resides in Tucson, Arizona. She has been called the first Native American woman novelist and holds an undisputed place in the western literary canon.

Although her collection of poetry, *Laguna Woman Poems* (1974), was her first major publication, it was *Ceremony,* published in 1977, that brought her the popular and critical attention that she enjoys today. This novel is inextricably intertwined with the landscape and stories of her homeland. The plot follows the healing journey of Tayo, a half-white, half-Native American man, returning to the reservation after fighting in World War II and witnessing his cousin's death during the Bataan Death March. Tayo's emotional and mental illnesses are linked to the "illness" of the drought-ridden land, the other "sick" young people of the tribe, who, like Tayo, have lost their connection to the traditional ways, and the world as a whole, which is being threatened by the "witchery" of nuclear war

and environmental destruction. Tayo visits a medicine man, who performs a healing ceremony, marking the beginning of Tayo's quest to recover his uncle's lost cattle and reject the violence of the returning veterans. This journey initiates Tayo's eventual return to health and signals the healing of the reservation and the defeat of the witchery.

The form of this novel is unique and illustrates Silko's connection to the tradition of Laguna storytelling. The plot is interspersed with poems that tell Tayo's own story as well as that of Nau'ts'ity'i, the Earth Mother, who grows angry and deserts the people after they become distracted by Ck'o'yo magic. The poems and the stories they tell are an integral part of Tayo's healing and Silko's vision. In following his uncle's lost cattle, meeting the mysterious woman Ts'eh, and rejecting the violence of the witchery, Tayo reenacts the ancient stories. Indeed, the stories themselves provide the necessary "medicine." As the opening poem states, "Don't be fooled./ They [the stories] are all we have, you see, all we have to fight off illness and death./ You don't have anything / if you don't have the stories." The stories, and the novel itself, become the ceremony through which Tayo, and the readers along with him, are reconnected to the ancient ways that emphasize harmony with the land.

Silko's next major piece continues to emphasize the importance of the Laguna storytelling tradition, and is aptly titled *Storyteller* (1981). This text, even more so than *Ceremony*, breaks generic conventions and mixes fictional short stories with poetry, autobiographical sections, and photos. Her writing here is not just an exercise in telling stories but also in linking her artistic expression to her cultural and personal history. Like all of her writing, her stories draw heavily on ancient myths and center on Native American individuals and communities. Several of the stories are critical of white exploitation of indigenous people and the environment, a theme she explores in most of her fiction.

Her epic and controversial novel, *Almanac of the Dead* (1991), takes up these and other ideas on a much grander scale. It covers several centuries and at least 50 different characters. Joy Harjo has said of this novel that it is "an exploded version of the same text [*Ceremony*], only now the terrain encompasses all of America." The "almanac" refers to an ancient Mayan writing that is being kept by a Native American psychic and predicts the end of European rule in the

Americas. The apocalyptic novel is peopled with drug dealers, pornographers, sadists, and practitioners of bestiality. This bleak vision and its gruesome violence have led to much criticism of *Almanac,* and challenge readers who are asked to be "witnesses" to the witchery that pollutes the world. However, as one critic suggests, this testing of readers' sensibilities is exactly what Silko intends. For "if we are truly horrified, we will take steps towards change. . . . Silko's mission in this novel is to present the horror in such a way that it cannot be shunted aside."

This transformative and haunting power is present in all of Silko's writing. As an artist and activist, she blends ancient traditions and wisdom with contemporary issues and images. Her writing is an important contribution to both Native American literature history and the southwestern American canon.

—Maureen Woodard Dana

SUGGESTED READINGS

Allen, Paula Gunn. "The Feminine Landscape of Leslie Marmon Silko's *Ceremony,*" in Paula Gunn Allen, ed., *Studies in American Indian Literature: Critical Essays and Course Designs.* New York: Modern Language Association, 1983.

Arnold, Ellen, ed. "Listening to the Spirits: An Interview with Leslie Marmon Silko," in *Conversions with Leslie Marmon Silko.* Jackson: University Press of Mississippi, 2000.

Powers, Janet. "Mapping the Prophetic Landscape in *Almanac of the Dead,*" in Louis Barnett, ed., *Leslie Marmon Silko: A Collection of Critical Essays.* Albuquerque: University of New Mexico, 1999.

Silko, Leslie Marmon. *Laguna Woman Poems.* New York: Greenfield Review Press, 1974.

Silko, Leslie Marmon. *Ceremony.* New York: Viking, 1977.

Silko, Leslie Marmon. *Storyteller.* New York: Seaver, 1981.

Silko, Leslie Marmon. *Almanac of the Dead: A Novel.* New York: Simon & Schuster, 1991.

Silko, Leslie Marmon. *Yellow Woman.* New Brunswick, NJ: Rutgers University Press, 1993.

SMITH, FERN M. (1933-)

Born in San Francisco in 1933, Fern M. Smith received her associate's degree from Foothill Community College in 1970. She transferred to Stanford, where she graduated with a bachelor of arts degree in 1972. Upon receiving her J.D. from Stanford Law School in 1975, she opened her private practice in San Francisco, where she stayed until 1986. From 1986 to 1988, she served as a judge on the San Francisco County Superior Court. On May 9, 1988, Ronald Reagan nominated her for the seat on the U.S. District Court for the Northern District of California vacated by Samuel Conti. The Senate confirmed her on July 26, 1988, and she received her commission on July 27, 1988. In 1999 she was named director of the Federal Judicial Center.

—Marcus J. Schwoerer

SUGGESTED READING

Fern M. Smith. Retrieved from air.fjc.gov/history/judges_frm.html. Source: History of the Federal Judiciary. http://www.fjc.gov. Web site of the Federal Judicial Center, Washington, D.C.

SNYDER, CHRISTINA A. (1947-)

In 1947 Christina A. Snyder was born in Los Angeles. She attended Pomona College, graduating with her B.A. in 1969. She studied law at Stanford Law School and received her J.D. in 1972. Immediately after graduation, she began her private practice in her home state and worked there for the next 25 years. When Edward Rafeedie vacated his seat on the U.S. District Court for the Central District of California, President Bill Clinton nominated her to fill the position on January 7, 1997. The Senate confirmed the nomination on November 7, 1997, and she received her commission on November 10, 1997.

—Marcus J. Schwoerer

SUGGESTED READING

Christina A. Snyder. Retrieved from air.fjc.gov/history/judges_frm.html. Source: History of the Federal Judiciary. http://www.fjc.gov. Web site of the Federal Judicial Center, Washington, D.C.

ST. JOHNS, ADELA ROGERS
(1894-1988)

Adela Rogers St. Johns was born in 1894, the daughter of noted criminal lawyer Earl Rogers. Her early childhood was characterized by frequent moves, as her father traversed the West Coast in pursuit of his legal career. In 1913, when she was 18, her father introduced her to William Randolph Hearst, and from that meeting she became the first female reporter for the *San Francisco Examiner.* She worked several beats, including crime, sports, city hall, and the hotel beat. She was transferred to the *Los Angeles Herald* in 1914, the same year she married William Ivan "Ike" St. Johns, a graduate of Stanford University and a copy editor for the *Herald.* In 1921 she went to work as a Hollywood columnist at *Photoplay* magazine but continued her work for the *Herald.* She quickly established herself as a Hollywood insider during the days when it was becoming the motion picture capital of the world.

Among the stories she covered for the Hearst papers were the Leopold and Loeb murder (1925), the assassination of Huey Long (1935), the trial of Bruno Hauptmann for the kidnapping and murder of the Lindbergh baby (1935), and the abdication of Edward VIII (1936). Though she retired from journalism in 1948, she returned to the *San Francisco Examiner* to cover the trial of Patty Hearst, her former employer's granddaughter, in 1976.

St. Johns was married three times, to Ike St. Johns from 1914 to 1927, to Richard Hyland from 1928 to 1934, and to F. Patrick O'Toole from 1936 to 1942. Each of her marriages ended in divorce. She had four children: two from her first marriage, one from her second, and one adopted child.

In addition to her work as a journalist, she wrote several screenplays, including *The Red Kimono* and *What Price Hollywood,* which was later remade as *A Star Is Born.* She also wrote several books, including a novel, *Tell No Man;* a book about her experiences in Hollywood, *Love, Laughter, and Tears: My Hollywood Story;* and her autobiography, *The Honeycomb.*

St. Johns also took an interest in spiritual matters, becoming involved with the Church of Religious Science. Among the books she wrote with a spiritual cast were *Affirmative Prayer in Action* and *No Goodbyes: My Search Into Life Beyond Death.* She was working on a book titled *The Missing Years of Jesus* at the time of her death.

—Scott Kesilis

SUGGESTED READINGS

Adela Rogers St. John. Retrieved from herstory.freehomepage.com/pages/rogersstjohn.html.

St. John, Adela Rogers. *The Honeycomb,* Garden City, NY: Doubleday, 1969.

STEWART, ELINORE PRUITT
(1876-1933)

Escaping a life of poverty in the Oklahoma Territory, Elinore Rupert headed to Denver in 1907 after losing her husband in a railroad accident. She hoped to find work to support herself and her 2-year-old daughter, Jerrine. She found work there as a housekeeper for a retired schoolteacher named Mrs. Juliet Coney, to whom she wrote letters after leaving for Wyoming in answer to an ad for a housekeeper for a rancher named Clyde Stewart and to claim a homestead of her own. Those letters are collected into a book called *Letters of a Woman Homesteader.* In Wyoming, she filed for a homestead of 147 acres and married Clyde Stewart soon after. Her letters include detailed descriptions of ranch life.

Elinore explores the wilderness around her with her family, and writes numerous descriptive letters about the various people and places that she visits. More of her works include *Letters on an Elk Hunt* (1915) and stories in the *Atlantic Monthly* titled "The Return of the Woman Homesteader" (1919) and "Snow: A Letter from the Woman Homesteader" (1923).

—Carolyn Stull

SUGGESTED READINGS

George, Susanne, Ph.D. "The Classic Journey of a Woman Homesteader: The Travel Theme in Elinore Pruitt Stewart." Retrieved from www.unk.edu/acad/english/faculty/bloomfields/Stewart/EPSTravel.htm.

Smith, Sherry L. "Single Women Homesteaders: The Perplexing Case of Elinore Pruitt Stewart." *Western Historical Quarterly* 22 (May 1991): 163-183.

STOTLER, ALICEMARIE
HUBER (1942-)

Alicemarie Huber was born on May 29, 1942, in Alhambra, California. She received her B.A. degree from the University of Southern California in 1964 and a J.D. from the same institution in 1967. While attending USC, she was honored as the winner of the Statewide Moot Court Competition, received the American Jurisprudence Award in Civil Procedure, and was a member of Kappa Alpha Theta.

Upon graduation, she served as deputy district attorney in Orange County, California. She married James Allen Stotler in September of 1971 and set herself up in private practice in the firm Stotler & Stotler of Santa Ana in 1973.

Stotler became municipal court judge of the Harbor Judicial District, Newport Beach, in 1976 and held that post for 2 years. She also served as justice pro tem for the Fourth District Court of Appeals in San Bernardino, California, and sat on the Orange County Superior Court.

Stotler returned to private practice for 2 years beginning in 1983, and is currently a U.S. District Court judge in Santa Ana, California. She resides in Southern California and spends her off time enjoying the outdoors with her husband.

—Neal Lynch

SUGGESTED READINGS

City News Service, December 6, 2000; January 22, 2001; February 6, 2002.

Los Angeles Times, May 26, 2000.

Reincke, Mary, and Jeaneen C. Wilhelmi, eds. *The American Bench*. Minneapolis, MN: Reginald Bishop Foster, 2001.

Stotler, Alicemarie Huber. Retrieved from air.fjc.gov/servlet/uGetInfo?jid=2304. Source: History of the Federal Judiciary. http://www.fjc.gov. Web site of the Federal Judicial Center, Washington, D.C.

SUMMERS, EMMA A. MCCUTCHEON (1858-1941)

Emma A. McCutcheon Summers, known as the Oil Queen of California, was born in Kentucky before the Civil War. She graduated from the New England Conservatory of Music and became a piano teacher. She moved west to Texas and then to Los Angeles with her husband, Alpha C. Summers. Summers saved the money she earned from piano lessons and began to invest in real estate. This was the turning point for Summers, for she would go on to help change the course of Los Angeles.

The oil boom in Los Angeles began when Edward L. Doheny and Charles A. Canfield struck oil in Crown Hill, at Colton Street and Glendale Boulevard. Summers took $700 from her savings and bought a half interest in a well at the site of today's civic center. She caught black fever, a term that has been used to describe people who became fanatical over the oil boom, and borrowed money so that she could invest in several more wells in Crown Hill. By 1897 the once quiet residential community of Crown Hill was filled with oil drills and derricks while homes and gardens were torn up in the search for more black gold.

Summers was known to go out to her wells and direct her workers during the day and at night give piano lessons in order to fund more drilling. By the early 1900s, Summers owned 14 wells, producing about 50,000 barrels a month. She sold her oil to hotels, factories, railroads, and the Pacific Light and Power Company. The price of oil peaked at $1.80 per barrel before it hit bottom at 15¢ in 1903. With prices so low, Summers began to buy out other operators, and patiently waited for the oil prices to rise again. By World War I, Summers's wait was over. The nation needed oil for wartime, and people in the Los Angeles area began to own and operate their own cars, which created a greater need in the local market.

Summers did not limit herself to oil; she also purchased theaters, apartment houses, a paint company, several ranches, an art collection, and a mansion on Wilshire Boulevard. But the oil boom in Los Angeles came to an end and the oil workers left Crown Hill to go on to Long Beach, Torrance, and other places in Southern California. Summers found herself in some financial difficulties. Wells went dry and she lost personal assets to satisfy her debts. Later she would move into a home on California Street, which she turned into a hotel that she named the Queen. She did not remain at the Queen, but lived at the Biltmore and Alexandria Hotels for a number of years. She ended her days in a Glendale nursing home and passed away in 1941 at the age of 83.

—Michelle A. Stretch

SUGGESTED READING

Rasmussen, Cecelia. "L.A., Then and Now: The Gush of Oil Was Music to Queen's Ear." *Los Angeles Times*, July 11, 1999, p. B3.

T

TAN, AMY (1952-)

Amy Tan was born in Oakland, California, on February 19, 1952, to parents John and Daisy Tan, who had come to America from China only years earlier. When she was 15, her father and brother both died of brain tumors and her mother moved the family to Montreux, Switzerland, where Tan attended high school. Upon graduation in 1969, Tan returned with her family to the United States, living in the San Francisco area.

Against her mother's wishes, Amy went to San Jose City College and transferred to San Jose State because she wanted to be closer to her boyfriend, Louis DeMattei. Amy received her bachelor's degree in English and linguistics in 1972 and her M.A. in linguistics in 1973, both from San Jose State. She worked as a consultant for disabled children from 1976 to 1981 and from 1981 to 1987 as a freelance technical writer for companies such as AT&T, IBM, and Pacific Bell. She married Lou DeMattei, now a tax attorney, in 1975. She currently resides in San Francisco.

In recent years, Tan joined the band Rock Bottom Remainders with other literary talents Dave Barry, Ridley Pearson, Barbara Kingsolver, and Stephen King. Tan's voice for the band shows yet another side of her contribution to the contemporary American West. The band's performances primarily benefit literary and First Amendment rights groups.

Although Tan is reputed as an Asian American writer who brought the Chinese American experience to the forefront of America's literary imagination, the universal themes of her work evidence her intention to create a work of art. She is the epitome of the great American storyteller using history, flashbacks, multiple narratives, poetry, and mysticism. She primarily depicts the ongoing struggle to resolve the conflict between Chinese heritage and the American lifestyle. Throughout her writings, she uses this clash of cultures to explore larger themes of womanhood, family, self-discovery, and personal identity.

THE JOY LUCK CLUB (1988)

Tan left her business as a technical writer to write fiction, producing a year later *The Joy Luck Club*. Originally intended to be a collection of short stories, it instantly became an international best-seller and lauded as an intricately woven novel of the Chinese American experience. It remained on the *New York Times* best-seller list for 40 weeks and won the National Book Award and the L.A. Book Award. Tan coauthored the screenplay with Ron Bass (*My Best Friend's Wedding* and *Snow Falling on Cedars*), and *The Joy Luck Club* was released in theaters in 1990.

In *The Joy Luck Club*, Amy Tan voices the Chinese American story of the American West told and retold through generations of immigrants. It is the story of American western history: the struggle, the sacrifice, and the pain of a war-torn homeland and the dreams and hopes for future generations that brought people out West. *The Joy Luck Club* tells the stories of four Chinese women and their daughters. The mothers lament the fact their daughters have become too Americanized and lost their Chinese heritage, yet they have not realized the American dream the mothers had so hoped for. The daughters, of course, resent their overbearing mothers and the high expectations, because they neither understand nor appreciate American culture or the difficulty of truly assimilating.

The novel begins with the story of Jing-Mei Woo, whose mother, Suyuan, founded the Joy Luck Club, a meeting of four women who play mah jong while feasting over Chinese dishes and discussing their stock market investments. Two months earlier, Suyuan died; Jing-Mei has been asked to take her mother's seat at the mah jong table. Her mother founded the Joy Luck Club over 30 years earlier in war-torn China as a defiant gesture against the Japanese. It became a refuge for the women where they could celebrate their perseverance and find strength and hope to face the unknown future. Shortly after the family arrived in San Francisco, Suyuan formed another Joy Luck Club. Although the entire four families gather for the Joy Luck Club meetings, only the four women play mah jong. Now that Suyuan has died, Jing-Mei assumes her mother's place at the table.

Although Suyuan shared parts of her story with Jing-Mei, she never finished it, and now the aunts feel compelled to complete her history. Finally, the aunts decide to pitch in to buy Jing-Mei a plane ticket to go to China to meet Suyuan's lost daughters, her half-sisters. For Jing-Mei, the journey reconciles her dual identities and she discovers an unknown part of herself upon learning her Chinese name.

As the stories unfold, the mothers speak of their past life in China and their struggles to maintain relationships with their daughters. Primarily, the mothers feel a strong sense of urgency to impart their stories to their daughters, since Suyuan died unexpectedly. The mothers' painful narratives recollect powerful and tragic memories with their own mothers and even grandmothers. Tan weaves in snapshots of multiple generations to show how brief moments leave significant and indelible thumbprints on the soul. All the mothers yearn for their daughters to understand them and learn how their tragic past defines them.

As the novel progresses, the division between mother and daughter grows deeper and the chasm is filled with silence, resentment, and shame. The daughters spend their lives running and hiding from their Chinese history and avoiding their Chinese identity, although in the process they have lost themselves. Living up to their mothers' high expectations is a repressive burden on each of the daughters, yet each of them seems to be driven by the desire to succeed and please their mothers. Waverly Jong achieves the most success, both as a child, winner of a national chess tournament, and as an adult, as a successful tax attorney; however, her life still falls short of the American dream her mother felt that coming to American was supposed to hold for her. Each of the daughters holds some deep-rooted fear of her Chinese identity because she cannot comprehend the power of such a complex, superstitious, culturally defined past; yet they all believe their own painfully divided lives as hyphenated Americans are equally misunderstood by their mothers.

At the heart of *The Joy Luck Club* is the Chinese belief in balance and the precariousness of the human condition. It is this desire for harmony with their daughters that compels the mothers to tell their stories, thereby helping the daughters learn to abandon their external striving for balance and look for a new harmony within themselves.

THE KITCHEN GOD'S WIFE (1991)

Amy Tan tells her mother's life story in *The Kitchen God's Wife* through the character Jiang Weili, or Winnie. The novel deals with similar themes as *The Joy Luck Club:* a mother-daughter relationship, secrets, a troubling, tragic past, and the renewal of family relationships. Upon learning of the death of her first husband, Winnie decides it is time for her daughter, Pearl, to hear her life story, a traumatic past she has kept secret for decades. Pearl sits in Winnie's kitchen and listens to her mother's story. Winnie relives her life story from 6 years old to the present and shares with her daughter the abuse and oppression she endured from her husband as well as the poverty, hunger, grief, and homelessness she experienced as a result of World War II.

As her mother shares her tremendous physical and psychological journey and Pearl begins to understand the sacrifice her mother has made, she recognizes her survivor instinct that compels her to reveal her own secret: Pearl has suffered with multiple sclerosis for the past 7 years. The spirit of hope and endurance is further reflected in Tan's incorporation of the Chinese folktale of the Kitchen God; however, Tan alters the ending to incorporate her own feminist reading. The Kitchen God reports to the emperor every year those who should be rewarded for enduring trials, and the wife emerges as a heroine for her own endurance and suffering. Thus, at the end of the novel, Winnie presents to Pearl a statue of the goddess, the Kitchen God's wife. Empowered by the revelation of their secrets, mother and daughter forge ahead with a renewed commitment to their relationship.

Tan's literary talent is clearly evident in this novel as she continues to use literary devices, themes, and symbols to depict Chinese history and the cultural tensions that exist between mother and daughter. Tan uses a frame device by opening the novel with Pearl's detailing the tension and rift between her and her mother. Pearl is a second-generation 40-year-old woman, married with two daughters. Like Waverly Jong, Pearl appears to be living the American dream, but is unhappy and apathetic about life. Winnie's criticism undermines Pearl's satisfaction with her career and often herself. Again, Tan revisits the theme of identity, both cultural and personal, in the characters of Winnie and Pearl. Winnie has lived in two cultures her whole life, but instead of embracing the duality, becomes unknown by the oppression of her first husband, and once again finds herself without identity when she comes to America. Pearl, who also experiences a lack of identity and is unwilling to embrace her Chinese heritage, comes to accept her Chinese history and must now claim her own new identity.

Food provides cultural associations and a rich language of imagery for Tan to illustrate the strength of character as well as Chinese history. The culinary traditions embody immigrant history. Winnie speaks of the foods she prepared and ate both in war and in celebration. She continually comments about food throughout her narrative with Pearl. The skills of food preparation symbolize another method of storytelling—passing tradition from generation to generation.

CHILDREN'S LITERATURE

After such a great welcome and acclaim by the literary critics for *The Joy Luck Club* and *The Kitchen God's Wife,* Tan devoted her energy to children's stories. She wrote *The Moon Lady* (1992) and *The Chinese Siamese Cat* (1994), now a PBS children's television series.

THE HUNDRED SECRET SENSES (1995)

In her third novel, Tan turns to the bond between sisters and further explores the conflict of identity and culture by creating two half-sisters, one whose father is Chinese and mother is white, Olivia, and the other,

Kwan, who is from Hakkia, a minority Chinese group. Upon the death of her father, Olivia learns of her half-sister, Kwan. Mother and daughter determine to bring Kwan to the United States from China. Kwan is 18 and believes she has yin eyes that let her see and speak to ghosts—a creation of Tan's and a new twist to this story, the magical and mystical.

Once again, Tan weaves a complex story of women's lives: half-sisters Olivia Bishop and Li Kwan and the friends Nelly Banner and Nunumu. These relationships share the hallmark of Tan's characters—complex and strained, filled with secrets, betrayal, and devotion. Olivia's childhood is marked by Kwan's stories of ghosts and a former life in 19th-century China. These stories develop into the tale of Nunumu and Nelly Banner, a story of their friendship and the betrayal that occurs as a result of a love relationship between Nelly Banner and Yiban. Kwan feels obligated to try and remedy the betrayal of Nunumu because she believes she was Nunumu in a previous life. Kwan's loyalties to her friend and to her sister compel her to take Olivia and her estranged husband, Simon, on a journey to China. In the homeland, Olivia discovers the heritage she was denying, and begins reconciliation with her husband, the reunion that Kwan was expecting.

This novel explores many of the same themes as in *The Joy Luck Club* and *The Kitchen God's Wife*: family relationships, ethnic identity, generational conflict, and the discovery of self-identity. Tan also uses her excellent storytelling skills to weave a complex narrative. Using Olivia's reflections upon her childhood as a frame device, Tan tells the story of Olivia and Kwan as sisters and, using Kwan's mystical flashbacks, constructs the story of Miss Banner and Nunumu. Tan employs the symbolism of food as both a vehicle to relive memories and a link to culture and heritage.

The Hundred Secret Senses illustrates Tan's literary talent. She received great acclaim for the character of Kwan as one of her most delightful, original, and memorable characters.

THE BONESETTER'S DAUGHTER (2001)

Her most recent work, *The Bonesetter's Daughter,* is an incredible story of mystery, superstition, self-discovery, ghosts, and secrets. It is the story of the American West in its preservation of personal history, of the family name, and the understanding of ancestral history through simple objects, such as towels that symbolize strife and perseverance. In the last weeks of Daisy Tan's life, Amy Tan learned her mother's birth name, and the family discovered many secrets about her former marriages, illegitimate children, and her birth date. So with the driving pain of grief, Tan rewrote a novel she had been working on for 5 years, but now with a flood of childhood memories and the inspiration of her grandmother's and mother's ghosts. This autobiographical novel is a story of discovery, revelation, and renewal.

The first part tells the story of Ruth, daughter of Lu Ling, whose 10-year relationship with Art is crumbling almost as quickly as her mother's mental and physical health. Once Ruth learns her mother has Alzheimer's disease, she becomes determined to translate the pages of her mother's history she had given her years before. She is on a quest to discover not only her heritage but, unbeknownst to her, also the Chinese identity that has eluded her for her whole life. The second part is the incredible story of Lu Ling from her childhood—secretly raised by her mother, Precious Auntie—to her immigration to the United States. It speaks of the strength and sacrifice of her mother and the personal tragedy she endures as well as the ambition to immigrate to the United States. Through discovery and revelation, the family relationships are strengthened and renewed. The final chapters reveal the mystery of their family history with the final discovery of the Bonesetter's name.

Tan is true to her reputation for strained mother/ daughter relationships as she continues to depict the affliction and affection between the Chinese mother and the American daughter. In *The Bonesetter's Daughter,* the bitter resentment is softened by the growing understanding and pride in personal heritage and an honest empathy for what parents are willing to sacrifice for their children, regardless of their bizarre rationalizations for shameful secrets and superstitions.

CONCLUSION

The Chinese immigrant experience depicts the difficulty of assimilation into an American culture that excludes, silences, and marginalizes those who do not conform to homogeneity. Tan as a voice of women of color breaks the silence of both the Chinese immigrant as well as the Chinese woman, creating an ethnic identity rooted in linguistic description. Her writing then asserts a politics of nonconformity

transcending definitions of ethnicity as well as undermining stereotypes of cultural expectations, especially the East-West dichotomy. Her works are clearly the vehicle for the expansion of American society.

Tan has achieved international acclaim. Her works have been widely anthologized, including her short essay "Mother Tongue" (1991), which was selected for the Best American Essays. Her literature lends itself to solid historical, feminist, cultural, and archetypal criticism. Moreover, she positions herself in the canon of American literature that redefines "American" not as the embodiment of the hyphenated experience but as the new American cultural identity, both self-aware and self-discovered and empowered by a unique and infinite inscription of personal cultural history transcribed onto the tapestry of American culture.

—Angela E. Henderson

SUGGESTED READINGS

Bloom, Harold. *Modern Critical Views: Amy Tan.* Philadelphia, PA: Chelsea House, 2000.

Caesar, Judith. "Patriarchy, Imperialism, and Knowledge in *The Kitchen God's Wife.*" *North Dakota Quarterly* 62(4, Fall 1994): 164-174.

Ho, Wendy Ann. "Mother and Daughter Writing and the Politics of Location in Maxine Hong Kingston's *The Woman Warrior* and Amy Tan's *The Joy Luck Club.*" *DAI* 54.7 (January 1994): DAI Number 9320902.

Huntley, Ed. *Amy Tan, A Critical Companion.* Westport, CT: Greenwood Press, 1998.

Ling, Amy, ed. *Between Worlds: Women Writers of Chinese Ancestry.* New York: Pergamon Press, 1990.

Shapiro, Laura. "Ghost Story." *Newsweek* (November 6, 1995): 91.

Shen, Gloria. "Born of a Stranger: Mother-Daughter Relationships and Storytelling in Amy Tan's *The Joy Luck Club,*" in Anne E. Brown and Marjanne E. Gooze, eds., *International Women's Writing: New Landscapes of Identity.* Westport, CT: Greenwood Press, 1995, 233-244.

The Spirit Within. The Salon Interview: Amy Tan. Retrieved from www.salon1999.com/12nov1995/feature/tan.html.

Wong, Sau-Ling Cynthia. "'Sugar Sisterhood': Situating the Amy Tan Phenomenon." *The Ethnic Canon: Histories, Institutions, and Interventions.* Minneapolis: University of Minnesota Press, 1995, 174-210.

TERASAWA, KUNIKO (1896-1991)

Kuniko Terasawa was born in Iida City, Naganoken, in Japan. She was the daughter of Kintaro and Yoshi Muramatsu. She married Uneo Terasawa in 1921 and they had two daughters, Kazuko and Haruko. She was the leader behind a newspaper, *The Utah Nippo,* that supplied information to first-generation Japanese who had migrated to the United States before World War II. The newspaper ran for 52 years and used metal type, which printed Japanese symbols.

Her death in 1991 marked the end of what is called in Japanese the Issei, meaning first-generation Japanese Americans. This ironically was the demographic that her writings were meant to reach out to. Her work in her advanced years earned her awards and recognition from her state of Utah and from the American Association of Retired Persons (AARP). The AARP featured her in its *Modern Maturity* magazine and on its television program as well.

While living, she received awards from Matsumoto City, where the premier female writer in Japan, Kamisaka Fuyoko, wrote a biography of Terasawa and printed a draft for television. Terasawa's fame was so great that her death was reported in newspapers in Japan before it was reported in the United States. She also received the Order of the Sacred Treasure, Zuihosho-5th Class, in the year 1968; she was rewarded by the Salt Lake Chapter of the Japanese American Citizens League for being the eldest donor to their cause; and she also accepted the Avon Josei Bunka Center award called the Million Yen.

She took over the newspaper from her husband, who died in 1939 from pneumonia. She guided the paper to about 10,000 subscribers, but subscriptions fell to about 700 near the time of her death. She remained the sole reporter, publisher, editor, and manager of the company that printed the delicate, old-fashioned way and celebrated its 75th anniversary in 1989. She had printed regularly until the bombing at Pearl Harbor, when the U.S. government ordered all printing in Japanese to cease. Soon after, she was used to inform the Japanese population about commands that came down from Washington about restrictions on the Japanese way of life during the war. She ended her life spending her Social Security earnings to sustain the paper and died a happy person, claiming that doing things the old way takes longer, but that those old things bring lots of joy.

—Kevin Christy

SUGGESTED READINGS

Arias, Ron. "Tireless Kuniko Terasawa Is the Force Behind a Newspaper Almost No One Can Read." *People Weekly* (September 25, 1989)

Thatcher, Leora. "Kuniko Muramatsu Terasawa: For 52 Years She Handset Type for a Unique Utah Newspaper." *Special Collections.* University of Utah. Retrieved from www.utahhistorytogo.org/utachiev.html.

U

ULFIG, CYNTHIA (1956-)

Cynthia Ulfig grew up in Woodland Hills, California, the daughter of a homemaker and a contractor. She earned her B.A. in political science from California State University, Northridge, and her law degree from Southwestern University School of Law in Los Angeles.

After graduating from law school, Ulfig went to work as a clerk for a personal injury firm. Shortly thereafter, she moved to the Los Angeles County District Attorney's Office in 1983, where she served as a trial attorney and later as a deputy district attorney. Her first child was born in 1990. Also in 1990 she first applied for a judgeship. In 1994, after the birth of her second child, she moved from trial work to filing cases within the District Attorney's Office in order to have a more stable schedule and to spend more time with her family.

On June 17, 1998, Ulfig became the first woman judge in the Santa Clarita Valley, presiding over the Newhall Municipal Court. Governor Pete Wilson appointed her to the position vacated by Judge H. Keith Bryham. Ulfig had applied for the job when she had heard that Bryham was retiring, and gained the support of many judges and prosecutors with whom she had worked over the years.

In 2000 the Newhall Municipal and Superior Courts merged, and Ulfig became the site judge of the superior court in the Santa Clarita Valley.

She currently lives in the Santa Clarita Valley with her husband, Don, and her children, Trevor and Allison.

—Scott Kesilis

SUGGESTED READINGS

Chambers, Carol, "Ulfig Appointed Newhall's First Woman Judge." *The Signal* (June 18, 1998).
Grossom, Janet, "A New Honor in Newhall." *The Signal* (July 15, 1998).

UNDERHILL, RUTH MURRAY (1883-1984)

Ruth Murray Underhill came to the field of anthropology as a middle-aged woman who had already tried marriage, social work, and novel writing. Born in 1883 to a Quaker family in Ossining, New York, she attended Vassar College and graduated in 1905 with an A.B. in English. Before World War I she was employed as a social worker in New York City. In 1920 she published her first novel, *White Moth,* about a successful businesswoman who must negotiate the strict gender roles of the workplace. After obtaining a divorce from Charles Crawford, she went directly to Columbia University, searching for a department that could help her to understand people. She landed in the Anthropology Department, in the office of Ruth Benedict.

At Columbia she also came under the influence of Franz Boas, who promoted anthropological study that endorsed cultural relativity and scientific objectivity. This quest for objectivity was manifested in an anthropological emphasis on precontact civilizations. Thus many Boasians sought informants who either remembered the old ways or continued to live without the corrupting influences of Christianity, modernization, and especially the English language. Although these studies often ignored contemporary political and economic situations in order to present a "purer" version of the past, Boasian anthropology ultimately encouraged closer contacts between natives and nonnatives.

Women Boas brought into anthropology and then sent into the field made many of these contacts. He sent his female students to work with native women and discover aspects of female ritual and life usually inaccessible to men. Boas thereby spawned a great deal of work by women anthropologists in the Southwest. Much of their work promoted Boas's agenda of cultural relativity by arguing for a uniquely female experience across cultural boundaries.

Thus in 1931 Underhill began her work with the Papago (Tohono O'Odham), using Maria Chona as her primary informant. After four trips to the Papago Reservation while in graduate school, she finished her fieldwork in 1934. She received her Ph.D. in 1935, and in 1939 she published her dissertation on *Social Organization of the Papago Indians.*

But Underhill's best-known work is her autobiography of Maria Chona, *Papago Woman* (1979), which originally appeared as Memoir No. 46 of the American Anthropological Association, "An Autobiography of Chona, a Papago Woman." In the original 1936 publication, Underhill expressed her interest in women's issues by emphasizing her informant's female perspective. The opening section describes Chona as a woman who, although immersed in her culture, challenged some of her culture's gender roles. Throughout the introductory material, Underhill interprets Chona's life from a feminist perspective and concludes that "on the whole, [her life] presents a fair picture of the crises which come to a Papago woman, heightened by a dynamic personality." In 1978, in the contextual material added to the autobiography, Underhill aligns herself with Papago women, making frequent references to "our women" and "we women." About the Sit-and-drink, she says that "here, the men officiated and we women stood in the background. It did not occur to me to resent this, for my companions did not."

Although she strove to get an exact transcription, Underhill was forced to use an interpreter for most of her work with Chona. She also says that she was obliged to edit the material to accommodate her white readers. Underhill thus arranged the life story in chronological order and cut out the repetitive

information because, she says, "Indian narrative style involves a repetition and a dwelling on unimportant details that confuse the white reader and make it hard for him to follow the story." She maintains, nonetheless, that she retained "the essentials" of the narrative and feels that the autobiography truly expresses Chona's thoughts, emotions, and narrative style.

In the following passage, for instance, Underhill uses Chona's emotion to structure the narrative:

> We always kept gruel in our house. It was in a big clay pot that my mother had made. She ground up seeds into flour. Not wheat flour—we had no wheat. But all the wild seeds, the good pigweed and the wild grasses. And corn, too! Some summers we could grow corn. All those things my mother kept in beautiful jars in our store-house. Every day she ground some more and added fresh flour to the gruel and some boiling water. That pot stood always ready so that whoever came in from running could have some. Oh, good that gruel was! I have never tasted anything like it. Wheat flour makes me sick! I think it has no strength. But when I am weak, when I am tired, my grandchildren make me gruel out of the wild seeds. That is *food.*

Chona seems to speak directly to her audience, expressing her enthusiasm for the old food and moving from thought to thought without clear connections. But the sense of togetherness and the sense of the past's presence form a circular cohesion that ties the threads of memories, explanation, and cultural details together. Contained within this discussion of gruel, Chona makes a not-so-oblique reference to the nasty foods white people eat (wheat flour), describes her culture's aesthetics (mother's useful yet beautiful jars), and argues for preservation of the old ways.

Because of her heavy-handed editorial work, many critics have questioned the ethnographic accuracy of Underhill's text. Others, however, praise her efforts at cross-cultural communication and admire the literary qualities of the autobiography. Interestingly, the text's collaborative nature, its explicit feminist agenda, and its recently added contextual material continue to compel teachers and students of anthropology, life writing, women's studies, cultural studies, and Native American studies. *Papago Woman* remains one of the most popular ethnographic books on the market.

For over a decade, Underhill worked as a consultant for the Bureau of Indian Affairs. Then she taught anthropology at the University of Denver, New York

State Teachers College in New Paltz, and Colorado Women's College. From 1956 until she died in 1984, she traveled, wrote, and consulted.

—Becky Jo (Gesteland) McShane

SUGGESTED READINGS

Babcock, Barbara A., and Nancy J. Parezo. *Daughters of the Desert: Women Anthropologists and the Native American Southwest, 1880-1980.* Albuquerque: University of New Mexico Press, 1988, 72-75.

Griffen, Joyce. "Ruth Murray Underhill," in Ute Gacs, Aisha Khan, Jerrie McIntyre, and Ruth Weinberg, eds., *Women Anthropologists: Selected Biographies.* Urbana: University of Illinois Press, 1989, 355-360.

U.S. AIR FORCE ACADEMY

One of the goals of the women's movement in the United States, from its beginnings during the late 19th century to the present day, has been equality in the workplace. In the military, officers who have had the benefit of a service academy education (at West Point, Annapolis, or the Air Force Academy) traditionally have a competitive edge when it comes time for promotions or consideration for desirable jobs. Until 1976 none of the service academies accepted women as cadets, which posed a problem for women who wanted to make a career in the military. At the academies, cadets not only learned the tools of their trade, but they also made important friendships that would help them later in their careers. Without this opportunity for networking, women who otherwise would have been very competitive often did not get the best jobs. Top military leaders opposed allowing women into the academies for various reasons, but perhaps the hardest to overcome was the traditional idea that the military is no place for a woman. Through the years, women have proven themselves capable of stepping up to the challenge of overcoming stereotypes and performing well in difficult situations.

ACADEMY LIFE

The Air Force Academy is a rigorous 4-year institution, academically similar to a civilian institution, where cadets earn a bachelor of science degree as well as complete an array of military training.

The Academy has excellent academic facilities, and in this area is on a par with schools such as Harvard, Princeton, and Stanford. It has been ranked the fifth "Toughest to Get Into" and fourth "Best Overall Academic Experience for Undergraduates" in the nation, according to the *Princeton Review*. Cadets take an average of 18 to 22 credit hours per semester and can choose any one of 28 academic majors, ranging from aeronautical engineering and mathematics to English and history.

Military training, however, is what sets the Air Force Academy apart from other academic institutions. This training begins on the very first day a cadet arrives at the Academy with a 6-week period known as basic cadet training (BCT), lovingly called "Beast" by the cadets. During this period, the cadets are introduced to the fundamental differences between military life and civilian life. They learn military customs and courtesies, such as saluting and flag decorum, and are given a series of character lessons. They also learn rifle drill, marching, and how to properly wear their uniforms. In the second phase of BCT, the cadets move out to an encampment on the Academy grounds, known as Jack's Valley, where the training becomes much more physical. They learn to operate the M-16 rifle and the M-9 handgun. They participate in athletic competitions, get their first taste of hand-to-hand combat training, and learn teamwork in stressful situations by participating in various obstacle courses and physical-conditioning exercises.

After BCT, cadets enter the academic year, but their military training does not end. They must keep their dorm rooms in immaculate condition, pass uniform inspections, and continue classes in character development, military tactics, and military history. Cadets also participate in what is called the "leadership laboratory." This is an essential part of the cadet experience that does not take place during a specific class period. In the leadership laboratory, cadets lead each other in the military operations of the cadet wing. This allows cadets to hone their leadership style and learn how to be effective followers before they are placed in an operational unit where mistakes would be more costly. In addition to all this, cadets must ensure that they remain in good enough physical condition so that they can pass the physical fitness tests that are administered every semester.

During the summer, academics cease, but other military training programs do not. These programs include leading the basic cadets in BCT and participating in introductory aviation programs, among many others. Cadets also have the opportunity to learn to fly gliders and master the techniques of free-fall parachuting. They participate in survival training and many other programs that build self-esteem, leadership, and military job skills.

With all the opportunities and challenges available to cadets, it is easy to see why women in the late 1960s and early 1970s saw their military careers impaired by their inability to attend the academies. During those times, academy graduates filled the higher ranks of all the branches almost entirely. This made opening the academies to women essential to equality in the military workforce.

THE FIGHT FOR ADMISSION

Women have served in the U.S. armed forces, in a restricted manner, since America's founding. During the Revolutionary War and the Civil War, women served in the armed forces as nurses. Many were actually on the battlefields fulfilling their duties. Even though men may have opposed their presence, the value of their service has never been questioned during times of national crisis. Each time the United States has gone to war, the role of women in war has increased. During World War I, the Navy and Marine Corps began enlisting women in their reserves. In World War II, the Women's Air Force Service Pilots (WASPs) flew transports and deliveries, freeing men for combat flying. By the 1950s and the Korean conflict, while women did not hold combat positions in the regular forces of the services, they did perform valuable administrative work. These expanding roles and the unquestioning value of the work women were doing in the armed forces made it difficult to argue effectively against giving women the excellent leadership training offered at the academies.

As women within the military pressed for an expanded role, which would lead to greater career opportunities and influence, the social movements of the 1960s and 1970s saw women in the military as a glaring example of women's inequity of opportunity. The Equal Rights Amendment, which would require complete equality between the sexes in the workplace, placed increasing pressure on Congress to voluntarily remove the existing barriers to women in the military in general and the service academies in particular.

Congress passed the Equal Rights Amendment on March 22, 1972, but it was never ratified by a sufficient number of states to become a part of the Constitution. This amendment applied especially in matters concerning education and employment. The appearance and passage of the amendment also made sex discrimination a highly visible issue. In addition to the pressures caused by this publicity, the Equal Rights Amendment also served as the basis for some of the most convincing arguments in support of women's admission to the academies, because education and employment opportunities were, and still are, some of the service academies' most potent recruiting tools.

In 1973 two young women applied for admission to the academies. Both the Naval and Air Force Academies flatly refused to consider the applications solely on the basis that the applicants were female. In response, Representatives Don Edwards (D-Calif.) and Jerome Waldie (D-Calif.) filed suit against the Secretary of Defense on the applicants' behalf. While the courts were not opposed to women's equality, they were, however, opposed to women in combat and were convinced that the service academies had been established for the sole purpose of training combat leaders. Thus, the courts ruled that since women could not serve in combat, they had no reason to attend military academies. These cases helped put the issue of women entering the service academies in the media spotlight.

There was heavy debate in Congress as the day to vote on the resolution that would become Public Law 94-106 came nearer. These debates reflected the same concerns that were brought up in the 1973 court cases. Besides a few relatively quiet members of Congress, the opposition to allowing women into the academies came mainly from the military itself. Military leaders stuck to the familiar combat argument. They said that the distinguished service of women in the military had traditionally been, and should remain, in support roles. They argued that sufficient training for these roles could already be found in the Reserve Officer Training Corps and Officer Training School. People such as Lt. Gen. A. P. Clark, then superintendent of the Air Force Academy, Col. Jacqueline Cochran, a pioneering female aviator, and even male cadets themselves, such as Cadet Capt. Stephen Townes, who was called to testify before Congress, voiced these ideas most loudly. Naval Academy officials cited the necessity of a two-track program should women be admitted. West Point officials said the addition of women would weaken their reserve of academy-trained combat officers.

Despite the strong military opposition and the arguments that were expressed in Congress and in the media, the hysteria behind the opposition was best expressed by Cadet Townes, who was a 4th-year cadet at West Point when these debates were taking place. When testifying before the house, he said that allowing women into the military service academies would forever weaken the morale of male cadets and destroy the "last bastion of military Puritanism."

Not all military men were opposed to the idea of women attending service academies. An article called "Solving the Controversy of Female Cadets" in the May 1972 issue of the *Talon,* a magazine written by and for cadets at the Air Force Academy, voiced this view. Here, Cadet Al Maurer expressed no reservations on allowing women into the Air Force Academy, citing women's higher academic performance statistics and the fact that an all-male school created an unrealistic worldview for the cadets. The constant use of the term "girls" and the joking tone of the article, however, gave the impression that this was an idea that was still not being taken quite seriously by cadets.

In general, military men opposed having women at the service academies by concentrating on the unsuitability of women for combat, while the supporters tended to concentrate their arguments around the Equal Rights Amendment that was in the process of being ratified by the states. To counter the strong opposition of prominent military figures, many women's organizations, such as the Defense Committee on Women in the Services (DACOWITS) and the National Organization for Women (NOW), testified in support of sending women to the service academies. People in Congress like Representative Pierre DuPont (R-Del.) and Representative Patricia Schroeder (D-Colo.) also supported this view because of the political visibility caused by the Equal Rights Amendment.

The first major argument in favor of allowing women to attend the Academy involved the value of an Academy education to promotion. Representative DuPont argued most convincingly in favor of the bill. DuPont's point rested on the demographics of the officer corps; at the second lieutenant level, academy graduates were a minority, but at the general officer level, almost 100% of officers at that time wore the ring. This, when considered along with the tremendous networking opportunities available to Academy graduates, begged the conclusion that since women were never given the opportunity to attend an academy, they were automatically put at a disadvantage when it came to promotion. This, DuPont argued, was a case of sex discrimination of the type forbidden by the Equal Rights Amendment.

Since opponents focused on the combat issue, supporters of sending women to the Academy focused their arguments on countering those claims. In the military, combat experience is almost essential to getting promoted to the highest ranks. By not allowing women into the academies and into combat positions, the military leaders were effectively limiting women's military careers to the lower ranks. Supporters of allowing women into the academies saw this thinking as restrictive and thus not legal for two main reasons. First, the services were moving toward an all-volunteer force. This made recruiting men more and more difficult. So DuPont, and many like him, turned to the increasing number of women who wanted a career in the military to fill the gaps in the ranks. A second major change in military culture was the new technology age into which warfare was advancing. This paradigm shift made it possible for women to hold nominally combat positions, such as missileers, who are stationed well within U.S. borders and have no more demanding physical tasks than pressing buttons. This point was extremely important, because not only had physical requirements been lowered in many fields, but it also directly rebutted the main argument in favor of the opposition, namely, that women could not hold combat positions because they were not physically strong enough. In today's military, being in combat does not necessarily mean carrying your buddy to safety while dodging bullets, so physical strength is no longer a critical requirement. In addition, many women, such as nurses, were on the front lines, even though they were technically in non-combat career fields. These changes in force structure meant that an academy education was just as essential for career female officers as it was for male officers.

In 1975 the Merchant Marine Academy opened its admissions to women voluntarily, again throwing the debate into the media spotlight. Because of this change, congressmen were particularly wary of being seen as sexist or backward, and so when it finally came time to vote, they passed Public Law 94-106 by a whopping 303 to 96 in the House and similar numbers in the Senate. The first women to attend the Air Force Academy entered in 1976 and graduated in 1980.

THE INTEGRATION

Despite his very vocal disapproval of the decision to admit women, Air Force Academy Superintendent Gen. A. P. Clark was in the process of developing a plan for the integration of women at the Air Force Academy. This plan, officially known as Ops Plan #7-73: Contingency Plan for Integration of Females into the Cadet Wing, unofficially known as the "Pink Plan," attempted to address all the issues of integrating women into the Academy. The Pink Plan set up the Air Training Officer (ATO) Program, which established female role models for the first female cadets, discussed the design of uniforms, outlined new physical standards, and proposed new dormitory arrangements.

The leadership at the Academy considered the ATO program to be the most essential program for the successful integration of women as cadets. The idea was to give the first women cadets female role models. This program was based on a similar program that was used at the Academy's inception when there were no upper-class cadets for male role models. Thus, junior women officers were put through a mock BCT and then assigned positions as ATOs. Despite General Clark's planning, these women quickly ran into trouble. Even though they performed well in the training scenarios, male cadets still did not believe that women were capable of being cadets. The training of the ATOs—which was conducted by upper-class men— also proved that men could indeed train women without the supervision of other women. So, ironically, the performance of the ATOs in BCT seemed to negate the need for their existence. Nonetheless, they remained a part of the Academy training environment throughout the first year of integration.

There was a great deal of animosity between the cadets (both men and the first women) and the ATOs. The ATOs saw themselves as the first women to go through the Academy, but they were officers already, and their 2-week training period was much shorter than that endured by the class of 1980. Thus, the female cadets saw their experience as fundamentally different from that of the ATOs. As Lt. Col. (Ret.) Nancy Snyder, class of 1980, said, "They were the first women to go through the Academy, but we were the first *girls* to go through the Academy." The male cadets had parallel feelings: they resented having close officer supervision of a type that had never been seen before at the Academy. The officers who work at the Academy, instructors and AOCs, all went home at night. This gave cadets a bit of freedom to experiment with leadership and have a little fun. In contrast, the ATOs lived in the dorms. This meant constant supervision and little time for cadets to unwind. Even today, there is a sense of grudging toleration between the former cadets of the class of 1980 and the ATOs.

A second major issue addressed by the Pink Plan was the differences in physical strength that existed between the women candidates and their male counterparts. These differences were especially important, considering the extremely physical nature of much of Academy training. No other colleges attempting integration had experienced such a problem. Several ways of addressing fitness testing were considered in the Pink Plan. The first option was leaving the tests as they were, and simply making the passing scores lower for women. Another option was lowering all the standards so that the women could keep up. Finally, they considered making separate scoring systems for women. In this system, for example, each individual push-up or pull-up would count for more when performed by a woman. In the end, the leadership decided that the last option would be the best. Upper-class male cadets resented lower standards for women.

Nevertheless, men in the class of 1980 came to respect their female classmates. Interviews conducted with both men and women of the class of 1980 show that a strong bond existed between all the cadets. During the first year of integration, there was an "us/them" mentality, but it was fourthclassmen versus upperclassmen, not men against women. According to many officers who graduated in the class of 1980, male and female alike, the bonding they experienced during fourth-class year helped to ease the transition.

Uniforms were a third problem. At the time of Public Law 94-106, there were no women cadets, and since the cadets traditionally wore uniforms that were different from those worn by other active duty personnel, new uniforms needed to be designed for the women cadets. Eventually, the writers of the Pink Plan decided that these uniforms would be designed at the Academy, by men, with an emphasis on cutting the cost of the uniforms. Another goal of the designers was to minimize the differences between the male and female uniforms, so that formations would not lose their appearance of continuity. The uniforms worn by the first women cadets were found to be inadequate— they were not cut well to fit the female figure. Poorly designed pockets often got caught in door handles during training. During the first year, skirts were required when wearing blues (the everyday uniform of cadets), which made physical training almost impossible. Eventually, new uniforms were designed, but while the initial problems have been laid to rest, many female cadets still complain about not feeling feminine in uniform and are bothered by the idea that the uniform is basically designed to make them look like men.

Probably foremost in the eyes of the planners was the problem of housing. In the interest of privacy, initial plans put women in completely separate sections of the dormitories. As the year went by, though, the male cadets began to see these arrangements as giving an unfair advantage to the women, since much of the training done by male cadets took place in the dormitories, and no upperclassmen were allowed in the female section of the dormitories. The women of the class of 1980 protested the separate housing—mostly because they wanted the respect of upperclassmen and at the beginning of the second semester the girls were given rooms in the same areas of the dormitories as their squadron mates.

According to the cadets of the class of 1980, one of the biggest problems in integrating women was not even mentioned in the Pink Plan. The Pink Plan did not even foresee, much less make preparations for, the massive press coverage of the first Air Force Academy class to include females. This attention created animosity between the men and women more than any other issue. Men were bitter because they were overcoming the same obstacles as the women and yet were receiving comparatively little attention, while women were praised and photographed for even the smallest successes. Women found completing their duties difficult when being followed around by a camera crew, and their friendship with their classmates made the men's bitterness difficult to bear. They wanted only the same recognition as the male cadets. Ignoring the media attention to be able to concentrate on their jobs as cadets was probably the biggest struggle for women in the class of 1980.

In 1976 the Academy leadership instituted a new training philosophy. This training philosophy shifted the emphasis from physical training to "positive reinforcement." To the upperclassmen, this made the training ordeal look "easier." For example, before 1976, when a fourthclassman made a mistake (e.g., forgetting to address an upperclassman by the title "sir" or not knowing required knowledge), the

upperclassman would yell at him and make him do push-ups or other physical punishment. Under the new training philosophy, this sort of negative reinforcement caused cadets to do things because of fear and not because they felt it was their duty. Since inspiring a sense of duty is one of the Academy's main objectives when it comes to character development, the leadership decided that the training philosophy had to change. Planners decided that encouragement and coaching should be the norm. This meant less physical training, which unfortunately coincided with what was considered to be a weak area for women. Because of this coincidence, the upperclassmen often blamed women for what they saw as a "degradation of standards."

Despite the mistakes made in the early plans, the "'80s Ladies," as the women of the class of 1980 came to be known, made it through their first year with flying colors. They had a significantly smaller attrition rate than their male counterparts, and they adapted well to the traditionally male environment. Despite the adversity of the Academy, both those challenges faced by all cadets as well as those that were placed solely upon the '80s Ladies and the women that followed them, the women went on to many astonishing accomplishments.

DISTINGUISHED WOMEN GRADUATES

Since the very first graduating class, the women graduates of the U.S. Air Force Academy have been proving, over and over again, that the decision to admit women was not a mistake. Below are just a few examples.

Lt. Col. Kathleen M. Conley, Class of 1980, was officially the first woman to graduate from the Air Force Academy. She went to graduate school at Cornell University, and her most recent assignment was as commander of a training squadron at Laughlin AFB, Texas.

Lt. Col. Susan J. Helms, Class of 1980, was the first female graduate to serve in the space program. She majored in aeronautical engineering and has flown three shuttle missions: one on the *Endeavor,* one on the *Discovery,* and another on the *Columbia.*

Maj. Debra J. Dubbe, Class of 1980, was the first female to return to the Air Force Academy and serve as an Air Officer Commander (AOC). An AOC commands a cadet squadron and supervises cadet military training. She is currently serving at the Pentagon.

Congresswoman Heather Wilson is an Academy graduate of the Class of 1982. She is the representative from the first congressional district of New Mexico and serves on the House Armed Services Committee. Congresswoman Wilson is the first woman veteran in U.S. history to serve in Congress.

The first female graduate to receive a Purple Heart was 1st Lt. Laura A. Piper, Class of 1992. She died on April 14, 1994, when the she was shot down over Iraq while traveling in a helicopter to help rebuild Kurdish villages in Turkey.

CONCLUSION

Women in the military are still "making waves," as one military training leader at the Academy phrased it, but every day and with every milestone, women are proving that they can do their jobs as well as their male counterparts. The women graduates of the Air Force Academy have overcome many challenges, and with the help of an Academy education, women are showing up in larger and larger numbers among the leaders of our nation.

—Jamie Rasmussen

SUGGESTED READINGS

Clark, Lt. Gen. A. P. "Women at the Service Academies and Combat Leadership." *Strategic Review* 5(4, Fall 1977): 64.

DeFleur, Dr. Lois B. *Four Years of Sex Integration at the United States Air Force Academy: Problems and Issues.* Colorado, 80840: Dean of Faculty, United States Air Force Academy, 1985.

Department of the Air Force, USAFA, Directorate of Plans and Programs, Deputy Chief of Staff for Operations. *Contingency Plan for Integration of Females into the Cadet Wing.* Operations Plan #7-73, December 10, 1973.

Dinsmore, Maj. John C., Air Command and Staff College. *Women as Cadets: An Analysis of the Issue.* Defense Technical Information Center. Alexandria, VA: Defense Logistics Agency, 1974.

Maurer, Al. "Solving the Controversy of Female Cadets." *Talon* (May 1973): 16-17.

Muenger, Dr. Betsy, 1st Lt. Laurel Scherer, Tech. Sgt. Ken Carter, and Christy Williams. *Women in Motion: Celebrating 20 Years at the Air Force Academy.* Colorado Springs, CO: USAFA Director of Public Affairs, 1996.

Stiehm, Judith Hicks. *Bring Me Men and Women: Mandated Change at the U.S. Air Force Academy.* Los Angeles: University of California Press, 1981.

"Vote to Admit Women to Service Academies." *Colorado Springs Gazette Telegraph.* January 6, 1975, p. 1.

Wallisch, William Joseph Jr. *The Admission and Integration of Women Into the United States Air Force Academy.* Los Angeles: University of Southern California, 1977.

"Women in Combat Key Issue of Bill." *Air Force Times* (June 19, 1974): 19.

"Women in the Academies Aired in Appeals Court." *Air Force Times* (November 27, 1974): 2.

VETERINARY MEDICINE

Veterinary medicine has been, as many fields, dominated by men for much of U.S. history. Like other fields, this has been true, in part, because of the very nature of gendered spheres of public and private space prior to World War II. Unlike others, however, veterinary medicine brought with it an additional hurdle for the entrance of women that is fundamental to the nature of the work—the proximity of women and large animals, which is particularly relevant to the problems of women entering this field in the West.

As we can see from rare sources such as the diary of Martha Ballard, midwives in 18th-century America often gave the primary medical care to humans and animals, both important residents on the farm. Besides aiding in childbirth, midwives had a limited, but experiential, knowledge of the processes of the human body and understood how to use herbs and poultices as cures. Livestock facing difficult births or having ailments similar to humans could receive the attention of the local midwife. As Laurel Thatcher Ulrich points out, patients trusted midwives often more so than the emerging male doctors. The female midwife, however, lost the ability to practice openly over time due to the professionalization of medicine in the 19th century. Although this primarily occurred in the East, it had great repercussions for the West, as easterners established this system that would eventually move west. Medicine and science, increasingly, became the domain of men. Colleges, universities, medical schools, and professional organizations worked to create a scientific community defined by education, licensure, and affiliation, excluding women almost entirely.

During the antebellum period, agricultural papers lamented the destruction of farm animals because of the lack of knowledge about animal physiology. The editor of the *Cultivator* complained in 1848, for instance, that ignorance on the part of farmers and healers led farmers to hire "vile quacks, knowing nothing of their business, and in their ignorance killing or ruining many a valuable animal." The agricultural leaders of this period promoted agricultural societies and papers and lobbied for agricultural colleges, all in order to increase the scientific knowledge that would destroy ignorance and lead to a better quality of farmer and, therefore, farm products. Livestock breeding and care (even simple things as building appropriate barns) were discussed in agricultural society meetings in the hope to eliminate the scrawny, unhealthy beasts that roamed the fields and forests around farms in the 19th century. It is important to remember that fences in this period were built to keep farm animals out, not in, and they were often left to forage for food on their own.

Americans generally moved west during the 19th century, and the Homestead Act facilitated this further. In the Midwest, the Great Plains, and the Far West, livestock raising became an important industry. In 1883 one author has estimated that there were 12 million horses and mules, 41 million head of cattle, 50 million sheep, and 44 million hogs. The shift from subsistence agriculture to commercial agriculture often meant that farmers and ranchers kept larger numbers of animals together in more confined spaces, increasing the instances of disease. During the late

19th century, diseases such as pleuropneumonia, hog cholera, scabies, anthrax, and Texas fever became major issues at a time when veterinary science still did not exist. Most of the men who treated animals at this time were farmers who read the available literature on animal health and had developed an experiential knowledge from working with their own livestock.

By this time, the gendered spaces of the farm and ranch focused the work of men in the field and barn and the work of women in the house and garden, generally only working with small animals such as poultry. The bifurcated nature of farm work persisted with individual adaptations even into the 20th century. As Thad Sitton and Dan K. Utley found in their research of cotton sharecroppers in Texas, the presence of a woman plow hand indicated the inability of the family's men to do the work. Not only was manhood threatened by women doing men's work, but also femininity was dishonored by a woman's proximity to the rear of the animal. These considerations notwithstanding, women did fill the places of men when needed, because the prosperity of the farm enterprise, whether owned or worked as sharecroppers, took precedence.

The division of labor seen here has also been documented among American Indian societies. Elizabeth A. Lawrence, a veterinary anthropologist, documented the spiritual and utilitarian relations between horses and various Plains Indians. She found that because men used the horses for the hunt, battle, and recreation (i.e., racing), men also became the healers, thus developing in some tribes a horse medicine cult. Young boys were also expected to give daily care such as watering and feeding. Women and girls, because of their experiences in and assisting with childbirth, could act as midwives to horses. One story tells of a girl who gave especially tender care to a pregnant mare, who then imparted a special wisdom to her about horses. As an important economic resource, horse care represented a practical need, one that entered the spiritual, ceremonial, and historical knowledge of such tribes as the Crow of Montana, who Lawrence studied.

During the 1880s on the ranches of the West, animal diseases became an economically destructive force that led to political, institutional, and scientific changes. Initially, ranchers attempted to deal with these problems on their own. The process to alleviate scabies and Texas fever remained male dominated, as can be seen from photos of these events from the late 19th century. Men constructed corrals and shoots to dip sheep and cattle in special baths to eliminate the mites and ticks from the skin that caused these diseases. This type of interaction with large animals in no way fell within what could be considered appropriate work for women.

During the 1880s livestock men in the West lobbied for governmental assistance with animal diseases such as Texas fever, and in 1884 the Bureau of Animal Industry (BAI) was created within the U.S. Department of Agriculture. The BAI needed trained veterinarians, and began to facilitate the professionalization of the field by only hiring graduates from specially approved institutions, all in the Midwest and West. Several prominent early veterinary schools were established at Iowa State University (1879), Western Veterinary College at Kansas City (1897), and Southwestern Veterinary College of Texas (1909). Individual states also encouraged the professional training of veterinarians through legislation requiring degrees to obtain licenses and establishing state veterinarians to combat livestock diseases. At this time in the West, veterinary medicine emerged as a narrow field to deal with economic problems in agricultural states.

The acceptance and establishment of veterinary medicine came late to the United States, and even later to the West. Even though livestock men wanted assistance with combating diseases, they often resisted the regulations imposed by states. The sustained effort, however, of professors and deans in the land grant universities built veterinary schools and colleges in states like Oklahoma, Kansas, Texas, Nebraska, and California. Little has been written about women in veterinary medicine, and male veterinarians, not historians, have written most of the history of the field. The histories of several university programs, however, indicate the increasing numbers of women in this emerging science as well as some of their struggles. In general, only a few women studied veterinary medicine prior to World War II. The war created a need for additional military and civilian veterinarians, opening spaces for women. Urbanization moved the dog and cat from the barn to the home, increasing small animal practices that provided women with acceptable workplaces. The real increase in numbers came after the civil rights movement. University administrators in the West attempting to comply with the Civil Rights Act of 1964 found it easier to recruit women students and faculty than to recruit minorities in any great number.

Despite this general pattern, each program grew at a different rate. One of the earliest women veterinarians in the West was Clara Lamplugh, who graduated from the San Francisco Veterinary College in 1917, yet the typical woman involved in veterinary medicine did so as the wife of a veterinarian, often acting as hospital attendants and anesthetists. These California wives organized the Women's Auxiliary to the California State Veterinary Medical Association in 1930 to advance research, support veterinary students, and provide a social outlet for professionals and their wives in the field. California veterinarian Mary K. Dunlap organized the Women's Veterinary Medical Association in 1947. By 1966 there were only 18 women veterinarians in the state.

Kansas State University also had an early woman graduate. Helen S. Richt, pictured with the class of 1932, ranks as one of the first women, along with Louise Sklar in 1934. Until the late 1960s, Kansas State consistently graduated one or two women. The numbers increased until women represented 30% of the graduating class in the 1980s. Helen Richt Irwin eventually went on to head the Small Animal section of the American Veterinary Medical Association in 1937, being the first woman elected to an office in this organization. Discussing Kansas State and other programs, Margaret Sloss, the first female Iowa State University veterinary student and faculty member, described some of the problems Richt faced as an early female student prior to 1939. The first female student was disregarded by faculty and even more so by fellow students. Her attendance was considered a joke in most cases. Universities barred women, by custom or rule, from particular courses such as ambulatory clinic, large animal clinic and surgery, and horseshoeing. Kansas State professors in the 1930s believed that women, if they had to enter the field, should do research, because their meticulousness with details prepared them for that type of work. Interestingly, this was an argument used in the 1840s by Maria Mitchell as a justification for women becoming astronomers. She equated the dexterity and detail orientedness needed for needlepoint with that needed to do astronomy. The Kansas dean R. R. Dykstra explicitly stated that training women was a waste of time because they married soon after graduation, contributing little to the advancement of the field. While women were barred from courses involving direct contact with live, large animals, female students found that professors teaching small animal courses were less hostile. Once graduated, women also found a greater acceptance among partners and clients if they pursued small animal practices.

Not all western veterinary schools advanced as well. The class of 1955 at Oklahoma A&M College was considered "unique" because June Iben became its first veterinary graduate. She remembers being shunned by the male students but asked to join the ladies auxiliary club. The ladies student auxiliary remained active even into the 1960s, demonstrating the expectation that veterinary medicine was still a man's sphere. The club offered an annual award for the "outstanding senior spouse," which has never been won by a man. Oklahoma State, as it was later known, was one of the schools that found it difficult to attract African American students and easier to attract women. Even then it did so slowly. Oklahoma State had one woman in the class of 1955, five in the class of 1965, and in 1986 the number finally increased to about a third of the graduating class.

Every program has its firsts, as these do, but this is not what is important about the entrance of women into the field of veterinary medicine. The American Veterinary Medical Association found that in 1999, 70% of veterinary students and 36% of practitioners were women, with the latter expecting to increase to 67% by 2015. With the importance of agriculture in the West and the number of pets that accompany the large urban populations in the area, western women will continue to play an important role in veterinary medicine. Research, as stated, has been limited and pursued mainly by retired veterinarians who disregarded female students in their universities and their histories. Yet rich information about the early years of these pioneering women can be found in the primary documentation in the university archives of land grant institutions. Because of the extreme resistance to women entering the field, this provides us with valuable insight into the struggles that women have faced entering the public sphere. Western values of individualism, rural conceptualizations of work and space, and farming exigencies all add to the complexity of the gendered division of life in the western United States.

—Alexandra Kindell

SUGGESTED READINGS

Arburua, Joseph M. *Narrative of the Veterinary Profession in California*. San Francisco: Joseph M. Arburua, 1966.

Association for Women Veterinarians. *Our History of Women in Veterinary Medicine: Gumption, Grace, Grit, and Good Humor.* Littleton, CO: Association of Women Veterinarians, 1997.

Dethloff, Henry C. *A Special Kind of Doctor: A History of Veterinary Medicine in Texas.* College Station: Texas A&M University Press, 1991.

Lemonds, Leo L. *A Century of Veterinary Medicine in Nebraska.* Hastings, NE: L. Lemonds, 1982.

Ludgate, Thomas B., and Janice Ludgate Kitzler. *The Prairie Practitioners: 20th Century South Dakota Veterinarians.* Freeman, SD: Pine Hill Press, 1996.

Sitton, Thad, and Dan K. Utley. *From Can See to Can't: Texas Cotton Farmers on the Southern Prairies.* Austin: University Press of Texas, 1997.

Stalheim, Ole H. V., ed. *Veterinary Medicine in the West.* Manhattan, KS: Sunflower University Press, 1988.

Trotter, Don M. *An 80 Year Review, 1905-1985: Kansas State University, College of Veterinary Medicine.* Manhattan: Kansas State University, 1985.

Ulrich, Laurel Thatcher. *A Midwife's Tale: The Life of Martha Ballard, Based on Her Diary, 1785-1812.* New York: Vintage Books, 1990.

Williams, Eric L. *A History of the Oklahoma State University College of Veterinary Medicine.* Stillwater: Oklahoma State University, 1986.

WARDLAW, KIM MCLANE (1954-)

Born in San Francisco in 1954, Kim McLane Wardlaw headed south to attend the University of California, Los Angeles. After graduating with an A.B. in 1976, she continued at her alma mater and received her J.D. from the UCLA School of Law in 1979. From 1979 to 1980, she served as a law clerk for Hon. William P. Gray, U.S. District Court, Central District of California. In 1980 she began her private practice in Los Angeles. She was a member of Justice Team I for the Department of Justice, Presidential Transition, in 1992-1993. In 1993 she also served as a member on the Mayoral Transition Committee for Los Angeles mayor-elect Richard Riordan. On August 10, 1995, President Bill Clinton nominated her for a seat vacated by David V. Kenyon on the U.S. District Court, Central District of California. Confirmed by the Senate on December 22, 1995, she received her commission on December 26, 1995.

On January 27, 1998, President Clinton nominated her for a seat, which had been vacated by J. Clifford Wallace, on the U.S. Court of Appeals for the Ninth Circuit. She received her commission on August 3, 1998, after being confirmed by the Senate on July 31 of that year.

—Marcus J. Schwoerer

SUGGESTED READING

Kim McLane Wardlaw. Retrieved from air.fjc.gov/history/ judges_frm.html. Source: History of the Federal Judiciary. http://www.fjc.gov. Web site of the Federal Judicial Center, Washington, D.C.

WATERS, MAXINE (1938-)

Maxine Waters is a woman who was born into poverty, lived in poverty, and now is a champion against poverty and for equality. Her mother raised her alone. She married Edward Waters after graduating from high school, and soon after, they moved west to California and settled in the Watts area of Los Angeles. They worked at a garment factory and a printing plant. Eventually, Maxine took a job working for the Pacific Telephone, but had to quit after she unfortunately had a miscarriage.

After this rocky start, Waters caught a break and started working for Head Start, a program that received financial aid from the federal government to help children who lived in low-income families. Due to her previous convictions and life experience, Waters was the one with the "head start" and quickly advanced in her new position. She used her time with the organization to motivate her to earn a B.A. degree from the University of California, Los Angeles, in sociology and as a step to being involved in politics. Due to a shady campaign mistake by Leon Ralph, she was able to enter the race for a chair in the California State Assembly. She won, and began down the road to political success.

She started a group called the Black Women's Forum, which was created in Los Angeles in 1978 as a springboard for the black female community to make sure that their needs were not overlooked when it came time to pass legislation. She also contributed to the creation of the Child Abuse Prevention Training Program, which was a pioneer in a field of great necessity.

She used her tenacity to push for a bill to be passed that would give pregnant women adequate time away from work to have their babies, with a guarantee that they would still have their job upon returning. She also pushed legislation that would respond to several stories from several women and children that they were being strip-searched for offenses as simple as missing a license for their dog. At first, she endorsed a prohibition on strip searches for all misdemeanors, but ran into resistance from groups that felt the law would hinder searches in jails. She also backed legislation that created a political gap between the United States and apartheid-plagued South Africa. Her ideas called for a separation from the country for its acts of racial discrimination against the people.

Waters was the first woman to hold the position of majority whip in the California State Assembly, the first woman in the Rules Committee, and the first person who did not possess a degree in the legal field to be in the Judiciary Committee for the assembly of the state. She also used her position to fight for minority rights when she served on the Ways and Means Committee's Subcommittee on Business Development and Consumer, Veterans, and Employment Issues. After 14 years in the California Assembly, Waters ran for national office.

Prior to winning her seat in the U.S. House of Representatives in 1988, Waters was since 1980 a member of the Democratic National Committee. With a seat in the national assembly, she continued her fight for the underclass in America and the interests of the 35th District. She was chair of the Congressional Black Caucus (1997-1998) and chief deputy whip in the 106th Congress. Today she continues her work for those who need the nation's help the most.

—Kevin Christy

SUGGESTED READINGS

Maxine Waters Official Biography. Retrieved from www.house.gov/waters/bio.htm.

Mills, Kay. "Maxine Waters: The Sassy Legislator Who Knows There Is More Than One Way to Make a Political Statement." *Governing 1*(6, March 1998): 26-33.

WEDDINGTON, SARAH RAGLE (1945-)

Sarah Ragle Weddington, lawyer, speaker, educator, and writer, was born in Abilene, Texas, on February 5, 1945, the daughter of Herbert Doyle and Lena Catherine Ragle. Weddington graduated magna cum laude from McMurry University in 1965; she received her J.D. from the University of Texas in 1967. She is most famous for her role as the plaintiff's counsel in the landmark case *Roe v. Wade.* In 1973 the suit successfully overturned antiabortion statutes in Texas and made abortion legal throughout the United States. She argued the case at the age of 26, only a few years out of law school.

In 1972 she became the first woman elected to the Texas House of Representatives from Austin, Travis County. She served three terms. Throughout her terms in the House, Weddington worked for women's rights, reforming rape statutes, passing an equal credit bill for women, and blocking antiabortion legislation. She served as the first female general counsel of the U.S. Department of Agriculture (1977-1978). She was special assistant to President Jimmy Carter (1979-1981), and chaired the Interdepartmental Task Force on Women for the Carter administration (1978-1981). She was the first female director of the Texas Office of State-Federal Relations (1983-1985).

In 1992 Weddington's book *A Question of Choice* was published. The book addresses the issues of abortion rights. She holds honorary doctorates from McMurry University, Hamilton College, Austin College, and Southwestern University.

She has received numerous honors and awards. In 1980 she received Planned Parenthood of America's highest honor, the Margaret award. In 1988 she was the recipient of Leadership America's Hummingbird award for contributions toward the advancement of women's leadership. In 1995 she was inducted into the Omicron Delta Kappa Society, the national leadership honor society. Through her organization, the Weddington Center, she works to get more women into higher leadership positions as well as encouraging more men and women to become involved in public and volunteer leadership. She is currently a lecturer of American studies and government at the University of Texas, Austin.

—Tiffany E. Dalpe

SUGGESTED READINGS

Godwin, Michelle Gerise. "The Progressive Interview: Sarah Weddington," *The Progressive* 64(8, August 2000. Retrieved from www.progressive.org.

The Weddington Center. Retrieved from www.sarahweddington.com.

Who's Who of American Women 2000-2001 Millennium Edition. Chicago: Marquis Who's Who, 2001.

WELLS, ALICE STEBBINS (1873-1957)

The history of the Los Angeles Police Department is one of rich tradition and time-honored commitment. While many recent problems have plagued the organization, such as the Rodney King beating in 1991, the Rampart scandal of 2000, and the contemporary replacement of Chief Bernard Parks, the force has been able to successfully police its citizens effectively and honestly. While the makeup of the LAPD has undergone many facelifts over the past 100 years, perhaps no other person was more influential at implementing changes in 1910 within the department than Alice Stebbins Wells, the first woman to serve in the Los Angeles Police Department. Without a doubt, Wells provided the vision and determination to allow women to achieve previously unattainable goals in terms of law enforcement, and she provided this impetus with calm assurance, coupled with staunch audacity.

The beginning of police work for women found its roots in juvenile detention facilities, where those who lacked the opportunity for advancement were usually relegated to watching over young offenders and guarding other female inmates. While the first American policewoman was Lola Baldwin in Portland, Oregon, serving in 1905, perhaps the most important female officer was Wells, who was appointed to the Los Angeles Police Department in 1910. She organized the International Association of Policewomen in 1915, and as a result, by 1919 over 60 police departments employed women, and 6 years after that, the number of departments with police-women reached 144. Even though the work was still based in juvenile and clerical duties, many hurdles had been cleared.

Wells was a graduate theological seminary student and diligent social worker in Los Angeles who found it puzzling that women had not gravitated to the realms of public service in the early 20th century. As a result, she felt that if women were to become more actively involved in public protection and crime prevention, then women and children would reap untold benefits, such as a better sense of well-being and a stronger sense of reliability. Because of her fiery demeanor and attractive personality, she decided to obtain a petition, signed by 100 citizens of Los Angeles, asking the mayor for an appointment as a police officer. The mayor was convinced of her determination, and the appointment was made in September of 1910.

While Wells has the notable title of the first regularly assigned "policewoman" in the United States, her main duties bordered on the mundane and inconsequential. Essentially, supervising skating rinks, penny arcades, picture shows, and other public recreational facilities was her modus operandi, and while seemingly unimportant, it proved to be an important first step. After the initial inroads traversed by Wells, many other cities in the United States decided that it was time to allow women to become a part of the force, and by mid-1910, Chicago, New York, and Philadelphia had secured the work of women in the institution. Wells began to speak at many functions concerning the implementation of women in the police force, resulting in newfound acceptance of extended duties, reaching farther than the rudimentary security duty that Wells initially found herself in charge of.

In fact, as Wells concluded her lecture circuit addressing the issues of the importance of allowing women in the police force, many departments around the country found it extremely difficult to defend their exclusion of women. Janis Appier claims that "the movement for women police was decentralized, localistic, and highly politicized," resulting in many police departments hiring women as a result of the pressure from women's groups rather than a sincere desire to include women. After Wells spoke to groups, many began to claim that hiring women would lead to safer streets, improved social conditions, and an increase in overall welfare of cities. It would be the women who would "clean up the town," and most felt that hiring policewomen was the key to any future success.

As the pressure mounted for Wells and others like her attempting to instill in urban centers the need for a force of women in the police ranks, the heckling and ridicule abounded. Many journalists addressed the controversial issue by representing policewomen as bony, muscular, masculine people carrying revolvers

Photo: Alice Stebbins Wells, Brooklyn, N.Y., as a Bible lecturer (LAPHS Archives).

and presenting themselves in a less than professional manner. Nevertheless, Wells and her supporters were able to shrug off the protests against her cause and to continue their work.

By 1916 Wells had spearheaded the change in over 25 cities to include women in their departments and also outside the United States. In 1914 the mayor of Milford, Ohio, even appointed Dolly Spencer as chief of police, an unprecedented move resulting in much controversy. Spencer was removed from the position when a new mayor took office.

Perhaps the most important event dealing with the women's police movement was the organization of the International Association of Policewomen (IAP), founded in 1915 by Wells, its first president. This group allowed women to play a viable role in the continual advancement of their cause, enlightening the general public with information concerning the force and the position that women were playing in the development of departments across the nation. As the well-being of women in law enforcement continued to increase, it was the help of organizations such as the IAP that allowed women to strive for additional advancements within the police force, as the years would pass.

In 1925 Wells organized the Los Angeles Policewomen's Association, and in 1928 she started the Women Peace Officers Association of California in San Bernardino. All of her achievements were accomplished while still serving in a full-time capacity as a police officer, an extremely commendable accomplishment. After 35 years of loyal service, Wells retired in 1945 at the age of 72. At this time, she continued to lecture on the constant need for policewomen and, until her last days, felt that women needed to be included in areas other than preventive work with women and children. On August 17, 1957, at the age of 84, Wells, the diminutive, outspoken woman who changed the mentality of police departments across America, died from a heart attack at her Glendale, California, home.

Without a doubt, Wells considerably paved the way for women in law enforcement. While problems in police departments still exist, many police administrators have reevaluated their use or nonuse of female officers in recent years. Various law enforcement agencies have also experienced substantial changes, which will eventually affect the entire American police community, and these changes concerning the role of policewomen are taking place not just in one department or area of the country or in just one type of department. All women can hand Wells a considerable amount of thanks for the incredible steps that she took to enable women of the 21st century to pursue a career in law enforcement.

—Charles Joseph Sedey

SUGGESTED READINGS

Appier, Janis. *Policing Women: The Sexual Politics of Law Enforcement and the LAPD.* Philadelphia, PA: Temple University Press, 1998.

Horne, Peter. *Women in Law Enforcement.* Springfield, IL: Charles C. Thomas Publishers, 1975.

Owings, Chloe. *Women Police: A Study of the Development and Status of the Women Police Movement.* Montclair, NJ: Patterson Smith, 1969.

Ryan, Gail F. "Policewoman One: Alice Stebbins Wells." *The Link* (February 2001). Retrieved from www.laphs.com/february2001articles-2.htm.

Walker, Samuel. *The Police in America: An Introduction.* San Francisco: McGraw-Hill, 1983.

WERDEGAR, KATHRYN M. (1936-)

Kathryn Mickle Werdegar has been a California Supreme Court justice since her appointment by Governor Pete Wilson in 1994. At the time of her appointment, she was the second woman serving on the Supreme Court bench. Her opinions have been conservative, yet she pays close attention to women's issues. Author of numerous articles, monographs, and other legal publications, Justice Werdegar is an established legal scholar.

Werdegar was educated at Wellesley College, finishing in 1955. She attended the University of California, Berkeley, Boalt Hall School of Law for 2 years and graduated from George Washington University School of Law in 1962.

She was a professor and associate dean for academic affairs at the University of San Francisco School of Law, senior staff attorney for the California Court of Appeals for the First District from 1981 to 1985, senior staff attorney to California Supreme Court Justice Edward

Panelli from 1985 to 1991, and became a state appellate court justice in 1991. Governor Wilson elevated her from the Court of Appeals to the Supreme Court in 1994. During her lengthy legal career, Werdegar has earned the Charles Glover Award for Highest Achievement in the field of Law. She also was the first woman elected as editor-in-chief of the University of California Boalt Hall *Law Review* and was also on the staff of the George Washington *Law Review.*

Werdegar is married to Dr. David Werdegar. They have two sons and reside in Ross, California.

—Lori S. Iacovelli

SUGGESTED READINGS

Kathryn Mickle Werdegar. Retrieved March 9, 2002, from www.courtinfo.ca.gov.

LexisNexis. Retrieved March 25, 2002, from web.lexis-nexis.com.

WIGGIN, KATE DOUGLAS SMITH (1856-1923)

Kate Douglas Smith Wiggin was a popular children's book author and also a pioneer in education, helping to create the first public, free kindergartens in California. She was born in Philadelphia, Pennsylvania, and was raised in a well-to-do New England family. They moved to California when she was a young woman to improve the health of her ailing father. While in California, she associated mainly with transplanted easterners of her class, and was occupied with social events, cotillions, and innocent flirtations. However, when her father was caught on the downside of a land speculation run, her family owed large amounts of money and was unable to pay. Upon the death of her father, Wiggin and her sister were forced to find work to maintain their lifestyle. At this hard time in her life, she wrote her first short story, and it was published, on its first submission, in the *St. Nicholas* magazine. The story, "Half a Dozen Housekeepers," was published in three installments, and she was paid the sum of $150, which helped ease the family's debts. However, instead of continuing to write, she felt the need to enter a career that would afford her the opportunity to learn about life outside her sphere. With very little practical book learning, she did not consider teaching an option; however, the new idea of a kindergarten was appealing to her.

Wiggin befriended women's reformer Caroline M. Severance, who had moved to Santa Barbara, California, from Boston and was interested in reforms for education. Severance, along with teacher Emma Marwedel, introduced the new idea of a free, public kindergarten for children under 7 years old. They also took on three teaching students in the hope that they could learn the method and begin schools of their own. Wiggin was one of the first three students and took a 9-month program that consisted of student teaching and learning a program of games, movement, and storytelling in the morning, followed by afternoon class sessions, studying psychology, history of education, and the methods of the movement's founder, Friedrich Froebel.

Wiggin went on to found her own school in Santa Barbara called the Swallow's Nest and then to start a free school in San Francisco called the Silver Street Kindergarten. After the success of the Silver Street school, she opened a teaching academy, and in a few short years had trained approximately 400 women in the method. Schools began to spread into Oregon and the Washington territory. The leaders of the kindergarten movement were educators but also social reformers. They hoped that by bringing free education to the urban poor, they would provide a positive early influence on the lives of neglected children. Their goal was to add the early age curriculum to that of the public school so that it would become the educational standard that it is today.

Wiggin later married and only worked with the schools on a part-time basis, commuting from her new home in New York. After the death of her husband, she decided to take a rest from the demands of teaching, training, and pioneering. She went on to travel and became a famous author of children's books such as *Rebecca of Sunnybrook Farm, A Summer in the Cañon, A Birds' Christmas Carol,* a series of books about the European travels of Penelope, and her autobiography, *My Garden of Memory.* The educational goals of Wiggin can still be seen in the West today, even as her books continue to be read.

—Michelle Bean

SUGGESTED READINGS

Cooper, Frederic Taber. *Some American Storytellers.* New York: Henry Holt, 1911.

Kate Douglas Wiggin. Knowledgerush Book Directory. Retrieved from www.knowledgerush.com/kr/jsp/db/ author.jsp?authorId=116.

Kate Douglas Wiggin. Retrieved from download.franklin. com/cgi-bin/franklin/ebookman_free_preview?vilwt10.

Wiggin, Kate Douglas. *Encyclopædia Britannica.* Retrieved from Encyclopædia Britannica Premium Service, www.britannica.com/eb/article?eu=78992.

Wiggin, Kate Douglas. *My Garden of Memory: An Autobiography.* Boston, MA: Houghton Mifflin, 1923.

WILKEN, CLAUDIA ANN (1949-)

Claudia Ann Wilken was born in Minneapolis, Minnesota, in 1949. After receiving her B.A. from Stanford University in 1971, she began to study law at Boalt Hall School of Law at the University of California, Berkeley. In 1975 she graduated with her J.D. and began as a staff attorney for the Federal Public Defender's Office in the Northern District of California. After 3 years, she opened her private practice in Berkeley, where she worked for the next 6 years. During this time, she was an adjunct professor at the Boalt Hall School of Law, and she also served as a professor at the New College School of Law from 1980 until 1985. In 1983 she became a U.S. magistrate for the U.S. District Court for the Northern District of California. On October 7, 1993, President Bill Clinton nominated her for a position as judge on the U.S. District Court for the Northern District of California when a new seat was created by 104 Stat. 5089. The Senate confirmed her nomination on November 20, 1993, and she received her commission on November 22, 1993.

—Marcus J. Schwoerer

SUGGESTED READING

Claudia Ann Wilken. Retrieved from air.fjc.gov/history/ judges_frm.html. Source: History of the Federal Judiciary. http://www.fjc.gov. Web site of the Federal Judicial Center, Washington, D.C.

WILLIAMS, JEANNE (1930-)

Jeanne Williams was born Dorothy Jean Kreie in Elkhart, Kansas, the daughter of Guy and Louella

Kreie. She is a writer of fiction under the numerous pseudonyms Megan Castell, Jeanne Crecy, Jeanne Foster, Kristin Michael, Deirdre Rowan, and J. R. Williams.

Williams's writing consists of juvenile fiction, Gothic novels, historical romances, and historical novels told from a feminine point of view. She was first published in 1952 while a student at the University of Oklahoma. Her writing has won many awards, including the Silver Spur and Golden Saddleman awards for *The Horse Talker.* She also has won the Juvenile Award of the Texas Institute of Letters and the University of Oklahoma Professional Writers' Award.

Williams married Lt. Col. Gene Williams in 1949, but they divorced in 1969. She then married John Creasey in 1970, but divorced him in 1973. She married Bob Morse in 1981 and now lives in Tucson, Arizona. They also have a home in England. She has two children.

—Lori S. Iacovelli

SUGGESTED READINGS

Commire, Anne. *Something About the Author: Facts and Pictures About Contemporary Authors and Illustrators of Books for Young People.* Detroit, MI: Gale Research, 1973.

Vinson, James, ed. *Twentieth-Century Western Writers.* Detroit, MI: Gale Research, 1982.

WILMANS, EDITH EUNICE THERREL (1882-1966)

Edith Eunice Therrel Wilmans, the first woman elected to the Texas legislature, was born on December 21, 1882, at Lake Providence, East Carroll Parrish, Louisiana. Her parents, Benjamin Franklin and Mary Elizabeth Grier Therrel, moved the family to Dallas, Texas, in 1885. Edith married Jacob Hall Wilmans on December 25, 1900, and the couple had three daughters. In 1914 Wilmans helped to organize the Dallas Equal Suffrage Association. She also helped to organize the Dallas Housewives League and the Democratic Women of Dallas County. She served as president of the Democratic Women's Association of Texas. Wilmans decided to go to law school to gain

a better understanding of the legal problems involved in improving the status of women and children.

Wilmans was admitted to the Texas bar in 1918, and in 1922 she was elected to the 38th Texas Legislature, representing Dallas County. Her husband passed away in 1923. During her one term in office, she endorsed legislation for child support and child care as well as the establishment of the Dallas County District Court of Domestic Relations. During her tenure, she became the first female Speaker of the Texas House of Representatives.

In 1925 Wilmans was appointed to the all-woman Supreme Court by Governor Neff to hear *Johnson v. Darr.* She was disqualified because she lacked, by just a few months, the necessary 7 years of legal experience. In 1929 she married Henry A. Born, but the marriage soon ended in divorce and she returned to Dallas to practice law. She ran for the legislature again in 1935 but was defeated. She ran for the Thirteenth District congressional seat in 1948 and again in a 1951 special election but lost both races. In 1958 she returned to Dallas, where she died on March 21, 1966.

—Tiffany E. Dalpe

SUGGESTED READINGS

Gilmour, Terry L. *A Difference: Women in the Texas Legislature.* Ph.D. dissertation. Texas Technical University, 1999.

The Handbook of Texas Online. Retrieved from www.tsha.utexas.edu/handbook/online.

"WINE, WOMEN, AND SONG"

Post-World War II Americas grew up with the hilarious television image of Lucille Ball crushing grapes with her bare feet. Audiences of all ages, to this day, continue to laugh as they watch Ball walk, run, fall, and fight her way through a grape-filled vat. Remarkably, this classic episode of *I Love Lucy* can also be used as a comedic parody of the role of American women in the economic, cultural, and social persona of wine. Across the centuries, male winemakers and enthusiasts relegated women to roles in food service and hospitality that enhanced viniculture. More importantly, this combination of wine and women took on a sexual guise whereby men entrenched women into wine roles as servers, hostesses, and seductresses that can be best described by the adage "wine, women, and song." Ball capitalized on this sexual image of women and winemaking and provided popular culture enthusiasts with a humorous means to reflect on the gender hurdles confronted by upwardly mobile women in the modern wine industry. Today, many wineries sponsor grape crush parties, complete with Lucy look-alike contests, where women crush grapes with their bare feet and, like Lucy, mock old images of women in wine and celebrate the ever-increasing movement of women into important roles in the American wine industry and the shattering of the wineglass barrier.

The world history of wine is a male story. This is somewhat confusing if one considers that "winemaking would seem to be a branch of the domestic arts." A dearth of career women in the top levels of winemaking is painfully evident by their absence from the written mainstream histories. As early as the time of the Greek symposium (men's drinking society), only token women were allowed to participate. Historically, women were burdened with "the paradox of being placed on pedestals on which they were obliged to stay—or risk disgrace." From the beginning, wine evolved into a wealthy male pastime, and female participants risked the loss of their virtue by associating with wine. This paradigm migrated with Western European culture to the Americas in the Age of Discovery.

Prior to the middle of the 20th century, American women served auxiliary roles in the nation's wine industry. The historical record to that time included male wine greats like Thomas Jefferson, Peter Legaux, John Adlum (father of the American Viticulture), Jean Jacques Dufour, Nicholas Longworth, Thomas Volney Munsen, Agoston Haraszthy, Eugene Hilgard, George Husmann, Gustave Niebaum, A. J. Winkler, Ernest and Julio Gallo, and Robert Mondavi. Notably absent from the roll call of wine greats are the names and stories of women. The narrative of the wine story glorifies white businessmen and politicians. For many years, America's wine experience relegated women to a submissive role to men in what has been referred to as the Cult of True Womanhood. Throughout most of the 19th and 20th centuries, virtuous wives tolerated male indulgence in the good life and the gentlemanly image of the wine culture and allowed men to live a life built on the slogan of "wine, women, and song." This code demanded that middle- and upper-class white women

hold the high moral ground and refrain from the excesses of alcohol that wreaked havoc on the women's spheres of her body, her family, and her home.

Most historians now concede that this was a myth and that working-class women vigorously partook in spirits in what historian W. J. Rorabaugh has aptly labeled the "Alcoholic Republic." Women served wine in taverns and family meals and many drank behind closed doors. These same women tended grapevines in the garden, made homemade wines, and drank wine for its medicinal properties. Thus, the story is much the same as women's total experience throughout the nation's early history. Women played a behind-the-scenes role to their men while at the same time actively participating in the wine culture in their private realm. The all-too-familiar result was a paucity of records, for the most part, and the predictable voiceless past for the story of women in wine.

During the 20th century, drinking males developed a more protective control of wine and alcohol as teetotaler women's groups sought to end the evils of alcohol and maintain their place on the moral pedestal. As a result, women became further removed from the wine record. Sadly, the reality was that alcohol did destroy many working-class homes, and progressive reform women had good reason to battle for limitation or termination of spirits that destroyed families and degraded women. Their determination helped produce the passage of the Nineteenth Amendment and the subsequent Volstead Act that prohibited the manufacture and distribution of alcoholic beverages. As a result, America lost its first juvenile wine culture to prohibition, although a few remaining wineries produced wine for religious ceremonies and grape growers provided immigrant families with wine grapes, a practice permitted by prohibition laws.

This turn of events produced a wine culture whereby many men, out of fear of loss of their wine supply, excluded women and institutionalized wine as a male-dominated realm. After all, it was considered improper for women to partake or be part of the production and distribution of alcohol. The cycle toughened as women's groups hardened their resolve to battle men who plied women with liquor for their sexual gratification. More disheartening was the fact that the trinity of "drinking, voting, and virility" planted powerful roadblocks in front of women's reform programs. This callous male attitude affirmed itself in the catchphrase "Candy is dandy, but liquor is quicker." In defiance, moral Christian women taught their daughters that "lips that touch liquor shall never touch mine."

These attitudes began to break down in the middle of the 20th century as enfranchised women used their newly won political powers to promote their struggle for gender equity. It is from these numerous women's movements that alcohol, among other advances, became a woman's right. Past stereotypes of vixen girls whose daughters frequented 1920s' speakeasies evolved into the 1950s', 1960s', and 1970s' liberated women, who publicly drank. Historian Catherine Murdock, in *Domesticating Drink,* documents this transition from the struggle to stop alcohol's degradation of women, at all costs, to a new generation of daughters who felt free to drink in public places. Consequently, drinking was one of many liberties acquired by modern women, and in Murdock's opinion, there is a legitimate relationship between "alcohol consumption and the women's rights movement." Women's gains in employment, birth control, suffrage, and divorce added to the clout of women's newfound freedom.

This combination of opportunities helped propel women into the American wine industry's general workforce and into positions as winery managers and owners. In addition, it made good business sense to have women drinking, because it doubled the size of the consumer market and greatly increased industry profits. Smart marketers in the new American century quickly learned to use feminine images to attract female drinkers. More important, management executives recognized that upwardly mobile liberated women were more likely to drink wine. Thus they directed marketing campaigns aimed at woman. What better strategy to market wine than to promote women winemakers who would produce wines for women or, for that matter, men. Included in the hard-gained rights were the acceptance of women in the workforce and the lowering, not removal, of the wineglass ceiling in the wine industry. Subsequently, oenophiles in the new millennium now interact with women who manage tasting rooms, serve as vineyard consultants and workers, sell wine at the retail and wholesale levels, write about wine, teach about viniculture and viticulture at colleges and universities, serve as winemakers, and own wineries.

Yet the gender inclusiveness of the wine industry is far from complete. Movies like *A Walk in the Clouds,* where actor Keanu Reeves's character Paul Sutton saves the virtue of Victoria Aragon, played by Aitana Sanchez-Gijon, and presumably helps run the male-dominated family winery, glorify past stereotypes. Many women wine advocates worry that a new feminization of wine is occurring as "the selling of wine draws heavily on the traditional feminine arts of making people feel welcome and at ease." Women's roles are again being defined by the culinary arts that complement the premium wines produced by male winemakers. Aggravating the problem is the continued use of the attitudes portrayed in the drinking songs of the Middle Ages that glorify the tavern pleasures of wine, women, and song. Incidents like these serve to remind us that equity for women in wine has rooted and hopefully, like premium wine, will improve with age. If one accepts Lucille Ball as an early entrant to modern femininity, it makes sense that her romp in the grapes helped crush the negative stereotypes of women and wine and thus serves as a precursor to the transition from wine as a man's hobby to wine as a people's drink.

This selection looks at the ever-increasing role of women in wine in the last half of the 20th century and purposefully limits its scope to examples that can be found in the California wine experience, which constitutes a lion's share of American wine production. While most are stories of great successes, it cannot be forgotten that women still make up a small percentage of the total numbers of those who earn a living from viticulture and viniculture.

WOMEN PIONEERS

As representative examples of female winemakers proliferate, it becomes easier to identify successful women winemakers. But this was not always the case. In the post-World War II era, one winery served as the training ground for the first wave of women pioneers in the California industry. It all started with Isabel Simi, who as a teenager inherited her Healdsburg winery just prior to prohibition. Simi opened one of the region's first tasting rooms and through the 1970s acted as a mentor and role model for the first wave of women. As early as 1974, Mary Ann Graf, first woman graduate of the University of California, Davis, enology program gained recognition as Simi's winemaker. In 1979 Graf helped start Vinquiry (a business specializing in chemical and microbiological analysis of wine). Zelma Long, Mike Grgich's protégé at the Robert Mondavi Winery in Oakville, became the next Simi winemaker and later became president of the winery. During her 20-year tenure at Simi, Long hired and launched numerous careers. Her practical women's wine university produced winemakers like Margaret Davenport of Wente Brothers and Clos Du Bois Winery and Carol Schelton of Windsor Vineyards. Add to this list Kristi Koford, winemaker of Alderbrook Winery, who, after graduating from the University of California, Santa Cruz, tutored under Zelma Long at Robert Mondavi Winery (1974-1984), after which she assumed the top Sonoma winemaker position at Alderbrook Winery, where she specialized in Zinfandel and Pinot Noir wines.

Dry Creek Valley has also nurtured its share of women pioneers. Milla Handley of Handley Cellars in Mendocino County grows grapes in the Dry Creek Valley and has received international recognition for her Sauvignon Blanc wines. Juliana Iantosca gained winemaking success as the winemaker for the valley's Lambert Bridge Winery.

One of the more conventional ways for women to enter the winery business has been through family tradition. Rashell (Shelly) Rafanelli followed this route when she became a third-generation (following in her mom's footsteps—Patty Rafanelli) winemaker for Rafanelli Winery. Another third-generation woman family winemaker is Gina Gallo, granddaughter of Julio Gallo. Gallo's family's wine fame and deep pockets provided her opportunities to produce award-winning wines and build her own brand recognition through her personal appearances in commercials and full-page advertisements in *Wine Spectator*. Mary Ann Sebastiani Cuneo of Sebastiani Vineyards and Winery has also followed this third-generation path that allows women to become spokespersons for the family business.

ORGANIZATIONS

In the 1990s, women concerned about their role in the wine industry formed the Women for Wine Sense (WWS) organization. Their main goal was to show women as a moderate voice in the wine industry that offered a balanced view of the social effects of wine drinking. In their words, they were "the flip side of the warning label. It's the opportunity to say that a glass of wine a day might be good for you." The two cofounders of WWS responded to Napa Valley Schools' MADD (Mothers Against Drunk Driving) program that taught that winery people were producing and selling "drugs."

Their mission exhibited their determination to provide "unbiased information about the cultural, social and health effects of moderate wine consumption, in order to protect the duty and the right of individuals to be responsible for their lifestyle decisions." From this statement, it is obvious that they were fighting the age-old battle that virtuous women do not drink. In a few years, the organization grew to include chapters in California, North Carolina, New York, Oregon, South Carolina, Texas, Washington State, and Wisconsin, and boasted members who were marketers, winery owners, winemakers, tasting room managers, journalists, university professors, bankers, consultants, and wine drinkers.

As a means to upgrade the image of women in wine, the group sponsored the Top Annual Women Winemaker Awards. In 1999 over 250 women celebrated, with wine, as Dawnine Dyer, vice president of winemaking at Domaine Chandon, received the Mentor of the Year award. From the 30 women winemakers serving wine at the dinner, Luisa Ponzi of Ponzi Vineyards, Celia Welch Masyczek of the Staglin Family Vineyards, and Gina Gallo of Gallo of Sonoma Valley received Rising Star Awards. The 2000 event seated 300 guests, and 45 women winemakers poured their wines while honoring Stacey Clark of Pine Ridge Winery, Marie-Eve Gilla of the Gordon Brothers Family Vineyards, Milla Handley of Handley Cellars, Ashley Heisey of Far Niente Winery, and Laurie Hook of Beringer Vineyards with the Rising Star awards.

SOMMELIER

The Court of Master Sommeliers, founded in England in 1969, oversees the testing and credentialing of the cream of the crop of liquor and beverage servers. The first woman recipient, Madeline Triffon, Michigan restaurateur, cracked the wine glass ceiling in 1987, although it would be another 8 years until Sally Mohr of Colorado Wine Merchant and Mary Ewing Mulligan, wine merchant, joined Triffon. By the year 2000, the United States had 29 of the world's 75 active master sommeliers, and women still made up less than 10% of the American Master Sommelier category.

Kim Caffrey, owner of Napa Valley Wine, Women & Laughs, believed this would change, since "women actually have an edge as far as tasting and subtleties because anthropologically, women are super tasters." But again it must be remembered that women have not achieved full recognition in the distribution end of the wine industry. A two-page Tinchero Winery of St. Helena, California, advertisement in *Wine Spectator* (June 2002) celebrated the winery's top 61 distribution executives with thumbnail photographs accompanied with name and company titles. Only one woman, Kathryn V. Folio of Can-Am Distributors of West Virginia, appeared on the California winery's thank-you list.

WOMEN FIND THEIR WAY

Rock 'n' roll great James Brown sang, "It's a Man's Man's World." Yet for wine, times were changing. A *San Francisco Examiner* article titled "Wine, Women and Strong" reflected this change. The article reported that a quick look at the 2001 Napa Valley Wine Auction showed "how prominent women" had become "in the once-male-dominated wine business." The auction illuminated the trend in California winemaking that "women have become a force." Michaela Rodeno, the auction's chairperson and CEO of St. Supery Winery in Rutherford, proudly announced that winemaker Celia Masyczek's Staglin Family Vineyards barrel lot had received the top auction price of $59,950 and wines from Delia Viader's Viader Winery in Deer Park, California, wine had received $5,100 in a silent auction bid. Heidi Barrett's (the event's hottest winemaker) Screaming Eagle (owned by Jean Phillips) and La Sirena (own label) wines drew the most attention and accolades for any winemaker—male or female.

These experiences suggest that women are beginning to make great inroads into the premium wine industry. Rodeno believed women's slow start would accelerate faster than the business world in general because the fine wine industry "didn't actually get started until about 30 years ago—so it didn't have time to build up as many barriers as the institutional industries have." This can be backed up with an ever-increasing list that includes women like Mia Klein of Selene Wines and Etude Winery, Helen Turley of Marcassin Wines and Bryant Family Winery, and Lorri Emmerich, general manager of Murphy-Goode Estate Winery and president of the Sonoma County Winemakers Association.

SANTA BARBARA WOMEN OF WINE: A CASE STUDY

The Santa Barbara wine region serves as a good case study of women's entrance into the wine industry in the late 20th century. The region's industry began its postprohibition rebirth in the 1960s and 1970s with the all-so-familiar list of male entrepreneurs like A. Brooks Firestone, Pierre La Fond, C. Frederick Brander, Jim Clendenen, Bob Miller, Harold Pfeiffer, Richard Sanford, and Dan Gainey, who helped establish the region as the Napa wine revolution spread to California's Central Coast. Again missing from the list were the names of women. This does not mean women were absent; it simply means that they were behind the scenes and supporting their winemaking husbands. Women like Margaret Houtz, Claire Bettencourt, Donna Marks, Geraldine Mosby, Fran Murray, and Jeanne Woods played major roles as tasting room managers, general hands, bookkeepers, and business partners in their husbands' new wine enterprises.

By the 1980s, the gender energy shifted and the region began to take note of numerous female wine stars. One of the first was Lane Tanner, who regarded her "femininity as an incredible asset" and used it to bring attention to her now famous Pinot Noir wines. The chemistry major from San Jose State University got her break in 1981 when California wine great Andre Tchelistcheff, credited by many for reviving quality winemaking after prohibition, helped her land an enologist (wine chemist) job at the Firestone Winery. Tanner began making her own wine in 1984 for her then husband Frank Ostini's Hitching Post Restaurant. In 1990 she opened Lane Tanner Winery with the help of wine distributor Larry Pearson, and today her wines command premium prices nationwide. Tanner also served as a role model for the growing numbers of future female winemakers. She took the role seriously and remembered the days when women were not allowed to "keep their femininity and still be winemakers," and takes pride in the fact that she could be "equal as a winemaker and still be incredibly feminine." She used her femininity to market her Pinot Noir wines and described them as the most feminine and difficult of all the grapes— "mostly finicky and fickle, and incredibly responsive." Tanner chose to stay small and oversee all aspects of her winery because she "can't stand the idea of someone else touching these babies."

Alison Green Doran, another Tchelistcheff protégé, started when her father, Russell H. Green, bought the Simi Winery in Healdsburg and hired Tchelistcheff as the winemaker consultant. The renowned winemaker quickly recognized Doran's knack for "discerning slight differences between various wines," and mentored her talents. In the meantime, her father provided her the perfect role model when he hired the first woman winemaker, Mary Ann Graff. Doran later became Firestone's winemaker and boasted that at the time there were only 25 women winemakers in California's over 800 wineries. Doran believed that there were more women succeeding because "women have such a special talent for blending and tasting." Firestone premium wines appeared in markets worldwide.

A. Brooks Firestone, of the Firestone Tire family, with his wife-partner Kate Boulton Firestone, London-trained ballerina, decided to expand their winery operations in 1987 by purchasing the small family-run Carey Cellars in the Santa Ynez Valley of Santa Barbara County. Kate assumed leadership of the winery and dedicated her energies to creating an intellectual and artistic winery, based on good business sense that would allow her to exploit her personal interests in wine and food. She successfully ensured the continuance of Firestone women in the family wine operations when she brought her daughter, Hayley Firestone Jessup, into the winery's daily operation. The Firestone women achieved their goal of leaving the "rat-race" for the active farming lifestyle.

Firestone was not the only woman to enter the industry through her husband's enterprise. In Santa Maria, California, Barbara Banke, along with her husband, winery megagiant Jess Jackson (Kendall-Jackson Winery; Kendall was his first wife's name), opened Cambria Winery and vineyard in 1988, and Banke later became president of the megaboutique winery. Jackson regarded his wife's Cambria Winery as a jewel in the Kendall-Jackson wine enterprise.

SANTA CRUZ WOMEN OF WINE: A CASE STUDY

A second case study of the post-1970s' entrance of women into the California wine industry can be found in the 40+ wineries of the Santa Cruz Mountains. According to *Santa Cruz Sentinel* reporter June Smith, in every winery in the region there is "at least one talented, dedicated woman involved in its success." Smith coined the phrase WOW (Women of Wine) to describe these female pioneers. As in previous examples, continuance of the family winemaking tradition was strong in the region. One such example of Smith's WOW was Beth Ahlgren of Ahlgren

Vineyard. In 2000 she became CEO for her parents' winery, and her only lament was that she missed "the camaraderie of other women winemakers." Ahlgren's husband, Dexter, entered the business as winemaker when (as he puts it) "things got out of control" and the winery took over their lives. Another woman following the family tradition was Beverly Bargetto of Bargetto Winery, who believed that the nurturing instinct of women brought new perspectives to the industry because women paid more attention "to detail" and have the "patience and emotional stamina" that coincides well with the "painstaking winemaking process and the many challenges each day brings." Bargetto also helped launch the career of her assistant winemaker, Deborah Elissagaray. The idea of family tradition also continued with fifth-generation Kathleen Rebhahn of Vinh-Rebhahn Vineyard, who rebuilt the late 1800s inherited family vineyard that had been destroyed by Pierce's disease.

As we have seen in previous cases, many women in Santa Cruz also made their winemaking fame by working side by side with their husbands. Jennifer Jackson of Equinox Methode Champenoise, along with her husband, Barry, continued their agricultural upbringing by producing sparkling wines through their "shared vision." Mount Eden Vineyards' winemaker/owner Jeffrey Patterson owed the success of his winery to his wife, Ellie. In 1985 the Pattersons reorganized their winery with Ellie's business expertise and marketing strategies. Christine Slatter of Hunter Hill Winery, who handled all the accounting and compliance reporting for her husband's wine enterprise, exemplified the husband-wife teamwork concept. Also included in this list would be Steve and Pamela Storrs of Storrs Winery and Greg and Kathleen Nolten of Zayante Vineyards.

The list of husband-wife teams continued to grow in the Santa Cruz Mountains. Anne Moulton and husband, David, worked hand in hand to create Burrell School Vineyards. The couple purchased the land in the 1970s and took their time developing the vineyards and winery until their children were older. Others included Sue Broadston and Max Maximovich of Thunder Mountain Winery and Brenda and Bill Murphy of Clos LaChance Winery.

University education and on-the-job training also provided an avenue for women to enter the business. Alison Crowe, with a University of California, Davis, bachelor's degree in fermentation science and a 1998 Outstanding Senior, used her internship experiences at

Chalone Vineyard in Soledad and Curtis Winery in Santa Ynez to begin her career as a temporary worker with winemaker Don Blackburn at Byington Winery in Los Gatos, California. In 2000 Crowe landed an enologist position at Bonny Doon Vineyard and was quickly elevated to associate winemaker, working directly under Randal Grahm. Other women in this category include Mary C. Ericson, Ph.D., research chemist, wine educator, and member of the Society of Wine Educators, who taught at the University of California, Santa Cruz, Extension wine program. Educated wine women like Kay Simon, UC Davis graduate, believed that more women would enter college and university programs in winemaking because "women have decided it's a fun career."

SALUD: TO YOUR HEALTH

Since wine has traditionally been a male-dominated activity—making and drinking—most health-related research on wine has centered on issues of alcoholism and male heart disease. As this story has shown, post-World War II women earned the right to publicly consume wine and assume positions in the wine industry, and a direct spin-off from this phenomenon has been that the medical community has begun to investigate and study the good and bad side effects of wine consumption for women. In other words, American society openly acknowledged that women would consume wine as part of their newfound strides toward equity.

Because women are generally smaller and weigh less than men, they become intoxicated easier because their stomachs produce less enzymes that break down alcohol. The resulting alcohol-laden blood delivers higher levels of alcohol to body systems. In the case of women, higher levels of body fat keep the alcohol in the body longer. Thus, women who consume three or more drinks a day face health risks that would not occur in men until they imbibe nine or more drinks a day. A study of 85,000 women who consumed one to three drinks a week revealed a significant decrease in mortality due to heart disease. Yet the same study showed three or more drinks a week resulted in higher death rates due to breast cancer and cirrhosis. A subsequent study with 322,000 women warned that two to five drinks a day increased breast cancer by 41%. Initial research led doctors to associate this increase with alcohol's ability to slow down the secretion and breakdown of estrogen. Those most at risk were women using contraceptives or estrogen replacement therapy. Most important for wine-drinking women was that medical researchers recognized women's involvement with and right to moderately drink wine and participate, guilt-free, in the wine industry.

Women in the American West have worked hard to break down the wineglass barrier that discouraged and at many times prevented their entrance into the pre-World War II wine industry. Gender inequity, war, prohibition, depression, and negative societal images of women and wine began to break down in the 1950s through 1970s as the modern women's movements attempted to bring political and economic equity to women. For women of wine, the women's movement paralleled the rebirth of the modern wine industry centered in California. As the two grew up together, the slogan "wine, women, and song" took on new meaning. Women were no longer just part of the pleasurable male-dominated ambiance of wine but had become an integral part of the business of viniculture and viticulture. As we have seen, the wineglass barrier had been cracked but not shattered. Lucille Ball's clownish depiction of women's old wine tradition marked the beginning of the new era where a woman could establish herself as a wine buyer, owner, grape grower, educator, business manager, winery hostess, or winemaker. The image of the pretty girl sensually crushing grapes with her bare feet has begun to give way to the Women of Wine.

—Victor W. Geraci

SUGGESTED READINGS

Barbara Banke interview by Rick Ryba, Cambria, California. Tape recording, Special Collections, University of California, Santa Barbara.

Barron, Cheryl Aimee. *Dreamers of the Valley of Plenty: A Portrait of the Napa Valley*. New York: Scribner, 1995.

Claire Bettencourt interview by Beverly Schwartzberg, Santa Ynez, California. Tape recording, Special Collections, University of California, Santa Barbara.

Folts, John, M.D., and Arthur Klatsky, M.D. *Wine's Heart Disease Benefits Most Pronounced in Women*. American College of Cardiology Meeting, March 1997 (Vol. 3, No. 8).

Franson, Paul. "Wine, Women and Strong." *San Francisco Examiner*, July 5, 2001.

Geraci, Victor W. *Grape Growing to Vintibusiness: A History of the Santa Barbara, California, Regional Wine Industry,*

1965-1995. Ph.D. dissertation. University of California, Santa Barbara, 1997. Forthcoming untitled monograph by the University of Nevada Press.

Geraldine Mosby interview by Susan Goldstein, January 28, 1994, Buellton, California. Tape recording, Special Collections, University of California, Santa Barbara.

Hayes, Tim, and John Koetzner. "Wine Tributaries." Retrieved November 28, 2001, from www.wines.com.

Hayley Firestone Jessup interview by Victor W. Geraci, February 3, 1994, Los Olivos, California. Tape recording, Special Collections, University of California, Santa Barbara.

Karlsberg, Elizabeth. "The Smell of Success." *Santa Barbara News-Press* Magazine (Fall 1997): 18-19, 22, 25.

Lee, Mike. "Women to Be Toast of Wine Event." *Tri-City Herald* (Washington State) (August 15, 2001).

Margaret Houtz interview by Sarah Case, January 28, 1994, Santa Ynez, California. Tape recording, Special Collections, University of California, Santa Barbara.

Matthews, Jayson. "Grape Expectations for Women in Wine." Retrieved November 28, 2001, from www.coastnews.com.

Murdock, Catherine Gilbert. *Domesticating Drink: Women, Men, and Alcohol in America, 1870-1940.* Baltimore, MD: Johns Hopkins University Press, 1998.

Peiss, Kathy. *Cheap Amusements: Working Women and Leisure in Turn-of-the-Century New York.* Philadelphia, PA: Temple University Press, 1986.

Pinney, Thomas. *A History of Wine in America: From Beginnings to Prohibition.* Los Angeles: University of California Press, 1989.

Schaefer, Dennis. "Grunge to Glamor." *Santa Barbara News-Press* Magazine (Fall 1997): 16-17, 27.

Smith, June. "Women of Wine: They Dared to Take a Great Leap of Faith." *Santa Cruz Sentinel* (March 14, 2001).

Women for Winesense. Retrieved from www.womenforwinesense.org.

WINNEMUCCA, SARAH (1840-1891)

Sarah Winnemucca was the granddaughter of Chief Truckee, a Paiute chief, and daughter of Chief Winnemucca, a shaman, and Tuboitony, Chief Truckee's daughter. She was a princess of the tribe at birth and became a spokesperson for the tribe and American Indians in general in the late 19th century. Both Chiefs Truckee and Winnemucca pursued a peace policy with the white settlers who swarmed through the Humbolt Sink, Pyramid Lake, and California, traditional Paiute ground. Sarah would continue to pursue peace and the interests of the Paiute people throughout her life.

Early in life, she experienced the terror of Indian-hunting whites who were seeking the extermination of all Indians, as well as the generosity of white settlers who traded with and befriended tribal members. Sarah was a gifted child who absorbed languages easily, learning English, Spanish, and several Indian dialects. She intuited that knowledge was power and sought the learning that the white population possessed. Given the opportunity to translate for Paiute leaders, she quickly turned her support role into a lead role as the eloquent voice of the Paiutes. She became, as LaVonne Ruoff has so succinctly put it, "the mightiest word warrior of her tribe." In November 1879 she started lecturing in San Francisco on behalf of the Paiute cause and against the injustices they suffered at the hands of the reservation system and its administrators. Best known for her *Life Among the Piutes: Their Wrongs and Claims* (1883), a tribal history, autobiography, and tract intended to win support and sympathy for the Paiutes as well as expose the corruption of the reservation system, Sarah was more than a gifted author.

Sarah gained credentials as a warrior, scout, messenger, and interpreter in the 1878 Bannock War. She infiltrated the Bannock camp on one occasion, created a ruse, and led her father's band from the camp to safety. She was an interpreter for General Oliver O. Howard and on one occasion took her uncle's place in battle. Her exploits included epic rides over vast distances carrying crucial orders. She was more than words; she was a warrior on Indian terms.

With her Indianness and her oratorical skills, she worked long and hard in the cause of justice for the Paiutes and all their tribal kin. She lectured in Boston and Washington, D.C., had an audience with the president, and continued her crusade throughout her life. In her time, she was unconventional as an Indian woman, both in white society and within her tribe. Her serial monogamy included several white men and produced no children, but a great deal of controversy. She was most at home with her people but uncomfortable in their environment. She was an important lobbyist in the American Indian cause, but even when a school in Reno, Nevada, was to be named for her in 1994, controversy stalked the public sphere. Yet more voices favored her and the school was named the Sarah Winnemucca Elementary School. Beyond the school, her legacy lives on in her attraction to scholars, with the most recent biography having come out in 2001.

—Gordon Morris Bakken

SUGGESTED READINGS

Brimlow, George. "The Life of Sarah Winnemucca: The Formative Years." *Oregon Historical Quarterly 53* (June 1952): 103-134.

Canfield, Gae Whitney. *Sarah Winnemucca of the Northern Paiutes.* Norman: University of Oklahoma Press, 1983.

Fowler, Catherine S. "Sara Winnemucca Northern Paiute, ca. 1844-1891." In Margot Liberty, ed., *American Indian Intellectuals.* St. Paul, MN: West Publishing, 1978.

Morrison, Dorothy N. *Chief Sarah: Sarah Winnemucca's Fight for Indian Rights.* 2nd ed. Portland: Oregon Historical Society Press, 1990.

Ruoff, A. LaVonne. "Nineteenth-Century American Indian Autobiographers: William Apes, George Copway, and Sarah Winnemucca." In LaVonne Ruoff and Jerry Ward, eds., *The New Literary History.* New York: Modern Language Association, 1991.

Trafzer, Clifford E. *Death Stalks the Yakama.* East Lansing: Michigan State University Press, 1997.

Zanjani, Sally. *Sarah Winnemucca.* Lincoln: University of Nebraska Press, 2001.

WOMAN SUFFRAGE IN THE WEST

The American fight for woman suffrage began in Seneca Falls, New York, in 1848. Seventy-two years later, the vote was finally secured when Tennessee ratified the Nineteenth Amendment in 1920. While the fight began and ended in the East, the story unfolded most significantly in the states west of the Mississippi River.

After adoption of the Fourteenth Amendment, which extended full citizenship to all American men, and arguably all women, a number of western territories and states considered amending their constitutions to extend the franchise to women. The most important of these early state campaigns occurred in Kansas in 1867. The Kansas legislature submitted two separate amendments for public approval: one extended the franchise to African American men and the other gave women the vote. Both amendments failed, despite heavy canvassing by eastern suffragists and extensive publicity.

The Kansas campaign had two long-term ramifications. First, in combination with stress originating from the Civil War, it split the fledgling women's rights movement. As a result, two competing organizations were formed. The National Woman Suffrage Association (NWSA) emphasized the primacy of women's vote, occasionally resorting to politically expedient, often racist, arguments to support their position. They advocated using their resources to secure a federal woman suffrage amendment. The American Woman Suffrage Association (AWSA) supported ratification of the Fifteenth Amendment, extending suffrage to African American men, and stressed the need to secure woman suffrage state by state. In the wake of the Kansas campaign, the completion of the transcontinental railroad in 1869 allowed prosuffrage literature, and activists riding the lecture circuit, to travel easily to the frontier. The eastern and western suffrage movements developed a mutually beneficial, if occasionally tense, relationship.

A second effect of the Kansas election was the proposal that women in all the territories be enfranchised. In 1867 and 1868 the U.S. Congress briefly considered legislation enfranchising territorial women as a suffrage experiment. It seemed a safe proposition. Territorial residents were not allowed to vote either for their own governors or for presidential electors. In addition, Congress could review the results of this democratic experiment when the various territories applied for statehood. Ultimately, Congress limited its test case to Utah, where using women to contain the Mormon practice of polygamy was a much larger issue. The woman suffrage experiment in Utah lasted from 1870 until 1887, when Congress enacted legislation disenfranchising Utah women. Despite congressional inaction, occasional outright prohibition, and general disapproval, the West became the laboratory in which woman suffrage was tested and found safe for democracy.

The western territories took a number of different developmental paths on the way to statehood. In general, states were most likely to extend suffrage to women if they had a territorial history of allowing married women at least partial property and economic rights. In the West, at least, contract theory seemed to necessitate the extension of political rights to protect economic interests. The more integrated women were in the economic life of a territory or state, the more likely the legislature was to offer some level of political participation. In short, property rights were more easily extended into voting rights in the newly developing states of the West. In a similar manner, in some territories—among them Washington—women's enfranchisement was cast partially as a reward for women's economic contributions. In addition, states were more likely to extend ballots to women in their constitutions if they had some previous territorial experience with female participation at the polls. Woman suffrage also gained support from women's involvement in Populism, the Grange, and other political communities.

Ultimately, however, historians agree that the western politicians who supported woman suffrage were motivated more by a variety of political ends than by ideology. Woman suffrage was seen as an incentive or lure to attract females to regions with unbalanced sex ratios, and in several states, legislators hoped to attract settlers by offering extensive rights. The female franchise was viewed as a means to recruit eastern support in campaigns for statehood; it also was seen as a potential force to either protect polygamy or to destroy it. Woman suffrage was used as a tool to embarrass opposing political parties. It was often seen as a way to offset the enfranchisement of black men under the Fifteenth Amendment. The quest for full suffrage gained additional support in the West in part because there was no significant organized opposition. States that did not have strong liquor lobbies moved to extend suffrage to women earlier and with less antisuffrage opposition. Each territory or state that moved to extend the franchise wove together several justifications for their suffrage legislation.

All four states that allowed women to vote by the end of the 19th century were west of the Mississippi River. Their widely divergent reasons for full democratic suffrage serve as good examples of the multiplicity of the western suffrage tradition. Wyoming was the first territory to extend the vote to women and the first state to protect female suffrage in its Constitution. Wyoming women were enfranchised in 1869 partially as a means of attracting investors and female settlers to the territory and partially to embarrass the Republican governor. Apparently unembarrassed, the governor refused to veto the act and later stopped a legislative attempt to repeal the law. When Wyoming petitioned for statehood, Congress balked at

the state constitution, which elevated full democratic suffrage to organic law. Wyoming legislators refused to amend the constitution and reported that Wyoming would stay out of the Union a hundred years rather than enter without their women. When admitted in 1890, Wyoming became the first state in the union to allow female citizens to vote in all elections.

The second state to extend full suffrage to women did so for vastly different reasons. In 1870 the Utah territorial legislature extended suffrage to women in an attempt to protect the Mormon Church and defend its practice of polygamy against growing agitation in the East. Initially, eastern politicians and suffragists supported the act, believing that women would not vote for their own marital enslavement and would therefore help undermine the institutional domination of the Mormon Church in the Utah territory. In addition, eastern suffragists believed the Mormons were providing a heaven-sent opportunity to show the civic benefits of female suffrage. Both groups were proved wrong when Mormon women voted their faith at the polls. In 1887 the U.S. Congress reacted by passing the Edmunds-Tucker Act, which, in addition to outlawing polygamy, disenfranchised women in Utah. In 1896 Utah successfully petitioned for statehood, having apparently complied with antipolygamy legislation. Like Wyoming, Utah built on its territorial experience, and its Constitution provided for female suffrage. This time the provision did not cause a congressional delay.

During the same time period, both Colorado and Idaho acted to expand their electorate. In 1893 Colorado amended its state constitution to include provisions for full female suffrage. Racist ideology played a major role in the long suffrage campaign, with proponents arguing as early as 1870 that if uneducated black men were allowed to vote, white women should be extended that privilege as well. Early supporters also maintained that women would have a special purifying influence on politics. In the end, support of prohibitionists, Populists, and Republicans led to the ratification of a special referendum, but only after 17 years of suffrage agitation.

The history of woman suffrage in Idaho contains elements found in each of the three preceding states' campaigns. Like Utah, the Mormon question complicated the issue of female suffrage in Idaho. Afraid of the taint of both woman suffrage and Mormonism, both groups were prohibited from voting despite the early introduction of suffrage bills into the territorial legislature and the tireless agitation of the suffragist Abigail Scott Duniway. As in Wyoming, concerns about future immigration figured into the legislative debates. And like Colorado, suffrage was secured after employing racist arguments supporting white women voting. They benefited as well from the political support from the Populists, Democrats, and Republicans, and from the Mormons and prohibitionists. Suffragists in Idaho also pointed out that women in surrounding states had gained the right to vote. They argued further that women's financial interests necessitated that they have the vote, reciting once again that there should be no taxation without representation. The campaign in Idaho benefited from the lack of significant opposition from liquor interests. Idaho finally adopted a woman suffrage amendment in 1896.

It was 14 years after Idaho's action before another state extended the franchise to women. The two national suffrage societies reunited in 1890. During this long dry stretch they rebuilt the National American Woman Suffrage Association (NAWSA) around new strategies. These included recruiting to the cause large numbers of middle- and upper-class women involved in the growing women's club movement as well as targeting socially prominent, politically influential, and professional women who could support the movement through financial contributions. The coalition leadership also decided to emphasize individual state campaigns, hoping to win enough state suffrage amendments that Congress would then be forced to approve a federal amendment for ratification. Despite new vitality, the suffrage movement faced considerable obstacles in the East and South. Powerful impediments to full female political participation included long-held cultural traditions of the separation of public and private spheres, the fear that female suffrage would destroy the foundations of the family and with it, the supposedly indivisible head of the household, widespread opposition to female jury service, and the more tangible formal antisuffrage organizations, including the formidable liquor lobby.

When the NAWSA was able once again to claim victories at the state level, they were once more predominately in the West. In 1910 Washington State enacted a provision protecting woman suffrage. The history of woman suffrage in Washington State was convoluted. It included two territorial provisions extending both voting rights and jury service to women in 1883 and a response from the territorial supreme court in 1885-1887 overturning these acts as unconstitutional. Following on Washington's heels, California allowed female enfranchisement in 1911 and Oregon in 1912. After a long history of granting women partial suffrage in school elections, Kansas allowed full suffrage through a constitutional amendment in 1912, as did Arizona. In 1913 Illinois was the first state east of the Mississippi to allow women to vote for presidential electors. A year later, Montana and Nevada adopted suffrage amendments on their first submission. The tide turned in 1917 when North Dakota, Nebraska, and Rhode Island secured presidential suffrage for women. In the same year, New York adopted a constitutional amendment extending the full vote to women. Despite a ticking clock that caused much last-minute anxiety, as time appeared to be running out on ratification of the national amendment, the die had been finally cast in favor of women's full political participation in the national polity.

—Debra A. Viles

SUGGESTED READINGS

Bakken, Gordon Morris. *Rocky Mountain Constitution Making, 1850-1912*. Westport, CT: Greenwood Press, 1987.

Beeton, Beverly. *Women Vote in the West: The Woman Suffrage Movement, 1869-1896*. New York: Garland, 1986.

Cole, Judith K. "A Wide Field for Usefulness: Women's Civil Status and the Evolution of Women's Suffrage on the Montana Frontier, 1864-1914." *American Journal of Legal History 34* (July 1990): 262-294.

Duniway, Abigail Scott. *Path Breaking: An Autobiographical History of the Equal Suffrage Movement in Pacific Coast States*. New York: Schocken Books, 1971.

Gordon, Sarah Barringer. *The Mormon Question: Polygamy and Constitutional Conflict in Nineteenth Century America*. Chapel Hill: University of North Carolina Press, 2002.

Kraditor, Aileen S. *The Ideas of the Woman Suffrage Movement: 1890-1920*. New York: Norton, 1981.

McBride, Genevieve. *On Wisconsin Women: Working for Their Rights From Settlement to Suffrage*. Madison: University of Wisconsin Press, 1994.

Petrik, Paula. *No Step Backward: Women and Family on the Rocky Mountain Mining Frontier, Helena, Montana, 1865-1900*. Helena: Montana Historical Society Press, 1987.

VanBurkleo, Sandra F. *"Belonging to the World": Women's Rights and American Constitutional Culture.* New York: Oxford University Press, 2001.

Wheeler, Marjorie Spruill, ed. *One Woman, One Vote: Rediscovering the Woman Suffrage Movement.* Troutdale, OR: New Sage Press, 1995.

WOMEN IN THE CRIPPLE CREEK DISTRICT

Women in the Cripple Creek, Colorado, gold-mining district, like women throughout the mining West, faced limited options in a place where men outnumbered women and the only industry employed only men. The richness of the mines, their rapid industrial development, and a high degree of labor union influence distinguished the District from other mining areas during its first tumultuous decade, all of which affected women and children as well as the mining workforce.

Deservedly called the World's Greatest Gold Camp, the Cripple Creek District, some 18 miles southwest of Colorado Springs, was a relatively late bonanza. Gold was discovered there in 1890, and the area rapidly developed into one of the world's major industrial gold-mining centers. Cripple Creek produced over $65 million in gold during its first decade, and over $20 million annually by the turn of the 20th century. By 1900 the district, only 6 miles square, held 32,000 residents and 10 towns: Cripple Creek, the commercial center and county seat of Teller county; Victor, the City of Mines in the heart of mining activity; the smaller residential towns of Anaconda, Elkton, Lawrence, Goldfield, Independence, Altman, and Cameron; and Gillett, a milling and railroad town at the northeast entrance to the District. A network of three railroads and interurban trains linked the towns and homes to over 700 producing mines, and hauled ore to the mills and smelters that refined the precious metal from the District's complex ores.

The richness of its ores and the rapid consolidation of the industry supported communities that offered steady employment for a predominantly working-class population. Four out of five adults were from the working class in 1900. Most men worked at the mines. Women managed households, ran boarding houses, or provided domestic services for wages as waitresses, cooks, laundry workers, and seamstresses. Others sold sex, dances, and companionship in the vice districts of Cripple Creek and Victor.

Women's status depended on their relationships to men—on whether they were married or single and whether they labored at home or in the respectable marketplace or sold entertainment and companionship in towns where most men were unmarried. Though sex workers were probably the largest group of women wage earners, Cripple Creek's communities were also known for the women who married and raised families there. Known as "good family towns," they drew experienced miners who settled, built schools, and established homes.

Women and children were more numerous in the District than in less prosperous and short-lived mining camps. Forty percent of the adult population in 1900 was female, a relatively high proportion compared to earlier gold rushes. Since there were roughly three men for each two women of marriageable age, most women married. Of all women 16 or older, 7 out of 10 were married in 1900 and lived with their husbands, compared with 42% of the men; 6% of the men were married but lived apart from their wives. Only 4% of the women remained single by age 31, compared with 62% of the men. Not until they were over 30 could most men support families and settle down. Married men were older, more skilled, and made more money than single men. They were skilled miners, skilled workers in other trades, salaried mine workers, professionals, and business owners. They frequently married women much younger than themselves. Age differences, coupled with diseases and accidents associated with mining, led to early widowhood. One woman in 10 in her 30s had lost her husband. By their 50s, over a fourth were widowed; over half of all women in their 60s coped alone or with the help of their families.

Women's options throughout their life cycles were tied to the local mining economy and, from 1894 to 1904, to the power of organized labor. For 10 years, between two crucial miners' strikes in 1894 and 1903-1904, the District was a stronghold of the militant Western Federation of Miners (WFM). The first strike won the right to union membership (but not a closed shop), an 8-hour day, and $3 minimum daily wage for all District miners. Miners' numbers, purchasing power, and control of the key local workforce gave them considerable leverage, and by 1902 nine WFM locals had helped organize a majority of all workers in all trades. At least 54 local unions existed.

Women wage workers belonged to the Retail Clerks, Laundry Workers, Cooks and Waiters, Hotel and Restaurant Employees, Dressmakers, Bakers and Confectioners, and Typographical locals. Labor endorsed equal pay for equal work, but there were few mixed-sex occupations. Women clerks and typographers, who most often had equal work and wages, benefited particularly from union membership. Most of the unions were male strongholds, and women generally earned less than men. For a 60-hour week, Cripple Creek laundry workers won a union wage of $8.50 for towel supply girls and $7.50 for mangle girls; in Victor, mangle girls earned $9 a week. Ten Cripple Creek waitresses hired temporarily to serve a convention overflow crowd staged a walkout in 1902 because they were paid the regular scale of $14 a week and board instead of the $3 a day and board usually paid temporary help.

Women union members were a minority of the District's women. Over 95% of District men listed occupations on the 1900 census; 19% of the women did. Paid occupations represented a fraction of women's work; most depended on male breadwinners and performed unpaid domestic labor. Many were proprietors of boarding and rooming houses, restaurants, and groceries. School teaching was the largest female profession. An unusual number of professional women practiced in the District—at least 4 physicians, 1 osteopath, 1 dentist, and 25 nurses in 1902. Married women, however, rarely worked outside the home. They might take in laundry, cook, clean, or manage boarding houses, but not work in public for pay.

Women who did not work for wages or belong to unions participated in the labor community, which exerted influence far beyond the workplaces and union halls, in social, educational, and political arenas. Many women belonged to the WFM women's auxiliaries. More attended union dances, socials, educational and political forums, and participated in the 3-day Labor Day celebrations. They benefited from the men's wages and union benefits. Many locals offered sick benefits, helped care for ill members, and buried those who died. Many, like the local lodges and fraternal associations, also offered charitable aid in hard times; some offered life insurance. Such benefits buffered the hazards of an unstable industry for working-class families.

Unions courted women's political and economic support. Colorado women won the vote in school elections when Colorado achieved statehood in 1876. In 1893, after years of suffrage campaigns and organizing, Colorado became the first state to enfranchise women by a vote of the male electorate. The major support came from Populist hard-rock metal miners. The Cripple Creek District ratified woman suffrage by a vote of 548 to 254, and the following year appointed the first women in Colorado to serve on a police court jury. Organized labor sought women's votes and their purchasing power, which was needed to support union-label products and labor boycotts. But the unions rarely addressed women's working conditions at unpaid household labor.

Family needs shaped women's work. Women were much more likely than men to live with families—92% as opposed to 69% of the male population. Only 2.4% of all women lived alone in 1900, or with unrelated adults, in circumstances where they could care for themselves alone. Over a third of all women cared for adults outside their immediate families. Twenty-one percent kept boarders; another 15.5% cared for extended family or other adults. They cared for children and old people as well. Roughly a fourth of the District's population consisted of children under age 16.

While families increased men's financial responsibilities, they intensified women's work at home. They tended vegetable gardens and small livestock, made clothing, did housework, and provided income by keeping boarders, cooking, or doing laundry. Few had running water, but hauled it to cook, clean, and bathe; they hauled wood and coal to cook food and heat water, and then hauled the ashes out. Besides their domestic tasks, women periodically buffered the instabilities of a mining economy when mine shutdowns, strikes, and accidents required them to produce income. A man's death meant that a woman must work for wages, take in boarders, or otherwise care for herself and her family.

The unions generally ignored women's household labor. But in 1899 they politically attacked the largest group of women wage workers, who earned their livings selling sex and companionship, and in 1902 the Cripple Creek District Trades and Labor Assembly attempted to expel members who worked in the District's dance halls, a position that most affected union musicians and bartenders.

Prostitutes performed wage labor, but perceptions of prostitutes' class status depended on their race and on the class of their clientele. Myers Avenue, Cripple Creek's red light district, reflected the racial and class hierarchy in its geography. Dance halls and "resorts" were located between Third and Fifth Streets, as well as the fancier parlor houses and a few one-woman cribs. Conventionally attractive younger white women worked in the big houses that served wealthier customers. The elite Old Homestead maintained a separate building where a few African American women worked behind the "big house." Further down Myers were smaller houses, two African American establishments, and the crib area, where French, Japanese, Chinese, Mexican, Indian, and African American women worked alone.

Besides sex, women sold dances, drinks, and companionship in dance halls, bars, and gambling houses. Women might choose such work to escape abusive homes, because it offered greater control or freedom than other options, and because it paid more than most work available to women in the District. One young woman worked in a Cripple Creek dance hall after her father developed silicosis, because she earned only $2.50 a week at her previous job in a Denver department store. Lillian Powers, who worked as a prostitute in Victor and Cripple Creek, said that she entered "the life" because it was her best option as an uneducated woman. She had earned only $2 a week as a domestic servant, and found that many laundry workers had to sell sex on the side to make ends meet. Working, by preference, out of her own crib, she charged a dollar a "date," and sold beer for a dollar a bottle.

The local unions never tried to organize the sex trade, but dance hall women went on strike in 1902 to oppose a 10% cut in their share of liquor sales and established a Dance Hall Girls' Protective Association. The strike succeeded, but the union was apparently short-lived. Nor could any union have protected the women from the hazards of the trade—from drugs and alcohol, venereal disease and pregnancy, exploitation by pimps, and violence from pimps and customers. Vice flourished as long as the District boomed; as the mines declined, a few aging sex workers grew old with their customers.

Cripple Creek women, then, faced a limited series of options throughout their lives. A young woman might work for wages for a short time before marriage, generally in service occupations that did not pay enough for her to live alone. Her choices became sex work or marriage. She was likely to marry before her mid-20s and to combine housecleaning and child care with some household production. She might supplement the family income by keeping boarders or doing cooking or laundry at home, but her world was largely domestic. That did not mean it was leisured. Quite the opposite was true. When she was widowed, her work would not change—she could support herself keeping a boarding house, do sewing or laundry, or depend on kin.

In such circumstances, labor's economic power and the fellowship of union socials and holidays did much to improve the quality of women's lives. That community ended with the 1903-1904 strike, called to support smelter workers who refined Cripple Creek ore in nearby Colorado City, and who were fired and blacklisted when they tried to form their own WFM local. During much of the strike, the area was under martial law. Troops commanded by a local mine superintendent harassed organized labor and invaded a meeting of the Victor WFM Women's Auxiliary. The strike ended violently. In the early morning of June 6, 1904, a dynamite explosion beneath the Independence train depot platform killed 13 nonunion miners. Mine owners and the military quickly ousted local elected officials, destroyed local union halls and stores, deported 238 union leaders to New Mexico and Kansas, violently drove hundreds of others from the District, and instituted a local blacklist that barred all union members from employment.

Responsibility for the Independence Depot explosion remains a contested issue. Harry Orchard, a former union member, later confessed to the deed and accused an "inner circle" of the WFM leadership of planning the disaster. The union insisted that mine owners hired the job done to justify martial law. The question may never be resolved, though it is certain that most union members and their families had nothing to do with it. But they were not strangers to violence—men were killed or injured daily in the mines, prize fighting was a ubiquitous male pastime, and men of all classes carried guns or hired them.

For the women of the Cripple Creek District, the strike defeat meant loss of union wages and benefits and of a supportive labor community. During the strike, as during wartime, it became acceptable for respectable women to act publicly. When the militia arrested the workforce of the prounion *Victor Record,* Emma Langdon, a union printer, sneaked into the building, printed the paper with the headline "Slightly Disfigured but Still in the Ring," and delivered it to the military commander. Hailed as a "Colorado Heroine," she became the first woman elected to honorary membership in the WFM. After the deportations, women raised bail bonds, fed imprisoned miners, and distributed strike relief in secret, despite a military ban. The militia harassed them, hauling auxiliary members to the military bullpen, and warning them to end their "insolent criticism and denunciation of the military."

Mining continued in the Cripple Creek District long after the 1904 strike defeat. Some union miners maintained households there and commuted from other camps to visit their families. Women's labor changed little, though over time they got running water, gas stoves, and electricity. Many mines never reopened, and the area never fully recovered, socially or economically. During World War II, the government closed the mines to move miners from gold to strategic metals. After the war, dwindling ore reserves and a volatile gold economy periodically closed down production. Most of the smaller mining towns were long since abandoned, and Cripple Creek and Victor shrank to a fraction of their boom period populations.

By the 1990s, the fluctuating gold market and heap leach mining revived some mining activity, as technology and cyanide made mining profitable again, but the new methods generated relatively few jobs compared to the boom days. The local workforce also depended on tourism and gambling, which became legal in Cripple Creek in 1991. Through all these fluctuations, the District remained home for former mining families and their descendants. Some women found employment in the gaming establishments and the hotels and restaurants established to serve tourists.

After the strike, women also inherited a special role. They became the keepers of memory. Many union records were destroyed by mobs in the brutal strike aftermath, and union miners were banned from the District. Memories of the labor community and the strike remained with wives who maintained homes in the District and with daughters who married young men who could work in the District because they had never belonged to unions. They kept the personal histories of labor's past.

—Elizabeth Jameson

SUGGESTED READINGS

Ellis, Anne. *The Life of an Ordinary Woman.* Boston, MA: Houghton Mifflin, 1929; rpt., Lincoln: University of Nebraska Press, 1980.

Feitz, Leland. *Myers Avenue: A Quick History of Cripple Creek's Red-Light District.* Denver, CO: Golden Bell Press, 1967.

Jameson, Elizabeth. *All That Glitters: Class, Conflict, and Community in Cripple Creek.* Urbana: University of Illinois Press, 1998.

Langdon, Emma F. *The Cripple Creek Strike: A History of Industrial Wars in Colorado.* Denver, CO: Great Western, 1904-1905; rpt., New York: Arno Press and the New York Times, 1969.

Lee, Mabel Barbee. *Cripple Creek Days.* Garden City, NY: Doubleday, 1958.

Suggs Jr., George G. *Colorado's War on Militant Unionism: James H. Peabody and the Western Federation of Miners.* Detroit, MI: Wayne State University Press, 1972.

WOMEN IN WESTERN MINING

The occupational structure of mining shaped the lives and labor of women in the hard-rock and coal mining communities of the American West. Women were barred from working underground until Title VII of the 1964 Civil Rights Act was implemented. Until then, women's options in mining towns largely consisted of providing domestic services and companionship for men, either within family households or in the marketplace. Their labor constituted an essential—if often unrecognized—component of mining's infrastructure.

The gendered division of labor distinguished the mining West from the mining regions of other times and places. The exclusion of women from western mines was so uniformly common that it came over time to appear natural. Yet Native American women had mined lead, copper, and precious metals before European colonization, and continued to labor in many Latin American mining regions after Spanish conquest. During the California Gold Rush, Miwok women adapted gold mining to their seasonal round of activities, using tightly woven baskets to pan the California streambeds as they accommodated to the diseases, disruption, and losses that came with Euro-American settlement.

Many immigrant miners knew that women had mined in their homelands. Japanese women labored in the Chikuho coal mines, most often in family groups, but also as single women and widows. Women were banned from working underground in England only in 1842, when the Mines and Collieries Act forbade the employment of boys under 10 and of all females in British mines. Their presence in the mines would have been a recent memory for men who traced their roots to the Welsh and Yorkshire coal fields and the Cornish tin, copper, and china clay mines. Women continued to perform hard labor for little pay in British surface workings after 1842. In Cornwall, older women hammered rude ore with stone mallets and then passed it on to the "bal maidens," adolescent girls who "bucked" it with iron hammers to the size of half-inch marbles.

Their daughters did no such work in the mines of the U.S. West. There, men considered it a positive achievement to exclude women from the mines and thus protect them from the dangers of the industry. Their ability to do so rested initially on the particular demography of western mining regions, which drew vastly more men than women, particularly in the early mining booms, and then on wages won with successful union organization.

Restricting women from the mines, however, did not protect the women from difficult toil. Women throughout the mining West confronted the limited personal and employment opportunities of a male-dominated industry. In the overwhelmingly working-class mining towns, most women worked hard for low wages or indirect support from working-class men. Their circumstances changed as mining developed, and their experiences varied according to what was being mined, the level of industrial development, the racial-ethnic composition of the local workforce, and local labor relations.

After the brief tumult of gold and silver rushes, western mining industrialized rapidly. Placer mining, a small-scale activity that sifted gold and silver from streams and gravel beds, quickly gave way to "lode" or "quartz" mining that tunneled into the earth from which placer metals had eroded, where the ore is not naturally separated from the rock, but must be milled and refined. Deep-shaft mining required considerable capital to finance underground development, milling and smelting facilities, and railroads to haul supplies to the mines and the ore to refining facilities. As industrial processes made it profitable to mine complex ores, and as new industries required new metals, the gold and silver of early prospectors' dreams expanded to include the shafts and pits that produced western coal, copper, zinc, molybdenum, and other base metals. In the industrial era, corporations owned the mines, mills, and transportation facilities, and their profits went largely to people who neither worked the mines nor lived in mining communities. Most mining

towns were overwhelmingly working class, with a smaller middle class of proprietors, professionals, and salaried mine managers. Women's roles followed the ownership, occupational, and household structures of the changing industry.

Women were most scarce in the early gold and silver placer booms. In California in 1850, a year after the Gold Rush began, the mining population was 97% male. Men outnumbered women 33 to 1 in the Southern Mines, 40 to 1 in the Northern Mines, 21 to 1 in the Klamath/Trinity diggings. By 1860 there was still only 1 woman per 20 men in California's mining areas. Ten years later, as the placers dwindled and quartz mining stabilized, the ratios became somewhat more balanced—almost 4 Californians in 10 were female. The deep-shaft mining center of Grass Valley housed 180 men per 100 women. California's gendered settlement pattern was repeated throughout the mining West. In Colorado, a year after the Pike's Peak boom of 1859, there were 1,650 men per 100 women. By 1900, in the two largest western industrial mining centers, Butte, Montana, and Colorado's Cripple Creek District, the ratio dropped to 3 men per 2 women.

The fact that they were outnumbered shaped women's options throughout their life cycles in western mining towns. In an economy that drew a disproportionately male population, women found a narrow set of options. Because there were vastly more men of marriageable age than women, particularly among immigrant miners, women tended to marry young. They were likely to be considerably younger than their husbands, who had to delay marriage until they had the skills and commanded the wages needed to support a family. Given age differences and the occupational diseases and underground dangers of mining, wives tended to outlive their husbands. They had to support their families when men were sick or disabled and after they died.

The persistence of a male majority throughout the mining West masked vast differences in the proportions of men and women among different ethnic migrants. In California, a decade after the Gold Rush, 30% of the white and free colored people were women, while Asian men outnumbered Asian women 20 to 1. The native-born population of California in 1870 was 43% female, but only 3 immigrants in 10 were women, and only 8% of all Chinese.

Although Chinese men worked the placers and built western railroads, neither capital nor labor welcomed

Chinese women, who, it was feared, would stabilize Chinese settlement and reproduce a Chinese workforce that would demand higher wages and better working conditions. The laws that restricted Chinese immigration and denied Chinese citizenship held particular consequences for women. The Page Law of 1875 sought to regulate the entry of Chinese prostitutes (but not prostitutes of any other nationality), while the 1882 Chinese Exclusion Act allowed only a privileged few women to emigrate, primarily the wives and daughters of Chinese merchants. Most of the Chinese women who were in the United States by 1882 were prostitutes, mostly impoverished peasant women imported to serve as sexual companions for Chinese men. Since Chinese could not legally marry people of other races, these few women became virtually the only available marriage partners for single Chinese laborers who remained in the United States. The "Gentleman's Agreement" of 1908 that restricted Japanese emigration resulted in similarly skewed sex ratios among Japanese in western coal camps.

Women's options changed as the short-lived placer camps gave way to mature industrial communities that promised steady employment and schools for working-class families. They varied, too, with the options for people of different racial and ethnic heritages in the regional mining economics. Native-born miners and western and northern European immigrants dominated the gold and silver camps of California, Nevada, Idaho, and Colorado. Chinese miners occupied a subordinate niche in the labor hierarchy of the early gold and silver camps. They were subjected to a discriminatory foreign miners' tax in California and were subsequently run out of mining towns throughout the West. Mexicans worked the placers of the Southern California mines; in the later zinc, copper, and coal mines of the Southwest, a dual labor system separated the work, wages, and living conditions of Anglo and Mexican miners. In addition to Euro-Americans, the Utah coal and copper camps employed Japanese, Greek, Slavic, Italian, and Mexican miners; Finns and eastern Europeans worked the copper and iron mines of Minnesota and Montana; eastern Europeans, Italians, and Greeks all mined coal in Wyoming and Colorado.

Each regional labor force created distinctions in the circumstances of women's domestic labor and intimate relationships. The different proportions of women in various ethnic groups affected the pressures on them to marry and to care for unmarried miners.

The vastly outnumbered Japanese wives might be contracted to feed and provide domestic services for large groups of Japanese miners, laboring and living in barracks that afforded little personal space, privacy, or other women's company. Anglo miners' wives in Arizona and New Mexico benefited from Anglo men's higher wages and from somewhat better housing than Mexican miners' families received. The women who lived in company-owned coal towns, like the Colorado Fuel and Iron (CF&I) camps of southern Colorado, kept house in company-owned houses, shopped at company stores, and were monitored by the company's Sociological Department. Only married women and a few men could keep boarders in the CF&I camps. This fact, coupled with lack of home ownership, meant that women heads of households could not easily survive there. Elsewhere, widows could run boarding houses in homes they owned or rented.

Women's conditions also varied with the success of mining organization. In the hard-rock West, miners began to organize as Nevada's Comstock Lode industrialized when the miners of Virginia City formed a Miners' Protective Association on May 30, 1863. Within 6 years, miners organized local unions in most of the major lode mining centers—in Grass Valley, California; Central City, Colorado; Silver City, Idaho; and Pioche, Nevada. Butte miners organized in 1878, and in 1889 four Idaho locals combined to form the Coeur d'Alene Executive Miners' Union. Then in 1893 representatives of 15 local unions met in Butte to form the Western Federation of Miners (WFM). From the 1890s, the United Mine Workers of America (UMW) organized western coal mines, while the WFM (later the International Union of Mine, Mill and Smelter Workers or IUMMSW) organized the hard-rock mines. When miners' unions were strong, they helped organize workers in smaller trades, so that in larger union communities like Butte, Anaconda, Bisbee, and Cripple Creek, women wage workers were also organized into local unions of retail clerks, typographers, cooks, waitresses, and laundry workers. Though women's wages were lower than union men's, mining town women benefited both directly and indirectly from organized labor. Women in union towns depended on the higher wages commanded by union men and on union services, like sick and death benefits and life insurance. They kept house in private family homes and shopped with private merchants.

Their lives, nonetheless, were hardly secure or leisured. Women grew vegetables in arid mining camps at high altitudes, preserved food and cooked it on wood or coal stoves, made clothing, and did laundry for extended households. Few had running water, but hauled and heated it for cooking, cleaning, and for baths for men covered with grime from the mines. They cared for the young, the old, the sick and infirm. Differences of degree more than kind distinguished mining town domesticity.

Mining town women's options varied by class, race, and marital status, by whether they labored at home, or earned "respectable" wages, or sold sex and companionship. Regardless of age or marital status, in the paid workforce or in their own households, women cooked, cleaned, laundered, sewed, waited tables, and provided companionship for men. Whether they were paid and what they were paid for distinguished reputable women from those who worked in the dance halls, saloons, and brothels of the mining West.

Before the 1920s, few respectable married women performed public wage work, and most of the larger mining communities accommodated segregated red light districts. Married women and widows might earn money and remain respectable in the privacy of family households. Many kept boarders or did laundry for single men, especially when illness, strikes, and unemployment jeopardized men's wages. Single women could work in the respectable marketplace as waitresses, laundry workers, domestic servants, and clerks. A small number found professional opportunities as teachers or nurses. Though numerically few, proportionately more women worked as doctors and lawyers, as well, in areas that needed their professional skills. Often the largest group of women wage earners consisted of those who sold sex, companionship, drinks, and dances throughout the mining West.

Women's options in all these arenas changed with time, as both mining towns and the women themselves matured and aged. The few women who joined the male influx of the early gold and silver rushes found their domestic skills in high demand. An unidentified woman wrote from San Francisco in 1850 that California was the only place she had seen "where a woman rec'd anything like a just compensation for work. I am perfectly contented and have no wish to return," she wrote. "I have been sewing ever since I came here but expect to change my business for some kind of housekeeping before long." She considered opening a boarding house, where she planned to care for 30 to 35 boarders, and pay a cook $150 a month. "People do not pretend to keep vary [sic] clean houses here," she commented. "But if the houses and streets are dirty the money is clean."

In early mining booms, women's domestic talents could provide the key to their families' fortunes. Luzena Stanley Wilson's Gold Rush odyssey began when a miner offered her $10 for biscuits baked by a woman. She found that the miners of Nevada City would pay a dollar for a meal. Her first restaurant there was so "well patronized," she wrote, that "I shortly after took my husband into partnership." Mrs. Wilson went on to operate hotels in Sacramento, Nevada City, and Vacaville. Other women did well selling vegetables, bread, butter, and other domestic amenities.

Some of the most significant women in the early mining booms were not the few exceptional ones who accompanied their husbands West or the even rarer souls who sought their independent fortunes. The male majorities in western mining camps left behind communities where "Gold Rush widows" managed farms and businesses in the absence of male guidance and authority. Women might have the help of their children, or of other family members, but for most women the men's absences left them responsible for family and business decisions they were not accustomed to handling on their own. Women far from the western streams and mine shafts underwrote men's labor in the western mines, just as their cooking, cleaning, and sewing enabled men to get up every morning and return to the diggings.

Economics and emotional meanings subtly distinguished the separations of different Gold Rush widows. The grass widows left behind when Chinese men sought their fortunes at the land they called Gold Mountain might remain dear in memory, but they faced separations that could last 10 years or a lifetime, depending on whether finances would enable a spouse to visit or return.

The boom years that placed a high premium on women's domestic talents were also the most prosperous for women sex workers, who found a narrow window of opportunity in the sex trade of the early gold and silver camps. In Helena, Montana, from 1865 to 1880, most prostitutes owned their own small houses, and worked independently. During the 1880s, several madams built and operated larger houses and rented space to other women. But their control crumbled after 1893, as pimps began to take control of the sex trade, and by 1900 women had lost control of their property and their labor.

Mining town vice was a stratified business. Sex workers' status depended on their youth, the class and race of their clientele, and the degree of discretion and control they were able to exercise over the conditions of their lives and labor. Prostitution could cover a range of transactions and living and working conditions. Mistresses might live in private homes outside the red light districts and be paid indirectly, much like respectable wives. Dance hall workers sold companionship and liquor. Paid by the dance and a share of the liquor sales, they might or might not also sell sex. A prostitute's status depended on how discreet or flagrant she was, how subtle about being paid, whether she sold talents other than impersonal sexual intercourse, whether she slept with many men or a few, what she charged, and the class of her clientele. The hierarchy ranged from madams and mistresses, to women who worked in elite houses, through those in smaller houses that catered to middle-class men, to women who worked independently from small one-woman cribs. Those on the lower rungs of the profession worked in small brothels or working-class saloons, or as streetwalkers. The lowest status went to older women, vagrants, and women of color, particularly Asian slaves or indentured prostitutes, who earned the least and had the least security and control. Regardless of their status, very few escaped the dangers of the trade: violence, venereal disease, pregnancy, drugs and alcohol, exploitation by pimps and customers, and declining status and wages as they aged.

Prostitution remained a constant of the mining landscape, seldom publicly approved, but regarded as a necessary evil, and exploited for the money that fines and compulsory medical exams brought to municipal coffers. For the women themselves, the sex trade was work—often the best-paid employment available for women among the limited options of the mining West.

As mining industrialized, more women joined the male majority in towns that offered steady work, union wages, schools, and sufficient stability to support families. The excitement of the Gold Rush miner who paid $10 for biscuits gave way to working-men's towns where women earned less than $10 a week doing domestic labor. Miners' daughters could look forward to working at home or in the paid workforce for a few years before they married, usually by their early 20s, then to years of domestic labor and childbearing, and to keeping boarders, taking in laundry, or depending on their children for support when they were widowed. Sex workers aged and often experienced downward mobility in the profession or suffered other dangers of their trade.

All western mines had one thing in common: mining is by nature an impermanent enterprise. Sooner or later the ore gives out. After the Sherman Silver Purchase Act was repealed in 1893, silver mines closed throughout the West and people fled the silver camps. That was only one dramatic instance of the mobility that characterized life in the mining West. Economic instability, strikes, and blacklists all fostered volatile movements from one mining camp to the next. As the minerals were depleted, mining communities shrank and their populations aged. The 1930s' Depression closed many mines, though gold mining prospered. During World War II, however, the U.S. government closed gold and silver mines to encourage miners to move to coal and metals needed for the war effort. During the war, women were allowed temporarily to enter some previously all-male workforces in the mining industry. Local women, for instance, were allowed into the smelters of Anaconda, Montana, a move that the local union community preferred to opening the jobs to outsiders. Not until the 1970s, however, would women join the mining workforce itself and share with men the dangers and instabilities of underground labor. More commonly, women of the 20th-century mining towns, like their predecessors, did domestic work at home and for pay, managed insecure family budgets, and tried to plan for periodic strikes. Their union communities were divided by Cold War red-baiting, and disrupted by periodic mine closures.

As the mines closed, former mining towns like Aspen, Park City, Breckenridge, and Telluride became ski resorts and tourist destinations. These enterprises, like the older mining communities, offered women low-paid service work in hotels and restaurants. Women's labor linked the diverse mining towns of the 19th-century West and connected the older mining West to the tourism that replaced it in 20th-century western boomtowns.

—Elizabeth Jameson

SUGGESTED READINGS

Chan, Sucheng, ed. *Entry Denied.* Philadelphia, PA: Temple University Press, 1991.

Deutsch, Darah. *No Separate Refuge: Culture, Class, and Gender on an Anglo-Hispanic Frontier in the American Southwest, 1880-1940.* New York: Oxford University Press, 1887.

Finn, Janet L. *Tracing the Veins of Copper, Culture, and Community From Butte to Chuquicamata.* Berkeley: University of California Press, 1998.

Goldman, Marion. *Gold Diggers and Silver Miners: Prostitution and Society on the Comstock Lode.* Ann Arbor: University of Michigan Press, 1981.

Jameson, Elizabeth. *All That Glitters: Class, Conflict, and Community in Cripple Creek.* Urbana and Chicago: University of Illinois Press, 1998.

John, Angela V. *By the Sweat of Their Brow: Women Workers at Victorian Coal Mines.* London: Croom Helm, 1980.

Johnson, Susan Lee. *Roaring Camp: The Social World of the California Gold Rush.* New York: Norton, 2000.

Levy, Jo Ann. *They Saw the Elephant: Women in the California Gold Rush.* 1990; rpt., Norman: University of Oklahoma Press, 1992.

Mann, Ralph Emerson. *After the Gold Rush: Society in Grass Valley and Nevada City, California, 1849-1870.* Stanford, CA: Stanford University Press, 1982.

Mercier, Laurie. *Anaconda: Labor, Community, and Culture in Montana's Smelter City.* Urbana: University of Illinois Press, 2001.

Murphy, Mary. *Mining Cultures: Men, Women, and Leisure in Butte, 1914-41.* Urbana: University of Illinois Press, 1997.

Owens, Kenneth N., ed. *Riches for All: The California Gold Rush and the World.* Lincoln: University of Nebraska Press, 2002.

Peavy, Linda, and Ursula Smith. *Women in Waiting in the Westward Movement: Life on the Home Frontier.* Norman: University of Oklahoma Press, 1994.

Petrik, Paula. *No Step Backward: Women and Family on the Rocky Mountain Mining Frontier, Ilelena, Montana, 1865-1900.* Helena: Montana Historical Society Press, 1987.

WOMEN'S EXPERIENCES ON THE WESTERN EMIGRANT TRAILS

During the western emigrant trails era, 1841-1869, an estimated 500,000 people traveled over a complex system of overland trails to western destinations, seeking a better life, economic opportunities, and religious freedom. The trails era is characterized by a succession of migrations, beginning with agricultural migration to the Pacific Northwest, followed by the Mormon migration to Utah, and finally gold rushes to California, Colorado, and Idaho-Montana. Each decade of the period exhibited distinct characteristics as the various types of migrations meshed and flowed together.

The proportion of men, women, and children varied greatly with the type of migration. Men dominated the mineral migrations (at least 80% and at times 95%), whereas a more balanced men/women ratio characterized agricultural migrations. Agricultural emigrants to the Pacific Northwest intended to settle on farms and build communities patterned on those they left behind. Nearly half of all agricultural overlanders traveled in parties based on kinship. In most cases, this was an extended family. Women comprised 15% to 20% of all travelers, and children an even higher percentage. Mormon settlement was a unique and distinct type of agricultural migration. While the Mormons went to develop available land, however difficult, they were interested in creating a new and different society, separate from the American mainstream. In the ensuing Mormon migration, the proportion of women and children rose dramatically.

The Gold Rushes—California, 1849-1852; Colorado, 1859-1862; and Idaho-Montana, 1863-1866—contrasted significantly with agricultural migration. Gold Rush emigrants traveled west for the economic opportunities in the goldfields. In contrast to the extended families who were the basis for agricultural migration, gold rushers tended to travel alone, in single-family units, or with acquaintances. Many intended to return home once they accumulated enough money, but others went to take advantage of commercial or professional opportunities in the mining camps and towns. Women made up only 5% to 10% of travelers in the gold rushes. Despite the greater proportion of men traveling to the mines during the peak Gold Rush years, the absolute number of families on the trails remained about the same throughout the emigrant trails era. Taking into account the fluctuations in the types of migration, women comprised 15% of the total migration for the entire period, or 75,000 women.

The diaries and journals written during overland journeys reveal that women had a wide range of experience on the trail. The kind of experience and the degree of comfort on the journey for an individual woman depended on physical, social, and personal factors. Much of the trail experience was determined by physical factors such as the natural environment, material culture, available resources, and the woman's health and fitness. A woman's experience was also shaped by the degree of support she received from her social network of family, in-laws, and friends. A significant factor was her personality type, or the way she viewed and interacted with her world. As a result, some women experienced the journey as unrelenting hardship and grief, others as totally easy and pleasant, but for most it was somewhere in between. Even for those in the middle range, some certainly experienced more difficulties, while others had an easier journey.

The majority of westering overlanders were white, middle-class Americans, although a large minority were immigrants, mostly from northern Europe and Canada. A small minority of blacks made the overland journey, and while their presence was not considered unusual, very little information is available about them. Thus, most overlanders throughout the era had the means to travel west, with the exception of large groups of Mormons who were subsidized. The poor could not afford the overland move, particularly to the coast, as the cost was substantial—$500 to $1,000 to outfit for the journey and more was needed during the journey and at trail's end.

The western migration also reflected another significant aspect of American national experience. Beginning in the colonial period, American expansion occurred as a regular process in a westward direction, spreading American society across the continent. Many overlanders had earlier moved to the states bordering the Mississippi and Missouri Rivers, demonstrating a predisposition toward mobility. Continuing this general pattern in westward migration, the majority of overlanders began their journeys from midwestern or Middle Atlantic states.

Since marriage was the accepted norm at the time, most of the adult westering women were married and traveled with their immediate families. Single women, young and old, traveled with kinship parties or at least a close relative. Although numerous brides or recently married women traveled west, virtually every other married woman traveled overland with children under 5. A single woman traveling alone was not just impractical, and it was considered to be improper. In spite of this, a few women resorted to extraordinary means to accomplish the journey outside the kinship norm.

Diarist Rebecca Ketcham traveled to Oregon in 1853 in the traveling company of a well-known Oregon missionary. She was unmarried, unaccompanied by any relatives, and yet received no censure. Perhaps she was accepted because she traveled more or less under the protection of the missionary. Friends and relatives loaned her the money to pay for her passage, which she intended to repay from her earnings as a teacher after she arrived. Nevertheless, discrimination marked her journey. She was still expected to fulfill domestic duties, but after she learned that she had been charged a great deal more than a young man who also paid for his passage, she heatedly recorded in her diary that from then on she would work less and find more time to write.

Other women who traveled alone did not fare so well. Overlanders tended to condemn or at least frown upon unattached single women who behaved outside the role of domesticity. In 1850 a young man reportedly smuggled a prostitute disguised as a man, causing dismay in the train when she was discovered. In 1864 another woman successfully disguised herself as a man and worked her way to Oregon as a wrangler. Her identity was not revealed until she was seen working as a waitress in Portland. It is unknown how many women disguised themselves as men, but clearly some did, as during this period instances are known of women serving in the Civil War disguised as men.

Gender roles and spheres of activity were the same during the journey as at home, reflecting the nature of gender in the larger society. Gender relations in the middle and upper classes in mid-19th-century America were characterized by an ideology of the private, domestic sphere of women in contrast to the public, business, political sphere of men. While both men and women had equally important responsibilities on the trail, their domains were distinct and separate. Nevertheless, trail conditions tended to blur gender boundaries for women. By necessity or choice, many women occasionally did what was usually men's work. Women pitched tents, gathered fuel for campfires, yoked oxen, rode horses, and drove teams and loose livestock. Sometimes they stood guard or joined their husbands to keep them company. Some women used firearms expertly. Yet even as they shared male tasks on the trail, women generally reverted to conventional roles in the more rigid society at trail's end.

Except in rare instances, women undertook the journey because their husbands, fathers, or other man in the family decided to go. The parameters of decision making on such matters fell into the circumscribed circle of family relations dominated by men. But as in all aspects of domestic life, an individual woman's influence on the decision varied with her situation. Some women had an active part in the decision to move west, but others had no say. Women who had the most influence on the decision to move often wished to join family members who had already migrated. Other factors, such as the desire for improved health or economic advantages, contributed to her influence. In spite of how the decision was made, leaving home was usually a highly emotional experience. Most women believed they would never again see family members and friends they were leaving behind. Only those who were traveling to join family members who preceded them westward were spared this anguish.

Outfitting for the journey was a universal necessity. Published emigrant guidebooks, newspaper articles, and experienced family members and friends provided information about what was necessary to take. Once again, the preparation responsibilities fell into two distinct areas. Men organized the wagons, draft animals, firearms, tools, and other equipment. Women gathered the provisions, bedding, clothing, and other domestic items. Then husbands and wives worked together to decide and pack what could be taken in the limited space. Many westering women were disappointed in having to leave cherished possessions behind, and others made poor decisions, only to later have to abandon such articles along the trail.

Women's preparations for the journey included sewing clothing, bedding, wagon covers, and tents; making soap; and baking, preserving, and packaging foods. The staple foods needed for the journey were flour, bacon, coffee, sugar, and salt. Additional supplies included smoked beef, shortening, soda crackers, rice, tea, dried beans, dried fruit and vegetables, fruit preserves and jams, saleratus (baking soda), vinegar, pickles, and condiments such as mustard and ketchup. In the later trail period, canned oysters provided a delicacy for trail meals. The basic kitchen articles were a kettle, frying pan, coffee pot, a tripod to hang cookware from, tin plates and cups, and cooking and eating utensils. Sheet-iron stoves were often taken, which were stored on a platform at the back of the wagon. Many such stoves were abandoned along the trail as women discovered it was easier to cook over a campfire.

Bedding included blankets, quilts, bedspreads, pillows, and feather or hair mattresses. Women were advised to make dark calico pillow covers and sheets, not white, for an overland journey. Quilts (often called comforters) were perhaps the most versatile and meaningful bedding articles. Primarily used for bedding, quilts were also used to line the walls of the wagons as protection against wind, rain, and cold. They were hung as privacy barriers to wall off sleeping and dressing areas in tents and wagons. Sometimes they were used as decorations in tents and wagons to relieve homesickness or create a homelike setting. When used as a burial shroud, a quilt provided reassurance to the living that a tangible connection to the family was left with the deceased.

Other domestic items to be packed included mosquito nets, towels and tablecloths, candles, matches, washtub, washboard, and soap. Overlanders also had a wide choice of India rubber articles, including blankets, air mattresses, coats, boots, and leggings. India rubber blankets or sheets were especially useful for wrapping food and ammunition to keep them dry. An assortment of medicines was an important part of the outfit. Quinine, blue mass (a mercury preparation), laudanum (opium), calomel, sugar of lead, paregoric, ipecac, and Epsom salts were regularly included in medicine chests. Whiskey for snakebites and citric acid for scurvy were also common additions. Women packed sewing items such as scissors, needles, pins, thread, scraps for patching, and knitting and quilting projects to work on during the journey.

Clothing for the journey was another important concern. Women needed shoes, stockings, nightgowns, two or three dresses, drawers and corsets, one or two petticoats, aprons, shoulder kerchiefs, sunbonnets, and a warm shawl or cape. Usually at least one good dress was packed away to be worn at the destination. Everyday dresses were made of wool, linen, linsey-woolsey (a durable combination of wool and linen), delaine (lightweight wool or cotton and wool), and cotton fabrics such as gingham, calico, and muslin. A pregnant woman wore a wrapper or loose-fitting dress. Underneath the dress a woman wore drawers, a chemise (slip), one or two petticoats, and a corset. Corsets were worn for foundation, not style, and were loosely laced. Some women did not wear drawers, but most did. Drawers were loose knee-length pants with an open crotch that allowed a woman to easily squat to relieve herself.

Sunbonnets were essential to protect the face and neck from sun, wind, and rain. For everyday wear they were made of gingham, calico, seersucker, or other

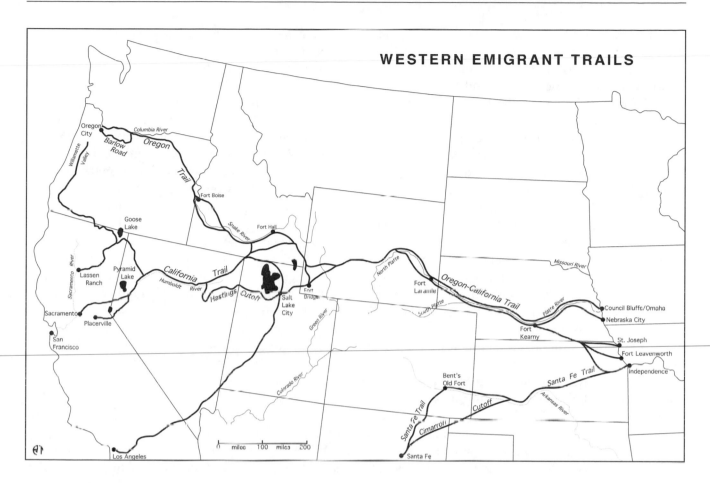

durable material, and lighter ones were worn for special occasions. The brim was 8 to 10 inches in length, made of a double thickness of fabric, and stiffened with narrow slats of wood or pasteboard. The slats stiffened the brim and held it out from the face but could be removed for laundering. The bonnet had an apron that hung down across the back ranging from 2 to 12 inches long, which protected the neck and upper back. And because suntanned skin was considered improper, some women also wore mitts with the fingers cut off to protect their hands. Shoes for the journey were especially important. Shoes of the time were made of leather, including the soles, and tended to wear out rapidly if the wearer walked most of the distance. Most women took several pairs, but many nevertheless ended up barefoot.

In the early to mid-1850s, the more adventurous women wore bloomers, the costume named for American social reformer Amelia Jenks Bloomer. The bloomer costume, or bloomers, was a knee-length skirt worn over long loose trousers that were gathered at the ankles. Bloomers declined in popularity in the late 1850s but had a revival in the mid-1860s. Bloomers

contradicted the accepted style of mid-19th-century women's clothing. Designed to control shape and hide body parts, particularly the legs, women's dresses were confining and concealing. Because bloomers allowed more freedom of movement and were closer to a man's attire than dresses, they were highly controversial among both men and women.

Overland travelers left their homes in early spring and headed for the departure places on the Missouri River known as jumping-off towns. The earliest travelers began arriving at the Missouri River at the end of March to wait for conditions on the trails to allow departure in early April. Those who hadn't outfitted at home did so in these towns. Before 1849 nearly all overlanders departed from Independence, Missouri. St. Joseph upstream was the center for the Gold Rush travelers in 1849 and 1850. By 1852 Council Bluffs, Iowa, was the primary emigrant outfitting town and departure point on the Missouri River, and continued to hold the lead through the end of the era. Once across the Missouri River, the overlanders traveled a number of feeder routes to the Platte River. These routes came together at Fort Kearny, and the trail continued up the Platte River along both banks in a corridor to South Pass. West of South Pass, routes diverged to destinations in Oregon, Utah, and California. Overlanders took 6 months to travel the 2,000 miles from the Missouri River to the Pacific Coast, less to closer destinations.

Once under way, trail life settled into a daily routine. Women generally got up about 4:00, at least a half hour before the men, to make the fire and begin cooking breakfast. If the family had a milk cow, it was milked before breakfast. Some women made butter in conventional churns, but most hung a bucket with cream on the wagon and the motion as it rolled along made butter. By the time breakfast was ready, the men had brought in the animals and were ready to eat. After breakfast, the women washed and put away the cooking equipment and packed the wagon. The usual morning drive was about 10 miles at 2 miles an hour with oxen, faster with horses and mules. A stop was made at midday for "nooning," for a meal and rest. The noon meal was known as dinner, although some diarists called it lunch. After nooning, another 10-mile drive was made to the evening camp. The actual distance traveled each day varied, depending on the kind of draft animals, terrain, and weather conditions.

Adequate water, fuel, and grass were important concerns for evening camp. Consequently, most travelers used the same campgrounds, and with overuse the necessary resources were often depleted. In addition, the availability of these resources varied greatly along the length of the trails, and many times overlanders faced shortages of one or more conditions. Water for people and animals and forage for animals were the most important requirements for the camp. Gathering fuel for the campfire was women's work. If trees were to be chopped, men did it, but more often women collected sagebrush, sticks, or buffalo chips along the trail during the day, which they placed in bags hanging on the sides of the wagons. Buffalo chips, dried buffalo dung, made a clean, hot fire. Cattle chips were also gathered when buffalo chips were not available.

The evening meal was called supper, or occasionally tea. Men's work ended when the animals were taken care of and they could relax in the evenings, but women continued cooking past the mealtime, preparing food for the next day's breakfast and dinner, and often working late in the night on other domestic chores. After supper, men relaxed, talked, and played cards around the campfires. Music was a common feature in the evening camps. All kinds of musical instruments were played, many by women. Young people danced, sang, and laughed boisterously. Women were mostly too occupied to participate in evening entertainments, although sometimes they completed their work and had time to socialize with other women before bedtime. Sleeping arrangements also varied on the plains. Men, women, and children generally slept in wagons or in tents, but some men slept under the wagons or in blankets on the ground.

During the day, women frequently rode in the wagons. The ride was not comfortable in the wagons with iron tires and no springs, so women also walked, and many women walked most of the time. While riding, they worked on mending, knitting, crocheting, or piecing quilts. Walking women visited from wagon to wagon, picked flowers, gathered fuel, or walked with friends. Women also rode horses, usually sidesaddle but sometimes astride.

Trains often laid over to observe the Sabbath or when weather or trail conditions forced them to. Whether or not to travel on Sundays was one of the most divisive issues in wagon trains. Laying by on Sundays served more than a time for religious observance, it also provided a sense of continuity with the familiar customs at home. Such layover days, whether Sunday or not, were an opportunity for women to do laundry; clean and air the wagons; dry the bedding, clothing, and provisions after a heavy rain or getting wet in a stream crossing; and repack the wagon loads. Women usually did their laundry in washtubs, heating water over a fire. When no fuel for a fire was available, the washing was done directly in the stream. Some women even ironed clothing after it dried.

Men and women's relations covered the same gamut on the trail as at home. The overland journey offered many opportunities for couples to meet, and courting was a common result. Sometimes courting caused trains to split up. One father did not approve of the young man who courted his daughter and took his family out of the train. The couple resorted to communicating through messages left on buffalo skulls beside the road using a pseudonym. Numerous weddings occurred on the trails, which were celebrated in a variety of ways—with dinners, breakfasts, dances, or not at all. One wedding typifies the often expedient nature of trail relations. A young woman married a man whose wife suddenly died, leaving him with six children. No officials were available for the ceremony, so they declared their mutual consent before a group of fellow travelers.

Intergender relations were not always harmonious during the journey. A few diaries mention abusive husbands, wives, and fathers. Other men in the train often publicly whipped abusive men, or at least threatened with a whipping if they abused again. Abusive women were more often the topic of gossip than punishment. Some women may have been quarrelsome and unpleasant by nature, but most instances mentioned in diaries were reactions to extreme stresses on the trail. One woman set the family wagon on fire and refused to go any farther. Diarists also recorded adultery, couples quarrelling, men or women who deserted their spouses, and homicides that involved arguments over women.

Health and hygiene, childbirth, disease, and death affected women on the overland trails. Although knowledge about what constituted good health and hygiene practices was limited at the time, diaries reveal that some women suspected the now-known causes of illness, particularly drinking water before it was boiled, eating contaminated food, or handling soiled clothing and linens. While men and women diarists often commented on the dirty, unkempt appearance of other overlanders, many attempted to keep as clean as possible under the circumstances. Women washed themselves and their children in the streams. One diarist bathed every chance she got, which was often. Most apparently washed their faces regularly. Mid-19th-century health was also enhanced with false teeth and eyeglasses, and a wooden, articulated false leg was found a hundred years later along the trail in Wyoming.

Discomfort, injury, and disease were constant threats on the trail. One diarist noted that women's work required stooping much of the time, which was hard on the back. Hands and faces were chapped or sunburned, and blisters and calluses were common. On the trail, broken bones, cuts, burns, and other injuries were caused by animals, falling under wagons, guns, stampedes, fires, and numerous other ways in an often-hazardous environment. Doctors were seldom available, but women made good use of their medicine chests or used whatever means were at hands to treat injuries. They applied axle grease to chapped skin, made splints for broken bones, and stitched cuts with needle and thread.

The most common medical problems on the overland trails were gastrointestinal illness—diarrhea and dysentery—and diseases such as cholera and typhoid fever. The most terrifying disease was cholera, with its sudden onset, rapid course, and high mortality rate.

Cholera was prevalent on the overland trails in 1849 through 1854, coinciding with its epidemic years in the United States. Mountain fever, smallpox, measles, tuberculosis, and diphtheria were also significant diseases on the trail. Other commonly occurring medical problems included infected insect bites, rattlesnake bites, boils, headache, toothache, scurvy, and a host of adverse effects of the conditions of overland travel.

Childbirth was a common occurrence on the overland trails, as one out of five women was pregnant at some time during her journey. Even under the best circumstances, childbirth was perilous in the mid-19th century. The mortality rate for deaths under the age of 1 year was more than 20 times that of today. Giving birth on the trail was even riskier for mother and infant than at home, as a result of little medical advice or care, inadequate nutrition, exposure, and limited access to water. If a midwife were not available, family members or other women in the train attended the birth. Sometimes the family or the train would camp for a day or more to await a birth and allow the mother to rest, but the more usual pattern was to resume traveling within hours. Perhaps because birth was commonplace while the journey was not, a number of women who gave birth on the trail named the babies after the place they were born—La Bonte, Platte, Columbia, or Nevada.

An estimated 25,000 people died on the journey during the emigrant trails era, or about 5% of the total number of emigrants. The chance of dying on the trail was nearly twice that if they stayed home; thus the journey clearly entailed risk. The majority of deaths on the trail were caused by disease. Cholera was overwhelmingly the leading cause of disease-related deaths, making it the leading cause of all deaths during the trails era. Other fatal diseases included dysentery, mountain fever, measles, and scurvy. The next significant cause of death was accidents. The leading cause of accidental deaths was drowning, followed by accidental gunshot wounds. A wide variety of other accidents also resulted in fatalities. Indians were the third most common cause of trail mortality. Lastly, homicides, starvation, complications from childbirth, and freezing accounted for a number of deaths.

The death of a loved one on the overland trail was worse than at home, where the gravesite could be visited and cared for. On the journey, the deceased was abandoned to the elements, animals, and possibly Indians, rarely to be seen again by grieving family and friends. Yet there were instances where family members traveling the same route at a later time found the grave of a loved one, undoubtedly based on information sent to them. In one case, the children of a deceased woman made a new headboard for her grave several years later. The numerous graves along the trail were a constant reminder of death, and they greatly affected some of the passing travelers. Particularly in the cholera years, overland diaries by women as well as men are filled with mentions of trailside graves. Many discussed at length their feelings about death on the plains. A few even recorded little else but the graves they passed by.

The overland journey exposed women to a new and unfamiliar natural environment. Women's diaries reveal they were affected by a wide range of severe weather conditions; were troubled by snakes, mosquitoes, and other troublesome insects; and viewed spectacular scenery. Typically, women's responses to the natural environment varied. Some barely noticed their changing surroundings, while others climbed rocks for the view from the top, explored unusual geological features, and visited trail landmarks such as Chimney Rock. Women's diaries contain exquisite descriptions of prairies, mountains, waterfalls, and rainbows. They note the varieties and colors of flowers, types of trees and rocks, and names of mountains.

The Indian tribes along the route comprised a significant aspect of the overland trail environment. Women's attitudes toward Indians depended on their preconceived ideas and biases as well as personality type. Some disliked or feared them, viewing them as inferior savages. Others were curious and interested in them, finding them colorful and exotic. Still others merely looked upon them with pity or condescension. Whatever impression they made, Indians were part of life on the trail, even though the majority of overlanders actually saw very few of them.

In the 1840s through the early 1850s, Indians were more of a nuisance than a serious danger to overland travelers. They demanded tribute or begged from them, traded with them, and visited their camps. Occasionally, they raided their stock, and a few emigrant men and Indians were killed, but no direct attacks were made against wagon trains. In the early 1850s tensions heightened between Indians and the encroaching whites, causing the Indian danger to increase. Indian attacks were mostly against isolated individuals or small trains, but as more army posts were established and military activity increased, the situation escalated. Before 1863, three quarters of

deaths from Indian attacks occurred on the trail west of South Pass. A major punitive campaign in January 1863 ended problems in that area, and the arena of aggression shifted to the eastern half of the trail.

Indian attacks against emigrants and swift and massive army reprisals continued the escalating spiral until Indian wars embroiled the northern plains until nearly the end of the emigrant trails era. Attacks against emigrants in Wyoming and a series of raids all along the road from Kansas to Colorado in summer 1864 resulted in a high number of casualties among emigrants, freighters, and settlers as well as notorious cases of Indian captivity. For the next few years, emigrant traffic continued, but under strict army observation and regulation. The last major year of overland traffic was 1866. As an immense post-Civil War emigration poured across the plains, a treaty council was attempted at Fort Laramie, the Indian wars on the northern plains began, and the first transcontinental railroad tracks were laid west from Omaha. In the mix of emigrants, Indians, and soldiers that summer, women encountered Indians in the same range of circumstances they previously had. They observed them, traded with them, and had loved ones killed by them.

The overland journey was a time of transition for women as they traveled to a new life. One way women accommodated to the insecurity and uncertainty of life on the road was to arrange their belongings in wagons and tents to create and maintain a homelike setting. Perpetuating familiar surroundings and activities on the journey forged a symbolic link between the home left behind and the one to be established at trail's end, even when the rigors of travel made this difficult. Above all, women's overland experience was the sum of the details of daily life as each woman in her unique way confronted and reacted to the journey.

—Susan Badger Doyle

SUGGESTED READINGS

Faragher, John Mack. *Women and Men on the Overland Trail.* New Haven, CT: Yale University Press, 1979.

Holmes, Kenneth L., ed. *Covered Wagon Women* (11 vols.). Spokane, WA: Arthur H. Clark, 1983-1993.

Myres, Sandra L., ed. *Ho for California! Women's Overland Diaries From the Huntington Library.* San Marino, CA: Huntington Library, 1980.

Schlissel, Lillian. *Women's Diaries of the Westward Journey.* New York: Schocken Books, 1982, 1992.

WOMEN OF THE SOUTHWEST

Women have lived in what is now New Mexico, Arizona, Texas, and California for thousands of years, yet their experiences varied tremendously depending upon era, environment, race, class, and ethnicity. The first inhabitants of the region appeared around 11500 B.C.E. and survived by hunting and gathering. Unmistakable desert culture groups appeared, such as the Hohokam, Mogollón, and Anasazi. Of them, the Mogollón most likely adopted the use of cultivated crops first, trading it further into the interior for other trade goods that they could not otherwise acquire. By approximately 2000 B.C.E., specialized tools for grinding grains like maize began to appear, indicative of a more sedentary, agricultural lifestyle. Women played a major role in food production and preparation, thereby possessing a key role in society. They assisted with the gardens, harvest, and even helped clean and repair irrigation ditches. They also augmented their family's diet by collecting wild foods like pine nuts. Women created beautifully decorated pottery to contain their family's surplus, and they became experts in finely woven baskets and textiles, which were traded for buffalo robes and jerked meat, for example. Between the first appearance of humans in the Southwest until the arrival of Europeans, women's roles evolved as the tribes became more culturally sophisticated.

The importance of women is evident in American Indian religion as well. For example, the Acoma creation story recounts how two corn mothers created life on earth. Chiricahua Apache creation stories abound of White Painted Woman, who, according to one version, created human beings. White Painted Woman also called for a puberty ceremony for young women—which is still celebrated to this day. Spiritual representations of females, such as Earth Mother, played an important role in many indigenous religious traditions.

By the 1500s, when the Spanish arrived in the Southwest, or more properly northwestern New Spain, numerous and very distinct Indian peoples lived throughout the region. For unnumbered generations, they had developed into hundreds of distinct tribes such as New Mexico's sedentary Pueblo Indians; semisedentary Pima Indians in Arizona; *rancherías* in California; as well as nomadic tribes like the Apache, Navajo, Ute, and Comanche. Distinguishable bands existed within the larger tribe—each developing gender roles based on such things as tradition, skill, ability, and need. Sometimes women and men expanded their roles to incorporate, or entirely encompass, gender roles prescribed for the opposite sex. Known by some as *berdaches,* these individuals held special prominence within the tribe.

The Spanish arrived in the Southwest not as mighty conquerors but as gaunt skeletons of warriors, washed ashore in their horsehide boats near Galveston, Texas—the result of a failed expedition to Florida in the 1520s. While no Spanish women participated in this venture, the tales of wealth in northern New Spain from this failed expedition caused the first viceroy, Antonio de Mendoza, to authorize an expedition into Pueblo Territory in 1540. Led by Francisco Vázquez de Coronado, the expedition explored the region as far east as the plains of Kansas. They hoped to find a new source of wealth to fuel the continued Christianization and settlement of the Americas, as well as the religious wars in Europe. Upon entering some villages, Spaniards bartered for necessary supplies where possible. When an agreement was not forthcoming, Spaniards took what they needed, and occasionally even raped Pueblo Indian women. Relations became strained and, after 2 years of fruitless searching for mineral wealth, Coronado and his men returned to Mexico City. During the postexpedition investigation, Francisca de Hozes, one of the three known women on Coronado's journey, spoke her mind. Apparently without restraint, she expounded on Coronado's abusive attitude toward her and the danger into which he placed her husband and the other soldiers.

The voices of Pueblo women, however, were not heard. Pueblo women and children reeled from the violent entrance of these newcomers who looked, dressed, and behaved strangely. These metal men were not at all like the raiding nomadic Indians whose attacks yielded Pueblo food surpluses and captives. As mothers, they likely agonized over their children who took ill and died from diseases that Coronado left behind—smallpox, influenza, and the common cold. But the Spaniards would not disappear forever.

Nearly 50 years later, Juan de Oñate won the contract to settle New Mexico as a proprietary colony. Women who joined the expedition as wives, mothers, daughters, and female servants approached the venture with as much resolve as did the men. In the late 1590s, as Oñate scurried about New Spain looking to fulfill his quota of 200 soldier-colonists, those men who had already contracted for the New Mexico venture remained impatiently at Santa Bárbara, California. When they tired of waiting, some threatening to break their contracts and leave, Doña Eufemia de Sosa chastised them into staying and thereby saved the expedition. By August 1598, 129 soldier-colonists and their families finally reached northern New Mexico. Unfortunately, one expeditionary force met with disaster at Acoma Pueblo shortly thereafter, and 70 men left the new Spanish community of San Juan de los Caballeros to conduct a retaliatory and punitive expedition against Acoma in January 1599. Doña Eufemia successfully rallied the women to patrol the rooftops of their homes to ward off impending Apache attacks.

Although women proved tough and courageous, they still attempted to turn the remote frontier into a civilized one. Before they left for New Mexico, they packed necessities, but also fine dresses and other luxury items. These extravagances allowed them to create a semblance of civilization on the frontier. As many western women's historians have argued, women attempted to re-create on the frontier the home atmosphere that they left behind.

Spanish civilization to Pueblo women, however, meant something very different. When Oñate's troops attacked Acoma, they killed several hundred Pueblo Indians and captured about 600, mostly women and children. Women above age 12 were sentenced to 20 years of personal servitude, and children under 12 were divvied out to two friars who would see to their Christian upbringing. This destruction of families, however, did not repress the spirit of the Acoma Indians. Within a relatively short time, Acoma Pueblo was reoccupied—some of its returning inhabitants had escaped from their Spanish captors. Yet while the Acoma and other Indian women captives lived among Spanish families, Spanish women learned important lessons about medicinal plants and herbs, remedies for specific maladies, use of fibrous plants like yucca for soap, and other environmentally specific knowledge that proved advantageous. In return, Spanish women shared knowledge and European tools, which upon release, Pueblo women took back to their communities.

Even while Spanish and Indian women exchanged useful knowledge, Franciscan friars were forcing Pueblo Indians to stop practicing their traditional religion by destroying ceremonial accoutrements and kivas. To make matters worse, a great drought hit New Mexico and the surpluses that the Pueblo women had saved for future use was usurped by the Spaniards under the *encomienda* system (grants of Indian tribute). Pueblo women followed the Spaniards' wagons that carted away the last of their corn, gathering up seeds that fell through the cracks of the wagon beds. By 1680 most Indian pueblos rebelled against the Spaniards and forced them into swift retreat to El Paso. The refugees had no time to gather supplies, food, or clothing. Historical documents revealed that in El Paso, Spanish women refused to attend mission services for want of clothing. Pueblo women in New Mexico suffered as well, for the drought continued. Apaches and Navajos renewed their raids in hopes of feeding their families, and European diseases continued to ravage the weakened populations. By 1693 Spanish men, women, and children, led by Don Diego de Vargas, returned to New Mexico with new hopes of establishing a frontier colony in which accommodation with Pueblo people would be a key to their survival.

Governor Vargas began issuing land grants to settlers so that they could survive without depending upon the Pueblo Indians or the mission supply wagons that arrived once a year from Mexico City. Ana Sandoval was one of the first individuals to receive a land grant; after all, Spanish law allowed for women to own, control, and will their land and property. While some women allowed their husbands, uncles, or older brothers to administer their assets, Spanish documents clearly articulated women's competence at managing their own properties. Records also illustrate that women mindfully willed property to their daughters or other female family members. At the same time in the English colonies, women had no property rights and married women had few rights at all—something that would continue for more than 200 years.

As settlement returned to New Mexico in the 1690s, the Spanish also expanded into other regions. Father Francisco Eusebio Kino extended his missions into Pimería Alta, or Arizona, where he hoped to Christianize the Pima Indians. Instead of bringing the Pima into mission communities, Kino went on *visitas*. The Pima, therefore, could maintain their homes, food, language, and way of life while adding the new element of Christianity to their religious structure. At the same time, the Pima learned more about Spanish religion, language, mode of dress, and trade items. Even though the Salvatierra Fund hoped to improve mission effectiveness, Indian uprisings periodically occurred in the region for almost 200 years. This uncertainty placed a great strain on mothers and wives, who never knew if their daughters or sons would become fatherless. Kinship ties continued to play a major role in nomadic and semisedentary tribes. Besides warfare, epidemics (which returned in approximately 30-year cycles) continued to depopulate indigenous communities.

By early 1700 Franciscan missionaries established some of the first missions in eastern Texas as a response to the failed La Salle expedition in the mid-1680s. Thirty colonists and their families founded Spanish Texas; in return, they received grants and privileges afforded by Spanish law. The settlers were awarded a salary and supplies, partly resulting from the colony's location near the Lipan Apaches, Comanches, and other nomadic Indian tribes. By the end of the 1710s, Spaniards had established a foothold in Texas. As in other portions of the Southwest, part of their success in the region was due to the dwindling numbers of American Indians who died in epidemics, conflicts, or simply fled. The rivers, fertile flood plains, and increased fortifications and missions enhanced communities in Texas, in particular San Antonio. While few women arrived with the earliest colonists, by the early 1730s the soldier-colonists had sent for their wives and their daughters of marrying age. Young women married into the established population, and soon more than half of the marriages in San Antonio involved locally performed ceremonies. These kinship ties between the new and the established settlers solidified the community. Population, however, grew slowly. While women had children, infant mortality rates were quite high—sometimes as many as 7 of 10 children in one family died before age 3. Spanish families emigrated from the Canary Islands, helping to boost the population. Some Spanish governors granted land lots to women, hoping to encourage new migration and population growth. Women in Texas were unmistakable partners in their family's successes and failures.

More than 170 years passed between the settlement of New Mexico and that of Alta California. In 1769 Father Junípero Serra and General Gaspar de Portolá moved north into Alta California to establish missions, set up outposts for the Spanish galleons returning from Asia, establish farms and ranches, and hedge their bets against the Russians, who had begun expanding beyond southeast Alaska and south along the Pacific Coast. Where Spaniards established missions, California natives reacted with caution. With few Spanish women in the region, soldiers periodically raped Indian women. (Rape occurred also in Russian, French, and English empires.) Perhaps Father Serra's permission for Spaniards to marry indigenous women curbed some improprieties; but more importantly, this miscegenation helped integrate Indians into Spanish culture. The Spanish crown also attempted to recruit Spanish couples and single women with incentives, hoping to augment its hegemony over California. By the early 1800s, families began to grow and more Spanish immigrants moved north into California.

Friars and soldiers, who had relocated Indians into missions, required them to perform menial labor in order to help support the mission. Indian women adjusted to the new lifestyle yet continued to prepare meals for their families using traditional recipes and methods. They also resumed weaving exquisite baskets. While indigenous populations tended to drop due to warfare, disease, and lack of resources, Spanish populations doubled twice—once by 1800 and again by 1821. Women in California had far better luck with fertility rates than Texas, and families grew in size. As children married, Spanish population expanded even further. Immigrants to California quickly adapted to the agricultural and pastoral economy, part of which fed the mining industry farther south in Mexico. Wealthy California women became matriarchs of their homes, doting on their children, overseeing servants, and serving as managers of the family's estate in the absence of husbands.

Even beyond 1821, when Mexico became independent, Spanish women continually adapted their life work to new innovations in technology, changes in political control, and shifts in family economic status—and they did so deliberately. They knew that their family's success depended upon them.

By 1821 Texans had established ranching and farming communities, sharing land and water resources according to Spanish law. Unlike New Mexico, which by 1750 had more than 50,000 Spanish settlers, Texas remained quite small. Therefore, Spain negotiated with some U.S. citizens to bring colonists into Texas as communities that would receive a large land grant (*empresario*), adhere to Spanish law, expand the population of Texas, and provide a buffer zone against nomadic Indians.

By the time that the first Anglo-American pioneers arrived in Texas, Mexico had gained independence from Spain. With them, some of the Anglos brought new attitudes: distrust of the others, at times bordering on racism. Yet some Anglo-American men married into the *Tejano* community; therefore, Spanish women became an important link between the two cultures. In New Mexico, Hispanas also served as cultural brokers during the Mexican period, marrying Anglo-Americans who had relocated to New Mexico as merchants and traders. Anglo men provided protection, security, companionship, and an important political connection that proved invaluable by the 1850s. In order to maintain or enhance the family's social and economic standing, parents negotiated their daughters' marriages to older, more powerful, economically stable men. In California, many young women loathed their fathers who had planned their nuptials years before they entered puberty. Some women chose not to marry, joining a convent or entering "spinsterhood." In all cases, the women retained autonomy. Yet for both, family connections remained very important.

Throughout the Southwest, however, some women experienced a tremendous loss of independence. Communities such as Taos, New Mexico, historically served as a buffer zone between Hispanos and nomadic tribes. They raided each other for supplies, captives, and revenge. Women who became captives of the Comanche, Apache, or other tribes incorporated themselves into the existing social and cultural structure of the tribe. These women learned to survive by adapting their lifestyle to that of their captors, oftentimes becoming a spouse and having children. Other times, tribes traded captive women in exchange for supplies to tribes as far away as the Pawnee Indians along the Loup and Platte Rivers of Nebraska. In order to redeem Spanish captives, the Spanish and later Mexican governments established a fund to ransom captives during *rescates,* or trade fairs. When they were repatriated, they were rarely shunned, but rather rejoined their families or reentered their communities.

By the mid-1840s, Mexico found itself buried in political turmoil. Mexican women and men recognized the danger that the Anglo-Americans posed to the Mexican state. Some bold women even warned their husbands and chided officials that U.S. imperialism would not stop with the Louisiana Purchase. In 1846 the United States invaded Mexican territory, and shortly thereafter, the Mexican War ended with the signing of the Treaty of Guadalupe Hidalgo in 1848. Although the treaty called for protection of all property owned by Mexican citizens, women began to lose some independence. Life would change especially for Native American women.

During the Spanish (1500s-1821) and Mexican (1821-1848) eras, women in the Southwest had very different experiences based on ethnicity, class, race, and cultural heritage. They were wives and mothers, miners and ranchers, businesswomen and matriarchs, captives and slave owners. After 1848 they tried to continue these roles, but the U.S. legal system was not geared to protect women's rights. Laws protecting women's inheritance and ownership became more confusing and difficult to interpret, forcing Hispanos to hire Anglo-American lawyers. In the past, simple wills served as legal transfers of property. Under U.S. hegemony, for example, women had to contend with probate courts when their husbands died intestate. No longer would half of a husband's property automatically fall to the widow. By the late 1800s, in many Southwestern territories, new provisions allowed for land and property to be distributed to children, longevity of the marriage had to be considered, and even more bewildering legalities applied. Women initiated long legal battles for rights that during the Spanish and Mexican periods had not been questioned.

While women lost some legal rights, they did actually gain some new opportunities in the United States. Women owned mines, filed homesteads, and staked land claims under the Timber Culture Act and the Desert Lands Act. Women also owned and operated gambling and dance halls, some of which became famous far beyond the Southwest. Anglo-Americans who met Hispana women often wrote disparagingly about them, describing them as lewd, cigar smokers, and having loose morals. Perhaps the legacy of women's rights under the Spanish system, as well as women's unwillingness to relinquish any of their independence or control, caused women to ignore the new Anglo social norms, which provided more stringent societal prescriptions for women. They chose to describe only public women, however, not the majority of women who lived as mothers, wives, and business associates. This sort of racism continued to surface, and still exists today.

At the end of the 1800s, men continued to outnumber women in the Southwest. Darlis Miller reported that in New Mexico, men outnumbered women by a ratio of 17 to 10 in the 1870s. In Arizona in 1870, it was 4 to 1. The numbers were even more out of balance in Colorado. Even though the numbers were unbalanced, men depended upon women to provide for their families by preparing meals, raising chickens, making butter and milk from the family's dairy cow, growing a garden, keeping the home clean, and making or mending clothing. When necessary, women assisted men in the fields by walking behind the plow, planting, cultivating, or harvesting. Women, therefore, played key roles in the success or failure of the family.

While Spaniards brought African servants into New Mexico, more came willingly after the Civil War. African American women followed the Buffalo Soldiers to western forts like Fort Stanton, New Mexico. Black women lived near the forts and served as laundresses or paid servants. Other African American women moved into the Southwest with their families in the late 19th and early 20th centuries as Exodusters. Towns like Hobbs, New Mexico, grew significantly as a result of black resettlement from the South. These women had similar experiences to those of other women in the desert Southwest: life consisted of hard work. Often they lived in 12-foot square adobe or wood frame homes with dirt floors, forcing them to constantly fight filthy working conditions, sometimes infiltrated by rattlesnakes, tarantulas, and even scorpions. The lower the social class, the worse the living conditions. Yet women attempted to create a home for their families and brought with them ideas and institutions from home.

Not only did African American, Hispanic American, Anglo-American, and Native American women occupy the West, however. So too did Asian, Russian, Czechoslovakian, and many others.

Asian American women began to appear in California's "Golden Mountain," due to the abundant resources in mineral wealth and farmland. Agricultural and economic conditions in China had forced some women from their families, and they ended up in California with hopes of finding a husband among the many Chinese miners and businessmen. Few women, however, achieved this dream. San Francisco turned bright-eyed and hopeful young girls into prostitutes in mining camps, saloons, or brothels, while others met their fate as servants. Some Protestant missions began to operate in San Francisco in an attempt to offer prostitutes a safe place if they chose to leave prostitution. Most, however, lived out their lives as captive slaves of men who abused their freedoms and bodies. A few Chinese women did escape this stereotypical role, however, to become agriculturalists and businesswomen, or to join their husbands in the gold fields.

Another non-European group that found its way into Northern California were Russian women, although relatively few in number. Russian women had not traveled to Russian America until well after the first stage of Russian exploitation in the Aleutian chain. In fact, not until the Russian American Company acquired a monopoly by 1800 did women arrive in perceivable numbers at all. By the 1810s the Russians had established farms in Northern California near Fort Hall in an attempt to make their American venture more self-sufficient.

Other often overlooked groups found their way into the Southwest. Czechoslovakian immigrants arrived beyond the Mississippi River by the 1850s, the majority of whom found their way mostly to the rural eastern half of Texas and south-central California. Czechs, like many other ethnic outsiders, coalesced into close-knit communities. They brought their agricultural skills to the Southwest and became excellent producers. Women played key roles in keeping alive traditions, language, crafts, as well as organizing community events and providing a sense of security. But while Czech women's experiences were also harsh and at times unbearable, "when they must bear any misfortune here, they do it without lamentations." Although their experience permeated portions of East Texas, relatively few of their stories have been published.

All women, regardless of ethnicity, era, or region, had to prepare themselves for the untimely passing of a spouse and being left without his labor and contributions to the family. The social safety network that helped them survive included family, friends, and caring neighbors. Susan McSween Barber, like many women who helped manage their family's estates, readily took over after the untimely death of her husband and turned a small farm and ranching operation into one of the largest in the territory by the time of her death. Her story is not atypical for the Southwest, or the West as a whole. Women were capable partners who, if necessary, bartered for services or tasks that they could not perform on their own. They clearly served as partners in family operations, to which their successful proprietary management abilities attest.

Not all women or girls had as fortunate experiences with the exchange to U.S. hegemony. Perhaps the most negative and drastic changes to women occurred to Native Americans. By the end of the 19th century, the United States had begun shipping Native American boys and girls off to boarding schools in cities all over the Southwest (and as far east as the Carlisle Industrial School in Pennsylvania). The United States used the schools to assimilate indigenous children by separating them from their parents and grandparents, culture, tradition, language, religion, and lifeways. Girls learned the basics of reading, writing, and basic math, but they also learned domestic chores like sewing, embroidery, and housework. Some young girls were even parceled out to nearby farm families in the summertime to hone their skills in the domestic arts. More importantly, they were kept from their families. Mothers tried desperately to protect their children from seizure by Indian agents who had quotas to fill, often hiding them or sending them to the homes of neighbors or relatives when the Indian agent arrived in the area.

By the end of the 19th century, women had learned how to become politically active in the only venue available to them—church associations and school organizations. Southwestern women learned the same lessons that other women did throughout the West regarding power. Society accepted their role as teachers and church event organizers, and through those roles, Southwestern women expanded their power. Anglo-American and Hispana women began to run for slots on the local school boards, and by the end of the 19th century, women served on school boards and as elected school superintendents. By 1924 most women acquired the right to vote. Historians of women tend to forget that Native Americans in New Mexico and Arizona were not allowed the right to vote until shortly after World War II.

For other women, World War II signaled a fearful change. The United States rounded up families of Asian ancestry, confiscated their property, and carted them off to internment camps farther inland. Even as some of their husbands fought against Japan in the Pacific Theater, women of Japanese descent found themselves living inside barracks surrounded by barbed wire and watchtowers occupied by men with menacing machine guns aimed at them. Only recently has the United States taken some financial responsibility for this abuse against people of Japanese and Asian heritage.

The World War II era brought many major changes for women in the Southwest, including the washing machine and the advent of air conditioners. Air conditioning made household tasks less debilitating for women. Prior to air conditioning, women toiled over hot stoves and ovens to prepare meals for sometimes large families, farm workers, or even extended families. They hand-scrubbed clothes in tanks or used hand crank wringers. They swept clean their homes of the endless dunes of dust and sand that blew in their open windows during spring windstorms. With air conditioning, they could close their windows and work without suffering exhaustion or even heat stroke.

Women did not always remain inside the home, however. During World War II, they answered the call for domestic war support. Anglo-American, Hispanic, African American, and other women worked in shipyards, munitions factories, and other war production factories across the Southwest. They became wage earners, which helped provide for their families. For some, additional wages helped move them to nicer neighborhoods or to a higher economic class; for others, it allowed them to buy luxuries like an air conditioner, washing machine, or other items that made women's work at home less time consuming. For even though women joined the wage labor force, they could not stop working at home. The balancing act between wage work and domestic labor had begun in earnest.

Women's roles also expanded beyond the economic and into the political realm. Their experience with school boards gave them the knowledge and experience to become involved in labor and political movements. Women took active roles in supporting male causes that, if not secured, would hurt the entire family. For example, when male workers protesting a major mine in New Mexico were forced off the picket line, their wives took up picket signs and marched in their place. In California, women played an active role in the development of canning and farm labor unions.

By the 1960s women began to rebel against social norms that stifled wage-earning women who demanded decision-making power at home. They also concerned themselves with environmental and social issues, such as stopping the creation of toxic waste facilities and prisons in East Los Angeles. They also demanded equal pay for equal work, school lunch programs, the building of youth centers, and the establishment of playgrounds and parks in inner-city neighborhoods. Women learned that if they worked together for a common community cause, they could influence males who continued to hold key positions of power in the local, regional, and state governments. Women now serve as city council members, mayors, and even U.S. senators of Southwestern states.

If one could draw conclusions from the experiences of Southwestern women, it might be this: they knew that family and community could not survive without them. Women often were the first to look beyond stereotypes and prejudice to learn from each other. They used that knowledge to enhance their family's station. They challenged the prescribed roles that society set for them, and at times shattered them. While women's experiences will continue to be incredibly diverse, one key element binds them together: they live in a region cherished for its environmental beauty and spiritual mystique.

—Sandra K. Matthews-Lamb

SUGGESTED READINGS

Bolton, Herbert Eugene. *Coronado, Knight of Prairie and Plain.* New York: Whittlesey House, 1949.

Chipman, Donald, and Harriett Denise Joseph. *Notable Men and Women of Spanish Texas.* Austin: University of Texas Press, 1999.

de la Teja, Jésus Frank. *San Antonio de Béxar: A Community on New Spain's Northern Frontier.* Albuquerque: University of New Mexico Press, 1995.

Jameson, Elizabeth, and Susan Armitage, eds. *The Women's West.* Norman: University of Oklahoma Press, 1987.

Jameson, Elizabeth, and Susan Armitage, eds. *Writing the Range: Race, Class, and Culture in the Women's West.* Norman: University of Oklahoma Press, 1997.

Jensen, Joan, and Darlis Miller, eds. *New Mexico Women: Intercultural Perspectives.* Albuquerque: University of New Mexico Press, 1986.

Kessell, John L. *Spain in the Southwest: A Narrative History of Colonial New Mexico, Arizona, Texas and California.* Norman: University of Oklahoma Press, 2002.

Korytová-Magstadt, Štepánka. *To Reap a Bountiful Harvest: Czech Immigration Beyond the Mississippi, 1850-1900.* Iowa City, IA: Rudi Publishing, 1993.

Mah, Adeline Yen. *Falling Leaves: The True Story of an Unwanted Chinese Daughter.* New York: Broadway Books, 1999.

Martin, Patricia Preciado. *Songs My Mother Sang to Me: An Oral History of Mexican American Women.* Tucson: University of Arizona Press, 1996.

Mills, Ava E., ed. *A Legacy of Words: Texas Women's Stories, 1850-1920.* San Angelo, TX: Doss Books, 1999.

Ravage, John W. *Black Pioneers: Images of the Black Experience on the North American Frontier.* Salt Lake City: University of Utah Press, 1997.

Rothschild, Mary Logan, and Pamela Claire Hronek. *Doing What the Day Brought: An Oral History of Arizona Women.* Tucson: University of Arizona Press, 1992.

Ruiz, Vicki. *Cannery Women, Cannery Lives: Mexican Women, Unionization, and the California Food Processing Industry, 1930-1950.* Albuquerque: University of New Mexico Press, 1987.

Stockel, H. Henrietta. *Chiricahua Apache Women and Children: Safekeepers of the Heritage.* College Station: Texas A&M Press, 2000.

Turner, Erin H. *More Than Petticoats: Remarkable California Women.* Helena, MT: TwoDot, 1999.

WOMEN RELIGIOUS

In the book *The Restructuring of American Religion,* the author, Robert Wuthnow, reports some significant statistics with regard to women and religion. According to the author, when surveyed, 46% of women say they have attended a religious service in the past 7 days, compared to 35% of men. Two thirds of women say they have read their Bible in the past month, compared to two fifths of men. In addition, 57% of women report giving a lot of thought to developing their faith, whereas only 37% of men report doing so.

Some historians have suggested, perhaps rightly so, that these differences may be because of the roles women play—mother, housekeeper, and guardian of traditional values—and therefore their affinity for religion may simply reflect their attachment to traditional family values. As an example, when faced with the uncertainties associated with uprooting their families and making the long journey west, many women chose to embark on the overland journey to keep their families together under their Christian obligation. Others simply had no choice but to emigrate due to economic circumstances, but still others were motivated to go by the possibility of free expression of religion. The overland journey was hard on women. Women usually traveled within the family structure. Men either went with their families or left their wives and children at home in the East. Uprooted from their lives and their homes, women faced horrendous challenges and hardships—accidents, illness (cholera), pregnancy, and childbirth. It became important for women to establish a social infrastructure for their life on the trail and in overland settlements. The trail journey resulted in women bonding to one another. They were companions for one another and caretakers of each other. For many, their religion sustained the arduousness of the journey.

Frederick Jackson Turner argued that the frontier influenced the development of the making of the character of the American people. Unconquered lands and development, according to Turner, fueled individualism, progress, and democracy. But Turner's thesis was applicable to men. It was women's activities that would fuel community development and the forging of communal identity.

Frontier women held to a simple faith in God and tended to dispense with dogmas and formal creeds as they dealt with the harsh realities of frontier life. Women on the frontier were predominantly Protestant from the Midwest. They held to a strong, solid faith in God that sustained them as they courageously and tenaciously dealt with the loneliness and deprivation inherent to frontier life. Despite their best efforts, the fabric of frontier family life was not stable, as sickness, death, and hardships posed constant threats to family unity. Women tapped into their inherent nurturing skills and soon realized that the community's survival would depend on their being mindful of their neighbor's needs in addition to their own.

In trying to make sense of the arduous life on the frontier, women looked to religion as a means of building community. They abandoned the worship of God as a wrathful father, which had been the hallmark of liberal Protestantism in the mid-19th century. Engaging in activities such as raising money to build schools, churches, and synagogues, holding bake sales, participating in sewing circles, and sponsoring raffles were all means to foster women's ties to organized religion and to their influence on communal development.

Kansas was a particularly physically challenging place for settlers. With its fierce extremes in weather, locusts, snakes, outlaws, horse thieves, and border wars, it was a breeding ground for producing a hardy people. Kansas women sought first to establish schools and places of worship. Kansas in 1860 was predominantly Protestant of various denominations. Worship services were held in homes as the population of communities increased. It was in this context that temperance emerged as an urgent issue to unite women. Seen as a moral issue, abstinence was viewed as the way to wipe out liquor as a destroyer of the home. Women ardently believed that prayer, education, and will power could overcome one's desire for alcohol.

In 1874 Kansas, the temperance movement achieved a cohesive edge. The Women's Christian Temperance Union (WCTU) expanded. Women congregants formed religious revivals and street-corner prayer meetings to evangelize about the dangers of alcohol. By the 1880s the WCTU was the largest organization of women in U.S. history. The year 1880 marked the passage of the first state prohibition amendment. From 1875 to 1900 the WCTU was the largest women's organization promoting woman suffrage. The WCTU purported that women had a basic right to extend their sphere of influence from the home to the public sector. There were chapters in every state and major city. Frances Willard served as president of the WCTU from 1879 to 1898 and oversaw the group's activities to work for prison reform, day care for children, medical clinics, reduced tobacco use, and, drawing on her religious beliefs, a stricter adherence to observing the Sabbath.

The WCTU was one group of women striving to make a difference in America in the late 1800s. The Sisters of St. Joseph were another. From 1600 to 1720 there were 90 congregations of uncloistered Roman Catholic nuns in France. These congregations were primarily service-oriented communities that were active in teaching, nursing, and charitable work. Most religious communities of women were involved in only one apostolate, but the Sisters of St. Joseph, founded in Le Puy, France, functioned in education, social service, and health care. In her book *Spirited Lives,* Carol Coburn provides a detailed record of the congregation of the Sisters of St. Joseph. Mother St. John Fontbonne superior of the community generated the first Sisters of St. Joseph of Carondela of St. Louis (CSJ) missionary foundation in North America by sending six sisters from Lyons to the newly created Catholic diocese of St. Louis, Missouri, in 1839. They were sent to the developing West to "convert the savages, to teach their children and those of Protestant families." Catholic bishops in North America saw European nuns as a potentially exploitable labor source and were, therefore, eager to employ them in missionary outreach. They would face gender issues, harsh living conditions, poverty, isolation, as well as religious and ethnic bigotry. And these new immigrant sisters would need to finance their own institutions and missionary endeavors, which in France had not been an issue for them because of the close association between church and state.

Despite the traits of piety, purity, and submissiveness inherent to Victorian ideology, missionary nuns were extremely resourceful. Well educated and active in the public sphere, the sisters could retain their Victorian aura and at the same time be extremely practical and inventive in trying to execute their missions. As an example, in 1839 the CSJs in St. Louis received money from local and state government to run their St. Joseph Institute for the Deaf. Local legislators had not been able to agree on funding and the location for a public school for the deaf, so the local bishop suggested that the government contract with the nuns until something else could be arranged. And in nearby Carondelet, Missouri, the sisters accepted children from families who could not afford to pay tuition, which ingratiated them with the local government, made up of both Catholics and Protestants.

The Sisters of St. Joseph continued their work, sending a group of sisters to St. Paul, Minnesota, in 1851, where, within 3 years, they had established an academy, an Indian school, and a hospital with an orphanage. Another group of sisters arrived in Kansas City in 1866, where they opened a clinic for indigents when a cholera epidemic struck the region, and in 1872, they opened St. Joseph's Hospital.

A major force in developing the community's missions in the Southwest was Sister Monica Corrigan. Monica Corrigan was born in 1843 in Canada and was raised in the Anglican faith tradition. She eloped with John Corrigan, a Catholic, and moved to Kansas with him. Diphtheria claimed the lives of their two children, and John, too, when Monica was a young 23 years of age. To support herself, she began teaching at St. Teresa's Academy and eventually converted to the Catholic faith of her deceased husband. Soon thereafter, Monica became a sister in the Congregation of the Sisters of St. Joseph.

A self-appointed archivist, Monica's diaries provide a vibrant portrait of the challenges and difficulties of pursuing missionary work on the frontier. On April 20, 1870, she and six other sisters embarked on a journey from St. Louis to Tucson. The seven sisters traveled by train to San Francisco, by ship from San Francisco to San Diego, by stagecoach, and finally, on foot to reach their destination. Of the trek from San Diego to Arizona, Corrigan writes, "We started early entering upon the most dangerous portion of our journey, as we were in danger of being attacked and massacred by the savages, at any moment; but placing ourselves in the hands of Providence to whom we have consecrated our lives, we courageously advanced." The final trek of the journey was the crossing of the Mojave Desert by foot in May. Dressed in full religious habit, the sisters suffered from extreme thirst and fatigue. They braved temperatures of 125 degrees and walked in the early morning hours and at night to avoid the scorching midday and afternoon sun. She writes,

"We started on our way at four o'clock a.m. and passed many recently made graves of persons who had been killed by the Indians." They themselves encountered some Pima Indians. One of the sisters wrote, "Mother . . . fell asleep. A troop of nude Indians came in the meantime, who were peaceable; they had the consideration to be quiet and let her sleep. S[ister]. Martha was resting on an old cowhide; a noble warrior perceiving her, stole softly up and sat down beside her as her Guardian Angel." Corrigan remarks that "the sides of the road were covered with teams of horses, oxen and cattle that had dropped dead trying to ascend."

Throughout the West, the CSJs would systematically go to railroad camps, mining camps, and military posts on regular paydays to beg for money for their missionary endeavors. In Tucson, the sisters established an orphanage that accommodated about 40 children. In 1902 the building was destroyed by a hurricane. Sister Angelica Byrne went off to the ore mines to beg for money where she was granted access to the mine shafts. Her total "earnings" on these journeys reaped the community an amazing $16,000. By 1880 the CSJs had built hospitals in Prescott and Tucson primarily to serve railroad and mine workers. And in Fort Yuma, where the CSJs ministered from 1886 to 1900, Sister Ambrosia O'Neill was appointed by the Department of the Interior to be superintendent of the Fort Yuma government school.

From 1840 through 1920, the CSJs established secondary academies in 11 states. They founded their first institution of higher learning, the College of St. Catherine, in St. Paul, Minnesota. Sister Antonia McHugh, the first dean of the college, expanded the curriculum to include subjects traditionally reserved for males: mathematics, history, English, and French. She bolstered the science subjects and downplayed the more traditional female areas of learning that included personal hygiene, physiology, and other gender-specific courses.

The presence of the CSJ community in the western United States helped to preserve, sustain, and shape American Catholic culture. By 1920, 2,300 Sisters of St. Joseph supported 175 schools, 2 schools for the deaf, 3 women's colleges, 10 hospitals, and 9 orphanages throughout the United States. Other congregations of Roman Catholic nuns also made significant contributions to the development of the West.

In Santa Fe, New Mexico, the Dominican sisters engaged the community to open a quarry, install a limekiln, and open a brickyard and a lumber mill to support the congregation's mission to establish a local trade school. Sister Joseph of the Sacred Heart, a Providence nun from Montreal, earned enough money in the Oregon territory as an architect and contractor to build 11 hospitals, 7 academies, 5 Indian schools, 2 orphanages, and an old-age home. Rosa Maria Segale, a Sister of Charity, went to Trinidad, Colorado, in 1872 to run a public school. While there, she had an occasion to tend to an ill member of Billy the Kid's gang. Thereafter, Billy the Kid showed kindness and benevolence toward the Sisters of Charity. In 1876 Segale went to Santa Fe, New Mexico, where she raised funds to build an industrial trade school for Indian girls, a hospital, and an orphanage.

In 1869 President Grant's peace policy included a board of mostly Protestant laymen who were appointed Indian commissioners to monitor government subsidies given to Indians. Religious denominations provided material goods to Indian schools in return for a fixed per capita appropriation from the federal government. Catholics created the Bureau of Catholic Indian Missions (BCIM) to fund and oversee Catholic mission schools. The largest financial support for the Indian mission schools came from Katharine Drexel, a Philadelphia heiress who founded the congregation of the Sisters of the Blessed Sacrament for Indian and Colored People in 1891. Mother Drexel did not want the church to be embarrassed by her fortune so she funneled funds through the BCIM. She contributed millions of dollars through the fund to support the movement.

In addition to the work with Indians, American nuns were among the first white women to take as their mission the formation of towns and settlements. There were more nuns than clerics available, so often the nuns functioned as surrogate priests. They entrenched themselves pastorally into a community and subsequently influenced the development of local culture and public life. Because of their charitable works of mercy, the sisters were able to contribute to the toning down of anti-Catholic sentiment prevalent on the developing frontier. Their services were welcomed and appreciated. The nuns also were forced into extensive secular interaction, as they had to deal with local governments and businesses. Their assertive manner coupled with their public good works ingratiated them with many, and they were able to gain the latitude they needed in fostering their missions.

Coburn argues that the rivalry between Catholic and Protestant women during the 19th century may have aided in the growth of female institution building. Separate denominational institutions were desirable, and there was indeed competition for clients. Catherine Beecher used both gender ideology and fear of Catholicism in her efforts to raise funds to build seminaries to train Protestant women teachers in order to combat the spreading presence of nuns in the West. Conversely, Catholic nuns as well as Catholic clergy used Protestant proselytizing and bigotry to raise funds from both American and European philanthropic sources.

Protestants did, however, recognize the extent of the contribution of Catholic nuns and often were direct recipients of their benevolence. For example, in mining towns, because of their own ethnic backgrounds, the sisters were able to reduce ethnic rivalries. Coburn writes that at Sister's Hospital in Georgetown, Colorado, the works of the sisters softened the harsh attitudes the Protestants had toward the nuns as well as the attitude toward the general Roman Catholic population. Through their care of and ministry to the sick, the sisters curried favor in the communities. Their visible contribution to communal welfare helped to reduce and alleviate Protestant suspicion and prejudice. And their own poverty and their lack of financial security helped to ingratiate them with the poor, as the poor did not see them as patronizing, unlike the view of many Protestant women's groups.

Like the Catholic nuns, Protestant women's organizations and benevolent societies also greatly served to influence communities in the developing West. As well, a number of Protestant women individually made some remarkable contributions.

Methodist Alma Bridwell White was the first female bishop of any Christian church in the United States. In 1901 in Denver, Colorado, she founded the Methodist fundamentalist sect. Sixteen years later, the sect became known as the Pillar of Fire Church. The sect was blatantly anti-Catholic and received financial support from the Ku Klux Klan (KKK), which it publicly endorsed.

Olympia Brown was the first woman ordained by the Universalist church. An ardent suffragist, Brown was also a charter member of the American Equal Rights Association. She sought to improve the political and social status of women. In 1884 she was elected president of the Wisconsin Woman Suffrage Association (WWSA). She eventually gave up her pastorate to devote herself full time to woman suffrage and stayed on as president of the WWSA for 18 years. She viewed suffrage as a woman's right as well as a way to improve communities and raise the level of political morality.

Mary Baker Eddy founded the Christian Science church. In the 1880s, a sect of Christian Science, Divine Science, emerged. Nona Lovell Brooks, founder of the sect, felt that Christian Science doctrine could be supplemented with additional religious beliefs. Brooks and her sister, Fannie James, opened the Divine Science College in Denver in 1898. One year later, Mary Baker Eddy was ordained within the sect and opened and pastored the denomination's first church, which opened in Denver.

Aimee Semple McPherson, an early 20th-century evangelist, preached across the United States. In 1918 she established the Angelus temple in Los Angeles, California. She was the first woman to receive an FCC radio license and was one of the earliest radio evangelizers. McPherson developed her foursquare instruction about the gospel, and her church eventually became the International Church of the Foursquare Gospel. Currently, there are 24,000 churches worldwide in the denomination, making it one of the major denominations of Pentecostalism. McPherson was kidnapped by the KKK in 1918 and was brought to a KKK meeting in Denver, where she spoke of love and tolerance. She managed to convert some members, who threw away their robes by the end of the meeting.

Mary Lucind Bobbey (1816-1900), a Baptist laywoman, advocated for Native American rights. Congress's 1879 proposal to allow settlers to occupy and possess land in Oklahoma that by treaty rightfully belonged to the Native Americans infuriated her. She circulated a petition and obtained 13,000 signatures and then sent the 300-foot-long document to then President Rutherford Hayes and to the Congress in 1880. She presented a second petition in 1881 advocating protection of Native American lands. On that petition, she obtained 50,000 signatures. The petition requested that Native Americans be given full rights under the law and for tribal lands to be allotted to individual native Americans and that sufficient schools be provided to every child of every tribe. Bobbey founded the Central Indian Committee in 1880, which in 1883 became the Women's National Indian Association. In addition to political advocacy, the organization sought to assist Native American

women with child care, English, and vocational and religious training.

Both Protestant and Catholic missionaries sought to take Native American children out of their tribal environment to educate them in schools where the pedagogy was traditional white ethnocentrism. Several Native American women, including Polingaysi Qoyawayma of the Hopi people, Maria Solares of the Chumash tribe, Buffalo Bird Woman of the Hidatsas, Mountain Wolf Woman of the Winnebagos, and Ruby Modesto of the Cahuilla people, sought to record, preserve, and pass on their unique tribal traditions. The practice of removing Native American children from their tribal families and placing them in nontribal schools did not end until passage of the Indian Child Welfare Act in 1978.

By 1830, 5 million Mormons had settled in the Utah territory. Dismayed by what he perceived as doctrinal dilution by Catholics and Protestants, Joseph Smith sought to establish a distinct religious commonwealth in order to reestablish God as the unquestionable source of religious authority. Smith also sought to reaffirm the father in the family unit as the single source of authority within the family. God, according to Smith, was a flesh and blood patriarch manifested in the male family head on earth. Women needed to marry in order to become close to such earthly divinity. The Mormons elevated marriage to a divine law. Polygamy was an exalted form of celestial marriage, but it is important to note that 90% of the Mormon population did not practice polygamy. Marriage, polygamous or monogamous, was not only necessary for one's personal salvation, but it was also necessary for the family's economic survival. Reproduction was important for providing workers to perpetuate the commonwealth.

Smith commissioned the Mormon Female Relief Society of Nauvoo in 1842. Founded to respond to the needs of the poor and the sick, the society called on the more affluent members of the community for support. By 1868 the society functioned as a well-organized semiindependent power within the Mormon Church and within the national women's movement. In 1892 the society incorporated as a legal entity under the name of the National Woman's Relief Society.

Concern about unruly young boys in Mormon communities who might not become "proper" husbands in their adult life prompted Aurelia Spencer Rogers to form what was known as a Primary Association. The goal of this organization was to organize the boys of the communities by age group, provide lessons in the benefit of obedience, faith in God, prayer, and proper etiquette. The movement spread quickly throughout Mormon settlements and wards. Rogers expanded her interests to support the issue of women's rights, and she served as Utah's delegate to the 1893 Woman's Suffrage Convention in Atlanta and to the National Council of Women meeting in Washington, D.C., in 1895.

Another prominent Mormon woman was Romania Pratt Penrose, who responded to Brigham Young's urging in 1873 for women to study medicine. She established a medical practice in Salt Lake City in 1879. She was also heavily involved with the woman suffrage movement and church relief societies. She was a speaker at the 1908 Women's International Suffrage Alliance meeting in Amsterdam.

In 1871 Eliza Young founded the *Woman's Exponent,* the first magazine published by and for women who were settled west of the Mississippi River. Young was also the first leader of the Mormon Young Ladies Retrenchment Association, which sought to answer Brigham Young's plea for simplicity and frugal economy. Referring to the message as the "organization gospel," Young traveled from ward to ward and established groups for the society that perpetuated Brigham Young's vision.

In 1878 Sarah A. Cook formed the Ladies' Anti-Polygamy Society in Utah and appealed to the entire nation for support. Cook based her antipolygamy arguments on issues of women's degradation, the enslavement of women, lust, incest, and consequential defects of polygamy progeny. Polygamy, Cook argued, caused disharmony within the family, thereby perpetuating its destruction as a social unit.

Eliza Snow, one of Joseph Smith's wives and later one of Brigham Young's, facilitated the proceedings of the largest gathering of Mormon women in Utah. There, in 1878, Mormon women assembled to protest against the interests of Cook's Ladies' Anti-Polygamy Society. Snow and her followers defended polygamy as being necessary to the redemption of the human family. Eventually the U.S. government would pass antipolygamy laws.

Susan Young Gates (1856-1933), the 41st child of Brigham Young, launched the *Young Woman's Journal* in 1897, which was the official magazine of the Young Ladies Mutual Improvement Association. She was also one of the founding organizers of genealogical research, which Mormons still conduct extensively today.

Jewish women also contributed to the development of community in the West. Jewish overland migration began in the 1820s to Texas. Later, migration extended to New Mexico and California. In addition to their second-class status as women, Jewish women faced an additional barrier, as they were a minority on the frontier.

Migrating Jewish women of Eastern European descent were in many cases adept at money-making skills. There were no rigid social structures on the frontier to impede their ambition. Free to allow their ambition to flourish, talented Jewish women developed identities of their own, apart from their husbands. Mary Prag, widowed at the age of 34, who had been married to a Forty-Niner, became one of San Francisco's first Jewish schoolteachers and vice principal of San Francisco's Girls' High School. At the age of 82, she was appointed to the San Francisco Board of Education.

Anna Solomon ran a family store in Solomonville, Arizona. In addition to her household duties and the running of the store, she opened a hotel to accommodate visiting friends and family that became a center of social life in the Gila Valley. Anna Rich Marks made her fortune in land and mining ventures. She invested money in diamonds and owned controlling interests in two mines. Never without her rifle, she was not afraid to threaten when necessary in order to get what she wanted.

Many Jewish families sought to settle in larger western cities because the smaller towns lacked educational, social, and religious institutions. Inherent to largely populous areas were problems of extreme poverty and need. In 1861 Frances Wisebart Jacobs enlisted the aid of the Hebrew Benevolent Ladies' Society and the Denver-wide Ladies' Relief Society to help provide funds for the indigent who were sick and in need of treatment. She spent a considerable amount of time in the slums and was known as the Queen of Charities. Fannie Lorber and Bessie Willens organized the Denver Sheltering Home to care for dependent children of destitute parents who were suffering from tuberculosis.

Similar groups provided assistance to the Jewish community in San Francisco. By 1880 there were 30 organizations serving the Jewish population there.

Two such organizations are the Women's Exchange and the Ladies' Protection and Relief Society.

Jessica Peixoto, the daughter of a prominent San Francisco Sephardic family, received her Ph.D. from the University of California, Berkeley, in 1900, the second woman to do so at the school. She was subsequently hired to teach social economics, and in 1918 she became the first woman to achieve the rank of full professor at her alma mater.

In Portland, Oregon, during the 1890s, the National Council of Jewish Women raised money along with other charitable groups to construct a Neighborhood House in the Jewish quarter to provide adult education and organized recreational activities. Terese Marx-Ferrin, president of the Hebrew Ladies Benevolent Society in Tucson, Arizona, in 1890, oversaw the planning of Temple Emmanuel, which still exists there today.

The story of American women's religious activities regardless of their religious beliefs or affiliation parallels the transformation of American society. American women have been instrumental in the evolution of the American religious experience beginning in an era that viewed women as only submissive wives through the tremendous social changes of the 19th and 20th centuries. American women made a difference and effected real social change under the umbrella of their religious beliefs. Some women worked for change by beginning a new religion. Some saw God's hand in the struggle for freedom, while others sought to relieve human suffering. There were also those women who built lasting institutions dedicated to education and the relief of suffering, as demonstrated by the work of the various orders of Catholic nuns. There can be no doubt that American women have had a long and proud history of involvement with religious issues, social activism, and the struggle for freedom.

—Mary M. McCulloch

SUGGESTED READINGS

Braude, Ann. *Women and American Religion.* New York: Oxford University Press, 2000.

Bushman, Claudia, ed. *Mormon Sisters: Women in Early Utah.* Logan: Utah State University Press, 1997.

Coburn, Carol K., and Martha Smith. *Spirited Lives: How Nuns Shaped Catholic Culture and American Life, 1836-1920.* Chapel Hill: University of North Carolina Press, 1999.

Keller, Rosemary Skinner, and Rosemary Radford Ruether, eds. *In Our Own Voices: Four Centuries of American Women's Religious Writing.* San Francisco: Harper, 1995.

Rochlin, Harriet, and Fred Rochlin. *Pioneer Jews: A New Life in the Far West.* Boston, MA: Houghton Mifflin, 1984.

Ruether, Rosemary Radford, and Rosemary Skinner Keller, eds. *Women and Religion in America: Vol. 1. The Nineteenth Century: A Documentary History.* New York: Harper & Row, 1982.

Ruether, Rosemary Radford, and Rosemary Skinner Keller, eds. *Women and Religion in America: Vol. 2. The Colonial and Revolutionary Periods. A Documentary History.* New York: Harper & Row, 1982.

Schlissel, Lillian. *Women's Diaries of the Westward Journey.* New York: Schocken Books, 1992.

WOODY, ELIZABETH (1959-)

Elizabeth Woody was born in Ganado, Arizona. Her childhood home was in Madras, Oregon, 14 miles from the Warm Springs Reservation. She is enrolled as a member of the Confederated Tribes of Warm Springs in Oregon. She is a noted Native American (Warm Springs Yakima/Wasco/Navajo) poet, having written several collections of poems, including *Hand into Stone,* published in 1988. This collection won her the American Book Award from the Before Columbus Foundation. Her other works include *Luminaries of the Humble* (1994) and *Seven Hands, Seven Hearts* (1994). She has received several other honors for her poetry, including the William Stafford Memorial Poetry Award in 1995. She earned her A.A. in 1983 at the Institute of American Indian Arts and her B.A. in humanities in 1991 from Evergreen State College in Olympia, Washington. She has also studied at Portland State University in Oregon. In addition to poetry, she is a visual artist, working in photography and several other media. Some of her works, including several collaborations with fellow artist Joe Fedderson, have received critical acclaim. She is a founding member of the Northwest Native American Writer's Association. She worked as a manager for Lillian Pitts Masks in Portland, Oregon, from 1985 to 1994. Woody has also worked as a professor of creative writing at the Institute of American Indian Arts from 1994 to 1996, is a program associate for Ecotrust, an environmental nonprofit association, in Portland, Oregon, and sits on the board of directors for the Crow's Shadow Institute in eastern Oregon.

—Scott Kesilis

SUGGESTED READINGS

Harjo, Joy, and Gloria Bird, eds. *Reinventing the Enemy's Language.* New York: Norton, 1997.

Matuz, Roger, ed. *St. James Guide to Native North American Artists.* Detroit, MI: St. James, 1998.

The Chronology of America and Its Women

1804- 1806	Lewis and Clark explore the West with the help of Sacagawea	1848	Women's Rights Convention held at Seneca Falls, New York
1821	Emma Willard founds the Troy Female Seminary; Mexico grants Stephen Austin the right to settle in Texas with 300 families	1849	Elizabeth Blackwell receives a medical degree from Geneva College; Gold Rush to California begins
1828	Sarah Josepha Hale founds the *American Ladies' Magazine*	1852	Vicar Apostolic Jean-Baptiste Lamy accompanies the first Sisters of Loretto to New Mexico with Mother Magdalen Hayden as their first superior
1829	Fannie Baker Darden, "The Poet Laureate of Columbus, Texas," born		
1832	Harriet Bunce Wright is teacher/cofounder of Wheelock Academy, Choctaw Nation, Indian Territory	1853	Sisters of Loretto open the Academy of Our Lady of Light in Santa Fe
		1855	Sara Robinson arrives in Lawrence, Kansas
1833	Lydia Maria Child publishes *An Appeal for That Class of Americans Called Africans*	1856	Elizabeth Fulton Hester, teacher/founder of Muskogee Day Nursery, begins 70 years of service to American Indian people in Oklahoma
1836	Sarah Josepha Hale becomes editor of *Godey's Lady's Book;* Eliza Hart Spalding and Narcissa Whitman become the first two white women to cross the Rocky Mountains on their way to Oregon; Emily Morgan (Emily D. West) becomes the Yellow Rose of Texas for her exploits in the Texas war with Mexico	1859	Mary Bridget Hayden named mother superior at Osage Mission School; Clear Creek, Colorado, and "Comstock Lode" in Nevada strikes continue migration to mining regions
		1864	Eliza Wood Burhans Farnham's *Woman and Her Era* published
1839	Mary Avery Loughridge becomes a teacher at the Koweta Manual Labor Boarding School, Cherokee Nation, Indian Territory	1865	The first all-women's college founded: Vassar
1841	Nancy Kelsey departs Missouri for California with the Bartleson/Bidwell Company	1867	Kansas legislature refuses to extend voting rights to women; Mollie Evelyn Moore Davis's *Minding the Gap* published; Young Women's Christian Association (YWCA) founded
1846	Susan Shelby Magoffin sets off down the Santa Fe Trail	1868	Laura de Force Gordon delivers her first speech for woman suffrage in California
1847	Tamsen Donner dies in Donner Pass, the victim of a man who would not ask for directions; Mary Bridget Hayden arrives at Osage Mission Government School	1869	Wyoming Territory passes a female suffrage statute; Eagle Woman takes over the Grand River Agency trading post; National Woman Suffrage

Association founded; American Woman Suffrage Association founded; Transcontinental Railroad completed

1870   Utah Territory passes a female suffrage statute

1871   Lawrence, Kansas, Friends in Council founded

1872   Kate Flint opens a brothel two blocks from Temple Square in Salt Lake City; Victoria Woodhull runs for president of the United States

1873   Abigail Scott Duniway named president of the Oregon Equal Suffrage Association; (*Women's*) *Home Companion* founded

1874   Women's Christian Temperance Union established; Occidental Mission Home for Girls opened by the Presbyterian church to minister to Asian females in San Francisco; Women's Christian Temperance Union (WCTU) emerges as a national organization from its midwestern roots

1876   Oakland Ebell Society founded; Annie Oakley outshoots Frank Butler in a demonstration of world-class marksmanship

1877   Salt Lake City Lady's Literary Society founded; Elizabeth Culver elected first female school superintendent in Hamilton County, Kansas

1878   Clara Shortridge Foltz is the first woman admitted to the California bar; Buffalo Calf Road leads Cheyenne in battle against the U.S. Army; Caroline M. Severance founds the Los Angeles Women's Club

1879   Frances Willard named president of the WCTU

1880   Mary E. Foy appointed the first Los Angeles City Librarian

1881   First suffrage bill introduced in Arizona Territorial Legislature

1882   Association of Collegiate Alumnae founded

1883   Washington Territory extends voting rights and jury service to women, but the statutes are declared unconstitutional by the Territorial Supreme Court; Sarah Winnemucca's *Life Among the Piutes* published; Mary Hallock Foote's *The Led-Horse Claim* published; *Ladies Home Journal* founded

1885   Mary Elizabeth "Hell Raising" Lease admitted to the Kansas bar; *Good Housekeeping* founded

1886   Rebecca Lee Dorsey opens a medical practice in Los Angeles

1887   Congress disfranchises women in Utah Territory with the Edmunds-Tucker Act

1889   Ella L. Knowles passes the Montana bar examination with distinction; Jane Addams and Ellen Gates Starr establish Hull House in Chicago

1890   Wyoming is admitted as a state with woman suffrage, the first in the nation; General Federation of Women's Clubs founded

1891   Sophie Alice Callahan's *Wynema* published; Friday Morning Club of Los Angeles founded; Katherine Drexel founded the Sisters of the Blessed Sacrament for Colored and Indian People

1893   Colorado amends its constitution to grant women the vote

1896   Utah enters the union with woman suffrage; Idaho adopts a woman suffrage amendment to the state constitution; woman suffrage lost at the polls in California

1898   Freda Ehmann starts the Ehmann Olive Company in Oroville, California

1900   Carrie Nation starts her prohibition campaign at the Cary Hotel in Wichita, Kansas; Donaldina MacKenzie Cameron becomes superintendent of the Mission Home of the Women's Occidental Board of Foreign Missions in San Francisco

1902   St. Frances Xavier Cabrini visits Denver

1903   Women first compete in rodeo at Cheyenne Frontier Days; Mary Hunter Austin's *The Land of Little Rain* published; Women's Trade Union League founded

1904   Annette Abbott Adams is the first woman to graduate from the University of California, Berkeley, Boalt Hall School of Law

1905   Alice Eastwood's *A Handbook of the Trees of California* published

1906   Elsie Clews Parson's *The Family* published; Bertha Muzzy Sinclair's *Chip, of the Flying U* published

1908   Woman's Club of Huntington Beach, California, founded

1910   Frances Marion signs a contract with Bosworth Studios; Alice Stebbins Wells becomes the first policewoman of the Los Angeles Police Department

1911   California extends the franchise to women; Triangle Shirtwaist fire in New York kills 146 workers, mostly women

1912   Kansas and Arizona extend the franchise to women

1913   Montana and Nevada extend the franchise to women; Willa Cather's *O Pioneers!* published

1914   Gloria Bullock graduates from the University of Southern California Law School

1915   Alice Stebbins Wells organizes the International Association of Policewomen; Woman's Peace Party founded

1916   Annie Webb Blanton becomes the first female president of the Texas State Teachers Association; Jeannette Rankin of Montana elected to the U.S. House of Representatives

1917   North Dakota and Nebraska extend presidential suffrage to women

1918   Minnie Grinstead becomes the first woman elected to the Kansas legislature

1920   Nineteenth Amendment ratified giving women the right to vote; Nellie Trent Bush elected to the Arizona Legislature; Hildegarde Flanner's *Younger Girl and Other Poems* published; Ruth Murray Underhill's *White Moth* published

1921   National Woman's Party starts a state-by-state campaign for an Equal Rights Bill; Sheppard-Towner Act passes in Congress to provide maternal and infant health education; Alice Mary Robertson (R-Okla.) elected to the U.S. House of Representatives

1923   Aimee Semple McPherson opens the Angelus Temple in Los Angeles; Mae Ella Nolan (R-Calif.) elected to the U.S. House of Representatives; Congress holds hearings on an Equal Rights Amendment

1924   Miriam "Ma" Amanda Wallace Ferguson elected governor of Texas

1925   Emma Grigsby Meharg appointed first female Secretary of State in Texas; Edith Eunice Therrel Wilmans appointed to the Texas Supreme Court; Florence Prag Kahn (R-Calif.) elected to the U.S. House of Representatives

1926   Margie Elizabeth Neal becomes the first woman elected to the Texas Senate; Laura Scudder introduces Mayflower Chips to California

1929   Florence "Pancho" Barnes wins the First Women's Air Race in Glendale, California; Ruth Leah Bunzel's *The Pueblo Potter* is published; Isabella Selmes Greenway (D-Ariz.) elected to the U.S. House of Representatives

1930   Jessie Daniel Ames helps found the Association of Southern Women for the Prevention of Lynching

1931   Ruth Winifred Brown elected president of the Oklahoma Library Association; Gloria Bullock is the first woman appointed to the California Superior Court bench

1932   Helen S. Richt graduates from the veterinary medicine program at Kansas State University; Ella Cara Deloria's *Dakota Texts* published; Amelia Earhart makes her solo flight over the Atlantic

1933   Kathryn O'Loughlin (McCarthy) (D-Kan.) elected to the U.S. House of Representatives

1934   Gladys Amanda Reichard's *Spider Woman* published

1935   Sarah Tilghman Hughes becomes first woman to serve as a Texas district judge; Mari Sandoz's *Old Jules* published

1936   Katherine Cheung obtains her commercial pilot's license; Nina Otero Warren's *Old Spain in Our Southwest* published; Mary McLeod Bethune named Negro Affairs Director of the National Youth Administration

1937   Nan Wood Honeyman (D-Ore.) elected to the U.S. House of Representatives

1938   Lorna Lockwood elected to the Arizona legislature

1939   Cleofas Martinez Jaramillo's *Cuentos del hogar/Spanish Fairy Tales* published; Elsie Clews Parson's *Pueblo Indian Religion* published

1940   Jeannette Rankin of Montana wins a seat in the U.S. House of Representatives a second time

1941   Agnes Morley Cleaveland's *No Life for a Lady* published

1942   Charlotte Winter King wins a seat on the South Pasadena City Council; Maria Tallchief becomes

America prima ballerina with Ballet Russe de Monte Carlo

1944   Mildred Jeffrey and Lillian Hatcher lead the United Auto Workers Women's Bureau

1945   Helen Gahagan Douglas (D-Calif.) elected to the U.S. House of Representatives

1947   Rose Hum Lee completes her doctorate at the University of Chicago; Georgia Lee Lusk (D-N.Mex.) elected to the U.S. House of Representatives

1948   Marie Callender starts selling her pies commercially to Long Beach, California eateries

1949   Georgia Neese Clark Gray named U.S. Treasurer; Reva Boone (D-Utah) elected to U.S. House of Representatives

1953   Ivy Baker Priest appointed U.S. Treasurer; *Kinsey Report* issued; Gracie Pfost (D-Idaho) elected to the U.S. House of Representatives

1955   Adlai Stevenson exhorts Smith College graduates to become republican mothers; Del Martin and Phyllis Lyon found the Daughters of Belitis in San Francisco; Rosa Parks refuses to sit in the "colored" section of a Montgomery, Alabama bus; Edith Green (D-Ore.) elected to the U.S. House of Representatives

1958   Donna Joy McGladrey starts teaching in Alaska

1959   Ruth Handler creates Barbie; Catherine Dean May (R-Wash.) elected to the U.S. House of Representatives

1960   Alice Ramsey named Woman Motorist of the Century; Julia Butler Hansen (D-Wash.) elected to the U.S. House of Representatives

1963   Betty Friedan's *The Feminine Mystique* published; Presidential Commission on the Status of Women, chaired by Eleanor Roosevelt, issues its report and only Marguerite Rewalt supports an Equal Rights Amendment; Equal Pay Act becomes law

1964   Civil Rights Act of 1964 becomes law

1966   Barbara Jordan elected to the Texas Senate; National Organization of Women founded; Ivy Baker Priest elected Treasurer of California; Lera Thomas (D-Tex.) elected to the U.S. House of Representatives

1968   Shirley Ann Mount Hufstedler appointed to the Ninth Circuit Court of Appeals; Kuniko Terasawa receives the Order of the Sacred Treasure, Zuiosho-5th Class

1969   Hattie Burnstad is named Washakie County, Wyoming, teacher of the year

1971   Octavia Butler's *Crossover* published

1972   Barbara Jordan elected to the U.S. House of Representatives; Sarah Ragle Weddington is the first woman elected to the Texas House of Representatives; Title IX of the Higher Education Act becomes law, increasing access to higher education for women, particularly athletics; Congresswoman Shirley Chisholm runs for president of the United States; the journal *Women's Studies* founded; the journal *Feminist Studies* founded; Equal Rights Amendment to the U.S. Constitution approved by Congress; Patricia Schroeder (D-Colo.) elected to the U.S. House of Representatives

1973   Sarah Ragle Weddington successfully argues *Roe v. Wade;* Billie Jean King defeats Bobby Riggs in a tennis match; Yvonne Brathwaite Burke (D-Calif.) and Barbara Jordan (D-Tex.) elected to the U.S. House of Representatives

1974   Leslie Marmon Silko's *Laguna Woman Poems* published; Mary Ann Graf is the first female graduate of the University of California, Davis, enology program; March Fong Eu elected California's first female Secretary of State

1975   The journal *Signs* founded; Congress mandates that U.S. military academies admit women; Shirley Pettis (R-Calif.), Martha Keys (D-Kan.), and Virginia Smith (R-Nev.) elected to the U.S. House of Representatives

1976   Maxine Hong Kingston's *The Warrior Woman* published

1977   Rose Elizabeth Bird becomes the first female Chief Justice of the California Supreme Court; United Nations International Women's Year declared; Phyllis Schlafly's *The Power of the Positive Woman* published

1978   Sally K. Ride joins NASA

1979   Mildred Imach Cleghorn named chair of Fort Sill Apache tribe; Dorothy Wright Nelson appointed to the Ninth Circuit Court of Appeals; Ruth Murray Underhill's *Papago Woman* published

1980 Kathleen M. Conley is the first woman to graduate from the U.S. Air Force Academy

1981 Margaret Coel's *Chief Left Hand: Southern Arapaho* published; Linda Hogan's *Daughters, I Love You* published; Molly Ivins takes a job with the *Dallas Times Herald;* Bobbi Fiedler (R-Calif.) elected to the U.S. House of Representatives

1982 A sufficient number of states fail to ratify the Equal Rights Amendment

1983 Barbara Boxer (D-Calif.), Sala Burton (D-Calif.), and Barbara Vucanocick (R-Nev.) elected to the U.S. House of Representatives; Sally K. Ride is first female in space on the shuttle *Challenger*

1984 Gloria Anzaldua's *Borderlands/La frontera: The New Mestiza* published; Cynthia Holcomb Hall appointed to the Ninth Circuit Court of Appeals

1985 Jan Meyers (R-Kan.) elected to the U.S. House of Representatives

1987 Linda M. Hasselstrom's *Going Over East* published; National Museum of Women in the Arts opens in Washington, D.C.; Wilma Mankiller becomes Principal Chief of the Cherokee Nation; Nancy Pelosi (D-Calif.) is elected to the U.S. House of Representatives

1988 Amy Tan's *The Joy Luck Club* published; Dr. Mae C. Jemison becomes first African American woman in space; Congress passes the Family Support Act to collect from "deadbeat dads"

1989 Joyce Kennard appointed to the California Supreme Court; Patricia Schroeder's *Champion of the Great American Family* published; Jolene Unsoeld (D-Wash.) elected to the U.S. House of Representatives

1990 Ann Richards elected governor of Texas; Maxine Waters elected to the U.S. House of Representatives

1991 Congresswoman Patricia Schroeder's rider to a Department of Defense bill leads to the assignment of women to combat aircraft

1992 Dianne Feinstein (D-Calif.) elected to the U.S. Senate

1993 Barbara Boxer (D-Calif.) elected to the U.S. Senate; Mary Crow Dog's *Ohitika Woman* published; Janet Campbell Hale's *Bloodlines* published; Karan English (D-Ariz.), Anna Eshoo (D-Calif.), Jane Harman (D-Calif.), Lucille Roybal-Allard (D-Calif.), Lynne Schenk (D-Calif.), Lynn Woolsey (D-Calif.), Elizabeth Furse (D-Ore.), Eddie Bernice Johnson (D-Tex.), Karen Sheperd (D-Utah), Maria Cantwell (D-Wash.), and Jennifer Dunn (D-Wash.) elected to the U.S. House of Representatives; Wilma Mankiller's *Mankiller: A Chief and Her People* published

1994 Kathryn M. Werdegar appointed to the California Supreme Court

1995 Eileen M. Collins of San Antonio, Texas, becomes first woman to fly the space shuttle; Zoe Lofgren (D-Calif.), Andrea Seastrand (R-Calif.), Juanita Millender-McDonald (D-Calif.), Helen Chenoweth (R-Idaho), Darlene Hooley (D-Ore.), Sheila Jackson-Lee (D-Tex.), Enid Green (Waldholtz) (R-Utah), Linda Smith (R-Wash.), and Barbara Cubin (R-Wyo.) elected to the U.S. House of Representatives

1996 Janice Rogers Brown appointed to the California Supreme Court

1997 Ellen Tauscher (D-Calif.), Loretta Sanchez (D-Calif.), Diana DeBette (D-Colo.), and Kay Granger (R-Tex.) elected to the U.S. House of Representatives; Maria Tallchief receives Kennedy Center Honor

1998 Patricia Schroeder's *24 Years of House Work . . . and the Place is Still a Mess* published; Lois Capps (D-Calif.), Mary Bono (R-Calif.), Barbara Lee (D-Calif.), and Heather Wilson (R-N.Mex.) elected to the U.S. House of Representatives

1999 Dawnine Dyer named Mentor of the Year by winemakers; Team USA wins Women's World Cup of soccer; Eileen M. Collins becomes the first woman space shuttle commander; Shelley Berkley (D-Nev.) and Grace Napolitano (D-Calif.) elected to the U.S. House of Representatives

2000   U.S. Senator Kay Bailey Hutchison (R-Tex.) named Border Texan of the Year

2001   Rosario Marin named U.S. Treasurer; Susan Davis (D-Calif.), Hilda Solis (D-Calif.), and Diane Watson (D-Calif.) elected to the U.S. House of Representatives

2002   Delphine Red Shirt's *Turtle Lung Woman's Granddaughter* published

2003   Representative Nancy Pelosi (D-Calif.) named House Democratic Whip

Women's Organizations

QUICK REFERENCE

Association of Black Women Historians
labwh.tcnj.edu

Berkshire Conference of Women Historians
www.berkconference.org

Coordinating Council for Women in History
theccwh.org

National Women's History Project
www.nwhp.org

Western Association of Women Historians
www.wawh.org

Women's Studies Section, Association
of College and Research Libraries,
American Library Association
www.ala.org/acrl/wss/wsshp.html

ADDITIONAL SITES OF INTEREST

Alice Paul Centennial Foundation
Director
PO Box 1376
Mt. Laurel, NJ
609-231-1885
609-231-4223 FAX

American Historical Association
Women & Minorities
400 A Street, SE
Washington, DC 20003
202-544-2422

Assoc. of Black Women Historians
Dr. Barbara Woods, Director
South Carolina State University
Department of History
Orangeburg, SC 29117
803-536-8672

Butte Women's Labor History Project
Ellen Crain, Director
Butte Silver Bow Public Archives
Box 81
Butte, MT 59703

Colorado Coalition for Women's History
c/o Marcia Goldstein
PO Box 673
1200 Madison
Denver, CO 80206
303-377-6315

Coordinating Committee for Women Historians
c/o Kimberly Jensen
Gender Studies
Western Oregon State University
Monmouth, OR 97361

Foundation for Women's Resources
Candace O'Keefe, Director
3500 Jefferson, Suite 210
Austin, TX 78731
512-459-1167

General Federation of Women's Clubs
Women's History and Resource Center
1734 N Street, NW
Washington, DC 20036
202-347-3168

International Women's Air and Space Museum
26 North Main Street
Centerville, OH 45459
513-433-6766

Italian-American Women's History Project
c/o Lola Rozzi
3531 Kutztown Road
Laureldale, PA 19605
215-929-4463

Montana Women's History Project
c/o Jennifer Hisatomi
University of Montana
University Center 210
Missoula, MT 59812

National Women's History Museum
Post Office Box 1296
Annandale, VA 22003
703-813-6209

National Cowgirl Museum and Hall of Fame
111 West 4th Street, # 300
Ft. Worth, TX 76102
817-336-4475

National Women's History Project
3345 Industrial Drive, Suite 3
Santa Rosa, CA 95403
www.nwhp.org
(707) 636-2888
(707) 636-2909 FAX
Email: nwhp@aol.com
On-line form: Order our free catalog

Nevada Women's History Project
c/o Jean Ford
1048 N Sierra, #A
Reno, NV 89503
702-784-1268

Pioneer Woman Museum
c/o Jan Prough
701 Monument Road
Ponca City, OK 74604
405-765-6108

Rogue Valley Women's History Project
c/o Marilyn Boje
PO Box 674
Ashland, OR 97520

Women's Heritage Museum
Elizabeth Colton, President
PO Box 642370
San Francisco, CA 94164-2370
415-775-1366
elcolton@aol.com

Women's History Reclamation Project
Mary Lou C. Sulentich, Exec. Director
2323 Broadway, Suite 103
San Diego, CA 92102
619-238-0754

Washington Women Historians
c/o Sarah Larson
1668 Wainwright Drive
Reston, VA 20190-3432
703-742-0578

Women's History Research Center
c/o American Heritage Center
University of Wyoming, Box 3924
Laramie, WY 82071-3924
307-766-4114

Researching Women's History

Access and Strategy in the Electronic Age

Over the last 3 decades, the academy has witnessed a proliferation of scholarship across the disciplines on women, and more recently, on gender. Along with the growth of women's studies as an academic discipline, women's history has increasingly filled the pages of books, journals, conference panels, and curricula. Women's historians now have colleagues and collaborators in area studies, anthropology, sociology, communications, literary criticism, and beyond. Historians of the American West, too, have been engaged in an active cross-disciplinary discussion.

The explosion of such varied historical scholarship in the last quarter century has coincided with rapid advances in information technologies and systems of information retrieval. Researchers face important challenges as they attempt to navigate this information arena—both inside the walls of libraries and special collections and in an increasingly electronic, Web-based environment. First, the terminology and classification schemes used to describe (and hence access) research materials are themselves historically constructed. Second, interdisciplinary research continues to be constrained by the highly structured internal organization of academic disciplines and the manner in which academic research is published. This essay will raise the reader's general awareness of the structure of information, impart concrete library skills, and introduce tools and resources for mediating the quest for interdisciplinary historical literature.

THE LITERATURE

Modern historical inquiry is based on the examination of primary documents—to analyze and tell stories about the past using its contemporaneous evidence. Historians rely on secondary source materials—books, journal articles, conference presentations, and other forms of published scholarly communication—to provide context and background for original investigations and to engage in interpretive dialogue. Bibliographies, abstracting and indexing services, and, increasingly, Web-based pathfinders make up a third category of tertiary literature—or sources that compile and otherwise direct students and scholars to primary and secondary material. The concurrence of electronic publishing and increased interdisciplinarity among women's historians and historians of the American West has influenced the access to and availability of all forms of historical literature. The savvy researcher will need to make use of new research strategies to identify, locate, and keep pace with it all.

Women's studies and social history are "high-scatter" fields—with needed information dispersed throughout many different journals and books, indexed by different databases, and recorded and preserved in different locales. Electronic databases, full-text journal articles, digitized archival and manuscript materials, and electronic books have emerged to serve history students and professional historians alike, and proficiency in accessing resources in electronic format is now essential. However, research strategies also must include an understanding of the physical arrangement and description of books, manuscripts, and other forms of printed scholarly text and communication, as some of these materials remain in printed form, and even as others are converted to digital formats. Historians must apply the same evaluative skills they use every day to determine the context and voice of *documents*, to understand the tools and terrain of the information and resources in which they are searching and browsing. Information by and about women itself has a history that shapes research strategy and success.

PRIMARY SOURCES

Traditionally the domain of archives, manuscript repositories, historical societies, and library special collections, unpublished primary source material is assembled, described, and preserved based on prevailing social and intellectual values and professional archival judgment. To locate source material, researchers can consult comprehensive finding aids such as the *National Union Catalog of Manuscript Collections (NUCMC)* and more specialized volumes such as *Women in the West: A Guide to Manuscript Sources,* which compile information about the scope and location of existing collections. The Internet has vastly expanded and facilitated the process of identifying and locating potential archival and manuscript collections for research and afforded smaller projects and sources increased visibility and access. Prominent examples of Web sites include the geographically arranged *Archival Sites for Women's Studies* (gwis2.circ. gwu.edu/~mfpankin/archwss.htm). Ken Middleton's American Women's History: A Research Guide (www.mtsu.edu/~kmiddlet/history/women.html) organizes sites by type or format of material. Middleton's extensive guide also includes practical tips on using online library catalogs to find published primary documents. Finally, online versions of *NUCMC* (www.loc.gov/coll/nucmc/nucmc.html) for the United States, and subscription products such as OCLC's union catalog *WorldCat* (international), Chadwyk-Healey's *ArchivesUSA,* and *RLG Archival Resources,* also figure prominently in the historian's electronic library by providing keyword access to cataloged archival and manuscript collections.

Some special collections and manuscript repositories have also digitized their collections, making scanned page images of unique materials available worldwide. Examples of fully digitized, online collections of primary source documents continue to grow, either through locally funded projects or national initiatives such as the Library of Congress *American Memory Project* (lcweb2.loc.gov/ammem/amhome. html). *American Memory* has spawned sites such as *History of the American West: 1860-1920,* a collection of photographs from the Denver Public Library. Among universities, the University of California, Berkeley's, Bancroft Library (bancroft.berkeley.edu/ collections) is distinguished for depth and breadth of research material on the American West available online, including the California Heritage Collection.

Finally, both free and commercial Web-based products not only make available full-text diaries, historical periodicals, court cases, statutes, speeches, census data, letters, and many other sources online, but they often integrate them and index them in ways that facilitate new kinds of historical inquiry. Noteworthy examples include Alexander Street Press's *North American Women's Letters and Diaries* and *Early Encounters.*

SECONDARY SOURCES

Monographs

Most academic libraries in the United States arrange their print collections using the Library of Congress Classification (LCC) system—which assigns an alphanumeric code (or call number) corresponding to subject arrangement and shelf location. Library of Congress Subject Heading (LCSH) terms *describe* the collections, and although that language has changed over time, LCSH terms chronically trail current academic vernacular. Its embedded gender hierarchies (e.g., "lawyers" and "women lawyers") also endure.

Since its development as a classification scheme at the turn of the 20th century, the LCC system has evolved to reflect the ordering of traditional academic disciplines. Research materials appropriate for women's history and other interdisciplinary studies are physically dispersed throughout the library, and can only be identified comprehensively by navigating the entire system—from A (General works) to Z (Bibliographies). Subject terms schematically link items in different classification ranges, and library users can search online catalogs by keyword (finding words in titles, multiple subject terms, and sometimes additional notes) to create lists of desired material. But literature on the information-seeking behavior of historians and other humanists suggests a strong penchant for browsing. If serendipitous identification of new works through browsing library stacks often leads to important new discoveries, it also takes place in a decidedly ordered, discipline-oriented context, which may obscure other useful materials from view. The most successful researchers will harness the power and functionality of online retrieval systems by combining keyword and subject searches, maintaining a productive skepticism of the way information is organized, and employing analytical and creative approaches to research.

Journals

Since the early 1970s, feminism as a social movement and women's studies as an academic discipline have influenced scholarship throughout the academy. As articles about women and gender increasingly appear in discipline-based journals (in the humanities and social sciences and, more recently, in the sciences), scholarship also is flourishing in women's studies periodicals such as *Signs* and *Feminist Studies.* Historians seeking recent interdisciplinary scholarship on women should therefore be aware of several challenges of bibliographic access to women's studies and women's history content in academic journals.

Scholars are often compelled by the tenure process to publish in the journals of their home discipline. Women's history and related articles might therefore appear in journals of anthropology, literature, and sociology, as well as economics, medicine, and beyond. A variety of online databases (the electronic counterparts of print indexing and abstracting services) associated with each academic subject will index these discipline-based journals. At the same time, scholars also publish articles of interest to women's historians in peer-reviewed women's studies journals. And while a wide range of discipline-based databases may index women's studies journals, they often do so selectively and in ways that reflect a more traditional disciplinary bias or perspective.

Women's studies databases such as *Women's Resources International* and the full-text *Contemporary Women's Issues* and *GenderWatch* provide more comprehensive access to women's studies journals, but cannot fully capture the gender-related content available from subject-specific periodical literature. Finally, at the intersection of what in interdisciplinary studies is separated into "women's history" and "ethnic studies" lies a rich literature on ethnic minority and international women, which is even further dispersed. Like women's studies journals, ethnic studies journals are themselves marginalized by traditional subject indexes, and access to content on women may be further scattered in their pages. While literature in many academic fields is scattered, such relatively new and inherently interdisciplinary categories of inquiry as gender or ethnicity increase the extent to which needed materials are located across literature in numerous disciplines.

TERTIARY SOURCES

Bibliographies and other tertiary sources of compiled research are standard tools for historians. Attempts to assemble citations from disparate disciplines and provide reviews and summaries in subject handbooks represent a critical component of the information infrastructure that facilitates comprehensive retrieval. Bibliographies also may be published as Web-based pathfinders to an integrated mix of print and electronic sources.

The principal online databases in history, ABC-CLIO's *Historical Abstracts* and *America: History & Life,* have greatly enhanced historians' access to history journals of recent decades, through sophisticated search interfaces and indexing appropriate to the structure of the discipline. As noted, however, interdisciplinary research projects in women's history require searching across multiple subject-oriented indexes in the social sciences, humanities, and sciences. As well as including different content, each database has its own indexing structure and set of subject terms to describe included material. Similar to library catalogs, online keyword access to these indexes obviates some of the need to master each database's unique set of subject terms, but successful searchers understand that subject terms exist to describe and link related materials, and use these to supplement keyword searches and expand retrieval.

Further complicating the picture are studies revealing that women's studies journals are generally underindexed by the discipline-based subject databases. For example, while databases such as *America: History & Life,* with its comparatively strong interdisciplinary content, yield citations from women's studies journals, they do not necessarily include all relevant articles from them. *Relevance* to the historical discipline may not always correspond to relevance to the individual researcher. From 1975 to 2000, *America: History & Life* contains 293 abstracts of articles from *Signs* an average of 12 articles per year, or slightly more than 10% of the articles published in *Signs* during that period. The articles selected for inclusion were identified for their significance to history and the database's geographic scope (United States and Canada). Articles not selected, however, still might be relevant to U.S. women's historians, based on topic, method, or approach. Researchers should be aware of the selection criteria of any information tool they consult, with consideration to limitations those criteria may place—disciplinary, geographic, etc.—on the interdisciplinary study of women and gender.

CONCLUSION

How information is produced, collected, preserved, categorized, and accessed reflects (and shapes) the society in which it originated. Successful researchers will be aware of these categories and critically interrogate the content and structure of the tools available to them. If libraries, online databases, Web sites, and other tools discussed in this article provide paths to needed research material, they themselves also constitute primary sources that reveal much about the social and political structure of information at the turn of the 21st century.

— Judy Ruttenberg

REFERENCES AND RECOMMENDED READING

Armitage, S. H. *Women in the West: A Guide to Manuscript Sources*. New York: Garland, 1991.

Dickstein, R., V. A. Mills, and E. J. Waite. *Women in LC's Terms: A Thesaurus of Library of Congress Subject Headings Relating to Women*. Phoenix, AZ: Oryx Press, 1988.

Garcia, S. A. "Indexing Patterns of Periodical Literature on African American Women and U.S. Latinas," in K. H. Gerhard, ed., *Women's Studies Serials: A Quarter Century of Development*. New York: Haworth Press, 1988, 167-196.

Gerhard, K. H., T. E. Jacobson, and S. G. Williamson. "Indexing Adequacy and Interdisciplinary Journals: The Case of Women's Studies." *College & Research Libraries* 54(2), 1993.

Intner, S. S., and E. Futas. "The Role and Impact of Library of Congress Classification on the Assessment of Women's Studies Collections." *Library Acquisitions: Practice & Theory, 20*(3), 269, 1996.

Lensink, J. N. "Beyond the Intellectual Meridian: Transdisciplinary Studies of Women." *Pacific Historical Review 61*, 1992

Limerick, P. N. "Going West and Ending Up Global." *Western Historical Quarterly, 32*(1), 2001.

Scott, A. F., S. M. Evans, S. K. Cahn, and E. Faue. "Women's History in the New Millennium" (Panel Discussion). *Journal of Women's History 11*, 1999.

Tibbo, H. R. *Abstracting, Information Retrieval and the Humanities: Providing Access to Historical Literature*. Chicago: American Library Association, 1993.

Westbrook, L. *Interdisciplinary Information Seeking in Women's Studies*. Jefferson, NC: McFarland, 1999.

Readings, Resources, and References

Abbott, Devon. "Ann Florence Wilson: Matriarch of the Cherokee Female Seminary." *Chronicles of Oklahoma* 67(4, Winter 1989-1990).

Abbott, Lawrence. "Nora Naranjo-Morse." *I Stand in the Center of the Good: Interviews of Contemporary North American Artists.* Lincoln: University of Nebraska Press, 1994.

Abernethy, Francis Edward, ed. *Legendary Ladies of Texas.* Denton: University of North Texas Press, 1994.

Abram, Ruth J., ed. *Send Us a Lady Physician. Women Doctors in America, 1835-1920.* New York: Norton, 1985.

Acheson, Sam Hanna, Herbert P. Gambrell, Mary Carter Toomey, and Alex M. Acheson Jr., eds. *Texian Who's Who: Vol. 1.* Dallas, TX: Texian, 1937.

Adela Rogers St. John: herstory.freehomepage.com/pages/rogerstjohn.html.

Agnew, Brad. "A Legacy of Education: The History of the Cherokee Seminaries." *Chronicles of Oklahoma* 63(2, Summer 1985).

Agonito, Rosemary, and Joseph Agonito. "Resurrecting History's Forgotten Women: A Case Study From the Cheyenne Indians." *Frontiers* 6(3).

Alexander, Thomas G. "An Experiment in Progressive Legislation: The Granting of Woman Suffrage in Utah in 1870." *Utah Historical Quarterly* 38 (Winter, 1970).

Alexander, Thomas G. *Utah, The Right Place.* Salt Lake City, UT: Gibbs-Smith, 1995.

Allen, Paula Gunn. "The Feminine Landscape of Leslie Marmon Silko's *Ceremony,*" in Paula Gunn Allen, ed., *Studies in American Indian Literature: Critical Essays and Course Designs.* New York: Modern Language Association, 1983.

Allen, Susan L. "Progressive Spirit: The Oklahoma and Indian Territory Federation of Women's Clubs." *Chronicles of Oklahoma* 66(1, Spring 1988): 4-19.

American Medical Association. *Physician Characteristics and Distribution in the U.S., 2003/2004 Edition.* www. ama-assn.org/ama/pub/print/article/168-185.html.

American Medical Association. www.ama-assn.org/ama/pub/print/article/168-191.html.

American Police Hall of Fame. "Officer of the Year 1996: Corporal Regina Bonny." www.aphf.org.

Appier, Janis. *Policing Women: The Sexual Politics of Law Enforcement and the LAPD.* Philadelphia, PA: Temple University Press, 1998.

Arburua, Joseph M. *Narrative of the Veterinary Profession in California.* San Francisco: Joseph M. Arburua, 1966.

Arias, Ron. "Tireless Kuniko Terasawa Is the Force Behind a Newspaper Almost no One Can Read." *People Weekly* (September 25, 1989).

Armitage, Susan, and Elizabeth Jamison, eds. *The Women's West.* Norman: University of Oklahoma Press, 1987.

Armitage, S. H. *Women in the West: A Guide to Manuscript Sources.* New York: Garland, 1991.

Arnold, Ellen, ed. "Listening to the Spirits: An Interview with Leslie Marmon Silko," in *Conversions with Leslie Marmon Silko.* Jackson: University Press of Mississippi, 2000.

Arnold, Marilyn. *Willa Cather's Short Fiction.* Athens: Ohio University Press, 1984.

Association for Women Veterinarians. *Our History of Women in Veterinary Medicine: Gumption, Grace, Grit, and Good Humor.* Littleton, CO: Association of Women Veterinarians, 1997.

Austin, Gail T., comp. "African-American Women in the Sciences and Related Disciplines." www.nau.edu/~wst/access/lcafam.html.

EDITORS' NOTE: Web sites may be listed by title and not necessarily by subject.

Autoshop Online. "Automotive 101, Automotive History." www.autoshoponline.com/auto101/histtext.html.

Babcock, Barbara A., and Nancy J. Parezo. *Daughters of the Desert: Women Anthropologists and the Native American Southwest, 1880-1980*. Albuquerque: University of New Mexico Press, 1988.

Babcock, Barbara Allen. "Clara Shortridge Foltz: 'First Woman.'" *Arizona Law Review 30* (1988).

Bakken, Gordon Morris. *Rocky Mountain Constitution Making, 1850-1912*. Westport, CT: Greenwood Press, 1987.

Bakken, Gordon Morris. *Practicing Law in Frontier California*. Lincoln: University of Nebraska Press, 1991.

Baldwin, Lou. *A Call to Sanctity: the Formation and Life of Mother Katherine Drexel*. Philadelphia, PA: Catholic Standard and Times, 1987.

Bangs, Pat. "Red Shirt, Delphine." *School Library Journal* (November 1998).

Barker Texas History Center, University of Texas, Austin.

Barnett, Stephen. "The Supreme Court of California 1981-1982 Forward: The Emerging Court." *California Law Review 71* (July 1983).

Barron, Cheryl Aimee. *Dreamers of the Valley of Plenty: A Portrait of the Napa Valley*. New York: Scribner, 1995.

Batalle, Gretchen, and Laurie Lisa, eds. *Native American Women: A Biographical Dictionary* (2d ed.). New York: Routledge, 2001.

Beal, Frances M. "Black Scholar Interview with Octavia Butler: Black Women and the Science Fiction Genre," *The Black Scholar: The Black Woman Writer and the Diaspora 29* (October 1985).

The Bear Flag Revolt: www.colusi.org/linked/html/bear_flag_revolt.htm

Beaton, Gail Marjorie. *The Literary Study and Philanthropic Work of Six Women's Clubs in Denver, 1881-1945*. Master's thesis. University of Colorado, 1987.

Beauchamp, Cari. *Without Lying Down: Frances Marion and the Powerful Women of Early Hollywood*. New York: Simon & Schuster,1997.

Beeton, Beverly. *Women Vote in the West: The Woman Suffrage Movement, 1869-1896*. New York: Garland, 1986.

Belcher, Dixie. "A Democratic School for Democratic Women." *Chronicles of Oklahoma 61*(4, Winter 1983-1984).

Bennett, Mildred. *The World of Willa Cather*. Lincoln: University of Nebraska Press, 1961.

Berner, Robert L. "Book Review of Mud Women: Poems from the Clay." *World Literature Today 67*(2, Spring 1993).

Bertram, Peggy Brooks. "Rescuing Drusilla: Drusilla Dunjee Houston": http://wings.buffalo.edu/dunjeehouston/history/bio.htm.

Berry, Carolyn. "Comenha." *Frontiers 6*(3).

Bhopal, Kalwant. *Gender, "Race" and Patriarchy: A Study of South Asian Women*. Aldershot, England: Ashgate, 1997.

Bibbs, Susheel. *The Legacies of Mary Ellen Pleasant—Mother of Human Rights in California*. San Francisco: MEP Productions, 1998.

Bird, Gloria. *Full Moon on the Reservation*. New York: Greenview Review Press, 1993

Bird, Gloria. *The River of History*. Portland, OR: Trask House Press, 1997.

Bird, Gloria, and Joy Harjo, eds. *Reinventing the Enemy's Language*. New York: Norton, 1997.

Bird, Gloria, and Karen Strom. "Gloria Bird": www.hanksville.org/storytellers/gbird.

Blackburn, Bob L. "Zelia Breaux and Bricktown: Crossroads of Commerce, Crossroads of Diversity, Crossroads of Renewal." Bricktown History: www.bricktownokc.com.

Blackstock, Joseph R. *Report on Laura Scudder*. Monterey Park, CA: Historical Society of Monterey Park, 1974.

Blair, Karen J. *The Clubwoman as Feminist: True Womanhood Redefined, 1868-1914*. New York: Holmes & Meier, 1980.

Bliss, Mary Lee, ed. *The American Bench: Judges of the Nation 1999-2000* (10th ed.). Sacramento, CA: Forster-Long, 1999.

Block, Judy Rachel. *The First Woman in Congress: Jeannette Rankin*. New York: C.P.I., 1978.

Bloom, Edward A., and Lillian Bloom. *Willa Cather's Gift of Sympathy*. Carbondale: Southern Illinois University Press, 1962.

Bloom, Harold. *Modern Critical Views: Amy Tan*. Philadelphia, PA: Chelsea House, 2000.

Blossom, Debbie. "African-American Businesswomen in Tulsa, Oklahoma, Head to Conference." *Tulsa World*, August 25, 2001.

Blumhoffer, Edith L. *Aimee Semple McPherson: Everybody's Sister*. Grand Rapids, MI: William B. Eerdman's, 1993.

Bolton, Herbert Eugene. *Coronado, Knight of Prairie and Plain*. New York: Whittlesey House, 1949.

Bookspan, Shelley. *A Germ of Goodness: The California State Prison System, 1851-1944*. Lincoln: University of Nebraska Press, 1991.

Bostic, E. McCurdy. "Elizabeth Fulton Hester." *Chronicles of Oklahoma 6*(4, December 1928): 449-452.

Boxer, Barbara. *Strangers in the Senate: Politics and the New Revolution of Women in America*. Washington, DC: National Press Books, 1994.

Boxer, Barbara: Official Website of U.S. Senator Barbara Boxer of California: http://boxer.senate.gov.

Brandenstein, Sherilyn. "The Colorado Cottage Home." *Colorado* magazine *53* (Summer 1976).

Braude, Ann. *Women and American Religion*. New York: Oxford University Press, 2000.

Brave Bird, Mary. *Ohitika Woman*. New York: Grove Press, 1993.

Brenton, Thaddeus Reamy. *An Exhibition of Rare Manuscripts and Books From the Library of Mrs. Edward Laurence Doheny*. Los Angeles: College Press, 1936.

Brimlow, George. "The Life of Sarah Winnemucca: The Formative Years." *Oregon Historical Quarterly 53* (June 1952).

Brown, E. K., with Leon Edel. *Willa Cather: A Critical Biography*. Lincoln: University of Nebraska Press, 1953.

Brown, Norman D. *Hood, Bonnet, and Little Brown Jug: Texas Politics, 1921-1928*. College Station: Texas A&M University Press, 1984.

Bryant, Edwin. *What I Saw in California: Being the Journal of a Tour, by the Emigrant Route and South Pass of the Rocky Mountains, Across the Continent of North America, the Great Desert Basin, and Through California, in the Years 1846-1847*. Minneapolis, MN: Ross & Haines, 1967.

Buck, Holly J. "'The Powerful Instrumentalities of Our Up-Building': The Woman's Study League of Pocatello, 1896-1916." *Pacific Northwest Quarterly 93* (1, 2001-02): 3-12.

Burnstad, Hattie. Personal papers, private collection in author's possession.

Burnstad, Hattie. *Summary of Wyoming Government*. Worland, WY: Valley Press, 1967.

Bushman, Claudia, ed. *Mormon Sisters: Women in Early Utah*. Logan: Utah State University Press, 1997.

Butler, Anne. *Daughters of Joy, Sisters of Misery: Prostitutes in the American West, 1865-90*. Urbana: University of Illinois Press, 1985.

Butler, Anne M. "Mother Katharine Drexel: Spiritual Visionary for the West," in Glenda Riley and Richard W. Etulain, eds., *By Grit and Grace: Eleven Women Who Shaped the American West*. Golden, CO: Fulcrum, 1997, 198-220.

Butler, Anne M. *Gendered Justice in the American West: Women Prisoners in Men's Penitentiaries*. Urbana: University of Illinois Press, 1997.

Caesar, Judith. "Patriarchy, Imperialism, and Knowledge in *The Kitchen God's Wife*." *North Dakota Quarterly 62*(4, Fall 1994): 164-174.

Cahn, Susan K. *Coming on Strong: Gender and Sexuality in Twentieth-Century Women's Sport*. New York: Free Press, 1994.

Calderon, Hector, and Jose David Saldivar. *Criticism in the Borderlands*. Durham, NC: Duke University Press, 1991.

California Bar Journal: www.calbar.org.

Barbara A. Caulfield: http://air.fjc.gov/newweb/jnetweb.nsf/fjc_bio.

Callander, Marilyn Berg. *Willa Cather and the Fairy Tale*. Ann Arbor: University of Michigan, 1989.

Canfield, Gae Whitney. *Sarah Winnemucca of the Northern Paiutes*. Norman: University of Oklahoma Press, 1983.

Cao, Jerry Finely. "The Los Angeles Public Library: Origins and Development." Ph.D. dissertation. University of Southern California, 1977.

Casey, Naomi Taylor. "Miss Edith Johnson, Pioneer Newspaper Woman." *Chronicles of Oklahoma 60*(1, Spring 1982).

Castillo, Edward. "The Impact of Euro-American Exploration and Settlement," in Robert F. Heizer, ed., *Handbook of North American Indians: Vol 8*. Washington, DC: Smithsonian Institution, 1978.

Carter Anon Museum, Anadarko, Oklahoma. *Dolls by Mildred Cleghorn: An Exhibition*. December 19, 1971-January 29, 1972.

Carter, Lyndia. "Nancy Kelsey, the First Woman to Cross Utah": www.utahhistorytogo.org/kelsey.html.

Carver, Sharon Snow. "Salt Lake City's Reapers' Club," *Utah Historical Quarterly 64* (Spring 1996).

Carver, Sharon Snow. *Club Women of the Three Intermountain Cities of Denver, Boise and Salt Lake City between 1893 and 1929*. Ph.D. dissertation. Brigham Young University, 2000.

Cather, Willa. *The Troll Garden*. 1905. In Sharon O'Brien, ed., *Early Novels and Stories*. New York: Library of America, 1987.

Cather, Willa. *Alexander's Bridge*. 1912. In Sharon O'Brien, ed., *Stories, Poems, and Other Writings*. New York: Library of America, 1992.

Cather, Willa. *O Pioneers!* 1913. In Sharon O'Brien, ed., *Early Novels and Stories*. New York: Library of America, 1987.

Cather, Willa. *The Song of the Lark*. 1915. In Sharon O'Brien, ed., *Early Novels and Stories*. New York: Library of America, 1987.

Cather, Willa. *My Ántonia*. 1918. In Sharon O'Brien, ed., *Early Novels and Stories*. New York: Library of America. 1987.

Cather, Willa. *Youth and the Bright Medusa.* 1920. In Sharon O'Brien, ed., *Stories, Poems and Other Writings.* New York: Library of America, 1992.

Cather, Willa. *One of Ours.* 1922. In Sharon O'Brien, ed., *Later Novels.* New York: Library of America, 1992.

Cather, Willa. *April Twilight and Other Poems.* 1923. In Sharon O'Brien, ed., *Stories, Poems, and Other Writings.* New York: Library of America, 1992.

Cather, Willa. *A Lost Lady.* 1923. In Sharon O'Brien, ed., *Later Novels.* New York: Library of America, 1990.

Cather, Willa. "Nebraska: The End of the First Cycle." *The Nation 117* (1923): 236-38.

Cather, Willa. *The Professor's House.* 1925. In Sharon O'Brien, ed., *Later Novels.* New York: Library of America, 1990.

Cather, Willa. *My Mortal Enemy.* 1926. In Sharon O'Brien, ed., *Stories, Poems, and Other Writings.* New York: Library of America, 1992.

Cather, Willa. *Death Comes for the Archbishop.* 1927. In Sharon O'Brien, ed., *Later Novels.* New York: Library of America, 1990.

Cather, Willa. *Shadows on the Rock.* 1931. In Sharon O'Brien, ed., *Later Novels.* New York: Library of America, 1990.

Cather, Willa. *Obscure Destinies.* 1932. In Sharon O'Brien, ed., *Stories, Poems, and Other Writings.* New York: Library of America, 1992.

Cather, Willa. *Lucy Gayheart.* 1935. In Sharon O'Brien, ed., *Later Novels.* New York: Library of America, 1990.

Cather, Willa. *Not Under Forty.* 1936. In Sharon O'Brien, ed., *Stories, Poems, and Other Writings.* New York: Library of America, 1992.

Cather, Willa. *Sapphira and the Slave Girl.* 1940. In Sharon O'Brien, ed., *Later Novels.* New York: Library of America, 1990.

Cather, Willa. *Willa Cather in Europe,* George N. Kates, ed. New York: Knopf, 1956.

Cather, Willa. *Willa Cather on Writing.* Stephen Tennant (Introduction). 1949. Lincoln: University of Nebraska Press, 1988.

Cather, Willa. *Early Stories of Willa Cather,* Mildred R. Bennett, ed. New York: Dodd, Mead, 1957.

Cather, Willa. *Willa Cather's Collected Short Fiction, 1892-1912,* Virginia Faulkner, ed. Mildred R. Bennett (Introduction). Lincoln: University of Nebraska Press, 1965.

Cather, Willa. *The Kingdom of Art: Willa Cather's First Principles and Critical Statements, 1893-1896,* Bernice Slote, ed. Lincoln: University of Nebraska Press, 1966.

Cather, Willa. *Willa Cather: 24 Stories,* Sharon O'Brien, ed. New York: Penguin Meridian, 1988.

Cather, Willa. *The Old Beauty and Others.* 1948. In Sharon O'Brien, ed., *Stories, Poems, and Other Writings.* New York: Library of America, 1992.

Cather, Willa. *Stories, Poems, and Other Writings,* Sharon O'Brien, ed. New York: Library of America, 1992.

"Cathy Martin: Functional Ceramic Art." Retrieved October 25, 2001, from members.aol.com/cmartin27.

Cekola, Anna. "Marie Callender; Turned Pie Shop Into Restaurant Chain." *Los Angeles Times,* November 12, 1995.

Celeste, Eric. "Molly Ivins Leaves the *Star-Telegram's* Staff, but Not Its Pages": www.dallasobserver.com/issues/2001-04-19/filler.html.

Chambers, Carol, "Ulfig Appointed Newhall's First Woman Judge." *The Signal* (June 18, 1998).

Chan, Sucheng, ed. *Entry Denied.* Philadelphia, PA: Temple University Press, 1991.

Chan, Sucheng. *Hmong Means Free: Life in Laos and America.* Philadelphia, PA: Temple University Press, 1994.

Chan, Sucheng. "Race, Ethnic Culture, and Gender in the Construction of Identities Among Second Generation Chinese Americans, 1880s to 1930s," in K. Scott Wong and Sucheng Chan, eds., *Claiming America: Constructing Chinese American Identities During the Exclusion Era.* Philadelphia, PA: Temple University Press, 1998.

Chaney, Lindsay. *The Hearsts: Family and Empire.* New York: Simon & Schuster, 1981.

Chipman, Donald, and Harriett Denise Joseph. *Notable Men and Women of Spanish Texas.* Austin: University of Texas Press, 1999.

Chow, Claire S. *Leaving Deep Water: The Lives of Asian American Women at the Crossroads of Two Cultures.* New York: Dutton, 1998.

Christianson, Gale E. *Edwin Hubble: Mariner of the Nebulae.* New York: Farrar, Straus & Giroux, 1995.

Christina A. Snyder. Retrieved from air.fjc.gov/history/judges_frm.html. Source: History of the Federal Judiciary. http://www.fjc.gov. Web site of the Federal Judicial Center, Washington, D.C.

Christman, Anastasia J. *The Best Laid Plans: Women's Clubs and City Planning in Los Angeles, 1890-1930.* Ph.D. dissertation. University of California, Los Angeles, 2000.

Chronicles of Oklahoma 59(2, Summer 1981).

Clark, Lt. Gen. A. P. "Women at the Service Academies and Combat Leadership." *Strategic Review 5*(4, Fall 1977): 64.

Clark, J. Stanley. "Carolyn Thomas Foreman." *Chronicles of Oklahoma 45*(4, Winter 1967-1968).

Claudia Ann Wilken: http://air.fjc.gov/history/judges_frm.html.

Cleaveland, Norman. *The Morleys—Young Upstarts on the Southwest Frontier*. Albuquerque, NM: Calvin Horn, 1971.

Coburn, Carol. "Ethnicity, Religion, and Gender: The Women of Block, Kansas, 1868-1940," in Frederick C. Luebke, ed., *European Immigrants in the American West: Community Histories*. Albuquerque: University of New Mexico Press, 1998.

Coburn, Carol K., and Martha Smith. *Spirited Lives: How Nuns Shaped Catholic Culture and American Life, 1836-1920*. Chapel Hill: University of North Carolina Press, 1999.

Coffman, Edward M. *The Old Army: A Portrait of the American Army in Peacetime, 1784-1898*. New York: Oxford University Press, 1986.

Cole, Judith K. "A Wide Field for Usefulness: Women's Civil Status and the Evolution of Women's Suffrage on the Montana Frontier, 1864-1914." *American Journal of Legal History 34* (July 1990): 262-294.

Comer, Krista. "Sidestepping Environmental Justice: 'Natural' Landscapes and the Wilderness Plot," in Sherrie Innes and Diana Royer, eds., *Breaking Boundaries: New Perspectives on Women's Regional Writing, 1997*. Iowa City: University of Iowa Press, 1997.

Commire, Anne, *Something About the Author: Facts and Pictures About Contemporary Authors and Illustrators of Books for Young People*. Detroit, MI: Gale Research, 1973.

Consuelo Bland Marshall: .http://air.fjc.gov/servlet/tGetInfo?jid=1485.

Cooper, Frederic Taber. *Some American Storytellers*. New York: Henry Holt, 1911.

Costello, Cynthia B. and Anne J. Stone. *The American Woman, 2001-2002: Getting to the Top*. New York: Norton, 2002.

Costello, David F. *The Prairie World*. Minneapolis: University of Minnesota Press, 1980.

Cottrell, Debbie Mauldin. *Pioneer Woman Educator: The Progressive Spirit of Annie Webb Blanton*. College Station: Texas A&M University Press, 1993.

Crane, Joan. *Willa Cather: A Bibliography*. Lincoln: University of Nebraska Press, 1982.

Crockett, Bernice Norman. "No Job for a Woman." *Chronicles of Oklahoma 61*(2, Summer 1983).

Croly, J. C. *The History of the Woman's Club Movement in America*. New York: Harry G. Allen, 1898.

Cunningham, Mary S. *The Woman's Club of El Paso: Its First Thirty Years*. El Paso: Texas Western Press, 1978.

Daiches, David. *Willa Cather: Critical Introduction*. Ithaca, NY: Cornell University Press, 1951.

Davidson, Cathy N., and Linda Wagner-Martin. *The Oxford Companion to Women's Writing in the United States*. New York: Oxford University Press, 1995.

Davidson, Sue. *A Heart in Politics: Jeannette Rankin and Patsy T. Mink*. Seattle, WA: Seal Press, 1994.

Dary, David. *The Santa Fe Trail*. New York: Alfred P. Knopf, 2001.

Davis, Marianna W., ed. *Contributions of Black Women to America: Vol. 2, Civil Rights, Politics and Government, Education, Medicine, Sciences*. Columbia, SC: Kenday Press, 1982.

Davies, Marion. *The Time We Had*. New York: Ballantine Books, 1975.

Deacon, Desley. *Elsie Clews Parsons: Inventing Modern Life*. Chicago: University of Chicago Press, 1997.

Debo, Angie. "Jane Heard Clinton." *Chronicles of Oklahoma 24*(1, Spring 1946).

DeFleur, Dr. Lois B. *Four Years of Sex Integration at the United States Air Force Academy: Problems and Issues*. Colorado, 80840: Dean of Faculty, United States Air Force Academy, 1985.

de Graaf, Lawrence B. "Race, Sex, and Region: Black Women in the American West, 1850-1920." *Pacific Historical Review 49*(2, 1980).

de la Teja, Jésus Frank. *San Antonio de Béxar: A Community on New Spain's Northern Frontier*. Albuquerque: University of New Mexico Press, 1995.

Delly, Lillian. "Ellen Howard Miller." *Chronicles of Oklahoma 26*(2, Summer 1948).

DeMarr, Mary Jean. *Barbara Kingsolver: A Critical Companion*. Westport, CT: Greenwood Press, 1999.

Dennis, Helen May, ed. *Willa Cather and European Cultural Influences*. Studies in American Literature 16. Lewiston, NY: Mellen,1996.

Department of the Air Force, USAFA, Directorate of Plans and Programs, Deputy Chief of Staff for Operations. *Contingency Plan for Integration of Females into the Cadet Wing*. Operations Plan #7-73, December 10, 1973.

Derr, Jill Mulvay, Janath Russell Cannon, and Maureen Ursenbach Beecher. *Women of Covenant: The Story of Relief Society*. Salt Lake City, UT: Deseret Book Company, 1992.

Dethloff, Henry C. *A Special Kind of Doctor: A History of Veterinary Medicine in Texas*. College Station: Texas A&M University Press, 1991.

Deutsch, Darah. *No Separate Refuge: Culture, Class, and Gender on an Anglo-Hispanic Frontier in the American*

Southwest, 1880-1940. New York: Oxford University Press, 1887.

Dewar, Helen. "Senate Starts to Act on Judicial Nominees; Party Leaders Reach Agreement That Breaks Impasse on Confirmation Process." *Washington Post.* October 2, 1999.

Dickson, Lynda Faye. *The Early Club Movement Among Black Women in Denver, 1890-1925.* Ph.D. dissertation. University of Colorado, Boulder, 1982.

Dickstein, R., V. A. Mills, and E. J. Waite. *Women in LC's Terms: A Thesaurus of Library of Congress Subject Headings Relating to Women.* Phoenix, AZ: Oryx Press, 1988.

DiDonato, Pietro. *Immigrant Saint: The Life of Mother Cabrini.* New York: McGraw-Hill, 1960.

Diggs, Nancy Brown. *Steel Butterflies: Japanese Women and the American Experience.* Albany: State University of New York Press, 1998.

Dillon, Richard. *California Caravan: The 1846 Overland Trail Memoir of Margaret M. Hecox.* San Jose, CA: Harlan-Young Press, 1966.

Dinsmore, Maj. John C., Air Command and Staff College. *Women as Cadets: An Analysis of the Issue.* Defense Technical Information Center. Alexandria, VA: Defense Logistics Agency, 1974.

Directory of American Poets and Fiction Writers. New York: Poets & Writers, 2001.

Dobbin, Muriel. "As Voters Try to Overrule a Top Judge." *U.S. News & World Report* (December 2, 1985): 71, 73.

Douglas, Deborah G. *United States Women in Aviation.* Washington, DC: Smithsonian Institution Press, 1990.

Downey, Lynn. "Laura de Force Gordon," *American National Biography.* New York: Oxford University Press, 1999.

Drew, William M. "Speeding Sweethearts, Part VI." *New York Dramatic Mirror,* September 1, 1915.

Drew, William M. "Speeding Sweethearts, Part VII." Mary Pickford, Answers to Correspondents, Daily Talks. *Detroit News,* December 11, 1915.

Drew, William M. "Speeding Sweethearts, Part I." Gloria Swanson, *Swanson on Swanson.* New York: Random House, 1980.

Drivers.com: www.drivers.com/Top_Driving_Women.html.

Drum, Stella M., ed. *Down the Santa Fe Trail and Into Mexico: The Diary of Susan Shelby Magoffin.* New Haven, CT: Yale University Press, 1926.

Duffey, Sister Consuela Marie. *Katherine Drexel: A Biography.* Bensalem, PA: Mother Katharine Drexel Guild, 1987.

Duniway, Abigail Scott. *Path Breaking: An Autobiographical History of the Equal Suffrage Movement*

in Pacific Coast States. New York: Schocken Books, 1971.

Elias, Paul. "Berzon's 9th Circuit Bid Looks Good." *The Recorder.* June 17, 1999.

Ellis, Anne. *The Life of an Ordinary Woman.* Boston, MA: Houghton Mifflin, 1929; rpt., Lincoln: University of Nebraska Press, 1980.

Emerson, F. W. *History of the Los Angeles Sheriff's Department, 1850-1940.* Pasadena, CA: Federal Writer's Project, 1940.

Encyclopedia Louisiana. "Louisiana Timeline, 1879": www.enlou.com/time/year1879.htm.

Endicott, William, and Robert Fairbanks. "Supreme Court Decision to Reverse Gun Law Reported." *Los Angeles Times,* November 7, 1978, p. 1.

Engh, Michael E. "Mary Julia Workman, the Catholic Conscience of Los Angeles." *California History* 72(Spring 1993).

Espiritu, Yen Le. *Asian American Women and Men: Labor, Laws, and Love.* Thousand Oaks, CA: Sage, 1997.

Eversole, Dana. "She Has Surely Done Her Share: Miss Bessie Huff and the Muskogee Junior College. *Chronicles of Oklahoma* 79(4, Winter 2001-2002).

Faragher, John Mack. *Women and Men on the Overland Trail.* New Haven, CT: Yale University Press, 1979.

Farrington, Brenda. "Banking on the Court and Congress," in Gordon Morris Bakken, ed., *Law in the Western United States.* Norman: University of Oklahoma Press, 2000.

Farrington-Myers, Brenda. *Rose Bird and the Rule of Law.* Thesis. California State University, Fullerton. 1991.

Farrington-Myers, Brenda. "Credibility and Crisis in California's High Court," in John W. Johnson, ed., *Historic U.S. Court Cases: An Encyclopedia.* New York: Routledge, 2001.

Fawcett, David M., and Teri McLuhan. "Ruth Leah Bunzel," in Ute Gacs, Aisha Khan, Jerrie McIntyre, and Ruth Weinberg, eds., *Women Anthropologists: Selected Biographies.* Urbana: University of Illinois Press, 1989, 29-36.

Feitz, Leland. *Myers Avenue: A Quick History of Cripple Creek's Red-Light District.* Denver, CO: Golden Bell Press, 1967.

Fergusson, Erna. *Mexican Cookbook.* Santa Fe, NM: Rydall, 1934.

Fergusson, Erna. *New Mexico: A Pageant of Three Peoples.* New York: Knopf, 1951.

Fern M. Smith. Retrieved from air.fjc.gov/history/judges_frm.html. Source: History of the Federal Judiciary. http://www.fjc.gov. Web site of the Federal Judicial Center, Washington, D.C.

Ferrar, Ann. *Hear Me Roar: Women, Motorcycles, and the Rapture of the Road* (2d ed.). North Conway, NH: Whitehorse Press, 2001.

Ferrar, Miranda H. *The Writers Directory 2001*. Detroit, MI: St. James Press, 2001.

Finn, Janet L. *Tracing the Veins of Copper, Culture, and Community From Butte to Chuquicamata*. Berkeley: University of California Press, 1998.

"First Female Astronaut Still Hoping to Go Up: Jerrie Cobb." *CNN Science-Technology:* www.cnn.com/TECH/space/9810/28/first.woman.astronaut.

Fisher-Sipuel, Ada Lois. *A Matter of Black & White: The Autobiography of Ada Lois Sipuel Fisher*. Norman: University of Oklahoma Press, 1996.

Flanner, Hildegarde. *Mansions: A Play in One Act*. Cincinnati, OH: Stewart & Kidd, 1920.

Flanner, Hildegarde. *Younger Girl and Other Poems*. San Francisco: Crocker, 1920.

Flanner, Hildegarde. *A Tree in Bloom and Other Verses*. San Francisco. Lantern Press, 1924.

Flanner, Hildegarde. *Time's Profile*. New York: Macmillan, 1929.

Flanner, Hildegarde. *The White Bridge: A Play in One Act*. New York: Appleton, 1938.

Flanner, Hildegarde. *A Vanishing Land*. Portola Valley, CA: No Dead Lines, 1980

Flanner, Hildegarde. *Brief Cherishing: A Napa Valley Harvest*. Santa Barbara, CA: John Daniel, 1985.

Flexner, Eleanor, and Ellen Fitzpatrick. *Century of Struggle: The Woman's Rights Movement in the United States*. London: Belknap Press, 1959.

Folts, John, M.D., and Arthur Klatsky, M.D. *Wine's Heart Disease Benefits Most Pronounced in Women*. American College of Cardiology Meeting, March 1997 (Vol. 3, No. 8).

Foote, Cheryl J. *Women of the New Mexico Frontier, 1846-1912*. Niwot: University Press of Colorado, 1990.

Foreman, Carolyn Thomas. "Aunt Eliza of Tahlequah." *Chronicles of Oklahoma* 9(1, March 1931).

Foreman, Carolyn Thomas. "Augusta Robertson Moore: A Sketch of Her Life and Times." *Chronicles of Oklahoma* 13(4, December 1935).

Foreman, Carolyn Thomas. "Mrs. Laura E. Harsha." *Chronicles of Oklahoma* 18(2, June 1940).

Foreman, Carolyn Thomas. "Alice Ross Howard." *Chronicles of Oklahoma* 23(3, Autumn 1945).

Foreman, Grant. "The Honorable Alice M. Robertson." *Chronicles of Oklahoma* 10(1, March 1932).

Fowler, Catherine S. "Sara Winnemucca Northern Paiute, ca. 1844-1891." In Margot Liberty, ed., *American Indian Intellectuals*. St. Paul, MN: West Publishing, 1978.

Franck, Irene M., and David M. Brownstone. *The Wilson Chronology of Women's Achievements*. New York: H. W. Wilson, 1998.

Franson, Paul. "Wine, Women and Strong." *San Francisco Examiner*, July 5, 2001.

Freedman, Estelle B. *Their Sister's Keepers: Women's Prison Reform in America, 1830-1930*. Ann Arbor: University of Michigan Press, 1981.

Friday, Chris. "Recasting Identities: American-born Chinese and Nisei in the Era of the Pacific War," in Richard White and John M. Findlay, eds., *Power and Place in the North American West*. Seattle: University of Washington Press, 1999.

Fryer, Judith. *Felicitous Space: The Imaginative Structures of Edith Wharton and Willa Cather*. Chapel Hill: University of North Carolina Press, 1986.

Funk, Wally. "The Ninety-Nines: Wally Funk, Air Safety Investigator": www.ninety-nines.org/funk.htm.

Gabriel, Barbara A. "In Their Footsteps: The First Women Physicians and the Pioneers Who Followed Them": www.aamc.org/newsroom/reporter/dec01/womenphysicians.htm.

Gale Group UXL Biographies. "Nancy Ward: Cherokee Tribal Leader 1738-1824," Celebrating Women's History Month 1996: www.roup.com/freresrc/womenhst/bio/ward.htm

Gall, Susan B., and Helen Zia. "Joyce Kennard." *Notable Asian Americans*. New York: Gale Research, 1995.

Garcia, S. A. "Indexing Patterns of Periodical Literature on African American Women and U.S. Latinas," in K. H. Gerhard, ed., *Women's Studies Serials: A Quarter Century of Development*. New York: Haworth Press, 1988, 167-196.

Gardner, Ann L. *Kansas Women*. Lawrence: Kansas Key Press, 1986.

Gates, Susa Young. *History of Young Ladie's Mutual Improvement Association of the Church of Jesus Christ of Latter Day Saints*. Salt Lake City, UT: Deseret News, 1911.

Gates, Susa Young. *The Life Story of Brigham Young*. New York: Macmillan, 1930.

Gayle, Mary Redus. *Glass Paperweights From the Estelle Doheny Collection at St. John's Seminary, Camarillo, California and St. Mary's of the Barrens Seminary, Perryville, Missouri*. Ephrata, PA: Science Press, 1971.

Gelfant, Blanche. "The Forgotten Reaping-Hook: Sex in *My Ántonia*." *American Literature* 43 (1971).

Geraci, Victor W. *Grape Growing to Vintibusiness: A History of the Santa Barbara, California, Regional Wine Industry, 1965-1995.* Ph.D. dissertation. University of California, Santa Barbara, 1997. Forthcoming untitled monograph by the University of Nevada Press.

Gerber, Philip L. *Willa Cather.* New York: Twayne, 1995.

Gerhard, K. H., T. E. Jacobson, and S. G. Williamson. "Indexing Adequacy and Interdisciplinary Journals: The Case of Women's Studies." *College & Research Libraries* 54(2), 1993.

George, Susanne, Ph.D. "The Classic Journey of a Woman Homesteader: The Travel Theme in Elinore Pruitt Stewart": www.unk.edu/acad/english/faculty/bloomfields/Stewart/EPSTravel.htm.

Gere, Anne Ruggles. *Intimate Practices: Literacy and Cultural Work in U.S. Women's Clubs, 1880-1920.* Urbana: University of Illinois, 1997.

Giannone, Richard. *Music in Willa Cather's Fiction.* Lincoln: University of Nebraska Press, 1968.

Gibson, A. M. "Prehistory of Oklahoma." *Chronicles of Oklahoma 43*(1, Spring 1965).

Giles, Kevin S. *Flight of the Dove: The Story of Jeannette Rankin.* Beaverton, OR: Lochsa Experience Publishers, 1980.

Gilmour, Terry L. *A Difference: Women in the Texas Legislature.* Ph.D. dissertation. Texas Technical University, 1999.

Godwin, Michelle Gerise. "The Progressive Interview: Sarah Weddington," *The Progressive 64*(8, August 2000.

Goldberg, Michael Lewis. *An Army of Women: Gender and Politics in Gilded Age Kansas.* Baltimore, MD: Johns Hopkins University Press, 1997.

Goldman, Marion. *Gold Diggers and Silver Miners: Prostitution and Society on the Comstock Lode.* Ann Arbor: University of Michigan Press, 1981.

Gordon, Lynn D. *Gender and Higher Education in the Progressive Era.* New Haven. CT: Yale University Press, 1990.

Goetz, Henry Kilian. "Kate's Quarter Section: A Woman in the Cherokee Strip." *Chronicles of Oklahoma 61(3,* Fall 1983).

Gordon, Sarah Barringer. *The Mormon Question: Polygamy and Constitutional Conflict in Nineteenth Century America.* Chapel Hill: University of North Carolina Press, 2002.

Gould, Florence C., and Patricia N. Pando. *Claiming Their Land: Women Homesteaders in Texas.* El Paso: Texas Western Press, 1991.

Graves, Carl R. "The Right to be Served: Oklahoma City's Lunch Counter Sit-Ins, 1958-1964." *Chronicles of Oklahoma 59(2,* Summer 1981).

Gravitt, Winnie Lewis. "Anna Lewis: A Great Woman of Oklahoma." *Chronicles of Oklahoma 40*(4, Winter 1962-1963).

Gray, Janet, ed. *She Wields a Pen: American Women Poets of the Nineteenth Century.* Iowa City: University of Iowa Press, 1997.

Gray, John S. "The Story of Mrs. Picotte-Galpin, a Sioux Heroine." *Montana: The Magazine of Western History 36* (Summer 1986).

Greeley, Horace. *Proceedings of the Women's Rights Convention, Cleveland, Ohio, 1853.* Cleveland, OH: Gray, Beardsley, Spear, 1854.

Griffen, Joyce. "Ruth Murray Underhill," in Ute Gacs, Aisha Khan, Jerrie McIntyre, and Ruth Weinberg. eds., *Women Anthropologists: Selected Biographies.* Urbana: University of Illinois Press, 1989.

Grossom, Janet, "A New Honor in Newhall." *The Signal* (July 15, 1998).

Grunwald, Michael. "Coming Up Short on an Appeals Circuit; Labor Lawyer's Nomination Is Latest Casualty of Ideological Fight, Clinton Woes." *Washington Post.* October 6, 1998.

Guide to Butte County. "Paradise in Northern California": www.paradisedirect.com/paradise/butte.html.

Gullett, Gayle. *Becoming Citizens: The Emergence and Development of the California Women's Movement, 1880-1911.* Urbana: University of Illinois Press, 2000.

Gullett, Gayle. "Women Progressives and the Politics of Americanization in California, 1915-1920." *Pacific Historical Review 64*(1, 1995): 71-94.

Haarsager, Sandra. *Organized Womanhood: Cultural Politics in the Pacific Northwest, 1840-1920.* Norman: University of Oklahoma Press, 1997.

Haas, Lisbeth. *Conquests and Historical Identities in California, 1769-1936.* Berkeley: University of California Press, 1995.

Hackett, Sheila. *Dominican Women in Texas: From Ohio to Galveston and Beyond.* Houston, TX: D. Armstrong, 1986.

Hale, Janet Campbell, and Karen M. Strom. "Janet Campbell Hale": www.hanksville.org/storytellers/jchale.

Hamburg, Jill. "Raising Oklahoma: A Devastated City Gets a New Look." *Working Woman* (October 1998).

Hamilton, Anne M. "A Daring Young Girl on the Flying Trapeze of Life." *Hartford Courant,* September 30, 2001, p. H2.

The Handbook of Texas Online. www.tsha.utexas.edu/handbook/online.

Handler, Ruth, with Jacqueline Shannon. *Dream Doll: The Ruth Handler Story*. Stamford, CT: Longmeadow Press, 1994.

Hansen, Debra, Karen F. Gracy, and Sheri D. Irvin. "At the Pleasure of the Board: Women Librarians and the Los Angeles Public Library, 1880-1905." *Libraries and Culture 34* (1999): 311-347.

Hardin, Margaret Ann. "Zuni Potters and the Pueblo Potter: The Contributions of Ruth Bunzel," in Nancy Parezo, ed., *Hidden Scholars: Women Anthropologists and the Native American Southwest*. Albuquerque: University of New Mexico Press, 1993, 259-69.

Harding, Jan, ed. *Perspective on Gender and Science*. London: Falmer Press, 1986.

Harjo, Joy, and Gloria Bird, eds. *Reinventing the Enemy's Language*. New York: Norton, 1997.

Harries, Keith D., and H. Wayne Morgan, eds. "Land and Climate." *World Book Encyclopedia*. 1999.

Harris, Katherine. *Long Vistas: Women and Families on Colorado Homesteads*. Niwot: University Press of Colorado, 1993.

Harris, Ted Carlton. *Jeannette Rankin: Suffragist, First Woman Elected to Congress, and Pacifist*. New York: Arno Press, 1982.

Harris, Walter. "Margie E. Neal: First Woman Senator in Texas." *East Texas Historical Journal 11* (Spring 1973).

Harvard University's Cather Web Site: http://lcg.harvard.edu/~cather/home.html.

Hasselstrom, Linda M. *Going Over East: Reflections of a Woman Rancher*. Golden, CO: Fulcrum, 1987.

Hawkins, Renee Frances. "Laura de Force Gordon: Fragments of a Feminist Pioneer": www.stanford.edu/group/WLHP/papers/gordon.html.

Hayes, Tim, and John Koetzner. "Wine Tributaries": www.wines.com.

Hearst Castle. "Phoebe Apperson Hearst": www.hearstcastle.org/history/phoebe_hearst.asp.

Hecox Family Miscellany. "Adna A. Hecox Family". http://home.earthlink.net/~butlers/hecox-misc.html.

Helen Sewell: http://webpages.marshall.edu/~irby1/laura/sewell.html.

Helm, Mark. "Boxer Forces Vote on Stalled Judicial Nominations; Lott Caves In When Friend Became a Casualty." *San Francisco Examiner*, November 13, 1999.

Herr, Pamela. "Reformer," in *Western Writers of America: Women Who Made the West*. Garden City, NY: Doubleday, 1980.

Hicks, Jack. *Literature of California*. Berkeley: University of California Press, 2000.

Herring, Rebecca. "Their Work Was Never Done: Women Missionaries on the Kiowa-Comanche Reservation." *Chronicles of Oklahoma 64*(1, Spring 1986): 68-83.

Hildenbrand, Kathleen. "Big Trouble in Little Tulsa: It Was One of the Nation's Worst Outbreaks of Racial Violence." *Alice 1*(1, January 31, 2000).

Hildenbrand, Suzanne. "A Historical Perspective on Gender Issues in American Librarianship." *Canadian Journal of Information Science 17* (September 1992).

Hildenbrand, Suzanne. *Reclaiming the Library Past: Writing the Women in*. Norwood, NJ: Ablex, 1996.

Hill, Anita. "Anita Hill," in Brian Lamb, ed., *Booknotes Life Stories: Notable Biographers on the People Who Shaped America*. New York: Times Books, 1992.

Hine, Darlene Clark, ed. *Black Women in America: An Historical Encyclopedia*, Vols. 1 & 2. New York: Carlson, 1993.

Hine, Robert V. *The American West: An Interpretive History*. New York: Little, Brown, 1975.

H-Net. Humanities and Social Sciences Online: www2.h-net.msu.edu/~women/blbs.

Ho, Wendy Ann "Mother and Daughter Writing and the Politics of Location in Maxine Hong Kingston's *The Woman Warrior* and Amy Tan's *The Joy Luck Club*." *DAI 54.7* (January 1994): DAI Number 9320902.

Hoder-Salmon, Marilyn. "Myrtle Archer McDougal: Leader of Oklahoma's Timid Sisters." *Chronicles of Oklahoma 60*(3, Fall 1982).

Hogan, Linda. *Calling Myself Home*. Greenfield Center, NY: Greenfield Review Press, 1978.

Hogan, Linda. *Mean Spirit*. New York: Atheneum. 1990.

Hogan, Linda. *Power*. New York: Norton. 1998.

Hogan, Linda. *The Woman Who Watches Over the World*. New York: Norton. 2001.

Hogsett, Vernetta Murchison. *The Golden Years: A History of the Idaho Federation of Women's Clubs*, 1905-1955. Caldwell, ID: Caxton, 1955.

Hoig, Stan. *Tribal Wars of the Southern Plains*. Norman: University of Oklahoma Press, 1993.

Holden, Eunah Temple. *Our Heritage in the Delta Kappa Gamma Society*. Austin, TX: Delta Kappa Gamma Society, 1960; rpt. 1970.

Holdredge, Helen. *Mammy Pleasant*. New York: Putnam, 1953.

Holdredge, Helen. *Mammy Pleasant's Partner*. New York: Putnam, 1954.

Holdredge, Helen. *Mammy Pleasant's Cookbook*. San Francisco: 101 Productions, 1970.

Holmes, Kenneth L., and David Duniway. *Covered Wagon Women: Diaries & Letters from the Western Trails, 1840-1849.* Glendale, CA: Arthur H. Clark, 1983.

Hornbein, Marjorie. "Frances Jacobs: Denver's Mother of Charities." *Western States Jewish Historical Quarterly 15*(2, 1983).

Horne, Peter. *Women in Law Enforcement.* Springfield, IL: Charles C. Thomas Publishers, 1975.

Horner, Louise L., ed. *Black Americans: A Statistical Sourcebook.* Palo Alto, CA: Information Publications, 1999.

Horton, Joey Dean. "'Girl' Lawyer Makes Good: The Story of Annette Abbott Adams": www.stanford.edu/group/WLHP/papers/aaahtml.html

Houghton, Eliza P. *Donner. The Expedition of the Donner Party and Its Tragic Fate.* Chicago: A. C. McClurg, 1911.

Howarth, William. "The Country of Willa Cather." Photos by Farrell Grehan. *National Geographic 162* (July 1982).

Huntley, E. D. *Maxine Hong Kingston: A Critical Companion.* Westport, CT: Greenwood Press, 2001.

Huntley, Ed. *Amy Tan, A Critical Companion.* Westport, CT: Greenwood Press, 1998.

Hutson, Jan. *The Chicken Ranch: The True Story of the Best Little Whorehouse in Texas.* Cranbury, NJ: Barnes, 1980.

Illston, Susan Yvonne. Retrieved from air.fjc.gov/servlet/tGetInfo?jid=1143. Source: *History of the Federal Judiciary.* http://www.fjc.gov. Web site of the Federal Judicial Center, Washington, D.C.

Indian Country Today: www.indiancountry.com/?author=44.

Intner, S. S., and E. Futas. "The Role and Impact of Library of Congress Classification on the Assessment of Women's Studies Collections." *Library Acquisitions: Practice & Theory, 20*(3), 1996.

Irma Elsa Gonzalez. Retrieved March 23, 2002, from air.fjc.gov/newweb/jnetweb.nsf/fjc_bio. Source: History of the Federal Judiciary. http://www.fjc.gov. Web site of the Federal Judicial Center, Washington, D.C.

Ireland, Norma Olin. *Index to Women of the World from Ancient to Modern Times: A Supplement.* Westwood, MA: F. W. Faxon, 1970.

Irwin, Mary Ann. "'Going About and Doing Good': The Politics of Benevolence, Welfare, and Gender in San Francisco, 1850-1880." *Pacific Historical Review 68*(3, 1999).

Ivins, Molly. "'Dissent' Is Not a Dirty Word": www.dfw.com/mld/startelegram/news/columnists/molly_ivins/3056069.ht . . ./printstory.js.

Jackson, Hugh. "The History of Volunteering in Wyoming." *Annals of Wyoming 59*(1, 1987).

Jackson, Joe. "Dr. Emma Estill-Harbour, 1884-1967." *Chronicles of Oklahoma 45*(2, Summer 1967).

Jacobs, Jane, ed. *A Schoolteacher in Old Alaska: The Story of Hanna Breece.* New York: Vintage Books, 1997.

Jaffe, A. J. *The First Immigrants from Asia: A Population History of the North American Indians.* New York: Plenum, 1992.

James Edward Ferguson Collection, Barker Texas History Center, University of Texas, Austin.

James, Louise Boyd. "The Woman Suffrage Issue in Oklahoma's Constitutional Convention." *Chronicles of Oklahoma 64*(4, Winter 1978-1979).

James, Parthena Louise. "Reconstruction in the Chickasaw Nation: The Freedmen Problem." *Chronicles of Oklahoma 45*(1, Spring 1967).

James, Ronald M., and Elizabeth C. Raymond, eds. *Comstock Women: The Making of a Mining Community.* Reno: University of Nevada Press, 1997.

Jameson, Elizabeth, and Susan Armitage, eds. *The Women's West.* Norman: University of Oklahoma Press, 1987.

Jameson, Elizabeth. *All That Glitters: Class, Conflict, and Community in Cripple Creek.* Urbana: University of Illinois Press, 1998.

Jensen, Joan M. "After Slavery: Caroline Severance in Los Angeles," *Southern California Quarterly 48* (June 1966).

Jensen, Joan, and Darlis Miller, eds. *New Mexico Women: Intercultural Perspectives.* Albuquerque: University of New Mexico Press, 1986.

Jensen, Richard L. "Forgotten Relief Societies, 1844-67." *Dialogue 16*(1, 1983).

John, Angela V. *By the Sweat of Their Brow: Women Workers at Victorian Coal Mines.* London: Croom Helm, 1980.

Johnson, Kristin. *Donner Party Bulletin, Issue No.1, September/October, 1997:* www.utahcrossroads.org/DonnerParty/Bulletin1.htm.

Johnson, Kristin. *Donner Party Bulletin, Issue No. 3, January/February, 1998.* www.utahcrossroads.org/DonnerParty/Bulletin1.htm.

Johnson, Susan Lee. *Roaring Camp: The Social World of the California Gold Rush.* New York: Norton, 2000.

Jordan, Barbara, and Shelby Hearon. *Barbara Jordan: A Self-Portrait.* Garden City, NY: Doubleday, 1979.

Jordan, Teresa. *Cowgirls: Women of the American West.* Lincoln: University of Nebraska Press, 1992.

Josephson, Hannah Geffen. *Jeannette Rankin, First Lady in Congress: A Biography.* Indianapolis, IN: Bobbs-Merrill, 1974.

Judicial Council of California. "Associate Justice Janice Rogers Brown": www.courtinfo.ca.gov/courts/supreme/justices/brown.htm.

Judith N. Keep: http://air.fjc.gov/servlet/tGetInfo?jid=1241.

Just the Beginning Foundation: www.jtbf.org.

Kammen, Robert, Frederick Lefthand, and Joe Marshall. *Soldiers Falling Into Camp: The Battles at the Rosebud and the Little Big Horn*. Encampment, WY: Affiliated Writers of America, 1992.

Kamp, Jim, and Telgen, Dianne. "Lourdes Baird." *Notable Hispanic American Women*. Detroit, MI: Gale Research, 1993.

Kansas State Historical Society, "People in Kansas History": www.kshs.org.

Karlsberg, Elizabeth. "The Smell of Success." *Santa Barbara News-Press* Magazine (Fall 1997): 18-19, 22, 25.

Kate Douglas Wiggin. Knowledgerush Book Directory: www.knowledgerush.com/kr/jsp/db/author.jsp?authorId=116.

Kate Douglas Wiggin: http://download.franklin.com/cgi-bin/franklin/ebookman_free_preview?vilwt10.

Kathleen E. O'Leary, Associate Justice: www.courtinfo.ca.gov/courts/courtsofappeal/4thDistrictDiv3/justices/oleary.htm.

Kathryn Mickle Werdegar: www.courtinfo.ca.gov.

Kaufman, Polly Welts, *Women Teachers on the Frontier*. New Haven, CT: Yale University Press, 1984.

Keller, Rosemary Skinner, and Rosemary Radford Ruether, eds. *In Our Own Voices: Four Centuries of American Women's Religious Writing*. San Francisco: Harper, 1995.

Kelly, Brendan. "Inspirations." *Variety* 368(10, October 13, 1997): 100.

Kelley, Mary L. *Private Wealth, Public Good: The Origins and Legacy of Foundation Philanthropy in Texas, 1920-1970*. Ph.D. dissertation. Texas Christian University, Fort Worth, Texas, 2000.

Kennedy, Ruth A. ed. *The American Bench: Judges of the Nation, 1997/1998* (9th ed.). Sacramento, CA: Forster-Long, 1997.

Kessell, John L. *Spain in the Southwest: A Narrative History of Colonial New Mexico, Arizona, Texas and California*. Norman: University of Oklahoma Press, 2002.

Kessler, Lauren. *Stubborn Twig: Three Generations in the Life of a Japanese Family*. New York: Random House, 1993.

Kessler, Lauren. *The Happy Bottoms Riding Club: The Life and Times of Pancho Barnes*. New York: Random House, 2000.

Kingsolver, Barbara. *The Bean Trees*. New York: Harper & Row, 1988.

Kingsolver, Barbara. *Homeland and Other Stories*. New York: Harper & Row, 1989.

Kingsolver, Barbara. *Animal Dreams*. New York: HarperCollins, 1990.

Kingsolver, Barbara. *Pigs in Heaven*. New York: HarperCollins, 1993.

Kingsolver, Barbara. *The Poisonwood Bible*. New York: HarperCollins, 1998.

Kingsolver, Barbara. *Prodigal Summer*. New York: HarperCollins, 2000.

Kisliuk, Bill. "Marsha Berzon Nominated to Ninth Circuit." *The Recorder*, January 28, 1998.

Kloppenberg, Lisa A. "A Mentor of Her Own": law.utoledo.edu/lawreview/publication_archives/v33_n1_fall2001/koppenberg.htm.

Knight, Lucian Lamar, ed. *Biographical Dictionary of Southern Authors*. Detroit, MI: Gale Research, 1978.

Knight, Oliver. *Life and Manners in the Frontier Army*. Norman: University of Oklahoma Press, 1978.

Korytová-Magstadt, Štepánka. *To Reap a Bountiful Harvest: Czech Immigration Beyond the Mississippi, 1850-1900*. Iowa City, IA: Rudi Publishing, 1993.

Kraditor, Aileen S. *The Ideas of the Woman Suffrage Movement: 1890-1920*. New York: Norton, 1981.

Kreider, Marie L., and Michael R. Wells, eds. "White Ribbon Women: The Women's Christian Temperance Movement In Riverside, California." *Southern California Quarterly 81* (Spring 1999).

La Botz, Dan. *Edward L. Doheny: Petroleum, Power, and Politics in the United States and Mexico*. New York: Praeger, 1991.

Lacayo, Richard. "Shaking the Judicial Perch." *Time* (September 15, 1986).

Lady Truck Drivers.com. "The First Lady Truck Driver": Retrieved from www.ladytruckdrivers.com/firstladytrck-driver.htm.

Lane, Rose Wilder. "Drive Like a Woman!" *Good Housekeeping*, January 1939.

Langdon, Emma F. *The Cripple Creek Strike: A History of Industrial Wars in Colorado*. Denver, CO: Great Western, 1904-1905; rpt., New York: Arno Press and the *New York Times*, 1969.

Langum, David J. *Law and Community of the Mexican California Frontier: Anglo-American Expatriates and the Clash of Legal Traditions, 1821-1846*. Norman: University of Oklahoma Press, 1987.

La Rocca, Linda. Review of *Bitter Creek Junction* by Linda M. Hasselstrom: www.cozine.com/archive/cc2000/00780448.htm.

Larralde, Carlos, and Richard Griswold del Castillo. "Luisa Moreno: A Hispanic Civil Rights Leader in San Diego." *Journal of San Diego History 41*(4, Fall 1995).

Larralde, Carlos, and Richard Griswold del Castillo. "Luisa Moreno and the Beginnings of the Mexican American

Civil Rights Movement." *Journal of San Diego History* 43(3, Summer 1997).

Leacock, Eleanor. "Gladys Amanda Reichard," in Ute Gacs, Aisha Khan, Jerrie McIntyre, and Ruth Weinberg, eds., *Women Anthropologists: Selected Biographies.* Urbana: University of Illinois Press, 1989.

Leckie, William H., and Shirley A. Leckie. *Unlikely Warriors: General Benjamin H. Grierson and His Family.* Norman: University of Oklahoma Press, 1984.

LeCompte, Mary Lou. *Cowgirls of the Rodeo: Pioneer Professional Athletes.* Urbana: University of Illinois Press, 1993.

Lee, Hermione. *Willa Cather: Double Lives.* Chapel Hill: University of North Carolina Press, 1989.

Lee, Joann Faung Jean. *Asian American Experiences in the United States: Oral Histories of First to Fourth Generation Americans from China, the Philippines, Japan, India, the Pacific Islands, Vietnam, and Cambodia.* Jefferson, NC: McFarland, 1991.

Lee, Josephine Ding. *Performing Asian America: Race and Ethnicity on the Contemporary Stage.* Philadelphia, PA: Temple University Press, 1997.

Lee, Mabel Barbee. *Cripple Creek Days.* Garden City, NY: Doubleday, 1958.

Lee, Mike. "Women to Be Toast of Wine Event." *Tri-City Herald* (Washington State) (August 15, 2001).

Lemonds, Leo L. *A Century of Veterinary Medicine in Nebraska.* Hastings, NE: L. Lemonds, 1982.

Lensink, J. N. "Beyond the Intellectual Meridian: Transdisciplinary Studies of Women." *Pacific Historical Review 61,* 1992

Levy, Joann. *They Saw the Elephant: Women in the California Gold Rush.* Hamden, CT: Archon Books, 1990.

Lewis, Anna. "Jane McCurtain." *Chronicles of Oklahoma 11*(4, December 1933).

Lewis, Daniel. Forensics II, "The Donner Party":http:// raiboy.tripod.com/Donner/id16.html.

Lewis, Edith. *Willa Cather Living.* Lincoln: University of Nebraska Press, 1953.

Liberty, Margot. "Hell Came With Horses: Plains Indian Women in the Equestrian Era." *Montana: The Magazine of Western History 32* (Summer 1982).

Lichtenstein, Grace. "The Evolution of a Craft Tradition: Three Generations of Navajo Women." *Ms. 11* (April 1983).

Limerick, P. N. "Going West and Ending Up Global." *Western Historical Quarterly, 32*(1), 2001.

Linda Hodge McLaughlin: http://air.fjc.gov/servlet/ tGetInfo?jid=1578.

Linda M. Hasselstrom: www.netwalk.com/~vireo/hasselstrom.html.

Lindgren, H. Elaine. *Land in Her Own Name: Women Homesteaders in North Dakota.* Fargo: North Dakota Institute for Regional Studies, 1991.

Lindeman, Marilee. *Willa Cather: Queering America.* New York: Columbia University Press, 1999.

Ling, Amy, ed. *Between Worlds: Women Writers of Chinese Ancestry.* New York: Pergamon Press, 1990.

Ling, Amy. "Maxine Hong Kingston and the Dialogic Dilemma of Asian American Writers." *Bucknell Review 39*(1, 1995).

"Local Women Named Outstanding Young Oklahomans." *Cherokee Advocate 22*(3-4, April 30, 1998).

Lodestar Olive Oil. "Tradition": www.lodestarfarms.com/ tradition/index.html.

"Lookout Named Vice President of Greenwood Systems." *Oklahoma Indian Times 6*(7, July 31, 2000).

Lothrop, Gloria Ricci. "Strength Made Stronger: The Role of Women in Southern California Philanthropy." *Southern California Quarterly 71*(2-3, 1989).

Lothrop, Gloria, and Thelma Lee Hubbell. "The Friday Morning Club: A Los Angeles Legacy," *Southern California Quarterly 50* (March 1968).

Lourdes G. Baird. Retrieved from air.fjc.gov/servlet/ tGetInfo?jid=77. Source: History of the Federal Judiciary. http://www.fjc.gov. Web site of the Federal Judicial Center, Washington, D.C.

Lowe, Jennifer. "Sweetie Pie." *Orange County Register,* November 11, 1998.

Lowe, Lisa. *Immigrant Acts: On Asian American Cultural Politics.* Durham, NC: Duke University Press, 1996.

Luchetti, Cathy. *Medicine Women: The Story of Early-American Women Doctors.* New York: Crown, 1998.

Luckingham, Bradford. "Benevolence in Emergent San Francisco: A Note on Immigrant Life in the Urban Far West." *Southern California Quarterly 55*(Winter 1973).

Ludgate, Thomas B., and Janice Ludgate Kitzler. *The Prairie Practitioners: 20th Century South Dakota Veterinarians.* Freeman, SD: Pine Hill Press, 1996.

Lykes, Aimée de Potter. "Phoenix Women in the Development of Public Policy: Territorial Beginnings," in G. Wesley Johnson Jr., ed., *Phoenix in the Twentieth Century: Essays in Community History.* Norman: University of Oklahoma Press, 1993.

Mabry, Russ. "Woodruff Elected New Mayor of Wilburton." *Latimer County News 106*(2, January 10, 2002).

Madsen, Carol Cornwall. "Decade of Detente: Mormon/ Gentile Female Relationship in Nineteenth Century Utah." *Utah Historical Quarterly 63* (Fall 1995).

Madsen, Deborah. *Literary Masters: Maxine Hong Kingston.* Vol. 9. Detroit, MI: Gale Group, 2000.

Mah, Adeline Yen. *Falling Leaves: The True Story of an Unwanted Chinese Daughter.* New York: Broadway Books, 1999.

Mainiero, Lisa. *American Women Writers: A Critical Reference Guide from Colonial Times to the Present.* New York: Ungar, 1979-1994.

Malinowski, Sharon, and George H. J. Abrams. *Notable Native Americans.* New York: Gale Research, 1995.

Malinowski, Sharon, and Simon Glickman, eds. *Native North American Biography.* New York: Gale Research, 1996.

Mann, Ralph Emerson. *After the Gold Rush: Society in Grass Valley and Nevada City, California, 1849-1870.* Stanford, CA: Stanford University Press, 1982.

March Fong Eu: A Career of Breaking Barriers: www.smartvoter.org/2002/03/05/ca/state/vote/eu_m/bio.html.

March, John. *A Reader's Companion to the Fiction of Willa Cather,* Marilyn Arnold, ed. Westport, CT: Greenwood, 1999.

Margie E. Neal Papers, Barker Texas History Center, University of Texas at Austin.

Marilyn Hall Patel: http://air.fjc.gov/servlet/tGetInfo?jid=1846.

Marilyn M. Huff: http://air.fjc.gov/servlet/tGetInfo?jid=1110.

Mark, Daniel. *Sister Aimee: The Life of Aimee Semple McPherson.* New York: Epstein Harcourt Brace Jovanovich, 1993.

Martin, Mart. *The Almanac of Women and Minorities in American Politics 2002.* Boulder, CO: Westview Press, 2001.

Martin, Patricia Preciado. *Songs My Mother Sang to Me: An Oral History of Mexican American Women.* Tucson: University of Arizona Press, 1996.

Mathes, Valerie Sherer. *Helen Hunt Jackson and Her Indian Reform Legacy.* Austin: University of Texas Press, 1990; Reprint with new preface, Norman: University of Oklahoma Press, 1997.

Mathes, Valerie Sherer. "Helen Hunt Jackson: Official Agent to the California Mission Indians," in Doyce B. Nunis Jr., ed., *Women in the Life of Southern California.* Los Angeles: Historical Society of Southern California, 1996.

Mathes, Valerie Sherer. *The Indian Reform Letters of Helen Hunt Jackson, 1879-1885.* Norman: University of Oklahoma Press, 1998.

Matthews, Jayson. "Grape Expectations for Women in Wine": www.coastnews.com.

Matsumoto, Valerie. *Farming the Home Place: A Japanese American Community in California, 1919-1982.* Ithaca, NY: Cornell University Press, 1993.

Matsumoto, Valerie J. "Japanese American Women and the Creation of Urban Nisei Culture in the 1930s," in Valerie J. Matsumoto and Blake Allmendinger. eds., *Over the Edge: Remapping the American West.* Berkeley: University of California Press, 1999.

Matuz, Roger, ed. *St. James Guide to Native North American Artists.* Detroit, MI: St. James, 1998.

Maurer, Al. "Solving the Controversy of Female Cadets." *Talon* (May 1973)

Maxine M. Chesney: http://air.fjc.gov/newweb/jnetweb.nsf/fjc_bio.

Maxine Waters Official Biography: www.house.gov/waters/bio.htm.

"Mayors Convene in Denver," *Sacramento Observer.* May 12, 1999, p. A12.

McBride, Genevieve. *On Wisconsin Women: Working for Their Rights From Settlement to Suffrage.* Madison: University of Wisconsin Press, 1994.

McCarthy, Kathleen D., ed. *Lady Bountiful Revisited: Women, Philanthropy, and Power.* New Brunswick, NJ: Rutgers University Press, 1990.

McConnell, Curt. *A Reliable Car and a Woman Who Knows It: The First Coast-To-Coast Auto Trips by Women, 1899-1916.* Jefferson, NC: McFarland, 2000.

McDonald, Joyce. *The Stuff of Our Forebears: Willa Cather's Southern Heritage.* Tuscaloosa: University of Alabama Press, 1998.

McFerren, Martha. *Women in Cars.* Kansas City, MO: Helicon Nine Editions, 1992.

McGlashan, Charles Fayette. *History of the Donner Party: A Tragedy of the Sierra.* Stanford, CA: Stanford University Press, 1968.

McMillan, Ethel. "Women Teachers in Oklahoma, 1820-1860." *Chronicles of Oklahoma* 27(1, Spring 1949).

Medsger, Emily. *Framed: The New Right Attack on Chief Justice Rose Bird and the Courts.* New York: Pilgrim Press, 1983.

Mercier, Laurie K. "We Are Women Irish: Gender, Class, and Ethnic Identity in Anaconda, Montana." *Montana: The Magazine of Western History* 44(1, 1994).

Mercier, Laurie. *Anaconda: Labor, Community, and Culture in Montana's Smelter City.* Urbana: University of Illinois Press, 2001.

Metropolitan News-Enterprise, March 29, 1996.

Miller, Bertha E. Mahony. *Illustrators of Children's Books 1744-1945.* Boston, MA: Horn Book, 1947.

Miller, Carol. "Mediation and Authority: The Native American Voices of Mourning Dove and Ella Deloria."

In James A. Banks, ed., *Multicultural Education, Transformative Knowledge, and Action*. New York: Teachers College Press, 1996.

Miller, Darlis A. *Mary Hallock Foote, Author-Illustrator of the American West*. Norman: University of Oklahoma Press, 2002.

Miller, Lucille V. *The Book as a Work of Art*. Los Angeles: Ward Ritchie, 1935.

Mills, Ava E., ed. *A Legacy of Words: Texas Women's Stories, 1850-1920*. San Angelo, TX: Doss Books, 1999.

Mills, Kay. "Maxine Waters: The Sassy Legislator Who Knows There Is More Than One Way to Make a Political Statement." *Governing 1*(6, March 1998).

Mills, Kenneth, and William B. Taylor, eds. *Colonial Spanish America: A Documentary History*. Wilmington, DE: Scholarly Books, 1998.

"Miss America Pageant": www.pressplus.com/missam/pastwinners.

Miss Margie Neal: www.carthagetexas.com/neal.htm.

Moline, Norman T. *Mobility and the Small Town 1900-1930*. Chicago: University of Chicago, 1971.

Molly Ivins to Speak at Smith College as One of Four Outstanding Alumnae to Be Honored: www.smith.edu/newsoffice/Releases/00-053.html.

Monaghan, Jay. *The Overland Trail*. Indianapolis, IN: Bobbs-Merrill, 1947.

Moon, Danelle. "Educational Housekeepers: Female Reformers and the California Americanization Program, 1900-1927," in Gordon Morris Bakken, ed., *California History: A Topical Approach*. Wheeling, IL: Harlan Davidson, 2002.

Morgan, H. Wayne, and Anne Hodges Morgan. *Oklahoma: A History*. Nashville, TN: Norton, 1977.

Morris, Celia. *Storming the Statehouse: Running for Governor with Ann Richards and Dianne Feinstein*. New York: Charles Scribner's Sons, 1992.

Morrison, Dorothy. *Ladies Were Not Expected: Abigail Scott Duniway and Women's Rights*. New York: Antheneum, 1977.

Morrison, Dorothy N. *Chief Sarah: Sarah Winnemucca's Fight for Indian Rights*. 2nd ed. Portland: Oregon Historical Society Press, 1990.

Mowry, George E. *The California Progressives*. Berkeley: University of California Press, 1951.

Moynihan, Ruth Baines. *Rebel for Rights: Abigail Scott Duniway*. New Haven, CT: Yale University Press, 1983.

Muenger, Dr. Betsy, 1st Lt. Laurel Scherer, Tech. Sgt. Ken Carter, and Christy Williams. *Women in Motion: Celebrating 20 Years at the Air Force Academy*. Colorado Springs, CO: USAFA Director of Public Affairs, 1996.

Muncy, Robyn. *Creating a Female Dominion in American Reform, 1890-1935*. New York: Oxford University Press, 1991.

Murdock, Catherine Gilbert. *Domesticating Drink: Women, Men, and Alcohol in America, 1870-1940*. Baltimore, MD: Johns Hopkins University Press, 1998.

Murphy, John J. *Critical Essays on Willa Cather*. Boston: Hall, 1984.

Murphy, John J. *Willa Cather: Family, Community, and History*. Provo, UT: Brigham Young University Humanities Publication Center, 1990.

Murphy, Mary. *Mining Cultures: Men, Women, and Leisure in Butte, 1914-41*. Urbana: University of Illinois Press, 1997.

Myres, Sandra L., ed. *Ho for California! Women's Overland Diaries From the Huntington Library*. San Marino, CA: Huntington Library, 1980.

Myers, Sandra L. *Westering Women and the Frontier Experience, 1800-1915*. Albuquerque: University of New Mexico Press, 1982.

Nagel, Joane. *American Indian Ethnic Renewal: Red Power and the Resurgence of Identity and Culture*. New York: Oxford University Press, 1996.

Nalle, Ouida Ferguson. *The Fergusons of Texas, or "Two Governors for the Price of One": A Biography of James Edward Ferguson and His Wife*. San Antonio, TX: Naylor, 1946.

Nam, Vickie. *Yell-Oh Girls! Emerging Voices Explore Culture, Identity, and Growing Up Asian American*. New York: HarperCollins, 2001.

Nancy Kelsey: http://gcclearn.gcc.cc.va.us/adams/pw2-kelsn.htm

Nakano, Mei. *Japanese American Women: Three Generations, 1890-1990*. Berkeley, CA: Mina Publishing; National Japanese Historical Society, 1990.

Naples, Nina A. *Grassroots Warriors: Activist Mothering, Community Work, and the War on Poverty*. New York: Routledge, 1998.

Naranjo-Morse. *Mud Women: Poems from the Clay*. Tucson: University of Arizona Press, 1992.

National Aeronautics and Space Administration. "Shannon W. Lucid: Astronaut," Lyndon B. Johnson Space Center: www.jsc.nasa.gov/Bios/htmlbios/lucid.html.

"The National Law Review Tenth Anniversary: Assistant District Attorneys," *National Law Review* (September 26, 1988).

Native American Authors Project: www.ipl.org.

Nauen, Elinor. *Ladies, Start Your Engines*. New York: Faber & Faber, 1996.

Nelson, Robert J. *Willa Cather and France: In Search of the Lost Language*. New York: Oxford University Press, 1988.

Nichols, Jeffrey. *Prostitution, Polygamy, and Power: Salt Lake City, 1847-1918*. Urbana and Chicago: University of Illinois Press, 2002.

Nielsen, Waldemar. *Inside American Philanthropy: The Dramas of Donorship*. Norman: University of Oklahoma Press, 1972.

Nielsen, Waldemar. *The Golden Donors: A New Anatomy of the Great Foundations*. New York: Columbia University Press, 1972.

"Ninth Circuit Judge to Take Senior Status." *Metropolitan News-Enterprise*. Capitol News Service, August 29, 1997.

Nora Margaret Manella: http://air.fjc.gov/servlet/tGetInfo?jid=2798.

Northern Wyoming Daily News. "Days of Remembrance. Hattie Burnstad" (video and pamphlet). United Methodist Church RER Building, Worland, Wyoming, September 27, 1984.

Nunis, Doyce B., ed. *The Bidwell-Bartleson Party: 1841 California Emigrant Adventure*. Santa Cruz, CA: Western Tanager Press, 1991.

O'Brien, Sharon. *Willa Cather: The Emerging Voice*. New York: Oxford University Press, 1987.

O'Connor, Margaret Anne. "Octavia E. Butler," in Thadious M. Davis and Trudier Harris, eds., *Dictionary of Literary Biography: Afro-American Fiction Writers After 1955. Vol. 33*. Detroit, MI: Gale Research, 1984.

O'Dea Schenken, Suzanne. *From Suffrage to the Senate: An Encyclopedia of American Women in Politics*. Santa Barbara, CA: ABC-CLIO, Inc., 1999.

Odendahl, Teresa. *Charity Begins at Home: Generosity and Self-Interest Among the Philanthropic Elite*. New York: Basic Books, 1990.

Oklahoma City Hall. "Biographies of City Council Members": www.okc-cityhall.org/Mayor-Council.

Oklahoma State University. "Chief Wilma P. Mankiller: Principal Chief, Cherokee Nation," Henry G. Bennett Distinguished Service Award Winners: www.library.okstate.edu.

Oklahoma State University. "Judge Juanita Kidd Stout: Judge of the Common Pleas Court, Philadelphia, Pennsylvania," Henry G. Bennett Distinguished Service Award Winners: www.library.okstate.edu.

Olive Heritage: www.calolive.org/foodservice/heritage.html.

Oppedisano, Jeannette M. *Historical Encyclopedia of American Women Entrepreneurs: 1776 to the Present*. Westport, CT: Greenwood Press, 2000.

Oregon Blue Book. "Notable Oregonians: Abigail Scott Duniway, Women's Rights Pioneer": http://bluebook.state.or.us/notable/notduniway.htm.

Oroville, California, Attractions. "Butte County Historical Society Ehmann Home": oroville.com/orovilleattractions.shtml.

Orozco, Cynthia E. "Beyond Machismo, La Familia, and Ladies Auxiliaries: A Historiography of Mexican-Origin Women's Participation in Voluntary Associations and Politics in the United States, 1870-1990." *Perspectives in Mexican American Studies* 5(1995). 1-34.

Osselaer, Heidi J. *'A Woman for a Woman's Job': Arizona Women in Politics, 1900-1950*. Ph.D. dissertation. Arizona State University, 2001.

Owens, Kenneth N. ed. *Riches for All: The California Gold Rush and the World*. Lincoln: University of Nebraska Press, 2002.

Owings, Chloe. *Women Police: A Study of the Development and Status of the Women Police Movement*. Montclair, NJ: Patterson Smith, 1969.

Pamela Ann Rymer: http://air.fjc.gov/servlet/tGetInfo?jid=2083.

Pardo, Mary. "Mexican American Women Grassroots Community Activists: Mothers of East Los Angeles." *Frontiers* 11(1, 1990): 1-7.

Paregien, Stan, ed. *Directory of Western Writers and Entertainers*. "Linda M. Hasselstrom." Retrieved from www.texmexx.net/H/h-as.html. Copyright © 2000 by Stan Paregien, Sr.

Parsons, Katherine B. *History of Fifty Years, Utah Federation of Women's Clubs*. Salt Lake City, UT: Arrow Press, 1927.

Parsons, Elsie Clews. "Mothers and Children at Laguna." *Man* 19 (1919): 34-38.

Parsons, Elsie Clews. *Pueblo Indian Religion*. Chicago: University of Chicago Press, 1939.

Pascoe, Peggy. *Relations of Rescue: The Search for Female Moral Authority in the American West, 1874-1939*. New York: Oxford University Press, 1990.

Passet, Joanne E. *Cultural Crusaders: Women Librarians in the American West, 1900-1917*. Albuquerque: University of New Mexico Press, 1994.

Peavy, Linda, and Ursula Smith. *Women in Waiting in the Westward Movement: Life on the Home Frontier*. Norman: University of Oklahoma Press, 1994.

Peffer, George Anthony. *If They Don't Bring Women Here: Chinese Female Immigration Before Exclusion*. Urbana: University of Illinois Press, 1999.

Peiss, Kathy. *Cheap Amusements: Working Women and Leisure in Turn-of-the Century New York.* Philadelphia, PA: Temple University Press, 1986.

Perry, Donna. *Backtalk: Women Writers Speak Out.* New Brunswick, NJ: Rutgers University Press, 1993.

Peters, Alexander. "Creating a Different Kind of Labor Practice; With a Long Roster of Union Clients, Altshuler, Berzon Has Established a Public Interest Practice That Pays the Rent." *The Recorder,* May 10, 1991.

Petrik, Paula. *No Step Backward: Women and Family on the Rocky Mountain Mining Frontier, Helena, Montana, 1865-1900.* Helena: Montana Historical Society Press, 1987.

Philanthropy in the Southwest. Austin, TX: The Hogg Foundation for Mental Health, 1965.

Phyllis J. Hamilton: http://air.fjc.gov/servlet/tGetInfo?jid=2863.

Pichardo, Nelson. "The Establishment and Development of Chicano Voluntary Associations in California, 1910-1930." *Aztlán 19*(2, 1988-1990).

Pinney, Thomas. *A History of Wine in America: From Beginnings to Prohibition.* Los Angeles: University of California Press, 1989.

Plummer, Louise. "Susa Young Gates," *Encyclopedia of Mormonism: Vol. 2.* New York: Macmillan, 1992.

Ponce, Mary Helen. "The Lives and Works of Five Hispanic New Mexican Writers, 1878-1991." *Southwest Hispanic Research Institute Working Paper No. 119.* Albuquerque: University of New Mexico Press, 1992.

Pounds, Kelley. "The Manifest Destiny of Susan Shelby Magoffin." *Calico Trails*, July 1997.

Powell, John Carroll. "Early Settlers of Sangamon County—1876": www.rootsweb.com/~ilsangam/1876/donnerg.htm.

Powers, Janet. "Mapping the Prophetic Landscape in *Almanac of the Dead,*" in Louis Barnett, ed., *Leslie Marmon Silko: A Collection of Critical Essays.* Albuquerque: University of New Mexico, 1999.

Putnam, Jackson K. *Modern California Politics* (4th ed). Sparks, NV: MTL, 1996.

The Quotable Ivins: www.salon.com/people/feature/2000/12/12/ivins_quotes/print.html.

Rader, Brian F. *The Political Outsiders: Blacks and Indians in a Rural Oklahoma County.* San Francisco, CA: R&E Research, 1978.

Raftery, Judith Rosenberg. *Land of Fair Promise: Politics and Reform in Los Angeles Schools, 1885-1941.* Stanford, CA: Stanford University Press, 1992.

Raftery, Judith. "Los Angeles Clubwomen and Progressive Reform," in William Deverell and Tom Sitton, eds., *California Progressivism Revisited.* Berkeley: University of California Press, 1994.

Randall, John H. *The Landscape and the Looking Glass: Willa Cather's Search for Value.* Boston, MA: Houghton,1960.

Rasmussen, Cecelia. "L.A., Then and Now: The Gush of Oil Was Music to Queen's Ear." *Los Angeles Times*, July 11, 1999, p. B3.

Ravage, John W. *Black Pioneers: Images of the Black Experience on the North American Frontier.* Salt Lake City: University of Utah Press, 1997.

Rebolledo, Tey Diana. Introduction. *Romance of a Little Village Girl.* By Cleofas Jaramillo. Albuquerque: University of New Mexico Press, 2000 (reprint of 1955 edition). xv-xxvii.

Red Shirt, Delphine. *Bead on an Anthill: A Lakota Childhood.* Lincoln: University of Nebraska Press, 1998.

Reichard, Gladys. *Another Look at the Navaho.* Ms. 29-37. Flagstaff: Museum of Northern Arizona.

Reichard, Gladys. *Books from a Shelf.* KTAR, KVOA, KYUM, Arizona. July 15, 1941. Ms 29-23-4. Flagstaff: Museum of Northern Arizona.

Reincke, Mary, and Jeaneen C. Wilhelmi, eds. *The American Bench.* Minneapolis, MN: Reginald Bishop Foster, 2001.

Reese, Linda W. "Dear Oklahoma Lady: Women Journalists Speak Out." *Chronicles of Oklahoma 67*(3, Fall 1989).

Reese, Linda. *Women of Oklahoma, 1890-1920.* Norman: University of Oklahoma Press, 1997.

Reuben, Paul P. "Chapter 7: Early Twentieth Century—Willa Cather." PAL: Perspectives in American Literature—A Research and Reference Guide: www.csustan.edu/english/reuben/pal/chap7/cather.html.

Richards, Ann, and Peter Knobler. *Straight From the Heart: My Life in Politics and Other Places.* New York: Simon & Schuster, 1989.

Riddlesperger, James W. *Sarah T. Hughes.* M.A. thesis. North Texas University, 1980.

Rice, Julian. *Deer Women and Elk Men: The Lakota Narratives of Ella Deloria.* Albuquerque: University of New Mexico Press, 1992.

Riley, Glenda. *The Female Frontier: A Comparative View of Women on the Prairie and the Plains.* Lawrence: University Press of Kansas, 1988.

Riley, Glenda. *The Life and Legacy of Annie Oakley.* Norman: University of Oklahoma Press, 1994.

Riley, Glenda. *Women and Nature: Saving the Wild West.* Lincoln: University of Nebraska Press, 1999.

Riley, Glenda, and Richard Etulain. *By Grit and Grace: Eleven Women Who Shaped the American West.* Golden, CO: Fulcrum Press, 1997.

Risjord, Norman J. *Jefferson's America, 1760-1815.* Madison, WI: Madison House, 1991.

Ritchie, Ward. *The Dohenys of Los Angeles.* Los Angeles: Dawson's Book Shop, 1974.

Robbins, Louise S. *The Dismissal of Miss Ruth Brown.* Norman: University of Oklahoma Press, 2000.

Robertson, Cara. "Bobbed-Haired Portia Takes the Bench": Judge Georgia Bullock and Her Campaign for the Los Angeles Superior Court (May 13, 1997): www.stanford.edu/group/WLHP/papers/georgia.html.

Robinson, Judith. *The Hearsts: An American Dynasty.* New York: Acon Books, 1991.

Rochlin, Harriet, and Fred Rochlin. *Pioneer Jews: A New Life in the Far West.* Boston, MA: Houghton Mifflin, 1984.

Rogers, Mary Beth. *Barbara Jordan: American Hero.* New York: Bantam, 1998

Rood, Karen L., ed. *American Literary Almanac.* New York: Facts on File, 1988.

Root, Marilyn. *Women at the Wheel: 42 Stories of Freedom, Fanbelts and the Lure of the Open Road.* Naperville, IL: Sourcebooks Trade, 1999.

Rosowski, Susan J. *The Voyage Perilous: Willa Cather's Romanticism.* Ithaca, NY: Cornell University Press, 1986.

Rosowski, Susan J. "Willa Cather's Ecology of Place." *Western American Literature 30* (1995).

Rothman, David J. *The Discovery of the Asylum: Social Order and Disorder in the New Republic.* Boston, MA: Little, Brown, 1971.

Rothschild, Mary Logan, and Pamela Claire Hronek. *Doing What the Day Brought: An Oral History of Arizona Women.* Tucson: University of Arizona Press, 1992.

Rubien, David. "Molly Ivins": www.salon.com/people/bc/2000/12/12/ivins/print.html.

Rubio, Philip F. *A History of Affirmative Action, 1619-2000.* Jackson: University Press of Mississippi, 2001.

Ruckman, Jo Ann. "'Knit, Knit, and Then Knit': The Women of Pocatello and the War Effort, 1917-1918." *Idaho Yesterdays 26* (Spring 1982): 26-36.

Ruether, Rosemary Radford, and Rosemary Skinner Keller, eds. *Women and Religion in America: Vol. 1. The Nineteenth Century: A Documentary History.* New York: Harper & Row, 1982.

Ruether, Rosemary Radford, and Rosemary Skinner Keller, eds. *Women and Religion in America: Vol. 2. The Colonial and Revolutionary Periods: A Documentary History.* New York: Harper & Row, 1982.

Ruiz, Vicky L. *Cannery Women: Cannery Lives: Mexican, Women, Unionization, and the California Food Processing Industry, 1930-1950.* Albuquerque: University of New Mexico, 1987.

Ruoff, A. LaVonne. "Nineteenth-Century American Indian Autobiographers: William Apes, George Copway, and Sarah Winnemucca." In LaVonne Ruoff and Jerry Ward, eds., *The New Literary History.* New York: Modern Language Association, 1991.

Ryan, Gail F. "Policewoman One: Alice Stebbins Wells." *The Link* (February 2001).

Ryan, Maureen. "Barbara Kingsolver's Lowfat Fiction." *Journal of American Culture 18*(4, Winter 1995).

Sage, Margaret Olivia. "Opportunities and Responsibilities of Leisured Women." *North American Review 181* (April 1913): 103-108.

Sammons, Vivian Ovelton, ed. *Blacks in Science and Medicine.* New York: Hemisphere, 1990.

Sanchez, George. "'Go After the Women': Americanization and the Mexican Immigrant Woman, 1915-1929," in Vicki L. Ruiz and Ellen Carol DuBois, eds., *Unequal Sisters: A Multicultural Reader in U.S Women's History* (2d ed.). New York: Rutledge, 1994.

Sandoz, Mari. *Old Jules.* New York: Blue Ribbon Press, 1935.

Sandoz, Mari. *Crazy Horse: The Strange Man of the Oglalas.* Lincoln: University of Nebraska Press, 1942.

Sandoz, Mari. *Cheyenne Autumn.* Lincoln: University of Nebraska Press, 1992.

Sandoz, Mari. *The Buffalo Hunters: The Story of the Hide Men.* New York: Hastings House, 1954.

Sandoz, Mari. *The Cattlemen From the Rio Grande Across the Far Marias.* New York: Hastings House, 1958.

Sandoz, Mari. *The Beaver Men: Spearheads of Empire.* New York: Hastings House, 1964.

Sandoz, Mari. *Sandhill Sundays and Other Recollections.* Lincoln: University of Nebraska Press, 1970.

Sarah T. Hughes Papers, University of North Texas Archives.

Sarah T. Hughes, Oral History Interviews, University of North Texas Archives.

Saundra Brown Armstrong: http://air.fjc.gov/servlet/tGetInfo?jid=59.

Schackel, Sandra. *Social Housekeepers: Women Shaping Public Policy in New Mexico, 1920-1940.* Albuquerque: University of New Mexico Press, 1992.

Schafer, Delbert F. "French Explorers in Oklahoma." *Chronicles of Oklahoma* 55(4, Winter 1977-1978).

Scharff, Virginia. *Taking the Wheel: Women and the Coming of the Motor Age.* Albuquerque: University of New Mexico Press, 1992.

Schlegell, Abbie J. von, and Joan M. Fisher. *Women as Donors, Women as Philanthropists (New Directions for Philanthropic Fundraising, Series No. 2).* New York: Jossey-Bass, 1993.

Schlissel, Lillian, Vicki L. Ruiz, and Janice Monk, eds. *Western Women: Their Land, Their Lives.* Albuquerque: University of New Mexico Press, 1988.

Schlissel, Lillian. *Women's Diaries of the Westward Journey.* New York: Schocken Books, 1982, 1992.

Schrems, Suzanne H. "Radicalism and Song." *Chronicles of Oklahoma* 62(2, Summer 1984): 190-205.

Schroeter, James, ed. *Willa Cather and Her Critics.* Ithaca, NY: Cornell University Press, 1967.

Schultz, Dorothy Moses. *From Social Worker to Crime-fighter: Women in United States Municipal Policing.* Westport, CT: Greenwood Press, 1995.

Schultz, Jeffrey D., and Laura van Assendelft, eds. *Encyclopedia of Women in American Politics.* Phoenix, AZ: Oryx Press, 1999.

Scott, A. F., S. M. Evans, S. K. Cahn, and E. Faue. "Women's History in the New Millennium" (Panel Discussion). *Journal of Women's History 11,* 1999.

Scott, Anne Firor. "Most Invisible of All: Black Women's Voluntary Association," *Journal of Southern History 56* (February 1990).

Scott, Anne Firor. *Natural Allies: Women's Associations in American History.* Urbana: University of Illinois Press, 1991.

Scott-Smith, Daniel. "Female Householding in Late Eighteenth Century America and the Problem of Poverty." *Journal of Southern History 28* (Fall 1994).

Seagraves, Anne. *Soiled Doves: Prostitution in the Early West.* Hayden, ID: Wesanne Publications, 1994.

Searcy, Howard. "Mrs. Howard Searcy: Pearl C. Moyer, 1875-1945." *Chronicles of Oklahoma* 24(1, Spring 1946).

Selcer, Richard F. *Hell's Half Acre.* Fort Worth: Texas Christian University Press, 1991.

Senier, Siobhan. *Voices of American Indian Assimilation and Resistance: Helen Hunt Jackson, Sarah Winnemucca and Victoria Howard.* Norman: University of Oklahoma Press, 2001.

Sergeant, Elizabeth Shepley. *Willa Cather: A Memoir.* Lincoln: University of Nebraska Press, 1963.

Schaefer, Dennis. "Grunge to Glamor." *Santa Barbara News-Press* Magazine (Fall 1997).

Shapiro, Laura. "Ghost Story." *Newsweek* (November 6, 1995).

Shein, Debra. *Feminist Voices and Visions,* "Abigail Scott Duniway Exhibit Text": http://libweb.uoregon.edu/exhibits/feminist-voices/duntext.html.

Shen, Gloria. "Born of a Stranger: Mother-Daughter Relationships and Storytelling in Amy Tan's *The Joy Luck Club,"* in Anne E. Brown and Marjanne E. Gooze, eds., *International Women's Writing: New Landscapes of Identity.* Westport, CT: Greenwood Press, 1995.

"Sherwin Miller Museum of Jewish History": www.jewish-museum.net/Museum/history.htm.

Shipek, Florence Connolly. *Pushed Into the Rocks: Southern California Indian Land Tenure, 1769-1986.* Lincoln: University of Nebraska Press, 1987.

Shropshire, Mike, and Frank Schaefer. *The Thorny Rose of Texas: An Intimate Portrait of Governor Ann Richards.* Secaucus, NJ: Carol Publishing Group, 1994.

Sicherman, Barbara, and Carol Hurd Green, eds. *Notable American Women: A Biographical Dictionary.* 4 vols. Cambridge, MA: Belknap, 1980.

Silko, Leslie Marmon. *Laguna Woman Poems.* New York: Greenfield Review Press, 1974.

Silko, Leslie Marmon. *Ceremony.* New York: Viking, 1977.

Silko, Leslie Marmon. *Storyteller.* New York: Seaver, 1981.

Silko, Leslie Marmon. *Almanac of the Dead: A Novel.* New York: Simon & Schuster, 1991.

Silko, Leslie Marmon. *Yellow Woman.* New Brunswick, NJ: Rutgers University Press, 1993.

Silvey, Anita. *Children's Books and Their Creators.* Boston: Houghton Mifflin, 1995.

Simmons, Diane. *Maxine Hong Kingston.* New York: Twayne, 1999.

Sinton, May L. *A History of the Women's Clubs of Denver, 1894-1915.* Master's thesis. University of Colorado, Denver, 1987.

Sitton, Thad, and Dan K. Utley. *From Can See to Can't: Texas Cotton Farmers on the Southern Prairies.* Austin: University Press of Texas, 1997.

Skaggs, Merrill Maguire. *After the World Broke in Two: The Later Novels of Willa Cather.* Charlottesville: University Press of Virginia, 1990.

Skandera-Trombley, Laura E., ed. *Critical Essays on Maxine Hong Kingston.* New York: G. K. Hall, 1998.

Skenazy, Paul, and Tera Martin, eds. *Conversations with Maxine Hong Kingston.* Jackson: University of Mississippi Press, 1998.

Sklar, Kathryn Kish. *Catherine Beecher: A Study in American Domesticity.* New Haven, CT: Yale University Press, 1973.

Slote, Bernice. *Willa Cather: A Pictorial Memoir.* Photographs by Lucia Woods and others. Lincoln: University of Nebraska Press, 1973.

Sloss, Robert Sloss. "What a Woman Can Do With an Auto," *Outing* (April, 1910).

Smith, Bridget E., ed. "Women Win the Right to Vote." *Historical Gazette (3)*5, August 20, 1925.

Smith, Jessie Carney, and Carrell Peterson-Horton, eds. *Historical Statistics of Black America: Media to Vital Statistics.* New York: Gale Research, 1995.

Smith, Norma. *Jeannette Rankin: America's Conscience.* Helena: Montana Historical Society Press, 2002.

Smith, Patricia Clark. "Achacans, Americanos, Prelates and Monsters: Willa Cather's *Death Comes for the Archbishop* as New World Odyssey," in E. A. Mares, ed., *Padre Martinez: New Perspectives from Texas*, 101-24. Taos, NM: Millicent Rogers Museum. 1988.

Smith, Jessie Carney, ed. *Notable Black American Women.* Detroit, MI: Gale Research, 1992.

Smith, June. "Women of Wine: They Dared to Take a Great Leap of Faith." *Santa Cruz Sentinel* (March 14, 2001)

Smith, Sherry Lynn. *The View From Officers' Row: Army Perceptions of Western Indians.* Tucson: University of Arizona Press, 1990.

Smith, Sherry L. "Single Women Homesteaders: The Perplexing Case of Elinore Pruitt Stewart," *Western Historical Quarterly* 22 (May 1991): 163-183.

Sonneborn, Liz. *A to Z of Native American Women.* New York: Facts on File, 1998

Southwestern University School of Law. "Hon. Kathleen O'Leary": www.swlaw.edu/alumni/oleary.html.

Specht, Robert. *Tisha: The Story of a Young Teacher in the Alaska Wilderness.* New York: Bantam Doubleday Dell, 1977.

The Spirit Within. The Salon Interview: Amy Tan: www.salon1999.com/12nov1995/feature/tan.html.

Sprague, William Forrest. *Women and the West: A Short Social History.* New York: Arno Press, 1972.

St. John, Adela Rogers. *The Honeycomb,* Garden City, NY: Doubleday, 1969.

Stallard, Patricia. *Glittering Misery: Dependents of the Indian Fighting Army.* Norman: University of Oklahoma Press, 1978, 1992.

Stanford Law School. "Clara Shortridge Foltz": www.law.stanford.edu/library/wlhbp/clara.

Stanley, John Joseph. "L.A. Behind Bars, 1847 to 1886: Establishing a Secure Institution," in Gordon Morris Bakken, ed., *California History: A Topical Approach.* Wheeling, IL: Harlan Davidson, 2003.

Stanley, Ruth Moore. "Alice M. Robertson: Oklahoma's First Congresswoman." *Chronicles of Oklahoma 45*(3, Autumn 1969): 278-288.

Stalheim, Ole H. V., ed. *Veterinary Medicine in the West.* Manhattan, KS: Sunflower University Press, 1988.

Starr, Kevin. *Material Dreams: Southern California Through the 1920s.* New York: Oxford University Press, 1990.

Steele, James, and Stephen Shennan, eds. *The Archaeology of Human Ancestry: Power, Sex and Tradition.* New York: Routledge, 1996.

Stefanco, Carolyn J. *Pathways to Power: Women and Voluntary Associations in Denver, Colorado, 1876-1893.* Ph.D. dissertation. Duke University, 1987.

Stein, Bill, and Easterling, Jayne, eds. "The Writings of Fannie Amelia Dickson Darden," *Nesbitt Memorial Library Journal: A Journal of Colorado County History* 9(3) (1999): 131-194.

Stewart, George Rippey. *Ordeal by Hunger: The Story of the Donner Party.* Boston, MA: Houghton Mifflin, 1960.

Stiehm, Judith Hicks. *Bring Me Men and Women: Mandated Change at the U.S. Air Force Academy.* Los Angeles. University of California Press, 1981.

Stineman, Esther. *American Political Women: Contemporary and Historical Profiles.* Littleton, CO: Libraries Unlimited, 1980.

Stockel, H. Henrietta. *Women of the Apache Nation: Voices of Truth.* Reno: University of Nevada Press, 1991.

Stockel, H. Henrietta. *Chiricahua Apache Women and Children: Safekeepers of the Heritage.* College Station: Texas A&M Press, 2000.

Stoeltje, Beverly. *Females in Rodeo: Private Motivation and Public Representation.* Kentucky Folklore Record 32 n.1-2 (1986): 46.

Stolz, Preble. *Judging Judges: The Investigation of Rose Bird and the California Supreme Court.* New York: Free Press, 1981.

Stotler, Alicemarie Huber. Retrieved from air.fjc.gov/servlet/uGetInfo?jid=2304. Source: History of the Federal Judiciary. http://www.fjc.gov. Web site of the Federal Judicial Center, Washington, D.C.

Stouck, David. *Willa Cather's Imagination.* Lincoln: University of Nebraska Press, 1975.

Stout, Janis P. *Willa Cather: The Writer and Her World.* Charlottesville: University Press of Virginia, 2000.

Stout, Janis P., ed. *A Calendar of the Letters of Willa Cather.* Lincoln: University of Nebraska Press, 2002.

Strickland, Rennard. "Oklahoma Indians." *The Native North American Almanac.* Detroit, MI: Gale Research, 1994.

Suggs Jr., George G. *Colorado's War on Militant Unionism: James H. Peabody and the Western Federation of Miners.* Detroit, MI: Wayne State University Press, 1972.

Swanton, John R. *The Indian Tribes of North America.* Washington, DC: Scholarly Press, 1978.

Tallchief, Maria, and Larry Kaplan. "Maria Tallchief: America's Prima Ballerina": www.washingtonpost.com

Tate, Grover Ted. *The Lady Who Tamed Pegasus: The Story of Pancho Barnes.* Bend, OR: Maverick, 1984.

Texas Settlement Region: www.tsir.org.

Thatcher, Leora. "Kuniko Muramatsu Terasawa: For 52 Years She Handset Type for a Unique Utah Newspaper." *Special Collections.* University of Utah: www.utahhistorytogo. org/utachiev.html.

Thomas, Lately. *The Vanishing Evangelist: The Aimee Semple McPherson Kidnapping Affair.* New York: Viking Press, 1959.

Thomas, Lately. *Storming Heaven: The Lives and Turmoils of Minnie Kennedy and Aimee Semple McPherson.* New York: William Morrow, 1970.

Tibbo, H. R. *Abstracting, Information Retrieval and the Humanities: Providing Access to Historical Literature.* Chicago: American Library Association, 1993.

Tolleson-Rinehart, Sue, and Jeanie R. Stanley. *Claytie and the Lady: Ann Richards, Gender, and Politics in Texas.* Austin: University of Texas Press, 1994.

Tomer, John S. "Edith Force Kassing: Scientist With a Gift for Teaching." *Chronicles of Oklahoma* 63(4, Winter 1985-1986).

Tong, Benson. *Unsubmissive Women: Chinese Prostitutes in Nineteenth-Century San Francisco.* Norman: University of Oklahoma Press, 1994.

Trafzer, Clifford E. *Death Stalks the Yakama.* East Lansing: Michigan State University Press, 1997.

Trafzer, Clifford E. *As Long as the Grass Shall Grow and Rivers Flow: A History of Native Americans.* New York: Harcourt, 2000.

Tran, Quin. "KFOR-TV News Channel 4 People: Quin Tran": www.kfor.com.

Traut, Carol Ann, and Craig F. Emmert. "Expanding the Integrated Model of Judicial Decision Making: The California Justices and Capital Punishment." *Journal of Politics, 60*(4). (November 1998).

Treese, Joel D., ed. *2001/Fall Congressional Staff Directory: 107th Congress, First Session* (62d ed.). Washington, DC: CQ Press, 2001.

Trimble, Steven. "Brown Earth and Laughter: The Clay People of Nora Naranjo Morse." *American Indian Art* 12 (Autumn 1987).

Trotter, Don M. *An 80 Year Review, 1905-1985: Kansas State University, College of Veterinary Medicine.* Manhattan: Kansas State University, 1985.

Truitt, Bess. "Jennie Harris Oliver." *Chronicles of Oklahoma* 22(2, Summer 1944).

Tubbs, Stephenie Ambrose. "Montana Women's Clubs at the Turn of the Century." *Montana: The Magazine of the West 36* (Winter 1986).

Turner, Erin H. *More Than Petticoats: Remarkable California Women.* Helena, MT: TwoDot, 1999.

Turner, William Bennett. "From the *Tanner* Hearings to the Brethren and Beyond: Judicial Accountability and Judicial Independence." *California State Bar Journal 55* (July 1980).

Tuska, Jon, and Vicki Piekarski. *Encyclopedia of Frontier and Western Fiction.* New York: McGraw-Hill, 1983.

Ulrich, Laurel Thatcher. *A Midwife's Tale: The Life of Martha Ballard, Based on Her Diary, 1785-1812.* New York: Vintage Books, 1990.

Underwood, June O. "Civilizing Kansas: Women's Organizations, 1880-1920." *Kansas History 7* (Winter 1984/85).

University of Minnesota Voices from the Gaps: Women Writers of Color. "Janet Campbell Hale": http://voices.cla. umn.edu/authors/HALEjanetcampbell.html.

University of Minnesota, American Indian Studies Department. "Carol Miller: Associate Professor American Studies and American Indian Studies": www.cla.umn. edu/amerind/staff/cmiller.html.

Urgo, Joseph R. *Willa Cather and the Myth of American Migration.* Urbana: University of Illinois Press, 1995.

U.S. Department of Transportation, Women in Transportation. "Bus Operators": www.fhwa.dot.gov/wit/ bus.htm.

Utah State Historical Society. "Utah History to Go": www.utahhistorytogo.org.

VanBurkleo, Sandra F. *"Belonging to the World": Women's Rights and American Constitutional Culture.* New York: Oxford University Press, 2001.

Van Dyke, Annette. "An Introduction to Wynema, A Child of the Forest, by Sophia Alice Callahan." *Studies in American Indian Literature* (Summer/Fall 1992).

Van Ghent, Dorothy. *Willa Cather.* Minneapolis: University of Minnesota Press, 1964.

Vargas, Zaragosa. "Tejana Radical: Emma Tenayuca and the San Antonio Labor Movement During the Great Depression. *Pacific Historical Review 66* (November 1997).

Vehik, Susan C. "Cultural Continuity and Discontinuity in the Southern Prairies and Cross Timbers," in Karl

H. Schlesier, ed., *Plains Indians, A.D. 500-1500: The Archaeological Past of Historical Groups.* Norman: University of Oklahoma Press, 1994.

Vinson, James, ed. *Twentieth-Century Western Writers.* Detroit, MI: Gale Research, 1982.

Virginia A. Phillips. Retrieved from air.fjc.gov/newweb/jnetweb.nsf/fjc_bio. Source: History of the Federal Judiciary. http://www.fjc.gov. Web site of the Federal Judicial Center, Washington, D.C.

"Vote to Admit Women to Service Academies." *Colorado Springs Gazette Telegraph.* January 6, 1975, p. 1.

Wagenknecht, Edward. *Willa Cather.* New York: Continuum, 1994.

Waite, Robert G. "The Woman's Club Movement in Idaho: A Document on the Early Years." *Idaho Yesterdays* 36(2, 1992).

Walker, Samuel. *The Police in America: An Introduction.* San Francisco: McGraw-Hill, 1983.

Wallisch, William Joseph, Jr. *The Admission and Integration of Women Into the United States Air Force Academy.* Los Angeles: University of Southern California, 1977.

Kim McLane Wardlaw: http://air.fjc.gov/history/judges_frm.html.

Wasserman, Loretta. *Willa Cather: A Study of the Short Fiction.* Boston, MA: Twayne, 1991.

Watson, Anita Ernst. *Into Their Own: Nevada Women Emerging Into Public Life.* Reno: Nevada Humanities Committee, 2000.

Watson, Wilbur H., ed. *Black Folk Medicine: The Therapeutic Significance of Faith and Trust.* New Brunswick, NJ: Transaction Books, 1988.

Weatherford, Doris. *A Chronology of American Woman's History.* New York: Facts on File, 1997.

Webber, Carl J. *A Thousand and One Fore-Edge Paintings.* Waterville, ME: Colby College Press, 1949.

Webber, David J. *The Spanish Frontier in North America.* New Haven, CT: Yale University Press, 1992.

Weber, Francis J. *Southern California's First Family.* Fullerton, CA: Lorson's Books and Prints, 1993.

Weimann, Jeanne Madeline. *The Fair Women.* Chicago: Academy Chicago, 1981.

Welch, Linda M. "Janet Campbell Hale Visit": http://nativenet.uthscsa.edu/archive/nn-dialogue/9911/0002.html.

Welch, Rosanne. *Encyclopedia of Women in Aviation and Space.* Santa Barbara, CA: ABC-CLIO, 1998.

Wellman, Paul I. "Cynthia Ann Parker." *Chronicles of Oklahoma* 12(2, June 1934).

Wells College News & Events. "Human Rights Advocate Will Give Wells Commencement Address": www.wells.edu/whatsnew/wnnwar31.htm.

Wenke, Robert J. *Patterns in Prehistory: Mankind's First Three Million Years.* New York: Oxford University Press, 1980.

Wentworth, Alicia. *The Ultimate Challenge.* City of Huntington Beach Miscellaneous Data, Special Collections, California State University, Fullerton.

Westfall, Connie. "Janet Campbell Hale—1946": www.ncteamericancollection.org/litmap/hale_janet_campbell_id.htm.

Westbrook, L. *Interdisciplinary Information Seeking in Women's Studies.* Jefferson, NC: McFarland, 1999.

Westwood, Richard E., *Woman of the River: Georgie White Clark: White Water Pioneer.* Logan: Utah State University Press, 1997.

Wharton, Joseph. "ABA Honors Shirley Hufstedler: Former Federal Judge Is First Woman to Be Awarded ABA Medal." *ABA Journal,* August 1995.

Wheeler, Marjorie Spruill, ed. *One Woman, One Vote: Rediscovering the Woman Suffrage Movement.* Troutdale, OR: New Sage Press, 1995.

White, Florence Meiman. *First Woman in Congress, Jeannette Rankin.* New York: J. Messner, 1980.

Whitman, Ruth. *Tamsen Donner: A Woman's Journey.* Cambridge, MA: Alice James Books, 1977.

Whitney, Catherine. *Nine and Counting: The Women of the Senate.* New York: HarperCollins, 2001.

Whitney, Colleen. *Worth Their Salt: Notable but Often Unnoted Women of Utah.* Logan: Utah State University Press, 1996.

Who's Who of American Women 2000-2001. New Providence, NJ: Marquis Who's Who, 2000.

Who's Who of American Women 2000-2001 Millennium Edition. Chicago: Marquis Who's Who, 2001.

Wiggin, Kate Douglas. *Encyclopædia Britannica.* Retrieved from Encyclopædia Britannica Premium Service, www.britannica.com/eb/article?eu=78992.

Wiggin, Kate Douglas. *My Garden of Memory: An Autobiography.* Boston, MA: Houghton Mifflin, 1923.

Willa Cather Pioneer Memorial Web Site: www.willacather.org.

Williams, Eric L. *A History of the Oklahoma State University College of Veterinary Medicine.* Stillwater: Oklahoma State University, 1986.

Wills, Kathy Lynn, and Virginia Artho. *Cowgirl Legends from the Cowgirl Hall of Fame.* Salt Lake City, UT: Gibbs-Smith, 1995.

Windbreak House. "Writing Retreats for Women with Author Linda M. Hasselstrom": www.windbreakhouse.com.

Wolf, Michele. "U.S. District Judge Elizabeth D. Laporte." *San Francisco Attorney Magazine,* April/May 1998.

Women Children's Book Illustrators. "Helen Moore Sewell": www.ortakales.com/illustrators/Sewell.html.

Women for Winesense: www.womenforwinesense.org.

"Women in Combat Key Issue of Bill." *Air Force Times* (June 19, 1974).

"Women in the Academies Aired in Appeals Court." *Air Force Times* (November 27, 1974).

"Women's Advancement New AAHOA Initiative for 1999," *India West.* September 4, 1998, p. A40.

Women's Clubs of Denver, Essays in Colorado History, No. 13. Denver, CO: Colorado Historical Society, 1993.

Wong, Sau-Ling Cynthia. "'Sugar Sisterhood': Situating the Amy Tan Phenomenon." *The Ethnic Canon: Histories, Institutions, and Interventions.* Minneapolis: University of Minnesota Press, 1995, 174-210.

Wong, Sau-Ling Cynthia. *Maxine Hong Kingston's The Woman Warrior: A Casebook.* New York: Oxford University Press, 1999.

Woodress, James. *Willa Cather: Her Life and Art.* Lincoln: University of Nebraska Press, 1970.

Woodress, James. *Willa Cather: A Literary Life.* Lincoln: University of Nebraska Press, 1987.

Wright, A. J. "Early Black and Female Physicians in Jefferson County: www.anes.uab.edu/jeffcodocs.htm.

Wright, Muriel H. "Choctaws and Chickasaws Were Allied With Confederacy," in Mattie Lloyd Wooten, ed., *Women Tell the Story of the Southwest.* San Antonio, TX: Naylor, 1940.

Your Car: A Magazine of Romance, Fact and Fiction, 1925.

Yu, Diana. *Winds of Change: Korean Women in America.* Silver Spring, MD: Women's Institute Press, 1991.

Yu, Henry. *Thinking Orientals: Migration, Contact, and Exoticism in Modern America.* New York: Oxford University Press, 2001.

Yung, Judy. *Unbound Feet: A Social History of Chinese Women in San Francisco.* Berkeley: University of California Press, 1995.

Zanjani, Sally. *Sarah Winnemucca.* Lincoln: University of Nebraska Press, 2001.

Zhu, Liping. *A Chinaman's Chance: The Chinese on the Rocky Mountain Mining Frontier.* Boulder: University Press of Colorado, 1997.

Index

6/23/04

REFERENCE